Lecture Notes in Computer Science 12478

More information about this series at http://www.springer.com/series/7407

Tiziana Margaria · Bernhard Steffen (Eds.)

Leveraging Applications of Formal Methods, Verification and Validation

Applications

9th International Symposium
on Leveraging Applications of Formal Methods, ISoLA 2020
Rhodes, Greece, October 20–30, 2020
Proceedings, Part III

 Springer

Editors
Tiziana Margaria ⓘ
University of Limerick and Lero
Limerick, Ireland

Bernhard Steffen ⓘ
TU Dortmund
Dortmund, Germany

ISSN 0302-9743   ISSN 1611-3349 (electronic)
Lecture Notes in Computer Science
ISBN 978-3-030-61466-9   ISBN 978-3-030-61467-6 (eBook)
https://doi.org/10.1007/978-3-030-61467-6

LNCS Sublibrary: SL1 – Theoretical Computer Science and General Issues

This Springer imprint is published by the registered company Springer Nature Switzerland AG
The registered company address is: Gewerbestrasse 11, 6330 Cham, Switzerland

Introduction

It is our responsibility, as general and program chairs, to welcome the participants to the 9th International Symposium on Leveraging Applications of Formal Methods, Verification and Validation (ISoLA), planned to take place in Rhodes, Greece, during October 20–30, 2020, endorsed by the European Association of Software Science and Technology (EASST).

This year's event follows the tradition of its symposia forerunners held in Paphos, Cyprus (2004 and 2006), Chalkidiki, Greece (2008), Crete, Greece (2010 and 2012), Corfu, Greece (2014 and 2016), and most recently in Limassol, Cyprus (2018), and the series of ISoLA workshops in Greenbelt, USA (2005), Poitiers, France (2007), Potsdam, Germany (2009), Vienna, Austria (2011), and Palo Alto, USA (2013).

Considering that this year's situation is unique and unlike any previous one due to the ongoing COVID-19 pandemic, and that ISoLA's symposium touch and feel is much unlike most conventional, paper-based conferences, after much soul searching we are faced with a true dilemma. "Virtualizing" the event, as many conferences have done, violates the true spirit of the symposium, which is rooted in the gathering of communities and the discussions within and across the various communities materialized in the special tracks and satellite events. Keeping with the physical meeting and holding it in a reduced form (as many may not be able to or feel comfortable with travel) under strict social distancing rules may also end up not being feasible. At the time of writing there is a resurgence of cases in several countries, many nations are compiling "green lists" of countries with which they entertain free travel relations, and these lists are updated – most frequently shortened – at short notice, with severe consequence for the travelers. Many governments and universities are again strengthening the travel restrictions for their employees, and many of us would anyway apply caution due to our own specific individual situation.

To be able to react as flexibly as possible to this situation, we decided to split ISoLA 2020 into two parts, one this year and one in October 2021, with the track organizers deciding when their track will take place. So far both dates have promoters, but it may still happen that, in the end, the entire event needs to move. All accepted papers are published in time, but some tracks will present their papers at the 2021 event.

As in the previous editions, ISoLA 2020 provides a forum for developers, users, and researchers to discuss issues related to the adoption and use of rigorous tools and methods for the specification, analysis, verification, certification, construction, test, and maintenance of systems from the point of view of their different application domains. Thus, since 2004, the ISoLA series of events serves the purpose of bridging the gap between designers and developers of rigorous tools on one side, and users in engineering and in other disciplines on the other side. It fosters and exploits synergetic relationships among scientists, engineers, software developers, decision makers, and other critical thinkers in companies and organizations. By providing a specific, dialogue-oriented venue for the discussion of common problems, requirements, algorithms, methodologies, and practices, ISoLA aims in particular at supporting researchers in their quest to improve the usefulness, reliability, flexibility, and efficiency of tools for building systems, and users in their search for adequate solutions to their problems.

The program of the symposium consists of a collection of special tracks devoted to the following hot and emerging topics:

- Reliable Smart Contracts: State-of-the-art, Applications, Challenges and Future Directions
  (Organizers: Gordon Pace, César Sànchez, Gerardo Schneider)
- Engineering of Digital Twins for Cyber-Physical Systems
  (Organizers: John Fitzgerald, Pieter Gorm Larsen, Tiziana Margaria, Jim Woodcock)
- Verification and Validation of Concurrent and Distributed Systems
  (Organizers: Cristina Seceleanu, Marieke Huisman)
- Modularity and (De-)composition in Verification
  (Organizers: Reiner Hähnle, Eduard Kamburjan, Dilian Gurov)
- Software Verification Tools
  (Organizers: Markus Schordan, Dirk Beyer, Irena Boyanova)
- X-by-Construction: Correctness meets Probability
  (Organizers: Maurice H. ter Beek, Loek Cleophas, Axel Legay, Ina Schaefer, Bruce W. Watson)
- Rigorous Engineering of Collective Adaptive Systems
  (Organizers: Rocco De Nicola, Stefan Jähnichen, Martin Wirsing)
- Automated Verification of Embedded Control Software
  (Organizers: Dilian Gurov, Paula Herber, Ina Schaefer)
- Automating Software Re-Engineering
  (Organizers: Serge Demeyer, Reiner Hähnle, Heiko Mantel)
- 30 years of Statistical Model Checking!
  (Organizers: Kim G. Larsen, Axel Legay)
- From Verification to Explanation
  (Organizers: Holger Herrmanns, Christel Baier)
- Formal methods for DIStributed COmputing in future RAILway systems (DisCoRail 2020)
  (Organizers: Alessandro Fantechi, Stefania Gnesi, Anne Haxthausen)
- Programming: What is Next?
  (Organizers: Klaus Havelund, Bernhard Steffen)

With the embedded events:

- RERS: Challenge on Rigorous Examination of Reactive Systems (Falk Howar, Markus Schordan, Bernhard Steffen)
- Doctoral Symposium and Poster Session (A. L. Lamprecht)
- Industrial Day (Falk Howar, Johannes Neubauer, Andreas Rausch)

Colocated with the ISoLA symposium is:

- STRESS 2020 – 5th International School on Tool-based Rigorous Engineering of Software Systems (J. Hatcliff, T. Margaria, Robby, B. Steffen)

Altogether the ISoLA 2020 proceedings comprises four volumes, Part 1: Verification Principles, Part 2: Engineering Principles, Part 3: Applications, and Part 4: Tools, Trends, and Tutorials, which also covers the associated events.

We thank the track organizers, the members of the Program Committee and their referees for their effort in selecting the papers to be presented, the local organization chair, Petros Stratis, and the EasyConferences team for their continuous and precious support during the entire two-year period preceding the events, and Springer for being, as usual, a very reliable partner for the proceedings production. Finally, we are grateful to Kyriakos Georgiades for his continuous support for the website and the program, and to Markus Frohme and Julia Rehder for their help with the editorial system Equinocs.

Special thanks are due to the following organization for their endorsement: EASST (European Association of Software Science and Technology) and Lero – The Irish Software Research Centre, and our own institutions – TU Dortmund University and the University of Limerick.

We wish you, as an ISoLA participant, a wonderful experience at this edition, and for you, reading the proceedings at a later occasion, valuable new insights that hopefully contribute to your research and its uptake.

August 2020   Tiziana Margaria
                                                               Bernhard Steffen

Organization

Symposium Chair

Tiziana Margaria   University of Limerick and Lero, Ireland

PC Chair

Bernhard Steffen   TU Dortmund University, Germany

PC Members

Christel Baier	Technische Universität Dresden, Germany
Maurice ter Beek	ISTI-CNR, Italy
Dirk Beyer	LMU Munich, Germany
Irena Bojanova	NIST, USA
Loek Cleophas	Eindhoven University of Technology, The Netherlands
Rocco De Nicola	IMT Lucca, Italy
Serge Demeyer	Universiteit Antwerpen, Belgium
Alessandro Fantechi	University of Florence, Italy
John Fitzgerald	Newcastle University, UK
Stefania Gnesi	CNR, Italy
Kim Guldstrand Larsen	Aalborg University, Denmark
Dilian Gurov	KTH Royal Institute of Technology, Sweden
John Hatcliff	Kansas State University, USA
Klaus Havelund	Jet Propulsion Laboratory, USA
Anne E. Haxthausen	Technical University of Denmark, Denmark
Paula Herber	University of Münster, Germany
Holger Hermanns	Saarland University, Germany
Falk Howar	Dortmund University of Technology and Fraunhofer ISST, Germany
Marieke Huisman	University of Twente, The Netherlands
Reiner Hähnle	Technische Universität Darmstadt, Germany
Stefan Jähnichen	TU Berlin, Germany
Eduard Kamburjan	Technische Universität Darmstadt, Germany
Anna-Lena Lamprecht	Utrecht University, The Netherlands
Peter Gorm Larsen	Aarhus University, Denmark
Axel Legay	Université Catholique de Louvain, Belgium
Heiko Mantel	Technische Universität Darmstadt, Germany
Tiziana Margaria	University of Limerick and Lero, Ireland
Johannes Neubauer	Materna, Germany
Gordon Pace	University of Malta, Malta
Cesar Sanchez	IMDEA Software Institute, Madrid, Spain

Ina Schaefer	TU Braunschweig, Germany
Gerardo Schneider	University of Gothenburg, Sweden
Markus Schordan	Lawrence Livermore National Laboratory, USA
Cristina Seceleanu	Mälardalen University, Sweden
Bernhard Steffen	TU Dortmund University, Germany
Bruce Watson	Stellenbosch University, South Africa
Martin Wirsing	Ludwig-Maximilians-Universität München, Germany
James Woodcock	University of York, UK

Reviewers

Aho, Pekka
Aichernig, Bernhard
Backeman, Peter
Baranov, Eduard
Basile, Davide
Beckert, Bernhard
Bensalem, Saddek
Bettini, Lorenzo
Beyer, Dirk
Bourr, Khalid
Bubel, Richard
Bures, Tomas
Casadei, Roberto
Castiglioni, Valentina
Ciatto, Giovanni
Cimatti, Alessandro
Damiani, Ferruccio
Di Marzo Serugendo, Giovanna
Duong, Tan
Filliâtre, Jean-Christophe
Fränzle, Martin
Gabor, Thomas
Gadducci, Fabio
Galletta, Letterio
Geisler, Signe
Gerostathopoulos, Ilias
Guanciale, Roberto
Heinrich, Robert
Hillston, Jane
Hnetynka, Petr
Hoffmann, Alwin

Hungar, Hardi
Inverso, Omar
Iosti, Simon
Jacobs, Bart
Jaeger, Manfred
Jensen, Peter
Johnsen, Einar Broch
Jongmans, Sung-Shik
Jähnichen, Stefan
Kanav, Sudeep
Konnov, Igor
Kosak, Oliver
Kosmatov, Nikolai
Kretinsky, Jan
Könighofer, Bettina
Lanese, Ivan
Lecomte, Thierry
Lluch Lafuente, Alberto
Loreti, Michele
Maggi, Alessandro
Mariani, Stefano
Mazzanti, Franco
Morichetta, Andrea
Nyberg, Mattias
Omicini, Andrea
Orlov, Dmitry
Pacovsky, Jan
Parsai, Ali
Peled, Doron
Piho, Paul
Pugliese, Rosario

Pun, Violet Ka I
Reisig, Wolfgang
Schlingloff, Holger
Seifermann, Stephan
Soulat, Romain
Steinhöfel, Dominic
Stolz, Volker
Sürmeli, Jan
Tiezzi, Francesco
Tini, Simone
Tognazzi, Stefano
Tribastone, Mirco

Trubiani, Catia
Tuosto, Emilio
Ulbrich, Mattias
Vandin, Andrea
Vercammen, Sten
Viroli, Mirko
Wadler, Philip
Wanninger, Constantin
Weidenbach, Christoph
Wirsing, Martin
Zambonelli, Franco

Contents – Part III

Automated Verification of Embedded Control Software

Formal methods for DIStributed COmputing in future RAILway systems

Reliable Smart Contracts: State-of-the-art, Applications, Challenges and Future Directions

Reliable Smart Contracts

Gordon J. Pace[1]([✉]), César Sánchez[2], and Gerardo Schneider[3]

[1] University of Malta, Msida, Malta
gordon.pace@um.edu.mt
[2] IMDEA Software Institute, Madrid, Spain
cesar.sanchez@imdea.org
[3] University of Gothenburg, Gothenburg, Sweden
gerardo@cse.gu.se

Abstract. The rise of smart contracts executed on blockchain and other distributed ledger technologies enabled trustless yet decentralised computation. Various applications take advantage of this computational model, including enforced financial contracts, self-sovereign identity and voting. But smart contracts are nothing but software running on a blockchain, with risks of malfunction due to bugs in the code. Compared to traditional systems, there is an additional risk in that erroneous computation or transactions triggered by a smart contract cannot be easily rolled back due to the immutability of the underlying execution model. This ISoLA track brings together a number of experts in the field of smart contract reliability and verification to discuss the state-of-the-art in smart contract dependability and discuss research challenges and future directions.

1 Blockchains and Smart-Contracts

Blockchains and Distributed Ledger Technologies (DLTs) are essentially a distributed ledger or database, running on multiple devices. The key elements which have generated the hype of this technology are (1) that the consistency of the data stored and the guarantees on updates are performed in a fully decentralised manner, and (2) to ensure immutability of information written. This provided a way of implementing the secure management of digital asset storage in a decentralised manner, enabling the implementation of trustless cryptocurrencies. In the paper which set all this in motion [4], Satoshi Nakamoto outlined how blockchain can be implemented and used to record ownership of cryptocurrency, and acted also as the launch of the Bitcoin blockchain which keeps track of ownership of Bitcoins.[1]

It was soon realised that such a ledger could easily be used to keep track of ownership of any digital asset, recorded on a particular blockchain or as a representation (or evidence) of ownership of any object, physical or otherwise, stored off the blockchain (e.g. music, art, intellectual property, votes). Also, such a trustless network can be used to script performance of agreements between parties on the blockchain. The immutable nature of the blockchain ensures that

---

[1] Confusingly, the term is used both for the network and the cryptocurrency.

© Springer Nature Switzerland AG 2020
T. Margaria and B. Steffen (Eds.): ISoLA 2020, LNCS 12478, pp. 3–8, 2020.
https://doi.org/10.1007/978-3-030-61467-6_1

such agreements are themselves permanent and immutable, thus safeguarding the rights of the parties involved. In this manner, blockchain has the potential to change in a fundamental way, not only with financial services, but also more generally with other applications, improving transparency and regulation.

The Ethereum [1] blockchain was the first widespread blockchain system to implement such smart contracts, allowing not only for transactions consisting of transfer of Ether (the native cryptocurrency) between parties, but also for transactions to deploy and interact with smart contracts. The underlying implementation ensured that the smart contracts are irrevocably written on the blockchain, and their invocations are executed autonomously and securely on the blockchain. On such a public blockchain, smart contracts are openly stored on the blockchain (i.e. they can be read and used by anyone).

Since smart contracts would thus have to be executed and verified automatically by the nodes of the underlying blockchain network, they have to be expressed in a formalism which has a deterministic operationalisation. Many DLTs enabling smart contract execution, including Ethereum, opted for supporting a full Turing-complete instruction set. The execution of smart contract invocations is performed, and the results recorded, on the blockchain network by nodes on the network acting as "miners", who are rewarded (in cryptocurrency) in return. The corresponding instructions in the smart contract may perform normal computation logic but also manipulate the local book-keeping of data (including cryptocurrency). In addition, smart contracts may act as other parties in that they can own and can transfer cryptovalues.

A smart contract can be seen as an embodiment of an agreement between different parties in order to automate the regulated exchange of value and information over the internet. Their promise is that of reducing costs of contracting, and of enforcing contractual agreements (*"robust [. . .] against sophisticated, incentive compatible breach"* [6]), and making payments, while at the same time ensuring trust and compliance, all in the absence of a central authority.

The challenge, however, lies in the fact that smart contracts, just like any other program, can have bugs and vulnerabilities. The agreement enforced can thus inadvertently not match the intended one, and may result in losses for the parties involved. In the literature, one can find reports on various bugs which resulted in the equivalent of millions of euros [2,3,5]. Reliability and correctness of smart contracts is, effectively, a question of reliability and correctness of programs, one of the Holy Grails of computer science. However, one may argue that the need for reliability is even more acute in smart contracts, where code is immutable[2] and critical in that it typically manipulates cryptocurrency. Writing a smart contract carries risk akin to a payment service provider implementing their software in hardware circuits which cannot (or are too expensive to) be updated. On the other hand, since in this setting the computation is performed in small, bite-sized chunks of code, smart contracts are more amenable to

---

[2] It shares, in a sense, the permanent nature of algorithms implemented as hardware circuits. Hardware led the efforts for automated verification in the 90s due to the high cost of potential bugs.

verification than traditional systems which may run into millions of lines of code. This calls for better programming languages for smart contracts with stronger security and privacy guarantees, achieved either through improved underlying DLT platforms, the design of programming languages better suited for smart contract programming or through verification techniques for smart contracts.

In the track we have collected new results and discussions related to:

- Research on different languages for smart contracts including their expressivity and reasoning methods.
- Research on the use of formal methods for specifying, validating and verifying smart contracts.
- Surveys and state-of-knowledge about security and privacy issues related to smart contract technologies.
- New applications based on smart contracts.
- Description of challenges and research directions to future development for better smart contracts.

2   Summary of Selected Articles

In this section we briefly summarise the articles invited to the ISoLA'20[3] track on "Reliable Smart Contracts: State-of-the-art, Applications, Challenges and Future Directions"[4], appearing in this volume.

- **Functional Verification of Smart Contracts via Strong Data Integrity**, by Wolfgang Ahrendt and Richard Bubel, presents an invariant-based static analysis approach and tool implementation for Solidity smart contracts. The approach is based on theorem proving and symbolic execution and was built upon the tool KeY. Unlike much of the other work being carried out in static analysis for smart contracts, the approach presented by the authors focuses on the business logic, the expected functionality of the smart contract in question, although it also addresses standard problems, in particular reentrancy.
- **Bitcoin Covenants Unchained**, by Massimo Bartoletti, Stefano Lande and Roberto Zunino, proposes an extension of the Bitcoin script language with "covenants", a set of script operators used to constrain how funds can be used by the redeeming transactions. Covenants can be recursive, extending the expressiveness of Bitcoin contracts. A formal model for covenants is given to show the expressiveness of the extension. Finally, the paper discuss how covenants could be integrated in a high-level language, in particular it is hinted how this could be done in the BitML language.
- **Specifying Framing Conditions for Smart Contracts**, by Bernhard Beckert and Jonas Schiffl, proposes a formalism to enrich smart contract specifications with frame conditions in order to specify what a smart contract

---

[3] http://isola-conference.org/isola2020.
[4] http://www.cs.um.edu.mt/gordon.pace/Workshops/RSC2020.

function cannot (and will not) do. The approach is based on the concept of dynamic frames. It proposes languages for specifying frame conditions for both Ethereum and Hyperledger Fabric.

- **Making Tezos Smart Contracts More Reliable with Coq**, by Bruno Bernardo, Raphaël Cauderlier, Guillaume Claret, Arvid Jakobsson, Basile Pesin and Julien Tesson, presents the Mi-Cho-Coq framework, a Coq library defining formal semantics of Michelson (the Tezos language to write smart contracts) as well as an interpreter, a simple optimiser and a weakest-precondition calculus to reason about Michelson smart contracts. The paper also introduces Albert, an intermediate language with a compiler written in Coq that targets Mi-Cho-Coq, illustrating how Mi-Cho-Coq can be used as a compilation target to generate correct code.

- **UTxO- vs Account-Based Smart Contract Blockchain programming paradigms**, by Lars Brünjes and Murdoch J. Gabbay, formalises and proves desirable properties of Cardano, most importantly that the effects of a transaction do not depend on the other transactions in the same block. A formalisation of Ethereum is given and contrasted in terms of smart contract language paradigm—Solidity and Plutus, vulnerability to DDoS attacks and in terms of propensity to certain errors (e.g. due to the effect of Ethereum transactions can change depending on the behaviour of other transactions in the same block, but not in Cardano).

- **Native Custom Tokens in the Extended UTXO Model**, by Manuel M.T. Chakravarty, James Chapman, Kenneth MacKenzie, Orestis Melkonian, Jann Müller, Michael Peyton Jones, Polina Vinogradova and Philip Wadler, presents an extension of user-defined tokens UTXO (present in blockchains like Bitcoin) and how this exstension can be used to define some smart-contract behavior. Extended UTXO allow to encode, pass and validate arbitrary data across multiple transactions which is sophisticated enough to validate runs with so-called Constraint Emitting machines (Mealy machine with data).

- **UTXO$_{ma}$: UTXO with Multi-Asset Support**, by Manuel M.T. Chakravarty, James Chapman, Kenneth MacKenzie, Orestis Melkonian, Jann Müller, Michael Peyton Jones, Polina Vinogradova, Philip Wadler and Joachim Zahnentferner, explores a design for the creation of user-defined tokens based on UTXO ledgers. Unlike platforms such as Ethereum, which allow for the implementation of such tokens using general scripting capabilities which comes with well-known risks, the authors propose an extension to the UTXO model to manage an unbounded number of user-defined, native tokens using a simple domain-specific language with bounded computational expressiveness. They formalise the model and its semantics using the Agda proof assistant.

- **Towards Configurable and Efficient Runtime Verification of Blockchain based Smart Contracts at the Virtual Machine Level**, by Joshua Ellul, studies the problem of alleviating the overhead imposed by monitoring the execution of smart-contracts, using low-level (virtual machine) infrastructure. The paper presents modifications of the VM level that permit enabling and disabling state variable monitoring and syscall monitoring dynamically, and compares the different approaches empirically, in terms of the reduction in the monitoring overhead obtained.

– **Compiling Quantitative Type Theory to Michelson for Compile-Time Verification & Run-time Efficiency in Juvix**, by Christopher Goes, uses quantitative type theory (QTT)—a typed lambda calculus equipped with resources using dependent types—to construct a theoretical basis of the core language within Juvix. The paper illustrate how this basis can be used to efficiently compile Juvix into efficient Michelson code, the execution language of the Tezos Blockchain ecosystem.

– **Efficient Static Analysis of Marlowe Contracts**, by Pablo Lamela Seijas, David Smith and Simon Thompson, discusses the authors' experience in the implementation and optimisation of static analysis for the smart contract language Marlowe which is designed specifically for self-enforcing financial smart-contracts. In particular, the authors look at the use of SMT solvers for the verification of properties written in this language.

– **Accurate Smart Contract Verification through Direct Modelling**, by Matteo Marescotti, Rodrigo Otoni, Leonardo Alt, Patrick Eugster, Antti E. J. Hyvärinen and Natasha Sharygina, presents a formal analysis engine used in the Solidity compiler. The verification is performed using the logic of constrained Horn clauses. The approach, evaluated on a set of smart contracts deployed in the Ethereum platform, is able to prove correctness and discover bugs in number of such contracts.

– **Smart Derivatives: On-chain Forwards for Digital Assets** by Alfonso D.D.M. Rius and Eamonn Gashier, introduces a framework to facilitate the development of on-chain forwards (and futures), based on smart contracts. The paper builds upon, and extends, previous work by the authors on on-chain options. The paper makes a connection between computer smart contracts and "real world" (financial) contracts.

– **The Good, the Bad and the Ugly: Pitfalls and Best Practices in Automated Sound Static Analysis of Ethereum Smart Contracts**, by Clara Schneidewind, Markus Scherer and Matteo Maffei, focuses on static analysis of smart contracts, particularly for Ethereum. It discusses the challenges of providing sound verification techniques, highlighting unsoundness of existing tools through concrete examples. The paper then proceeds to give details about eThor, a tool developed by the authors, and outline its use for addressing the reentrancy problem.

References

1. Ethereum. https://www.ethereum.org
2. Hern, A.: $300 m in cryptocurrency accidentally lost forever due to bug. Appeared at The Guardian. https://www.theguardian.com/technology/2017/nov/08/cryptocurrency-300m-dollars-stolen-bug-ether. Accessed Nov 2017
3. Mix: Ethereum bug causes integer overflow in numerous erc20 smart contracts (update). Appeared at HardFork (2018). https://thenextweb.com/hardfork/2018/04/25/ethereum-smart-contract-integer-overflow/

4. Nakamoto, S.: Bitcoin: A Peer-to-Peer Electronic Cash System (2009). White Paper https://bitcoin.org/bitcoin.pdf
5. Qureshi, H.: A hacker stole \$31M of Ethereum – how it happened, and what it means for Ethereum. Appeared at FreeCodeCamp (2017). https://medium. freecodecamp.org/a-hacker-stole-31m-of-ether-how-it-happened-and-what-it-means-for-ethereum-9e5dc29e33ce
6. Szabo, N.: Smart contracts: building blocks for digital markets. Extropy (16) **18**(2) (1996)

Functional Verification of Smart Contracts via Strong Data Integrity

Wolfgang Ahrendt[1]($\boxtimes$) and Richard Bubel[2]($\boxtimes$)

[1] Chalmers Technical University, Gothenburg, Sweden
ahrendt@chalmers.se
[2] Technical University Darmstadt, Darmstadt, Germany
bubel@cs.tu-darmstadt.de

Abstract. We present an invariant-based specification and verification methodology that allows us to conveniently specify and verify strong data integrity properties for Solidity smart contracts. Our approach is able to reason precisely about arbitrary usage of the contracts, which may include re-entrance, a common security pitfall in smart contracts. We implemented the approach in a prototype verification tool, called SolidiKeY, and applied it successfully to a number of smart contracts.

1 Introduction

Distributed ledger technology (DLT) has been around since the incarnation of Bitcoin by Satoshi Nakamoto. The crucial idea was to publicly agree on, and irreversibly record, the content and order of transactions. The backbone of DLT is an immutable list data-structure called blockchain. The concept of *smart contracts* was coined by Nick Szabo prior to the rise of DLT. Their DLT incarnation, however, is based on the realisation that the blockchain concept can also store programs, as well as their runtime state in between transactional units of execution. These programs are called (smart) contracts because they are meant to form an agreement of procedure between all parties which choose to engage with them. The first, and still major, DLT framework which supports smart contracts was Ethereum [16], with its built-in cryptocurrency Ether. The virtual machine on which smart contracts are run is called Ethereum Virtual Machine (EVM). In Ethereum not only the users, but also the contracts themselves can receive, own, and send Ether. Sending Ether to a contract, and calling the contract, is the same thing in this framework. Sending funds to a contract without passing control to the receiver is not possible.

Ethereum miners look for transaction requests on the network. A transaction request contains the address of a contract to be called, the call data, and the amount of Ether to be sent. Miners are paid for their efforts with units of "gas", to be paid by the address which requested the transaction. Each EVM instruction has an assigned cost. If the execution runs out of gas, the currently executing transaction is aborted, discarded, and the state is reverted to before the start of the transaction (except for the depleted gas). Lack of gas is only one of numerous

T. Margaria and B. Steffen (Eds.): ISoLA 2020, LNCS 12478, pp. 9–24, 2020.
https://doi.org/10.1007/978-3-030-61467-6_2

causes for aborting and reverting a transaction. Others are attempts to send unbacked funds, or failing runtime checks.

Even if contracts can be written directly in EVM bytecode [16], there are several higher level languages that are compiled into EVM bytecode. The most popular one is Solidity [6], which has been inspired by C++, Python, and JavaScript.

One important difference between traditional programs and Ethereum smart contracts is that the latter do not only pass around information, but assets, in particular crypto funds. Many interesting, contract specific properties, on which users want to rely, depend on the flow of assets, and the interaction of the asset flow with the internal state of the contracts. In this work, we put the spotlight on the *relation between the flow of Ether and the data of the contract*.

We report on a methodology, logic, and calculus for Solidity source code verification. Invariants describe the expected relation between the Ether flow and the contract's data. These invariants should hold independent of usage scenarios (intended or malicious) and cover every behaviour. Our approach guarantees *strong data-integrity* properties, and supports full functional verification. The calculus keeps track of ingoing and outgoing payments, in order to prove that the payment-data-invariant is intact at critical points. The precise points, where such invariants have to hold, and where they can be assumed again, must fully reflect the subtleties of Solidity and the EVM. We must ensure that data integrity is independent of the (potentially hostile) environment.

A central feature, for specification and verification, will be easy access to the *financial net* (difference between incoming and outgoing funds) which the examined contract has with every address in its environment. We specify invariants and postconditions with help of the financial net, and verify them in a calculus which knows when and how to manipulate the net.

The methodology has been implemented in a prototype of what is going to become a fully fledged verification tool for smart contracts written in Solidity, called SolidiKeY. It is based on the state-of-the-art deductive verification system KeY [1]. We also report on the successful application of SolidiKeY on example contracts. Although the calculus does not yet cover Solidity fully, the methodology, and most aspects of the calculus, will remain valid for future developments of the approach and tool.

2   Background

2.1   Solidity

We cannot afford a proper introduction to Solidity. Many things become clear when discussing examples (Figs. 1 and 4). Here, we only mention a few concepts.

Solidity follows largely an object-oriented paradigm. The equivalent to object fields is called state variables, but we call them fields throughout this paper. External users and contract instances—think of the latter as objects—share the same type, address. (More precisely, contracts are convertible to address.) Each address owns Ether (possibly 0), can send Ether to other addresses, and receive Ether. The type address **payable** is like address, but with the additional members `transfer` and `send`, used for receiving Ether. For instance, `a.transfer` (v) transfers the amount of v Ether to a. Contracts can be called by every address (incl. contracts), receiving Ether along with the call. What is called method in object-orientation is called function in Solidity. Built-in data types include unsigned integer (`uint`), dynamic and fixed-size arrays, enums, structs, and mappings. Mappings associate keys with values. For instance, the declaration `mapping (address => uint) public balances` declares a field `balances` which contains a mapping from addresses to unsigned integers. Storing and lookup in mappings uses array-like syntax. The modifier `public` does *not* mean that the field is writable by anyone. Instead, it means that a public getter function for `balances[x]` is automatically provided. The current caller, and the amount of Ether sent with the call, are always available via `msg.sender` and `msg.value`, respectively. Only `payable` functions accept payments. `require(b)` and `assert(b)` check the boolean expression b, and abort (and revert) when b is false. Apart from how much gas is kept, behaviour is the same. However, what differs is the implication of a failure to program correctness. A failing `require(b)` is considered the caller's problem ("If you call me like that, there is nothing I can do for you."). In contrast, `assert(b)` is a claim of the contract's implementer that b will always be true at this point. Breaking such an assertion indicates a bug in the implementation. Solidity features programmable *modifiers*, offering some kind of delta-oriented programming. This will be explained in Sect. 5. Finally, in Solidity terminology, *storage* refers to the data stored in the fields of a contract, whereas *memory* refers to local variables and their values.

2.2 Dynamic Logic

To verify that programs adhere to their specification, we use *dynamic logic* (DL), a program logic which, like Hoare logic, expresses properties of programs, and the programs themselves, inside the same formula. We follow the tradition of the KeY approach and system [1], which targets object-oriented programs. KeY is a particular good fit as Solidity's contract-oriented approach shares many principles with object-orientation.

The calculus and the prototype of the verification system SolidiKeY do not yet cover full Solidity. Further features will be covered in future work. For now, we refer to our calculus as a 'calculus for Solidity Light' (see Sect. 4). Solidity Light features a simpler memory model (no distinction of storage and memory, reference semantics for all assignments to non-primitive types, like in Java), and unbounded integers. This allows us to focus, for now, on the main contribution of this paper, namely a general specification and verification methodology for smart contracts to ensure strong data integrity. The simpler memory model does not impact provability as long as we refrain from assignments to non-primitive typed fields as a whole. Solidity's bounded (round-robin) integers can be easily added in the future, following the lines of KeY's existing support for Java's round-robin integers. Both limitations will be addressed in future work.

Syntax. Dynamic logic (DL) for Solidity is an extension of first-order logic (FOL) by the box *modality* and by *updates*. Every FOL formula is a DL formula. The *box* modality $[\cdot_1]\cdot_2$ takes as first argument (a fragment of) a Solidity program, and as second argument another DL formula. The formula $[s]$post means: *if s terminates successfully* (i.e., s does not revert), then the property post holds in the reached final state. An important special case of DL formulas is the pattern pre $\rightarrow [s]$post, which in Hoare triple notation would be $\{$pre$\}s\{$post$\}$.

In order to enable symbolic execution as a proof principle, KeY style DLs are further extended with *updates*. An update $v_1 := t_1 \| \ldots \| v_n := t_n$ consists of a program variable $v_1, \ldots, v_n$ and a terms $t_1, \ldots, t_n$. (n can be 1.) Updates represent state changes and are essentially explicit substitutions. An update u can be applied to a formula ϕ, written $\{u\}\phi$, resulting again in a formula. Evaluating $\{v_1 := t_1 \| \ldots \| v_n := t_n\}\phi$ in a state s is equivalent to evaluating ϕ in a state s', where s' coincides with s except that each v_i is mapped to the value of t_i. (Different occurrences of identical v_i, v_j are resolved by "right-win".)

Example 1. Let x,y, and z be program variables. The meaning of the DL formula $x \leq y \rightarrow [\text{t=x;x=y;y=z;}]y \leq x$ is that if the three assignments are executed in a state where $x \leq y$, then $y \leq x$ holds after the execution. Turning the first assignment into an update, we get the formula $x \leq y \rightarrow \{$t := x$\}[$x=y;y=z;$]y \leq x$. After processing the other two assignments in the same way, we get the formula $x \leq y \rightarrow \{$t := x$\}\{$x := y$\}\{$y := z$\}y \leq x$. Applying the updates to each other, composing the substitutions, we get $x \leq y \rightarrow \{$t := x$\|$x := y$\|$y := x$\}y \leq x$. Applying the (now single) update, as a substitution, to the postcondition, results in $x \leq y \rightarrow x \leq y$, which is trivially true.

Calculus. To reason about the validity of formulas, we use a *sequent calculus*. A *sequent* $\phi_1, \ldots, \phi_n \implies \psi_1, \ldots, \psi_m$ consists of two sets of formulas called antecedent ($\phi_1, \ldots, \phi_n$) and succedent ($\psi_1, \ldots, \psi_m$). Its meaning is equivalent to the formula $\bigwedge_{i=1..n} \phi_i \rightarrow \bigvee_{i=1..m} \psi_i$. Calculus rules are denoted as rule schemata

$$\text{name} \ \frac{\overbrace{\Gamma_1 \implies \Delta_1 \quad \ldots \quad \Gamma_n \implies \Delta_n}^{premises}}{\underbrace{\Gamma \implies \Delta}_{conclusion}}$$

where $\Gamma, \Delta, \Gamma_i, \Delta_i$ with $i = 1..n$ are schemavariables denoting sets of formulas.

A proof is a tree whose nodes are labelled with sequents. For each inner node there is a rule r such that its conclusion matches the node's sequent and the node's children are labelled with the instantiated premises of r. Applying a rule with no premises closes the branch. A proof is closed if all branches are closed. Our calculus design follows the symbolic execution paradigm. The rules realise a symbolic interpreter by step-wise rewriting the first statement of a program into a sequence of simpler statements until an *atomic* statement is reached, which is then translated into logic possibly using updates and proof branching.

We illustrate this approach with the following two sequent rules:

ifThenElse
$$\frac{\Gamma, \{u\}(b = \text{true}) \implies \{u\}[s1; \omega]\phi, \Delta \qquad \Gamma, \{u\}(b = \text{false}) \implies \{u\}[s2; \omega]\phi, \Delta}{\Gamma \implies \{u\}[\text{if } (b) \,\{\, s1; \,\}\,\text{else}\,\{\, s2; \,\}\, \omega]\phi, \Delta}$$

assign
$$\frac{\Gamma \implies \{u\}\{v := se\}[\omega]\phi, \Delta}{\Gamma \implies \{u\}[v = se; \omega]\phi, \Delta}$$

Schemavariable ω matches the remainder of the program, schemavariable u matches the leading update, b, v match program variables, and se matches on simple expressions without side-effects. In the above rules, u represents the condensed effect of symbolically executing the program up to now, and the next statement to be symbolically executed is the if-statement, or assignment, respectively.

Storage Modelling. Solidity Light distinguishes between storage, which consists of the fields and their values, and local variables. Unlike Solidity, it uses reference semantics for all assignments. This does not affect the paper's main contribution for which the storage details are orthogonal. We model the storage as data structure of type **Storage** axiomatised as an algebra of arrays. If a program accesses a field, symbolic execution reads from, or writes to, the data structure referred to by the global program variable **storage**.

3   Verifying Strong Data Integrity of Smart Contracts

Consider the Solidity contract **Auction** given in Fig. 1, realising an auction dealing with, and remembering, multiple bidders and their bids. The implementation choices (including the violation of some best practices) serve the upcoming discussion. The contract can be used by anyone to place or increase a bid with the same function. Bidders can also withdraw their (accumulated) bid at any time. The auction owner can close the auction, in which case the highest bid is sent to the owner, and all bidders, except the highest bidder, are reimbursed.

The implementation of **Auction** is centred around the field **balances**, a mapping from addresses to (unsigned) integer. **balances** *is meant to store the accumulated funds sent by each bidder, minus anything that has been sent back.* This property, let us call it I, is what the implementer aimed to keep intact, by increasing or decreasing **balances[x]** whenever funds flow from or to x, respectively. Also, the users' expectations on the contract are based on I. For instance, the bidder's expectation to get back all the investments when **withdrawing** (see line 27) is based on the understanding that I is kept intact throughout the lifetime of the contract. The same holds for the expectation of the auction owner to receive the investments of the winner, and all (non-winning) bidders' expectation of getting back their investments in **closeAuction** (see lines 35, 39).

It is the fulfilment of such expectations which we call *functional correctness* of a contract. In turn, functional correctness depends on keeping properties, such as I in our example, intact. Such properties form a relation between internal

```
 1 contract Auction {
 2 address payable private auctionOwner;
 3 mapping (address => uint) public balances;
 4 mapping (address => bool) private bidded;
 5
 6 uint numberOfBidders;
 7 address payable [100] public bidders;
 8
 9 constructor() public
10 { auctionOwner = msg.sender; }
11
12 function placeOrIncreaseBid()
13 public payable {
14   balances[msg.sender] =
15   balances[msg.sender] + msg.value;
16   // If caller didn't bid yet,
17   // add her to bidders
18   if (!bidded[msg.sender]) {
19     bidders[numberOfBidders] = msg.sender;
20     numberOfBidders = numberOfBidders + 1;
21     bidded[msg.sender] = true;
22   }
23 }
```

```
24 function withdraw() public {
25 // A bidder can withdraw all her money
26 require(bidded[msg.sender]);
27 msg.sender.transfer(balances[msg.sender]);
28 balances[msg.sender] = 0;
29 }
30
31 function closeAuction() public {
32 // Determine highestBid and winner
33 ...
34 // Transfer the money to the auction owner
35 auctionOwner.transfer(highestBid);
36 balances[winner] = 0;
37 // Reimburse everyone else
38 for(i = 0; i < numberOfBidders; i = i + 1) {
39   bidders[i].transfer(balances[bidders[i]]);
40   balances[bidders[i]] = 0;
41 }
42 }
43 }
```

Fig. 1. Contract auction

data (fields) and the history of payments. This paper is mostly concerned with proving that these relations between data and history are invariants. This means that they are established at program points where control is potentially passed to another contract (and reentrance may occur). This allows us to safely assume the validity of these relations once control is regained. In other words, we prove that no usage of the contract can break these relations no matter if by a simple programming error or an attack. The invariance of such properties is what we call *strong data integrity*. And we call the properties themselves *invariants*.

Let us look closer at the informal invariant I: "balances *stores for each bidder the accumulated funds sent by the bidder, minus anything that has been sent back*." As a step towards formalising this invariant, we could express I as:

$$\forall a \in \text{address.}$$
$$\text{balances}[a] = \sum \{\text{msg.value} \mid \text{msg.sender} = a\} - \sum \{v \mid a.\text{transfer}(v)\} \quad (1)$$

Note that we are not really using a formal language here, just mathematical notation to convey the meaning of I a bit more precise than in natural language. Formula (1) says that, for all addresses a, the value stored in the map balances, under key a, corresponds to the difference of two sums. The first sum adds up all payments sent by a up to now, in the history of this contract's existence. The second sum adds up all values that have been sent to a, via transfer, up to now. The difference between the two is what is supposed to be stored in balances[a]. This holds even for addresses which did not bid (yet), as maps with integer value type are implicitly initialised to value 0. However, (1) does not actually hold for the winner or auction owner after closing the auction. We will come back to that.

As we said before, the functional correctness of the contract relies on I being an invariant of the contract. To verify this, with a verification tool, we need a language to specify such properties, and to reason about them in a suitable logic and calculus. One could base such a language on concepts which are present in (1), however being more explicit and precise. Such a language would have as a datatype the history of call (i.e., payment) events. Also, it would allow to project out specific call events, like in the set comprehension in (1), select values of interest, and feed them to a computation, like the summations in (1). This can be done, and has been done in the compositional verification of functional properties of distributed programs (see, e.g., [3,7]). Unfortunately, the experience with compositional deductive verification approaches where the call history is an explicit piece of data shows that specifications tend to get complex, and verification meets challenges concerning efficiency and usability.

While information about past (in- and out-going) calls is essential, we believe that the full power of the call/payment history will typically not be necessary to formulate and verify strong data integrity, and with that, the implied functional properties. It can suffice to reason about the financial *net*, i.e., the difference between in- and out-going payments, which a contract has with any other address. For that, our logic uses the built-in mapping $\mathtt{net}$: address $\rightarrow \mathbb{Z}$ to keep track of the money flow between this contract and other addresses, with

$$\mathtt{net}(a) = \text{money received from } a - \text{money sent to } a$$

With the help of the $\mathtt{net}$ mapping, property (1) becomes simply:

$$\forall a \in \text{address. } \mathtt{balances}[a] = \mathtt{net}(a) \tag{2}$$

Now that we can express formulas more concisely, let us get the data integrity property of $\mathtt{Auction}$ more precise. As indicated earlier, the above invariant does not always hold for the highest bidder hb, neither for the auction owner. We refine the invariant (2) accordingly, exploiting again the power of the $\mathtt{net}$ mapping:

$$\exists hb \in \text{address. } \forall a \in \text{address. } \mathtt{balances}[hb] \geq \mathtt{balances}[a]$$
$$\wedge \; (\; a \neq hb \wedge a \neq \mathtt{auctionOwner} \rightarrow \mathtt{balances}[a] = \mathtt{net}(a) \;) \tag{3}$$
$$\wedge \; \mathtt{balances}[hb] = \mathtt{net}(hb) + \mathtt{net}(\mathtt{auctionOwner})$$

The last line captures different situations at once. All the way until closing the auction, $\mathtt{net}(\mathtt{auctionOwner})$ is 0, and $\mathtt{balances}[hb] = \mathtt{net}(hb)$, just like for other bidders. After closing the auction, $\mathtt{net}(\mathtt{auctionOwner})$ is $-\mathtt{net}(hb)$, as the investment of the highest bidder were sent to the owner, and $\mathtt{balances}[hb]$ is 0.

For a given contract, once we capture the specific notion of data integrity in a formula I, how can we verify that I indeed *is* an invariant of the contract? Where does an invariant need to hold? Obviously, such invariants do not need to hold at each point in time. For instance, consider a situation where $\mathtt{placeOrIncreaseBid()}$ has just been called, the payment has been received, and the program counter is at line 15 (Fig. 1), i.e., the assignment has not been executed yet. At this point, the invariant is not intact. The relation between payments and the contract data is out of sync, but that is all right, because it is repaired (by executing line 15) before control is given away again.

A verification methodology needs to make sure that the invariant of contract C holds whenever control is *outside* C, like after C has been created, and before and after each transition executing C, but also during a transition while some other contract executes. We visualise the invariant verification discipline in Fig. 2. It shows schematically the code of a function f (of the contract C we want to verify). f contains two calls to other contracts, $c1.f1()$ and $c2.f2()$. We assume the invariant I to hold *before* f is called and funds are passed to C. After the funds were passed, I may be broken, which is fine as long as we show that I is intact again when $c1$ gains control, *after* funds were passed to $c1$. (If instead we showed I before funds were passed, I would not be intact once $c1$ gains control.) We assume I when $c1.f1()$ returns, and have to show I once funds were passed to $c2$, and assume it again when $c2.f2()$ returns. Finally, we have to show that I holds at the end of f. If we follow such a principle for all **public/external** functions of C (and in

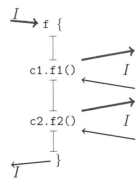

Fig. 2. Assuming and proving invariant I

addition show that the **constructor** establishes I), we have proven that I is intact whenever control is outside C, in particular after each transaction on C. Note that this reasoning also covers the case where, in the above example, $c1.f1()$ calls back into any function of C. In fact, the proof principle does not rely on any particular ordering of code snippets (between gaining and releasing control). Hence, verified invariants, and implied functional properties, cannot be compromised by re-entrancy.

It is important to note that $a.transfer(v)$ is a *call* (of a special kind) to a. Therefore, invariants also need to be shown when executing $a.transfer(v)$ (but after v has been passed, see above). We discuss a possible weakening later on.

So can we verify the invariance of property (3) in **Auction** with this discipline? The answer is no. Let us assume (3) holds when **withdraw** is called (line 24). Thereby, **balances**[msg.sender] = **net**(msg.sender) holds before executing line 27. But when executing line 27, in between sending money to **msg.sender** and the return of **transfer**, the **net**(msg.sender) is 0, whereas **balances**[msg.sender] is unchanged, which breaks the invariant (3). If for instance **msg.sender**, before returning from **transfer**, calls back into **Auction**, the assumption, intuitive or formal, that contract data and payments are in sync at the beginning of each function has become a harmful illusion. **Auction** does not feature strong data integrity! This can be repaired, by updating **balances**[a] *before* sending funds to a. With that, (3) can be shown correct after the passing of funds, and our verification discipline guarantees data integrity for **Auction**.

Note that only successful, non-reverting code execution needs to maintain the invariant of a contract. The reason is that reverting executions (with for instance unbacked payments, or failing **requires**) are discarded, and the state is reset to before the failing transaction, where we can assume the invariant again.

4 A Calculus for Solidity Light

4.1 From Specification to Proof-Obligation

To verify that a contract satisfies its specification, we construct, for each function, a dynamic logic formula (called *proof obligation*) from the function and the specification. If all functions (plus the constructor) of a contract have been verified, then the contract as a whole adheres to its specification. In the current SolidiKeY prototype, however, specifications are manually translated to proof obligations in Solidity dynamic logic. (In a mature verification system, specifications will be automatically translated to proof obligations.)

```
1 contract C {
2   //@ invariant I;
3
4   T field₁;
5   ...
6   T fieldₙ;
7
8   /*@ requires
9     @   pre
10    @ after_success
11    @   post
12    @*/
13  function f(T args)
14           modifiers { body }
15 }
```

Fig. 3. Contract w/ specification

In order to explain how the proof obligation is constructed, consider a contract C, annotated with specification, as shown in Fig. 3. The annotated contract specifies a *contract invariant* I, as well as *function specifications* for functions, here f. The function specification states that if f is called in a state satisfying precondition *pre*, and in which I holds (for the storage and payment history of this contract object), then the execution of f, if successful, guarantees that postcondition *post* and invariant I are satisfied in the post-state.

The contract's semantics can now be expressed by instantiating the proof obligation schemata (4) with the concrete specification:

$$\texttt{msg.value} \geq 0 \ \wedge \ I \ \wedge \ pre \ \rightarrow$$
$$\{\texttt{old} := \texttt{storage}\}\{\texttt{net}(\texttt{msg.sender}) := \texttt{net}(\texttt{msg.sender}) + \texttt{msg.value})\}$$
$$[\texttt{result} = f(\texttt{msg}, \overline{args})@C\,;](I \wedge post) \qquad (4)$$

The variable `old` saves the storage before the function is called and can be used in the postcondition to refer to values of fields (incl. arrays, structs, and mappings) in the pre-state. This allows us for instance to express that the value of a field got increased by some value. Each function has an additional argument `msg` used to pass the address of the caller and the amount of passed Ether. The update on `storage` reflects that the net of the callee changes due to the payment which comes with the call. As explained in Sect. 3 the invariant is assumed before the transfer of the Ether. In case of a non-payable function f, the proof obligation is strengthened by changing `msg.value` ≥ 0 to `msg.value` $= 0$.

4.2 Symbolic Execution Rules for Contract Execution

To prove the formula valid, we use a sequent calculus as outlined in Sect. 2.2. Here, we focus on the symbolic execution rules for Solidity, highlighting where the specific pitfalls lie when the underlying virtual machine is blockchain based. Symbolic execution of a function consists of:

1. left-to-right evaluation of the function arguments,
2. symbolic execution of the function implementation.

As for built-in "functions" (e.g., `assert` and `require`), their meaning is reflected by providing specific rules in the calculus.

Left-to-right evaluation of the function call arguments is realised by rule unfoldArgument. The rule rewrites a function call with complex arguments into a sequence of statements. For each argument a new local variable of compatible type is introduced and initialised with the corresponding argument expression. The assignment order ensures the correct evaluation order of the arguments. The arguments in the method call are replaced by the fresh variables:

$$\text{unfoldArgument} \quad \frac{\Gamma \Longrightarrow \{u\}[T\ x;\ x = e;\ m(x);\ \omega]\phi, \Delta}{\Gamma \Longrightarrow \{u\}[m(e);\ \omega]\phi, \Delta} \quad e \text{ complex}$$

Built-in functions `require` *and* `assert`. Both built-in functions `require` and `assert` check whether the Boolean expression given as argument evaluates to true, and abort if otherwise, with the state being reverted.

Although their operational semantics is identical (except for gas handling), their pragmatics differ in the sense that `require` is used as a kind of refusal to execute a certain call unless the caller made sure that a certain condition holds. Failing `require`s are not considered harmful, and nothing is wrong with the inspected code. (If there is any blame, than it is on the callers side.) In contrast, `assert` is used as a claim that a certain property always holds at a specific code position. Failing `assert`s manifest an error in the inspected code base, and our calculus treats it accordingly. Here comes the rule for `require`:

$$\text{require} \quad \frac{\Gamma, \{u\}\texttt{b} = \text{true} \Longrightarrow [\omega]\phi, \Delta}{\Gamma \Longrightarrow \{u\}[\texttt{require(b)};\ \omega]\phi, \Delta} \quad \texttt{b} \text{ simple}$$

Turning `b` into an assumption is sound as we are only examining successful transactions (partial correctness), and thus a reverted transaction is trivially correct. In particular, a reverted transaction maintains every invariant, because it is undone and has no effect (other than gas consumption, which we do not talk about in the invariants). This observation is important for the overall invariant verification discipline, and carries over to other statements which may possibly lead to reverting a transaction, like the attempt to send unbacked funds with `transfer`, see below.

In contrast the rule for `assert`

$$\text{assert} \quad \frac{\Gamma \Longrightarrow \{u\}\texttt{b} = \text{true}, \Delta \qquad \Gamma, \{u\}\texttt{b} = \text{true} \Longrightarrow [\omega]\phi, \Delta}{\Gamma \Longrightarrow \{u\}[\texttt{assert(b)};\ \omega]\phi, \Delta} \quad \texttt{b} \text{ simple}$$

splits the proof, and demands proving that `b` is true in the current symbolic state, while continuing symbolic execution on the second branch under the (then justified) assumption that `b` is true. This semantics prevents us from closing a proof if an assertion does not hold, thereby detecting further programming errors.

Function Calls Transferring Ether. Transfer of resources, for instance cryptocurrencies (here: Ether), is central to most distributed ledger frameworks. In Solidity, Ether is transferred to a contract by calling one of its `payable` functions. Any function declared in a contract can be marked `payable` by using the eponymous modifier. Calling these functions is usually done using the `call` statement, with the syntax `c.call{value: v}(data)`, where c specifies the contract to which to send the amount v of Ether by calling the payable function whose signature as well as the passed arguments are provided in `data`.[1]

The predefined payable functions `transfer` and `send` that can be called in a more readable manner `c.transfer(v)` or `b = c.send(v)`. For sake of simplicity, we give the calculus rules for function calls along these functions.

The calculus rule for symbolically executing the `transfer` function is

$$\text{transfer (w/ callback)} \quad \frac{\Gamma, c \neq \text{this} \Longrightarrow \{u\}\{\text{net}(c) := \text{net}(c) - v\}I, \Delta \qquad \Gamma, c \neq \text{this} \Longrightarrow \{u\}\{\text{havoc}(\text{storage})\}(I \to [\omega]\phi), \Delta}{\Gamma, c \neq \text{this} \Longrightarrow \{u\}[c.\text{transfer}(v);\ \omega]\phi, \Delta}$$

which splits the proof into two branches. The first branch establishes that invariant I of the calling contract `this` holds, before we actually execute the call, but after transferring the Ether, which is represented by updating the `net`-value of the target contract c. Establishing the invariant ensures that the calling contract `this` is in a consistent state when control is handed over to the called contract, and thus behaves well even in case of a callback by c may occur. The transfer of Ether is guaranteed by the EVM and happens before control is passed. The second branch continues symbolic execution after the calling contract regains control. Upon resuming control, we can assume that the contract's invariant holds, but we have to eliminate all knowledge about the whole storage, as nothing can be assumed about the actions of the called contract c before `transfer` returns. This elimination is achieved by performing a havoc operation using an update (for details how to construct such updates, see [1, Chap. 3.7.1]).

Remark 1. To prevent certain callbacks, which often lead to security holes, the current release of the Ethereum platform limits the amount of gas passed when calling `transfer`, such that the receiver is not provided with enough gas to call back. Under this assumption, the rule simplifies to

transfer (w/o callback)
$$\frac{\Gamma, c \neq \text{this} \Longrightarrow \{u\}\{\text{net}(c) := \text{net}(c) - v\}\{\text{havoc}(c)\}[\omega]\phi, \Delta}{\Gamma, c \neq \text{this} \Longrightarrow \{u\}[c.\text{transfer}(v);\ \omega]\phi, \Delta}$$

As no callbacks can happen, we do not have to ensure that the invariant of `this` holds when passing control. Hence, the rule has only one premise on which symbolic execution continued directly after `transfer` returns. The only visible effect is that the `net`-value of the called contract c has been updated accordingly.

---

[1] If the external called contract is defined in the same file, or an imported file, one can also invoke a payable function via `c.f{value:v}(args)`, but that is rarely the case.

```
 1 contract OneAuction {
 2 /*@ invariant
 3  @    address(this) != owner,
 4  @    address(this) != bidder,
 5  @    bid == net(bidder)+net(owner),
 6  @    (\forall address a;
 7  @     (a != owner && a != bidder
 8  @      && a != address(this))
 9  @                ==> net(a) == 0),
10  @    net(owner) <= 0,
11  @    mode==Open ==> net(owner) == 0;
12  @*/
13 // Handling mode of the auction
14 enum AuctionMode {NeverStarted, Open, Closed}
15 // Handling auction information
16 AuctionMode mode;
17 address payable owner;
18 address payable bidder;
19 uint bid;
20
21 // Modifier to check mode
22 modifier inMode(AuctionMode m) {
23  require (mode == m);
24  _;
25 }
```

```
26 modifier notBy(address c) {
27  require (msg.sender != c);
28  _;
29 }
30 ...
31 /*@ requires msg.sender != address(this);
32  @ after_success
33  @   bid > \old(bid),
34  @   net(bidder) == msg.value,
35  @   \old(bidder) != msg.sender ==>
36  @              net(\old(bidder)) == 0;
37  @*/
38 function makeBid() public payable
39  inMode(AuctionMode.Open)
40  notBy(owner) {
41    require (msg.value > bid);
42    // Transfer the old bid
43    // to the old bidder
44    uint tmp = bid;
45    bid = 0;
46    bidder.transfer(tmp);
47    // Set the new bid
48    bid = msg.value;
49    bidder = msg.sender;
50  }
51 }
```

Fig. 4. Contract OneAuction

Because the invocation of `transfer` on c did not receive enough gas for external calls, we only need to eliminate the knowledge about the state of c. However, we can maintain all other information about the storage, in particular about the value of the fields of `this`. Nevertheless, the problem with callbacks persists as function calls via `call` can still receive enough gas which permit callbacks.

5 Tool and Experiments

We implemented our approach as a prototype, called SolidiKeY, based on the KeY tool [1]. The user can choose between two variants of the calculus, one where `transfer` allows callbacks and one where it does not. Translating the specification into a proof-obligation is not yet automatic and has to be done manually.

We performed several experiments, to get first insights into the practical usage of our approach. We discuss one example in more detail, and give some statistical information for other examples. SolidiKeY and the examples are available at https://www.key-project.org/isola2020-smart/. Figure 4 shows a simple contract implementing the business logic for an auction that can be used to sell a single item. The contract can be in one of three states (lines 14–16). It keeps track of the **owner** selling the item, and the **bidder** who gave the highest **bid** so far.

The invariant states that the contract itself can never own itself or be the highest bidder. Further, it states that the sum of what has been payed into the contract by the highest bidder and what has been payed out to the contract's owner equals **bid**. As long as the auction is open, the equation holds because nothing has been payed out (`net(owner)==0`). Once the auction is closed, the contract transfers the bid to the owner and sets `bid` to zero, thus re-establishing the equality. Last not least, the financial net of the contract to everyone else except for the owner and the *current* highest bidder is zero, always.

The modifiers `inMode()` and `notBy()` (lines 22–29) implement checks whether the contract is in a given mode or the caller of a method is not identical to a given address, respectively. The placeholder statement `_;` is original Solidity syntax, and refers to the body of the function to which the modifier is attached. For example, function `makeBid()` has both modifiers and their effect is the same as when inserting the two statements `require(mode==AuctionMode.Open); require(msg.sender!=owner);` at the beginning of the function body.

Function `makeBid()` is called if someone wants to place a bid. Its precondition together with the modifiers and require-check state that placing a bid is only successful if the auction is open, the bid is neither from the contract itself nor from the owner and it is higher than the previously highest bid. In that case the function shall guarantee that, after successful termination, the field `bid` has been updated to the higher bid, the caller is the new highest `bidder`, the amount of money we owe to the caller is exactly the new bid, and that we have a financial net of 0 with the previous highest bidder (unless she overbidded herself).

If `transfer()` allows callbacks, then method `makeBid()` cannot be proven correct. Neither the invariant is guaranteed to be preserved, nor the postcondition can be proven. For instance, when calling transfer to return the money to the former highest bidder, the former bidder could callback to place a higher bid. Then, once the original call resumes, that bid is overwritten. Hence, the former bidder will not get her money back. In the variant

```
function makeBid() ... {
  require (msg.value > bid);
  uint oldBid = bid;
  uint oldBidder = bidder;
  bid = msg.value;
  bidder = msg.sender;
  oldBidder.transfer(oldBid);
}
```

Fig. 5. Fixed `makeBid()`

where function `transfer()` cannot call back, the function specification (incl. the invariant) can be proven. Rewriting the function `makeBid()` as shown in Fig. 5, where the call to `transfer()` is the last statement, fixes the problem.

Table 1 lists several of our verification experiments (auction-last is the fixed version of the above example). All proofs were done fully automatically. Proofs that could not be closed did point to a problem in the contract.

6   Related Work

We discuss some approaches to the analysis and verification of smart contracts.

In [10], an executable, SOS-style semantics of EVM byte code is defined in the framework K, which also generates a program verifier. The specifications and proofs are quite low level, talking about byte code, and about the artefacts of the SOS formalisation. There is ongoing work about a K semantics for Solidity.

In [4] the authors present a calculus for TINYSOL, a Solidity-like but much reduced language. They give a formal big-step style operational semantics that allows one to study the intricacies of Solidity semantics concerning external function calls (and hence, re-entrance) and transfer of currency. In contrast to

Table 1. Verification Results

Name	Method	Invariant verified		Postcondition verified	
		w/	w/o	w/	w/o
auction-last	transfer	✓	✓	✗	✓
auction	transfer	✗	✓	✗	✓
auction-wd	makeBid	✓	✓	✓	✓
auction-wd	withdraw	✓	✓	✗	✓
escrow	placeInEscrow	✓	✓	✓	✓
escrow	withdrawFrom	✗	✓	✗	✓
piggyBank	addMoney	✓	✓	✓	✓
piggyBank	break	✓	✓	✗	✓

✓: Proof closed, ✗: Proof open   w/: transfer with callbacks, w/o: transfer without callbacks

Verification times:
(1) w/ callbacks (median/avg/min/max): 807 ms/1623 ms/272 ms/8450 ms
(2) wo callbacks (median/avg/min/max): 646 ms/1179 ms/278 ms/3593 ms
All experiments performed on macOS with an 8-core Intel i9, 2.3 GHz & warm Open-JDK 14.0.1 VM

us, they do not target verification of contracts and do not provide a program logic to explicitly specify a property about a contract to be proven.

Linters like SOLCHECK (https://git.io/fxXeu), SOLIUM (https://git.io/fxXe) and others are lightweight static-analysis tools that check mainly for the occurrence of vulnerability patterns and are used to find 'smells', which may indicate bugs. They are not able to check functional correctness properties.

OYENTE [12], MAYAN [14], MANTICORE [13], and SLITHER [8] are symbolic execution based static analysis tools, of which some are able to check for user-specified properties. They aim to support bug finding and are in contrast to us not compositional, less expressive and bound in the symbolic execution depth. In contrast, our approach is compositional, allowing verification independent of the behaviour of external contracts.

VERX [15] is an automatic CEGAR-based verifier for Solidity contracts. They use an LTL-style specification language and their invariants must hold throughout the function execution, while ours can be invalidated in between and only must be established at certain points. For re-entrance safety they rely on checking effective external callback freedom for a given bundle. This check requires that all external contracts are known a priori.

VERISOL [11] and SOLC [9] are verification tools for Solidity both based on Boogie. Like us, these works perform deductive verification of Solidity source code, however without our focus on the payment history.

In [5] the authors extend KeY [1] to support verification of Hyperledger Fabric contracts written in Java. They focus on modelling Hyperledger's storage of objects, which is a database of serialized objects. Unlike Etherem, Hyperledger does not have a built-in payment mechanism.

JAVADITY [2] which we co-authored, translates Solidity contracts into Java programs that can be specified with JML and verified with out-of-the-shelf verification systems like KeY. While the approach worked in principle, the translation overhead significantly impacted automation, and partly motivated verification that reasons directly about Solidity source code in the current work.

To our understanding, none of the above approaches provides built-in support to reason about the history of money flow. For some of them this may still be possible by manually inserting ghost annotations, which however can be prone to errors.

7   Conclusion

The smart contract domain makes up a challenging combination of different architectural principles. On the one hand, the software ecosystem is very open and highly decentralised, with different parts of the code base written by parties with potentially conflicting interests. On the other hand, the execution of the contracts remains entirely sequential, even if multiple contracts, following different goals, are involved. For the functional verification of smart contracts, it is therefore natural to use concepts which are based on principles used in both worlds: functional verification of distributed programs (e.g., [3,7]), and functional verification of sequential programs (e.g., KeY [1]). From the distributed world, we use the theme that the history of communication (in our domain, the history of payments) is a central vehicle for compositional, functional verification. At the same time, many lessons from sequential modular deductive program verification carry over to smart contracts. Two distinguished challenges are re-entrance and transfer of resources. We presented an approach that tackles both. By keeping book of the net transfer of Ether between two contracts, it is possible to elegantly specify strong data properties. By using local invariants, we keep the reasoning process modular and maintain data integrity even when calling unknown external contracts, taking into account arbitrary behaviour of the environment.

We implemented the approach in a prototype tool, SolidiKeY, and performed successful experiments to evaluate the practicality of our approach. Note that the successful proofs show more than the absence of—harmful—re-entrance attacks. They verify the invariance of contract specific relations between payment and data, which other properties, like postconditions, rely on.

More research is to be done to get a better coverage and usability, higher expressivity, and general accessibility, of formal methods for smart contracts.

Acknowledgements. We thank Gordon Pace for many fruitful discussions about Solidity verification, and for providing us with Solidity contracts on which we based our experiments. We want to highlight that we have deliberately introduced problems into these examples that were not present in Gordon's contracts.

References

1. Ahrendt, W., Beckert, B., Bubel, R., Hähnle, R., Schmitt, P.H., Ulbrich, M. (eds.): Deductive Software Verification - The KeY Book - From Theory to Practice. LNCS, vol. 10001. Springer, Heidelberg (2016). https://doi.org/10.1007/978-3-319-49812-6

2. Ahrendt, W., et al.: Verification of smart contract business logic. In: Hojjat, H., Massink, M. (eds.) FSEN 2019. LNCS, vol. 11761, pp. 228–243. Springer, Cham (2019). https://doi.org/10.1007/978-3-030-31517-7_16

3. Ahrendt, W., Dylla, M.: A system for compositional verification of asynchronous objects. Sci. Comput. Program. **77**(12), 1289–1309 (2012)

4. Bartoletti, M., Galletta, L., Murgia, M.: A minimal core calculus for solidity contracts. In: Pérez-Solà, C., Navarro-Arribas, G., Biryukov, A., Garcia-Alfaro, J. (eds.) DPM/CBT -2019. LNCS, vol. 11737, pp. 233–243. Springer, Cham (2019). https://doi.org/10.1007/978-3-030-31500-9_15

5. Beckert, B., Schiffl, J., Ulbrich, M.: Smart contracts: application scenarios for deductive program verification. In: Sekerinski, E., et al. (eds.) FM 2019. LNCS, vol. 12232, pp. 293–298. Springer, Cham (2020). https://doi.org/10.1007/978-3-030-54994-7_21

6. Chittoda, J.: Mastering Blockchain Programming with Solidity. Packt (2019)

7. Din, C.C., Owe, O.: A sound and complete reasoning system for asynchronous communication with shared futures. J. Logical Algebraic Methods Program. **83**(5), 360–383 (2014)

8. Feist, J., Grieco, G., Groce, A.: Slither: A static analysis framework for smart contracts. In: Proceedings of the 2nd International Workshop on Emerging Trends in Software Engineering for Blockchain, WETSEB@ICSE 2019, pp. 8–15. IEEE/ACM (2019)

9. Hajdu, Á., Jovanović, D.: SOLC-VERIFY: a modular verifier for solidity smart contracts. In: Chakraborty, S., Navas, J.A. (eds.) VSTTE 2019. LNCS, vol. 12031, pp. 161–179. Springer, Cham (2020). https://doi.org/10.1007/978-3-030-41600-3_11

10. Hildenbrandt, E., et al.: KEVM: a complete semantics of the Ethereum virtual machine. In: 2018 IEEE 31st Computer Security Foundations Symposium. IEEE (2018)

11. Lahiri, S.K., Chen, S., Wang, Y., Dillig, I.: Formal specification and verification of smart contracts for Azure blockchain. CoRR abs/1812.08829 (2018)

12. Luu, L., Chu, D., Olickel, H., Saxena, P., Hobor, A.: Making smart contracts smarter. In: Weippl, E.R., Katzenbeisser, S., Kruegel, C., Myers, A.C., Halevi, S. (eds.) Proceedings of of the 2016 ACM SIGSAC Conference on Computer and Communications Security, pp. 254–269. ACM (2016)

13. Mossberg, M., et al.: Manticore: a user-friendly symbolic execution framework for binaries and smart contracts. In: 34th IEEE/ACM International Conference on Automated Software Engineering, ASE 2019, pp. 1186–1189. IEEE (2019)

14. Nikolic, I., Kolluri, A., Sergey, I., Saxena, P., Hobor, A.: Finding the greedy, prodigal, and suicidal contracts at scale. In: Proceedings of the 34th Annual Computer Security Applications Conference, ACSAC 2018, pp. 653–663. ACM (2018)

15. Permenev, A., Dimitrov, D., Tsankov, P., Drachsler-Cohen, D., Vechev, M.: VerX: safety verification of smart contracts. In: 2020 IEEE Symposium on Security and Privacy (SP), pp. 414–430. IEEE (2020)

16. Wood, G.: Ethereum: a secure decentralised generalised transaction ledger. Ethereum Proj. Yellow Pap. **151**, 1–32 (2014)

Bitcoin Covenants Unchained

Massimo Bartoletti[1(✉)], Stefano Lande[1(✉)], and Roberto Zunino[2(✉)]

[1] Università degli Studi di Cagliari, Cagliari, Italy
`{bart,lande}@unica.it`
[2] Università degli Studi di Trento, Trento, Italy
`roberto.zunino@unitn.it`

Abstract. Covenants are linguistic primitives that extend the Bitcoin script language, allowing transactions to constrain the scripts of the redeeming ones. Advocated as a way of improving the expressiveness of Bitcoin contracts while preserving the simplicity of the UTXO design, various forms of covenants have been proposed over the years. A common drawback of the existing descriptions is the lack of formalization, making it difficult to reason about properties and supported use cases. In this paper we propose a formal model of covenants, which can be implemented with minor modifications to Bitcoin. We use our model to specify some complex Bitcoin contracts, and we discuss how to exploit covenants to design high-level language primitives for Bitcoin contracts.

1 Introduction

Bitcoin is a decentralised infrastructure to transfer cryptocurrency between users. The log of all the currency transactions is recorded in a public, append-only, distributed data structure, called blockchain. Bitcoin implements a model of computation called *Unspent Transaction Output (UTXO)*: each transaction holds an amount of currency, and specifies conditions under which this amount can be redeemed by a subsequent transaction, which spends the old one. Compared to the *account-based* model, implemented e.g. by Ethereum, the UTXO model does not require a shared mutable state: the current state is given just by the set of unspent transaction outputs on the blockchain. While, on the one hand, this design choice fits well with the inherent concurrency of transactions, on the other hand the lack of a shared mutable state substantially complicates leveraging Bitcoin to implement *contracts*, i.e. protocols which transfer cryptocurrency according to programmable rules.

The literature has shown that Bitcoin contracts support a surprising variety of use cases, including e.g. crowdfunding [1,10], lotteries and other gambling games [7,10,17,20,30,32], contingent payments [13], micro-payment channels [10,37], and other kinds of fair computations [9,29]. Despite this apparent richness, the fact is that Bitcoin contracts cannot express most of the use cases that are mainstream in other blockchain platforms (e.g., decentralised finance). There are several factors that limit the expressiveness of Bitcoin contracts. Among them, the crucial one is the script language used to express the

© Springer Nature Switzerland AG 2020
T. Margaria and B. Steffen (Eds.): ISoLA 2020, LNCS 12478, pp. 25–42, 2020.
https://doi.org/10.1007/978-3-030-61467-6_3

redeeming conditions within transactions. This language only features a limited set of logic, arithmetic, and cryptographic operators, but its has no loops, and it cannot access parts of the spent and of the redeeming transaction.

Several extensions of the Bitcoin script language have been proposed, with the aim to improve the expressiveness of Bitcoin contracts, while adhering to the UTXO model. Among these extensions, *covenants* are a class of script operators that allow a transaction to constrain how its funds can be used by the redeeming transactions. Covenants may also be recursive, by requiring the script of the redeeming transaction to contain the same covenant of the spent one. As noted by [35], recursive covenants would allow to implement Bitcoin contracts that execute state machines, by appending transactions to trigger state transitions.

Although the first proposals of covenants date back at least to 2013 [31], and that they are supported by Bitcoin fork "Bitcoin Cash" [28], their inclusion into Bitcoin is still uncertain, mainly because of the extremely cautious approach to implement changes to Bitcoin [27]. Still, the emerging of Bitcoin layer-2 protocols, like e.g. the Lightning Network [37], has revived the interest in covenants, as witnessed by a recent Bitcoin Improvement Proposal (BIP 119 [38,40]), and by the incorporation of covenants in Liquid's extensions to Bitcoin Script [34].

Since the goal of the existing proposals is to show how implementing covenants would impact on the performance of Bitcoin, they describe covenants from a low-level, technical perspective. We believe that a proper abstraction and formalization of covenants would also be useful, as it would simplify reasoning on the behaviour of Bitcoin contracts and on their properties.

Contributions. We summarise our main contributions as follows:

- we introduce a formal model of Bitcoin covenants, inspired by the informal, low-level presentation in [33].
- we use our formal model to specify complex Bitcoin contracts, which largely extend the set of use cases expressible in pure Bitcoin;
- we discuss how to exploit covenants in the design of high-level language primitives for Bitcoin contracts.

2   The Pure Bitcoin

We start by illustrating the Bitcoin transaction model. To this purpose we adapt the formalization in [12], omitting the parts that are irrelevant for our subsequent technical development.

Transactions. In its simplest form, a Bitcoin transaction allows a user to transfer cryptocurrency (the *bitcoins*, ₿) to someone else. For this to be possible, bitcoins must be created at first. This is obtained through *coinbase* transactions (i.e., the first transaction of each mined block), whose typical form is:

T_0
in: $\bot$
wit: $\bot$
out: $\{\mathsf{scr} : \mathsf{versig}(pk_\mathsf{A}, \mathsf{rtx.wit}), \mathsf{val} : 1\mathring{\mathrm{B}}\}$

We identify T_0 as a coinbase transaction by its in field, which does not point to any other previous transaction on the blockchain (formally, we model this as the undefined value $\bot$). The out field contains a pair, whose first element is a *script*, and the second one is the amount of bitcoins that will be redeemed by a subsequent transaction which points to T_0 and satisfies its script. In particular, the script versig(pk_A, rtx.wit) verifies the signature in the wit field of the redeeming transaction (rtx) against A's public key pk_A.

Assume that T_0 is on the blockchain, and that A wants to transfer 1Ƀ to B. To do this, A can append to the blockchain a new transaction, e.g.:

T_1
in: T_0
wit: $sig_{sk_A}(T_1)$
out: {scr : versig(pk_B, rtx.wit), val : 1Ƀ}

The in field points to T_0, and the wit field contains A's signature on T_1 (but for the wit field itself). This witness makes the script within T_0.out evaluate to true, hence the redemption succeeds, and T_0 is *spent*.

The transactions T_0 and T_1 above only use part of the features of Bitcoin. More in general, transactions can collect bitcoins from many inputs, and split them between many outputs; further, they can use more complex scripts, and specify time constraints. Following the formalization in [12], we represent transactions as records with the following fields:

- in is the list of *inputs*. Each of these inputs is a *transaction output* (T, i), referring to the i-th output field of T.
- wit is the list of *witnesses*, of the same length as the list of inputs. Intuitively, for each (T, i) in the in field, the witness at the same index must make the i-th output script of T evaluate to true.
- out is the list of *outputs*. Each output is a record {scr : e, val : v}, where e is a script, and v is a currency value.
- absLock is a value, indicating the first moment in time when the transaction can be added to the blockchain;
- relLock is a list of values, of the same length as the list of inputs. Intuitively, if the value at index i is n, the transaction can be appended to the blockchain only if at least n time units have passed since the input transaction at index i has been appended.

We let f range over transaction fields, and we use the standard dot notation to access the fields of a record. For a transaction output (T, i) and f $\in$ {scr, val}, we write (T, i).f for T.out(i).f. For uniformity, we assume that absLock is a list of unit length; we omit null values in absLock and relLock. When graphically rendering transactions, we usually write f$(1) : \ell_1 \cdots$ f$(n) : \ell_n$ for f $: \ell_1 \cdots \ell_n$, or just f $: \ell_1$ when $n = 1$ (as in T_0 and T_1 above). When clear from the context, we just write the name A of a user in place of her public/private keys, e.g. we write versig(A, e) for versig(pk_A, e), and $sig_A(T)$ for $sig_{sk_A}(T)$.

$$[\![v]\!]_{\mathsf{T},i} = v \qquad [\![e \circ e']\!]_{\mathsf{T},i} = [\![e]\!]_{\mathsf{T},i} \circ_\perp [\![e']\!]_{\mathsf{T},i} \quad (\circ \in \{+,-,=,<\})$$

$$[\![e.e']\!]_{\mathsf{T},i} = [\![e_j]\!]_{\mathsf{T},i} \text{ if } e = e_1 \cdots e_k,\ [\![e']\!]_{\mathsf{T},i} = j, \text{ and } 1 \leq j \leq k$$

$$[\![\text{if } e_0 \text{ then } e_1 \text{ else } e_2]\!]_{\mathsf{T},i} = \textit{if } [\![e_0]\!]_{\mathsf{T},i} \textit{ then } [\![e_1]\!]_{\mathsf{T},i} \textit{ else } [\![e_2]\!]_{\mathsf{T},i} \qquad [\![\text{rtx.wit}]\!]_{\mathsf{T},i} = \mathsf{T}.\text{wit}(i)$$

$$[\![|e|]\!]_{\mathsf{T},i} = size([\![e]\!]_{\mathsf{T},i}) \qquad [\![\mathsf{H}(e)]\!]_{\mathsf{T},i} = H([\![e]\!]_{\mathsf{T},i})$$

$$[\![\text{versig}(e_1 \cdots e_n, e'_1 \cdots e'_m)]\!]_{\mathsf{T},i} = \text{ver}_{[\![e_1]\!]_{\mathsf{T},i} \cdots [\![e_n]\!]_{\mathsf{T},i}}([\![e'_1]\!]_{\mathsf{T},i} \cdots [\![e'_m]\!]_{\mathsf{T},i}, \mathsf{T}, i)$$

$$[\![\text{absAfter } e : e']\!]_{\mathsf{T},i} = \textit{if } \mathsf{T}.\text{absLock} \geq [\![e]\!]_{\mathsf{T},i} \textit{ then } [\![e']\!]_{\mathsf{T},i} \textit{ else } \perp$$

$$[\![\text{relAfter } e : e']\!]_{\mathsf{T},i} = \textit{if } \mathsf{T}.\text{relLock}(i) \geq [\![e]\!]_{\mathsf{T},i} \textit{ then } [\![e']\!]_{\mathsf{T},i} \textit{ else } \perp$$

Fig. 1. Semantics of Bitcoin scripts.

Scripts. Bitcoin scripts are small programs written in a non-Turing equivalent language. Whoever provides a witness that makes the script evaluate to "true", can redeem the bitcoins retained in the associated (unspent) output. In our model, scripts are terms with the following syntax, where $\circ \in \{+,-,=,<\}$, and where we write sequences of scripts in bold notation:

$$e ::= v \mid e \circ e \mid \quad e.e \quad \mid \text{if } e \text{ then } e \text{ else } e \mid \quad \text{rtx.wit} \quad \mid$$
$$|e| \mid \mathsf{H}(e) \mid \text{versig}(e, e) \mid \quad \text{absAfter } e : e \mid \text{relAfter } e : e$$

Besides values v and the basic arithmetic/logical operators, scripts feature operators to access the elements of a sequence ($e.e$), to access the witnesses of the redeeming transaction (rtx.wit), to compute the size $|e|$ of a bitstring and its hash $\mathsf{H}(e)$. The script $\text{versig}(e, e')$ evaluates to true iff the sequence of signatures resulting from the evaluation of e' (say, of length m) is verified by using m out of the n keys resulting from the evaluation of e. The expressions $\text{absAfter } e : e'$ and $\text{relAfter } e : e'$ define absolute and relative time constraints: they evaluate as e' if the constraints are satisfied, otherwise their semantics is undefined. We assume a basic type system which rules out ill-formed scripts.

We define in Fig. 1 the semantics of scripts. The script evaluation function $[\![\cdot]\!]_{\mathsf{T},i}$ takes two parameters: T is the redeeming transaction, and i is the index of the redeeming input/witness. We denote with H a public hash function, with $size(n)$ the size (in bytes) of an integer n, and with ver a multi-signature verification function (see [12] for the definition of these semantic operators). All the operators are *strict*, i.e. they evaluate to $\perp$ if some of their operands is $\perp$. We use syntactic sugar for scripts, e.g. *false* denotes $1 = 0$, *true* denotes $1 = 1$, while e and e' denotes if e then e' else *false*, and e or e' denotes if e then *true* else e'.

Blockchains. We model a blockchain **B** as a sequence of transactions $\mathsf{T}_0 \cdots \mathsf{T}_n$. For simplicity, we abstract from the fact that Bitcoin groups transactions into time-stamped blocks, and we identify the time-stamp of a transaction with its position in the blockchain. We say that the j-th output of the transaction T_i in the blockchain is *spent* iff there exists some transaction $\mathsf{T}_{i'}$ in the blockchain (with $i' > i$) and some j' such that $\mathsf{T}_{i'}.\text{in}(j') = (\mathsf{T}_i, j)$.

$$e ::= \cdots \mid \mathsf{ctxo}(e).\mathsf{f} \qquad \text{access part of the current transaction}$$

	$\mid \mathsf{rtxo}(e).\mathsf{f}$	access part of the redeeming transaction
	$\mid \mathsf{outidx}$	index of the redeemed output
	$\mid \mathsf{inidx}$	index of the redeeming input
	$\mid \mathsf{verscr}(e, e)$	covenant
	$\mid \mathsf{verrec}(e)$	recursive covenant

Fig. 2. Extended Bitcoin scripts ($\mathsf{f} \in \{\mathsf{arg}, \mathsf{scr}, \mathsf{val}\}$).

A transaction T_n is *valid* with respect to the blockchain $\mathbf{B} = \mathsf{T}_0 \cdots \mathsf{T}_{n-1}$ whenever the following conditions hold:

1. for each input i of T_n, if $\mathsf{T}_n.\mathsf{in}(i) = (\mathsf{T}', j)$ then:
   (a) $\mathsf{T}' = \mathsf{T}_h$, for some $h < n$ (i.e., T' is one of the transactions in $\mathbf{B}$);
   (b) the j-th output of T_h is not spent in $\mathbf{B}$;
   (c) $[\![\mathsf{T}_h.\mathsf{out}(j)]\!]_{\mathsf{T}_n,i} = true$;
   (d) $n - h \geq \mathsf{T}_n.\mathsf{relLock}(i)$;
2. $n \geq \mathsf{T}_n.\mathsf{absLock}$;
3. the sum of the amounts of the inputs of T_n is greater or equal to the sum of the amount of its outputs (the difference between the amount of inputs and that of outputs is the *fee* paid to miners).

The Bitcoin consensus protocol ensures that each T_i in the blockchain (except the coinbase T_0) is valid with respect to the sequence of past transactions $\mathsf{T}_0 \cdots \mathsf{T}_{i-1}$.

3   Extending Bitcoin with Covenants

To extend Bitcoin with covenants, we amend the transaction model of the previous section as follows:

- we add to each output a field $\mathsf{arg} : \boldsymbol{a}$, where $\boldsymbol{a}$ is a sequence of values. Intuitively, the extra field can be used to encode a state within transactions.
- we add script operators to access the outputs of the current transaction and of the redeeming one (by contrast, pure Bitcoin scripts can only access the whole redeeming transaction, but not its parts).
- we add script operators to check whether the output scripts in the redeeming transaction match a given script, or a given output of the current transaction (by contrast, in pure Bitcoin the redeeming transaction is only used when verifying signatures).

We extend the syntax of scripts in Fig. 2, and in Fig. 3 we define their semantics. As in pure Bitcoin, the script evaluation function takes as parameters the redeeming transaction T and the index i of the redeeming input/witness. From them, it is possible to infer the current transaction $\mathsf{T}' = fst(\mathsf{T}.\mathsf{in}(i))$, and the index $j = snd(\mathsf{T}.\mathsf{in}(i))$ of the redeemed output. The script $\mathsf{ctxo}(k).\mathsf{f}$

$\llbracket \mathsf{rtxo}(e).\mathsf{f} \rrbracket_{\mathsf{T},i} = (\mathsf{T}, \llbracket e \rrbracket_{\mathsf{T},i}).\mathsf{f}$ $\llbracket \mathsf{ctxo}(e).\mathsf{f} \rrbracket_{\mathsf{T},i} = (\mathit{fst}\ \mathsf{T}.\mathsf{in}(i), \llbracket e \rrbracket_{\mathsf{T},i}).\mathsf{f}$

$\llbracket \mathsf{inidx} \rrbracket_{\mathsf{T},i} = i$ $\llbracket \mathsf{outidx} \rrbracket_{\mathsf{T},i} = \mathit{snd}\ \mathsf{T}.\mathsf{in}(i)$

$\llbracket \mathsf{verscr}(e, e') \rrbracket_{\mathsf{T},i} = (\mathsf{T}, \llbracket e \rrbracket_{\mathsf{T},i}).\mathsf{scr} \equiv e'$ $\llbracket \mathsf{verrec}(e) \rrbracket_{\mathsf{T},i} = (\mathsf{T}, \llbracket e \rrbracket_{\mathsf{T},i}).\mathsf{scr} \equiv \mathsf{T}.\mathsf{in}(i).\mathsf{scr}$

Fig. 3. Semantics of extended scripts.

evaluates to the field f of the k-th output of the current transaction; similarly, $\mathsf{rtxo}(k).\mathsf{f}$ operates on the redeeming transaction. The symbols outidx and inidx evaluate, respectively, to the index of the redeemed output and to that of the redeeming input. The last two scripts specify covenants, in basic and recursive form. The basic covenant $\mathsf{verscr}(k, e')$ checks that the k-th output script of the redeeming transaction is syntactically equal to e' (note that e' is *not* evaluated). The recursive covenant $\mathsf{verrec}(k)$ checks that the k-th output of the redeeming transaction is syntactically equal to the redeemed output script.

4   Use Cases

We illustrate the expressive power of our extension through a series of use cases, which, at the best of our knowledge, cannot be expressed in Bitcoin. We denote with $\mathsf{U}_{\mathsf{A}}^{v}$ an unspent transaction output $\{\mathsf{arg} : \varepsilon, \mathsf{scr} : \mathsf{versig}(\mathsf{A}, \mathsf{rtx.wit}), \mathsf{val} : v\mathsf{B}\}$, where ε denotes the empty sequence (we will usually omit arg when empty).

4.1   Crowdfunding

Assume that a start-up Z wants to raise funds through a crowdfunding campaign. The target of the campaign is to gather at least $v\mathsf{B}$ by time t. The contributors want the guarantee that if this target is not reached, then they will get back their funds after the expiration date. The start-up wants to ensure that contributions cannot be retracted before time t, or once $v\mathsf{B}$ have been gathered.

   We implement this use case without covenants, but just constraining the val field of the redeeming transaction. To fund the campaign, a contributor A_i publishes the transaction T_i in Fig. 4 (left), which uses the following script:

$$CF = \begin{array}{l} (\mathsf{versig}(\mathsf{Z}, \mathsf{rtx.wit})\ \mathsf{and}\ \mathsf{rtxo}(1).\mathsf{val} \geq v)\ \ \mathsf{or} \\ \mathsf{absAfter}\ t : \mathsf{versig}(\mathsf{A}_i, \mathsf{rtx.wit}) \end{array}$$

This script is a disjunction between two conditions. The first condition allows Z to redeem the bitcoins deposited in this output, provided that the output at index 1 of the redeeming transaction pays at least $v\mathsf{B}$ (note that this constraint, rendered as $\mathsf{rtxo}(1).\mathsf{val} \geq v$, is not expressible in pure Bitcoin). The second condition allows A_i to get back her contribution after the expiration date t.

T_i
in: $U_{A_i}^{v_i}$
wit: $\cdots$
out: $\{$arg $: \varepsilon$, scr $: CF$, val $: v_i\text{B}\!\!\!\!/\,\}$

T_Z
in: $(T_1, 1) \cdots (T_n, 1)$
wit: $sig_Z(T_Z) \cdots sig_Z(T_Z)$
out: $\{$arg $: \varepsilon$, scr $:$ versig$(Z, $rtx.wit$)$, val $: v'\text{B}\!\!\!\!/\,\}$

Fig. 4. Transactions for the crowdfunding contract.

T_0
in: U_A^1
wit: $sig_A(T_0)$
out: $\{$arg $: A$, scr $: NFT$, val $: 1\text{B}\!\!\!\!/\,\}$

T_1
in: $(T_0, 1)$
wit: $sig_A(T_1)$
out: $\{$arg $: B$, scr $: NFT$, val $: 1\text{B}\!\!\!\!/\,\}$

Fig. 5. A creates a token with T_0, and transfers it to B with T_1.

Once contributors have deposited enough funds (i.e., there are n transactions $T_1, \ldots, T_n$ with $v' = v_1 + \cdots v_n \geq v$), Z can get $v'\text{B}\!\!\!\!/\,$ by appending T_Z to the blockchain. Note that, compared to the assurance contract in the Bitcoin wiki [1], ours offers more protection to the start-up. Indeed, while in [1] any contributor can retract her funds at any time, this is not possible here until time t.

4.2 Non-fungible Tokens

A non-fungible token represents the ownership of a physical or logical asset, which can be transferred between users. Unlike fungible tokens (e.g., ERC-20 tokens in Ethereum [2]), where each token unit is interchangeable with every other unit, non-fungible ones have unique identities. Further, they do not support split and join operations, unlike fungible tokens.

We start by implementing a subtly flawed version of the non-fungible token. Consider the transactions in Fig. 5, which use the following script:

$$NFT = \text{versig}(\text{ctxo}(1).\text{arg}, \text{rtx.wit}) \text{ and } \text{verrec}(1) \text{ and } \text{rtxo}(1).\text{val} = 1$$

User A mints a token by depositing $1\text{B}\!\!\!\!/\,$ in T_0: to declare her ownership over the token, she sets out(1).arg to her public key. To transfer the token to B, A appends the transaction T_1, setting its out(1).arg to B's public key.

To spend T_0, the transaction T_1 must satisfy the conditions specified by the script NFT: (i) the wit field must contain the signature of the current owner; (ii) the script at index 1 must be equal to that at the same index in T_0; (iii) the output at index 1 must have $1\text{B}\!\!\!\!/\,$ value, to preserve the integrity of the token. Once T_1 is on the blockchain, B can transfer the token to another user, by appending a transaction which redeems T_1.

The script NFT has a design flaw, already spotted in [33]: we show how A can exploit this flaw in Fig. 6. Suppose we have two unspent transactions: T_A and T_A', both representing a token owned by A (in their first and only output). The transaction T_2 can spend both of them, since it complies with all the validity conditions: indeed, NFT only constrains the script in the first output of the

$\mathsf{T_2}$
in: $(\mathsf{T_A}, 1)$ $(\mathsf{T'_A}, 1)$
wit: $sig_\mathsf{A}(\mathsf{T_2})$ $sig_\mathsf{A}(\mathsf{T_2})$
out(1): $\{\mathsf{arg} : \mathsf{A},\ \mathsf{scr} : NFT,\ \mathsf{val} : 1\mathring{B}\}$
out(2): $\{\mathsf{arg} : \varepsilon,\ \mathsf{scr} : \mathsf{versig}(\mathsf{A}, \mathsf{rtx.wit}),\ \mathsf{val} : 1\mathring{B}\}$

Fig. 6. A exploits the flaw to destroy a token, redeeming its value.

redeeming transaction, while the other outputs are only subject to the standard validity conditions (in particular, that the sum of their values does not exceed the value in input). Actually, $\mathsf{T_2}$ destroys one of the two tokens, and removes the covenant from the other one.

To solve this issue, we can amend the NFT script as follows:

$$NFT' = \mathsf{versig}(\mathsf{ctxo}(\mathsf{outidx}).\mathsf{arg}, \mathsf{rtx.wit}) \text{ and } \mathsf{verrec}(\mathsf{inidx}) \text{ and } \mathsf{rtxo}(\mathsf{inidx}).\mathsf{val} = 1$$

The amended script correctly handles the case of a transaction which uses different outputs to store different tokens. NFT' uses $\mathsf{ctxo}(\mathsf{outidx}).\mathsf{arg}$, instead of $\mathsf{ctxo}(1).\mathsf{arg}$ in NFT, to ensure that, when redeeming a given output, the signature of the owner of the token at *that* output is checked. Further, NFT' uses $\mathsf{verrec}(\mathsf{inidx})$, instead of $\mathsf{verrec}(1)$ in NFT, to ensure that the covenant is propagated exactly to the transaction output which is redeeming that token (i.e., the one at index inidx). Notice that the amendment would make $\mathsf{T_2}$ invalid: indeed, the script in $\mathsf{T'_A}.\mathsf{out}(1)$ would evaluate to false:

$$\begin{aligned}
[\![NFT']\!]_{\mathsf{T_2},2} &= [\![\mathsf{verrec}(\mathsf{inidx})]\!]_{\mathsf{T_2},2} \wedge \cdots \\
&= (\mathsf{T_2}, [\![\mathsf{inidx}]\!]_{\mathsf{T_2},2}).\mathsf{scr} \equiv \mathsf{T_2}.\mathsf{in}(2).\mathsf{scr} \wedge \cdots \\
&= (\mathsf{T_2}, 2).\mathsf{scr} \equiv (\mathsf{T'_A}, 1).\mathsf{scr} \wedge \cdots \\
&= \mathsf{versig}(\mathsf{A}, \mathsf{rtx.wit}) \equiv NFT' \wedge \cdots \\
&= \mathit{false}
\end{aligned}$$

An alternative patch, originally proposed in [33], is to add a unique identifier id to each token, e.g. by amending the NFT script as follows:

$$NFT \text{ and } id = id$$

This allows to mint distinguishable tokens. For instance, if the tokens in $\mathsf{T_A}$ and $\mathsf{T'_A}$ are distinguishable, $\mathsf{T_2}$ cannot redeem both of them.

4.3 Vaults

Transaction outputs are usually secured by cryptographic keys (e.g. through the script $\mathsf{versig}(pk_\mathsf{A}, \mathsf{rtx.wit})$). Whoever knows the corresponding private key (e.g., sk_A) can redeem such an output: in case of key theft, the legitimate owner is left without defence. Vault transactions, introduced in [33], are a technique to mitigate this issue, by allowing the legitimate owner to abort the transfer.

T_V	T_S	T
in: U^1_A wit: $\cdots$ out: $\{\mathsf{scr} : V, \mathsf{val} : 1\dot{B}\}$	in: T_V wit: $sig_A(T_S)$ out: $\{\mathsf{arg} : B, \mathsf{scr} : S, \mathsf{val} : 1\dot{B}\}$	in: T_S wit: $sig_B(T)$ out: $\{\mathsf{scr} : \mathsf{versig}(B, \mathsf{rtx.wit}), \mathsf{val} : 1\dot{B}\}$ relLock: t

Fig. 7. Transactions for the basic vault.

T_V	T_S	T_R
in: U^1_A wit: $\cdots$ out: $\{\mathsf{arg} : 0, \mathsf{scr} : R, \mathsf{val} : 1\dot{B}\}$	in: T_V wit: $sig_A(T_S)$ out: $\{\mathsf{arg} : 1B, \mathsf{scr} : R, \mathsf{val} : 1\dot{B}\}$	in: T_S wit: $sig_{Ar}(T_R)$ out: $\{\mathsf{arg} : 0, \mathsf{scr} : R, \mathsf{val} : 1\dot{B}\}$

Fig. 8. Transactions for the recursive vault.

To create a vault, A deposits $1\dot{B}$ in a transaction T_V with the script V:

$$V = \mathsf{versig}(A, \mathsf{rtx.wit}) \text{ and } \mathsf{verscr}(1, S)$$
$$S = \big(\mathsf{relAfter}\ t : \mathsf{versig}(\mathsf{ctxo}(\mathsf{outidx}).\mathsf{arg}, \mathsf{rtx.wit})\big) \text{ or } \mathsf{versig}(Ar, \mathsf{rtx.wit})$$

The transaction T_V can be redeemed with the signature of A, but only by a *de-vaulting* transaction like T_S in Fig. 7, which uses the script S. The output of the de-vaulting transaction T_S can be spent by the user set in its arg field, but only after a certain time t (e.g., by the transaction T in Fig. 7). Before time t, A can cancel the transfer by spending T_S with her recovery key Ar.

A Recursive Vault. The vault in Fig. 7 has a potential issue, in that the recovery key may also be subject to theft. Although this issue is mitigated by hardware wallets (and by the infrequent need to interact with the recovery key), the vault modelled above does not discourage any attempt at stealing the key.

The issue can be solved by using a recursive covenant in the vault script R:

```
if ctxo(1).arg.1 = 0                              // current state: vault
      then versig(A, rtx.wit) and verrec(1) and
      rtxo(1).arg.1 = 1                           // next state: de-vaulting
else (relAfter t : versig(ctxo(1).arg.2, rtx.wit)) or  // current state: de-vaulting
      versig(Ar, rtx.wit) and verrec(1) and
      rtxo(1).arg.1 = 0                           // next state: vault
```

In this version of the contract, the vault and de-vaulting transactions (in Fig. 8) have the same script. The first element of the arg sequence encodes the contract state (0 models the vault state, and 1 the de-vaulting state), while the second element is the user who can receive the bitcoin deposited in the vault. The recovery key Ar can only be used to append the re-vaulting transaction T_R, locking again the bitcoin into the vault.

Note that key theft becomes ineffective: indeed, even if both keys are stolen, the thief cannot take control of the bitcoin in the vault, as A can keep re-vaulting.

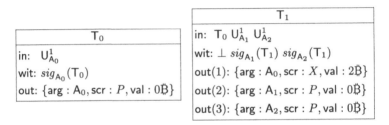

Fig. 9. Transactions for the pyramid scheme.

4.4 A Pyramid Scheme

Ponzi schemes are financial frauds which lure users under the promise of high profits, but which actually repay them only with the investments of new users. A pyramid scheme is a Ponzi scheme where the scheme creator recruits other investors, who in turn recruit other ones, and so on. Unlike in Ethereum, where several Ponzi schemes have been implemented as smart contracts [14,26], the limited expressive power of Bitcoin contract only allows for off-chain schemes [41].

We design the first "smart" pyramid scheme in Bitcoin using the transactions in Fig. 9, where:

$$P = \mathsf{verscr}(1, X) \text{ and } \mathsf{rtxo}(1).\mathsf{arg} = \mathsf{ctxo}(\mathsf{outidx}).\mathsf{arg} \text{ and } \mathsf{rtxo}(1).\mathsf{val} = 2$$
$$\text{and } \mathsf{verrec}(2) \text{ and } \mathsf{verrec}(3)$$
$$X = \mathsf{versig}(\mathsf{ctxo}(\mathsf{outidx}).\mathsf{arg}, \mathsf{rtx}.\mathsf{wit})$$

To start the scheme, a user A_0 deposits $1\mathsf{B}$ in the transaction T_0 (we burn this bitcoin for uniformity, so that each user earns at most $1\mathsf{B}$ from the scheme). To make a profit, A_0 must convince other two users, say A_1 and A_2, to join the scheme. This requires the cooperation of A_1 and A_2 to publish a transaction which redeems T_0. The script P ensures that this redeeming transaction has the form of T_1 in Fig. 9, i.e. $\mathsf{out}(1)$ transfers $2\mathsf{B}$ to A_0, while the scripts in $\mathsf{out}(2)$ and $\mathsf{out}(3)$ ensure that the same behaviour is recursively applied to A_1 and A_2.

Overall, the contract ensures that, as long as new users join the scheme, each one earns $1\mathsf{B}$. Of course, as in any Ponzi scheme, at a certain point it will no longer be possible to find new users, so those at the leaves of the transaction tree will just lose their investment.

4.5 King of the Ether Throne

King of the Ether Throne [3] is an Ethereum contract, which has been popular for a while around 2016, until a bug caused its funds to be frozen. The contract is initiated by a user, who pays an entry fee v_0 to become the "king". Another user can usurp the throne by paying $v_1 = 1.5v_0$ fee to the old king, and so on until new usurpers are available. Of course this leads to an exponential growth of the fee needed to become king, so subsequent versions of the contract introduced

T_0	T_1
in: $U_{A_0}^{v_0}$	in: $(T_0, 1)\ U_{A_1}^{v_1}$
wit: $sig_{A_0}(T_0)$	wit: $\bot\ sig_{A_1}(T_1)$
out(1): $\{\mathsf{arg} : A_0, \mathsf{scr} : K, \mathsf{val} : 0\math3B\}$	out(1): $\{\mathsf{arg} : A_1, \mathsf{scr} : K, \mathsf{val} : 0\math3B\}$
out(2): $\{\mathsf{arg} : A_0, \mathsf{scr} : \mathsf{versig}(A_0, \mathsf{rtx.wit}), \mathsf{val} : v_0\math3B\}$	out(2): $\{\mathsf{arg} : A_0, \mathsf{scr} : X, \mathsf{val} : v_1\math3B\}$

Fig. 10. Transactions for King of the Ether Throne.

mechanisms to make the current king die if not ousted within a certain time. Although the logic to distribute money substantially differs from that in Sect. 4.4, this is still an instance of Ponzi scheme, since investors are only paid with the funds paid by later investors.

We implement the original version of the contract, fixing the multiplier to 2 instead of 1.5, since Bitcoin scripts do not support multiplication. The contract uses the transactions in Fig. 10 for the first two kings, A_0 and A_1, where:

$$K = \mathsf{verrec}(1)\ \text{and}\ \mathsf{rtxo}(2).\mathsf{arg} = \mathsf{ctxo}(1).\mathsf{arg}\ \text{and}$$
$$\mathsf{rtxo}(2).\mathsf{val} \geq \mathsf{ctxo}(2).\mathsf{val} + \mathsf{ctxo}(2).\mathsf{val}\ \text{and}\ \mathsf{verscr}(2, X)$$
$$X = \mathsf{versig}(\mathsf{ctxo}(2).\mathsf{arg}, \mathsf{rtx.wit})$$

We use the arg field in out(1) to record the new king, and that in out(2) for the old one. The clause $\mathsf{rtxo}(2).\mathsf{arg} = \mathsf{ctxo}(1).\mathsf{arg}$ in K preserves the old king in the redeeming transaction. The clause $\mathsf{rtxo}(2).\mathsf{val} \geq \mathsf{ctxo}(2).\mathsf{val} + \mathsf{ctxo}(2).\mathsf{val}$ ensures that his compensation is twice the value he paid. Finally, verscr guarantees that the old king can redeem his compensation via out(2).

5   Implementing Covenants on Bitcoin

We now discuss how to implement covenants in Bitcoin, and their computational overhead. First, during the script verification, we need to access both the redeeming transaction and the one containing the output being spent. This can be implemented by adding a new data structure to store unspent or partially unspent transaction outputs, and modifying the entries of the UTXO set to link each unspent output to the enclosing transaction.

The language primitives that check the redeeming transaction script, verscr and verrec, can be implemented through an opcode similar to CheckOutputVerify described in [33]. While [33] uses placeholders to represent variable parts of the script, e.g., versig(<*pubKey*>, rtx.wit), we use operators to access the needed parts of a transaction, e.g., versig(ctxo(1).arg, rtx.wit). Thus, to check if two scripts are the same we just need to compare their hashes, while [33] needs to instantiate the placeholders. Similarly, we can use the hash of the script within verscr. The work [35] implements covenants without introducing operators to explicitly access the redeeming transaction. Instead, they exploit the current implementation of versig, which checks a signature on data that is build by implicitly accessing the redeeming transaction, to define a new operator CheckSigFromStack.

The arg part of each output can be stored at the beginning of the output script, without altering the structure of pure Bitcoin transactions. Similarly to the implementation of parameters in Balzac [6,12], the arguments are pushed on the alternative stack at the beginning of the script, then duplicated and copied in the main stack before the actual output script starts. Note that arguments need to be discharged when hashing the script for verrec/verscr. For this, it is enough to skip a known-length prefix of the script.

Even though the use cases in Sect. 4 extensively use non-standard scripts, they can be encoded as standard transactions using P2SH [5], as done in [6,12]. Crucially, the hash also covers the arg field, which is therefore not malleable.

6   Using Covenants in High-Level Contract Languages

As witnessed by the use cases in Sect. 4, crafting a contract at the level of Bitcoin transactions can be complex and error-prone. To simplify this task, the work [18] has introduced a high-level contract language, called BitML, with a secure compiler to pure Bitcoin transactions. BitML has primitives to withdraw funds from a contract, to split a contract (and its funds) into subcontracts, to request the authorization from a participant A before proceeding with a subcontract C (written $A : C$), to postpone the execution of C after a given time t (written after $t : C$), to reveal committed secrets, and to branch between two contracts (written $C + C'$). A recent paper [16] extends BitML with a new primitive that allows participants to (consensually) renegotiate a contract, still keeping the ability to compile into pure Bitcoin.

Despite the variety of use cases shown in [11,15], BitML has known expressiveness limits, given by the requirement to have pure Bitcoin as its compilation target. For instance, BitML cannot specify recursive contracts (just as pure Bitcoin cannot), unless all participants agree to perform the recursive call [16]. In this section we discuss how to improve the expressiveness of BitML, assuming to use Bitcoin with covenants as compilation target. We illustrate our point by a couple of examples, postponing the formal treatment of this extended BitML and of its secure compilation to future work.

Covenants allow us to extend BitML with the construct:

$$?\boldsymbol{x} \text{ if } b. \, \mathtt{X}(\boldsymbol{x})$$

Intuitively, the prefix $?\boldsymbol{x}$ if b can be fired whenever a participant provides a sequence of arguments $\boldsymbol{x}$ and makes the predicate b true. Once the prefix is fired, the contract proceeds as the continuation $\mathtt{X}(\boldsymbol{x})$, which will reduce according to the equation defining $\mathtt{X}$.

Using this construct, we can model the "King of the Ether Throne" contract of Sect. 4.5 (started by A with an investment of 1₿) as $\mathtt{X}(A, 1)$, where:

$$\mathtt{X}(a, v) \;=\; ?b \text{ if } \mathsf{val} \geq 2v. \, \mathtt{Y}(a, b, \mathsf{val})$$
$$\mathtt{Y}(a, b, v) \;=\; \mathtt{split} \left(0 \rightarrow \mathtt{X}(b, v) \mid v \rightarrow \mathtt{withdraw} \, a\right)$$

```
 1  def arg.1 = q        // state    0 = <X(A,-),1>
 2                       // state    1 = <Y(a,b,v),v>
 3                       // state    2 = <X(b,v),0> | <withdraw a,v>
 4  def arg.2 = oldK     // old King
 5  def arg.3 = newK     // new king
 6  def arg.4 = v        // paid fee
 7
 8  verrec(1) and                           // out(1) preserves covenant
 9  if ctxo(1).q = 0 then                   // state 0
10        rtxo(1).q = 1                     // state transition 0 -> 1
11    and rtxo(1).oldK = ctxo(1).newK       // usurp the throne
12    and rtxo(1).val >= ctxo(1).val + ctxo(1).val // fee at least doubled
13    and rtxo(1).v = rtxo(1).val           // instantiate v
14  else if ctxo(1).q = 1 then              // state 1
15        rtxo(1).q = 2                     // state transition 1 -> 2
16    and rtxo(1).newK = ctxo(1).newK       // preserve new king
17    and rtxo(1).v = ctxo(1).v             // preserve v
18    and rtxo(1).val = 0                   // reset value in out(1)
19    and rtxo(2).oldK = ctxo(1).oldK       // set old king
20    and verscr(2,versig(ctxo(2).oldK,rtx.wit)) // covenant to pay old king
21    and rtxo(2).val = ctxo(1).val         // preserve value in out(2)
22  else if ctxo(1).q = 2 then              // state 2
23        rtxo(1).q = 1                     // state transition 2 -> 1
24    and rtxo(1).oldK = ctxo(1).newK       // usurp the throne
25    and rtxo(1).val >= ctxo(1).v + ctxo(1).v // fee at least doubled
26    and rtxo(1).v = rtxo(1).val           // update v
```

Fig. 11. Script for King of the Ether Throne, obtained by compiling BitML.

The contract $X(a, v)$ models a state where a is the current king, and v is his investment. The guard val $\geq 2v$ becomes true when some participant injects funds into the contract, making its value (val) greater than $2v$. This participant can choose the value for b, i.e. the new king. The contract proceeds as $Y(a, b, \text{val})$, which has two parallel branches. The first branch makes val ฿ available to the old king; the second branch has zero value, and it reboots the game, recording the new king b and his investment.

A possible computation of A starting the scheme with 1฿ is the following, where we represent a contract C storing v฿ as a term $\langle C, v฿ \rangle$:

$$
\begin{aligned}
\langle X(A, -), 1฿ \rangle &\to \langle Y(A, B, 2), 2฿ \rangle & &\text{(B pays 2฿ fee)} \\
&\to \langle X(B, 2), 0฿ \rangle \mid \langle \text{withdraw } A, 2฿ \rangle & &\text{(contract splits)} \\
&\to \langle X(B, 2), 0฿ \rangle \mid \langle A, 2฿ \rangle & &\text{(A redeems 2฿)} \\
&\to \langle Y(B, C, 4), 4฿ \rangle \mid \langle A, 2฿ \rangle & &\text{(C pays 4฿ fee)} \\
&\to \langle X(C, 4), 0฿ \rangle \mid \langle \text{withdraw } B, 4฿ \rangle \mid \langle A, 2฿ \rangle & &\text{(contract splits)} \\
&\to \langle X(C, 4), 0฿ \rangle \mid \langle B, 4฿ \rangle \mid \langle A, 2฿ \rangle & &\text{(B redeems 4฿)}
\end{aligned}
$$

Executing a step of the BitML contract corresponds, in Bitcoin, to appending a transaction containing in out(1) the script in Fig. 11. The script implements a state machine, using arg.1 to record the current state, and the other parts of arg for the old king, the new king, and v. The verrec(1) at line 8 preserves the script in out(1). To pay the old king, we use the verscr at line 20, which constrains the script in out(2) of the transaction corresponding to the BitML state $\langle X(b, v), 0฿ \rangle \mid \langle \text{withdraw } a, v฿ \rangle$.

We now apply our extended BitML to specify a more challenging use case, i.e. a recursive coin-flipping game where two players A and B repeatedly flip coins, and the one who wins two consecutive flips takes the pot. The precondition to stipulate the contract requires each player to deposit 1Ḃ as a bet. The game first makes each player commit to a secret, using a timed-commitment protocol [21]. The secrets are then revealed, and the winner of a flip is determined as a function of the two secrets. The game starts another flip if the current winner is different from that of the previous flip, otherwise the pot is transferred to the winner.

We model the recursive coin-flipping game as the (extended) BitML contract $X_A(C)$, where $C \neq A, B$, using the following defining equations:

$$X_A(w) \ = \ A : ?h_A . X_B(w, h_A) \ + \ \texttt{afterRel}\, t : \texttt{withdraw}\ B$$
$$X_B(w, h_A) \ = \ B : ?h_B . Y_A(w, h_A, h_B) \ + \ \texttt{afterRel}\, t : \texttt{withdraw}\ A$$
$$Y_A(w, h_A, h_B) \ = \ ?s_A \ \texttt{if}\ H(s_A) = h_A . Y_B(w, s_A, h_B)$$
$$+\ \texttt{afterRel}\, t : \texttt{withdraw}\ B$$
$$Y_B(w, s_A, h_B) \ = \ ?s_B \ \texttt{if}\ H(s_B) = h_B \ \texttt{and}\ 0 \leq s_B \leq 1 . W(w, s_A, s_B)$$
$$+\ \texttt{afterRel}\, t : \texttt{withdraw}\ A$$
$$W(w, s_A, s_B) \ = \ \texttt{if}\ s_A = s_B \ \texttt{and}\ w = A : \texttt{withdraw}\ A \qquad \textit{// A won twice}$$
$$+\ \texttt{if}\ s_A = s_B \ \texttt{and}\ w \neq A : X_A(A) \qquad \textit{// A won last flip}$$
$$+\ \texttt{if}\ s_A \neq s_B \ \texttt{and}\ w = B : \texttt{withdraw}\ B \qquad \textit{// B won twice}$$
$$+\ \texttt{if}\ s_A \neq s_B \ \texttt{and}\ w \neq B : X_A(B) \qquad \textit{// B won last flip}$$

The contract $X_A(w)$ models a state where w is the last winner, and A must commit to her secret. To do that, A must authorize an input h_A, which represents the hash of her secret. If A does not commit within t, then the pot can be redeemed by B as a compensation (here, the primitive $\texttt{afterRel}\, t : C$ models a relative timeout). Similarly, $X_B(w)$ models B's turn to commit. In $Y_A(w, h_A, h_B)$, A must reveal her secret s_A, or otherwise lose her deposit. The contract $Y_B(w, s_A, h_B)$ is the same for B, except that here we additionally check that B's secret is either 0 or 1 (this is needed to ensure fairness, as in the two-player lottery in [18]). The flip winner is A if the secrets of A and B are equal, otherwise it is B. If the winner is the same as the previous round, the winner can withdraw the pot, otherwise the game restarts, recording the last winner.

This coin flipping game is fair, i.e. the expected payoff of a *rational* player is always non-negative, notwithstanding the behaviour of the other player.

7   Conclusions and Future Work

We have proposed a formalisation of Bitcoin covenants, and we have exploited it to present a series of use cases which appear to be unfeasible in pure Bitcoin. We have introduced high-level contract primitives that exploit covenants to enable recursion, and allow contracts to receive new funds and parameters at runtime.

Known Limitations. Most of the scripts crafted in our use cases would produce non-standard transactions, that are rejected by Bitcoin nodes. To produce standard transactions from non-standard scripts, we can exploit P2SH [5]. This requires the transaction output to commit to the hash of the script, while the actual script is revealed in the witness of the redeeming transaction. Since, to check its hash, the script needs to be pushed to the stack, and the maximum size of a stack element is 520 bytes, longer scripts would be rejected. This clearly affects the expressiveness of contracts, as already observed in [11]. In particular, since the size of a script grows with the number of contract states (see e.g. Fig. 11), contracts with many states would easily violate the 520 bytes limit. The introduction of Taproot [36] would mitigate this limit. For scripts with multiple disjoint branches, Taproot allows the witness of the redeeming transaction to reveal just the needed branch. Therefore, the 520 bytes limit would apply to branches, instead of the whole script. Another expressiveness limit derives from the fact that covenants can only constrain the scripts of the redeeming transaction. While this is enough to express non-fungible tokens (see Sect. 4.2), fungible ones seem to require more powerful mechanisms, because of the join operation. An alternative technique to enhancing covenants is to implement fungible tokens natively [24,25], or to enforce their logic through a sidechain [34].

Verification. Although designing contracts in the UTXO model seems to be less error-prone than in the shared memory model, e.g. because of the absence of reentrancy vulnerabilities (like the one exploited in the Ethereum DAO attack [4]), Bitcoin contracts may still contain security flaws. Therefore, it is important to devise verification techniques to detect security issues that may lead to the theft or freezing of funds. Recursive covenants make this task harder than in pure Bitcoin, since they can encode infinite-state transition systems, as in most of our use cases. Hence, model-checking techniques based on the exploration of the whole state space, like the one used in [8], cannot be applied.

High-Level Bitcoin Contracts. The compiler of our extension of BitML is just sketched in Sect. 6, and we leave as future work its formal definition, as well as the extension of the computational soundness results of [18], ensuring the correspondence between the symbolic semantics of BitML and the underlying computational level of Bitcoin. Continuing along this line of research, it would be interesting to study new linguistic primitives that fully exploit the expressiveness of Bitcoin covenants, and to extend accordingly the verification technique of [19]. Note that our extension of the UTXO model is more restrictive than the one in [23], as the latter abstracts from the script language, just assuming that scripts denote any pure functions [42]. This added flexibility can be exploited to design expressive high-level contract languages like Marlowe [39] and Plutus [22].

Acknowledgements. Massimo Bartoletti is partially supported by Aut. Reg. of Sardinia project "Sardcoin". Stefano Lande is partially supported by P.O.R. F.S.E. 2014–2020. Roberto Zunino is partially supported by MIUR PON 2018 "Distributed Ledgers for Secure Open Communities" ARS01_00587.

References

1. Bitcoin Wiki - contracts - assurance contracts (2012). https://en.bitcoin.it/wiki/Contract#Example_3:_Assurance_contracts
2. ERC-20 token standard (2015). https://github.com/ethereum/EIPs/blob/master/EIPS/eip-20.md
3. King of the Ether Throne (2016). https://web.archive.org/web/20160211005112/https://www.kingoftheether.com/
4. Understanding the DAO attack, June 2016. http://www.coindesk.com/understanding-dao-hack-journalists/
5. Bitcoin Wiki - Pay-to-Script Hash (2017). https://en.bitcoinwiki.org/wiki/Pay-to-Script_Hash
6. BALZaC: Bitcoin abstract language, analyzer and compiler (2018). https://blockchain.unica.it/balzac/
7. Andrychowicz, M., Dziembowski, S., Malinowski, D., Mazurek, Ł.: Fair two-party computations via Bitcoin deposits. In: Böhme, R., Brenner, M., Moore, T., Smith, M. (eds.) FC 2014. LNCS, vol. 8438, pp. 105–121. Springer, Heidelberg (2014). https://doi.org/10.1007/978-3-662-44774-1_8
8. Andrychowicz, M., Dziembowski, S., Malinowski, D., Mazurek, L.: Modeling Bitcoin contracts by timed automata. In: Legay, A., Bozga, M. (eds.) FORMATS 2014. LNCS, vol. 8711, pp. 7–22. Springer, Cham (2014). https://doi.org/10.1007/978-3-319-10512-3_2
9. Andrychowicz, M., Dziembowski, S., Malinowski, D., Mazurek, L.: Secure multi-party computations on Bitcoin. In: IEEE S&P, pp. 443–458 (2014). https://doi.org/10.1109/SP.2014.35
10. Atzei, N., Bartoletti, M., Cimoli, T., Lande, S., Zunino, R.: SoK: unraveling Bitcoin smart contracts. In: Bauer, L., Küsters, R. (eds.) POST 2018. LNCS, vol. 10804, pp. 217–242. Springer, Cham (2018). https://doi.org/10.1007/978-3-319-89722-6_9
11. Atzei, N., Bartoletti, M., Lande, S., Yoshida, N., Zunino, R.: Developing secure Bitcoin contracts with BitML. In: ESEC/FSE (2019). https://doi.org/10.1145/3338906.3341173
12. Atzei, N., Bartoletti, M., Lande, S., Zunino, R.: A formal model of Bitcoin transactions. In: Meiklejohn, S., Sako, K. (eds.) FC 2018. LNCS, vol. 10957, pp. 541–560. Springer, Heidelberg (2018). https://doi.org/10.1007/978-3-662-58387-6_29
13. Banasik, W., Dziembowski, S., Malinowski, D.: Efficient zero-knowledge contingent payments in cryptocurrencies without scripts. In: Askoxylakis, I., Ioannidis, S., Katsikas, S., Meadows, C. (eds.) ESORICS 2016. LNCS, vol. 9879, pp. 261–280. Springer, Cham (2016). https://doi.org/10.1007/978-3-319-45741-3_14
14. Bartoletti, M., Carta, S., Cimoli, T., Saia, R.: Dissecting Ponzi schemes on Ethereum: identification, analysis, and impact. Future Gener. Comput. Syst. **102**, 259–277 (2020). https://doi.org/10.1016/j.future.2019.08.014
15. Bartoletti, M., Cimoli, T., Zunino, R.: Fun with Bitcoin smart contracts. In: ISoLA, pp. 432–449 (2018). https://doi.org/10.1007/978-3-030-03427-632
16. Bartoletti, M., Murgia, M., Zunino, R.: Renegotiation and recursion in Bitcoin contracts. In: Bliudze, S., Bocchi, L. (eds.) COORDINATION 2020. LNCS, vol. 12134, pp. 261–278. Springer, Cham (2020). https://doi.org/10.1007/978-3-030-50029-0_17
17. Bartoletti, M., Zunino, R.: Constant-deposit multiparty lotteries on bitcoin. In: Brenner, M., et al. (eds.) FC 2017. LNCS, vol. 10323, pp. 231–247. Springer, Cham (2017). https://doi.org/10.1007/978-3-319-70278-0_15

18. Bartoletti, M., Zunino, R.: BitML: a calculus for Bitcoin smart contracts. In: ACM CCS (2018). https://doi.org/10.1145/3243734.3243795
19. Bartoletti, M., Zunino, R.: Verifying liquidity of Bitcoin contracts. In: Nielson, F., Sands, D. (eds.) POST 2019. LNCS, vol. 11426, pp. 222–247. Springer, Cham (2019). https://doi.org/10.1007/978-3-030-17138-4_10
20. Bentov, Iddo, Kumaresan, Ranjit: How to use Bitcoin to design fair protocols. In: Garay, Juan A., Gennaro, Rosario (eds.) CRYPTO 2014. LNCS, vol. 8617, pp. 421–439. Springer, Heidelberg (2014). https://doi.org/10.1007/978-3-662-44381-1_24
21. Boneh, D., Naor, M.: Timed commitments. In: Bellare, M. (ed.) CRYPTO 2000. LNCS, vol. 1880, pp. 236–254. Springer, Heidelberg (2000). https://doi.org/10.1007/3-540-44598-6_15
22. Brünjes, L., Gabbay, M.J.: UTxO- vs account-based smart contract blockchain programming paradigms. CoRR abs/2003.14271 (2020)
23. Chakravarty, M.M.T., Chapman, J., MacKenzie, K., Melkonian, O., Peyton Jones, M., Wadler, P.: The extended UTXO model. In: Bernhard, M., et al. (eds.) FC 2020. LNCS, vol. 12063, pp. 525–539. Springer, Cham (2020). https://doi.org/10.1007/978-3-030-54455-3_37
24. Chakravarty, M.M., et al.: Native custom tokens in the extended UTXO model. In: ISoLA (2020). To appear
25. Chakravarty, M.M., et al.: UTXO$_{ma}$: UTXO with multi-asset support. In: ISoLA (2020). To appear
26. Chen, W., Zheng, Z., Cui, J., Ngai, E., Zheng, P., Zhou, Y.: Detecting Ponzi schemes on Ethereum: towards healthier blockchain technology. In: WWW, pp. 1409–1418. ACM (2018). https://doi.org/10.1145/3178876.3186046
27. Dashjr, L.: BIP 0002 (2016). https://en.bitcoin.it/wiki/BIP_0002
28. Kalis, R.: Cashscript – writing covenants (2019). https://cashscript.org/docs/guides/covenants/
29. Kumaresan, R., Bentov, I.: How to use Bitcoin to incentivize correct computations. In: ACM CCS, pp. 30–41 (2014). https://doi.org/10.1145/2660267.2660380
30. Kumaresan, R., Moran, T., Bentov, I.: How to use Bitcoin to play decentralized poker. In: ACM CCS, pp. 195–206 (2015). https://doi.org/10.1145/2810103.2813712
31. Maxwell, G.: CoinCovenants using SCIP signatures, an amusingly bad idea (2013). https://bitcointalk.org/index.php?topic=278122.0
32. Miller, A., Bentov, I.: Zero-collateral lotteries in Bitcoin and Ethereum. In: EuroS&P Workshops, pp. 4–13 (2017). https://doi.org/10.1109/EuroSPW.2017.44
33. Möser, M., Eyal, I., Sirer, E.G.: Bitcoin covenants. In: Financial Cryptography Workshops. LNCS, vol. 9604, pp. 126–141. Springer (2016). https://doi.org/10.1007/978-3-662-53357-4_9
34. Nick, J., Poelstra, A., Sanders, G.: Liquid: a Bitcoin sidechain (2020). https://blockstream.com/assets/downloads/pdf/liquid-whitepaper.pdf
35. O'Connor, R., Piekarska, M.: Enhancing Bitcoin transactions with covenants. In: Brenner, M., et al. (eds.) FC 2017. LNCS, vol. 10323, pp. 191–198. Springer, Cham (2017). https://doi.org/10.1007/978-3-319-70278-0_12
36. Wuille, P., Nick, J., Towns, A.: Taproot: SegWit version 1 spending rules, BIP 341 (2020). https://github.com/bitcoin/bips/blob/master/bip-0341.mediawiki
37. Poon, J., Dryja, T.: The Bitcoin Lightning Network: Scalable off-chain instant payments (2015). https://lightning.network/lightning-network-paper.pdf

38. Rubin, J.: CHECKTEMPLATEVERIFY, BIP 119 (2020). https://github.com/bitcoin/bips/blob/master/bip-0119.mediawiki
39. Lamela Seijas, P., Thompson, S.: Marlowe: financial contracts on blockchain. In: Margaria, T., Steffen, B. (eds.) ISoLA 2018. LNCS, vol. 11247, pp. 356–375. Springer, Cham (2018). https://doi.org/10.1007/978-3-030-03427-6_27
40. Swambo, J., Hommel, S., McElrath, B., Bishop, B.: Bitcoin covenants: three ways to control the future. CoRR abs/2006.16714 (2020)
41. Vasek, M., Moore, T.: There's no free lunch, even using Bitcoin: tracking the popularity and profits of virtual currency scams. In: Böhme, R., Okamoto, T. (eds.) FC 2015. LNCS, vol. 8975, pp. 44–61. Springer, Heidelberg (2015). https://doi.org/10.1007/978-3-662-47854-7_4
42. Zahnentferner, J.: An abstract model of UTxO-based cryptocurrencies with scripts. Cryptology ePrint Archive 2018/469 (2018). https://eprint.iacr.org/2018/469

Specifying Framing Conditions for Smart Contracts

Bernhard Beckert[(✉)] and Jonas Schiffl[(✉)]

Karlsruhe Institute of Technology, Karlsruhe, Germany
{beckert,jonas.schiffl}@kit.edu

Abstract. Smart contracts are programs which run in conjunction with distributed ledgers. They often manage valuable assets, but, like all programs, they contain errors which can be exploited by an attacker. This makes them are a prime target for formal methods. Many formal analysis methods require the contracts' program code to be annotated with formal specifications. In this paper, we propose an approach and a formalism to enrich specifications with *frame conditions*, i.e., a specification of what a smart contract function *cannot* resp. *will not* do. We discuss the storage models of two smart contract platforms, Ethereum and Hyperledger Fabric, and propose languages for specifying frame conditions for both of them, based on the theory of dynamic frames.

Keywords: Smart contract verification · Frame conditions · Dynamic frames · Solidity · Hyperledger Fabric

1 Introduction

Smart contracts are a prime target for formal methods because they manage resources, bugs cannot be fixed easily, and they are relatively small. Many formal analysis methods require the contracts's program code to be annotated with formal specifications (invariants, pre- and postconditions). These may express the top-level functional requirements for the contract that are to be analysed, verified, or checked at runtime. Or they are auxiliary specifications of components to facilitate a modular analysis.

In this paper, we propose an approach and a formalism to enrich specifications with *frame conditions*, i.e., a specification of what a function *cannot* resp. *will not* do. Even though this information can also be given as part of a postcondition, frame conditions focus on a particular kind of information, namely which parts of the storage is changed – as opposed to specifying how it is changed.

Note that it is usually much easier to specify which parts of the state a function (potentially) changes (its frame) than specifying what is not changed. The changed part is closely tied to its functionality and in most cases is much smaller than the unchanged part.

Simple, intuitive frame annotations can help programmers express their expectations as to the effect of a function, and a proof that a function actually

© Springer Nature Switzerland AG 2020
T. Margaria and B. Steffen (Eds.): ISoLA 2020, LNCS 12478, pp. 43–59, 2020.
https://doi.org/10.1007/978-3-030-61467-6_4

adheres to its frame – whether successful or not – will give valuable feedback concerning the correctness of an implementation.

The idea of dynamic frames, which we use in our approach, aims to solve the frame problem by making location sets first-class citizens in the specification language, so that a programmer can refer to such sets directly. This allows proofs that two such sets are disjoint, or that one location is not part of a given set of locations. A dynamic frame is an abstract set of locations; it is "dynamic" in the sense that the set of locations to which it evaluates can change during program execution.

Smart contract networks can be categorized according to the general availability of their services: In a public platform, everyone can set up a node to replicate the ledger and validate the correctness of all transactions. And there are no limitations as to who may make a transaction. In contrast, private networks are set up to serve a group of stakeholders; setting up a node requires permission of some sort, and access to smart contract functions is regulated. This also implies the necessity of an identity management. For our approach to smart contract frame specifications, we select representatives of both categories: Ethereum [20] as the most relevant public blockchain platform, and Hyperledger Fabric [4] as a permission-based approach that targets industrial applicability. In Sects. 3 and 4, we discuss the relevant properties of Ethereum resp. Hyperledger Fabric, define languages for specifying frame conditions that fit these properties, respectively, define their semantics, and show some examples.

Even though our main focus is on the specification language, we give some hints as to how the frame specifications can be translated into assertion statements and can thus be analysed and verified (Sect. 5).

2 Motivation

Smart contracts are computer programs, written in turing-complete, high-level programming languages, which offer services to clients in distributed, decentralized networks. The services are made available through public function calls. The main benefit of smart contracts is that they ensure deterministic and reproducible execution despite the inherently decentralized architecture.

Though there is no universally accepted definition for what constitutes a smart contract, the general consensus is that they run on a blockchain infrastructure, i.e., they work in conjunction with a distributed, immutable ledger; they can take control over assets on that ledger; and they do so in an automated and deterministic fashion, thereby enabling parties who do not necessarily trust each other to rely on them. Depending on the platform, a smart contract can be deployed either by every network participant, or by the network administration. Interaction with a smart contract is done by calling its (public) functions. Reading from and writing to the distributed ledger is possible only through smart contracts.

Since their inception, smart contracts have been a prime target for research in the area of formal methods, for two main reasons: First, the main use cases of smart contracts, i.e., managing resources in networks in which participants do not trust each other, means that programming errors can have severe consequences. Furthermore, once discovered, bugs in the code cannot be fixed as easily as with other programs, since smart contracts are either immutable once deployed, or require the explicit consent of all concerned parties for every change to the code. This makes static proofs of correctness before deployment highly desirable. Second, the characteristics of smart contracts make them rewarding targets for formal specification and verification: smart contracts are usually short, do not have many dependencies on outside libraries, and tend to refrain from using complex program structures (to the point where unbounded loops are considered bad practice [7]). This makes functional verification of single smart contract functions feasible [2]. However, verifying the correctness of a smart contract application, i.e., a set of functions operating on the same part of the state, is still challenging. As others have noted [16], smart contract applications should be viewed to have an implicit enclosing loop, within which functions and parameters are nondeterministically chosen (while smart contract architectures eventually create a shared order of transactions, it is not possible to statically predict that order). This encourages a modular approach to formal verification in the style of design-by-contract, where function calls are abstracted through pre- and postconditions.

Even if verifying the functional correctness of a single smart contract function may be within reach due to the lack of complex control structures and data types, two difficulties remain: (a) reasoning about calls from one smart contract function to other functions, (b) proving that an invariant of a smart contract application is maintained by all its functions. We argue that these difficulties should be approached by modularisation of the verification effort: Smart contract functions should be annotated with pre- and postconditions. Correctness properties of a smart contract application are formulated as an invariant. A proof of correctness for a function must then include a proof that it preserves the invariant. However, proofs of this kind often require some sort of reasoning about a frame condition, i.e., a specification of what a function *cannot* resp. *will not* do. As a very simple motivating example, consider a smart contract with only two functions, one called `pay` that accepts a positive amount of currency, and another one called `lookup` which allows anyone to observe the accumulated amount. A plausible invariant states that the accumulated amount never decreases. However, that the invariant is preserved by `lookup` may not immediately follow from `lookup`'s postcondition, which typically does not mention any changes to the contract's balance. This can be solved by a frame annotation which states that `lookup` does not change the state at all.

3   Frame Conditions for Solidity

3.1   Relevant Features of Solidity

Ethereum is a distributed computing platform for smart contracts, which are executed on the Ethereum Virtual Machine (EVM). There are several higher-level languages that can be compiled into EVM bytecode; the most popular representative of these languages is Solidity[1]. Execution of bytecode instructions on the EVM consumes a resource called *gas*. The caller of a smart contract function has to provide sufficient gas. If the execution costs exceed the provided amount of gas, the execution is aborted and has no effect.

In Ethereum, there are two types of accounts: External accounts, which only have the functionality to send and receive money, and contract accounts, which can have arbitrary functions. Every account has a balance in the built-in *Ether* cryptocurrency.

Each account in Ethereum has an address in the form of a 160-bit integer. For contract accounts, this address also serves as a namespace where the contract's state is stored.

In the Solidity programming language, the balance of a contract with address `addr` is obtained with `addr.balance`. The address of the contract to which a function belongs is accessed with `address(this)`; the address of the caller of a function is accessed with the Ethereum built-in `msg.sender` construct.

Solidity differentiates between *memory* and *storage*. Memory is not persistent between function calls; it is used, e.g., for function parameters and temporary variables. Storage refers to the data persisted on the blockchain. In our approach for frame specifications, frames only contain locations in the persistent memory. In which way a function may or may not have affected the volatile memory is irrelevant after its termination anyway. In the following, we therefore always refer to `storage`.

Solidity has two kinds of variables types: *value types* of a fixed size, like booleans, integers, fixed-size arrays etc., and *reference types*, including dynamically sized arrays, mappings, and structs. Variables of reference type point to a location (in the namespace of their contract).

3.2   Syntax and Semantics of Frame Conditions for Solidity

We define a specification language for frame analysis of Solidity smart contracts. The basic building blocks are frame conditions, which can be attached to a function and define its frame. A frame condition starts with the keyword `modifies`, which is followed by one or more location expressions or the `nothing` keyword. A location expression is a combination of an address expression and a variable expression. We also call these frame conditions *modifies clauses*.

As for addresses, `msg.sender` and `this` are special address expressions. Furthermore, expressions of `int`, `contract` and `bytes20` types can be cast to addresses.

As for variable expressions, simple variables are referred to by their name. In addition, for array, struct, and mapping expressions we allow suffixes that denote which part of the data structure may be modified: `arr` would express that the pointer to the array can be modified, while `arr[4]` refers to the fourth entry in the array to which `arr` points. `arr[0..5]` allows the modification of the

---

[1] https://solidity.readthedocs.io.

first through fifth entry of the array. Finally, `arr[*]` includes all elements of the array. Similar short-hand constructs exist for structs and mappings.

The full syntax for our Solidity frame-condition language is given in Table 1. There,

- *addrExpr* is any Solidity expression of type address. This includes address literals as well as compositional expressions like `this.x` where `x` is a variable of type address, such that `this.x.y` becomes a valid location expression.
- *primitiveTypeVarName* is any name of a variable of primitive static type (boolean, integer, address).
- *fixedSizeArrayVarName* is any name of a variable of a fixed-sized (static) array type.
- *refToArrayExpr, refToMapExpr, refToStructExpr* are any Solidity expressions that evaluate to a reference of the appropriate (dynamic) type.

Table 1. Syntax of the Solidity frame condition language

`modifies` *locExpr*+ | `nothing`		
locExpr	::=	*addrExpr* . *loc-identifier*
loc-identifier	::=	*primitiveTypeVarName* | *fixedSizeArrayVarName arraySuffix* |
		refToArrayExpr | *refToArrayExpr arraySuffix* |
		refToMapExpr | *refToMapExpr mapSuffix* |
		refToStructExpr | *refToStructExpr structSuffix*
arraySuffix	::=	`[`*intExpr*`]` | `[`*intExpr* .. *intExpr*`]` | `[*]`
mapSuffix	::=	`[`*mapKey*`]` | `[*]`
structSuffix	::=	. *struct-member* | `.*`

Note that there is a difference between dynamic and static arrays (fixed-sized byte arrays): If `arr` is dynamic, then 'modifies arr' and 'modifies arr[i]' are both valid modifies clauses, while only the latter is allowed for static arrays. The reason is that the reference to a static array cannot be changed. If a user were to write 'modifies arr' for a static array, then either that clause would be redundant or it would have meant to be 'modifies arr[*]' – both an indication of some misconception on the user's part.

To formalise the semantics of modifies clauses, we first define the set $\mathbb{L}$ of *locations* and, based on that, the concept of *state*.

Definition 1. *The set of Solidity locations is*

$$
\begin{aligned}
\mathbb{L} = \mathbb{N}_{160} \times (\,& primitiveTypeVarName \cup \\
& (fixedSizeArrayVarName \times int) \cup \\
& ptr \cup \\
& (ptr \times (arrayIndices \times mapKeySet \times structMemberSet)))
\end{aligned}
$$

where

- $\mathbb{N}_{160}$ *is the set of 160-bit numbers (addresses),*
- *primitiveTypeVarName is the set of all names of variables of primitive type,*
- *ptr is the set of all references to storage,*
- *arrayIndices = int is the set of possible array indices (integers), mapKeySet is the set of all possible map keys (all primitive types), and structMemberSet contains the names of all struct members.*

A state is a function

$$state : \mathbb{L} \to \mathbb{V}$$

that assigns values to locations, where the set of possible values $\mathbb{V}$ contains all primitive types as well as the elements of ptr, i.e., the references to storage.

Instead of the set $\mathbb{L}$ from Definition 1, we could alternatively have used $\mathbb{N}_{160} \times ptr$ as the set of locations, staying closer to the Ethereum semantics. With our more structured definition, however, we encode in the structure of locations that certain location expressions cannot alias to the same position in storage while others can.

Consider for example the location expression this.arr[4]. It represents the location $(17, (25, 4))$ if this has the address 17 and a is a variable of dynamic array type that refers to an array at position 25 in the storage of this. Depending on the type of a, the value of that location can be a primitive value, say 42, but it can also be a pointer to, e.g., a particular struct in storage if arr is an array of structs. We can immediately conclude – without further analysis of the state – that the location expression this.a[5] evaluates to $(17, (25, 5))$ and is, therefore, a different location (no aliasing). The location expression this.b[4], on the other hand, may or may not evaluate to the same location as this.a[4], depending on the values of a and b in the particular state (aliasing possible). Similarly, if x and y are variables of static primitive type, then this.x and this.y evaluate to $(17, x)$ resp. $(17, y)$ and are, thus, different independently of the state. If, on the other hand, x and y are variables of dynamic type, their locations are of the form $(17, 25)$ (the second component is a pointer), and they may be the same.

The full semantics of the location expression lists which occur in modifies clauses is defined by the function $\llbracket \cdot \rrbracket^s$:

Definition 2. *Given a state s, the evaluation*

$$\llbracket \cdot \rrbracket^s : LocationExpressions \to \mathbb{L}$$

of lists of location expressions is defined by the rules shown in Table 2.

In these rules, $\llbracket e \rrbracket^s_{Eth}$ denotes Ethereum's evaluation function that evaluates an expression e in a state s according to Ethereum's semantics.

Note that, in the above definition, $\llbracket \cdot \rrbracket^s$ evaluates to a set of locations, while $\llbracket \cdot \rrbracket^s_{Eth}$ returns a single value (a primitive value, and address, or a storage pointer). The function $\llbracket \cdot \rrbracket^s_{Eth}$ is also responsible for giving values for the special expressions

Table 2. Rules for the evaluation function $[\![\cdot]\!]^s$ (see Definition 2)

If Exc is any expression that throws an exception:

$[\![Exc]\!]^s$ $:= \emptyset$

Otherwise:

$[\![nothing]\!]^s$	$:= \emptyset$
$[\![locExpr_1, locExpr_2]\!]^s$	$:= [\![locExpr_1]\!]^s \cup [\![locExpr_2]\!]^s$
$[\![addrExpr.loc\text{-}identifier]\!]^s$	$:= ([\![addrExpr]\!]^s_{Eth}, [\![loc\text{-}identifier]\!]^s)$
$[\![primitiveTypeVarName]\!]^s$	$:= \{\, primitiveTypeVarName \,\}$
$[\![fixedSizeArrayVarName\ \ arraySuffix]\!]^s$	$:= \{\, fixedSizeArrayVarName \,\} \times [\![arraySuffix]\!]^s$
$[\![refToArrayExpr]\!]^s$	$:= \{\, [\![refToArrayExpr]\!]^s_{Eth} \,\}$
$[\![refToArrayExpr\ \ arraySuffix]\!]^s$	$:= \{\, [\![refToArrayExpr]\!]^s_{Eth} \,\} \times [\![arraySuffix]\!]^s$
$[\![refToMapExpr]\!]^s$	$:= \{\, [\![refToMapExpr]\!]^s_{Eth} \,\}$
$[\![refToMapExpr\ \ mapSuffix]\!]^s$	$:= \{\, [\![refToMapExpr]\!]^s_{Eth} \,\} \times [\![mapSuffix]\!]^s$
$[\![refToStructExpr]\!]^s$	$:= \{\, [\![refToStructExpr]\!]^s_{Eth} \,\}$
$[\![refToStructExpr\ structSuffix]\!]^s$	$:= \{\, [\![refToStructExpr]\!]^s_{Eth} \,\} \times [\![structSuffix]\!]^s$
$[\![[intExpr]]\!]^s$	$:= \{\, [\![intExpr]\!]^s_{Eth} \,\}$
$[\![[intExpr_1 .. intExpr_2]]\!]^s$	$:= \{\, i \in int \mid [\![intExpr_1]\!]^s_{Eth} \leq i \,\wedge$
	$\qquad\qquad i \leq [\![intExpr_2]\!]^s_{Eth} \,\}$
$[\![[*]]\!]^s$	$:= int \cup mapKeySet$
$[\![.*]\!]^s$	$:= structMemberSet$
$[\![mapKey]\!]^s$	$:= \{\, mapKey \,\}$

`this`, `msg.sender`, `msg.value` etc., which we evaluate according to Ethereum's semantics.

Finally, we can define what it means for a function be correct w.r.t. a modifies clause:

Definition 3. *A Solidity smart contract function f is correct w.r.t. a modifies clause 'modifies locExpr' iff the following holds:*

For all preState, postState $\in$ states such that f terminates in postState when started in preState,

$$\forall l \in \mathbb{L} : preState(l) \neq postState(l) \implies l \in [\![locExpr]\!]^s$$

Note that the correctness condition of the above definition is equivalent to

$$\{l \mid preState(l) \neq postState(l)\} \subseteq [\![locExpr]\!]^s$$

According to the first line in Table 2, if a location expression throws an exception, such as division by zero or out-of-bounds array access, its semantics is the empty set. This is useful in the context of Ethereum, because if such an exception occurs, the function is rolled back and has no effect. In this case, no location is modified, and the modifies clause is trivially satisfied.

Modifies clauses are always evaluated in the prestate of a function execution, not in the state in which an assignment happens during the execution. For example, if the modifies clause contains `this.a[i]` and `this.i`, then the assignments 'a[i] = a[i]+1; i = i+1;' are fine, but 'i = i+1; a[i] = a[i]+1;' violates the clause. The latter would need `this.a[i+1]` to be included.

We do not allow pointer arithmetic in modifies clauses, i.e., `(a+n)[1]` cannot be used to refer to `a[2]` for any n. Modifies clauses with pointer arithmetic would be confusing, a source of errors, and a way of obfuscating the clauses for malicious programmers. Moreover, pointer arithmetic is notoriously hard to analyse for verification tools.

3.3   Example: A Simple Solidity Bank Contract

The example in Listing 1 shows a simple version of a Solidity contract for a bank, where clients can deposit and withdraw their money. When someone deposits their funds, the money is transferred to the bank contract, and their balance with the bank is adapted (in the `bals` mapping).

The modifies clauses of `deposit` and `withdraw` include `bals[msg.sender]` to indicate that one – and only one – entry of the `bals` mapping is changed; the other entries of the mapping remain unchanged, which is important for checking the '`this.balance == \sum(bals)`' (see Sect. 5).

The modifies clauses also mention the contract's as well as the caller's balance (`this.balance` and `msg.sender.balance`), which are modified because the function either accepts funds (because it is `payable`) or transfers funds to the caller.

A modifies clause has also been added to function `lookup` to specify that *only* the deposit and withdraw methods can change the bookkeeping balance, and `lookup` modifies `nothing`.

3.4   Example: Uninitialized Pointers in Ethereum

The example in Listing 2 illustrates one of the pitfalls of the solidity programming language (or, more precisely, a recent version of Ethereum).

The `Surprise` contract declares a struct `Thing`, a public integer variable x and a mapping `things`. The function `addThing` declares a variable t of the `Thing` type, but does not initialize it (which is problematic); afterwards, the struct's boolean field is set to false, and the new thing is added to the contract's `things` mapping. Unintuitively, calling this function overwrites x: Since t is an uninitialized storage pointer, it automatically points to slot 0 of the contract's storage, which in fact is also the position of the storage variable x. The boolean value `false` is cast to the type of x, i.e. `uint`, which yields 0. The `addThing` function modifies the value of a variable that it does not syntactically refer to, which is not what a programmer would expect. A framing condition that clearly states which locations a method may modify (along with a tool to prove that the function indeed fulfills the specification) would render errors of this kind harmless (of course, the tool needs to know about the intricacies of the memory model). In the example, the function is annotated with a `modifies` clause stating that only the `things` mapping at the key of the newly created object may be modified. A proof of correctness against this specification would fail, leading the programmer to detect the error. A programmer may then have the (wrong) idea that the problem can be fixed by adding t to the modifies clause; but that would

```
contract bank {
  //@ invariant this.balance == \sum(bals);
  mapping (address => uint) private bals;

  //@ postcondition
  //@      this.balance == \old(this.balance) + amt
  //@      && \bals[msg.sender] == \old(bals[msg.sender]) + amt);
  //@
  //@ modifies bals[msg.sender], this.balance, msg.sender.balance;
  function deposit() public payable returns (uint) {
    bals[msg.sender] += msg.value;
    return bals[msg.sender];
  }

  //@ postcondition bals[msg.sender] >= amt
  //@   ==> (this.balance == \old(this.balance) - amt
  //@      && \bals[msg.sender] == \old(bals[msg.sender]) - amt);
  //@ postcondition bals[msg.sender] < amt
  //@   ==> (this.balance == \old(this.balance)
  //@      && \bals[msg.sender] == \old(bals[msg.sender]));
  //@
  //@ modifies bals[msg.sender], this.balance, msg.sender.balance;
  function withdraw(uint amt) public returns (uint) {
    if (amt <= bals[msg.sender]) {
      bals[msg.sender] -= amt;
      msg.sender.transfer(amt);
    }
    return bals[msg.sender];
  }

  //@ modifies \nothing;
  function lookup() public returns (uint) {
    return bals[msg.sender];
  }
}
```

Listing 1. A simple bank contract written in Solidity

lead to a syntax error because the modifies clause is not within the scope of t's declaration.

Beginning with solidity version 0.5 (Nov. 2018), uninitialized storage pointers lead to a compiler error, because the behaviour described above was considered too dangerous and unintuitive. Nevertheless, the example shows that modifies clauses help in cases where a programmer has a misconception of what a function does. Moreover, a programming language does not even have to be unintuitive; mistakes always happen. Framing specifications can help to uncover these mistakes before they cause potentially serious errors.

```
contract Surprise {

  struct Thing {
    bool b;
  }

  uint public x = 100;
  mapping(string => Thing) public things;

  //@ modifies things[name];
  function addThing(string name) public {
    Thing storage t;
    t.b = false;
    things[name] = t;
  }
}
```

Listing 2. An example (This example is inspired by a similar example in [10].) of unintuitive behaviour in Ethereum

4   Frame Conditions for Hyperledger Fabric

4.1   Relevant Features of Hyperledger Fabric

Hyperledger Fabric emerged as one of the projects from the Linux Foundation's Hyperledger umbrella project. It aims to offer an "operating system for permissioned blockchains" [4]. Unlike Ethereum, a Fabric network consists of agents who know each other's identity. Fabric smart contracts are programs written in one of a number of languages, e.g., Go, Java, or Javascript. Function calls are regulated by access control and submitted to a number of nodes. If these nodes compute the same results, the resulting state changes are submitted to an ordering service in the form of a read/write set (i.e., a set of locations and values that are read or written, along with versions in order to detect read/write conflicts), and finally broadcast to all participating nodes.

Hyperledger Fabric has its own storage nomenclature. The fundamental data structure is a blockchain which stores the assignments made as a result of smart contract function calls. However, the data structure that a smart contract developer interacts with is not the blockchain, but an abstraction called the *world state*. The world state is a database that holds the current values of the ledger state, expressed as key-value pairs. The world state at key s is defined as the value of the last assignment to s in the blockchain. The *ledger* is the combination of the blockchain and the world state determined by the blockchain.

In the following, we consider the world state that represents the storage of one fabric network. Our frame condition language for Fabric allows for less granularity than the one for Solidity: It does not mention specific data structures (like structs or arrays) nor does it allow field access. This is due to the fact that Fabric chaincode can be written in one of several programming languages with different characteristics and built-in structures. We want our proposed language to capture the process of accessing the world state, which is similar in the different APIs. Our language can then be instantiated (i.e., refined) for the actual chaincode programming languages.

In Fabric, data is (only) stored in the form of byte arrays. Thus, all data structures have to be serialised before they can be written to the ledger, and deserialized after reading. This does not immediately lead to problems because we treat the data stored at one location as a monolithic block, and do not allow expressions accessing subunits of data structures (like fields of a stored object, or elements of a stored array). This has the drawback that, if more fine-grained information about which parts of a data structure are changed is required, this has to be achieved through cumbersome auxiliary specifications that refer to serialization and deserialization (see Sect. 4.3).

In the Java API for Fabric, basic storage access is provided by the `getState`, `putState` and `delState` methods. The ledger object on which these methods operate is passed as a parameter of each chaincode function. Range access is also possible: `getStateByRange(String start, String end)` returns all keys which are lexicographically between the two parameters, and the corresponding values. This is reflected in our specification language. We allow location expressions to end with an asterisk * to express that all locations with a given prefix may be modified. Furthermore, we allow expressions that evaluate to sets of strings, such as lists or arrays.

Composite keys are another way of storing and querying data in Fabric. A composite key consists of a list of attributes, and a string which denotes the types of these attributes. For example, an item in an auction (cf. Sect. 4.3) could be represented as a Java struct with two fields for the ID of the item (`itemID`) and the ID of the owner (`ownerID`). A composite key for one specific item could have the form (`itemID~ownerID, 42, "john"`). This enables queries for either the ID of the item or the owner; in this example, it would allow a function to retrieve all items belonging to a particular ID without having to read all items from the state and filter them by their owner. Since the composite key mechanism is present in the APIs for all chaincode programming languages, it is included in our specification language in the string set expressions.

In Hyperledger Fabric, the caller of a function is obtained via the CID (for Client Identification) interface, which guarantees that each agent in the network is identifiable by a unique ID.

4.2   Syntax and Semantics of Frame Conditions for Fabric

In Fabric, a location is uniquely described by a string. Our specification language (see Table 3) therefore consists of the `modifies` keyword followed by one or more expressions which return strings or sets of strings, such as string ranges (e.g., "`modifies itemA .. itemZ`" would express that all locations whose identifiers are lexicographically between `itemA` and `itemZ` can be modified), prefix expressions using the asterisk (e.g., "`modifies item*`" would include all locations

Table 3. Syntax of the Fabric frame condition language

$$\texttt{modifies}\ locExpr+\ |\ \texttt{nothing}$$

$locExpr$	$::=$	$strExpr\ |\ rangeExpr\ |\ starExpr\ |\ strSetExpr$
$rangeExpr$	$::=$	$strExpr\ ..\ strExpr$
$starExpr$	$::=$	$strExpr\ *$

where the key starts with "item"), and side-effect-free expressions that return a string or a collection of strings (such as string arrays in Java or Go).

The full syntax for our Fabric frame-condition language is given in Table 3. There,

- $strExpr$ is expression in the programming language that evaluates to a string,
- $strSetExpr$ is any expression that evaluates to a collection or set of strings (e.g., string arrays).

To formalise the semantics of modifies clauses, we again have to define a concept of state. The definition is similar to that for Solidity frame conditions (Definition 1), except that now locations are strings, and their values are byte arrays.

Definition 4. *The set of Fabric locations is*

$$\mathbb{L}\ =\ String$$

where String is the set of all strings. A state *is a function*

$$state : \mathbb{L} \to \mathbb{V}$$

that assigns values to locations, where the set of possible values $\mathbb{V}$ *is the set of all (finite) byte arrays.*

The semantics of location expression lists, which occur in modifies clauses is again defined by giving rules for the function $[\![\cdot]\!]^s$:

Definition 5. *Given a state* s, *the evaluation*

$$[\![\cdot]\!]^s : LocationExpressions \to \mathbb{L}$$

of lists of location expressions is defined by the rules shown in Table 4.

In these rules, $[\![e]\!]^s_{Fab}$ *denotes the evaluation function that evaluates an expression* e *in a state* s *according to the semantics of the programming language that is used to write Fabric contracts.*

The definition of when a contract function satisfies its modifies clause is the same as that for Solidity (Definition 3):

$$\forall l \in \mathbb{L} : preState(l) \neq postState(l) \implies l \in [\![locExpr]\!]^s$$

Table 4. Rules for the evaluation function $\llbracket \cdot \rrbracket^s$ (see Definition 5)

If Exc is any expression that throws an exception or whose evaluation is undefined:

$$\llbracket Exc \rrbracket^s \qquad\qquad := \emptyset$$

Otherwise:

$$\llbracket nothing \rrbracket^s \qquad\qquad := \emptyset$$
$$\llbracket locExpr_1, locExpr_2 \rrbracket^s \quad := \llbracket locExpr_1 \rrbracket^s \cup \llbracket locExpr_2 \rrbracket^s$$
$$\llbracket strExpr \rrbracket^s \qquad\qquad := \{ \llbracket strExpr \rrbracket^s_{Fab} \}$$
$$\llbracket strSetExpr \rrbracket^s \qquad\quad := \{ s \in String \mid s \text{ is in the collection } \llbracket strSetExpr \rrbracket^s_{Fab} \}$$
$$\llbracket strExpr_1 .. strExpr_2 \rrbracket^s := \{ s \in String \mid \llbracket strExpr_1 \rrbracket^s_{Fab} \leq s \text{ and } s \leq \llbracket strExpr_2 \rrbracket^s_{Fab}$$
$$\text{in the lexicographic ordering on strings} \}$$
$$\llbracket strExpr* \rrbracket^s \qquad\qquad := \{ s \in String \mid strExpr \text{ is a syntactical prefix of } s \}$$

```
public class Auction extends ChaincodeBase {

  //@ modifies auctionID, itemLocs;
  Response createAuction(...) {
    ...
  }

  //@ modifies
  //@    auctionID,
  //@    ((Auction) deserialize(ledger.getState(auctionID))).itemLocs
  Response closeAuction(String auctionID, ChaincodeStub ledger) {
    Auction a = deserialize(ledger.getState(auctionID));
    if (getCurrentTime() < a.ending) return newErrorResponse();
    a.closed = true;
    for (String s: a.itemLocs) {
      Item i = deserialize(ledger.getState(s));
      i.owner_id = a.highestBidderID;
      i.auctionID = "";
      ledger.putState(i.itemID, serialize(i));
    }
    ledger.putState(auctionID, serialize(a));
    return newSuccessResponse();
  }
  ...
}
```

Listing 3. Fabric chaincode from an auction contract

4.3   Example: A Fabric Auction Contract

In Listing 3, excerpts of an auction smart contract are shown. Items that can be bought or sold are represented as structs with fields for their own ID, the ID of their owner, and the ID of the auction in which the item is offered (if any).

Besides items, auction objects are stored on the ledger. They declare a list of strings which signify the locations of the items that are sold in the auction. Furthermore, they have an ID, a minimum bid, and an ending time. When an auction is created, it is checked that all items actually belong to the caller of the function, i.e., the identity which creates the auction. If all checks succeed, the items are given a non-empty auction ID, signifying they are currently being auctioned and cannot be offered in another auction.

When an auction is closed, the ownership of all its items is transferred to the highest bidder, and the auction ID of the items is set to the empty string, signifying that they are currently not being auctioned. The `closeAuction()` function can modify the auction object referred to in parameter `auctionID`. It also can modify all the items which are being sold in this auction object. However, there is no direct way to refer to this set of items, since their locations are not directly passed as parameters but only indirectly as a field of the auction object. Thus, to refer to the item list in the `modifies` clause, the object stored at the location of the `auctionID` string needs to be read from the ledger with `getState`, deserialized, and cast to an object of the auction type: '`(Auction) deserialize(ledger.getState(auctionID))`'. The `itemLocs` field of this object yields a list and, thus, constitutes a string set expression as defined by our specification language. If this frame condition is proven to be correct, it can then be used to prove more complex properties of the auction smart contract, e.g., that items can only be modified with consent of their current owner.

5   Towards Analysis and Verification of Frame Conditions

Though the focus of this paper is on the specification of frame conditions, we give short overview of how they can be analysed and verified, and how frame conditions can be used in the analysis and verification of other formal specifications such as invariants and pre-/postconditions.

The most obvious way to express what needs to be proved to establish correctness of a smart contract function f w.r.t. its frame condition is to use the formula from Definition 3 as a postcondition and to prove that it holds after all executions of f:

$$\forall l \in \mathbb{L} : preState(l) \neq postState(l) \implies l \in [\![locExpr]\!]^s \tag{1}$$

That is actually what is typically done in deductive verification tools with an expressive program logic such as the KeY tool [1], which supports both automatic and interactive verification of Java code with annotations such as pre-/postconditions and modifies clauses. KeY's support for user interaction allows verification w.r.t. expressive specifications, but proving frame conditions can require a lot of effort for interactive proof construction.

For systems based on software (bounded) model checking or runtime checking, formula (1) is problematic because it quantifies over all locations and, moreover, requires to store the prestate values of locations so that they can be compared to their poststate values. For such systems, it is better to add an assertion for each assignment such that the assertion fails if the assignment writes to a location not mentioned in the frame condition (for simplicity, we only consider assignments but this approach is applicable to other state-changing operations as well). Notice that only assignments to storage locations need to be covered, as assignment to volatile memory is always legal.

Consider, for example, the assignment 'bals[msg.sender] += msg.value;' in function deposit (Listing 1). It leads to the assertion that $[\![bals[msg.sender]]\!]^s$ must be an element of the locations in the modifies clause, where s is the state in which the assignment happens and the modifies clause is evaluated in the prestate of the function. This assertion is true, but note that even in this simple case the two states (s and the prestate) are not the same as the function is payable, and the transfer of funds happens before the assignment deposit is executed. Still, checking this assertion is easier then proving formula (1), as the assertion does not contain a universal quantifier and the set of locations in the modifies clause is much smaller than the set of all locations mentioned in formula (1). An implementation that generates the appropriate assertions needs to be aware and make use of the evaluation $[\![\cdot]\!]^s$ for modifies clauses (Definition 2).

Note, that an analysis which checks every assignment may actually raise false alarms. According to our definition, an assignment to a storage locations is allowed – even if the location is not mentioned in the modifies clause – if it has no effect (e.g., 'x=x+0') or is temporary (e.g., 'x=x+1;x=x-1'). However, such false alarms are rare in practice and mostly indicate redundant code or bad programming style even if they do not actually violate the modifies clause.

Once the correctness of a function w.r.t. a modifies clause has been established, that knowledge can be used in further correctness proofs. For example, consider the invariant shown at the beginning of contract bank (Listing 1). To prove that this invariant is preserved by function deposit, one can analyse deposit's implementation. But if deposit has already been shown to satisfy its specification, the proof can be modularised, i.e., one can prove that the invariant is implied by the specification. That requires to prove that (a) the invariant implies the precondition and that (b) the postcondition implies the invariant. The latter step, however, is only possible using the modifies clause. The postcondition alone is not sufficient as it only expresses what the function does, not what it does not do. The postcondition does not say anything about the elements of bals[c] for $c \neq msg.sender$ in the poststate. But the modifies clause comes to the rescue: since these locations are not mentioned in the modifies clause they must be unchanged, which implies that their value from the prestate is preserved.

6 Related Work

Several approaches to security analysis and formal verification of smart contracts have been proposed. They range from simple static analysis for detecting known anti-patterns (e.g., [14]), over dynamic approaches (e.g., [9]), trace properties [16] and functional specification and verification [5,6]) to full formalizations of the

Ethereum virtual machine in the Isabelle/HOL framework [3] (see [17] for a recent overview).

Frame analysis is an established field of research, and several logic frameworks have been proposed. The two most prominent approaches are *separation logic* [18] and *dynamic frames* [12].

Separation logic is an extension of Hoare Logic which enables reasoning about programs with complex pointer structures. It has been used for verification and program analysis in a variety of tools, such as jStar [8], a verification tool for Java programs, or the RustBelt project [11] for verification of the core of the Rust programming language.

The theory of dynamic frames has been widely used for program verification; for example, the Java Modeling Language [13] (and, subsequently, verification tools that build upon it) use a dynamic-frames approach (see [1]).

Combinations of both approaches have also been proposed [19]. For example, *Chalice* [15] is a language and program verifier for reasoning about concurrent programs with built-in specification constructs written in the style of implicit dynamic frames.

Our proposed specification languages for smart contracts use the dynamic frames approach. This has the advantage that the programmer can write the specification in the same terms that they need to know to write the program code. There is no additional learning required; the specification language is very similar to the programming language itself. This is a difference to separation logic, which requires more knowledge about the logic behind the specification.

From our experience, this does not make the proofs of correctness more difficult: While separation logic may have an advantage for reasoning about complex pointer data structures, these do not occur in the reality of smart contracts. Therefore, we can use the simple, intuitive specification language of dynamic frames without sacrificing expressive power or efficient proofs.

7 Conclusion

In this paper, we argue that formal specification and verification of smart contracts would benefit from frame conditions. We propose framing specification languages for two smart contract platforms, Ethereum and Hyperledger Fabric.

We plan to implement verification support by translating the proposed modifies clauses into a standard assertion language supported by existing tools. That will allow to automatically generate and then discharge proof obligations from our frame annotations. An implementation that generates the appropriate assertions needs to be aware and make use of the evaluation function $\llbracket \cdot \rrbracket^s$ for modifies clauses (Definition 2).

For Fabric specification, it would also be useful to support more complex location expressions. Regular expressions, which many programmers are familiar with, would make a useful addition. This would, however, also bring new challenges for the verification of the resulting proof obligations.

References

1. Ahrendt, W., Beckert, B., Bubel, R., Hähnle, R., Schmitt, P.H., Ulbrich, M. (eds.): Deductive Software Verification - The KeY Book: From Theory to Practice. LNCS 10001. Springer, Heidelberg (2016). https://doi.org/10.1007/978-3-319-49812-6
2. Ahrendt, W., Pace, G.J., Schneider, G.: Smart contracts: a killer application for deductive source code verification. Principled Software Development, pp. 1–18. Springer, Cham (2018). https://doi.org/10.1007/978-3-319-98047-8_1
3. Amani, S., Bégel, M., Bortin, M., Staples, M.: Towards verifying ethereum smart contract bytecode in Isabelle/HOL. In: CPP 2018, pp. 66–77. ACM (2018)
4. Androulaki, E., et al.: Hyperledger fabric: a distributed operating system for permissioned blockchains. In: EuroSys 2018. ACM (2018)
5. Beckert, B., Herda, M., Kirsten, M., Schiffl, J.: Formal specification and verification of Hyperledger Fabric chaincode. In: The 3rd Symposium on Distributed Ledger Technology. SDLT 2018 (2018)
6. Bhargavan, K., et al.: Formal verification of smart contracts: short paper. In: PLAS 2016, pp. 91–96. ACM Press, Vienna (2016)
7. ConsenSys Diligence: Known attacks: ethereum smart contract best practices (2020). https://consensys.github.io/smart-contract-best-practices/known_attacks/. Accessed 26 May 2020
8. Distefano, D., Parkinson, M.J.: jStar: towards practical verification for Java. ACM SIGPLAN Not. **43**(10), 213–226 (2008)
9. Ellul, J., Pace, G.J.: Runtime verification of ethereum smart contracts. In: EDCC, pp. 158–163. IEEE (2018)
10. Hitchens, R.: Storage Pointers in Solidity. B9lab blog, November 2018
11. Jung, R., Jourdan, J.H., Krebbers, R., Dreyer, D.: RustBelt: securing the foundations of the Rust programming language. In: POPL, pp. 66:1–66:34, December 2017
12. Kassios, I.T.: Dynamic frames: support for framing, dependencies and sharing without restrictions. In: Misra, J., Nipkow, T., Sekerinski, E. (eds.) FM 2006. LNCS, vol. 4085, pp. 268–283. Springer, Heidelberg (2006). https://doi.org/10.1007/11813040_19
13. Leavens, G.T., Cheon, Y.: Design by contract with JML (2006). jmlspecs.org
14. Luu, L., Chu, D.H., Olickel, H., Saxena, P., Hobor, A.: Making smart contracts smarter. In: CCS 2016, pp. 254–269. ACM Press, Vienna (2016)
15. Parkinson, M.J., Summers, A.J.: The relationship between separation logic and implicit dynamic frames. Logical Methods Comput. Sci. **8**(3) (2012)
16. Permenev, A., Dimitrov, D., Tsankov, P., Drachsler-Cohen, D., Vechev, M.: VerX: safety verification of smart contracts. In: IEEE Symposium on Security & Privacy (2020)
17. Praitheeshan, P., Pan, L., Yu, J., Liu, J., Doss, R.: Security analysis methods on ethereum smart contract vulnerabilities: a survey. arXiv:1908.08605 (2019)
18. Reynolds, J.: Separation logic: a logic for shared mutable data structures. In: LICS, pp. 55–74. IEEE, July 2002
19. Smans, J., Jacobs, B., Piessens, F.: Implicit dynamic frames: combining dynamic frames and separation logic. In: Drossopoulou, S. (ed.) ECOOP 2009. LNCS, vol. 5653, pp. 148–172. Springer, Heidelberg (2009). https://doi.org/10.1007/978-3-642-03013-0_8
20. Wood, G.: Ethereum: a secure decentralised generalised transaction ledger. Ethereum Proj. Yellow Pap. **151**, 1–32 (2014)

Making Tezos Smart Contracts More Reliable with Coq

Bruno Bernardo(✉), Raphaël Cauderlier, Guillaume Claret, Arvid Jakobsson, Basile Pesin, and Julien Tesson

Nomadic Labs, Paris, France
{bruno.bernardo,raphael.cauderlier,guillaume.claret,arvid.jakobsson,
basile.pesin,julien.tesson}@nomadic-labs.com

Abstract. Tezos is a smart-contract blockchain. Tezos smart contracts are written in a low-level stack-based language called Michelson. This article gives an overview of efforts using the Coq proof assistant to have stronger guarantees on Michelson smart contracts: the Mi-Cho-Coq framework, a Coq library defining formal semantics of Michelson, as well as an interpreter, a simple optimiser and a weakest-precondition calculus to reason about Michelson smart contracts; Albert, an intermediate language that abstracts Michelson stacks with a compiler written in Coq that targets Mi-Cho-Coq.

Keywords: Certified programming · Certified compilation · Programming languages · Blockchains · Smart contracts

1 Introduction

Tezos [5,15,16] is a public blockchain launched in June 2018. An open-source implementation of a Tezos node in OCaml is available [2]. Tezos has smart-contracts capabilities, a proof-of-stake consensus algorithm, and a voting mechanism that allows token holders to vote for changes to a subset of the codebase called the *economic protocol*. This subset contains, amongst other elements, the voting rules themselves, the consensus algorithm, and the interpreter for Michelson, the language for Tezos smart contracts.

Michelson [1] is a stack-based Turing-complete domain-specific language with a mix of low-level and high-level features. Low-level features include stack manipulation instructions. High-level features are high-level data types (option types, sum types, product types, lists, sets, maps, and anonymous functions) as well as corresponding instructions. Michelson is strongly typed: data, stacks and instructions have a type. Intuitively the type of a stack is a list of the types of its values, and the type of an instruction is a function type from the input stack to the output stack. The combination of high and low level features is the result of a trade-off between the need to meter resource consumption (computation *gas* and storage costs) and the willingness to have strong guarantees on the Michelson programs.

T. Margaria and B. Steffen (Eds.): ISoLA 2020, LNCS 12478, pp. 60–72, 2020.
https://doi.org/10.1007/978-3-030-61467-6_5

Michelson has been designed with formal verification in mind: its strong type system guarantees that there can be no runtime error apart from explicit failure and *gas* or token exhaustion. Furthermore, its OCaml implementation uses GADTs [25] which gives subject reduction for free. In this article, we describe a couple of efforts using Coq to make Tezos smart contracts more reliable. The first one is Mi-Cho-Coq, a Coq library that implements a Michelson interpreter, a weakest precondition calculus enabling the functional verification of Michelson programs as well as a very simple optimiser.

The second one is Albert, an intermediate language that abstracts Michelson stacks into records with named variables, for which we have implemented a compiler in Coq that targets Mi-Cho-Coq. Because of its low-level aspects, it is hard to write Michelson programs, and as a consequence, higher-level languages compiling to Michelson, such as LIGO [4] or SmartPy [7] have been developed in the Tezos ecosystem. Ideally, there would be certified compilers from these high-level languages to Michelson, and formal proofs of smart-contracts would be done directly at the higher level and not at the Michelson level, as it is done with Mi-Cho-Coq. The goal of Albert is to facilitate the implementation of certified compilers to Michelson by being used as a target for certified compilers from high-level languages.

This article is organised as follows: in Sect. 2 we illustrate the Michelson language with an example, we describe the Mi-Cho-Coq library in Sect. 3 and Albert in Sect. 4. Future and related work is discussed in Sect. 5.

2   Example of a Michelson contract

The goal of this section is to give the reader an intuitive feeling of the Michelson language. Our explanations will be illustrated by an example of a Michelson program, a voting contract, presented in Fig. 1a. This contract allows any voter to vote for a predefined set of choices. Voting requires a fee of 5 tez. It is possible to vote multiple times. The predefined set of choices is the initial storage chosen at the deployment of the contract. In this example, we assume that we want to vote for our favourite proof assistant amongst Agda, Coq and Isabelle (cf. Fig. 1b). Initially, each tool has obviously 0 vote.

Smart contracts are accounts that can contain code and storage. Calls to a smart-contract provokes the execution of the code contained in the account with the data sent during the transaction as input arguments for the code. The execution of the code can lead to a modification of the storage, it can also generate other transactions. The storage must be initialised when the contract is deployed on the chain.

A Michelson program is thus composed of three fields: `storage`, `parameter` and `code` that respectively contain types of the *storage* of the account, of the *parameter* that is sent during the transaction, or the *code* contained in the account.

In the case of the voting contract, the `storage` (l.1) is a map from strings to integers: the keys are the different choices for the vote, the values are the number of votes for a given choice. The `parameter` (l.2) is a string that represents the ballot that has been chosen by the caller of the contract.

As mentioned in the introduction, Michelson is a stack based language. The calling convention of Michelson is the following: the initial stack contains one element that is a pair of which the left member is the parameter sent by the transaction and the right element is the initial storage. At the end of the execution of a Michelson script, the stack must have one element that is a pair containing on the left a list of operations (*e.g.* a transaction) that will be executed afterwards and on the right the updated storage. Each instruction takes an input stack and rewrites it into an output stack. In the comments of the example are written the content of the stack before and after the execution of some groups of instructions. The program starts by verifying that enough tokens were sent by the voters. This is implemented in lines 5 to 8. The amount sent by the voter is pushed to the stack (`AMOUNT`) followed by the minimum amount required (5000000 *μtez i.e* 5 *tez*). `COMPARE` pops the two amounts and pushes $1, 0, -1$ whether the 5 *tez* threshold is greater, equal or smaller than the amount sent by the voter. If the threshold is greater then the contract will `FAIL`: the execution of the contract is stopped and the transaction is cancelled. Lines 9 to 11 contain stack manipulations that duplicate (with instruction `DUP`) the ballot and the current vote count. `DIP {code}` protects the top of the stack by executing `code` on the stack without its top element. The next block, from line 12 to 18, tries to `UPDATE` (l.18) the map with an incremented number of votes for the chosen candidate. This only happens if a candidate is a valid one, that is, if it is equal to one of the keys of the map. Indeed, in line 13 `GET` tries to retrieve the number of votes: it returns None if the chosen candidate is not in the list or Some i if the candidate is in the list and has i votes. `ASSERT_SOME` will fail if None is at the top of the stack and will pop Some i and push i at the top. The incrementation by one of the number of votes for the chosen candidate is done in l.15.

3   Mi-Cho-Coq: Defining Clear Semantics of Michelson

Mi-Cho-Coq [8] is a Coq library that contains an implementation of the Michelson syntax and semantics as well as a weakest precondition calculus that facilitates functional verifcation of Tezos smart contracts. Also, we have recently implemented a certified optimiser that performs basic simplifications of Michelson programs.

Mi-Cho-Coq has already been presented in [8] and we refer the reader to this publication for more details. Here we present Mi-Cho-Coq more succintly and focus on high-level additions and changes, as the implementation has evolved significantly.

```
1   storage (map string int); # candidates
2   parameter string; # chosen
3   code {
4     # (chosen, candidates):[]
5     AMOUNT; # amount:(chosen, candidates):[]
6     PUSH mutez 5000000; COMPARE; GT;
7     # (5 tez > amount):(chosen, candidates):[]
8     IF { FAIL } {}; # (chosen, candidates):[]
9     DUP; DIP { CDR; DUP };
10    # (chosen, candidates):candidates:candidates:[]
11    CAR; DUP; # chosen:chosen:candidates:candidates:[]
12    DIP { # chosen:candidates:candidates:[]
13        GET; ASSERT_SOME;
14        # candidates[chosen]:candidates:[]
15        PUSH int 1; ADD; SOME
16        # (Some (candidates[chosen]+1)):candidates:[]
17      }; # chosen:(Some (candidates[chosen]+1)):candidates:[]
18    UPDATE; # candidates':[]
19    NIL operation; PAIR # (nil, candidates'):[]
20  }
```

(a)

```
{Elt "Agda" 0 ; Elt "Coq" 0 ; Elt "Isabelle" 0}
```

(b)

Fig. 1. A simple voting contract a and an example of initial storage b

3.1 Syntax, Typing and Semantics of Michelson in Coq

Syntax and Typing. The data stored in the stacks have a type defined in the type inductive. The type of a stack is a list of type. Instructions are defined in the instruction inductive type. instruction is indexed by the type of the input and output stacks. This indexing implies that only well-typed Michelson instructions are representable in Mi-Cho-Coq.[1] A full contract is a sequence of instructions respecting the calling convention of Michelson mentioned above:

```
instruction ((pair params storage) :: nil) ((pair (list operation) storage) :: nil).
```

where storage is the type of the storage of the contract and params the type of its parameter.

Implementation-wise, Coq's canonical structures are used to deal with the ad-hoc polymorphism of some Michelson instructions (*e.g* ADD that can add integers to timestamp or mutez or integers). Coq's notations make contracts'appearance in Mi-Cho-Coq very close to actual contracts.

Also a lexer, parser and typechecker have been implemented, making it possible to generate a Mi-Cho-Coq AST from a string representing a Michelson contract. Support for Michelson entry-points and annotations has been added.

---

[1] This is also the case in the OCaml Michelson interpreter via the use of GADTs.

Semantics. An interpreter for Michelson has been implemented as an evaluator eval. Its simplified type is forall {A B : list type}, instruction A B → nat → stack A → M (stack B). Intuitively the interpreter takes a sequence of instructions and an input stack and returns an output stack. Since Michelson programs can explicitly fail the output stack is embedded in an error monad M. A *fuel* argument is added to enforce termination of the interpreter. This argument will decrease every time in any recursive call to eval. Note that the notion of *fuel* is different from *gas*, which measures computation costs.

3.2   Functional Verification of Michelson Smart Contracts

We have verified the functional correctness of Michelson contracts with Mi-Cho-Coq, including complex ones such as a multisig contract (cf. section 4 of [8]) or a daily spending limit contract[2] used in the Cortez mobile wallet[3]. Our correctness results are statements that condition successful runs of a contract with the respect of a specification:

```
Definition correct_smart_contract {A B : stack_type}
    (i : instruction A B) min_fuel spec : Prop :=
    forall (input : stack A) (output : stack B) fuel,
      fuel >= min_fuel input →
        eval i fuel input = Return (stack B) output <→
          spec input output.
```

For example, for the voting contract described in Sect. 2, the specification would be that (preconditions) the amount sent is greater than or equal to 5 tez, the chosen candidate is one of the possible choices and that (postconditions) the evaluation of the contract generates no operation, and modifies only the votes count by incrementing by 1 the number of votes of the chosen candidate.

In order to facilitate these functional proofs, a weakest precondition calculus eval_precond is implemented. Its type is forall {fuel A B}, instruction A B → (stack B → Prop) → (stack A → Prop) that for an instruction and a postcondition (a predicate over the output stack) returns the weakest precondition (a predicate over the input stack).

The correctness of eval_precond has been proven:

```
Lemma eval_precond_correct {A B} (i : instruction A B) fuel st psi :
    eval_precond fuel i psi st <→
      match eval i fuel st with Failed _ _ => False | Return _ a => psi a end.
```

Intuitively, eval_precond_correct states that (left to right) the predicate computed by eval_precond is a precondition and that (right to left) it is the weakest. This lemma is heavily used in the proofs of correctness.

---

[2] https://blog.nomadic-labs.com/formally-verifying-a-critical-smart-contract.html.
[3] https://gitlab.com/nomadic-labs/cortez-android.

3.3 Optimiser

A Michelson optimiser has been implemented in Mi-Cho-Coq. The purpose of this optimiser is to simplify Michelson programs, thus reducing the gas costs of executing them, without modifying their semantics. Simplifications are basic at the moment: the goal is mainly to clean programs generated from higher level languages by removing useless stack manipulation instructions.

Optimisations are defined in one file, `optimizer.v`. A first step (`dig0dug0`) removes useless instructions (DROP 0, DIG 0 and DUG 0), needless uses of DIP (DIP 0 i is replaced with i) and replaces DIG 1 and DUG 1 with SWAP. A second step (`digndugn`) removes DIG n; DUG n sequences. A third step (`swapswap`) removes SWAP ; SWAP sequences. A fourth step (`push_drop`) removes PUSH ; DROP 1 and rewrites PUSH ; DROP n+1 into DROP n (for n > 0). The `visit_instruction` function, similarly to the Visitor Pattern [12], traverses a Michelson sequence of instructions and applies one optimisation received as an argument. Finally, the `cleanup` function applies the four optimisations (in the order of their presentation above) to a sequence of instructions.

We prove that the semantics of Michelson instructions are preserved by the optimisations. This is implemented in `typed_optimizer.v`. The main theorem `optimize_correct` states that if an instruction sequence can by typechecked then its optimised version can also be typechecked with the same type; furthermore if the initial sequence runs successfully on some stack, then the optimised version runs also successfully on the same stack and they both return the same value.

4   Albert

Albert is an intermediate language for Tezos smart contracts with a compiler written in Coq and that targets Mi-Cho-Coq.

We present in this section a high level overview of Albert's design and features. A more detailed presentation of Albert's syntax, typing rules and semantics can be found in [9].

4.1 Design Overview

The key aspect of Albert's design is the abstraction of Michelson stacks by records with named fields. This gives two practical benefits: unlike in Michelson, in Albert we do not need to care about the order of the values and we can bind variables to names. Also, unlike Michelson where contracts can only contain one sequence of instructions, it is possible in Albert to define multiple functions, thus giving the possibility to implement libraries. An important limitation of Albert is that resources are still being tracked: variables are typed by a linear type system that enforces that each value cannot be consumed twice. A **dup** operation duplicates resources that need to be consumed multiple times. A next step would be to generate these operations in order to abstract data consumption.

In a nutshell, each expression or instruction is typed by a pair of record types whose labels are the variables touched by the instruction or expression. The first record type describes the consumed values and the second record type describes the produced values. Thanks to the unification of variable names and record labels, records in Albert generalise both the Michelson stack types and the Michelson pair type.

Albert offers slightly higher-level types than Michelson: records generalise Michelson's pairs and non-recursive variants generalise Michelson's binary sum types as well as booleans and option types. Variants offer two main operations to the user: constructing a variant value using a constructor, and pattern-matching on a variant value.

The semantics of the Albert base language is defined in big-step style.

We present in Fig. 2 the translation in Albert of the voting contract described in Sect. 2. The storage of the contract is a record with two fields: a `threshold` that represents the minimum amount that must be transferred, and an associative map, `votes`, with strings as keys (the options of the vote) and integers as values (the number of votes for each associated key). The contract contains a `vote` function that checks that the parameter sent is one of the available options, fails if not and otherwise updates the vote count. The main function `guarded_vote` verifies that the amount of tokens sent is high enough and if so, calls `vote`.

4.2   Implementation Overview

Albert is formally specified with the Ott tool [24] in a modular way (one `.ott` file per fragment of the language). From the Ott specification the Albert lexer and parser as well as typing and semantic rules are generated in Coq. The type checker is a Coq function that uses an error monad to deal with ill-typed programs. There is no type inference, which should not be a problem since Albert is supposed to be used as a compilation target.

The Albert compiler is written in Coq, as a function from the generated Albert grammar to the Michelson syntax defined in Mi-Cho-Coq. The compiler is extracted to OCaml code, which is more efficient and easier to use as a library. Compilation of types, data and instructions are mostly straightforward, apart from things related to records or variants. Records are translated into nested pairs of values, variants into a nesting of sum types. Projections of record fields are translated into a sequence of projections over the relevant components of a pair. Pattern matching over variants are translated into a nesting of IF_LEFT branchings. A mapping from variable names to their positions in the stack exists at every point in the program. This mapping is currently naive, variables are ordered by the lexicographic order of their names. This mapping is used in the translation of assignment instructions.

```
1    type storage_ty = { threshold : mutez; votes: map string nat }
2
3    def vote :
4        { param : string ; store : storage_ty } →
5        { operations : list operation ; store : storage_ty } =
6            {votes = state; threshold = threshold } = store ;
7            (state0, state1) = dup state;
8            (param0, param1) = dup param;
9            prevote_option = state0[param0];
10           { res = prevote } = assert_some { opt = prevote_option };
11           one = 1; postvote = prevote + one; postvote = Some postvote;
12           final_state = update state1 param1 postvote;
13           store = {threshold = threshold; votes = final_state};
14           operations = ([] : list operation)
15
16   def guarded_vote :
17       { param : string ; store : storage_ty } →
18       { operations : list operation ; store : storage_ty } =
19           (store0, store1) = dup store;
20           threshold = store0.threshold;
21           am = amount;
22           ok = am >= threshold0;
23           match ok with
24               False f →failwith "you_are_so_cheap!"
25            | True t →drop t;
26               voting_parameters = { param = param ; store = store1 };
27               vote voting_parameters
28       end
```

Fig. 2. A voting contract, in Albert

5   Future and Related Work

5.1   Towards Stronger Guarantees in the OCaml Michelson Interpreter

The OCaml implementation of Tezos contains an interpreter for Michelson. This interpreter is implemented with GADTs in a way that gives subject reduction for free: well-typed Michelson programs cannot go wrong: with the calling convention, we have the guarantee that well-typed programs will always be executed with stacks of the right length with data of the right type.

Nonetheless, because of the limitations of the logic implemented in OCaml, we are unable to reason directly about this interpreter. In this section, we sketch two possible solutions to this problem that we are currently exploring.

From Coq to OCaml. An obvious solution is to use Coq's extraction to produce OCaml code. Coq's extraction mechanism relies on well-studied theoretical grounds [20, 21], has been implemented for many years [18, 19] and has even been partially certified [13, 14]. However, OCaml code produced by Coq's extraction can contain `Obj.magic` to circumvent OCaml's less expressive type-system. That is in particular the case for Coq code that uses dependent types, such as Mi-Cho-Coq's interpreter.

Replacing the current OCaml Michelson interpreter with an extracted version containing `Obj.magic` occurrences would be problematic. The Michelson interpreter is part of the economic protocol which is sandboxed by a small subset of OCaml modules that, for obvious safety reasons, does not contain `Obj.magic`. Lifting this restriction would lower the guarantees provided by the OCaml type system and is not a path we would like to take.

A better solution would be to implement a second Michelson interpreter in Coq that would use simpler types so that its extraction is safe and compiles in the economic protocol sandboxing environment. In this second implementation, instructions' types would not be indexed by the input and output stacks and, as a consequence, the interpreter would be much more verbose, as all the ill-cases (e.g. executing `ADD` on a stack with only one element) would need to be dealt with. Proofs of equivalence between the typed interpreter and untyped interpreter would be needed, as the reference implementation would be the typed one, that uses dependent types, as the use of richer types would make it safer. It is also worth noting that any changes to the Michelson interpreter have to be approved by a community vote as it is part of the economic protocol that can be amended.

From OCaml to Coq with coq-of-ocaml. A reverse approach is to use the coq-of-ocaml [10] tool to mechanically translate the OCaml Michelson interpreter into Coq code and then to manually prove in Coq the equivalence of the two interpreters.

coq-of-ocaml [10] is a work in progress effort to compile OCaml code to Coq. As a simple example to illustrate coq-of-ocaml, let us consider a polymorphic tree and a sum function that sums the values of a tree of integers. The OCaml code and its coq-of-ocaml translations are respectively in Fig. 3) and Fig. 4. Notice that in Coq, the type of the values stored in the trees appears in the type of the tree, as the rich type system of Coq does not allow this to remain implicit. It is possible to reason about the generated Coq program. For example one could prove manually that the sum of a tree containing only positive integers is positive (Fig. 5). The Michelson interpreter is much more complex than this simple example and makes a heavy use of advanced OCaml features, such as GADTs. At the moment of writing, features such as side-effects, extensible types, objects and polymorphic variants, are not supported yet by coq-of-ocaml. Regarding GADTs, currently coq-of-ocaml translates them but in a way that generates axioms for casting. Work is being done to try to have an axiom-free translation. We have managed to translate the whole economic protocol of the Babylon[4] version of Tezos into Coq using coq-of-ocaml with the caveat that Coq axioms

---

[4] Babylon is the codename of the second amendment to the economic protocol voted by the Tezos community. It has been superseded by Carthage in March 2020.

are needed and that OCaml annotations were added. As the Michelson interpreter is part of the economic protocol, this means we have a Coq translation of the OCaml interpreter. A next step would be to prove the equivalence of the translated interpreter with the Mi-Cho-Coq one.

```
1  type 'a tree =
2  | Leaf of 'a
3  | Node of 'a tree * 'a tree
4
5  let rec sum tree =
6    match tree with
7    | Leaf n → n
8    | Node (tree1, tree2) → sum tree1 + sum tree2
```

Fig. 3. Sum of a tree, in OCaml

```
1   Inductive tree (a : Type) : Type :=
2   | Leaf : a → tree a
3   | Node : (tree a) → (tree a) → tree a.
4
5   Arguments Leaf {_}.
6   Arguments Node {_}.
7
8   Fixpoint sum (tree : tree Z) : Z :=
9     match tree with
10    | Leaf n ⇒ n
11    | Node tree1 tree2 ⇒ Z.add (sum tree1) (sum tree2)
12    end.
```

Fig. 4. Sum of a tree, in Coq

```
1   Inductive pos : tree Z → Prop :=
2   | PosLeaf : forall z, z > 0 → pos (Leaf z)
3   | PosNode : forall t1, t2, pos t1 → pos t2 → pos (Node t1 t2).
4
5   Fixpoint positive_sum (t : tree Z) (H : pos t) : sum t > 0.
6   Proof.
7     destruct H; simpl.
8     − trivial.
9     − assert (sum t1 > 0).
10      now apply positive_sum.
11      assert (sum t2 > 0).
12      now apply positive_sum.
13      lia.
14  Qed.
```

Fig. 5. The sum of a positive tree is positive, manual proof in Coq

5.2   Improvements to Mi-Cho-Coq and Albert

Mi-Cho-Coq. Mi-Cho-Coq has axioms for domain specific opcodes that are harder to implement such as instructions to query the blockchain environment for relevant information (amount sent during the transaction, current time, sender of the transaction,...), data serialisation and cryptographic primitives. Work is being done to decrease the number of axioms being used. Another useful addition would be to extend the expressivity of the framework by supporting mutual calls and calls to other contracts, as well as reasoning on the lifetime of a contract. Another issue that would need to be dealt with would be to implement the gas model in Mi-Cho-Coq. A better or longer term solution would be to replace gas accounting with static computation of execution costs *à la* Zen Protocol [3].

Albert. Albert is very much a work in progress. Next steps would be to have a smarter implementation of the compiler that would produce optimised code, as well as to prove the compiler correctness and meta-properties of the Albert language such as subject reduction. Longer term, we would like to implement a certified decompiler from Michelson to Albert as well as a weakest-precondition calculus to Albert in order to reason about Albert programs.

5.3   Related Work

Despite the novelty of the field, many works regarding formal verification of smart contracts have been published or announced. The K framework has been used to formalise semantics of smart-contracts languages for Cardano[5], Ethereum[6] and Tezos[7]. Concordium has developed the ConCert certification framework [6], implemented in Coq, that permits to reason on the lifetime of a contract. Scilla [22,23], the smart-contract language of Zilliqa has been formalised in Coq as a shallow embedding. Its formalisation supports inter-contract interaction and multiple calls over the lifetime of the contract.

Several high-level languages for Tezos smart contracts are being developed [4,7,11,17]. Programs in the Archetype language [11] can contain security properties assertions or specifications expressed in logic formulae that are translated to the Why3 platform and then verified by automatic provers such as Alt-ergo, CVC or Z3. Juvix [17] implements a variant of the quantitative type theory which enables to track resources, similarly to Albert, as well as to specify and verify smart contracts.

References

1. Michelson: the language of Smart Contracts in Tezos. https://tezos.gitlab.io/whitedoc/michelson.html
2. Tezos code repository. https://gitlab.com/tezos/tezos

---

[5] https://github.com/kframework/plutus-core-semantics.

[6] https://github.com/kframework/evm-semantics.

[7] https://github.com/runtimeverification/michelson-semantics.

3. An introduction to the Zen protocol (2017). https://www.zenprotocol.com/files/zen_protocol_white_paper.pdf

4. Alfour, G.: LIGO: a friendly smart-contract language for Tezos. https://ligolang.org. Accessed 12 May 2020

5. Allombert, V., Bourgoin, M., Tesson, J.: Introduction to the Tezos blockchain (2019)

6. Annenkov, D., Nielsen, J.B., Spitters, B.: ConCert: a smart contract certification framework in Coq. In: Blanchette, J., Hritcu, C. (eds.) Proceedings of the 9th ACM SIGPLAN International Conference on Certified Programs and Proofs, CPP 2020, New Orleans, LA, USA, 20–21 January 2020, pp. 215–228. ACM (2020). https://doi.org/10.1145/3372885.3373829

7. Arena, S.C.: SmartPy. https://smartpy.io. Accessed 12 Dec 2019

8. Bernardo, B., Cauderlier, R., Hu, Z., Pesin, B., Tesson, J.: Mi-Cho-Coq, a framework for certifying Tezos smart contracts. In: Proceedings of the First Workshop on Formal Methods for Blockchains (to be published). FMBC 2019 (2019). https://arxiv.org/abs/1909.08671

9. Bernardo, B., Cauderlier, R., Pesin, B., Tesson, J.: Albert, an intermediate smart-contract language for the Tezos blockchain. In: Proceedings of the 4th Workshop on Trusted Smart Contracts (to be published) (2020)

10. Claret, G.: Program in Coq. Theses, Université Paris Diderot - Paris 7, September 2018. https://hal.inria.fr/tel-01890983

11. Duhamel, G., Rognier, B., Sturb, P.Y.: Edukera: Archetype: a Tezos smart contract development solution dedicated to contract quality insurance. https://docs.archetype-lang.org. Accessed 12 Dec 2019

12. Gamma, E., Helm, R., Johnson, R., Vlissides, J.: Design Patterns: Elements of Reusable Object-Oriented Software. Addison-Wesley Professional Computing Series, Pearson Education (1994)

13. Glondu, S.: Extraction certifiée dans coq-en-coq. In: Schmitt, A. (ed.) JFLA 2009, Vingtièmes Journées Francophones des Langages Applicatifs, Saint Quentin sur Isère, France, 31 January–3 February 2009. Proceedings. Studia Informatica Universalis, vol. 7.2, pp. 383–410 (2009)

14. Glondu, S.: Vers une certification de l'extraction de Coq. (Towards certification of the extraction of Coq). Ph.D. thesis, Paris Diderot University, France (2012). https://tel.archives-ouvertes.fr/tel-01798332

15. Goodman, L.M.: Tezos: A self-amending crypto-ledger. Position paper (2014). https://tinyurl.com/tezospp

16. Goodman, L.M.: Tezos: A self-amending crypto-ledger. White paper (2014). https://tinyurl.com/tezoswp

17. Labs, C.: Juvix: a more elegant language for a more civilized age. https://github.com/cryptiumlabs/juvix. Accessed 31 May 2020

18. Letouzey, P.: Programmation fonctionnelle certifiée - L'extraction de programmes dans l'assistant Coq. Ph.D. thesis, Université Paris-Sud, July 2004

19. Letouzey, P.: A new extraction for Coq. In: Geuvers, H., Wiedijk, F. (eds.) TYPES 2002. LNCS, vol. 2646, pp. 200–219. Springer, Heidelberg (2003). https://doi.org/10.1007/3-540-39185-1_12

20. Paulin-Mohring, C.: Extracting F_ω's programs from proofs in the calculus of constructions. In: Sixteenth Annual ACM Symposium on Principles of Programming Languages. ACM, Austin, January 1989

21. Paulin-Mohring, C.: Extraction de programmes dans le Calcul des Constructions. Thèse d'université, Paris 7, January 1989. http://www.lri.fr/~paulin/PUBLIS/these.ps.gz

22. Sergey, I., Kumar, A., Hobor, A.: Scilla: a smart contract intermediate-level language. CoRR abs/1801.00687 (2018). http://arxiv.org/abs/1801.00687
23. Sergey, I., Nagaraj, V., Johannsen, J., Kumar, A., Trunov, A., Hao, K.C.G.: Safer smart contract programming with Scilla. PACMPL **3**(OOPSLA), 185:1–185:30 (2019). https://doi.org/10.1145/3360611
24. Sewell, P., Nardelli, F.Z., Owens, S.: Ott. https://github.com/ott-lang/ott
25. Xi, H., Chen, C., Chen, G.: Guarded recursive datatype constructors. SIGPLAN Not. **38**(1), 224–235 (2003). https://doi.org/10.1145/640128.604150

UTxO- vs Account-Based Smart Contract Blockchain Programming Paradigms

Lars Brünjes[1] and Murdoch J. Gabbay[2]([⊠])

[1] IOHK, Hong Kong, People's Republic of China
[2] Heriot-Watt University, Edinburgh, Scotland, UK
http://www.gabbay.org.uk

Abstract. We implement two versions of a simple but illustrative smart contract: one in Solidity on the Ethereum blockchain platform, and one in Plutus on the Cardano platform, with annotated code excerpts and with source code attached. We get a clearer view of the Cardano programming model in particular by introducing a novel mathematical abstraction which we call Idealised EUTxO. For each version of the contract, we trace how the architectures of the underlying platforms and their mathematics affects the natural programming styles and natural classes of errors. We prove some simple but novel results about alpha-conversion and observational equivalence for Cardano, and explain why Ethereum does not have them. We conclude with a wide-ranging and detailed discussion in the light of the examples, mathematical model, and mathematical results so far.

1 Introduction

In the context of blockchain and cryptocurrencies, smart contracts are a way to make the blockchain programmable. That is: a smart contract is a program that runs on the blockchain to extend its capabilities.

For the smart contract, the blockchain is just an abstract machine (database, if we prefer) with which it programmatically interacts. Basic design choices in the blockchain's design can affect the smart contract programming paradigm which it naturally supports, and this can have far-reaching consequences: different programming paradigms are susceptible to different programming styles, and different kinds of program errors.

Thus, a decision in the blockchain's design can have lasting, unavoidable, and critical effects on its programmability. It is worth being very aware of how this can play out, not least because almost by definition, applications of smart-contracts-the-programming-paradigm tend to be safety-critical.

In this paper we will consider a simple but illustrative example of a smart contract: a fungible tradable token issued by an issuer who creates an initial supply and then retains control of its price—imitating a government-issued fiat currency, but run from a blockchain instead of a central bank.

We will put this example in the context of two major smart contract languages: Solidity, which runs on the Ethereum blockchain, whose native token is

© Springer Nature Switzerland AG 2020
T. Margaria and B. Steffen (Eds.): ISoLA 2020, LNCS 12478, pp. 73–88, 2020.
https://doi.org/10.1007/978-3-030-61467-6_6

ether; and Plutus, which runs on the Cardano blockchain, whose native token is *ada*.[1] We compare and contrast the blockchains in detail and exhibit their respective smart contracts. Both contracts run, but their constructions are different, in ways that illuminate the essential natures of the respective underlying blockchains and the programming styles that they support.

We will also see that the Ethereum smart contract is arguably buggy, in a way that flows from the underlying programming paradigm of Solidity/Ethereum. So even in a simple example, the essential natures of the underlying systems are felt, and with a mission-critical impact.

Definition 1.1. We will use Solidity and Plutus to code a system as follows:

1. An issuer `Issuer` creates some initial supply of a tradable token on the blockchain at some location in `Issuer`'s control; call this the *official portal*.
2. Other parties buy the token from the official portal at a per-token ether/ada *official price*, controlled by the issuer.[2]
   Once other parties get some token, they can trade it amongst themselves (e.g. for ether/ada), independently of the official portal and on whatever terms and at whatever price they mutually agree.
3. The issuer can update the ether/ada official price of the token on the official portal, at any time.
4. For simplicity, we permit just one initial issuance of the token, though tokens can be redistributed as just described.

2   Idealised EUTxO

2.1   The Structure of an Idealised Blockchain

We start with a novel mathematical idealisation of the EUTxO (Extended UTxO) model on which Cardano is based [1,2].

Notation 2.1. Suppose X and Y are sets. Then:

1. Write $\mathbb{N} = \{0, 1, 2, \dots\}$ and $\mathbb{N}_{>0} = \{1, 2, 3, \dots\}$.
2. Write *fin*(X) for the finite powerset of X and *fin*$_!(X)$ for the pointed finite powerset (the $(X', x) \in$ *fin*$(X) \times X$ such that $x \in X'$).[3]
3. Write *pow*(X) for the powerset of X, and $X \overset{fin}{\rightharpoonup} Y$ for finite maps from X to Y (finite partial functions).

Definition 2.2. Let the **types** of **Idealised EUTxO** be a solution to the equations in Fig. 1.[4] For diagrams and examples see Example 2.6.

---

[1] Plutus and Cardano are IOHK designs. The CEO and co-founder of IOHK, Charles Hoskinson, was also one of the co-founders of Ethereum.

[2] Think: central bank, manufacturer's price, official exchange rate, etc.

[3] This use of 'pointed' is unrelated to the 'points to' of Notation 2.4.

[4] We write 'a solution of' because Fig. 1 does not specify a unique subset for Validator. *Computable* subsets is one candidate, but our mathematical abstraction is agnostic to this choice. This is just the same as function-types not being modelled by *all* functions, or indeed as models of set theory can have different powersets (e.g. depending on whether a powerset includes the Axiom of Choice).

$$\text{Redeemer} = \text{CurrencySymbol} = \text{TokenName} = \text{Position} = \mathbb{N}$$
$$\text{Chip} = \text{CurrencySymbol} \times \text{TokenName}$$
$$\text{Datum} \times \text{Value} = \mathbb{N} \times (\text{Chip} \xrightarrow{fin} \mathbb{N}_{>0})$$
$$\text{Validator} \subseteq pow(\text{Redeemer} \times \text{Datum} \times \text{Value} \times \text{Context})$$
$$\text{Input} = \text{Position} \times \text{Redeemer}$$
$$\text{Output} = \text{Position} \times \text{Validator} \times \text{Datum} \times \text{Value}$$
$$\text{Transaction} = fin(\text{Input}) \times fin(\text{Output})$$
$$\text{Context} = fin_!(\text{Input}) \times fin(\text{Output})$$

Fig. 1. Types for Idealised EUTxO

```
1    data Chip = MkChip
2      { cSymbol  ::  ! CurrencySymbol
3      , cName    ::  ! TokenName }
4
5    data Config = MkConfig
6      { cIssuer                  ::  ! PubKeyHash
7      , cTradedChip, cStateChip  ::  ! Chip }
8
9    tradedChip :: Config → Integer → Value
10   tradedChip MkConfig{..} n  =  singletonValue cTradedChip n
11
12   data Action =
13       SetPrice  ! Integer
14     | Buy       ! Integer
15
16   transition   ::  Config → State Integer → Action
17                    → Maybe (TxConstraints Void Void, State Integer )
18   transition c s (SetPrice p)            – ACTION: set price to p
19     | p < 0       =  Nothing             – p negative? ignore!
20     | otherwise   =  Just                – otherwise
21       ( mustBeSignedBy (cIssuer c)       – issuer signed?
22       , s{stateData = p})                – set new price!
23   transition c s (Buy m)                 – ACTION: buy m chips
24     | m ≤ 0       =  Nothing             – buy negative quantity? ignore!
25     | otherwise   =  Just                – otherwise
26       ( mustPayToPubKey (cIssuer c) value'  – issuer been paid?
27       , s{stateValue = stateValue s − sold}) – sell chips!
28     where
29     value'  =  lovelaceValueOf (m ∗ stateData s)  – final value buyer pays
30     sold    =  tradedChip c m             – no. chips buyer gets
31
32   guarded  ::  HasNative s ⇒ Config → Integer → Integer
33               → Contract s Text ()
34   guarded c n maxPrice =
35     void $ withError $ runGuardedStep (client c) (Buy n) $
36     λ_ p _ → if p ≤ maxPrice then Nothing else Just ()
```

Fig. 2. Plutus implementation of the tradable token

Remark 2.3. 1. Think of $r \in$ Redeemer as a key, required as a necessary condition by a validator (below) to permit computation.

2. A chip $c = (d, n)$ is intuitively a currency unit (£, $, ...), where $d \in$ CurrencySymbol is assumed to Gödel encode[5] some predicate defining a **monetary policy** (more on this in Remark 2.8(2) and $n \in$ TokenName is just a symbol (Ada has special status and is encoded as $(0, 0)$).

3. Datum is any data; we set it to be $\mathbb{N}$ for simplicity. A value $v \in$ Value is intuitively a multiset of tokens; $v\,c$ is the number of cs in v.
   - We may abuse notation and define $v\,c = 0$ if $c \notin dom(v)$.
   - If $dom(v) = \{c\}$ then we may call v a **singleton** value (note $v\,c$ need not equal 1). See line 10 of Fig. 2 for the corresponding code.

4. A transaction is a set of inputs and a set of outputs (either of which may be empty). In a blockchain these are subject to consistency conditions (Definition 2.5); for now we just say its inputs 'consume' some previous outputs, and 'generate' new outputs. A context is just a transaction viewed from a particular input (see next item).

5. Mathematically a validator $V \in$ Validator is the set of Redeemer × Datum × Value × Transaction tuples it validates *but* in the implementation we intend that V is represented by code V such that
   - from V we cannot efficiently compute a tuple t such that $V(t)$=True, and
   - from V and t, we can efficiently check if $V(t)$=True.[6]
   We use a *pointed* transaction (Notation 2.1(2)) because a Validator in an Output in a Transaction is always invoked by some particular Input in a later Transaction (see Definition 2.5(2&3)), and that invoking input is identified by using Context. If $t \in V$ then we say V **validates** t.

Notation 2.4. 1. If $tx = (I, O) \in$ Transaction and $o \in$ Output, say o **appears in** tx and write $o \in tx$ when $o \in O$; similarly for an input $i \in$ Input. We may silently extend this notation to larger data structures, writing for example $o \in \mathit{Txs}$ (Definition 2.9(1)).

2. If i and o have the same position then say that i **points to** o.

3. If $tx = (I, O) \in$ Transaction and $i \in I$ then write $tx@i$ for the context $((I, i), O)$ obtained by pointing I at $i \in I$.

Definition 2.5. A **valid blockchain**, or just **blockchain**, of idealised EUTxO is a finite sequence of transactions Txs such that:

1. Distinct outputs appearing in Txs have distinct positions.
2. Every input i in some tx in Txs points to a unique output in some earlier transaction — it follows from this and condition 1 of this Definition, that distinct inputs appearing in Txs also have distinct positions. Write this unique output $\mathit{Txs}(i)$.
3. If $i = (p, k)$ appears in tx in Txs and points to an earlier output $\mathit{Txs}(i) = (p, V, s, v)$, then $(k, s, tx@i) \in V$ (@ from Notation 2.4(3)).

---

[5] Gödel encoding refers to the idea of enumerating a countable datatype (in some arbitrary way) so that each element is represented by a unique numerical index.

[6] The 'crypto' in 'cryptocurrency' lives here.

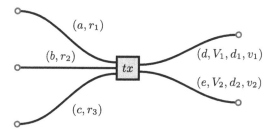

Fig. 3. A transaction tx with three inputs and two outputs, positions a, b, c, d, e, redeemers r_i, validators V_j, data d_j and values v_j

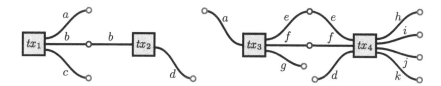

Fig. 4. A blockchain $\mathcal{B} = [tx_1, tx_2, tx_3, tx_4]$

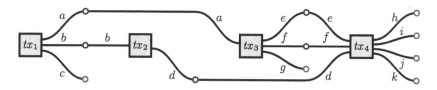

Fig. 5. B chopped up as a blockchain $[tx_1, tx_2]$ and a chunk $[tx_3, tx_4]$

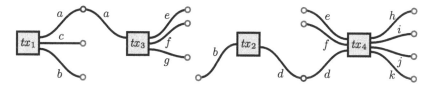

Fig. 6. B chopped up as a blockchain $[tx_1, tx_3]$ and a chunk $[tx_2, tx_4]$

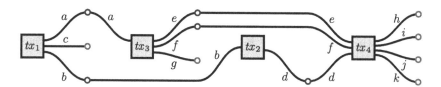

Fig. 7. The blockchain $\mathcal{B}' = [tx_1, tx_3, tx_2, tx_4]$

Example 2.6. Example transactions, blockchains, and chunks are illustrated in Figs. 3, 4, 5, 6, and 7.

We leave it as an exercise to the reader to verify that: $\mathcal{B}$, $\mathcal{B}'$, $[tx_1, tx_2]$ and $[tx_1, tx_3]$ are blockchains; and $[tx]$, $[tx_3, tx_4]$ and $[tx_2, tx_4]$ are chunks but not blockchains. Also, e.g. $[tx_2, tx_1]$ is neither blockchain nor chunk, though it is a list of transactions, because the b-input of tx_2 points to the later b-output of tx_1.

Notation 2.7. *Txs* will range over finite sequences of transactions, and $\mathcal{B}$ will range over blockchains. We write *valid*(*Txs*) for the assertion "*Txs* is a blockchain".

Remark 2.8. In words: *A sequence of transactions is a blockchain when every input points to an earlier validating output.* Note that output and inputs of a transaction may be empty, and this matters because any blockchain must contain a so-called *genesis block*, which is a transaction without inputs. We call Fig. 1 and Definition 2.5 *Idealised EUTxO* because:

1. The implementation has bells and whistles which we omit for simplicity:
   (a) There is a second type of output for making payments to people.
   (b) Values represent 'real money' and so are preserved—the sum of input values must be equal to the sum of output values—unless they are not preserved, e.g. due to fees (which reduce the sum of outputs) or forging (creating) tokens (which increase it).
   (c) Transactions can be made time-sensitive using *slot ranges* (Remark 2.18); a transaction can only be accepted into a block whose slot is inside the transaction's slot range.
   All of the above is important for a working blockchain but for our purposes it would just add complexity.
2. We continue the discussion in Remark 2.3(2). If we consider a chip $c = (d, n)$, the currency symbol d is not aritrary: it is (a Gödel encoding of) a *monetary policy* predicate. In the implementation, only transactions which satisfy all pertinent monetary policies are admissible.
   This is relevant to our example in Sect. 3 because we will assume a *state chip* with a monetary policy which enforces that it is affine (zero or one chips on the blockchain; see Remark 3.3). Explaining the mechanics of how this works is outside the scope of this paper; here we just note it exists.
3. In the implementation, a transaction is a pair of a set of inputs and a *list* of outputs. This is because an implementation concerns a run on a particular concrete blockchain $\mathcal{B}$, and we want to assign concrete positions for outputs in $\mathcal{B}$; so with a list the output located at the jth output of ith transaction could get position $2^i 3^j$.
   However, we care here about the theory of blockchains (plural). It is better to use sets and leave positions abstract, since if positions are fixed by their location in a blockchain then in Theorem 2.17 and the lemmas leading up to it, when we rearrange transactions in a blockchain (e.g. proving an observational equivalence) we could have to track an explicit reindexing of positions in the statement of the results. More on this in Subsect. 2.3.

2.2 UTxOs and Observational Equivalence

We will be most interested in Definition 2.9 when Txs and Txs' are blockchains $\mathcal{B}$ and $\mathcal{B}'$. However, it is convenient for Lemma 2.15(1) if we consider the more general case of any finite sequences of transactions Txs and Txs':

Definition 2.9. 1. Call an output $o \in Txs$ **spent** (in Txs) when a later input points to it, and otherwise call o **unspent** (in Txs).
2. Write $UTxO(Txs)$ for the set of unspent outputs in Txs.
3. If $UTxO(Txs) = UTxO(Txs')$ then write $Txs \approx Txs'$ and call Txs and Txs' **observationally equivalent**.

Notation 2.10. Given Txs and a tx, write $Txs; tx$ for the sequence of transactions obtained by appending tx to Txs. We will mostly care about this when Txs and $Txs; tx$ are blockchains, and if so this will be clear from context.

Lemma 2.11. *Validity (Definition 2.5) is closed under initial subsequences, but not necessarily under final subsequences:*

1. *$valid(Txs; tx)$ implies $valid(Txs)$.*
2. *$valid(tx; Txs)$ does not necessarily imply $valid(Txs)$.*

Proof. For part 1: removing tx cannot invalidate the conditions in Definition 2.5. For part 2: it may be that an input in Txs points to an output in tx; if we then remove tx we would violate condition 2 of Definition 2.5 that every input must point to a previous output.

A special case of interest is when two transactions operate on non-overlapping parts of the preceding blockchain:

Notation 2.12. Suppose tx and tx' are transactions. Write $tx \# tx'$ when the positions mentioned in the inputs and outputs of tx, are disjoint from those mentioned in tx', and in this case call tx and tx' **apart**. Similarly for $tx \# Txs$.

Lemma 2.13. $tx \# tx' \Longleftrightarrow tx' \# tx$.

Proof. An easy structural fact.

Remark 2.14. In Lemma 2.15 and Theorem 2.17 below, note that:

- $valid(\mathcal{B}; tx)$ (Notations 2.7 and 2.10) can be read as the assertion "it is valid to append the transaction tx to the blockchain $\mathcal{B}$".
- $valid(\mathcal{B}; Txs)$ can be read as "it is valid to extend $\mathcal{B}$ with Txs".
- If $tx \# tx'$ then they mention disjoint sets of positions, so they cannot point to one another and the UTxOs they point to are guaranteed distinct.

Lemma 2.15. *1. If $tx \# tx'$ then we have $valid(\mathcal{B}; tx; tx') \Longleftrightarrow valid(\mathcal{B}; tx'; tx)$ and $\mathcal{B}; tx; tx' \cong \mathcal{B}; tx'; tx$.[7] Intuitively: if two transactions are apart then it is valid to commute them.*

---

[7] We don't necessarily know $\mathcal{B}; tx; tx'$ is a blockchain, which is why we stated Definition 2.9 for sequences of transactions.

2. If $valid(\mathcal{B}; tx'; tx)$ then $valid(\mathcal{B}; tx) \Longleftrightarrow tx \# tx'$. (Some real work happens in this technical result, and we use this work to prove Theorem 2.17.)

Proof. 1. By routine checking Definition 2.5.

2. Suppose $\neg(tx \# tx')$, so some position p is mentioned by tx and tx'. If p is in an input in both tx and tx', or an output in both, then $valid(\mathcal{B}; tx'; tx)$ is impossible because each input must point to a unique earlier output, and each output must have a unique position. If p is in an input in tx and an output in tx' then $\neg valid(\mathcal{B}; tx)$, because now this input points to a nonexistent output. If p is in an output in tx and an input in tx' then $valid(\mathcal{B}; tx'; tx)$ is impossible, since each input must point to an *earlier* output.

Conversely suppose $tx \# tx'$. Then tx' must point only to outputs in $\mathcal{B}$ and removing tx cannot disconnect them and so cannot invalidate the conditions in Definition 2.5.

Remark 2.16. Theorem 2.17 below gives a sense in which UTxO-based accounting is 'stateless'. With the machinery we now have the proof looks simple, but this belies its significance, which we now unpack in English:

Suppose we submit tx to some blockchain $\mathcal{B}$. Then *either* the submission of tx fails and is rejected (e.g. if some validator objects to it)—*or* it succeeds and tx is appended to $\mathcal{B}$.

If it succeeds, then even if other transactions Txs get appended first—e.g. they were submitted by other actors whose transactions arrived first, so that in-between us creating tx and the arrival of tx at the main blockchain, it grew from $\mathcal{B}$ to $\mathcal{B}; Txs$—then the result $\mathcal{B}; Txs; tx$ is *up to observational equivalence* equivalent to $\mathcal{B}; tx; Txs$, which is what *would* have happened *if* our tx had arrived at $\mathcal{B}$ instantly and before the competing transactions Txs.

In other words: if we submit tx to the blockchain, then at worst, other actors' actions might prevent tx from getting appended, however, *if* our transaction gets onto the blockchain somewhere, then we obtain our originally intended result up to observational equivalence.

Theorem 2.17. *Suppose* $valid(\mathcal{B}; Txs; tx)$ *and* $valid(\mathcal{B}; tx)$. *Then*

1. $valid(\mathcal{B}; tx; Txs)$ and
2. $\mathcal{B}; tx; Txs \cong \mathcal{B}; Txs; tx$.

Proof. Using Lemma 2.15(2) $tx \# Txs$. The rest follows using Lemma 2.15(1).

Remark 2.18. The Cardano implementation has *slot ranges* (Remark 2.8(1c)). These introduce a notion of time-sensitivity to transactions which breaks Theorem 2.17(1), because Txs might be time-sensitive. If we enrich Idealised EUTxO with slot ranges then a milder form of the result holds which we sketch as Proposition 2.19 below.

Proposition 2.19. *If we extend our blockchains with slot ranges, which restrict validity of transactions to defined time intervals, then Theorem 2.17 weakens to:*

If $valid(\mathcal{B}; tx; Txs)$ *and* $valid(\mathcal{B}; Txs; tx)$ *then* $\mathcal{B}; tx; Txs \cong \mathcal{B}; Txs; tx$.

Proof. As for Theorem 2.17, noting that slot ranges are orthogonal to UTxOs, provided the transactions concerned can be appended.

2.3 α-Equivalence and More on Observational Equivalence

Our syntax for $\mathcal{B}$ in Definition 2.5 is *name-carrying*; outputs are identified by unique markers which—while taken from $\mathbb{N}$; see "Position=$\mathbb{N}$" in Fig. 1—are clearly used as *atoms* or *names* to identify binding points on the blockchain, to which at most one later input may bind. Once bound this name can be thought of graphically as an edge from an output to the input that spends it, so clearly the choice of name/position—once it is bound—is irrelevant up to permuting our choices of names. This is familiar from α-equivalence in syntax, where e.g. $\lambda a.\lambda b.ab$ is equivalent to $\lambda b.\lambda a.ba$. We define:

Definition 2.20. 1. Write $\mathcal{B} =_\alpha \mathcal{B}'$ and call $\mathcal{B}$ and $\mathcal{B}'$ **α-equivalent** when they differ only in their choice of positions of spent output-input pairs (Definition 2.9(1)).[8] It is a fact that this is an equivalence relation.
2. If $\varPhi$ is an assertion about blockchains, write "up to α-equivalence, $\varPhi$" for the assertion "there exist α-equivalent forms of the arguments of $\varPhi$ such that $\varPhi$ is true of those arguments".

Lemma 2.21 checks that observational equivalence interacts well with being a valid blockchain and appending transactions. We sketch its statement and its proof, which is by simple checking. In words it says: *extensionally, a blockhain up to α-equivalence is just its UTxOs*:

Lemma 2.21. *1. $\mathcal{B}\cong\mathcal{B}' \wedge valid(\mathcal{B};tx) \wedge valid(\mathcal{B}';tx)$ implies $\mathcal{B};tx\cong\mathcal{B}';tx$.*
2. If $\mathcal{B} =_\alpha \mathcal{B}'$ then $\mathcal{B} \cong \mathcal{B}'$.
3. Up to α-equivalence, if $\mathcal{B} \cong \mathcal{B}'$ then $valid(\mathcal{B};tx) \iff valid(\mathcal{B}';tx)$.
4. Up to α-equivalence, if $\mathcal{B} \cong \mathcal{B}' \wedge valid(\mathcal{B};tx)$ then $\mathcal{B}; tx \cong \mathcal{B}';tx$.

Remark 2.22. We need α-conversion in cases 3 and 4 of Lemma 2.21 because $valid(\mathcal{B};tx)$ might fail due to *accidental name-clash* between the position assigned to a spent output in $\mathcal{B}$, and a position in an unspent output of tx. We need α-conversion to rename the bound position and avoid this name-clash.

This phenomenon is familiar from syntax, e.g. we know to α-convert a in $(\lambda a.b)[b{:=}a]$ to obtain (up to α-equivalence) $\lambda a'.a$.

There are many approaches to α-conversion: graphs, de Bruijn indexes [4], name-carrying syntax with an equivalence relation as required (used in this paper), the *nominal abstract syntax* of the second author and others [5], and the type-theoretic approach in [6]. Studying what works best for a structural theory of blockchains is future research.

In this paper we have used raw name-carrying syntax, possibly quotiented by equivalence as above; a more sophisticated development might require more. Note the implementation solution discussed in Remark 2.8(3) corresponds to a de Bruijn index approach, and for our needs in this paper, this does *not* solve all problems, as discussed in that Remark (see 'messy reindexing').

---

[8] Positions of unspent outputs (UTxOs) cannot be permuted. If we permute a UTxO position in $\mathcal{B}$, we obtain a blockchain $\mathcal{B}'$ with a symmetric equivalence to $\mathcal{B}$ but not observationally equivalent to it (much as $-i$ relates to i in $\mathbb{C}$). More on this in [3].

3   The Plutus Smart Contract

Definition 3.1. Relevant parts of the Plutus code to implement Definition 1.1 are in Fig. 2. Full source is at https://arxiv.org/src/2003.14271/anc.

Remark 3.2. 1. Chip corresponds to *Chip* from Fig. 1.
2. Config stores configuration: the issuer (given by a hash of their public key), the chip traded, and the state chip (see Remark 3.3).
3. tradedChip packages up n of cTradedChip in a value (think: a roll of quarters).
4. Action is a datatype which stores labels of a transition system, which in our case are either 'buy' or 'set price'.
5. State Integer corresponds to Datum in Fig. 1. stateData s on line 29 retrieves this datum and uses it as the price of the token.
6. value' (lines 26 and 29) is the amount of ada paid to the Issuer.[9]

Remark 3.3 (STATE CHIP).   In Remark 2.16 we described in what sense Idealised EUTxO (Fig. 1) is stateless. Yet Definition 1.1(3) specifies that Issuer can set a price for the traded chip. This is seems stateful. How to reconcile this?

We create a *state chip* cStateChip, whose monetary policy (Remark 2.8(2)) enforces that it is *affine* and *monotone increasing*, and thus *linear* once created. The Issuer issues an initial transaction to the blockchain which sets up our trading system, and creates a unique UTxO that contains this state chip in its value, with the price in its Datum field.

The UTxO with the state chip corresponds to the *official portal* from Definition 1.1, and its state datum corresponds to the *official price*.

Monetary policy ensures this is now an invariant of the blockchain as it develops, and anybody can check the current price by looking up the unique UTxO distinguished by carrying precisely on cStateChip, and looking at the value in its Datum field.[10] The interested reader can consult the source code.

Remark 3.4 (EXPRESSIVITY OF OFF-CHAIN CODE).   The Plutus contract is a *state machine*, whose transition function transition is compiled into a Validator function, and so is explicitly *on-chain*. The function guarded lives *off-chain*; e.g. in the user's wallet. It can construct and send a Buy-transaction to (a UTxO with the relevant validator on) the blockchain, after checking that the price is acceptable.

If accepted, the effect of this transaction is independant of concurrent actions of other users, in senses we have made mathematically precise (cf. Remarks 2.16 and 4.4). This gives Plutus off-chain code a power that Solidity off-chain code cannot attain.

---

[9] We call it value because it directly corresponds with msg.value in Fig. 9, whose name is fixed in Solidity. We add a dash to avoid name-clash with value, an existing function from the Plutus Ledger library.

[10] This technique was developed by the IOHK Plutus team.

4   The Solidity Smart Contract

4.1   Description

Remark 4.1. The Ethereum blockchain is account-based: it can be thought of as a state machine whose transitions modify a global state of contracts containing functions and data. We propose in Fig. 8 a type presentation of Idealised Ethereum, parallel to the Idealised EUTxO of Fig. 1. In brief:

1. Sender, Address, and Value are natural numbers $\mathbb{N}$. Datum is intended to be structured data which we Gödel encode for convenience. FunctionName and ContractName are names, which again for simplicity we encode as $\mathbb{N}$.
2. A contract has a name and a finite set of functions (Notation 2.1(2)).
3. A function has a name and maps an input to a blockchain transformer.
4. A blockchain is a finite collection of contracts, to each of which is assigned a state of a value (a balance of ether) and some structured data. We intend that a valid blockchain satisfy some consistency conditions, including that each contract in it have a distinct name.

Thus the contract Changing (line 1 of Fig. 9), once deployed, is located on the Ethereum blockchain, with its functions and state. This contract and its state are 'in one place' on the blockchain; not spread out across multiple UTxOs as in Cardano. There is no need for the state-chip mechanism from Remark 3.3.

Remark 4.2. We now briefly read through the code:

1. address is an address for the Issuer. It is payable (it can receive ether) and public (its value can be read by any other function on the blockchain).[11]
2. constructor is the function initialising the contract. It gives issuer (who triggers the contract) all the new token.
3. send is a function to send money to another address. Note that this is not in the Plutus code; this is because we got it 'for free' as part of Cardano's in-built support for currencies (this is also why Idealised EUTxO has the type Value in Fig. 1).
4. buy on line 20 is analogue to the Buy transition in Fig. 2.

4.2   Discussion

Remark 4.3. In line 21 of Fig. 9 we calculate the tokens purchased using a division of value (the total sum paid) by price.

In contrast, in line 29 of Fig. 2 we calculate the sum by multiplying the number of tokens by the price of each token.

---

[11] Any data on the Ethereum blockchain is public in the external sense that it can be read off the binary data of the blockchain as a file on a machine running it. However, not all data is public in the internal sense that it can be accessed from any code running on the Ethereum virtual machine.

$$\text{Sender} = \text{FunctionName} = \text{ContractName} = \text{Datum} = \text{Value} = \mathbb{N}$$
$$\text{Transaction} = \text{ContractName} \times \text{FunctionName} \times \text{Sender} \times \text{Value} \times \text{Datum}$$
$$\text{Contract} = \text{ContractName} \times \mathit{fin}(\text{Function})$$
$$\text{Function} \subseteq \text{FunctionName} \times ((\text{Sender} \times \text{Value} \times \text{Datum}) \to \text{Blockchain} \to \text{Blockchain})$$
$$\text{Blockchain} = \text{Contract} \xrightarrow{\mathit{fin}} (\text{Value} \times \text{Datum})$$

Fig. 8. Types for Idealised Ethereum

```
1   contract Changing {
2       address payable public issuer ;           // issues the token
3       uint public price ;                        // current price
4       mapping (address ⇒ uint) public balances;  // tracks who owns how many tokens
5
6       constructor (uint _count, uint _ price) public {
7           require (_count > 0, "count must be positive");
8           require (_ price > 0, " price must be positive");
9           issuer              = msg.sender;
10          price               = _ price ;
11          balances[msg.sender] = _count;
12      }
13
14      function send(address _ receiver , uint _amount) public {
15          require (_amount ≤ balances[msg.sender], "balance too low");
16          balances[msg.sender] −= _amount;
17          balances[_ receiver ] += _amount;
18      }
19
20      function buy() public payable {
21          uint _tokens = msg.value / price ;
22          require (_tokens ≤ balances[ issuer ], "not enough tokens");
23          issuer . transfer (msg.value);
24          balances[ issuer ]       −= _tokens;
25          balances[msg.sender] += _tokens;
26      }
27
28      function setPrice (uint _newPrice) public {
29          require (msg.sender == issuer , "only issuer can set price");
30          price = _newPrice;
31      }
32  }
```

Fig. 9. Solidity implementation of the tradable coin

There is a reason for this: we cannot perform the multiplication in the Solidity buy code because we do not actually know the price per token at the time the function acts to transition the blockchain. We can access a price at the time of invoking buy by querying Changing.price(), but by the time that invocation reaches the Ethereum blockchain and acts on it, the blockchain might have undergone transitions, and the price might have changed.

Because Ethereum is stateful and has nothing like Remark 2.16 and Theorem 2.17, this cannot be fixed.

Remark 4.4. One might counter that this could indeed be fixed, just by changing buy to include an extra parameter which is the price that the buyer expects to pay, and if this expectation is not met then the function terminates. However, the issuer controls the contract (issuer = msg.sender on line 9 of Fig. 9), including the code for buy, so this safeguard can only exist at the *issuer's* discretion—and our issuer, whether through thoughtlessness or malice, has not included it.

In Cardano the buyer has more control, because by Theorem 2.17 a party issuing a transaction knows (up to observational equivalence) precisely what the inputs and outputs will be; the only question is whether it successfully attaches to the blockchain (cf. Remark 2.16 and Subsect. 2.3).

Another subtle error in the Ethereum code is that the / on line 21 is integer division, so there may be a rounding error.[12]

Remark 4.5. The Ethereum code contains two errors, but the emphasis of this discussion is not that it is possible to write buggy code (which is always true) rather, we draw attention to how and why the underlying accounts-based structure of Ethereum invites and provides cover for certain errors *in particular*.

On the other hand, the Plutus code is more complex than the Ethereum code. Plutus is arguably conceptually beautiful, but the pragmatics as currently implemented are fiddly and the amount of boilerplate required to get our Plutus contract running much exceeds that required for our Ethereum contract. This may improve as Plutus matures and libraries improve—Plutus was streamlined as this paper was written, in at least one instance because of a suggestion from this paper[13]—but it remains to be seen if the gap can be totally closed.

So Ethereum is simple, direct and alluring, but can be dangerous, whereas Plutus places higher burdens on the programmer but enjoys some good mathematical properties which can enhance programmability. This is the tradeoff.

Remark 4.6. (CONTRACTS ON THE BLOCKCHAIN). It is convenient to call the code referred to in Figs. 2 and 9 *contracts*, but this is in fact an imprecise use of the term: a contract is an entity on the blockchain, whereas the figures describe *schemas* or *programs* which, when invoked with parameters, attempt to push a contract onto the blockchain.

– For Plutus, each time we invoke the contract schema for some choice of values for Config, the schema tries to creates a transaction on the blockchain which generates a UTxO which carries a state-chip *and* an instance of the contract. The contract is encoded in the monetary policy of the state-chip

---

[12] It would be unheard of for such elementary mistakes to slip into production code; and even if it did happen, it is hardly conceivable that such errors would happen repeatedly across a wide variety of programming languages.

That was sarcasm, but the point may bear repeating: programmer error and programming language design are two sides of a single coin.

[13] —the need for runGuardedStep.

(which enforces linearity once created) and in the Validator of that UTxO. The issuer's address is encoded in the Validator field of the UTxO. A mathematical presentation of the data structures concerned is in Fig. 1.

- For Ethereum, Fig. 9 also describes a schema which deploys a contract to the blockchain. Each time we invoke its constructor we generate a specific instance of Changing. Configuration data, given by the constructor arguments, is simply stored as values of the global state variables of that instance, such as issuer (line 2 of Fig. 9).

Remark 4.7. (STATE & POSSIBLE REFINEMENTS). In Solidity, state is located in variables in contracts. To query a state we just query a variable in a contract of interest, e.g. price or balances in contract Changing in Fig. 9.

In Plutus, state can be more expensive. State is located in unspent outputs; see the Datum and Value fields in Output in Fig. 1. In a transaction that queries or modifies state, we consume any UTxOs containing state to which we refer, and produce new UTxOs with new state. Even if our queries are read-only, they destroy the UTxOs read and create new UTxOs.[14]

Suppose a UTxO contains some popular state information, so multiple users submit transactions referencing it. Only one transaction can succeed and be appended and the other transactions will *not* link to the new state UTxO which is generated—even if it contains the same state data as the older version. Instead, the other transactions will fail, because the particular incarnation of the state UTxO to which they happened to link, has been consumed.

This could become a bottleneck. In the specific case of our Plutus contract, it could become a victim of its own success if our token is purchased with high enough frequency, since access to the state UTxO and the tokens on it could become contested and slow and expensive in user's time. The state UTxO becomes, in effect, constantly locked by competing users—though note the the blockchain would still be behaving correctly in the sense that nobody can lose tokens.

For a more scaleable scenario, some library for parallel redundancy with a monetary policy for the state chip(s) implementing a consensus or merging algorithm, might be required. This is future work.

One more small refinement: every token ever bought must go through the contract at the official price—even if it is the issuer trying to withdraw it (recall from Definition 1.1(4) that we allow only one issuance). In practice, the issuer might want to code a way to get their tokens out without going through buy.

Remark 4.8. (RESISTING DOS ATTACKS). An aside contrasting how Cardano and Ethereum manage fees to prevent denial-of-service (DOS) attacks: In Cardano, users add transactions to the blockchain for a fee of $a + bx$ where a and b are constants and x is the size of the transaction in bytes. This prevents DOS attacks because e.g. if we flood the blockchain with n transactions containing

---

[14] This is distinct from a user inspecting the contents of UTxOs from outside the blockchain, i.e. by reading state off the hard drive of their node or Cardano wallet.

tiny balances, we pay $\geq na$ in fees. In Ethereum, storage costs a fee (denominated in gas); if we inflate balances—which is a finite but unbounded mapping from addresses to integers—with n tiny balances, we may run out of gas.

4.3 Summary of the Critical Points

1. The errors in the Solidity code are not necessarily obvious.
2. The errors cannot be defended against without rewriting the contract, which requires the seller's cooperation (who controls the contract and might even have planted the bug).
3. In Plutus, the *buyer* creates a transaction and determines its inputs and outputs. A transaction might be rejected if the available UTxOs change—but if it succeeds then the buyer knows the outcome. Thus if the user of a contract anticipates an error (or attack) then they can guard against it independently of the contract's designer.

   In Ethereum this is impossible: a buyer can propose a transition to the global virtual machine by calling a function on the Ethereum blockchain, but the designer of the contract designed that function—and because of concurrency, the buyer cannot know the values of the inputs to this function at the time of its execution on the blockchain.

5 Conclusions

We hope this paper will provide a precise yet accessible entry point for interested readers, and a useful guide to some of the design considerations in this area.

We have seen that Ethereum is an accounts-based blockchain system whereas Cardano (like Bitcoin) is UTxO-based, and we have implemented a specification (Definition 1.1) in Solidity (Sect. 4) and in Plutus (Sect. 3), and we have given a mathematical abstraction of Cardano, *idealised EUTxO* (Sect. 2). These have raised some surprisingly non-trivial points, both quite mathematical (e.g. Subsect. 2.3) and more implementational (e.g. Subsect. 4.2), which are discussed in the body of the paper.

The accounts-based paradigm lends itself to an imperative programming style: a smart contract is a *program* that manipulates a global state mapping global variables ('accounts') to values. The UTxO-based paradigm lends itself to a functional programming style: the smart contract is a *function* that takes a UTxO-list as its input, and returns a UTxO-list as its output, with no other dependencies. See Theorem 2.17 and the preceding discussion and lemmas in Subsect. 2.2 for a mathematically precise rendering of this intuition, and Subsect. 2.3 for supplementary results.

Smart contracts are naturally concurrent and must expect to scale to thousands, if not billions, of users,[15] but the problems inherent to concurrent imperative programming are well-known and predate smart contracts by decades. This

---

[15] How to reach distributed consensus in such an environment is another topic, with its own attack surface. Cardano uses Ouroboros consensus [7].

is an issue with Ethereum/Solidity and it is visible even in our simple example. Real-life examples, like the infamous DAO hack[16], are clearly related to the problem of transactions having unexpected consequences in a stateful, concurrent environment.

Cardano's UTxO-based structure invites a functional programming paradigm, and this is reflected in Plutus. The price we pay is arguably an increase in conceptual complexity. More generally, in Remarks 4.6 and 4.7 we discussed how state is handled in Plutus and its UTxO model: further clarification of the interaction of state with UTxOs is important future work.

In summary: accounts are easier to think about than UTxOs, and imperative programs are easier to read than functional programs, but this ease of use makes us vulnerable to new classes of errors, *especially* in a concurrent safety-critical context. Such trade-offs may be familiar to many readers with a computer science or concurrency background.

References

1. Chakravarty, M.M.T., Chapman, J., MacKenzie, K., Melkonian, O., Peyton Jones, M., Wadler, P.: The extended UTXO model. In: Bernhard, M., et al. (eds.) FC 2020. LNCS, vol. 12063, pp. 525–539. Springer, Cham (2020). https://doi.org/10.1007/978-3-030-54455-3_37

2. Coutts, D., de Vries, E.: A formal specification of the Cardano wallet, Technical report, IOHK, Version 1.2, July 2018

3. Gabbay, M.: Equivariant ZFA and the foundations of nominal techniques. J. Log. Comput. **30**(2), 525–48 (2020)

4. de Bruijn, N.G.: Lambda calculus notation with nameless dummies, a tool for automatic formula manipulation, with application to the Church-Rosser theorem. Indagationes Math. **5**(34), 381–392 (1972)

5. Gabbay, M.J., Pitts, A.M.: A new approach to abstract syntax with variable binding. Formal Aspects Comput. **13**, 341–363 (2001)

6. Allais, G., Atkey, R., Chapman, J., McBride, C., McKinna, J.: A type and scope safe universe of syntaxes with binding: their semantics and proofs. In: PACMPL, vol. 2, no. ICFP, pp. 90:1–90:30 (2018)

7. Kiayias, A., Russell, A., David, B., Oliynykov, R.: Ouroboros: a provably secure proof-of-stake blockchain protocol. In: Katz, J., Shacham, H. (eds.) CRYPTO 2017. LNCS, vol. 10401, pp. 357–388. Springer, Cham (2017). https://doi.org/10.1007/978-3-319-63688-7_12

8. Atzei, N., Bartoletti, M., Cimoli, T.: A survey of attacks on Ethereum smart contracts (SoK). In: Maffei, M., Ryan, M. (eds.) POST 2017. LNCS, vol. 10204, pp. 164–186. Springer, Heidelberg (2017). https://doi.org/10.1007/978-3-662-54455-6_8

---

[16] The DAO hack stole approximately 70 million USD from Ethereum, which chose to revert the theft using a hard fork of the Ethereum blockchain [8].

Native Custom Tokens in the Extended UTXO Model

Manuel M. T. Chakravarty[1]([⊠]), James Chapman[2]([⊠]),
Kenneth MacKenzie[3]([⊠]), Orestis Melkonian[3,7]([⊠]), Jann Müller[4]([⊠]),
Michael Peyton Jones[5]([⊠]), Polina Vinogradova[6]([⊠]), and Philip Wadler[3,7]([⊠])

[1] IOHK, Utrecht, The Netherlands
`manuel.chakravarty@iohk.io`
[2] IOHK, Glasgow, UK
`james.chapman@iohk.io`
[3] IOHK, Edinburgh, UK
`{kenneth.macKenzie,orestis.melkonian,philip.wadler}@iohk.io`
[4] IOHK, Mannheim, Germany
`jann.muller@iohk.io`
[5] IOHK, London, UK
`michael.jones@iohk.io`
[6] IOHK, Ottawa, Canada
`polina.vinogradova@iohk.io`
[7] University of Edinburgh, Edinburgh, UK
`orestis.melkonian@ed.ac.uk, wadler@inf.ed.ac.uk`

Abstract. *User-defined tokens*—both fungible ERC-20 and non-fungible ERC-721 tokens—are central to the majority of contracts deployed on Ethereum. User-defined tokens are *non-native* on Ethereum; i.e., they are not directly supported by the ledger, but require custom code. This makes them unnecessarily inefficient, expensive, and complex.

The *Extended UTXO Model (EUTXO)* [5] has been introduced as a generalisation of Bitcoin-style UTXO ledgers, allowing support of more expressive smart contracts, approaching the functionality available to contracts on Ethereum. Specifically, a bisimulation argument established a formal relationship between the EUTXO ledger and a general form of state machines. Nevertheless, *transaction outputs* in the EUTXO model lock integral quantities of a single native cryptocurrency only, just like Bitcoin.

In this paper, we study a generalisation of the EUTXO ledger model with *native* user-defined tokens. Following the approach proposed in a companion paper [4] for the simpler case of plain Bitcoin-style UTXO ledgers, we generalise transaction outputs to lock not merely coins of a single cryptocurrency, but entire *token bundles,* including custom tokens whose forging is controlled by *forging policy scripts*. We show that this leads to a rich ledger model that supports a broad range of interesting use cases.

Our main technical contribution is a formalisation of the multi-asset EUTXO ledger in Agda, which we use to establish that the ledger with custom tokens is strictly more expressive than the original EUTXO

T. Margaria and B. Steffen (Eds.): ISoLA 2020, LNCS 12478, pp. 89–111, 2020.
https://doi.org/10.1007/978-3-030-61467-6_7

ledger. In particular, we state and prove a transfer result for inductive and temporal properties from state machines to the multi-asset EUTXO ledger, which was out of scope for the single-currency EUTXO ledger. In practical terms, the resulting system is the basis for the smart contract system of the Cardano blockchain.

Keywords: Blockchain · UTXO · Tokens · Functional programming · State machines · Bisimulation

1 Introduction

If we look at contracts on Ethereum in terms of their use and the monetary values that they process, then it becomes apparent that so-called *user-defined* (or *custom*) *tokens* play a central role in that ecosystem. The two most common token types are *fungible tokens*, following the ERC-20 standard [17], and *non-fungible* tokens, following the ERC-721 standard [7].

On Ethereum, ERC-20 and ERC-721 tokens are fundamentally different from the native cryptocurrency, Ether, in that their creation and use always involves user-defined custom code—they are not directly supported by the underlying ledger, and hence are *non-native*. This makes them unnecessarily inefficient, expensive, and complex. Although the ledger already includes facilities to manage and maintain a currency, this functionality is replicated in interpreted user-level code, which is inherently less efficient. Moreover, the execution of user-code needs to be paid for (in gas), which leads to significant costs. Finally, the ERC-20 and ERC-721 token code gets replicated and adapted, instead of being part of the system, which complicates the creation and use of tokens and leaves room for human error.

The alternative to user-level token code is a ledger that supports *native tokens*. In other words, a ledger that directly supports (1) the creation of new user-defined token or asset types, (2) the forging of those tokens, and (3) the transfer of custom token ownership between multiple participants. In a companion paper [4], we propose a generalisation of Bitcoin-style UTXO ledgers, which we call UTXO$_{ma}$("ma" for "multi-asset"), adding native tokens by way of so-called *token bundles* and domain-specific *forging policy scripts*, without the need for a general-purpose scripting system.

Independently, we previously introduced the *Extended UTXO Model* (EUTXO) [5] as an orthogonal generalisation of Bitcoin-style UTXO ledgers, enabling support of more expressive smart contracts, with functionality similar to contracts on Ethereum. To support user-defined tokens or currencies on EUTXO, we could follow Ethereum's path and define standards corresponding to ERC-20 and ERC-721 for fungible and non-fungible tokens, but then we would be subject to the same disadvantages that non-native tokens have on Ethereum.

In this paper, to avoid the disadvantages of non-native tokens, we investigate the combination of the two previously mentioned extensions of the plain UTXO model: we add $UTXO_{ma}$-style token bundles and asset policy scripts to the EUTXO model, resulting in a new $EUTXO_{ma}$ ledger model.

We will show that the resulting $EUTXO_{ma}$ model is strictly more expressive than both EUTXO and $UTXO_{ma}$ by itself. In particular, the constraint-emitting state machines in [5] can not ensure that they are initialised correctly. In $EUTXO_{ma}$, we are able to use non-fungible tokens to trace *threads* of state machines. Extending the mechanised Agda model from [5] allows us to then prove inductive and temporal properties of state machines by induction over their traces, covering a wide variety of state machine correctness properties.

Moreover, the more expressive scripting functionality and state threading of EUTXO enables us to define more sophisticated asset policies than in $UTXO_{ma}$. Additionally, we argue that the combined system allows for sophisticated access-control schemes by representing roles and capabilities in the form of user-defined tokens.

In summary, this paper makes the following contributions:

- We introduce the multi-asset $EUTXO_{ma}$ ledger model (Sect. 2).
- We outline a range of application scenarios that are arguably better supported by the new model, and also applications that plain $UTXO_{ma}$ does not support at all (Sect. 3).
- We formally prove a transfer result for inductive and temporal properties from constraint emitting machines to the $EUTXO_{ma}$ ledger, an important property that we were not able to establish for plain EUTXO (Sect. 4).

We discuss related work in Sect. 5. Due to space constraints, the formal ledger rules for $EUTXO_{ma}$ are in Appendix A. A mechanised version of the ledger rules and the various formal results from Sect. 4 is available as Agda source code.[1]

On top of the conceptual and theoretical contributions made in this paper, we would like to emphasise that the proposed system is highly practical. In fact, $EUTXO_{ma}$ underlies our implementation of *Plutus Platform,* the smart contract system of the Cardano blockchain.[2]

2 Extending Extended UTXO

Before discussing applications and the formal model of $EUTXO_{ma}$, we briefly summarise the structure of EUTXO, and then informally introduce the multi-asset extension that is the subject of this paper. Finally, we will discuss a short-coming in the state machine mapping of EUTXO as introduced in [5] and illustrate how the multi-asset extension fixes that shortcoming.

2.1 The Starting Point: Extended UTXO

In Bitcoin's UTXO ledger model, the ledger is formed by a list of transactions grouped into blocks. As the block structure is secondary to the discussion in

---

[1] https://github.com/omelkonian/formal-utxo/tree/2d32.
[2] https://github.com/input-output-hk/plutus.

this paper, we will disregard it in the following. A transaction tx is a quadruple (I, O, r, S) comprising a set of *inputs* I, a list of *outputs* O, a *validity interval* r, and a set of signatures S, where inputs and outputs represent cryptocurrency value flowing into and out of the transaction, respectively. The sum of the inputs must be equal to the sum of the outputs; in other words, transactions preserve value. Transactions are identified by a collision-resistant cryptographic hash h computed from the transaction.[3]

An input $i \in I$ is represented as a pair (out_{ref}, ρ) of an *output reference* out_{ref} and a *redeemer value* ρ. The output reference out_{ref} uniquely identifies an output in a preceding transaction by way of the transaction's hash and the output's position in the transaction's list of outputs.

In plain UTXO, an output $o \in O$ is a pair of a *validator script* ν and cryptocurrency value *value*. In the Extended UTXO model (EUTXO) [5], outputs become triples $(\nu, value, \delta)$, where the added *datum* δ enables passing additional information to the validator.

The purpose of the validator is to assess whether an input i of a subsequent transaction trying to spend (i.e., consume) an output o should be allowed to do so. To this end, we execute the validator script to check whether $\nu(\rho, \delta, \sigma) = \mathsf{true}$ holds. Here σ comprises additional information about the *validation context* of the transaction. In the plain UTXO model that contextual information is fairly limited: it mainly consists of the validated transaction's hash, the signatures S, and information about the length of the blockchain. In the EUTXO model, we extend σ to include the entirety of the validated transaction tx as well as all the outputs spent by the inputs of tx.

2.2   Token Bundles

In UTXO and EUTXO, the *value* carried by an output is represented as an integral value denoting a specific quantity of the ledger's native cryptocurrency. As discussed in more detail in the companion paper [4], we can generalise *value* to carry a two-level structure of *finitely-supported functions*. The technicalities are in Appendix A; for now, we can regard them as nested finite maps to quantities of tokens. For example, the value $\{\mathsf{Coin} \mapsto \{\mathsf{Coin} \mapsto 3\}, g \mapsto \{t_1 \mapsto 1, t_2 \mapsto 1\}\}$ contains 3 Coin coins (there is only one (fungible) token Coin for a payment currency also called Coin), as well as (non-fungible) tokens t_1 and t_2, both in asset group g. Values can be added naturally, e.g.,

$$\{\mathsf{Coin} \mapsto \{\mathsf{Coin} \mapsto 3\}, g \mapsto \{t_1 \mapsto 1, t_2 \mapsto 1\}\}$$
$$+ \{\mathsf{Coin} \mapsto \{\mathsf{Coin} \mapsto 1\}, g \mapsto \{t_3 \mapsto 1\}\}$$
$$= \{\mathsf{Coin} \mapsto \{\mathsf{Coin} \mapsto 4\}, g \mapsto \{t_1 \mapsto 1, t_2 \mapsto 1, t_3 \mapsto 1\}\} .$$

In a bundle, such as $g \mapsto \{t_1 \mapsto 1, t_2 \mapsto 1, t_3 \mapsto 1\}$, we call g an *asset group* comprising a set of tokens t_1, t_2, and t_3. In the case of a fungible asset group, such as Coin, we may call it a *currency*. In contrast to fungible tokens, only a single instance of a non-fungible token may be minted.

---

[3] We denote the hash of some data d as $d^{\#}$.

2.3 Forging Custom Tokens

To enable the introduction of new quantities of new tokens on the ledger (*minting*) or the removal of existing tokens (*burning*), we add a *forge field* to each transaction. The use of the forge field needs to be tightly controlled, so that the minting and burning of tokens is guaranteed to proceed according to the token's *forging policy*. We implement forging policies by means of scripts that are much like the validator scripts used to lock outputs in EUTXO.

Overall, a transaction in EUTXO_{ma} is thus a sextuple $(I, O, r, forge, fpss, S)$, where *forge*, just like *value* in an output, is a token bundle and *fpss* is a set of *forging policy scripts*. Unlike the value attached to transaction outputs, *forge* is allowed to contain negative quantities of tokens. Positive quantities represent minted tokens and negative quantities represent burned tokens. In either case, any asset group ϕ that occurs in *forge* (i.e., $forge = \{\ldots, \phi \mapsto toks, \ldots\}$) must also have its forging policy script in the transaction's *fpss* field. Each script π in *fpss* is executed to check whether $\pi(\sigma) = \text{true}$, that is whether the transaction, including its *forge* field, is admissible. (In fact we have a slightly different σ here, which we elaborate on in Appendix A.)

2.4 Constraint Emitting Machines

In the EUTXO paper [5], we explained how we can map *Constraint Emitting Machines* (CEMs) —a variation on Mealy machines—onto an EUTXO ledger. A CEM consists of its type of states S and inputs I, predicates $\text{initial}, \text{final} : \text{S} \rightarrow \mathbb{B}$ indicating which states are initial and final, respectively, and a valid set of transitions, given as a partial function $\text{step} : \text{S} \rightarrow \text{I} \rightarrow \text{Maybe}\,(\text{S} \times \text{TxConstraints})$ from source state and input symbol to target state and constraints. (The result may be Nothing, in case no valid transitions exist from a given state/input.) One could present CEMs using the traditional five-tuple notation $(Q, \Sigma, \delta, q_0, F)$, but we opt for functional notation to avoid confusion with standard *finite state machines* (see [5] on how CEMs differ from FSMs), as well as being consistent with our other definitions.

A sequence of CEM state transitions, each of the form $s \xrightarrow{i} (s', tx^{\equiv})$, is mapped to a sequence of transactions, where each machine state s is represented by one transaction tx_s. Each such transaction contains a *state machine output* o_s whose validator ν_s implements the CEM transition relation and whose datum δ_s encodes the CEM state s.

The transition $tx_{s'}$, representing the successor state, spends o_s with an input that provides the CEM input i as its redeemer ρ_i. Finally, the constraints $tx^{\equiv}$ generated by the state transition need to be met by the successor transition $tx_{s'}$. (We will define the correspondence precisely in Sect. 4.)

A simple example for such a state machine is an on-chain n-of-m multisignature contract. Specifically, we have a given amount $value_{\text{msc}}$ of some cryptocurrency and we require the approval of at least n out of an *a priori* fixed set of $m \geq n$ owners to spend $value_{\text{msc}}$. With plain UTXO (e.g., on Bitcoin), a multisignature scheme requires out-of-band (off-chain) communication to collect all n

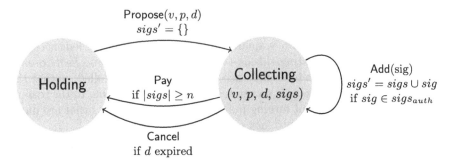

Fig. 1. Transition diagram for the multi-signature state machine; edges labelled with input from redeemer and transition constraints.

signatures to spend $value_{\mathrm{msc}}$. On Ethereum, and also in the EUTXO model, we can collect the signatures on-chain, without any out-of-band communication. To do so, we use a state machine operating according to the transition diagram in Fig. 1, where we assume that the threshold n and authorised signatures $sigs_{\mathrm{auth}}$ with $|sigs_{\mathrm{auth}}| = m$ are baked into the contract code.

In the multi-signature state machine's implementation in the EUTXO model, we use a validator function ν_{msc} accompanied by the datum δ_{msc} to lock $value_{\mathrm{msc}}$. The datum δ_{msc} stores the machine state, which is of the form Holding when only holding the locked value or Collecting($value, \kappa, d, sigs$) when collecting signatures $sigs$ for a payment of $value$ to κ by the deadline d. The initial output for the contract is $(\nu_{\mathrm{msc}}, value_{\mathrm{msc}}, \mathsf{Holding})$.

The validator ν_{msc} implements the state transition diagram from Fig. 1 by using the redeemer of the spending input to determine the transition that needs to be taken. That redeemer (state machine input) can take four forms: (1) Propose($value, \kappa, d$) to propose a payment of $value$ to κ by the deadline d, (2) Add(sig) to add a signature sig to a payment, (3) Cancel to cancel a proposal after its deadline expired, and (4) Pay to make a payment once all required signatures have been collected. It then validates that the spending transaction tx is a valid representation of the newly reached machine state. This implies that tx needs to keep $value_{\mathrm{msc}}$ locked by ν_{msc} and that the state in the datum δ'_{msc} needs to be the successor state of δ_{msc} according to the transition diagram.

While the state machine in Fig. 1 is fine, its mapping to EUTXO transactions comes with a subtle caveat: what if, for a 2–of–3 contract, somebody posts a transition tx_{bad} corresponding to the state Collecting($value, \kappa, d, \{sig_1, sig_2\}$) onto the chain *without* going through any of the previous states, including without starting in Holding? Given that Pay merely checks $|sigs| \geq 2$, the payment would be processed when requested on tx_{bad}, even if $\{sig_1, sig_2\}$ are invalid signatures. We would not have been allowed to add the invalid signatures sig_1 and sig_2 by way of Add(sig) since its state transition checks signature validity, but by initialising the state machine in an intermediate state s with initial(s) = false, we were able to circumvent that check.

In the plain EUTXO model, there is no simple way for the validator implementing a state machine to assert that the state it is operating on arose out of a succession of predecessor states rooted in an initial state. As a consequence of this limitation, the formal result presented in the EUTXO paper [5] is not as strong as one might hope. More precisely, this previous work did establish soundness and completeness for a weak bisimulation between CEMs and transactions on a EUTXO ledger; however, it fell short in that it did not show that an inductive property met by the states of a CEM may also be asserted for the corresponding states on the ledger. The reason for this omission is precisely the problem we just discussed: for a ledger-representation of a CEM state, we can never be sure that it arose out of a transaction sequence rooted in an initial CEM state.

2.5 Token Provenance

In the present work, we solve the problem described above. We will show that non-fungible tokens can be used to identify a unique trace of transactions through an $EUTXO_{ma}$ ledger that corresponds to all the states of the corresponding CEM. Moreover, we introduce a notion of *token provenance* that enables us to identify the first CEM state in such a trace and to ensure that it is a state accepted by initial : $S \rightarrow \mathbb{B}$. Together, these allow a state machine validator to ensure that a current CEM state indeed arose out of a trace of transactions rooted in a transaction corresponding to an initial CEM state merely by checking that the non-fungible token associated with this state machine instance is contained in the *value* of the state machine output that it locks: this would be $value_{msc}$ for the multi-signature contract of Sect. 2.4.

3   Applications

The functionality and applications discussed in the companion paper [4] on $UTXO_{ma}$ are all still possible in the extended $EUTXO_{ma}$ model discussed here. In fact, some of the applications can even be realised more easily by using the added EUTXO functionality, for example by using a state machine to control the behaviour of a forging policy over time. On top of that, we can realise new applications and move some of the functionality that needed to be implemented by an off-chain trusted party in $UTXO_{ma}$ into on-chain script code in $EUTXO_{ma}$.

3.1   State Thread Tokens

As discussed in Sect. 2, many interesting smart contracts can be implemented by way of state machines. However, without custom tokens, the implementation of state machines on an EUTXO ledger suffers from two problems:

- Multiple instances of a single state machine (using the same validator code) generate state machine outputs that look alike. Hence, for a given output locked by the state machine's validator, we cannot tell whether it belongs to one or another run of that state machine.

– The issue raised in Sect. 2.4: a validator cannot tell whether the state machine was started in one of its initial states or whether somebody produced out of thin air a state machine in the middle of its execution.

We can work around the first problem by requiring all transactions of a particular state machine instance to be signed by a particular key and checking that as part of state machine execution. This is awkward, as it requires off-chain communication of the key for a multi-party state machine. In any case these two problems open contracts up to abuse if they are not carefully implemented.

We can solve both of these problems with the help of a unique non-fungible token, called a *state thread token,* which is minted in an initial CEM state. From the initial state on, it uniquely identifies the transaction sequence implementing the progression of one specific instance of the token's state machine. The state thread token is passed from one transition to the next by way of the state machine output of each transaction, where the presence of the state thread token is asserted by the state machine validator. More precisely, assuming a validator ν_s implementing the state machine and a matching forging policy ϕ_s, the state thread token of the ϕ_s policy is used as follows:

– The forging policy ϕ_s checks that
  • the transaction mints a unique, non-fungible token tok_s and
  • the transaction's state machine output is locked by the state machine validator ν_s and contains an admissible initial state of the state machine in its datum field.
– The state machine validator ν_s, in turn, asserts that
  • the standard state machine constraints hold,
  • the value locked by ν_s contains the state thread token tok_s, and
  • if the spending transaction represents a final state, it burns tok_s. (We ignore burning in the formalisation in Sect. 4. It is for cleaning up and not relevant for correctness.)

This solves both problems. The uniqueness of the non-fungible token ensures that there is a single path that represents the progression of the state machine. Moreover, as the token can only be minted in an initial state, it is guaranteed that the state machine must indeed have begun in an initial state. In Sect. 4 we formalise this approach and we show that it is sufficient to give us the properties that we want for state machines.

3.2   Tokenised Roles and Contracts

Custom tokens are convenient to control ownership and access to smart contracts. In particular, we can turn *roles* in a contract into tokens by forging a set of non-fungible tokens, one for each role in the contract. In order to take an action (for example, to make a specific state transition in a state machine) as that role, a user must present the corresponding *role token*.

For example, in a typical financial futures contract we have two roles: the buyer (long), and the seller (short). In a tokenised future contract, we forge tokens which provide the right to act as the long or short position; e.g., in order to settle the future and take delivery of the underlying asset, an agent needs to provide the long token as part of that transaction.

Trading Role Tokens. Tokenised roles are themselves *resources* on the ledger, and as such are tradeable and cannot be split or double spent, which is useful in practice. For example, it is fairly typical to trade in futures contracts, buying or selling the right to act as the long or short position in the trade. With tokenised roles, this simply amounts to trading the corresponding role token.

The alternative approach is to identify roles with public keys, where users *authenticate* as a role by signing the transaction with the corresponding key. However, this makes trading roles much more cumbersome than simply trading a token; an association between roles and keys could be stored in the contract datum, but this requires interacting with the contract to change the association. Moreover, when using public keys instead of role tokens, we cannot easily implement more advanced use cases that require treating the role as a resource, such as the derivatives discussed below.

The lightweight nature of our tokens is key here. To ensure that roles for all instances of all contracts are distinct, every instance requires a unique asset group with its own forging policy. If we had a global register with all asset groups and token names, adding a new asset group and token for every set of role tokens we create would add significant overhead.

Derivatives and Securitisation. Since tokenised roles are just tokens, they are themselves assets that can be managed by smart contracts. This enables a number of derivative (higher-order) financial contracts to be written in a generic way, without requiring a hard-coded list of tokens as the underlying assets.

For example, consider interest, a contract from which payments can be extracted at regular intervals, based on some interest rate. We can tokenise this by issuing a token for the *creditor* role that represents the claim to those payments: if someone wishes to claim the payment then they must present that token.

If we have several instances of interest (perhaps based on different interest rates), we can lock their creditor tokens in a new contract that bundles the cash flows of all the underlying contracts. The payments of this new contract are the sum of the payments of the interest contracts that it collects. The tokens of the interest contracts cannot be traded separately as long as they are locked by the new contract.

This kind of bundling of cash flows is called *securitisation*. Securitisation is commonly used to even out variations in the payment streams of the underlying contracts and to distribute their default risk across different risk groups (tranches). Derivative contracts, including the example above, make it possible to package and trade financial risks, ultimately resulting in lower expenditure and higher liquidity for all market participants. Our system makes the cost of creating derivatives very low, indeed no higher than making a contract that operates on any other asset.

3.3   Fairness

Tokens can be used to ensure that *all* participants in some agreement have been involved. For example, consider a typical ICO setup in which a number of participants pay for the right to buy the token during an initial issuance phase. A naive implementation is as follows:

- Contributors lock their contributions with a validator ν and a datum δ, where δ contains their public key and ν requires that an appropriate part of the forged tranche be sent to the public key address corresponding to δ.
- The forging policy ϕ requires that the sum of the inputs exceeds a predetermined threshold T, and allows forging of n units of the token, which must be allocated to the input payers in proportion to their contribution.

Unfortunately, this is not *fair*, in that participants can be omitted by the party who actually creates the forging transaction, as long as the other participants between them reach the threshold.

We can fix this by issuing (fungible) *participation tokens*, representing the right to participate in the ICO. First, we forge l participation tokens, and then we distribute them to the participants (in return for whatever form of payment we require). Finally, in order to issue the main tranche of tokens, we require (in addition to the previous conditions) that some appropriate fraction of the issued participation tokens are spent in that transaction. That means we cannot omit (too many of) the holders of the participation tokens—and the forging policy ensures that all participants are compensated appropriately. As a bonus, this makes the right to participate in the ICO itself tradeable as a tokenised role. In other words, participation tokens make roles into *first-class* assets.

A similar scheme is being used in the Hydra head protocol [6], which implements a layer-2 scalability solution. *Hydra heads* enable groups of participants to advance an a priori locked portion of the mainchain UTXO set in a fast off-chain protocol with fast settlement in a manner that provides the same level of security as the mainchain. The mainchain portion of the protocol, which is based on $EUTXO_{ma}$, uses custom tokens to ensure that it is impossible for a subgroup of the participants to collude to exclude one or more other participants.

3.4   Algorithmic Stablecoins

In [4], we described how to implement a simple, centralised stablecoin in the $UTXO_{ma}$. However, more sophisticated stablecoin designs exist, such as the Dai of MakerDAO [9].

Stablecoins where more of the critical functionality is validated on-chain can be realised within the $EUTXO_{ma}$ model. For example, we can use a state machine that acts as a *market maker* for a stablecoin by forging stablecoins in exchange for other assets. Mechanisms to audit updates to the current market price, or to suspend trading if the fund's liabilities become too great, can also be implemented programmatically on-chain.

4 Meta-theoretical Properties of EUTXO$_{\text{ma}}$

In [5], we characterised the expressiveness of EUTXO ledgers by showing that we can encode a class of state machines—*Constraint Emitting Machines* (CEMs)—into the ledger via a series of transactions. Formally, we showed that there is a weak bisimulation between CEM transitions and their encoded transitions in the ledger.

However, as we have seen from the example in Sect. 2.4 above, this result is not sufficient to allow us to reason about the properties of the state machine. Even if we know that each individual step is valid, there may be some properties that are only guaranteed to hold if we started from a proper initial state. Specifically, we will not be able to establish any inductive or temporal property unless we cover the base case corresponding to initial states. Since our earlier model did not prevent us from starting the ledger in an arbitrary (and perhaps non-valid) state, such properties could not be carried over from the state machines to the ledger.

In this section we extend our formalisation to map CEMs into threaded ledgers. By formalising some of the properties of EUTXO$_{\text{ma}}$, we can guarantee that a ledger was started from a valid initial state, and thus carry over inductive and temporal properties from state machines. All the results in this section have been mechanised in Agda, extending the formalisation from [5].

4.1 Token Provenance

Given a token in a EUTXO$_{\text{ma}}$ ledger, we can ask "where did this token *come from?*" Since tokens are always created in specific forging operations, we can always trace them back through their transaction graph to their *origin*.

We call such a path through the transaction graph a *trace*, and define the *provenance* of an asset at some particular output to be a trace leading from the current transaction to an origin which forges a value containing the traced tokens.

In the case of fungible tokens, there may be multiple possible traces: since such tokens are interchangeable, if two tokens of some asset are forged separately, and then later mingled in the same output, then we cannot say which one came from which forging.

Let $\blacklozenge = (p, a)$ denote a particular Asset a controlled by a Policy p, and $v^{\blacklozenge} = v(p)(a)$ the quantity of $\blacklozenge$ tokens present in value v. Trace$(l, o, \blacklozenge, n)$ is the type of sequences of transactions $t_0, \ldots, t_i, t_{i+1}, \ldots, t_k$ drawn from a ledger l such that:

– the origin transaction t_0 forges at least n $\blacklozenge$ tokens: $t_0.forge^{\blacklozenge} \geq n$
– every pair (t_i, t_{i+1}) has an input/output connection in the ledger that transfers at least n $\blacklozenge$ tokens: $\exists o' \in t_{i+1}.inputs.outputRef.(t_i.outputs [o'.index].value^{\blacklozenge} \geq n)$
– the last transaction t_k carries the traced tokens in output o

We define $\mathsf{Provenance}(l, o, \blacklozenge)$ to be a set of traces $\dots \mathsf{Trace}(l, o, \blacklozenge, n_i) \dots$, such that $\sum n_i \geq o.value^{\blacklozenge}$.

To construct an output's provenance, with respect to a particular policy and asset, we aggregate all possible traces containing a token of this asset from the transaction's inputs as well as from the value that is currently being forged. Thus our tracing procedure will construct a sound over-approximation of the actual provenance.

$$\frac{o \in \{t.outputs \mid t \in l\}}{provenance(l, o, \blacklozenge) : \mathsf{Provenance}(l, o, \blacklozenge)} \text{ PROVENANCE}$$

4.2   Forging Policies Are Enforced

One particular meta-theoretical property we want to check is that each token is created properly: there is an origin transaction which forges it and is checked against the currency's forging policy.

Proposition 1 (Non-empty Provenance). *Given any token-carrying output of a valid ledger, its computed provenance will be inhabited by at least one trace.*

$$\frac{o \in \{t.outputs \mid t \in l\} \quad o.value^{\blacklozenge} > 0}{|provenance(l, o, \blacklozenge)| > 0} \text{ PROVENANCE}^+$$

However, this is not enough to establish what we want: due to fungibility, we could identify a single origin as the provenance for two tokens, even if the origin only forges a single token!

To remedy this, we complement (non-empty) token provenance with a proof of *global preservation*; a generalisation of the local validity condition of *value preservation* from Rule 4 in Appendix A.

Proposition 2 (Global Preservation). *Given a valid ledger l:*

$$\sum_{t \in l} t.forge = \sum_{o \in \mathsf{unspentOutputs}(l)} o.value$$

The combination of non-empty token provenance and global preservation assures us that each token is created properly and there is globally no more currency than is forged.

To prove these properties we require transactions to be unique throughout the ledger, which is not implied by the validity rules of Fig. 5 in Appendix A. In practice though, one could derive uniqueness from any ledger that does not have more than one transaction with no inputs, since a transaction would always have to consume some previously unspent output to pay its fees. For our purposes, it suffices to assume there is always a single *genesis* transaction without any inputs:

$$\frac{}{|\{t \in l \mid t.inputs = \emptyset\}| = 1} \text{ GENESIS}$$

Then we can derive the uniqueness of transactions and unspent outputs.

4.3   Provenance for Non-fungible Tokens

However, our approach to threading crucially relies on the idea that a non-fungible token can pick out a *unique* path through the transaction graph.

First, we define a token $\blacklozenge$ to be *non-fungible* whenever it has been forged at most once across all transactions of an existing valid ledger l. (This really is a property of a particular ledger: a "non-fungible" token can become fungible in a longer ledger if other tokens of its asset are forged. Whether or not this is possible will depend on external reasoning about the forging policy.) Then we can prove that non-fungible tokens have a singular provenance; they really do pick out a unique trace through the transaction graph.

Proposition 3 (Provenance for Non-fungible Tokens). *Given a valid ledger l and an unspent output carrying a non-fungible token $\blacklozenge$:*

$$\frac{o \in \{t.outputs \mid t \in l\} \quad o.value^{\blacklozenge} > 0 \quad \sum_{t \in l} t.forge^{\blacklozenge} \leq 1}{|provenance(l, o, \blacklozenge)| = 1} \text{ NF-Provenance}$$

4.4   Threaded State Machines

Armed with the provenance mechanism just described, we are now ready to extend the previously established bisimulation between CEMs and state machines in ledgers, so that it relates CEMs with support for initial states to *threaded* state machines in ledgers. That is, in addition to creating an appropriate validator as in [5], we also create a forging policy that forges a unique *thread token* which is then required for the machine to progress (and is destroyed when it terminates). Crucially, the forging policy also checks that the machine is starting in an initial state.

For the sake of brevity, we refrain from repeating the entirety of the CEM model definitions from [5]. Instead, we focus only on the relevant modifications and refer the reader to the mechanised model for more details.

First, we omit the notion of final states altogether, i.e., there is no final predicate in the definition of a CEM. (Note that this also simplifies the bisimulation propositions proven in [5], since we no longer need to consider the special case of final states. Other than that, the statements stay exactly the same.) We follow Robin Milner who observed, "What matters about a sequence of actions is not whether it drives the automaton into an accepting state but whether the automaton is able to perform the sequence interactively." [12] Formally, this corresponds to prefix closure: if an automaton accepts a string s then it accepts any initial part of s (Definition 2.6 [12]). Our state machines are not classical state machines which accept or reject a string—rather they are *interactive processes* which respond to user input. However, it might be useful to re-introduce final states in the future if we support burning of the thread token.

On the other hand, we now include the notion of initial state in the predicate function initial : $S \rightarrow \mathbb{B}$, which characterises the states in which a machine can start from. This enables us to ensure that multiple copies of the machine with the same thread token cannot run at once and the machine cannot be started in an intermediate state. State machines whose execution must start from an initial state are also referred to as *rooted* state transition systems [8].

To enforce non-fungibility of the forged token, we require that the forging transaction spends a specific output, fixed for a particular CEM instance $\mathcal{C}$ and supplied along with its definition as a field origin. Therefore, since no output can be spent twice, we guarantee that the token cannot be forged again in the future.

The CEM's forging policy checks that we only forge a single thread token, spend the supplied origin, and that the state propagated in the outputs is initial:

$$\text{policy}_\mathcal{C}(\textit{txInfo}, c) = \begin{cases} \text{true} & \textit{if } \textit{txInfo.forge}^\blacklozenge = 1 \\ & \textit{and } \text{origin} \in \textit{txInfo.outputRefs} \\ & \textit{and } \text{initial}(\textit{txInfo.outputs}^\blacklozenge) \\ \text{false} & \textit{otherwise} \end{cases}$$

where $\blacklozenge = \{\text{validator}_\mathcal{C}^\# \mapsto \{\text{policy}_\mathcal{C}^\# \mapsto 1\}\}$ is the thread token and $\textit{txInfo.outputs}^\blacklozenge$ looks up the output which carries the newly-forged thread token and is locked by the same machine's validator, returning the datum decoded as a value of the state type S.

We extend the previous definition of a CEM's validator (displayed in grey) to also check that the thread token is attached to the source state s and propagated to the target state s':

$$\text{validator}_\mathcal{C}(s, i, \textit{txInfo}) = \begin{cases} \text{true} & \textit{if } s \xrightarrow{i} (s', \textit{tx}^=) \\ & \textit{and } \text{satisfies}(\textit{txInfo}, \textit{tx}^=) \\ & \textit{and } \text{checkOutputs}(s', \textit{txInfo}) \\ & \textit{and } \text{propagates}(\textit{txInfo}, \blacklozenge, s, s') \\ \text{false} & \textit{otherwise} \end{cases}$$

This is sufficient to let us prove a key result: given a threaded ledger state (i.e., one that includes an appropriate thread token), that state *must* have evolved from a valid initial state. Since we know that the thread token must have a singular provenance, we know that there is a unique ledger trace that begins by forging that token—which is guaranteed to be an initial CEM state.

Proposition 4 (Initiality). *Given a valid ledger l and an unspent output carrying the thread token $\blacklozenge$, we can always trace it back to a single origin, which forges the token and abides by the forging policy:*

$$\frac{o \in \{t.outputs \mid t \in l\} \quad o.value^\blacklozenge > 0}{\exists tr.\ \text{provenance}(l, o, \blacklozenge) = \{tr\} \ \wedge\ \text{policy}_\mathcal{C}(\text{mkPolicyContext}(tr_0, \text{validator}_\mathcal{C}^\#, l^{tr_0})) = \text{true}} \text{ INITIALITY}$$

where tr_0 denotes the origin of trace tr, and l^t is the prefix of the ledger up to transaction t. The proof essentially relies on the fact that the thread token is non-fungible, as its forging requires spending a unique output. By NF-PROVENANCE, we then get the unique trace back to a *valid* forging transaction, which is validated against the machine's forging policy.

4.5 Property Preservation

Establishing correct initialisation is the final piece we need to be able to show that properties of abstract CEMs carry over to their ledger equivalents. It is no longer possible to reach any state that cannot be reached in the abstract state machine, and so any properties that hold over traces of the state machine also hold over traces of the ledger.

Intuitively, looking at the ledger trace we immediately get from INITIALITY, we can discern an underlying CEM trace that throws away all irrelevant ledger information and only keeps the corresponding CEM steps. After having defined the proper notions of property preservation for CEM traces, we will be able to transfer those for on-chain traces by virtue of this extraction procedure.

A simple example of a property of a machine is an invariant. We consider predicates on states of the machine that we call state-predicates.

Definition 1. *A state-predicate P is an* invariant *if it holds for all reachable states of the machine. i.e., if it holds for the initial state, and for any s, i, s' and $tx^{\equiv}$ such that $s \xrightarrow{i} (s', tx^{\equiv})$, if it holds for s then it holds for s'.*

Traces of State Machine Execution. We have traced the path of a token through the ledger. We can also trace the execution of a state machine. We consider rooted traces that start in the initial state, and refer to them as just *traces*. A trace records the history of the states of the machine over time and also the inputs that drive the machine from state to state.

Definition 2. *A* trace *is an inductively defined relation on states:*

$$\frac{\text{initial}(s) = \text{true}}{s \rightsquigarrow^* s} \text{ root} \qquad \frac{s \rightsquigarrow^* s' \quad s' \xrightarrow{i} (s'', tx^{\equiv})}{s \rightsquigarrow^* s''} \text{ snoc}$$

This gives us a convenient notion to reason about temporal properties of the machine, such as those which hold at all times, at some time, and properties that hold until another one does. In this paper we restrict our attention to properties that always hold.

Properties of Execution Traces. Consider a predicate P on a single step of execution. A *step-predicate* $P(s, i, s', tx^{\equiv})$ refers to the incoming state s, the input i, the outgoing state s' and the constraints $tx^{\equiv}$. A particularly important lifting of predicates on steps to predicates on traces is the transformer that ensures the predicate holds for every step in the trace.

Definition 3. *Given a step-predicate P, a trace tr satisfies $\text{All}(P, tr)$ whenever every step $s \xrightarrow{i} (s', tx^{\equiv})$ satisfies $P(s, i, s', tx^{\equiv})$.*

A predicate transformer lifting state-predicates to a predicate that holds everywhere in a trace can be defined as a special case: $\text{All}^S(P, tr) = \text{All}(\lambda s\ i\ s'\ tx^{\equiv}.\ P(s) \wedge P(s'),\ tr)$.

We are not just interested in properties of CEM traces in isolation, but more crucially in whether these properties hold when a state machine is compiled to a contract to be executed on-chain.

We observe that the on-chain execution traces precisely follow the progress of the thread token. We use the same notion of token provenance to characterise on-chain execution traces. To facilitate reasoning about these traces, we can *extract* the corresponding state machine execution traces and reason about those. This allows us to confine our reasoning to the simpler setting of state machines.

Proposition 5 (Extraction). *Given a valid ledger l and a singular provenance of the (non-fungible) thread token $\blacklozenge$, we can extract a rooted state machine trace.*

$$\frac{\mathsf{provenance}(l, o, \blacklozenge) = \{tr\}}{tr.source \leadsto^* tr.destination} \ \text{EXTRACTION}$$

where $tr.source, tr.destination$ are the states associated with the endpoints of the trace tr.

Proof. It is straightforward to show this holds, as a corollary of INITIALITY. For the base case, knowing that the origin of the trace abides by the forging policy ensures that it forges the thread token and outputs an initial state (root). In the inductive step, knowing that the validator runs successfully guarantees that there is a corresponding CEM step (snoc). □

Corollary 1. *Any predicate that always holds for a CEM trace also holds for the one extracted from the on-chain trace.*

We will write $\mathsf{extract}(tr)$ whenever we want to extract the CEM trace from the on-chain trace tr.

Example 1. Consider a CEM representing a simple counter that counts up from zero:

$$(\mathbb{Z}, \{\mathsf{inc}\}, \mathsf{step}, \mathsf{initial}) \quad \textbf{where} \quad \mathsf{step}(i, \mathsf{inc}) = \mathsf{just}(i + 1); \quad \mathsf{initial}(0) = \mathsf{true}$$

A simple property that we want to hold is that the state of the counter is never negative.

Property 1. The counter state c is non-negative, i.e., $c \geq 0$.

Lemma 1. *Property 1 is an invariant, i.e., it holds for all reachable states:*

1. $\forall c.\ \mathsf{initial}(c) \rightarrow c \geq 0$
2. $\forall c\ c'.\ c \xrightarrow{i} (c', tx^\equiv) \rightarrow c \geq 0 \rightarrow c' \geq 0$

Proposition 6. *In all reachable states, both off-chain and on-chain, the counter is non-negative.*

1. $\forall c\ c'\ (tr : c \leadsto^* c').\ \mathsf{All}^\mathsf{S}(\lambda x.\ x \geq 0,\ tr)$
2. $\forall l\ o\ tr.\ \mathsf{provenance}(l, o, \blacklozenge) = \{tr\} \rightarrow \mathsf{All}^\mathsf{S}(\lambda x.\ x \geq 0, \mathsf{extract}(tr))$

Proof. (1) follows from Lemma 1. (2) follows from (1) and Corollary 1.   □

Example 2. We return to the n–of–m multi-signature contract of Sect. 2. We pass as parameters to the machine a threshold number n of signatures required and a list of m owner public keys *signatories*. The states of the machine are given by $\{\mathsf{Holding}, \mathsf{Collecting}\}$ and the inputs are given by $\{\mathsf{Pay}, \mathsf{Cancel}, \mathsf{Add}, \mathsf{Propose}\}$, along with their respective arguments. The only initial state is $\mathsf{Holding}$ and we omit the definition of step which can be read off from the picture in Fig. 1.

First and foremost, the previous limitation of starting in non-initial states has now been overcome, as proven for all state machines in Proposition 5. Specifically, this holds at any output in the ledger carrying the $\mathsf{Collecting}$ state, therefore it is no longer possible to circumvent the checks performed by the Add input.

Property 2. It is only possible to cancel after the deadline.

We define a suitable step predicate Q on inputs and constraints for a step. If the input is Cancel then the constraints must determine that the transaction can appear on the chain only after the deadline. If the input is not Cancel then the predicate is trivially satisfied.

$$Q(s, i, \_, tx^\equiv) = \begin{cases} \mathsf{false} \ \textit{if}\ i = \mathsf{Cancel}\ \textit{and}\ s = \mathsf{Propose}(\_,\_,d)\ \textit{and}\ tx^\equiv.\mathsf{range} \neq d\ldots+\infty \\ \mathsf{true}\ \textit{otherwise} \end{cases}$$

Note that we could extend Q to include cases for correctness properties of other inputs such as ensuring that only valid signatures are added and that payments are sent to the correct recipient.

Lemma 2. *Q holds everywhere in any trace. i.e. $\forall s\ s'\ (tr : s \leadsto^* s').\ \mathsf{All}(Q,\ tr)$.*

Proof. By induction on the trace tr.   □

Proposition 7. *For any trace, all cancellations occur after the deadline.*

Proof. Follows from Lemma 2 and the fact that the validator ensures all constraints are satisfied.   □

Beyond Safety Properties. All the properties presented here are *safety* properties, i.e., they hold in every state and we express them as state predicates. However, a large class of properties we would like to prove are *temporal*, as in relating different states (also known as *liveness* or *progress* properties [2,10]).

Scilla, for instance, provides the `since_as_long` temporal operator for such purposes [15], which we have also encoded in our framework using a straightforward inductive definition. However, one may need to move to infinitary semantics to encode the entirety of *Linear Temporal Logic* (LTL) or *Computational Tree Logic* (CTL), in contrast to reasoning only about finite traces. In our setting, we would need to provide a *coinductive* definition of traces to encode the temporal operators of the aforementioned logics, as done in [13] in the constructive setting of the Coq proof assistant. We leave this exploration for future work.

5   Related Work

We discuss other efforts to use state machines to model smart contracts in our previous paper [5] and we compare our approach to a multi-asset ledger with other systems (including Waves [18], Stellar [16], and Zilliqa [14]) in the companion paper [4]. Here we focus on approaches that reason formally about the properties of such contracts as state machines, which is the essence of this paper's main contribution. We do not know of any other approaches that use tokens as state threads.

Scilla. Scilla [15] is a intermediate-level language for writing smart contracts as state machines. The Scilla authors have used Coq to reason about contracts written in Scilla, proving a variety of temporal properties such as safety, liveness, and others; hence their goals are similar to ours. Since our meta-theory enjoys property preservation over any trace predicate, we can also formally prove these temporal properties.

However, we are targeting a very different ledger model. This means that we need to do additional work: the major contribution of this paper is using tokens to provide state machine instances with an "identity", which comes for free on Ethereum. Another Ethereum feature that widens the gap between our approaches is support for asynchronous message passing, which renders Scilla unsuitable as a source language for a UTXO-based ledger, and explains the different choice of *communicating automata* [14] as the backbone of its model. Nonetheless, it would be interesting to develop a Scilla-like language that was suitable for our ledger model.

BitML. The *Bitcoin Modelling Language* (BitML) [3] allows the definition of smart contracts running on Bitcoin by means of a restricted class of state machines. The BitML compilation process has been proven to be computationally sound (although this proof has not yet been mechanised), which allows trace-based properties about the BitML contract to be transferred to the implementation, as in our system. This proof is used, for example, in [1] to prove and transfer LTL properties of BitML contracts to their implementations. Most importantly, LTL formulas can be automatically verified using a dedicated *model checker*.

Again, our work is closely related in spirit, although our ledger model is different and we use a more expressive class of state machines. In the future, we plan to add support for LTL formulas in our framework.

VeriSolid. VeriSolid [11] synthesises Solidity smart contracts from a state machine specification, and verifies temporal properties of the state machine using CTL. They use this to prove safety, liveness, deadlock-freedom, and others. Again, we expect to support CTL formulas in the near future.

In contrast, the present work focuses on establishing a formal connection between the state machine model and the real implementation on the ledger—in particular, our proofs are mechanised. We also target a UTXO ledger model, whereas VeriSolid targets the Ethereum ledger. Finally, our approach is agnostic about the logic or checker used to prove the properties that we assert on state machines and, by way of the results in this paper, transfer to an EUTXO$_{\mathrm{ma}}$ implementation of the same state machine.

Acknowledgments. We thank Gabriele Keller for comments on an earlier version of this paper.

A   Complete formal definition of EUTXO$_{\mathrm{ma}}$

A.1   Finitely-Supported Functions

If K is any type and M is a monoid with identity element 0, then a function $f : K \to M$ is *finitely supported* if $f(k) \neq 0$ for only finitely many $k \in K$. More precisely, for $f : K \to M$ we define the *support* of f to be $\mathsf{supp}(f) = \{k \in K : f(k) \neq 0\}$ and $\mathsf{FinSup}[K, M] = \{f : K \to M : |\mathsf{supp}(f)| < \infty\}$.

If $(M, +, 0)$ is a monoid then $\mathsf{FinSup}[K, M]$ also becomes a monoid if we define addition pointwise $((f + g)(k) = f(k) + g(k))$, with the identity element being the zero map. Furthermore, if M is an abelian group then $\mathsf{FinSup}[K, M]$ is also an abelian group under this construction, with $(-f)(k) = -f(k)$. Similarly, if M is partially ordered, then so is $\mathsf{FinSup}[K, M]$ with comparison defined pointwise: $f \leq g$ if and only if $f(k) \leq g(k)$ for all $k \in K$.

It follows that if M is a (partially ordered) monoid or abelian group then so is $\mathsf{FinSup}[K, \mathsf{FinSup}[L, M]]$ for any two sets of keys K and L. We will make use of this fact in the validation rules presented later (see Fig. 5).

Finitely-supported functions are easily implemented as finite maps, with a failed map lookup corresponding to returning 0.

A.2   Ledger Types

The formal definition of the EUTXO$_{\mathrm{ma}}$ model integrates token bundles and forge fields from the plain UTXO$_{\mathrm{ma}}$ model [4] into the single currency EUTXO model definition, while adapting forging policy scripts to enjoy the full expressiveness of validators in EUTXO (rather than the limited domain-specific language of UTXO$_{\mathrm{ma}}$). Figures 2 and 3 define the ledger types for EUTXO$_{\mathrm{ma}}$.

A.3   Transaction Validity

Finally, we provide the transaction validity rules, which among other things state how forging policy scripts affect transaction validity. To this end, we replace the notion of an integral Quantity for values by the token bundles discussed in Sect. 2.2 and represented by values of the type Quantities.

As indicated in Sect. 2.1, validator scripts get a context argument, which includes the validated transaction as well as the outputs that it consumed, in EUTXO. For EUTXO$_{\mathrm{ma}}$, we need two different such context types. We have

BASIC TYPES

$\mathbb{B}, \mathbb{N}, \mathbb{Z}$	the type of Booleans, natural numbers, and integers
$\mathbb{H}$	the type of bytestrings: $\bigcup_{n=0}^{\infty}\{0,1\}^{8n}$
$g(\phi_1 : T_1, \ldots, \phi_n : T_n)$	a record type with fields $\phi_1, \ldots, \phi_n$ of types $T_1, \ldots, T_n$
$t.\phi$	the value of ϕ for t, where t has type T and ϕ is a field of T
$\mathsf{Set}[T]$	the type of (finite) sets over T
$\mathsf{List}[T]$	the type of lists over T, with $\_[\_]$ as indexing and $|\_|$ as length
$h :: t$	the list with head h and tail t
$\mathsf{Interval}[A]$	the type of intervals over a totally-ordered set A
$\mathsf{FinSup}[K, M]$	the type of finitely supported functions from a type K to a monoid M

LEDGER PRIMITIVES

Quantity	an amount of an assets
Asset	a type consisting of identifiers for individual asset classes
Tick	a tick
Address	an "address" in the blockchain
Data	a type of structured data
DataHash	the hash of a value of type Data
dataHash : Data → DataHash	computes the hash of an value of typeData
TxId	the identifier of a transaction
txId : Tx → TxId	computes the identifier of a transaction
lookupTx : Ledger × TxId → Tx	retrieves the unique transaction with a given identifier
Script	the (opaque) type of scripts
$\llbracket \_ \rrbracket$: Script → Data × ⋯ × Data → $\mathbb{B}$	applies a script to its arguments
scriptAddr : Script → Address	the address of a script

DEFINED TYPES

$$\mathsf{Policy} = \mathsf{Address}$$
$$\mathsf{Signature} = \mathbb{H}$$

$$\mathsf{Quantities} = \mathsf{FinSup}[\mathsf{Policy}, \mathsf{FinSup}[\mathsf{Asset}, \mathsf{Quantity}]]$$

$$\mathsf{Output} = (addr : \mathsf{Address}, value : \mathsf{Quantities}, datumHash : \mathsf{DataHash})$$

$$\mathsf{OutputRef} = (id : \mathsf{TxId}, index : \mathsf{Int})$$

$$\mathsf{Input} = (outputRef : \mathsf{OutputRef},$$
$$validator : \mathsf{Script},$$
$$datum : \mathsf{Data},$$
$$redeemer : \mathsf{Data})$$

$$\mathsf{Tx} = (inputs : \mathsf{Set}[\mathsf{Input}],$$
$$outputs : \mathsf{List}[\mathsf{Output}],$$
$$validityInterval : \mathsf{Interval}[\mathsf{Tick}],$$
$$forge : \mathsf{Quantities},$$
$$forgeScripts : \mathsf{Set}[\mathsf{Script}],$$
$$sigs : \mathsf{Set}[\mathsf{Signature}])$$

$$\mathsf{Ledger} = \mathsf{List}[\mathsf{Tx}]$$

Fig. 2. Primitives and basic types for the $\mathrm{EUTXO}_{\mathrm{ma}}$ model

ValidatorContext for validators and PolicyContext for forging policies. The difference is that in ValidatorContext we indicate the input of the validated transaction that consumes the output locked by the executed validator, whereas for forging policies, we provide the policy script hash. The latter makes it easy for the policy script to look up the component of the transaction's forging field that it is controlling.

$$
\begin{aligned}
\mathsf{OutputInfo} \;=\; (& \mathit{value} : \mathsf{Quantities}, \\
& \mathit{validatorHash} : \mathsf{Address}, \\
& \mathit{datumHash} : \mathsf{DataHash})
\end{aligned}
$$

$$
\begin{aligned}
\mathsf{InputInfo} \;=\; (& \mathit{outputRef} : \mathsf{OutputRef}, \\
& \mathit{validatorHash} : \mathsf{Address}, \\
& \mathit{datumHash} : \mathsf{DataHash}, \\
& \mathit{redeemerHash} : \mathsf{DataHash}, \\
& \mathit{value} : \mathsf{Quantities})
\end{aligned}
$$

$$
\begin{aligned}
\mathsf{TxInfo} \;=\; (& \mathit{inputInfo} : \mathsf{List[InputInfo]}, \\
& \mathit{outputInfo} : \mathsf{List[OutputInfo]}, \\
& \mathit{validityInterval} : \mathsf{Interval[Tick]}, \\
& \mathit{forge} : \mathsf{Quantities}, \\
& \mathit{forgeScripts} : \mathsf{Set[Script]}, \\
& \mathit{sigs} : \mathsf{FinSet[Signature]})
\end{aligned}
$$

$$
\begin{aligned}
\mathsf{ValidatorContext} \;&=\; (\mathsf{TxInfo}, \mathbb{N}) \\
\mathsf{PolicyContext} \;&=\; (\mathsf{TxInfo}, \mathsf{Policy})
\end{aligned}
$$

$\mathsf{mkValidatorContext} : \mathsf{Tx} \times \mathsf{Input} \times \mathsf{Ledger} \rightarrow \mathsf{ValidatorContext}$

summarises a transaction for a validator script in the context of an input and
a ledger state

$\mathsf{mkPolicyContext} : \mathsf{Tx} \times \mathsf{Policy} \times \mathsf{Ledger} \rightarrow \mathsf{PolicyContext}$

summarises a transaction for a forging
policy script in the context of an currency and a ledger state

Fig. 3. The Context types for the $\mathrm{EUTXO}_{\mathrm{ma}}$ model

$\mathsf{unspentTxOutputs} : \mathsf{Tx} \rightarrow \mathsf{Set[OutputRef]}$
$\mathsf{unspentTxOutputs}(t) \;=\; \{(\mathsf{txId}(t), 1), \ldots, (\mathsf{txId}(id), |t.outputs|)\}$

$\mathsf{unspentOutputs} : \mathsf{Ledger} \rightarrow \mathsf{Set[OutputRef]}$
$\mathsf{unspentOutputs}([]) \;\;\;= \{\}$
$\mathsf{unspentOutputs}(t :: l) = (\mathsf{unspentOutputs}(l) \setminus t.inputs) \cup \mathsf{unspentTxOutputs}(t)$

$\mathsf{getSpentOutput} : \mathsf{Input} \times \mathsf{Ledger} \rightarrow \mathsf{Output}$
$\mathsf{getSpentOutput}(i, l) \;\;= \mathsf{lookupTx}(l, i.outputRef.id).outputs[i.outputRef.index]$

Fig. 4. Auxiliary functions for $\mathrm{EUTXO}_{\mathrm{ma}}$ validation

The validity rules in Fig. 5 define what it means for a transaction t to be valid
for a valid ledger l during the tick currentTick. (They make use of the auxiliary
functions in Fig. 4.) Of these rules, Rules 1, 2, 3, 4, and 5 are common to the two
systems (EUTXO and UTXO$_{\mathrm{ma}}$) that we are combing here; Rules 6 and 7 are

1. **The current tick is within the validity interval**

$$\mathsf{currentTick} \in t.validityInterval$$

2. **All outputs have non-negative values**

$$\text{For all } o \in t.outputs, \ o.value \geq 0$$

3. **All inputs refer to unspent outputs**

$$\{i.outputRef \,|\, i \in t.inputs\} \subseteq \mathsf{unspentOutputs}(l).$$

4. **Value is preserved**

$$t.forge + \sum_{i \in t.inputs} \mathsf{getSpentOutput}(i, l) = \sum_{o \in t.outputs} o.value$$

5. **No output is double spent**

$$\text{If } i_1, i \in t.inputs \text{ and } i_1.outputRef = i.outputRef \text{ then } i_1 = i.$$

6. **All inputs validate**

$$\text{For all } i \in t.inputs, \ [\![i.validator]\!](i.datum, i.redeemer, \mathsf{toData}(\mathsf{mkValidatorContext}(t, i, l))) = \mathsf{true}$$

7. **Validator scripts match output addresses**

$$\text{For all } i \in t.inputs, \ \mathsf{scriptAddr}(i.validator) = \mathsf{getSpentOutput}(i, l).addr$$

8. **Datum objects match output hashes**

$$\text{For all } i \in t.inputs, \ \mathsf{dataHash}(i.datum) = \mathsf{getSpentOutput}(i, l).datumHash$$

9. **Forging**
   A transaction with a non-zero *forge* field is only valid if either:
   (a) the ledger l is empty (that is, if the transaction is the initial transaction).
   (b) for every key $h \in \mathsf{supp}(t.forge)$, there exists $s \in t.forgeScripts$ with $\mathsf{scriptAddr}(s) = h$.

10. **All forging policy scripts validate**

$$\text{For all } s \in t.forgeScripts, \ [\![s]\!](\mathsf{toData}(\mathsf{mkPolicyContext}(t, \mathsf{scriptAddr}(s), l))) = \mathsf{true}$$

Fig. 5. Validity of a transaction t in the $\mathrm{EUTXO_{ma}}$ model

similar in both systems, but we go with the more expressive ones from EUTXO. The crucial changes are to the construction and passing of the context types mentioned above, which appear in Rules 6 and 10. The later is the main point as it is responsible for execution of forging policy scripts.

A ledger l is *valid* if either l is empty or l is of the form $t :: l'$ with l' valid and t valid for l'.

References

1. Atzei, N., Bartoletti, M., Lande, S., Yoshida, N., Zunino, R.: Developing secure Bitcoin contracts with BitML. In: Proceedings of the 2019 27th ACM Joint Meeting on European Software Engineering Conference and Symposium on the Foundations of Software Engineering, pp. 1124–1128 (2019)
2. Baier, C., Katoen, J.: Principles of Model Checking. MIT Press, Cambridge (2008)

3. Bartoletti, M., Zunino, R.: BitML: a calculus for Bitcoin smart contracts. In: Proceedings of the 2018 ACM SIGSAC Conference on Computer and Communications Security, pp. 83–100. ACM (2018)
4. Chakravarty, M.M.T., et al.: UTXO$_{ma}$: UTXO with multi-asset support. In: Margaria, T., Steffen, B. (eds.) ISoLA 2020. LNCS, vol. 12478, pp. 112–130. Springer, Heidelberg (2020). https://omelkonian.github.io/data/publications/utxoma.pdf
5. Chakravarty, M.M.T., Chapman, J., MacKenzie, K., Melkonian, O., Peyton Jones, M., Wadler, P.: The extended UTXO model. In: Bernhard, M., et al. (eds.) FC 2020. LNCS, vol. 12063, pp. 525–539. Springer, Cham (2020). https://doi.org/10.1007/978-3-030-54455-3_37
6. Chakravarty, M.M.T., Coretti, S., Fitzi, M., Gazi, P., Kant, P., Kiayias, A., Russell, A.: Hydra: Fast isomorphic state channels. Technical report, Cryptology ePrint Archive, Report 2020/299 (2020). https://eprint.iacr.org/2020/299
7. Entriken, W., Shirley, D., Evans, J., Sachs, N.: ERC-721 non-fungible token standard. Ethereum Foundation (2018). https://eips.ethereum.org/EIPS/eip-721
8. Kröger, F., Merz, S.: Temporal Logic and State Systems. Springer, Heidelberg (2008). https://doi.org/10.1007/978-3-540-68635-4
9. Maker Team: The Dai stablecoin system (2017). https://makerdao.com/whitepaper/DaiDec17WP.pdf
10. Manna, Z., Pnueli, A.: The Temporal Logic of Reactive and Concurrent Systems - Specification. Springer, Heidelberg (1992). https://doi.org/10.1007/978-1-4612-0931-7
11. Mavridou, A., Laszka, A., Stachtiari, E., Dubey, A.: VeriSolid: correct-by-design smart contracts for ethereum. In: Goldberg, I., Moore, T. (eds.) FC 2019. LNCS, vol. 11598, pp. 446–465. Springer, Cham (2019). https://doi.org/10.1007/978-3-030-32101-7_27
12. Milner, R.: Communicating and Mobile Systems: the π-Calculus. Cambridge University Press, Cambridge (1999)
13. Nakata, K., Uustalu, T., Bezem, M.: A proof pearl with the fan theorem and bar induction. In: Yang, H. (ed.) APLAS 2011. LNCS, vol. 7078, pp. 353–368. Springer, Heidelberg (2011). https://doi.org/10.1007/978-3-642-25318-8_26
14. Sergey, I., Kumar, A., Hobor, A.: Scilla: a smart contract intermediate-level language. arXiv preprint arXiv:1801.00687 (2018)
15. Sergey, I., Nagaraj, V., Johannsen, J., Kumar, A., Trunov, A., Hao, K.C.G.: Safer smart contract programming with Scilla. Proc. ACM Program. Lang. **3**(OOPSLA), 185 (2019)
16. Stellar Development Foundation: Stellar Development Guides (2020). https://solidity.readthedocs.io/
17. Vogelsteller, F., Buterin, V.: ERC-20 token standard. Ethereum Foundation (Stiftung Ethereum), Zug, Switzerland (2015). https://eips.ethereum.org/EIPS/eip-20
18. Waves Team: Waves blockchain documentation (2020). https://docs.wavesprotocol.org/

UTXO$_{ma}$: UTXO with Multi-asset Support

Manuel M. T. Chakravarty[1(✉)], James Chapman[2(✉)], Kenneth MacKenzie[3(✉)],
Orestis Melkonian[3,7(✉)], Jann Müller[4(✉)], Michael Peyton Jones[5(✉)],
Polina Vinogradova[6(✉)], Philip Wadler[3,7(✉)], and Joachim Zahnentferner[8]

[1] IOHK, Utrecht, The Netherlands
manuel.chakravarty@iohk.io
[2] IOHK, Glasgow, UK
james.chapman@iohk.io
[3] IOHK, Edinburgh, UK
{kenneth.macKenzie,orestis.melkonian,philip.wadler}@iohk.io
[4] IOHK, Mannheim, Germany
jann.muller@iohk.io
[5] IOHK, London, UK
michael.jones@iohk.io
[6] IOHK, Ottawa, Canada
polina.vinogradova@iohk.io
[7] University of Edinburgh, Edinburgh, UK
orestis.melkonian@ed.ac.uk, wadler@inf.ed.ac.uk
[8] Wan Chai, Hong Kong
chimeric.ledgers@protonmail.com

Abstract. A prominent use case of Ethereum smart contracts is the creation of a wide range of *user-defined tokens* or *assets* by way of smart contracts. User-defined assets are *non-native* on Ethereum; i.e., they are not directly supported by the ledger, but require repetitive custom code. This makes them unnecessarily inefficient, expensive, and complex. It also makes them insecure as numerous incidents on Ethereum have demonstrated. Even without stateful smart contracts, the lack of perfect fungibility of Bitcoin assets allows for implementing user-defined tokens as layer-two solutions, which also adds an additional layer of complexity.

In this paper, we explore an alternative design based on Bitcoin-style UTXO ledgers. Instead of introducing general scripting capabilities together with the associated security risks, we propose an extension of the UTXO model, where we replace the accounting structure of a single cryptocurrency with a new structure that manages an unbounded number of user-defined, native tokens, which we call *token bundles*. Token creation is controlled by *forging policy scripts* that, just like Bitcoin validator scripts, use a small domain-specific language with bounded computational expressiveness, thus favouring Bitcoin's security and computational austerity. The resulting approach is lightweight, i.e., custom asset creation and transfer is cheap, and it avoids use of any global state in the form of an asset registry or similar.

© Springer Nature Switzerland AG 2020
T. Margaria and B. Steffen (Eds.): ISoLA 2020, LNCS 12478, pp. 112–130, 2020.
https://doi.org/10.1007/978-3-030-61467-6_8

The proposed UTXO$_{ma}$ model and the semantics of the scripting language have been formalised in the Agda proof assistant.

Keywords: Blockchain · UTXO · Native tokens · Functional programming

1   Introduction

Distributed ledgers began by tracking just a single asset—money. The goal was to compete with existing currencies, and so they naturally started by focusing on their own currencies—Bitcoin and its eponymous currency, Ethereum and Ether, and so on. This focus was so clear that the systems tended to be identified with their primary currency.

More recently, it has become clear that it is possible and very useful to track other kinds of asset on distributed ledger systems. Ethereum has led the innovation in this space, with ERC-20 [15] implementing new currencies and ERC-721 [8] implementing unique non-fungible tokens.

These have been wildly popular—variants of ERC-20 are the most used smart contracts on Ethereum by some margin. However, they have major shortcomings. Notably, custom tokens on Ethereum are not native. This means that tokens do not live in a user's account, and in order to send another user ERC-20 tokens, the sender must interact with the governing smart contract for the currency. That is, despite the fact that Ethereum's main purpose is to track ownership of assets and perform transactions, users have been forced to build their own *internal ledger* inside a smart contract.

Other systems have learned from this and have made custom tokens native, such as Stellar, Waves, Zilliqa, and more. However, these typically rely on some kind of global state, such as a global currency registry, or special global accounts that must be created. This is slow, and restricts creative use of custom tokens because of the high overhead in terms of time and money. There have also been efforts to introduce native multi-assets into UTXO ledgers [19], a precursor to our work.

We can do better than this through a combination of two ideas. Firstly, we generalise the value type that the ledger works with to include *token bundles* that freely and uniformly mix tokens from different custom assets, both fungible and non-fungible. Secondly, we avoid any global state by "eternally" linking a currency to a governing forging policy via a hash. Between them this creates a multi-asset ledger system (which we call UTXO$_{ma}$) with native, lightweight custom tokens.

Specifically, this paper makes the following contributions:

- We introduce token bundles, represented as finitely-supported functions, as a uniform mechanism to generalise the existing UTXO accounting rules to custom assets including fungible, non-fungible, and mixed tokens.

- We avoid the need for global state in the form of a currency registry by linking custom forging policy scripts by way of their script hash to the name of asset groups.
- We support a wide range of standard applications for custom assets without the need for general-purpose smart contracts by defining a simple domain-specific language for forging policy scripts.
- We provide a formal definition of the $UTXO_{ma}$ ledger rules as a basis to formally reason about the resulting system, along with a mechanised version in Agda.[1]

Creating and transferring new assets in the resulting system is lightweight and cheap. It is lightweight as we avoid special setup transactions or registration procedures, and it is cheap as only standard transaction fees are required—this is unlike the Ethereum gas model, where a script must be run each time a custom asset is transferred, which incurs gas costs.

The proposed multi-asset system is not merely a pen and paper exercise. It forms the basis of the multi-asset support for the Cardano blockchain. In a related work [4], we further modify the native multi-asset ledger presented in this paper to an extended UTxO ledger model, which additionally supports the use of Plutus (Turing complete smart contract language) to define forging policies. This ledger model extension allows the use of stateful smart contracts to define state machines for output locking.

2   Multi-asset Support

In Bitcoin's ledger model [2,10,18], transactions spend as yet *unspent transaction outputs (UTXOs)*, while supplying new unspent outputs to be consumed by subsequent transactions. Each individual UTXO locks a specific *quantity* of cryptocurrency by imposing specific conditions that need to be met to spend that quantity, such as for example signing the spending transaction with a specific secret cryptographic key, or passing some more sophisticated conditions enforced by a *validator script*. Quantities of cryptocurrency in a transaction output are represented as an integral number of the smallest unit of that particular cryptocurrency—in Bitcoin, these are Satoshis. To natively support multiple currencies in transaction outputs, we generalise those integral quantities to natively support the dynamic creation of new user-defined *assets* or *tokens*. Moreover, we require a means to forge tokens in a manner controlled by an asset's *forging policy*.

We achieve all this by the following three extensions to the basic UTXO ledger model that are further detailed in the remainder of this section.

1. Transaction outputs lock a *heterogeneous token bundle* instead of only an integral value of one cryptocurrency.
2. We extend transactions with a *forge* field. This is a token bundle of tokens that are created (minted) or destroyed (burned) by that transaction.

---

[1] https://github.com/omelkonian/formal-utxo/tree/ed72.

3. We introduce *forging policy scripts* (*FPS*) that govern the creation and destruction of assets in forge fields. These scripts are not unlike the validators locking outputs in UTXO.

2.1 Token Bundles

We can regard transaction outputs in an UTXO ledger as pairs (*value*, ν) consisting of a locked value *value* and a validator script ν that encodes the spending condition. The latter may be proof of ownership by way of signing the spending transaction with a specific secret cryptography key or a temporal condition that allows an output to be spent only when the blockchain has reached a certain height (i.e. a certain number of blocks have been produced).

To conveniently use multiple currencies in transaction outputs, we want each output to be able to lock varying quantities of multiple different currencies at once in its *value* field. This suggests using finite maps from some kind of *asset identifier* to an integral quantity as a concrete representation, e.g. Coin $\mapsto$ 21. Looking at the standard UTXO ledger rules [18], it becomes apparent that cryptocurrency quantities need to be monoids. It is a little tricky to make finite maps into a monoid, but the solution is to think of them as *finitely supported functions* (see Sect. 3 for details).

If want to use *finitely supported functions* to achieve a uniform representation that can handle groups of related, but *non-fungible* tokens, we need to go a step further. In order to not lose the grouping of related non-fungible tokens (all house tokens issued by a specific entity, for example) though, we need to move to a two-level structure—i.e., finitely-supported functions of finitely-supported functions. Let's consider an example. Trading of rare in-game items is popular in modern, multi-player computer games. How about representing ownership of such items and trading of that ownership on our multi-asset UTXO ledger? We might need tokens for "hats" and "swords", which form two non-fungible assets with possibly multiple tokens of each asset—a hat is interchangeable with any other hat, but not with a sword, and also not with the currency used to purchase these items. Here our two-level structure pays off in its full generality, and we can represent currency to purchase items together with sets of items, where some can be multiples, e.g.,

$$\{\text{Coin} \mapsto \{\text{Coin} \mapsto 2\}, \text{Game} \mapsto \{\text{Hat} \mapsto 1, \text{Sword} \mapsto 4\}\}$$
$$+ \{\text{Coin} \mapsto \{\text{Coin} \mapsto 1\}, \text{Game} \mapsto \{\text{Sword} \mapsto 1, \text{Owl} \mapsto 1\}\}$$
$$= \{\text{Coin} \mapsto \{\text{Coin} \mapsto 3\}, \text{Game} \mapsto \{\text{Hat} \mapsto 1, \text{Sword} \mapsto 5, \text{Owl} \mapsto 1\}\} \ .$$

2.2 Forge Fields

If new tokens are frequently generated (such as issuing new hats whenever an in-game achievement has been reached) and destroyed (a player may lose a hat forever if the wind picks up), these operations need to be lightweight and cheap. We achieve this by adding a forge field to every transaction. It is a token bundle (just like the *value* in an output), but admits positive quantities (for minting new tokens) and negative quantities (for burning existing tokens). Of course, minting and burning needs to be strictly controlled.

$$
\begin{aligned}
\mathbb{B} &\quad \text{the type of Booleans} \\
\mathbb{N} &\quad \text{the type of natural numbers} \\
\mathbb{Z} &\quad \text{the type of integers} \\
\mathbb{H} &\quad \text{the type of bytestrings: } \bigcup_{n=0}^{\infty}\{0,1\}^{8n}
\end{aligned}
$$

$(\phi_1 : T_1, \ldots, \phi_n : T_n)$ a record type with fields $\phi_1, \ldots, \phi_n$ of types $T_1, \ldots, T_n$

$t.\phi$ the value of ϕ for t, where t has type T and ϕ is a field of T

$\mathsf{Set}[T]$ the type of (finite) sets over T

$\mathsf{List}[T]$ the type of lists over T, with $\_[\_]$ as indexing and $|\_|$ as length

$h :: t$ the list with head h and tail t

$x \mapsto f(x)$ an anonymous function

$c^{\#}$ a cryptographic collision-resistant hash of c

$\mathsf{Interval}[A]$ the type of intervals over a totally-ordered set A

$\mathsf{FinSup}[K, M]$ the type of finitely supported functions from a type K to a monoid M

Fig. 1. Basic types and notation

2.3 Forging Policy Scripts

The script validation mechanism for locking UTXO outputs is as follows: in order to for a transaction to spend an output $(value, \nu)$, the validator script ν needs to be executed and approve of the spending transaction. Similarly, the forging policy scripts associated with the tokens being minted or burned by a transaction are run in order to validate those actions. In the spirit of the Bitcoin Miniscript approach, we chose to include a simple scripting language supporting forging policies for several common usecases, such as single issuer, non-fungible, or one-time issue tokens, etc. (see Sect. 4 for all the usecases).

In order to establish a permanent association between the forging policy and the assets controlled by it, we propose a hashing approach, as opposed to a global registry lookup. Such a registry requires a specialized access control scheme, as well as a scheme for cleaning up unused entries. In the representation of custom assets we propose, each token is associated with the hash of the forging policy script required to validate at the time of forging the token, eg. in order to forge the value $\{\mathsf{HASHVALUE} \mapsto \{\mathsf{Owl} \mapsto 1\}\}$, a script whose hash is $\mathsf{HASHVALUE}$ will be run.

Relying on permanent hash associations to identify asset forging policies and their assets also has its disadvantages. For example, policy hashes are long strings that, in our model, will have multiple copies stored on the ledger. Such strings are not human-readable, take up valuable ledger real estate, and increase transaction-size-based fees.

3 Formal Ledger Rules

Our formal ledger model follows the style of the UTXO-with-scripts model from [18] adopting the notation from [5] with basic types defined as in Fig. 1.

Finitely-Supported Functions. We model token bundles as finitely-supported functions. If K is any type and M is a monoid with identity element 0, then a function $f : K \to M$ is *finitely supported* if $f(k) \neq 0$ for only finitely many

$k \in K$. More precisely, for $f : K \to M$ we define the *support* of f to be $\mathsf{supp}(f) = \{k \in K : f(k) \neq 0\}$ and $\mathsf{FinSup}[K, M] = \{f : K \to M : |\mathsf{supp}(f)| < \infty\}$.

If $(M, +, 0)$ is a monoid then $\mathsf{FinSup}[K, M]$ also becomes a monoid if we define addition pointwise (i.e., $(f+g)(k) = f(k)+g(k)$), with the identity element being the zero map. Furthermore, if M is an abelian group then $\mathsf{FinSup}[K, M]$ is also an abelian group under this construction, with $(-f)(k) = -f(k)$. Similarly, if M is partially ordered, then so is $\mathsf{FinSup}[K, M]$ with comparison defined pointwise: $f \leq g$ if and only if $f(k) \leq g(k)$ for all $k \in K$.

It follows that if M is a (partially ordered) monoid or abelian group then so is $\mathsf{FinSup}[K, \mathsf{FinSup}[L, M]]$ for any two sets of keys K and L. We will make use of this fact in the validation rules presented later in the paper (see Fig. 4). Finitely-supported functions are easily implemented as finite maps, with a failed map lookup corresponding to returning 0.

3.1 Ledger Types

Figure 2 defines the ledger primitives and types that we need to define the UTXO$_{ma}$ model. All outputs use a pay-to-script-hash scheme, where an output is locked with the hash of a script. We use a single scripting language for forging policies and to define output locking scripts. Just as in Bitcoin, this is a restricted domain-specific language (and not a general-purpose language); the details follow in Sect. 4. We assume that each transaction has a unique identifier derived from its value by a hash function. This is the basis of the lookupTx function to look up a transaction, given its unique identifier.

Token Bundles. We generalise per-output transferred quantities from a plain Quantity to a bundle of Quantities. A Quantities represents a token bundle: it is a mapping from a policy and an *asset*, which defines the asset class, to a Quantity of that asset.[2] Since a Quantities is indexed in this way, it can represent any combination of tokens from any assets (hence why we call it a token *bundle*).

Asset Groups and Forging Policy Scripts. A key concept is the *asset group*. An asset group is identified by the hash of special script that controls the creation and destruction of asset tokens of that asset group. We call this script the *forging policy script*.

Forging. Each transaction gets a *forge* field, which simply modifies the required balance of the transaction by the Quantities inside it: thus a positive *forge* field indicates the creation of new tokens. In contrast to outputs, Quantities in forge fields can also be negative, which effectively burns existing tokens.[3]

---

[2] We have chosen to represent Quantities as a finitely-supported function whose values are themselves finitely-supported functions (in an implementation, this would be a nested map). We did this to make the definition of the rules simpler (in particular Rule 8). However, it could equally well be defined as a finitely-supported function from tuples of PolicyIDs and Assets to Quantitys.

[3] The restriction on outputs is enforced by Rule 2. We simply do not impose such a restriction on the *forge* field: this lets us define rules in a simpler way, with cleaner notation.

LEDGER PRIMITIVES

Quantity	an amount of currency, forming an abelian group (typically $\mathbb{Z}$)
Asset	a type consisting of identifiers for individual asset classes
Tick	a tick
Address	an "address" in the blockchain
TxId	the identifier of a transaction
txId : Tx $\to$ TxId	a function computing the identifier of a transaction
lookupTx : Ledger $\times$ TxId $\to$ Tx	retrieve the unique transaction with a given identifier
verify : PubKey $\times$ $\mathbb{H}$ $\times$ $\mathbb{H}$ $\to$ $\mathbb{B}$	signature verification
Script	forging policy scripts
scriptAddr : Script $\to$ Address	the address of a script
[$\cdot$] : Script $\to$ (Address $\times$ Tx $\times$ Set[Output]) $\to$ $\mathbb{B}$	apply script inside brackets to its arguments

LEDGER TYPES

$$\text{PolicyID} = \text{Address} \qquad \text{(an identifier for a custom currency)}$$
$$\text{Signature} = \mathbb{H}$$

$$\text{Quantities} = \text{FinSup}[\text{PolicyID}, \text{FinSup}[\text{Asset}, \text{Quantity}]]$$

$$\text{Output} = (addr : \text{Address}, value : \text{Quantities})$$

$$\text{OutputRef} = (id : \text{TxId}, index : \text{Int})$$

$$\text{Input} = (outputRef : \text{OutputRef}$$
$$validator : \text{Script})$$

$$\text{Tx} = (inputs : \text{Set}[\text{Input}],$$
$$outputs : \text{List}[\text{Output}],$$
$$validityInterval : \text{Interval}[\text{Tick}],$$
$$forge : \text{Quantities}$$
$$scripts : \text{Set}[\text{Script}],$$
$$sigs : \text{Set}[\text{Signature}])$$

$$\text{Ledger} = \text{List}[\text{Tx}]$$

Fig. 2. Ledger primitives and basic types

Additionally, transactions get a *scripts* field holding a set of forging policy scripts: Set[Script]. This provides the forging policy scripts that are required as part of validation when tokens are minted or destroyed (see Rule 8 in Fig. 4). The forging scripts of the assets being forged are executed and the transaction is only considered valid if the execution of the script returns true. A forging policy script is executed in a context that provides access to the main components of the forging transaction, the UTXOs it spends, and the policy ID. The passing of the context provides a crucial piece of the puzzle regarding self-identification: it includes the script's own PolicyID, which avoids the problem of trying to include the hash of a script inside itself.

Validity Intervals. A transaction's *validity interval* field contains an interval of ticks (monotonically increasing units of "time", from [5]). The validity interval states that the transaction must only be validated if the current tick is within the interval. The validity interval, rather than the actual current chain tick value, must be used for script validation. In an otherwise valid transaction, passing the current tick to the evaluator could result in different script validation outcomes at different ticks, which would be problematic.

unspentTxOutputs : Tx $\rightarrow$ Set[OutputRef]
unspentTxOutputs(t) = {(txId(t), 1), . . . , (txId(id), |$t.outputs$|)}

unspentOutputs : Ledger $\rightarrow$ Set[OutputRef]
unspentOutputs([])   = {}
unspentOutputs($t :: l$) = (unspentOutputs(l) \ $t.inputs$) $\cup$ unspentTxOutputs(t)

getSpentOutput : Input $\times$ Ledger $\rightarrow$ Output
getSpentOutput(i, l)   = lookupTx($l, i.outputRef.id$)$.outputs[i.outputRef.index]$

Fig. 3. Auxiliary validation functions

Language Clauses. In our choice of the set of predicates p1, . . . , pn to include in the scripting language definition, we adhere to the following heuristic: we only admit predicates with quantification over finite structures passed to the evaluator in the transaction-specific data, i.e. sets, maps, and lists. The computations we allow in the predicates themselves are well-known computable functions, such as hashing, signature checking, arithmetic operations, comparisons, etc.

The gamut of policies expressible in the model we propose here is fully determined by the collection of predicates, assembled into a single script by logical connectives &&, ||, and Not. Despite being made up of only hard-coded predicates and connectives, the resulting policies can be quite expressive, as we will demonstrate in the upcoming applications section. When specifying forging predicates, we use tx._ notation to access the fields of a transaction.

3.2 Transaction Validity

Figure 4 defines what it means for a transaction t to be valid for a valid ledger l during the tick currentTick, using some auxiliary functions from Fig. 3. A ledger l is *valid* if either l is empty or l is of the form $t :: l'$ with l' valid and t valid for l'.

The rules follow the usual structure for an UTXO ledger, with a number of modifications and additions. The new **Forging** rule (Rule 8) implements the support for forging policies by requiring that the currency's forging policy is included in the transaction—along with Rule 9 which ensures that they are actually run! The arguments that a script is applied to are the ones discussed earlier.

When forging policy scripts are run, they are provided with the appropriate transaction data, which allows them to enforce conditions on it. In particular, they can inspect the *forge* field on the transaction, and so a forging policy script can identify how much of its own currency was forged, which is typically a key consideration in whether to allow the transaction.

We also need to be careful to ensure that transactions in our new system preserve value correctly. There are two aspects to consider:

- We generalise the type of value to Quantities. However, since Quantities is a monoid (see Sect. 3), Rule 4 is (almost) identical to the one in the original

1. **The current tick is within the validity interval**

$$\mathsf{currentTick} \in t.validityInterval$$

2. **All outputs have non-negative values**

$$\text{For all } o \in t.outputs, \ o.value \geq 0$$

3. **All inputs refer to unspent outputs**

$$\{i.outputRef : i \in t.inputs\} \subseteq \mathsf{unspentOutputs}(l).$$

4. **Value is preserved**

$$t.forge + \sum_{i \in t.inputs} \mathsf{getSpentOutput}(i, l) = \sum_{o \in t.outputs} o.value$$

5. **No output is double spent**

$$\text{If } i_1, i \in t.inputs \text{ and } i_1.outputRef = i.outputRef \text{ then } i_1 = i.$$

6. **All inputs validate**

$$\text{For all } i \in t.inputs, \ [\![i.validator]\!](\mathsf{scriptAddr}(i.validator), t, \{\mathsf{getSpentOutput}(i, l) \mid i \in t.inputs\}) = \mathsf{true}$$

7. **Validator scripts match output addresses**

$$\text{For all } i \in t.inputs, \ \mathsf{scriptAddr}(i.validator) = \mathsf{getSpentOutput}(i, l).addr$$

8. **Forging**
A transaction with a non-zero *forge* field is only valid if either:
(a) the ledger l is empty (that is, if it is the initial transaction).
(b) for every key $h \in \mathsf{supp}(t.forge)$, there exists $s \in t.scripts$ with $h = \mathsf{scriptAddr}(s)$.

9. **All scripts validate**

$$\text{For all } s \in t.scripts, \ [\![s]\!](\mathsf{scriptAddr}(s), t, \{\mathsf{getSpentOutput}(i, l) \mid i \in t.inputs\}) = \mathsf{true}$$

Fig. 4. Validity of a transaction t in a ledger l

UTXO model, simply with a different monoid. Concretely, this amounts to preserving the quantities of each of the individual token classes in the transaction.

– We allow forging of new tokens by including the forge field into the balance in Rule 4.

4   A Stateless Forging Policy Language

The domain-specific language for forging policies strikes a balance between expressiveness and simplicity. It particular, it is stateless and of bounded computational complexity. Nevertheless, it is sufficient to support the applications described in Sect. 5.

Semantically Meaningful Token Names. The policy ID is associated with a policy script (it is the hash of it), so it has a semantic meaning that is identified with that of the script. In the clauses of our language, we give semantic meaning to the names of the tokens as well. This allows us to make some judgements about them in a programmatic way, beyond confirming that the preservation

$[\![\text{JustMSig(msig)}]\!]$(h, tx, utxo) = checkMultiSig(msig, tx)

$[\![\text{SpendsOutput(o)}]\!]$(h, tx, utxo) = o $\in$ { i.outputRef : i $\in$ tx.inputs }

$[\![\text{TickAfter(tick1)}]\!]$(h, tx, utxo) = tick1 $\leq$ min(tx.validityInterval)

$[\![\text{Forges(tkns)}]\!]$(h, tx, utxo) = (h $\mapsto$ tkns $\in$ tx.forge) && (h $\mapsto$ tkns $\geq$ 0)

$[\![\text{Burns(tkns)}]\!]$(h, tx, utxo) = (h $\mapsto$ tkns $\in$ tx.forge) && (h $\mapsto$ tkns $\leq$ 0)

$[\![\text{FreshTokens}]\!]$(h, tx, utxo) =
   $\forall$ pid $\mapsto$ tkns $\in$ tx.forge, pid == h $\Rightarrow$
     $\forall$ t $\mapsto$ q $\in$ tkns,
      t == hash(indexof(t, tkns), tx.inputs) && q == 1

$[\![\text{AssetToAddress(addr)}]\!]$(h, tx, utxo) =
   $\forall$ pid $\mapsto$ tkns $\in$ utxo.balance, pid == h $\Rightarrow$
     addr == _ $\Rightarrow$ (h, pid $\mapsto$ tkns) $\in$ utxo
   $\wedge$ addr $\neq$ _ $\Rightarrow$ (addr, pid $\mapsto$ tkns) $\in$ utxo

$[\![\text{DoForge}]\!]$(h, tx, utxo) = h $\in$ supp(tx.forge)

$[\![\text{SignedByPIDToken}]\!]$(h, tx, utxo) =
   $\forall$ pid $\mapsto$ tkns $\in$ utxo.balance, pid == h $\Rightarrow$
     $\forall$ s $\in$ tx.sigs, $\exists$ t $\in$ supp(tkns),
      isSignedBy(tx, s, t)

$[\![\text{SpendsCur(pid)}]\!]$(h, tx, utxo) =
   pid == _ $\Rightarrow$ h $\in$ supp(utxo.balance)
   $\wedge$ pid $\neq$ _ $\Rightarrow$ pid $\in$ supp(utxo.balance)

Fig. 5. Forging policy language

of value holds, or which ones are fungible with each other. For example, the FreshTokens constructor gives us a way to programmatically generate token names which, by construction, mean that these tokens are unique, without ever checking the global ledger state.

Forging Policy Scripts as Output-Locking Scripts. As with currency in the non-digital world, it is a harder problem to control the transfer of assets once they have come into circulation (see also Sect. 7). We can, however, specify directly in the forging policy that the assets being forged must be locked by an output script of our choosing. Moreover, since both output addresses and policies are hashes of scripts, we can use the asset policy ID and the address interchangeably. The AssetToAddress clause is used for this purpose.

Language Clauses. The various clauses of the validator and forging policy language are as described below, with their formal semantics as in Fig. 5. In this figure, we use the notation x $\mapsto$ y to represent a single key-value pair of a finite map. Recall form Rule 9 that the arguments passed to the validation function $[\![s]\!]$ h are: the hash of the forging (or output locking) script being validated, the transaction tx being validated, and the ledger outputs which the transaction tx is spending (we denote these utxo here).

- JustMSig(msig) verifies that the m-out-of-n signatures required by s are in the set of signatures provided by the transaction. We do not give the multi-signature script evaluator details as this is a common concept, and assume a procedure checkMultiSig exists.
- SpendsOutput(o) checks that the transaction spends the output referenced by o in the UTXO.
- TickAfter(tick1) checks that the validity interval of the current transaction starts after time tick1.
- Forges(tkns) checks that the transaction forges exactly tkns of the asset with the policy ID that is being validated.
- Burns(tkns) checks that the transaction burns exactly tkns of the asset with the policy ID that is being validated.
- FreshTokens checks that all tokens of the asset being forged are non-fungible. This script must check that the names of the tokens in this token bundle are generated by hashing some unique data. This data must be unique to both the transaction itself and the token within the asset being forged. In particular, we can hash a pair of
  1. some *output* in the UTXO that the transaction consumes, and
  2. the *index* of the token name in (the list representation of) the map of tokens being forged (under the specific policy, by this transaction). We denote the function that gets the index of a key in a key-value map by indexof.
- AssetToAddress(addr) checks that all the tokens associated with the policy ID that is equal to the hash of the script being run are output to an UTXO with the address addr. In the case that no addr value is provided (represented by _), we use the addr value passed to the evaluator as the hash of the policy of the asset being forged.
- DoForge checks that this transaction forges tokens in the bundle controlled by the policy ID that is passed to the FPS script evaluator (here, again, we make use of the separate passing of the FPS script and the policy ID).
- SignedByPIDToken(pid) verifies the hash of every key that has signed the transaction.
- SpendsCur(pid) verifies that the transaction is spending assets in the token bundle with policy ID pid (which is specified as part of the *constructor*, and may be different than the policy ID passed to the evaluator).

5   Applications

UTXO$_{ma}$ is able to support a large number of standard use cases for multi-asset ledgers, as well as some novel ones. In this section we give a selection of examples. There are some common themes: (1) Tokens as resources can be used to reify many non-obvious things, which makes them first-class tradeable items; (2) cheap tokens allow us to solve many small problems with *more tokens*; and (3) the power of the scripting language affects what examples can be implemented.

5.1 Simple Single Token Issuance

To create a simple currency SimpleCoin with a fixed supply of s = 1000 SimpleCoins tokens, we might try to use the simple policy script Forges(s) with a single forging transaction. Unfortunately, this is not sufficient as somebody else could submit another transaction forging another 1000 SimpleCoins.

In other words, we need to ensure that there can only ever be a single transaction on the ledger that successfully forges SimpleCoin. We can achieve that by requiring that the forging transaction consumes a specific UTXO. As UTXOs are guaranteed to be (1) unique and (2) only be spent once, we are being guaranteed that the forging policy can only be used once to forge tokens. We can use the script:

```
simple_policy(o, v) = SpendsOutput(o) && Forges(v)
```

where o is an output that we create specifically for this purpose in a preceding setup transaction, and v = s.

5.2 Reflections of Off-Ledger Assets

Many tokens are used to represent (be backed by) off-ledger assets on the ledger. An important example of this is *backed stablecoins*. Other noteworthy examples of such assets include video game tokens, as well as service tokens (which represent service provider obligations).

A typical design for such a system is that a trusted party (the "issuer") is responsible for creation and destruction of the asset tokens on the ledger. The issuer is trusted to hold one of the backing off-ledger assets for every token that exists on the ledger, so the only role that the on-chain policy can play is to verify that the forging of the token is signed by the trusted issuer. This can be implemented with a forging policy that enforces an m-out-of-n multi-signature scheme, and no additional clauses:

```
trusted_issuer(msig) = JustMSig(msig)
```

5.3 Vesting

A common desire is to release a supply of some asset on some schedule. Examples include vesting schemes for shares, and staged releases of newly minted tokens. This seems tricky in our simple model: how is the forging policy supposed to know which tranches have already been released without some kind of global state which tracks them? However, this is a problem that we can solve with more tokens. We start building this policy by following the single issuer scheme, but we need to express more.

Given a specific output o, and two tranches of tokens tr1 and tr2 which should be released after tick1 and tick2, we can write a forging policy such as:

```
vesting = SpendsOutput(o) && Forges({"tr1" ↦ 1, "tr2" ↦ 1})
       || TickAfter(tick1) && Forges(tr1bundle) && Burns({"tr1" ↦ 1})
       || TickAfter(tick2) && Forges(tr2bundle) && Burns({"tr2" ↦ 1})
```

This disjunction has three clauses:

- Once only, you may forge two unique tokens tranche1 and tranche2.
- If you spend and burn tr1 and it is after tick1, then you may forge all the tokens in tr1bundle.
- If you spend and burn tr2 and it is after tick2, then you may forge all the tokens in tr2bundle.

By reifying the tranches as tokens, we ensure that they are unique and can be used precisely once. As a bonus, the tranche tokens are themselves tradeable.

5.4   Inventory Tracker: Tokens as State

We can use tokens to carry some data for us, or to represent state. A simple example is inventory tracking, where the inventory listing can only be modified by a set of trusted parties. To track inventory on-chain, we want to have a single output containing all of the tokens of an "inventory tracking" asset. If the trusted keys are represented by the multi-signature msig, the inventory tracker tokens should always be kept in a UTXO entry with the following output:

```
(hash(msig) , {hash(msig) ↦ {hats ↦ 3, swords ↦ 1, owls ↦ 2}})
```

The inventory tracker is an example of an asset that should indefinitely be controlled by a specific script (which ensures only authorized users can update the inventory), and we enforce this condition in the forging script itself:

```
inventory_tracker(msig) = JustMSig(msig) && AssetToAddress(_)
```

In this case, inventory_tracker(msig) is both the forging script and the output-locking script. The blank value supplied as the argument means that the policy ID (and also the address) are both assumed to be the hash of the inventory_tracker(msig) script. Defined this way, our script is run at initial forge time, and any time the inventory is updated. Each time it only validates if all the inventory tracker tokens in the transaction's outputs are always locked by this exact output script.

5.5   Non-fungible Tokens

A common case is to want an asset group where *all* the tokens are non-fungible. A simple way to do this is to simply have a different asset policy for each token, each of which can only be run once by requiring a specific UTXO to be spent.

However, this is clumsy, and typically we want to have a set of non-fungible tokens all controlled by the same policy. We can do this with the `FreshTokens` clause. If the policy always asserts that the token names are hashes of data unique to the transaction and token, then the tokens will always be distinct.

5.6 Revocable Permission

An example where we employ this dual-purpose nature of scripts is revocable permission. We will express permissions as a *credential token*.

The list of users (as a list of hashes of their public keys) in a credential token is composed by some central accreditation authority. Users usually trust that this authority has verified some real-life data, e.g. that a KYC accreditation authority has checked off-chain that those it accredits meet some standard.[4] Note here that we significantly simplify the function of KYC credentials for brevity of our example.

For example, suppose that exchanges are only willing to transfer funds to those that have proved that they are KYC-accredited.

In this case, the accreditation authority could issue an asset that looks like

```
{KYC_accr_authority ↦ {accr_key_1 ↦ 1, accr_key_2 ↦ 1, accr_key_3 ↦ 1}}
```

where the token names are the public keys of the accredited users. We would like to make sure that

- only the authority has the power to ever forge or burn tokens controlled by this policy, and it can do so at any time,
- all the users with listed keys are able to spend this asset as on-chain proof that they are KYC-accredited, and
- once a user is able to prove they have the credentials, they should be allowed to receive funds from an exchange.

We achieve this with a script of the following form:

```
credential_token(msig) = JustMSig(msig) && DoForge
                       || AssetToAddress(_) && Not DoForge && SignedByPIDToken(_)
```

Here, forges (i.e. updates to credential tokens) can only be done by the `msig` authority, but every user whose key hash is included in the token names can spend from this script, provided they return the asset to the same script. To make a script that only allows spending from it if the user doing so is on the list of key hashes in the credential token made by `msig`, we write

```
must_be_on_list(msig) = SpendsCur(credential_token(msig))
```

In our definition of the credential token, we have used all the strategies we discussed above to extend the expressivity of an FPS language. We are not yet using the UTXO model to its full potential, as we are just using the UTXO

---

[4] KYC stands for "know your customer", which is the process of verifying a customer's identity before allowing the customer to use a company's service.

to store some information that cannot be traded. However, we could consider updating our credential token use policy to associate spending it with another action, such as adding a pay-per-use clause. Such a change really relies on the UTXO model.

6 Related Work

Ethereum. Ethereum's ERC token standards [8,15] are one of the better known multi-asset implementations. They are a non-native implementation and so come with a set of drawbacks, such as having to implement ledger functionality (such as asset transfers) using smart contracts, rather than using the underlying ledger.

Augmenting the Ethereum ledger with functionality similar to that of the model we present here would likely be possible. Additionally, access to global contract state would make it easier to define forging policies that care about global information, such as the total supply of an asset.

Waves. Waves [16] is an account-based multi-asset ledger, supporting its own smart contract language. In Waves, both accounts and assets themselves can be associated with contracts. In both cases, the association is made by adding the associated script to the account state (or the state of the account containing the asset). A script associated with an asset imposes conditions on the use of this asset, including minting and burning restrictions, as well as transfer restrictions.

Stellar. Stellar [13] is an account-based native multi-asset system geared towards tracking real-world item ownership via associated blockchain tokens. Stellar is optimised to allow a token issuer to maintain a level of control over the use of their token even once it changes hands. The Stellar ledger also features a distributed exchange listing, which is used to facilitate matching (by price) exchanges between different tokens.

Zilliqa. Zilliqa is an account-based platform with an approach to smart contract implementation similar to that of Ethereum [12]. The Zilliqa fungible and non-fungible tokens are designed in a way that mimics the ERC-20 and ERC-721 tokens, respectively. While this system is designed to be statically analysable, it does not offer new solutions to the problem of dependency on the global state.

DAML. DAML [7] is a smart contract language designed to be used on the DAML ledger model. The DAML ledger model does not support keeping records of asset ownership, but instead, only stores current contract states in the following way: a valid transaction interacting with a contract results in the creation of new contracts that are the next steps of the original contract, and removal of the original contract from the ledger.

Only the contracts with which a transaction interacts are relevant to validating it, which is similar to our approach of validation without global context. Although this system does not have built-in multi-asset support (or any ledger-level accounting), the transfer of any type of asset can be represented on the ledger via contracts. Due to the design of the system to operate entirely by listing contracts on the ledger, each action, including accepting funds transferred by a contract, requires consent. This is another significant way in which this model is different from ours.

Bitcoin. Bitcoin popularised UTXO ledgers, but has neither native nor non-native multi-asset support on the main chain. The Bitcoin ledger model does not appear to have the accounting infrastructure or sufficiently expressive smart contracts for implementing multi-asset support in a generic way. There have been several layer-two approaches to implementing custom Bitcoin assets. Because each mined Bitcoin is unique, a particular Bitcoin can represent a specific custom asset, as is done in [3]. A more sophisticated accounting strategy is implemented in another layer-two custom asset approach [11]. There have also been attempts to implement custom tokens using Lightning network channels [1].

Tezos. Tezos [9] is an account-based platform with its own smart contract language. It has been used to implement an ERC-20-like fungible token standard (FA1.2), with a unified token standard in the works (see [14]). The custom tokens for both multi-asset standards are non-native, and thus have shortcomings similar to those of Ethereum token standards.

Nervos CKB. Nervos CKB [17] is a UTXO-inspired platform that operates on a broader notion of a Cell, rather than the usual output balance amount and address, as the value stored in an entry. A Cell entry can contain any type of data, including a native currency balance, or any type of code. This platform comes with a Turing-complete scripting language that can be used to define custom native tokens. There is, however, no dedicated accounting infrastructure to handle trading custom assets in a similar way as the base currency type.

7   Discussion

7.1   General Observations

Asset Registries and Distributed Exchanges. The most obvious way to manage custom assets might be to add some kind of global *asset registry*, which associates a new asset group with its policy. Once we have an asset registry, this becomes a natural place to put other kinds of infrastructure that rely on global state associated with assets, such as decentralised exchanges.

However, our system provides us with a way to associate forging policies and the assets controlled by them *without* any global state. This simplifies the ledger implementation in the concurrent and distributed environment of a blockchain. Introducing global state into our model would result in disrupted synchronisation (on which [6] relies to great effect to implement fast, optimistic settlement), as well as slow and costly state updates at the time of asset registration. Hence, on balance we think it is better to have a stateless system, even if it relegates features like decentralised exchanges to be Layer 2 solutions.

Spending Policies. Some platforms we discussed provide ways to express restrictions on the *transfer* of tokens, not just on their forging and burning, which we refer to as *spending policies*. Unlike forging policies, spending polices are not a native part of our system. We have considered a number of approaches to adding spending policies, but we have not found a solution that does not put an undue burden on the *users* of such tokens, both humans and programmatic users such as layer-two protocols (e.g. Lightning). For example, it would be necessary to ensure that spending policies are not in conflict with forging or output-locking scripts (any time the asset is spent).

Forging tokens requires a specific action by the user (providing and satisfying a forging policy script), but this action is always taken knowingly by a user who is specifically trying to forge those tokens. *Spending* tokens is, however, a completely generic operation that works over arbitrary bundles of tokens. Indeed, a virtue of our system is that custom tokens all look and behave uniformly. In contrast, spending policies make custom tokens extremely difficult to handle in a generic way, in particular for automated systems.

These arguments do not invalidate the usefulness of spending policies, but instead highlight that they are not obviously compatible with trading of native assets in a generic way, and an approach that addresses these issues in an ergonomic way is much needed. This problem is not ours alone: spending policies in other systems we have looked at here (such as Waves), do not provide universal solutions to the issues we face with spending policies either.

Viral Scripts. One way to emulate spending policies in our system is to lock all the tokens with a particular script that ensures that they *remain* locked by the same script when transferred. We call such a script a "viral" script (since it spreads to any new outputs that are "infected" with the token).

This allows the conditions of the script to be enforced on every transaction that uses the tokens, but at significant costs. In particular such tokens can never be locked by a *different* script, which prevents such tokens from being used in smart contracts, as well as preventing an output from containing tokens from two such viral asset groups (since *both* would require that their validator be applied to the output!). In some cases, however, this approach is exactly what we want. For example, in the case of credential tokens, we want the script locking the credential to permanently allow the issuer access to the credential (in order to maintain their ability to revoke it).

Global State. There are limitations of our model due to the fact that global information about the ledger is not available to the forging policy script. Many global state constraints can be accommodated with workarounds (such as in the case of provably unique fresh tokens), but some cannot: for example, a forging policy that allows a variable amount to be forged in every block depending on the current total supply of assets of another policy. This is an odd policy to have, but nevertheless, not one that can be defined in our model.

7.2   Conclusions

We present a multi-asset ledger model which extends a UTXO-based ledger so that it can support custom fungible and non-fungible tokens. We do this in a way that does not require smart contract functionality. We add a small language with the ability to express exactly the logic we need for a particular set of usecases. Our UTXO$_{ma}$ ledger together with this language allows us to use custom assets to support a wide variety of usecases, even those that are not normally based on "assets", while still remaining deterministic, high-assurance, and analysable.

Our design has a number of limitations, some of which have acceptable workarounds, and some that do not. In particular, access to global state in a general way cannot be supported, and spending policies are not easy to implement. It is also not possible to explicitly restrict payment to an address. We consider these worthy directions for future improvements to our model.

References

1. Lightning Network multi-asset channels (2016). https://github.com/lightningnetwork/lightning-rfc/pull/72
2. Atzei, N., Bartoletti, M., Lande, S., Zunino, R.: A formal model of bitcoin transactions. In: Meiklejohn, S., Sako, K. (eds.) FC 2018. LNCS, vol. 10957, pp. 541–560. Springer, Heidelberg (2018). https://doi.org/10.1007/978-3-662-58387-6_29
3. Buterin, V., Hakim, L., Rosenfeld, M., Lev, R.: Liquid: a bitcoin sidechain (2012)
4. Chakravarty, M.M.T., et al.: Native custom tokens in the extended UTXO model. In: Margaria,T., Steffen, B. (eds) ISoLA 2020. LNCS, vol. 12478, pp. 89–111. Springer, Heidelberg (2020). https://omelkonian.github.io/data/publications/eutxoma.pdf
5. Chakravarty, M.M.T., Chapman, J., MacKenzie, K., Melkonian, O., Peyton Jones, M., Wadler, P.: The extended UTXO model. In: Bernhard, M., et al. (eds.) FC 2020. LNCS, vol. 12063, pp. 525–539. Springer, Cham (2020). https://doi.org/10.1007/978-3-030-54455-3_37
6. Chakravarty, M.M.T., et al.: Hydra: fast isomorphic state channels. Technical report, Cryptology ePrint Archive, Report 2020/299 (2020). https://eprint.iacr.org/2020/299
7. DAML Team: DAML SDK documentation (2020). https://docs.daml.com/
8. Entriken, W., Shirley, D., Evans, J., Sachs, N.: ERC-721 non-fungible token standard. Ethereum Foundation (2018). https://eips.ethereum.org/EIPS/eip-721
9. Goodman, L.: Tezos–a self-amending crypto-ledger white paper (2014)
10. Nakamoto, S.: Bitcoin: a peer-to-peer electronic cash system (2008). https://bitcoin.org/en/bitcoin-paper
11. Nick, J., Poelstra, A., Sanders, G.: Liquid: a bitcoin sidechain (2020)
12. Sergey, I., Kumar, A., Hobor, A.: Scilla: a smart contract intermediate-level language. arXiv preprint arXiv:1801.00687 (2018)
13. Stellar Development Foundation: Stellar Development Guides (2020). https://solidity.readthedocs.io/
14. Tezos Team: Digital Assets on Tezos (2020). https://assets.tqtezos.com/docs/intro/

15. Vogelsteller, F., Buterin, V.: ERC-20 token standard. Ethereum Foundation (Stiftung Ethereum), Zug, Switzerland (2015). https://eips.ethereum.org/EIPS/eip-20
16. Waves Team: Waves blockchain documentation (2020). https://docs.wavesprotocol.org/
17. Xie, J.: Nervos CKB: a common knowledge base for crypto-economy (2018). https://docs.daml.com/
18. Zahnentferner, J.: An abstract model of UTxO-based cryptocurrencies with scripts. IACR Cryptology ePrint Archive 2018, 469 (2018). https://eprint.iacr.org/2018/469
19. Zahnentferner, J.: Multi-currency ledgers (2018). https://eprint.iacr.org/2020/895

Towards Configurable and Efficient Runtime Verification of Blockchain Based Smart Contracts at the Virtual Machine Level

Joshua Ellul$^{(\boxtimes)}$ (iD)

Centre for Distributed Ledger Technologies and Department of Computer Science,
University of Malta, Msida, Malta
joshua.ellul@um.edu.mt

Abstract. Runtime Verification in both traditional systems and smart contracts has typically been implemented at the application level. Such systems very often run on Virtual Machines which execute their application logic. Conditional monitoring is often implemented to enable for certain monitors to be switched off in aim of reducing execution overheads once certain levels of assurance have been provided. Even when turned off such application level conditional monitoring still incurs added overheads to execute the conditional statement related operations. In this paper, we propose methods to support conditional runtime verification of applications at the virtual machine level. We demonstrate that such an approach can provide lower overheads in terms of both execution and gas.

Keywords: Virtual machines · Runtime verification · Smart contracts · Blockchain

1 Introduction

Although runtime verification is typically touted as a *lightweight* verification technique [2], the term is often associated to high overheads associated with the verification process in comparison to other techniques such as model checking and symbolic execution, despite the fact that the cost, no matter how lightweight, is induced post-deployment. From an end user perspective, the technique is, in comparison, more heavyweight than predeployment techniques which do not have any discernible impact on the live system. Such additional costs in terms of resources, typically time and space, may render the use of runtime verification impractical in the context of reactive systems working in a realtime environment.

In the context of smart contracts [8] on public Blockchain and other Distributed Ledger Technology (DLT) recent work demonstrates the costs of runtime verification [6]. The very nature and mission of smart contracts is that of providing guaranteed regulated behaviour between parties—which, until a

© Springer Nature Switzerland AG 2020
T. Margaria and B. Steffen (Eds.): ISoLA 2020, LNCS 12478, pp. 131–145, 2020.
https://doi.org/10.1007/978-3-030-61467-6_9

decade ago, was only possible through the adoption of a trusted third party to execute the code. Public blockchains, and DLTs in general, however, provided a means of decentralising this central point-of-trust by delegating trust to the underlying peer-to-peer network and protocol used to record transactions. The solution lies in having the miner which successfully mines a block to execute the logic of the smart contract and store the result, but having the other nodes replicate the work to ensure that the recorded information is, in fact, sound. Without measures in place, anyone could bring a network to a grinding halt by providing non-terminating (or computationally expensive) logic to be executed by the miners. Various solutions were proposed and adopted, from drastically limiting the expressive power of smart contracts (e.g. Bitcoin script which allows for non-Turing complete computation as part of transactions on Bitcoin [7]), to placing a cost on the computation (e.g. systems like Ethereum [10] and Neo[1] which require transaction initiators to pay for 'gas', a resource used to store data on and execute smart contracts). In this context, the additional cost due to runtime verification becomes more concerning—not only may the users be actively directly paying for the extra computation, but all mining and verifying nodes are performing the extra computation to verify the block written by the successful miner. The larger the underlying network, the larger the effective extra computation performed.

Much work has recently appeared in literature concerning the reduction of runtime verification overheads in general (i.e. not just for smart contract monitoring). Most of the work relies on static analysis techniques to prove as much of the specification as possible, and use that information to reduce the runtime verification overheads.

Other approaches have advocated monitoring which can be switched on and off at will, sometimes allowing for the choice between synchronous and asynchronous monitoring according to runtime flags. These approaches reduce overheads, leaving nothing but checks to the monitoring flag when switched off. Still, one retains some overhead, depending on the number of instrumentation points in the code.

In this paper we present an alternative to the latter approach which allows for monitoring to be enabled or disabled at a granular level at runtime whilst minimising execution overhead by pushing down monitoring into the Virtual Machine (VM) level. It is, however, worth adding that the former monitoring optimisation techniques mentioned are orthogonal to this work in that as mentioned the approach aims to minimise runtime overheads when monitoring is switched on as well as when they are switched off.

Given that most smart contract platforms execute on a virtual machine, we argue that a prime use of our approach is in this domain. We illustrate the use of our approach on the Neo blockchain[2], to demonstrate the benefits of using our proposed virtual machine level approach as opposed to application level monitoring. To the best of our knowledge this is the first proposed approach

---

[1] https://docs.neo.org/docs/en-us/basic/whitepaper.html.
[2] https://neo.org/.

to investigate runtime verification of applications implemented at the virtual machine level.

2   Background/Related Work

Many techniques aiming to reduce runtime verification overheads which have appeared in the literature e.g. [1,3,4] mostly focus on the use of static analysis to (i) simplify the property that will be monitored; (ii) reduce the number of instrumentation points in the main system which will not affect the specification; or (iii) simplify the monitoring logic generated to monitor the property. Our approach is orthogonal to such techniques, in that we do not attempt to reduce overheads, but rather enable switching off monitoring in such a manner so as to leave no residual costs.

Colombo et al. have considered allowing for switching between different runtime verification modes e.g. synchronous, asynchronous or offline, in [5]. However, unlike the approach we present here, even switching monitoring off completely would still leave small overheads when checking the flag denoting whether monitoring is to be performed. On the other hand, here we simply allow for switching off monitoring, whereas in the other work enables a finer grained monitoring control e.g. switching to asynchronous monitoring at peak times of the system under scrutiny in order to avoid performance degradation. In order to ensure that asynchronous monitoring be able to catch up with the system (to be able to switch back to synchronous monitoring), Colombo et al. use fast-forwarding function which allow faster consumption of buffered events at the cost of over or under approximate results. In contrast, here we characterise specification languages localised to single transactions, and show that, using these, any runtime verification of a transaction is sound and complete no matter if monitoring was switched off for other transactions earlier on.

Also closely related to our approach is that of Wonisch et al. [9], in which the authors present an approach which replicates code to reduce runtime monitoring overheads to zero. By branching whenever an event relevant to the monitoring occurs, the authors show how overheads can be removed altogether. From such a perspective, our approach can be seen as a way of replicating aspects of the virtual machine interpreter, some of which use monitoring, and others which do not. This ensures that the replication is tractable and built into the virtual machine directly. Just like our approach, whenever monitoring is not required, the system does not even check whether or not an event should be propagated to the monitor. However, that is where the approaches similarities stop.

Finally, we note that although there is work out there that instruments monitoring at the bytecode level (e.g. the aspect-oriented programming language ApsectJ, which various runtime verification tools use, injects code at the JVM level), such instrumentation is still at the application level, including any specification-level choice on when to monitor and when not to. In contrast, our approach allows us to instrument this choice at the VM runtime and interpreter level, allowing the VM to have a native notion of monitoring.

3   Virtual Machine Design and Implementation

Traditional application level conditional runtime verification (RV) instils extra overheads required to check whether a monitor is active. When active such a condition increases the monitoring substantially. When disabled the condition itself leaves the residual condition statement execution overhead. In this work we aim to minimise such overheads by pushing down RV into the VM level.

In aim of investigating whether configurable runtime verification can be achieved with minimal execution overheads we will now propose and discuss Virtual Machine (VM) design related solutions. Virtual Machines are not designed with runtime verification in mind. Therefore, below we will discuss changes that can be implemented on existing VMs to support configurable runtime verification for applications. We have implemented our work on NeoVM[3]. Whilst, we will present the solution in a VM architecture agnostic manner as much as possible, indeed the approach presented herein would be more easily implemented on similar architectures (stack based interpreter VMs) however changes to the design may be required for other architectures (e.g. Ahead-of-Time and Just-in-Time compilation based VMs). For the scope of this work we have altered the NeoVM source for version 3.0.0-preview2 available on github[4].

3.1   Bytecode

We introduce the following new bytecode operations: (i) two new bytecode operations to provide required functionality to control whether monitoring is switched on or off at runtime on either a smart contract global level, or for a particular monitor; and (ii) a bytecode operation that explicitly states that a specific system call invocation will trigger a monitor. Further details regarding the full execution engine mechanisms are described in Sect. 3.2. The operations follow.

Operation:	MON
Parameters:	\<id> \<state>
Effect on Stack:	→
Description:	This operation will disable monitor \<id> if \<state> is set to 0, otherwise it will enable it.

Operation:	AMON
Parameters:	\<state>
Effect on Stack:	→
Description:	This operation will disable all monitoring for the smart contract if \<state> is set to 0, otherwise individual monitors will be enabled or disabled based upon their individual setting using MON.

---

[3] https://docs.neo.org/docs/en-us/basic/technology/neovm.html.

[4] https://github.com/neo-project/neo-vm/tree/v3.0.0-preview2.

Operation: SYSCALLM
Parameters: as required per specific SYSCALL operation
Effect on Stack: as per specific SYSCALL operation
Description: This operation will perform the standard implementation of the
                     SYSCALL operation, but will invoke a monitored version of the
                     SYSCALL implementation.

3.2   Execution Engine

We will now highlight functionality implemented in order to provide configurable application runtime verification at the VM level which provides for both smart contract global and granular monitoring configurability. In this work we evaluate global state monitoring as a first means of investigation of VM-level application monitoring. We present two approaches, one which allows for monitoring to be switched on/off at the smart contract and state variable levels, and another which allows for bytecode operations to initiate monitors and allows for the bytecode to be patched accordingly at runtime.

NeoVM implements global state storage operations (as well as other runtime functionality including serialization, blockchain and cryptography operations) through a system call interface provided via the SYSCALL bytecode operation[5]. Upon a system call being raised the application execution engine translates the system call operation identifier to the respective operation handler's implementation.

Enabling Configurable State Variable Monitoring: Global smart contract state variables are accessed and set (in the Neo blockchain platform) using runtime Storage function calls to Get and Put respectively. These runtime function calls get compiled down to SYSCALL bytecode operations. When encountering such instructions, the VM will process the SYSCALL bytecode operation, decode the system call number to identify the respective handler implementation and transfer execution to the handler. We implement a new handler for the Put runtime function, PutAndMonitor, which undertakes the original functionality yet also checks if a monitor is enabled for the given state variable being set and if so executes the monitor. Through such an approach, a monitor can be switched on or off at the level of a specific state variable. Functionality and logic allowing for users (or developers) to enable or disable monitoring can be coded into the smart contract using the MON bytecode operation presented herein. The implementation here investigates the use of monitors for global state variables by checking whether a particular monitor is enabled within the Put runtime function. The same could be done for other types of monitors that require inspection within runtime libraries and should be investigated in future work.

---

[5] https://docs.neo.org/v3/docs/en-us/reference/Neo_vm.html.

Enabling Configurable Smart Contract Monitoring: Specific monitors can be enabled or disabled through a check implemented in the runtime implementation of the Put function as described above. In order to avoid having to check for active monitors in invocations to Put for smart contracts not using monitoring, the AMON bytecode operation is introduced which sets whether monitoring is enabled or not for a specific smart contract. When a smart contract is invoked the VM can thereafter wire up the system to either handle monitoring or not for the specific smart contract. The full mechanism is depicted in Fig. 1.

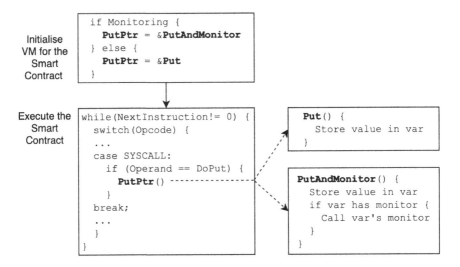

Fig. 1. The VM wires up either a path that includes monitoring or not dependent upon whether monitoring is enabled.

Optimisation: Initialising the VM for each smart contract call may incur extra overhead. In fact the actual implementation in Neo does not involve just pointer updating but is implemented using a process that requires hashing the function signature, and updating a dictionary reference. In order to minimise such overheads (which are executed every smart contract transaction) we implemented an optimisation that will only undertake this 'costly' reference update if it is needed. If the 'pointer' is already pointing to the correct function required (i.e. the monitored version or the unmonitered version) for the specific smart contract invocation, then there's no need to update the 'pointer'.

Bytecode Operation Level Monitoring: Together the smart contract wide and state variable specific monitoring mechanisms described above allows for runtime configurability of runtime verification which minimises monitoring to only those smart contracts that have enabled it, and also to only the specific state variables for which it is enabled on. Whilst this minimises potential over-heads, it still does incur overheads for: (i) all smart contract invocations in order to determine whether monitoring should be switched on; and (ii) for all `Put` invocations for smart contracts with enabled monitoring in order to determine whether the specific state variable is being monitored. Herein we are further investigating another approach which enables for monitoring to be specified at the bytecode operation level which can do away with all such overheads as well – at the expense of a more complex Bytecode rewriting procedure when required.

We introduce the `SYSCALLM` operation which implements the standard `SYSCALL` functionality and also executes an associated monitor. By allowing for monitoring to be explicitly selected at the Bytecode level overheads associated with determining whether monitoring is enabled (at both the smart contract and specific function level) can be eliminated. Figure 2 depicts the required change to the VM execution engine loop which has both implementations for `SYSCALL` and to `SYSCALLM`. When a system call is intended to invoke the runtime's `Put` function the `SYSCALL` operation will always call the original handler implementation, but for the `SYSCALLM` instruction an altered `PutAndMonitor` implementation will be called. Note that even the condition in `PutAndMonitor` from Fig. 1 is removed since the `SYSCALLM` instruction explicitly states that it is to call the associated monitor.

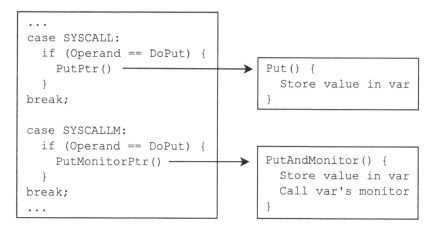

Fig. 2. Depending upon the Bytecode specified within the smart contract the VM will use either operations that do or do not include monitoring. The intention is that such operations can be patched at runtime.

Here we have presented a solution to enable for monitoring of global state variables (using `SYSCALL`), however this approach could similarly be applied to other monitoring points of interest including: `CALLs` to both monitor before calling a function and the beginning of execution of a function; `RET` to both monitor before returning from a function and also after returning; `LDs` and `STs` for loading and storing of variables and fields; amongst others.

Whilst this method does require less overhead, it does involve patching all Bytecode operations when monitoring is enabled or disabled for the specific monitors (in this case monitoring of specific state variables). This raises some challenges in regards to the blockchain's smart contract storage implementation, since if the Bytecode in the smart contract were to change then the hash for the smart contract and respective block would no longer be valid. We leave this challenge for future work. This also raises questions of the smart contract's immutability and determinism which we now discuss.

Issues of Immutability and Determinism: Enabling or disabling smart contract wide monitoring and/or specific monitors does not affect determinism of the smart contract nor allow for any logic to be changed that was not 'agreed upon' or visible to the various smart contract users. The reason being is that the AMON and MON bytecode operations need to be (implemented and) executed from within the smart contract itself. Therefore, the various users agreeing to the smart contract are explicitly agreeing to the 'terms' that define when monitoring can be enabled and disabled. More so, the specific monitor code is part of the smart contract itself.

When it comes to enabling and disabling of explicit monitor triggering bytecode such as SYSCALLM (proposed herein) thought needs to go into how the bytecode operations can be stored and updated without breaking the hashes associated with the smart contract and respective block. This is left as future work. From a user point of view, as long as the semantics specify that particular bytecode operations could (or could not) trigger monitors, then the same argument above applies in regards to determinism and inability to change its logic.

4   Evaluation

To evaluate the approach proposed herein and in order to provide granular performance results of the costs of virtual machine based application runtime verification, execution costs of monitoring a single global state variable will be presented to motivate further work towards pushing runtime verification of applications down to the virtual machine layer.

4.1   The Application Being Monitored

As an initial evaluation metric let's consider a trivial invariant. Let's assume that we need to ensure that a particular global state variable, V, should never go below 1. The NEO smart contract (template) that we'll use to evaluate performance is presented in Listing 1.1. Line 7, which sets the value of V, is the line that should trigger monitoring. A comment on line 6 is used in this paper to highlight where monitoring is to be undertaken.

```
1  [Features(ContractFeatures.HasStorage)]
2  public class MonitorInvariant : SmartContract {
3      public static bool Main(string operation, object[] args)
          {
4          if (Runtime.Trigger == TriggerType.Application) {
5              if (operation == "s") {
6                  //*application level monitoring placeholder
7                  Storage.Put("V", 1);
8              }
9              return true;
10          }
11          return false;
12      }
13  }
```

Listing 1.1. Smart contract code which sets the storage variable "V" being monitored.

Indeed our use case involves nothing more than setting the global state variable which is being monitored. Therefore, our evaluation results will be highlighting the direct overheads of monitoring at a granular level independent of a typical application. When applied to real applications the proportional monitoring overhead would be much lower. In future work we will demonstrate the performance gains not just on a granular level but on typical applications.

4.2   The Monitor

The monitoring code is presented in Listing 1.2, which checks if the variable V is ever set below 1 (or is 0, since it is a byte), and if the property is not held then an exception is thrown (which ensures that the state is reverted).

```
1  byte b = Storage.Get("V")[0];
2  if (b == 0) {
3      throw new InvalidOperationException("V is zero!!");
4  }
```

Listing 1.2. Application level monitoring code used (whether inlined or in a separate function).

4.3   Experiment Setup

We will first compare different configurations that do not undertake any monitoring, following by different configurations that do implement monitoring in aim of establishing the various overheads for the different methods. The experiments were conducted on a Microsoft Surface Book running Windows 10 Pro with an Intel Core i7-8650U CPU equipped with 16 GB of physical memory. A private Neo chain was used which was configured for a single node.

The smart contract code was invoked 1,000,000 times for each configuration and the result averaged to determine the (average) execution cost for a single run. This was undertaken since the node implementation is responsible for more than just the execution of the smart contracts. The gas consumed was recorded for a single run (which is deterministic).

4.4   Evaluating When Monitoring Is Off

We first compare various methods that do not monitor the running code that make use of either: (i) virtual machine-level monitoring (the work being proposed herein) or application-level monitoring; (ii) inlined monitoring code or monitors implemented as separate functions; and (iii) no monitoring, hard-coded monitoring or conditional monitoring. We compare 6 cases listed in Table 1 where no monitoring is implemented or where conditional monitoring is disabled. The two approaches proposed in this paper are listed as VMMon which makes use of the VM runtime smart contract wide monitoring, and specific monitor conditional settings and implementation; and the VM SYSCALLM approach which makes use of explicit bytecode operations that explicitly require monitoring post-bytecode operation execution. The average execution time, and gas consumption for configurations that do not result in monitoring of the global state variable as presented in Fig. 3.

Table 1. Different configurations that do not result in monitoring of the global state variable.

Method	Level	Form	Monitoring
None	–	–	–
App Fn Cond Off	Application	Separate Function	Conditional and disabled
App Inline Cond Off	Application	Inlined	Conditional and disabled
VMMon On Fn Cond Off	VM Runtime	Separate Function	Conditional and disabled
VMMon On Fn Cond Off Opt	VM Runtime	Separate Function	Optimised for conditional and disabled
VM SYSCALLM Off	VM Bytecode	Separate Function	Conditional and disabled

It is important to highlight that overhead associated with conditional statements implemented in the VM to check whether a particular smart contract has monitoring enabled or whether a global state variable was being monitored was not assigned any gas overheads. The question of how much gas should be associated with internal VM operations is indeed an interesting question, however not one which we aim to answer here. Therefore, the gas consumption of the two VM configurations may be required to be slightly higher (based upon the gas requirement that would eventually by assigned to such VM-level monitoring functionality). The above applies as well below when comparing configurations that have monitoring enabled. The VM SYSCALLM Off implementation does not incur any additional overheads when monitoring is switched off, as the bytecode executed is exactly the same to that of an application that has not implemented monitoring—this however does not apply when monitoring is enabled and the

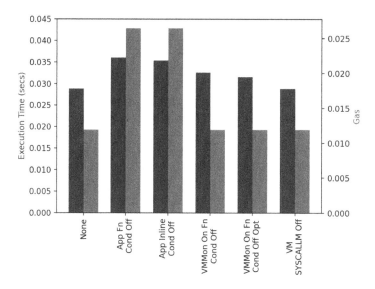

Fig. 3. The average execution time, and gas consumption for various methods that do not result in monitoring of the global state variable listed in Table 1.

SYSCALLM bytecode operation is used (though the extra overhead only involves a direct call to the monitor).

The execution time for running the code is a better indicator for performance as it includes both the execution overheads of the smart contract logic as well as the VM execution overheads, and does not rely on external factors to establish costs associated with instructions.

From the results above for the various configurations that do result in monitoring of the global state variable, we highlight the following observations:

- Introducing conditional monitoring that is disabled at the application level introduces 24% execution overheads for both when implemented for inlined code (App Inline Cond Off) or as a separate function (App Fn Cond Off) since the code executed for both remains the same since the condition to execute the monitor never holds. Gas consumption is relatively higher since the conditional statement has to be evaluated within the application (and the application does little else more).
- Conditional monitoring implemented in the VM that is enabled for the specific smart contract, but disabled for the global state variable in question results in 13% and 9% higher overheads (compared to an application that does not allow for monitoring) for the non-optimised VM runtime monitoring implementation and the optimised implementation respectively. It is unlikely that in a real environment hosting many different applications that either represent the reality, however they represent the maximum and minimum execution costs.

- Conditional monitoring implemented using the Bytecode-level approach proposed herein results in 0% execution overhead when monitoring is disabled, since the execution paths both within the VM and the application remain the same.
- The gas consumption for the VM-based approaches result in the same gas consumption as for the 'None' configuration that does not implement monitoring (nor conditional). For the VMMon approaches it may well be the case that such a platform designer may require some gas consumption for having to check whether the specific monitor is on or not. However, for the SYSCALLM implementation, the bytecode executed and all instructions executed within the VM remain exactly the same. So, for this configuration zero-overheads are introduced for monitoring when it is disabled.

4.5   Evaluating When Monitoring Is On

We now compare the various methods that enable monitoring of the global state variable. For comparison, we include the 'None' configuration.

Similar to the evaluation for when monitoring is off, here we evaluate the various configurations when monitoring is switched on. We compare 7 configurations with the 'None' configuration as listed in Table 2. The average execution time, and gas consumption for configurations that result in monitoring of the global state variable as presented in Fig. 4.

In our implementations VM-level runtime verification was only implemented using a separate function to act as the monitoring code. Given the overheads incurred to call a function, including requiring the VM to set up the function's stack frame and to return from the function, further work could be undertaken to have the VM execute the monitor code as though it is inlined in the same function to further minimise overheads.

Table 2. Different configurations that result in monitoring of the global state variable and the 'None configuration'.

Method	Level	Form	Monitoring
None	–	–	–
App Fn	Application	Separate Function	Always On
App Inline	Application	Inlined	Always On
App Fn Cond On	Application	Separate Function	Conditional and enabled
App Inline Cond On	Application	Inlined	Conditional and enabled
VMMon On Fn Cond On	VM Runtime	Separate Function	Conditional and enabled
VMMon On Fn Cond On Opt	VM Runtime	Separate Function	Optimised for conditional and enabled
VM SYSCALLM On	VM Bytecode	Separate Function	Conditional and enabled

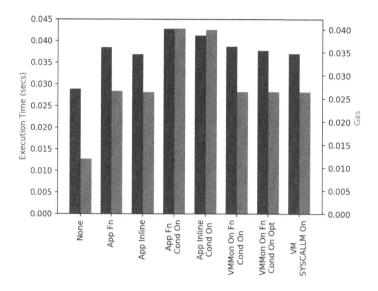

Fig. 4. The average execution time, and gas consumption for various methods that result in monitoring of the global state variable listed in Table 2.

Given the overheads noted above, calling a separate function as opposed to an inlined version could result in around 5% in execution overhead reductions. In fact, such an approach would be desirable to provide both benefits to both minimizing monitoring code to a single location (and therefore saving on gas storage costs) and also to minimise execution costs as previously discussed.

From the results above we highlight the following observations:

- Introducing monitoring to the application level introduces 33% and 28% execution overheads when implemented as a separate function or as inlined code respectively (when compared to the 'None' configuration—no monitoring).
- Application level conditional monitoring that is enabled results in 48% and 43% overheads for a separate function and inlined monitor implementations when compared to no monitoring; and 11% and 12% overheads when compared to their unconditional monitoring counterparts. Gas consumption is sufficiently higher for application level conditional monitoring as well compared to unconditional monitoring counterparts.
- Conditional monitoring implemented in the VM that is enabled for the specific smart contract and enabled for the global state variable in question for the non-optimised and optimised versions results in: 34% and 31% higher overheads compared to no monitoring at all; 5% and 2% more execution time than hardcoded application level monitoring that is inlined, and 1% overheads when compared to the application level hardcoded implementation that makes use of a monitor implemented in a separate function; however they are 7% and 9% faster than the application level conditional inlined monitoring configuration, and 11% and 13% faster than the conditional separate function

application level implementation. As previously discussed these two versions implement the best case and worst case scenarios for overheads that would be incurred for the VM level runtime monitoring approach.

- Conditional active monitoring using the Bytecode-level approach results in the following execution overheads: 28% compared to no monitoring; 1% extra overhead compared to the application level hardcoded inlined monitoring code and yet is 4% faster than the hardcoded separate monitor implementation; it is 11% and 15% faster than the conditional application level monitoring for the inlined and separate function implementations respectively.
- Gas consumption for the VM-based approaches result in slightly less gas consumption than for the hardcoded application level monitoring configurations. This is due to the lack of the application level conditional statement, and for the SYSCALLM implementation due to the explicit instruction that the monitor is to be executed. Nonetheless, such system designers may factor in some gas costs for these overheads, however as demonstrated through the execution time overheads such gas overheads should not be as high as the application level counterparts.

As demonstrated through the results presented above runtime verification implemented in the VM level can result in zero overheads when monitoring is disabled (as demonstrated using the SYSCALLM bytecode operation approach), and similarly zero to minimal gas overheads (depending upon the gas associated by the platform designers). Comparing when monitoring is enabled a VM level approach can implement monitoring with similar to minimal execution overheads when compared with hardcoded application level monitoring. More so, when compared to application level conditional monitoring, the VM monitoring approaches largely outperform the application level conditional monitoring implementations. We did not implement an inlined monitor implementation for the VM based versions which would incur even more speedups. Comparing the hardcoded application inlined version with the separate monitor function version this could result in up to 4% execution speed ups which would make the VM level based implementations that much faster than they already are compared to the application level conditional monitoring implementations.

5   Conclusions

In this paper an initial investigation in application runtime verification at the VM level was undertaken. It is to the author's best knowledge that this is the first proposed work that looks into VM level monitoring of application code.

Two approaches were proposed, one which requires the VM to keep track of whether monitoring is enabled at the smart contract level and also for each monitor. This approach enables for a convenient method to make changes primarily within the VM's runtime and requires minimal changes to the bytecode instruction set and compiler. However, this introduces additional checks required for each smart contract invocation. It should be noted that this approach may be better suited to VM's that host single applications, like private blockchain systems and also for non-blockchain based traditional VMs. This approach nonetheless results in better performance to application level conditional monitoring.

Another approach proposed is to include new instructions that both execute operations that are the same as other operations (which would be likely to require monitoring) and also explicitly trigger monitoring related to the same instruction. This approach results in zero-overheads when monitoring is disabled, and similar overheads to hardcoded application level monitoring. This approach however requires more work to be conducted within the compiler and tools to support enabling and disabling of monitoring at runtime. This approach also enables for finer grained monitoring to be enabled/disabled for specific monitors at exact locations within application code.

References

1. Azzopardi, S., Colombo, C., Pace, G.J.: A technique for automata-based verification with residual reasoning. In: Model-Driven Engineering and Software Development - 8th International Conference, MODELSWARD 2020, Valletta, Malta, 25–27 February 2020 (2020)
2. Bartocci, E., Falcone, Y., Francalanza, A., Reger, G.: Introduction to runtime verification. In: Bartocci, E., Falcone, Y. (eds.) Lectures on Runtime Verification. LNCS, vol. 10457, pp. 1–33. Springer, Cham (2018). https://doi.org/10.1007/978-3-319-75632-5_1
3. Bodden, E., Lam, P., Hendren, L.: Clara: a framework for partially evaluating finite-state runtime monitors ahead of time. In: Barringer, H., et al. (eds.) RV 2010. LNCS, vol. 6418, pp. 183–197. Springer, Heidelberg (2010). https://doi.org/10.1007/978-3-642-16612-9_15
4. Chimento, J.M., Ahrendt, W., Pace, G.J., Schneider, G.: StaRVOOrS: a tool for combined static and runtime verification of Java. In: Bartocci, E., Majumdar, R. (eds.) RV 2015. LNCS, vol. 9333, pp. 297–305. Springer, Cham (2015). https://doi.org/10.1007/978-3-319-23820-3_21
5. Colombo, C., Pace, G.J.: Fast-forward runtime monitoring — an industrial case study. In: Qadeer, S., Tasiran, S. (eds.) RV 2012. LNCS, vol. 7687, pp. 214–228. Springer, Heidelberg (2013). https://doi.org/10.1007/978-3-642-35632-2_22
6. Ellul, J., Pace, G.J.: Runtime verification of Ethereum smart contracts. In: 2018 14th European Dependable Computing Conference (EDCC), pp. 158–163. IEEE (2018)
7. Nakamoto, S.: Bitcoin: a peer-to-peer electronic cash system (2009). http://www.bitcoin.org/bitcoin.pdf
8. Szabo, N.: Formalizing and securing relationships on public networks. First Monday 2(9) (1997)
9. Wonisch, D., Schremmer, A., Wehrheim, H.: Zero overhead runtime monitoring. In: Hierons, R.M., Merayo, M.G., Bravetti, M. (eds.) SEFM 2013. LNCS, vol. 8137, pp. 244–258. Springer, Heidelberg (2013). https://doi.org/10.1007/978-3-642-40561-7_17
10. Wood, G.: Ethereum: a secure decentralised generalised transaction ledger. Ethereum Proj. Yellow Paper 151, 1–32 (2014)

Compiling Quantitative Type Theory to Michelson for Compile-Time Verification and Run-time Efficiency in Juvix

Christopher Goes[(✉)]

Metastate AG, Zug, Switzerland
cwgoes@metastate.dev

Abstract. Michelson, the stack-based virtual machine of the Tezos blockchain, integrates type-checking for program execution completion but not program correctness. Manual stack tracking is efficient but less ergonomic to write in than a higher-level lambda calculus with variables. Compiling McBride's Quantitative Type Theory to Michelson allows for compile-time verification of semantic predicates and automatic stack optimisation by virtue of the type-theoretic usage accounting system.

Keywords: qtt · Michelson · Tezos · Juvix

1 Introduction and Prior Work

Smart contracts running on distributed ledgers are an archetypal example of a security-critical application, and one where the popular conceit of security-through-obscurity cannot serve since contract code is public, yet results so far from languages such as Solidity [1], the contract language most popular on the Ethereum blockchain [2], have not been promising. Numerous hacks and losses numbering in the hundreds of millions [3,4] have resulted from often quite simple bugs in contracts.

Michelson is the smart contract language of Tezos [5]. The Michelson language is stack-based, with high-level data types & primitive functions. A Michelson program consists of a series of instructions, each of which describes a state transition rule which re-writes the stack. At compile-time, static type-checking ensures that the instruction sequence has the correct stack types by starting with the initial stack type & walking through the start & return stack types of each instruction. An run-time, instructions are executed in sequence according to the rewrite rules, with input values provided by the caller (e.g. as arguments to a smart contract call). Michelson's static type checking provides for verification of executability but not for verification of semantic correctness—it can say nothing about how the start & end storage values of a contract relate to each other or to the arguments provided in the contract call.

© Springer Nature Switzerland AG 2020
T. Margaria and B. Steffen (Eds.): ISoLA 2020, LNCS 12478, pp. 146–160, 2020.
https://doi.org/10.1007/978-3-030-61467-6_10

Due to its stack-based nature, pure Michelson is not particularly ergonomic to develop in—the contract author must mentally track which stack position corresponds to what value at each instruction in the sequence of instructions which together comprise the contract, and limited facilities exist for function abstraction and avoidance of code duplication. For this reason, prior efforts have build intermediate languages for Michelson, such as Albert [6], which allow the programmer to use a higher-level syntax to define functions which operate on named variables, and automatically handle the conversion to Michelson operation sequences by tracking the relationship between variables names & stack positions during compilation. Due to the higher-level abstraction, however, these techniques frequently come at a cost in runtime efficiency, since the automatic translation cannot easily take into account whether a variable used as an argument to a function will need to be used later (and so must be kept around on the stack) or is only used once (and so can be safely discarded), as a programmer might do mentally when writing low-level Michelson by hand.

Prior efforts to bring semantic verification to Michelson, in particular Nomadic Labs' *Mi-Cho-Coq* [7] framework for the verification of Michelson contracts in Coq, have provided verification capabilities by expressing the semantics of Michelson in an existing theorem prover. This allows for precise verification of contract behavioural semantics, but requires that such verification be done at the low-level of Michelson instruction sequences—so if a developer writes a contract in a higher-level language which compiles to Michelson, they will need to perform verification on the translated Michelson output, instead of in the higher-level language itself. Furthermore, the verification must operate at the level of Michelson stack semantics—one cannot, for example, express invariants about the behaviour of functions with named variables written in the higher-level language, but must instead reason about values at particular stack positions. Of course, this has the advantage of guarding against mistakes in the translation from the higher-level language to Michelson, but requires this verification overhead in every analysis performed—ideally, one would express properties of each unique contract in the semantics of the higher-level language, verify (once) the compiler transformation to the semantics of Michelson, and thereby obtain an equivalent level of assurance.

Outside the Tezos ecosystem, Edstrom & Pettersson's prior effort to realise dependently-typed smart contracts [8] achieved high-level semantic verification, but found the output code to be too inefficient to execute. They wrote an Idris [9] backend targeting Ethereum's LLL language [10]. Our approach shares a similar goal of high-level verification, but utilises a bespoke compilation pipeline—their approach handicapped itself by compiling to LLL instead of directly to EVM opcodes, and Idris' lack of linearity meant that they had to perform expensive memory-management operations in output contracts.

Conor McBride's Quantitative Type Theory (QTT) [11] elegantly melds full-spectrum dependent-type semantics with precise usage accounting. In our high-level smart contract language Juvix, we alter QTT to include the semantics of built-in Michelson operations in the higher-level language so that semantic verification can be performed in the language in which the developer is writing, and we utilise the precise usage information to optimise the output code produced by our Michelson compilation pipeline. Juvix also includes a high-level frontend language, datatype system, pattern matching, etc., but those abstractions can be desugared to the core representation, so this paper describes only the core altered quantitative type theory & the variable-usage stack accounting used in the Michelson compilation pipeline. We expect that this fundamental approach could also be reused with other frontends or other stack-based virtual machines without much difficulty.

2 Core Language

Our core syntax & type theory is based on QTT, altered to include additional primitives, and instantiated over the semiring of the natural numbers plus ω for maximum granularity in expressing usage information.

2.1 Preliminaries

A *semiring* R is a set R with binary operations $+$ (addition) and $\cdot$ (multiplication), such that $(R, +)$ is a commutative monoid with identity 0, $(R, \cdot)$ is a monoid with identity 1, multiplication left and right distribute over addition, and multiplication by 0 annihilates R.

The core type theory must be instantiated over a particular semiring. Choices include the boolean semiring $(0, 1)$, the zero-one-many semiring $(0, 1, \omega)$, and the natural numbers with addition and multiplication.

We instantiate the type theory over the semiring of natural numbers plus ω, which is the most expressive option—terms can be 0-usage ("contemplated"), n-usage ("computed n times"), or ω-usage ("computed any number of times").

Let S be a set of sorts (i, j, k) with a total order.

Let K be the set of primitive types, C be the set of primitive constants, and $\overset{.}{:}$ be the typing relation between primitive constants and primitive types, which must assign to each primitive constant a unique primitive type and usage. When instantiated for compiling to Michelson, these sets are the sets of built-in types & values in the Michelson language [12].

Let F be the set of primitive functions, where each f is related to a function type, including an argument usage annotation, by the $\overset{.}{:}$ relation and endowed with a reduction operation $\overset{\rightarrow}{} f$, which provided an argument of the function input type computes an argument of the function output type. When instantiated for compiling to Michelson, this set is the set of built-in operations in the Michelson language, e.g. ADD, MUL, NOT, etc., endowed with appropriate types.

Primitive types, primitive constants, and primitive functions are threaded-through to the untyped lambda calculus to which the core language is erased, so they must be directly supported by the low-level execution model, in this case Michelson. The core type theory and subsequent compilation pathways are parameterised over K, C, F, $\overset{.}{:}$, and the reduction operations $\overset{\rightarrow}{} f$, which are assumed to be available as implicit parameters.

2.2   Syntax

Our syntax is inspired by the bidirectional syntax of Conor McBride in I Got Plenty o' Nuttin' [13].

Let R, S, T, s, t be types & terms and d, e, f be eliminations, where types can be synthesised for eliminations but must be specified in advance for terms (Fig. 1).

$$
\begin{array}{lll}
R, S, T, s, t ::= & *_i & \text{sort } i \\
& \mid \kappa \in K & \text{primitive type} \\
& \mid (x \overset{\pi}{:} S) \to T & \text{function type} \\
& \mid (x \overset{\pi}{:} S) \otimes T & \text{dependent multiplicative conjunction type} \\
& \mid \lambda x.t & \text{abstraction} \\
& \mid e & \text{elimination}
\end{array}
$$

$$
\begin{array}{lll}
d, e, f ::= & x & \text{variable} \\
& \mid c \in C & \text{primitive constant} \\
& \mid f \in F & \text{primitive function} \\
& \mid f s & \text{application} \\
& \mid (s, t) & \text{multiplicative conjunction} \\
& \mid let\ (x, y) = d\ in\ e & \text{dependent multiplicative conjunction pattern match} \\
& \mid s \overset{\pi}{:} S & \text{type \& usage annotation}
\end{array}
$$

Fig. 1. Core syntax

Sorts $*_i$ are explicitly levelled. Dependent function types, dependent conjunction types, and type annotations include a usage annotation π.

Judgements have the following form:

$$
x_1 \overset{\rho_1}{:} S_1, \ldots, x_n \overset{\rho_n}{:} S_n \vdash M \overset{\sigma}{:} T
$$

where $\rho_1 \ldots \rho_n$ are elements of the semiring and σ is either the 0 or 1 of the semiring.

Further define the syntactic categories of usages ρ, π and precontexts Γ:

$$
\rho, \pi \in R
$$

$$
\Gamma := \diamond \mid \Gamma, x \overset{\rho}{:} S
$$

The symbol $\diamond$ denotes the empty precontext.

Precontexts contain usage annotations ρ on constituent variables. Scaling a precontext, $\pi\Gamma$, is defined as follows:

$$\pi(\diamond) = \diamond$$

$$\pi(\Gamma, x \overset{\rho}{:} S) = \pi\Gamma, x \overset{\pi\rho}{:} S$$

Usage annotations in types are not affected.

By the definition of a semiring, 0Γ sets all usage annotations to 0.

Addition of two precontexts $\Gamma_1 + \Gamma_2$ is defined only when $0\Gamma_1 = 0\Gamma_2$:

$$\diamond + \diamond = \diamond$$

$$(\Gamma_1, x \overset{\rho_1}{:} S) + (\Gamma_2, x \overset{\rho_2}{:} S) = (\Gamma_1 + \Gamma_2), x \overset{\rho_1+\rho_2}{:} S$$

Contexts are identified within precontexts by the judgement $\Gamma \vdash$, defined by the following rules:

$$\frac{}{\diamond \vdash} \; \text{Emp}$$

$$\frac{\Gamma \vdash \qquad 0\Gamma \vdash S}{\Gamma, x \overset{\rho}{:} S \vdash} \; \text{Ext}$$

$0\Gamma \vdash S$ indicates that S is well-formed as a type in the context of 0Γ. Emp, for "empty", builds the empty context, and Ext, for "extend", extends a context Γ with a new variable x of type S and usage annotation ρ. All type formation rules yield judgements where all usage annotations in Γ are 0—that is to say, type formation requires no computational resources).

Term judgements have the form:

$$\Gamma \vdash M \overset{\sigma}{:} S$$

where $\sigma \in 0, 1$.

Primitive constant term judgements have the form:

$$\vdash M \overset{\gamma}{:} S$$

where γ is any element in the semiring.

A judgement with $\sigma = 0$ constructs a term with no computational content, while a judgement with $\sigma = 1$ constructs a term which will be computed with.

For example, consider the following judgement:

$$n \overset{0}{:} Nat, x \overset{1}{:} Fin(n) \vdash x \overset{\sigma}{:} Fin(n)$$

When $\sigma = 0$, the judgement expresses that the term can be typed:

$$n \overset{0}{:} Nat, x \overset{1}{:} Fin(n) \vdash x \overset{0}{:} Fin(n)$$

Because the final colon is annotated to zero, this represents contemplation, not computation. When type checking, n and x can appear arbitrary times. Computational judgement:

$$n \overset{0}{:} Nat, x \overset{1}{:} Fin(n) \vdash x \overset{1}{:} Fin(n)$$

Because the final colon is annotated to one, during computation, n is used exactly 0 times, x is used exactly one time. x can also be annotated as ω, indicating that it can be used (computed with) an arbitrary number of times.

2.3 Typing Rules

2.3.1 Universe (Set Type)

Let S be a set of sorts i, j, k with a total order.

2.3.1.1 Formation Rule

$$\frac{0\Gamma \vdash \qquad i < j}{0\Gamma \vdash *_i \overset{0}{:} *_j} \ *$$

2.3.1.2 Introduction Rule

$$\frac{0\Gamma \vdash V \overset{0}{:} *_i \qquad 0\Gamma, x \overset{0}{:} V \vdash R \overset{0}{:} *_i}{\Gamma \vdash (x \overset{\pi}{:} V) \to R \overset{0}{:} *_i} \ \text{*-Pi}$$

Sorts can be contemplated (typed in the $\sigma = 0$ fragment) only.

2.3.2 Primitive Constants

2.3.2.1 Formation and Introduction Rule

$$\frac{c \in C \qquad \kappa \in K \qquad \dot{c}{:}(\gamma, \kappa)}{\vdash c \overset{\gamma}{:} \kappa} \ Prim - Const$$

Primitive constants are typed according to the primitive typing relation, and they can be produced in any computational quantity wherever desired.

2.3.3 Primitive Functions

2.3.3.1 Formation and Introduction Rule

$$\frac{f \in F \qquad f : (\gamma, (x \overset{\pi}{:} S) \to T)}{\vdash f \overset{\gamma}{:} (x \overset{\pi}{:} S) \to T} \ \text{Prim-Fn}$$

Primitive functions are typed according to the primitive typing relation, and they can be produced in any computational quantity wherever desired. Primitive functions can be dependently-typed—in the case of Michelson, polymorphic primitives such as ADD will be represented in the core language as dependently typed, i.e. `add : (t: Type) -> t -> t`, where `t` is restricted to the primitive types for which Michelson supports ADD.

2.3.3.2 Elimination Rule
Primitive functions use the same elimination rule as native lambda abstractions.

2.3.4 Dependent Function Types
Function types $(x \overset{\pi}{:} S) \to T$ record usage of the argument.

2.3.4.1 Formation Rule

$$\frac{0\Gamma \vdash S \qquad 0\Gamma, x \overset{0}{:} S \vdash T}{0\Gamma \vdash (x \overset{\pi}{:} S) \to T} \; \text{Pi}$$

2.3.4.2 Introduction Rule

$$\frac{\Gamma, x \overset{\sigma\pi}{:} S \vdash M \overset{\sigma}{:} T}{\Gamma \vdash \lambda x.M \overset{\sigma}{:} (x \overset{\pi}{:} S) \to T} \; \text{Lam}$$

The usage annotation π is not used in judgement of whether T is a well-formed type. It is used in the introduction and elimination rules to track how x is used, and how to multiply the resources required for the argument, respectively:

2.3.4.3 Elimination Rule

$$\frac{\Gamma_1 \vdash M \overset{\sigma}{:} (x \overset{\pi}{:} S) \to T \qquad \Gamma_2 \vdash N \overset{\sigma'}{:} S \qquad 0\Gamma_1 = 0\Gamma_2 \qquad \sigma' = 0 \Leftrightarrow (\pi = 0 \vee \sigma = 0)}{\Gamma_1 + \pi\Gamma_2 \vdash MN \overset{\sigma}{:} T[x := N]} \; \text{App}$$

$0\Gamma_1 = 0\Gamma_2$ means that Γ_1 and Γ_2 have the same variables with the same types.

In the introduction rule, the abstracted variable x has usage $\sigma\pi$ so that non-computational production requires no computational input.

In the elimination rule, the resources required by the function and its argument, scaled to the amount required by the function, are summed.

The function argument N may be judged in the 0-use fragment of the system if and only if we are already in the 0-use fragment $(\sigma = 0)$ or the function will not use the argument $(\pi = 0)$.

2.3.5 Dependent Multiplicative Conjunction (Tensor Product)
Multiplicative conjunctions, colloquially referred to as "pair" type, can be dependent.

2.3.5.1 Formation Rule

$$\frac{0\Gamma \vdash A \qquad 0\Gamma, x \overset{0}{:} S \vdash T}{0\Gamma \vdash (x \overset{\pi}{:} S) \otimes T} \; \otimes$$

Type formation does not require any resources.

2.3.5.2 Introduction Rule

$$\frac{\Gamma_1 \vdash M \overset{\sigma}{:} S \qquad \Gamma_2 \vdash N \overset{\sigma}{:} T[x := M] \qquad 0\Gamma_1 = 0\Gamma_2}{\pi\Gamma_1 + \Gamma_2 \vdash (M, N) \overset{\sigma}{:} (x \overset{\pi}{:} S) \otimes T}$$

This is similar to the introduction rule for dependent function types above.

2.3.5.3 Elimination Rules

$$\frac{\Gamma \vdash M \overset{0}{:} (x \overset{\pi}{:} S) \otimes T}{\Gamma \vdash fst_\otimes M \overset{0}{:} S}$$

$$\frac{\Gamma \vdash M \overset{0}{:} (x \overset{\pi}{:} S) \otimes T}{\Gamma \vdash snd_\otimes M \overset{0}{:} T[x := fst_\otimes(M)]}$$

Under the erased ($\sigma = 0$) part of the theory, projection operators can be used as normal.

$$\frac{0\Gamma_1, z \overset{0}{:} (x \overset{\pi}{:} S) \otimes T \vdash U \quad \Gamma_1 \vdash M \overset{\sigma}{:} (x \overset{\pi}{:} S) \otimes T \quad \Gamma_2, x \overset{\sigma\pi}{:} S, y \overset{\sigma}{:} T \vdash N \overset{\sigma}{:} U[z := (x, y)] \quad 0\Gamma_1 = 0\Gamma_2}{\Gamma_1 + \Gamma_2 \vdash let\ (x, y) = M\ in\ N \overset{\sigma}{:} U[z := M]}\ \otimes\ \text{Elim}$$

Under the resourceful part, both elements of the conjunction must be matched and consumed.

2.3.6   Variable and Conversion Rules

The variable rule selects an individual variable, type, and usage annotation from the context:

$$\frac{\vdash 0\Gamma, x \overset{\sigma}{:} S, 0\Gamma'}{0\Gamma, x \overset{\sigma}{:} S, 0\Gamma' \vdash x \overset{\sigma}{:} S}\ \text{Var}$$

The conversion rule allows conversion between judgmentally equal types:

$$\frac{\Gamma \vdash M \overset{\sigma}{:} S \qquad 0\Gamma \vdash S \equiv T}{\Gamma \vdash M \overset{\sigma}{:} T}\ \text{Conv}$$

Note that type equality is judged in a context with no resources.

2.3.7   Equality Judgements

Types are judgmentally equal under beta reduction:

$$\frac{\Gamma \vdash S \qquad \Gamma \vdash T \qquad S \to_\beta T}{\Gamma \vdash S \equiv T}\ \equiv\text{-Type}$$

Terms with the same type are judgmentally equal under beta reduction:

$$\frac{\Gamma \vdash M \overset{\sigma}{:} S \qquad \Gamma \vdash N \overset{\sigma}{:} S \qquad M \to_\beta N}{\Gamma \vdash M \equiv N \overset{\sigma}{:} S}\ \equiv\text{-Term}$$

As primitive types, values, and functions are included in the type theory, proofs about behavioural semantics can then be created in the usual fashion.

2.4   Erasure

Terms which are merely contemplated (in the $\sigma = 0$ fragment) are erased at compile-time, and thereby incur no runtime cost.

Define the core erasure operator $\blacktriangleright$.

Erasure judgements take the form $\Gamma \vdash t \overset{\sigma}{:} S \; \blacktriangleright \; u$ with $t \overset{\sigma}{:} S$ a core judgement and u an erased core term.

Computationally relevant terms are preserved, while terms which are only contemplated are erased.

Note that $\sigma / = 0$ must hold, as the erasure of a computationally irrelevant term is nothing.

2.4.1   Primitives and Lambda Terms

$$\frac{c \overset{\sigma}{:} S \qquad \sigma/ = 0}{c \overset{\sigma}{:} S \; \blacktriangleright \; c} \; \text{Prim-Const-Erase-+}$$

$$\frac{f \overset{\sigma}{:} S \qquad \sigma/ = 0}{f \overset{\sigma}{:} S \; \blacktriangleright \; f} \; \text{Prim-Fun-Erase-+}$$

$$\frac{\vdash 0\Gamma, x \overset{\sigma}{:} S, 0\Gamma' \qquad \sigma/ = 0}{0\Gamma, x \overset{\sigma}{:} S, 0\Gamma' \vdash x \overset{\sigma}{:} S \; \blacktriangleright \; x} \; \text{Var-Erase-+}$$

$$\frac{t \overset{\sigma}{:} T \blacktriangleright u \qquad \sigma\pi = 0}{\lambda x.t : (x \overset{\pi}{:} S) \to T \blacktriangleright u} \; \text{Lam-Erase-0}$$

$$\frac{t \overset{\sigma}{:} T \blacktriangleright u \qquad \sigma\pi/ = 0}{\lambda x.t : (x \overset{\pi}{:} S) \to T \blacktriangleright \lambda x.u} \; \text{Lam-Erase-+}$$

$$\frac{\Gamma_1 \vdash M \overset{\sigma}{:} (x \overset{\pi}{:} S) \to T \blacktriangleright u \qquad \Gamma_2 \vdash N \overset{0}{:} S \qquad \sigma\pi = 0}{\Gamma_1 \vdash MN \overset{\sigma}{:} T[x := N] \blacktriangleright u} \; \text{App-Erase-0}$$

$$\frac{\Gamma_1 \vdash M \overset{\sigma}{:} (x \overset{\pi}{:} S) \to T \blacktriangleright u \qquad \Gamma_2 \vdash N \overset{\sigma\pi}{:} S \blacktriangleright v \qquad \sigma\pi/ = 0}{\Gamma_1 + \Gamma_2 \vdash MN \overset{\sigma}{:} T[x := N] \blacktriangleright u\,v} \; \text{App-Erase-+}$$

$$\frac{\Gamma \vdash s \overset{\pi}{:} S \qquad s \; \blacktriangleright \; u \qquad \pi/ = 0}{\Gamma \vdash s \overset{\pi}{:} S \; \blacktriangleright \; u} \; \text{Ann-Erase-+}$$

In the *Lam-Erase-0* rule, the variable x bound in t will not occur in the corresponding u, since it is bound with usage 0, with which it will remain regardless of how the context splits, so the rule *Var-Erase-+* cannot consume it.

2.4.2   Multiplicative Conjunction

2.4.2.1 Constructor

$$\frac{\Gamma \vdash (s,t) \overset{\sigma}{:} (x \overset{\pi}{:} S) \otimes T \qquad \sigma/ = 0 \qquad \pi/ = 0 \qquad s \blacktriangleright u \qquad t \blacktriangleright v}{\Gamma \vdash (s,t) \overset{\sigma}{:} (x \overset{\pi}{:} S) \otimes T \blacktriangleright (u,v)} \otimes\text{-Erase-}{+}{+}$$

If the first element of the pair is used, the constructor is erased to the untyped constructor.

$$\frac{\Gamma \vdash (s,t) \overset{\sigma}{:} (x \overset{\pi}{:} S) \otimes T \qquad \sigma/ = 0 \qquad \pi = 0 \qquad t \blacktriangleright v}{\Gamma \vdash (s,t) \overset{\sigma}{:} (x \overset{\pi}{:} S) \otimes T \blacktriangleright v} \otimes\text{-Erase-}0{+}$$

If the first element of the pair is not used, the constructor is erased completely.

2.4.2.2 Destructor

$$\frac{\Gamma_1 \vdash s \overset{\sigma}{:} (x \overset{\pi}{:} S) \otimes T \quad \Gamma_1 + \Gamma_2 \vdash let\ (x,y) = s\ in\ t \overset{\sigma'}{:} M[z := (x,y)] \quad \sigma, \sigma'/ = 0 \quad s \blacktriangleright u \quad t \blacktriangleright v}{\Gamma_1 + \Gamma_2 \vdash let\ (x,y) = s\ in\ t \overset{\sigma'}{:} M[z := (x,y)] \blacktriangleright let\ (x,y) = u\ in\ v} \text{let-Erase-}{+}{+}$$

If the pair is used, the destructor is erased to the untyped destructor.

$$\frac{\Gamma_1 \vdash s \overset{\sigma}{:} (x \overset{\pi}{:} S) \otimes T \quad \Gamma_1 + \Gamma_2 \vdash let\ (x,y) = s\ in\ t \overset{\sigma'}{:} M[z := (x,y)] \quad \sigma = 0 \wedge \sigma'/ = 0 \quad t \blacktriangleright v}{\Gamma_1 + \Gamma_2 \vdash let\ (x,y) = s\ in\ t \overset{\sigma'}{:} M[z := (x,y)] \blacktriangleright v} \text{let-Erase-}0{+}$$

If the pair is not used, the destructor is erased completely.

2.5   Reduction Semantics

Contraction is $(\lambda x.t : (\pi x : S) \to T)\ s \leadsto_\beta (t : T)[x := s : S]$.

De-annotation is $(t : T) \leadsto_\nu t$.

The reflexive transitive closure of $\leadsto_\beta$ and $\leadsto_\nu$ yields beta reduction $\to_\beta$ as usual.

2.5.1   Parallel-Step Reduction

Let parallel reduction be $\triangleright$, operating on usage-erased terms, by mutual induction.

2.5.1.1 Basic Lambda Calculus

$$\frac{}{*_i \vartriangleright *_i}$$

$$\frac{}{x \vartriangleright x}$$

$$\frac{S \vartriangleright S' \qquad T \vartriangleright T'}{(x : S) \to T \vartriangleright (x : S') \to T'}$$

$$\frac{t \vartriangleright t'}{\lambda x.t \vartriangleright \lambda x.t'}$$

$$\frac{f \vartriangleright f' \qquad s \vartriangleright s'}{fs \vartriangleright f's'}$$

$$\frac{t \vartriangleright t' \qquad T \vartriangleright T'}{t : T \vartriangleright t' : T'}$$

$$\frac{t \vartriangleright t' \qquad S \vartriangleright S' \qquad T \vartriangleright T' \qquad s \vartriangleright s'}{(\lambda x.t : (x : S) \to T)s \vartriangleright (t' : T')[x := s' : S']}$$

2.5.1.2 Multiplicative Conjunction

$$\frac{S \vartriangleright S' \qquad T \vartriangleright T'}{(x : S) \otimes T \vartriangleright (x : S') \otimes T'}$$

$$\frac{s \vartriangleright s' \qquad t \vartriangleright t'}{(s,t) \vartriangleright (s',t')}$$

$$\frac{z \vartriangleright (m,n) \qquad m \vartriangleright m' \qquad n \vartriangleright n' \qquad s \vartriangleright s'}{let \ (x,y) \ = \ z \ in \ s \vartriangleright s'[x := m', y := n']}$$

Reduction takes place inside a multiplicative conjunction.

2.5.1.3 Primitives

$$\frac{\kappa \in K}{\kappa \vartriangleright \kappa}$$

$$\frac{c \in C}{c \vartriangleright c}$$

Primitive types and primitive constants reduce to themselves.

$$\frac{f \in F \qquad x \vartriangleright x' \qquad x' \to_f y}{fx \vartriangleright y}$$

Primitive functions reduce according to the reduction operation defined for the function according to the Michelson semantics [12].

2.6   Examples

2.6.1   SKI Combinators

2.6.1.1 S Combinator The dependent S ("substitution") combinator can be typed as (Fig. 2):

$$\vdash \lambda t1.\lambda t2.\lambda t3.\lambda x.\lambda y.\lambda z.xz(yz) \overset{1}{:} (x \overset{1}{:} ((a \overset{1}{:} t1) \to (b \overset{1}{:} t2) \to t3)) \to (y \overset{1}{:} ((a \overset{1}{:} t1) \to t2)) \to (z \overset{2}{:} t1) \to t3$$

Fig. 2. S combinator

This will also typecheck if the x, y, and z argument usages are replaced with ω (instead of 1 and 2).

2.6.1.2 K Combinator The dependent K ("constant") combinator can be typed as (Fig. 3):

$$\vdash \lambda t1.\lambda t2.\lambda x.\lambda y.x \overset{1}{:} (t1 \overset{0}{:} *_i) \to (t2 \overset{0}{:} *_i) \to (x \overset{1}{:} t1) \to (y \overset{0}{:} t2) \to t1$$

Fig. 3. K combinator

This will also typecheck if the x and y argument usages are replaced with ω (instead of 1 and 0).

2.6.1.3 I Combinator The dependent I ("identity") combinator can be typed as (Fig. 4):

$$\vdash \lambda t.\lambda x.(x \overset{1}{:} t) \overset{1}{:} (t \overset{0}{:} *_i) \to (x \overset{1}{:} t) \to t$$

Fig. 4. I combinator

This will also typecheck if the x argument usage is replaced with ω (instead of 1).

2.6.2   Church-Encoded Natural Numbers

The dependent Church-encoded natural n, where the successor function s is applied n times, can be typed as (Fig. 5):

$$\vdash \lambda t.\lambda s.z.s...sz \overset{1}{:} (s \overset{n}{:} ((a \overset{1}{:} t) \to t)) \to (z \overset{1}{:} t) \to t.$$

Fig. 5. Church-encode n

This will also typecheck if the s argument usage is replaced with ω (instead of n for some specific n).

3   Towards Compilation to Michelson

The erased core language can be compiled to Michelson by fairly standard procedure, with accommodations for the particular cost model of Michelson—the main addition is the more efficient stack manipulation enabled by usage accounting.

3.1   Stack Tracking

As is standard for compilation of the lambda calculus to stack machines, we track a virtual symbolic stack which maps variable names to stack positions. When a function call is compiled, such as:

```
let f x y = x * y
```

x and y are fetched from their positions in the stack and the body of f is inlined (suppose x is at stack position 3 and y is at stack position 4:

```
{DUG 3; DUP; DIG 4; DUG 5; DUP; DIG 6; MUL}
```

Lambdas in Michelson are quite expensive—each can take only one argument, so multiple-argument functions compiled to lambdas must tuple their arguments before calling the function, and the function body must un-tuple them—so we inline aggressively and also track virtual closures on the stack to avoid compiling to LAMBDA whenever possible. All of this is standard fare.

3.2   Usage Accounting

Consider the following indicative example—compilation of the identity function:

```
let f x = x
```

In a normal compilation of the lambda calculus to a stack machine without quantitative type theory or any notion of linearity, x must be kept on the stack in case it is used elsewhere and only dropped after the computation is complete, so f must be compiled to:

```
{DUG 5; DUP; DIG 6}
```

With quantitative type theory, the compiler can lookup the usage annotation for x, and if x is only used once, then x can simply be moved from lower in the stack instead:

```
{DUG 5}
```

This technique easily generalises to multi-argument functions and any usage on the semiring—in cases of usage ω, the non-quantitative behaviour is preserved, and x is instead dropped after the computation is complete.

3.3   Usage Propagation

Consider the following function which uses its argument twice:

```
let f x = x * x
```

Suppose that x is five slots down in the stack, with a total usage of 3. A naive implementation without lookup caching might fetch x twice:

```
{DUG 5; DUP; DIG 6; DUG 6; DUP; DIG 7; MUL}
```

Or, alternatively, with lookup caching but without linearity, x might be duplicated more than necessary (as each lookup must treat the variable as possibly being used elsewhere):

```
{DUG 5; DUP; DIG 6; DUP; DUP; DIG 2; MUL; DIP {DROP}}
```

Instead, with usage annotations, we can propagate two usages of x upwards immediately and avoid both the double-fetch and the unnecessary duplication/cleanup:

```
{DUG 5; DUP; DIG 6; DUP; MUL}
```

4   Future Work

4.1   Improved Usage Accounting with ANF

As detailed in a blog post [14], we plan to add an administrative normal form transformation, such that all functions take primitives—for example, ANF would transform

```
f a (x + y) b
```

into

```
let xy0 = x + y in f a xy0 b
```

This would allow all usages of variables to be moved forward to the top of the stack when used and remaining uses to be moved back, instead of moving all usages but one forward, which is currently required.

4.2   First-Class Usages

Work is in progress to add dependent usages [15], where terms can be lifted into usages and usages can be converted to terms, such that usages can depend on terms in the usual dependent-type-theory sense. This will allow more precise usage accounting in cases where an annotation of ω would otherwise be required, such as where the usage of one argument to a function depends on the value of another argument, although it requires more complex accounting in the compiler.

Acknowledgements. This paper describes part of the ongoing research work being undertaken to develop the Juvix smart contract language [16,17] by the Juvix team at Metastate, including Marty Stumpf, Jeremy Ornelas, Andy Morris, and April Goncalves. Thanks to an anonymous reviewer for comments and suggestions.

References

1. S. Developers, Solidity: An object-oriented, high-level language for implementing smart contracts. https://solidity.readthedocs.io/en/v0.6.8/
2. Wood, G.: Ethereum: A secure decentralised generalised transaction ledger. https://gavwood.com/paper.pdf
3. Parity Technologies: A postmortem on the parity multi-sig library self-destruct. https://www.parity.io/a-postmortem-on-the-parity-multi-sig-library-self-destruct/
4. 0x Core Team, "Post-mortem: 0x v2.0 exchange vulnerability." https://blog.0xproject.com/post-mortem-0x-v2-0-exchange-vulnerability-763015399578
5. Goodman, L.M.: Tezos - a self-amending crypto-ledger, September 2014. https://tezos.com/static/white_paper-2dc8c02267a8fb86bd67a108199441bf.pdf
6. Bernardo, B., Cauderlier, R., Pesin, B., Tesson, J.: Albert, an intermediate smart-contract language for the tezos blockchain (2020). https://arxiv.org/abs/2001.02630
7. Bernardo, B., Cauderlier, R., Hu, Z., Pesin, B., Tesson, J.: Mi-cho-coq, a framework for certifying tezos smart contracts. https://arxiv.org/abs/1909.08671 (2019)
8. Pettersson, J.: Safer smart contracts through type-driven development. https://publications.lib.chalmers.se/records/fulltext/234939/234939.pdf
9. Brady, E.: IDRIS - systems programming meets full dependent types. In: PLPV 2011 - Proceedings of the 5th ACM Workshop on Programming Languages Meets Program Verification, pp. 43–54 (2011)
10. Edgington, B.: Ethereum lisp like language. https://lll-docs.readthedocs.io/en/latest/lll_introduction.html
11. Atkey, R.: Syntax and semantics of quantitative type theory. In: Proceedings of the 33rd Annual ACM/IEEE Symposium on Logic in Computer Science, pp. 56–65 (2018)
12. N. Labs: Michelson: The language of smart contracts in tezos. https://tezos.gitlab.io/whitedoc/michelson.html
13. McBride, C.: I got plenty o' Nuttin'. In: Lindley, S., McBride, C., Trinder, P., Sannella, D. (eds.) A List of Successes That Can Change the World. LNCS, vol. 9600, pp. 207–233. Springer, Cham (2016). https://doi.org/10.1007/978-3-319-30936-1_12
14. Ornelas, J.: Compiling Juvix to Michelson, May 2020. https://research.metastate.dev/juvix-compiling-juvix-to-michelson/
15. Goes, C., Morris, A.: Usage polymorphism and dependent usages in Juvix, September 2019. https://github.com/cryptiumlabs/juvix/issues/87
16. Goes, C.: The why of Juvix: on the design of smart contract languages, January 2020. https://research.metastate.dev/the-why-of-juvix-part-1-on-the-design-of-smart-contract-languages/
17. Goes, C.: The why of Juvix: Ingredients & architecture, January 2020. https://research.metastate.dev/the-why-of-juvix-ingredients-architecture/

Efficient Static Analysis of Marlowe Contracts

Pablo Lamela Seijas[1](✉)[iD], David Smith[1][iD], and Simon Thompson[1,2][iD]

[1] IOHK, Wan Chai, Hong Kong
{pablo.lamela,simon.thompson}@iohk.io, david.smith@tweag.io
[2] School of Computing, University of Kent, Canterbury, UK
s.j.thompson@kent.ac.uk

Abstract. SMT solvers can verify properties automatically and efficiently, and they offer increasing flexibility on the ways those properties can be described. But it is hard to predict how those ways of describing the properties affect the computational cost of verifying them.

In this paper, we discuss what we learned while implementing and optimising the static analysis for Marlowe, a domain specific language for self-enforcing financial smart-contracts that can be deployed on a blockchain.

1 Introduction

Thanks to static analysis, we can automatically check beforehand whether any payments promised by a Marlowe [12,13] contract can be fulfilled in every possible execution of the contract. If a Marlowe contract has passed the static analysis, we will have a very high assurance that whenever the contract says it will make a payment, the contract will indeed have enough money available.

Marlowe's static analysis relies on SMT solvers, which are able to check efficiently whether a set of constraints is satisfiable. The main property for us is whether a contract will have enough money for all payments to be made in full.

Thanks to state of the art libraries like SBV [7], we can describe those constraints in a high level language. In the case of SBV, we can write properties as Haskell functions, with few restrictions on how those functions are implemented; SBV automatically translates those functions to SMTLib format [3], a language many SMT solvers understand. However, high level abstractions often have a tradeoff with efficiency, and static analysis can become very expensive computationally if implemented naïvely, because it is NP-complete in the general case.

This paper contributes a number of approaches that can be used when optimising static analysis, with examples extracted from a case-study where we applied these approaches. Our approach aims to ensure correctness of the optimisations by combining the use of property-based testing and with verification in an automated theorem prover to establish properties of the optimisations. We also present empirical data that measures the effect of some of the optimisations on the implementation of our Marlowe case-study.

© Springer Nature Switzerland AG 2020
T. Margaria and B. Steffen (Eds.): ISoLA 2020, LNCS 12478, pp. 161–177, 2020.
https://doi.org/10.1007/978-3-030-61467-6_11

The techniques described helped us reduce the analysis time of an implementation that followed the semantics closely and took a couple of minutes to analyse contracts with a source code of a few kilobytes, to one where the same contract takes less than a second to analyse, and where a four-person crowdfunding contract that fully expanded occupies about 19 MB, can be analysed in around 10 min. We have classified optimisation techniques as lightweight and heavyweight.

Lightweight modifications are local and can be done without fundamentally changing the implementation. We consider three main ideas:

- **Removing unnecessary parts from the analysis.** If they do not affect the property that is being verified then we can just remove them.
- **Avoiding high level abstractions.** High level abstractions aid reasoning and avoid errors, but also introduce complexity that may not be necessary.
- **Reducing the search space by normalising parameters.** If there are several ways of representing some inputs, and the different representations have no impact on the analysis, we can remove all but one for analysis.

Heavyweight modifications are more fundamental approaches that require considerable changes to the structure of the implementation. But these optimisations can also translate in important reductions to execution time and memory usage, as shown by the experiments we report in Sect. 6. We consider two main ideas:

- **Reducing the search space by using normalised execution paths relevant to the property.** Instead of using the search space to model inputs, we use it to model possible executions, and we only represent each equivalence class of executions once, i.e: we represent them in a normal form.
- **Minimizing the representation of inputs and outputs.** We encode inputs and outputs as concisely as possible, discarding inferable information.

In the following sections, we introduce the semantics of Marlowe as a case study (Sect. 2), and we cover a general approach to static analysis (Sect. 3). We then, in Sect. 4 explore in Section the lightweight and heavyweight optimisation techniques in more detail, and illustrate them with examples of how they apply to Marlowe static analysis. In Sect. 5, we illustrate the use of property based testing on the implementation with heavyweight optimisations. Finally, we present empirical results that show the effect of heavyweight optimisations on the execution time and memory usage of Marlowe's static analysis (Sect. 6).

2   Marlowe Design and Semantics

Firstly, we introduce the semantics of Marlowe, the guarantees that are offered implicitly by the semantics, and how the design choices facilitate static analysis and make it decidable. A more detailed explanation can be found in [12].

2.1   Structure of Marlowe Contracts

The Marlowe language is realised as a set of mutually recursive Haskell data types. Marlowe contracts regulate interactions between a finite number of participants, determined before the contract is deployed.

Marlowe contracts are able to receive payments, store money and tokens, ask for input from its participants, and redistribute stored money and tokens among participants. A contract determines when and which of these actions may be carried out. Participants may correspond to either individual public keys or to tokens (Roles). In turn, Roles may be controlled by other contracts.

The main data type in Marlowe is called Contract, and it represents the logic and actions that the contract allows or enforces. The outmost constructs of the Contract represent the actions that will be enforced first and, as those constructs become enforced, the Contract will evolve into one of its continuations (subcontracts), and the process will continue until only the construct Close remains.

There are 5 constructs of type Contract:

- Close – signals the end of the life of a contract. Once it is reached, all the money and tokens stored in the accounts of the contract will be refunded to the owner of each of the respective accounts.
- If – immediately decides how the contract must continue from between two possibilities, depending on a given Boolean condition that we call an Observation. An Observation may depend on previous choices by participants, on amounts of money and tokens in the contract, or other factors.
- Let – immediately stores a Value for later use. Expressions of type Value in Marlowe are evaluated to integer values and they depend on information available to the contract at the time of evaluation. For example, a Let construct record the amount of money in an account at a point in time.
- When – waits for an external input. The When construct also specifies a timeout slot[1]: after this slot has been reached, the When construct expires, and no longer accepts any input. There are three kinds of input:
  - Deposit – Waits for a participant to deposit an amount of money or tokens (specified as a Value) in an account of the contract.
  - Choice – Waits for a participant to make a choice. A choice is represented as an integer number from a set specified by the contract.
  - Notify – Waits for an Observation to be true. Because contracts are reactive (they cannot initiate transactions), it is necessary for an external actor (not necessarily a participant) to Notify the contract.
- Pay – immediately makes a payment between accounts of the contract, or from an account of the contract to a given participant. The amount transferred is specified as a Value.

2.2   Semantics

As we mentioned in the previous section, Marlowe contracts are passive: their code is executed as part of the validation of transactions that are submitted

---

[1] Slots are blockchain's proxy for time, they are added to the blockchain periodically.

to the blockchain. Transactions need to be submitted by participants or their representatives (e.g. user wallets) and validation is atomic and deterministic.

Each transaction may include a list of inputs, a set of signatures, a slot interval, a set of input UTxOs (incoming money and tokens), and a set of outputs (outgoing money and tokens). We use a slot interval because it is very difficult to know the exact slot in which the transaction will be included in practice. For a transaction to be valid in Marlowe, the transaction must have the same effect for every slot within that slot interval (be deterministic). For example, if a transaction has a minimum slot number lower than timeout, and a maximum slot that is greater, then the transaction will fail with the error AmbiguousSlotInterval.

A key aspect of the Marlowe semantics is that it checks that a particular transaction is valid given the current state and contract. Because transactions are deterministic, there should be no reason why someone accidentally sends a transaction that is invalid for a given State and Contract, since it will only result in a cost to that participant. However, it is still possible that, due to a race condition, a participant will send a transaction that no longer applies to a running Contract and State, but such a transaction would simply be ignored by the blockchain.

The type signature of the transaction validation function is:

```
computeTransaction :: TransactionInput -> State -> Contract
                      -> TransactionOutput
```

This function can be factored into four main functions:

- reduceContractStep - this function executes the topmost construct that does not require an input to be executed (i.e: anything but a When that has not expired or a Close when accounts are empty). It only simplifies the When construct if it has expired (i.e. the timeout specified in the When is less than or equal to the minimum slot number). In the case of the Close contract, it only refunds one of the accounts at each invocation.
- reduceContractUntilQuiescent - this function calls reduceContractStep repeatedly until it has no further effect,
- applyInput - this function processes one single input. The topmost construct must be a When that is expecting that particular input and has not expired.
- applyAllInputs - this function processes a list of inputs. It calls applyInput for each of the inputs in the list, and calls reduceContractUntilQuiescent before and after every call to applyInput.

The State stores information about the amount of money and tokens in the contract at a given time, together with the choices made, Let bindings made, and a lower bound for the current slot:

```
data State = State { accounts    :: Map AccountId Money
                   , choices     :: Map ChoiceId ChosenNum
                   , boundValues :: Map ValueId Integer
                   , minSlot     :: Slot }
```

2.3   Extra Considerations

Many of the design decisions behind Marlowe have been made with the aim of preventing potential errors. For example:

- **Classification of money and tokens into accounts** separates concerns. A Marlowe contract will never spend more money or tokens than there are in an account, even if there is more available in the contract. But a payment for more than there is will not fail, it will pay as much as is available, in order to remain as close as possible to the original intention of the contract.
- **Account identifiers include an account owner.** An account owner is a participant that will get the money or tokens remaining in an account when a contract terminates. At the same time, the only construct that can pause the execution of a contract is the `When` construct, which has a timeout, this ensures that all contracts eventually expire and terminate. Together, these properties ensure that no money or tokens are locked in the contract forever.
- **No negative deposits or payments.** Marlowe treats negative amounts in deposits and payments as zero. At the same time, if there happens to be a request for a deposit with a negative amount, the contract will still wait for a null deposit to be made, and it will continue as if everything is correct. This way execution of the contract is disturbed as little as possible.
- **Upper limit in the number of inputs** that a Marlowe contract can accept throughout its lifetime. This limit is implied by the path with maximum number of nested `When` constructs in the contract, since only one input per `When` can be accepted. At the same time, transactions with no effect on the contract are invalid, thus there is a limit on the maximum number of transactions a contract can accept throughout its life too. This bound prevents DoS attacks, and it makes static analysis easier. We discuss further in Sect. 3.

3   Making Marlowe Semantics Symbolic

In this section, we briefly present and reflect on a technique that can be used to convert a concrete implementation of a Haskell function into a symbolic one by using the SBV library [7], and to use this symbolic implementation for static analysis. In particular, we explore this technique in the context of the Marlowe.

This approach corresponds to our first attempt at implementing static analysis for Marlowe contracts, and it is a systematic approach that can be carried out with very few assumptions.

The SBV library supports implementing Haskell functions in a way that the same implementation can be used:

- With concrete parameters, as a normal Haskell function.
- With symbolic parameters, so that properties can be checked for satisfiability using an SMT solver.
- As part of QuickCheck properties, for random testing.

Parameters that can be used symbolically are wrapped in a monad called SBV. Values that depend on symbolic values must also be wrapped in the SBV monad. Our semantics transaction processing function would thus become:

```
computeTransaction :: SBV TransactionInput -> SBV State
                   -> SBV Contract -> SBV TransactionOutput
```

We just need a function playTrace that takes a list of transactions and calls computeTransaction for each. We can then write our property to state that the output of playTrace does not have any failed payments (or other warnings). We can ask SBV to find an input transaction list that breaks the property. However, there are a couple of issues with this approach, we review them in Sect. 3.1.

3.1   Additional Considerations

At the time of writing, SBV does not fully support complex custom data types, but it provides symbolic versions for Either and Tuple types. Our original implementation of Marlowe's static analysis overcomes this limitation by generating conversion functions using Template Haskell [16]. This allows static analysis to remain similar to the semantics. For example, the following data structure:

```
data Input = IDeposit AccountId Party Money
           | IChoice ChoiceId ChosenNum
           | INotify
```

Would be translated to the following type synonym:

```
type SInput = SBV (Either (AccountId, Party, Money)
                          (Either (ChoiceId, ChosenNum)
                           ()))
```

But this approach cannot address recursive datatypes, let alone mutually recursive datatypes. And the Contract definition uses mutual recursion.

Even if we could use symbolic corecursive datatypes, SMT solvers have another general limitation: if termination of a function is not bounded by a concrete value, SMT solvers may not terminate when determining the satisfiability of a property about the function. We discuss how to address this in Sect. 3.2.

3.2   Adapting the Semantics

In order to guarantee termination of the analysis, we need a concrete bound. Related work often addresses this problem by manually establishing an artificial bound on the amount of computation, e.g: limiting the number of computation steps analysed, the number of times loops are unrolled [5,8,9].

Marlowe has natural bounds, given a concrete contract, we can infer:

- The maximum number of inputs that can have an effect on the contract
- The maximum number of transactions that can have an effect on the contract
- All of the account, choice, and Let identifiers that will be used in the contract
- The number of participants that will participate in the contract

From this data, we can also deduce an upper bound for:

- The number of times that computeTransaction, reduceContractStep, and applyInput may be called.
- The number of accounts that the contract will use, and the number of elements there may be in each of the associative maps that comprise the State of the contract at any given point of the execution.

Marlowe Contracts are finite, and every call to reduceContractStep will either make no progress or remove one of the constructs, with the exception of Close. In the case of Close, every call to reduceContractStep refunds one account, and the number of accounts is also bounded, since each needs to be mentioned in the Contract. Thus, the symbolic transaction processing function becomes:

```
computeTransaction :: SBV TransactionInput -> SBV State
                   -> Contract -> SBV TransactionOutput
```

There is one more problem: the output Contract returned by the function, which is wrapped inside the TransactionOutput, is symbolic, since it depends on the current TransactionInput and State, which are both symbolic.

We get around this by using a continuation style. Instead of returning the TransactionOutput, we take a continuation function that takes the concrete Contract and the symbolic version of TransactionOutput without the Contract.

Thus, the symbolic transaction processing function will look something like:

```
computeTransaction :: SymVal a => SBV TransactionInput
                   -> SBV State -> Contract
                   -> (SBV TransactionOutput -> Contract -> SBV a)
                   -> SBV a
```

In practice, we also include some extra information about bounds, and we make some other parts of TransactionOutput concrete.

4 Making Static Analysis More Efficient

In this section, we explain the optimisation techniques in more detail, and we illustrate them with examples of their application to Marlowe's static analysis.

4.1 Lightweight Modifications

Lightweight modifications are local, which means it is less likely that we will introduce reasoning errors when implementing them.

Removing Unnecessary Parts from the Analysis. When we use the same or similar code for both the analysis and the implementation, we may end up including code that is not relevant to the analysis.

In the case of Marlowe, this was the case of the `Close` construct. The `Close` construct refunds all the money and tokens remaining in the accounts. The number of times that `reduceContractStep` needs to be called depends on how many accounts have money left, and because this information is symbolic, there are many potential ways in which execution can unfold. All these paths need to be represented as constraints, which makes analysing `Close` very costly.

Fortunately, as it turns out, we do not need to analyse `Close` at all. Because it is impossible for the `Close` construct to produce a failed payment or any other warning (we have proven this[2] using Isabelle [15]). `Close` only pays as much as available, so we can safely remove it from the analysis.

Avoiding High Level Abstractions. High level libraries like SBV, and even standards like SMTLib, support the use and construction of high level abstractions, e.g: custom data-types, list, sets… Unfortunately, even though high level abstractions aid reasoning about code, they often prevent optimisations, since they abstract out aspects that in our particular case may be concrete.

For example, in the case of Marlowe's static analysis, we initially implemented a *symbolic* associative map primitive with the only limitation that it needed a concrete bound in the number of elements. This is straightforward to realise using the symbolic implementation of list and tuple, both provided by SBV. However, because we assumed keys were symbolic, looking up a single element required constraints that compared the element with every key up to the maximum capacity of the associative map.

Nevertheless, in Marlowe we know the values of all the keys that we are going to use in maps, because the contract is concrete, and only `Account`, `Choice`, and `Let` identifiers that are mentioned in the contract will ever make it into the `State`. So we do not need keys of the associative map to be symbolic, we can use a concrete associative map with symbolic values.

Reducing the Search Space by Normalising Parameters. The higher the number of degrees of freedom of the input, the larger the search space, and the higher the load we are putting on the SMT solver. But, if two or more different inputs have the same effect on the property we only need to include one of them.

For example, in the case of Marlowe's static analysis, Marlowe allows several inputs to be combined into a single transaction. This functionality is important because each transaction requires the issuer to pay fees. On the other hand, it also means that static analysis must consider many more possibilities, since the number of ways of partitioning inputs is exponential in the number of inputs.

However, we can devise a normal form for input traces, in which there is a maximum of one input per transaction. We only need to make sure that, for

---

[2] https://github.com/input-output-hk/marlowe/blob/master/isabelle/CloseSafe.thy (Accessed on 04 April 2020).

every trace, if it produces a warning, there exists a trace with only one input per transaction that also produces a warning. Using the automated proof assistant Isabelle [15], we have shown that, indeed, splitting transactions into transactions with single inputs and the same slot interval as the original transactions does not modify the effect of those transactions on a contract[3].

This optimization reduces the search space, but transactions may still have either one or zero inputs, so there are still many ways of distributing the inputs in transactions. We explain how we reduced the search space further in Sect. 4.2.

4.2   Heavyweight Modifications.

When optimising, if our solution is a local minimum, small changes to the parameters will not grant any improvement to the result. For that reason, in this section, we explore ways of optimising that may imply considerable rewriting of our properties, constraints, and static analysis implementation in general.

Unfortunately, not following the concrete implementation closely is much more error prone, since there are many more assumptions that we need to make and reason about. In Sect. 5, we explore ways of mitigating this issue.

Reducing the Search Space by Using Normalised Execution Paths Relevant to the Property.   Instead of modelling the execution symbolically, we can focus on modelling the property. We do not even need to consider the representation of the counterexamples (we will discuss that in the next section), but only in what are the conditions for the property to be false.

For example, the main property we want to check is whether there is any possible execution that produces a failed payment. Thus, we only write constraints for executions in which this can happen instead of modelling all possibilities. The most complicated construct in terms of execution is the When construct, since it allows for transactions that are separate in time to have different effects depending on when they are issued, all other constructs will get resolved atomically in one way or another. Without loss of generality, we can structure possible executions as shown in Fig. 1: we can conceptually break the contract tree into subtrees, where each subtree has a When construct as its root, with the exception of the subtree at the root of the original tree.

Each level of subtrees corresponds to a potential transaction, i.e: the root subtree will correspond to the first transaction, the set of subtrees that are children of the first subtree (in the original tree) will correspond to the second transaction, and so on. There may be paths which require fewer transactions/subtrees because they traverse fewer When constructs.

We split transactions like this because if the maximum slot number of a transaction is lower than the slot number in the timeout of a When it will stop before executing that When. Since the When and its continuation may be executed by a different transaction, the slot numbers for that segment of execution may be

---

[3] https://github.com/input-output-hk/marlowe/blob/master/isabelle/SingleInputTr
ansactions.thy (Accessed on 29 April 2020).

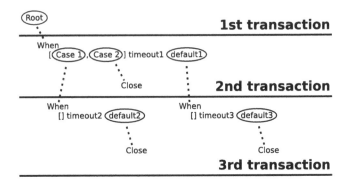

Fig. 1. Distribution of transactions with respect to a contract

different, which means the values of Values may be different, which means the amounts in payments and deposits may be different, and thus the warnings issued may be different as if both segments were executed by the same transaction.

However, there is an edge case: a transaction may execute past a When if the minimum slot number in the transaction is greater or equal than the timeout of the When. If the transaction expires the When we can no longer separate the execution before the When and after the When into two different transactions, because we know that the timeout branch of the When will be executed as part of the first transaction, and thus it will use the slot interval of the first transaction (same used for the first segment).

This is not only true for the timeout branch, if we include an input that is allowed by a When, then the first transaction will continue into the corresponding When branch, and we will not use a second transaction.

We cannot just constrain the maximum slot number of the first transaction to be less than the timeout in the When because, if we do that, then we will miss executions where one transaction expires several When in a row, or where it expires one When and provides the right input for a later When. And we cannot just not constrain the maximum slot number of the first transaction because then we will be considering impossible executions.

We get around this problem by allowing the slot numbers of the first and second transactions to be equal. If this happens, we will find out that one of the transactions will be marked as UselessTransaction by the semantics when we look at the counterexample. So we just need to filter out all transactions that produce UselessTransaction warnings in the final result.

To sum up, in Sect. 4.1, we already limited the number of inputs per transaction to a maximum of one. But now we have also assigned each of the transactions to a part of the contract, so we no longer need a symbolic list of transactions, we can use a finite concrete list of symbolic transactions.

One detail we found out during testing is that, even though a When belongs to the beginning of a transaction, the environment used by the Observations in the Notify cases of the When correspond to the State before the When is executed (except for the slot interval). The same is true for the `Value` in the `Deposit` cases, since the amount to deposit must be calculated without considering the effects of the deposit itself.

Minimizing the Representation of Inputs and Outputs. When we initially implemented the efficient version of static analysis for Marlowe, we did not pay any attention to the inputs and outputs. The first version would simply take a concrete `Contract` as input, and it would return a symbolic Boolean that determined whether the `Contract` was valid or not. However, if a `Contract` turns out to be invalid, we will also want to know why, so we later modified the property to give a counterexample that illustrated what went wrong. The original implementation still used some intermediate symbolic variables, but they were anonymous, and they were created during the exploration of the contract.

A simple way of obtaining a counterexample is to modify the output of the function to return the offending trace using the symbolic `Maybe` type. Surprisingly, this change increases the time required by the symbolic analysis severalfold.

An efficient way of extracting counterexample information was to pass a symbolic fixed-size list, as input to the static analysis, where each element corresponds to a transaction and consists of a tuple with four symbolic integers:

1. An integer representing the minimum slot
2. An integer representing the maximum slot
3. An integer representing the `When` case whose input is being included in the transaction, where zero represents the timeout branch (and no input).
4. An integer representing the amount of money or tokens (if the input is a `Deposit`), or the number chosen (if the input is a `Choice`)

For short branches (that require fewer transactions) we pad the end of the list with dummy transactions with all four numbers set to -1.

In order to translate this sequence of numbers into a proper list of transactions that is human readable and we can use to report the counter example, we need to use the concrete semantics together with the information obtained from the static analysis to *fill the gaps*, by iterating through the list and looking at the evolution of the contract with each transaction. This provides us with the rest of necessary information, such as the type of a transaction input (e.g: whether it is a `Deposit` or a `Choice`). We also use this process to filter transactions with no effect, i.e: they produce `UselessTransaction` as we mentioned in Sect. 4.2.

We also use this separation of concerns between static analysis and concrete semantics as an opportunity for applying property based testing.

5   Testing for Consistency and Equivalence

The more different the static analysis implementation and the concrete implementation are, the harder it is to ensure they are consistent with each other. To ensure that heavyweight optimisations remain consistent, we combine the use of automated proof assistants and the use of property based testing.

5.1   Testing for Consistency

If our static analysis does not replicate all the functionality of the semantics, we can use potential discrepancies as an opportunity for testing, as shown in Fig. 2. We generate random contracts and we apply the static analysis to them in order to try to find a counterexample that produces warnings. If we cannot find any counterexamples then the test passes, but if we find one, we can test it on the semantics and see whether the counterexample indeed produces warnings in the semantics too, if it does not we have found a problem in either the static analysis or the semantics.

A limitation of this approach is that it only tests for false positives; false negatives can be detected by testing for equivalence (see Sect. 5.2).

In addition, we can add assertions to the process. In the case of Marlowe, if the counterexample causes errors during the execution or is formed incorrectly, it would also mean that there is a problem with the static analysis. For example, it may be that the counterexample refers to a `Case` of a `When` that does not exist, or that it has invalid or ambiguous intervals. If it has `UselessTransactions` that is ok, because we are doing that on purpose, as we mentioned in Sect. 4.2.

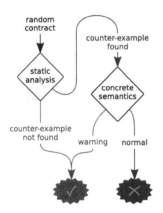

Fig. 2. Testing for consistency

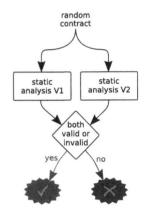

Fig. 3. Testing for equivalence

5.2   Testing for Equivalence

Given two implementations of the static analysis, we have another opportunity for testing. We have one efficient implementation that is very different from the semantics and one inefficient implementation that is much closer to the semantics, and we can compare the results of the two, as shown in Fig. 3.

We generate random contracts using a custom QuickCheck [4] generator, feed them to both implementations, and compare the results. If the results are same then test passes, if they are different then one of the implementations is wrong. This approach covers both types of errors, i.e: false positives and false negatives (for both of the implementations), but the execution time of the tests is bounded from below by the slower of the two implementations. The consistency approach is thus more efficient in finding false positives.

6   Measurements

In our experiments, the heavyweight optimisations considerably reduced the requirements of both processing time and memory for Marlowe's static analysis. We present below the results of measuring the performance of static analysis on four example contracts, before[4] and after[5] the heavyweight optimisations. We could not obtain data for some of the experiments because they required more RAM than there was available or too much processing time.

Unfortunately, at the time of writing, we do not have a completely unoptimised version of the static analysis that we can use to compare, because the semantics of Marlowe have changed since we implemented that version. However, our impression from manual testing is that the impact of lightweight optimisations was much more modest than the impact of heavyweight optimisations.

Using the `perf` tool [1], we measured the execution time[6] and the overhead of the generation of the constraints and their solution by Z3 [6]. We also measured the peak RAM usage of the whole process using GNU's `time` tool [10].

In all cases the implementation with the heavyweight optimisations performs much better and scales further. In the case of the *auction* and *crowdfunding* contracts, whose size grows exponentially, both approaches quickly overwhelm the resources available in the execution environment. In the case of *rent* and *coupon bond* contracts, which grow linearly, when using the lightweight version the problem becomes intractable much faster than with the heavyweight one.

Auction contract − `Auction.hs`

Num. participants	1	2	3	4	5
Contract size (chars)	275	3,399	89,335	4,747,361	413,784,559
Lightweight optimisations					
Execution time	0.2205s	4m 45.2015s	N/A	N/A	N/A
Generation overhead	76.61%	96.40%	N/A	N/A	N/A
× execution time	0.1689s	4m 34.9342s	N/A	N/A	N/A
Z3 overhead	23.39%	3.60%	N/A	N/A	N/A
× execution time	0.0516s	10.2673s	N/A	N/A	N/A
RAM usage peak	44,248KB	1,885,928KB	N/A	N/A	N/A
Heavyweight optimisations					
Execution time	0.01198s	0.0289s	1.1138s	1h 5m 45.1377s	N/A
Generation overhead	16.27%	29.64%	24.09%	80.86%	N/A
× execution time	0.001949s	0.008566s	0.268314s	53m 10.038344s	N/A
Z3 overhead	83.73%	70.36%	75.91%	19.14%	N/A
× execution time	0.010031s	0.020334s	0.845486s	12m 35.099356s	N/A
RAM usage peak	17,020KB	17,740KB	49,668KB	2,364,500KB	N/A

---

[4] https://github.com/input-output-hk/marlowe/blob/master/src/Language/Marlowe /Analysis/FSSemantics.hs [Accessed 19 May 2020].

[5] https://github.com/input-output-hk/marlowe/blob/master/src/Language/Marlowe /Analysis/FSSemanticsFastVerbose.hs [Accessed 19 May 2020].

[6] The experiments were run on a laptop computer with a i9-9900K (3.6 GHz) processor and two modules of 16 GB of SODIMM DDR4 RAM at 2400 MHz.

Crowdfunding contract – `CrowdFunding.hs`

Num. participants	1	2	3	4	5
Contract size (chars)	857	12,704	364,824	19,462,278	1,690,574,798
Lightweight optimisations					
Execution time	0.6298s	50m 53.4597s	N/A	N/A	N/A
Generation overhead	85.02%	99.82%	N/A	N/A	N/A
× execution time	0.5356s	50m 47.9635s	N/A	N/A	N/A
Z3 overhead	14.98%	0.18%	N/A	N/A	N/A
× execution time	0.0943s	5.4962s	N/A	N/A	N/A
RAM usage peak	111,980KB	5,641,056KB	N/A	N/A	N/A
Heavyweight optimisations					
Execution time	0.0125s	0.041s	1.0515s	32m 15.4478s	N/A
Generation overhead	16.68%	25.36%	37.23%	69.83%	N/A
× execution time	0.0021s	0.0104s	0.3915s	22m 31.5232s	N/A
Z3 overhead	83.32%	74.64%	62.77%	30.17%	N/A
× execution time	0.0104s	0.0306s	0.6600s	9m 43.9246s	N/A
RAM usage peak	17,016KB	18,768KB	62,108KB	3,715,020KB	N/A

Rent contract – `Rent.hs`

Num. months	1	2	3	4	5
Contract size (chars)	339	595	852	1,109	1,366
Lightweight optimisations					
Execution time	0.2850s	3.0303s	2m 53.2458s	3h 22m 13.0122s	N/A
Generation overhead	77.55%	91.25%	99.18%	99.94%	N/A
× execution time	0.2210s	2.7651s	2m 51.8252s	3h 22m 5.7324s	N/A
Z3 overhead	22.45%	8.75%	0.82%	0.06%	N/A
× execution time	0.0640s	0.2652s	1.4206s	7.2798s	N/A
RAM usage peak	42,052KB	221,960KB	1,237,092KB	9,160,616KB	N/A
Heavyweight optimisations					
Execution time	0.0114s	0.0111s	0.01132s	0.01124s	0.01255s
Generation overhead	11.55%	11.95%	13.65%	13.69%	21.00%
× execution time	0.0013s	0.0013s	0.0015s	0.0015s	0.0026s
Z3 overhead	88.45%	88.05%	86.35%	86.31%	79.00%
× execution time	0.0101s	0.0098s	0.0098s	0.0097s	0.0099s
RAM usage peak	15,536KB	15,364KB	15,400KB	15,364KB	15,540KB

Coupon bond contract - `CouponBond.hs`

Num. months	2	3	4	5	6
Contract size (chars)	479	635	791	947	1,103
Lightweight optimisations					
Execution time	0.8293s	5.8887s	1m 35.3930s	26m 36.4585s	9h 50m 22.3418s
Generation overhead	76.57%	74.91%	89.29%	72.34%	76.66%
× execution time	0.6350s	4.4112s	1m 25.1764s	19m 14.8781s	7h 32m 34.7672s
Z3 overhead	23.43%	25.09%	10.71%	27.66%	23.34%
× execution time	0.1943s	1.4775s	10.2166s	7m 21.5804s	2h 17m 47.5746s
RAM usage peak	74,180KB	209,724KB	940,924KB	3,283,384KB	13,483,908KB
Heavyweight optimisations					
Execution time	0.0092s	0.0095s	0.0097s	0.0102s	0.0105s
Generation overhead	14.51%	15.50%	15.51%	19.71%	19.69%
× execution time	0.0013s	0.0015s	0.0015s	0.0020s	0.0021s
Z3 overhead	85.49%	84.50%	84.49%	80.29%	80.31%
× execution time	0.0079s	0.0080s	0.0082s	0.0082s	0.0085s
RAM usage peak	15,636KB	15,816KB	15,788KB	15,780KB	15,760KB

Another conclusion that can be derived from the experiments is that, in the version with lightweight optimisations, most of the processing time seems to be spent generating of the constraints, and solving is done relatively quickly by Z3; while the opposite happens for the version with heavyweight optimisations.

These results suggest that the SBV library is able to generate constraints in a way that they are handled efficiently by Z3, but the process itself can be costly. However, the execution time required by Z3 is also lower in the case of the heavyweight optimisations as well as growing more slowly, which suggests that the optimisations described here affect both parts of the process.

7 Related Work

Work in [14] documents a similar effort to ensure correctness of control software in Haskell using the SBV library; the authors also discuss performance of the analysis and apply this approach to non-functional requirements.

The idea of using constraint solvers for finding bugs is not new, and there have been a number of initiatives that have explored its application to the verification of assertions in programs written using general purpose programming languages [8,9]; as well as for the compliance with protocols [2,17].

[11] also applies constraint solvers for detecting problems in the usage of DSLs. The authors observe that SMT solvers have limited support for nonlinear constraints such as exponentiation. This problem does not affect the current design of Marlowe because it does not support multiplication by arbitrary variables, and because all inputs are integer and bounded finitely.

8 Conclusion

In this paper we have summarized our work on optimising the static analysis for Marlowe contracts. We have seen that there are two distinct approaches to static analysis using SMT, both have advantages and disadvantages. One is less error prone and straightforward, but inefficient and hard to test; the other is much more efficient, versatile, and testable, but more error prone. We have also seen that many specific properties and restrictions characteristic of the target DSL can be utilized both as optimisation opportunities and, in our case, for completeness of the analysis. Symbolic execution of a Turing-complete language, would be intractable, and would require us to manually set a bound; but this is not in the case for Marlowe.

In the end, we have illustrated how to counteract the main disadvantage of the optimised approach – its propensity to errors – by using property based testing. This way we have obtained a static analysis implementation that is efficient, versatile, testable, and reliable. On the other hand, for the static analysis of Marlowe contracts, we found out that when running statistics on the equivalence testing property, most of the bugs were false negatives in the straightforward implementation, and the optimised implementation seems to be more reliable thanks to the consistency tests that we run beforehand.

Another advantage of the optimised implementation is that, because it relies on fewer and simpler features, it is compatible with more SMT solvers which, in turn, means that it is less reliant on the correctness or efficiency of a single solver. If one solver fails to give an answer, we can try another; if we want further evidence that a contract is valid, we can test it with several solvers.

In the future, we would like to extend static analysis to cover other potential problems in Marlowe contracts and to aid their development. We plan to use static analysis to locate unreachable subcontracts, to allow developers to provide custom assertions and check their satisfiability, and to allow users to inspect the possible maximum and minimum values that particular expressions can reach.

References

1. Performance analysis tools for Linux. https://github.com/torvalds/linux/tree/master/tools/perf. Accessed 20 May 2020
2. Ball, T., Rajamani, S.K.: Automatically validating temporal safety properties of interfaces. In: Dwyer, M. (ed.) SPIN 2001. LNCS, vol. 2057, pp. 102–122. Springer, Heidelberg (2001). https://doi.org/10.1007/3-540-45139-0_7
3. Barrett, C., Stump, A., Tinelli, C., et al.: The SMT-LIB standard: version 2.0. In: Proceedings of the 8th International Workshop on Satisfiability Modulo Theories (2010)
4. Claessen, K., Hughes, J.: QuickCheck: a lightweight tool for random testing of Haskell programs. In: Proceedings of the ACM SIGPLAN International Conference on Functional Programming, ICFP, vol. 46 (2000)
5. Clarke, E., Kroening, D., Lerda, F.: A tool for checking ANSI-C programs. In: Jensen, K., Podelski, A. (eds.) TACAS 2004. LNCS, vol. 2988, pp. 168–176. Springer, Heidelberg (2004). https://doi.org/10.1007/978-3-540-24730-2_15
6. de Moura, L., Bjørner, N.: Z3: an efficient SMT solver. In: Ramakrishnan, C.R., Rehof, J. (eds.) TACAS 2008. LNCS, vol. 4963, pp. 337–340. Springer, Heidelberg (2008). https://doi.org/10.1007/978-3-540-78800-3_24
7. Erkök, L.: SBV: SMT based verification in Haskell. Software library (2019)
8. Gulwani, S., Srivastava, S., Venkatesan, R.: Program analysis as constraint solving. In: Proceedings of the 29th ACM SIGPLAN Conference PLDI (2008)
9. Jackson, D., Vaziri, M.: Finding bugs with a constraint solver. ACM SIGSOFT Softw. Eng. Notes **25**(5), 14–25 (2000)
10. Keppel, D., MacKenzie, D., Juul, A.H., Pinard, F.: GNU time tool (1998). https://www.gnu.org/software/time/. Accessed 20 May 2020
11. Keshishzadeh, S., Mooij, A.J., Mousavi, M.R.: Early fault detection in DSLs using SMT solving and automated debugging. In: Hierons, R.M., Merayo, M.G., Bravetti, M. (eds.) SEFM 2013. LNCS, vol. 8137, pp. 182–196. Springer, Heidelberg (2013). https://doi.org/10.1007/978-3-642-40561-7_13
12. Lamela Seijas, P., Nemish, A., Smith, D., Thompson, S.: Marlowe: implementing and analysing financial contracts on blockchain. In: Workshop on Trusted Smart Contracts (2020, to appear)
13. Lamela Seijas, P., Thompson, S.: Marlowe: financial contracts on blockchain. In: Margaria, T., Steffen, B. (eds.) ISoLA 2018. LNCS, vol. 11247, pp. 356–375. Springer, Cham (2018). https://doi.org/10.1007/978-3-030-03427-6_27

14. Mokhov, A., Lukyanov, G., Lechner, J.: Formal verification of spacecraft control programs (experience report). In: Proceedings of the 12th ACM SIGPLAN International Symposium on Haskell (2019)
15. Nipkow, T., Paulson, L.C., Wenzel, M.: Isabelle/HOL: A Proof Assistant for Higher-Order Logic, vol. 2283. Springer, Heidelberg (2002). https://doi.org/10.1007/3-540-45949-9
16. Sheard, T., Jones, S.P.: Template meta-programming for Haskell. In: Proceedings of the 2002 ACM SIGPLAN Workshop on Haskell (2002)
17. Xie, Y., Aiken, A.: Saturn: a SAT-based tool for bug detection. In: Etessami, K., Rajamani, S.K. (eds.) CAV 2005. LNCS, vol. 3576, pp. 139–143. Springer, Heidelberg (2005). https://doi.org/10.1007/11513988_13

Accurate Smart Contract Verification
Through Direct Modelling

Matteo Marescotti[1(✉)], Rodrigo Otoni[1(✉)], Leonardo Alt[2(✉)],
Patrick Eugster[1(✉)], Antti E. J. Hyvärinen[1(✉)], and Natasha Sharygina[1(✉)]

[1] Università della Svizzera italiana, Lugano, Switzerland
{matteo.marescotti,rodrigo.benedito.otoni,patrick.thomas.eugster,
antti.hyvaerinen,natasha.sharygina}@usi.ch
[2] Ethereum Foundation, Zug, Switzerland
leo@ethereum.org

Abstract. Smart contracts challenge the existing, highly efficient techniques applied in symbolic model checking of software by their unique traits not present in standard programming models. Still, the majority of reported smart contract verification projects either reuse off-the-shelf model checking tools resulting in inefficient and even unsound models, or apply generic solutions that typically require highly-trained human intervention. In this paper, we present the solution adopted in the formal analysis engine of the official Solidity compiler. We focus on the accurate modeling of the central aspects of smart contracts. For that, we specify purpose-built rules defined in the expressive and highly automatable logic of constrained Horn clauses, which are readily supported by an effective solving infrastructure for establishing sound safety proofs or finite-length counterexamples. We evaluated our approach on an extensive set of smart contracts recently deployed in the Ethereum platform. The reported results show that the approach is able to prove correctness and discover bugs in significantly more contracts than comparable publicly available systems.

1 Introduction

Smart contracts are programs designed to manage and enforce contract transactions without relying on trusted parties but instead exploiting the blockchain technology to achieve consensus. The safety of smart contracts is increasingly important: in the past years millions of US Dollars were lost due to bugs [4,6], and currently the smart contracts deployed in the widely used Ethereum platform control increasing amounts of wealth in the order of billions of dollars. This issue is even more pronounced because once deployed in the blockchain, the source code of smart contracts is immutable, complicating the task of fixing errors with new releases.

Ethereum [17] nowadays is the most popular platform for writing smart contracts. High-level languages for implementing smart contracts such as Solidity [3] and Vyper [5] are compiled to the low-level Ethereum Virtual Machine (EVM)

© Springer Nature Switzerland AG 2020
T. Margaria and B. Steffen (Eds.): ISoLA 2020, LNCS 12478, pp. 178–194, 2020.
https://doi.org/10.1007/978-3-030-61467-6_12

that is deployed in the blockchain. In this paper we introduce the *direct modeling* for Solidity smart contracts automatic verification implemented inside the Solidity compiler [18] in collaboration with the Ethereum Foundation. The proposed direct modelling uses constrained Horn clauses (CHCs) [11] for modelling contract behaviours based on the control-flow. Besides being convenient to model transition systems, CHCs benefit from the current active area of research on their solving. Recent efforts produced several efficient sequential and parallel solvers [13,33] that can be directly exploited. Our algorithm for creating formal models of Solidity smart contracts produces models that are solver-independent (any theorem prover supporting CHCs can be used to solve them), and accurate (the models properly encode the semantic traits specific of smart contracts). Additionally, solving the model automatically provides *contract invariants* that prove unbounded safety, or a finite-length *counterexample* that concretely shows property violation. Contract invariants can also be used by developers to confirm the intents of the code. Specifically, they represent conditions over the contract variables that always hold after any possible transaction. Counterexamples show the interactions with the contract that lead to a violation of the safety properties. This is achieved by providing the list of transactions that produce an assertion error. All these features are implemented in the module (called Solicitous – Solidity contract verification using constrained Horn clauses) of the SMTChecker formal engine inside the official Solidity compiler [18].

In our experiments, our tool solves the CHCs generated with Spacer [29], the IC3 [14] engine of the SMT solver Z3 [35]. We compared Solicitous with Solc-Verify [24,25], VeriSol [30] and Mythril [15], and report an extensive experimental evaluation verifying 6138 smart contracts currently deployed on the Ethereum blockchain. We show that Solicitous outperforms the other tools both for proving safety and for discovering bugs. To summarize, this paper provides the following contributions:

- a direct formal modeling of smart contracts using CHCs that enables fully automated verification using generic theorem provers (Sect. 3),
- an industrial implementation inside the Solidity compiler (Sect. 4), and
- an extensive verification experimentation over thousands of real-world contracts which demonstrates the effectiveness of our technique (Sect. 5).

We further discuss related work in Sect. 6, and conclude the paper in Sect. 7. An extended version of this paper including an end-to-end example of the entire verification process, from the Solidity source code to the counterexample, is available at http://verify.inf.usi.ch/research/fvsc.

2   Background

Smart contracts consist of a *storage* and a set of *functions*. The storage is a persistent memory space used to store variables whose values represent the contract state. Functions are the interface by which users interact with the contract. Functions are allowed to access the storage both in read and write modes, and their behavior is defined by the corresponding EVM instructions, stored persistently in a separate memory residing within the blockchain. The Ethereum yellow paper [17] provides further details of the semantics of the EVM bytecode. Solidity[1] is a Turing-Complete language specifically designed for smart contracts targeting EVM. A Solidity contract is a structure similar to a class in object-oriented programming languages. Contracts have data types such as integers, Boolean, array, map, etc. and either external or internal functions depending on whether they can be called directly by the user. Solidity supports control structures that are common in programming languages, such as conditionals and loops.

A control-flow graph (CFG) is a graph representation of the execution paths of a program, and it is commonly used for static analysis. The graph nodes represent *basic blocks*, that is, sequences of program statements that do not change the control flow of the program. Common programming constructs that modify the control flow are branching, loops, and function calls. Moving from one block to the next is a *jump*. Here we consider that the edges in a CFG are labeled with a Boolean expression that must be true for the jump to occur.

The interaction with a contract is performed by calling one of its external functions. During a function execution both external and internal functions can be called. Each individual function call is an *atomic* transaction, i.e., it either executes without exceptions committing the changes, or rolls back completely if an exception occurs, leaving the state unchanged. Contrarily, in standard programming languages all the changes made in the heap by a function prior to throwing an exception are preserved.

In [12] the *Existential Positive Least Fixed-Point logic* (E+LFP) is proven to logically match Hoare logic [27] and is therefore useful for determining partial correctness of programs. Following [11], in this work we use a specialization of E+LFP called *constrained Horn clauses* (CHC) due to the intuitive syntax in representing transition systems with loops, and the efficient decision procedures available for them. We give here a characterisation of CHC based on first-order logic and the fixed-point operator adapted from [12]. Let ψ be a first-order formula over a theory T with free variables $\boldsymbol{x}$, and a finite set $\{P_1, \ldots, P_n\}$ be predicates over $\boldsymbol{x}$ not appearing in ψ. We denote by $\bigcup_{i=1}^{n} \{\Delta_{P_i}\} \models_T \psi(\boldsymbol{x}) \wedge P_1(\boldsymbol{x}) \wedge \ldots \wedge P_n(\boldsymbol{x})$ the satisfiability of $\psi(\boldsymbol{x}) \wedge P_1(\boldsymbol{x}) \wedge \ldots \wedge P_n(\boldsymbol{x})$ in theory T when the interpretations of P_i are Δ_{P_i}.

Given a set of predicates $\mathcal{P}$, a first-order theory T, and a set of variables $\mathcal{V}$, a *system of CHCs* is a set S of clauses of form

$$H(\boldsymbol{x}) \leftarrow \exists \boldsymbol{y}. \, \phi(\boldsymbol{x}, \boldsymbol{y}) \wedge P_1(\boldsymbol{y}) \wedge \ldots \wedge P_m(\boldsymbol{y}) \text{ for } m \geq 0 \qquad (1)$$

where ϕ is a first-order formula over $\boldsymbol{x}, \boldsymbol{y} \subseteq \mathcal{V}$ with respect to the theory T; $\boldsymbol{x}$ is the tuple of distinct variables free in ϕ; $H \in \mathcal{P}$ a predicate with arity matching $\boldsymbol{x}$; $P_i \in \mathcal{P}$ predicates with arities matching $\boldsymbol{y}$; and no predicate in $\mathcal{P}$ appears in ϕ. For a clause c we write $head(c) = H$ and $body(c) = \exists \boldsymbol{y}. \, \phi(\boldsymbol{x}, \boldsymbol{y}) \wedge P_1(\boldsymbol{y}) \wedge \ldots \wedge P_m(\boldsymbol{y})$. For each predicate $P \in \mathcal{P}$ we define the transfinite sequence Δ_P^α given by

---

[1] Solidity official documentation is available at https://solidity.readthedocs.io.

$$\Delta_P^0 = \emptyset$$
$$\Delta_P^{\alpha+1} = \Delta_P^\alpha \cup \{\boldsymbol{a} \mid \bigcup_{Q \in \mathcal{P}} \{\Delta_Q^\alpha\} \models_T \bigvee_{c \in S, head(c) = P} body(c)[\boldsymbol{a}/\boldsymbol{x}]\}$$
$$\Delta_P^\lambda = \bigcup_{\alpha < \lambda} \Delta_P^\alpha \text{ for limit ordinals } \lambda.$$

Since the sequence Δ_P^α is monotonic, there is a value for α such that $\Delta_P^\alpha = \Delta_P^{\alpha+1} = \Delta_P$.

In the context of modeling and verification, in this paper we are in addition interested in determining whether the $\Delta_\perp$ of the predicate $\perp \in \mathcal{P}$ is empty. In particular the CHC solver we use guarantees that if $\Delta_\perp$ is nonempty then the model of a program violates a safety property and the solver is able to map the construction to an execution. Conversely, if $\Delta_\perp$ is empty, the solver either does not terminate, or provides quantifier-free first-order formulas $\psi_P(\boldsymbol{x})$ in T for each $P \in \mathcal{P}$ that serve as safe inductive invariants in the following sense. First, each ψ_P over-approximate the interpretations Δ_P, that is, $\{\Delta_P\} \models_T P(\boldsymbol{x}) \implies \psi_P(\boldsymbol{x})$. Second, for each clause $c \in S$ of the form (1) where $head(c) \neq \perp$, $\models_T \phi(\boldsymbol{x}, \boldsymbol{y}) \wedge \psi_{P_1}(\boldsymbol{y}) \wedge \ldots \wedge \psi_{P_m}(\boldsymbol{y}) \implies \psi_H(\boldsymbol{x})$. Third, if $head(c) = \perp$, then $\models_T \neg(\phi(\boldsymbol{x}, \boldsymbol{y}) \wedge \psi_{P_1}(\boldsymbol{y}) \wedge \ldots \wedge \psi_{P_m}(\boldsymbol{y}))$. We use the terminology from [11] and call a set of CHCs *satisfiable* if $\Delta_\perp$ is empty, and *unsatisfiable* otherwise.

In presenting the clauses we use some conventions that make reading them easier. First, we omit the existential quantifier since its scope is clear from the arguments of the body for a given clause. Second, we do not write variables that do not appear in the formulas. Third, we often omit superfluous equalities: if an element y_i of $\boldsymbol{y}$ is equated with an element x_j of $\boldsymbol{x}$ in a top-level conjunct of ϕ, we do not write the equality but instead substitute y_i for x_j in the head.

3   The Model

We define a contract C with the triplet $\langle \boldsymbol{s}, I(\boldsymbol{s}), F \rangle$, where $\boldsymbol{s}$ is the set of state variables, $I(\boldsymbol{s})$ is the initial state of $\boldsymbol{s}$, and F is the set of all functions in the contract. The disjoint subsets F^+ and F^- of F denote respectively the sets of external and internal functions of F. Given a function $f(\boldsymbol{a}) \to \boldsymbol{r} \in F$, where $\boldsymbol{a}$ is the set of function arguments and $\boldsymbol{r}$ is the set of return variables, the CFG of f is the tuple $\langle G, \alpha, \omega, \rho \rangle$. $G = (V, E, \lambda, \mu, S)$ is a node- and edge-labeled directed graph, where V is the set of CFG blocks; $E \subseteq V \times V$ is the set of control flow *jumps*; λ_v is the set that contains, for all $v \in V$, the set of instructions performed by v; μ_e is, for all $e \in E$, the condition under which the jump e is performed; and $S \subseteq V$ is the set of *safety blocks*, each representing a safety property. During the execution of f only local variables are manipulated. Therefore the labelings λ and μ, respectively, of each block and jump, are instructions performed only over a set of local variables $\boldsymbol{l}$ of f. The CFG blocks $\alpha, \omega \in V$ are respectively the entry block and the exit block. The injection $\rho : \boldsymbol{s} \cup \boldsymbol{a} \cup \boldsymbol{r} \to \boldsymbol{l}$ maps every state variable, function argument and return variable to a distinct local variable accessed by the instructions in each block and jump. We extend the function notation to sets in the natural way: for a given set of variables $\boldsymbol{z}$, $\rho(\boldsymbol{z}) = \{\rho(x) \mid x \in \boldsymbol{z}\}$.

A safety property in the CFG is represented by a safety block. In Solidity, safety properties are specified with the `assert` keyword. Safety properties failing during the execution cause the function to revert and return immediately. To achieve this behaviour, for every safety block $b \in S$ there exists the jump $e = \langle b, \omega \rangle$ where the condition μ_e is the negation of the property. This ensures a direct jump to the exit block in case the safety property is violated. A jump to the exit block ω from a safety block requires ω to revert by restoring the state prior the function's execution. In order to provide ω with the information that a safety property has been broken, λ_b sets the special variable $\tilde{r} \in l$ to a value that uniquely identifies the violated safety property.

Consider functions f and f' (which can be the same), represented by CFGs G and G' respectively. Function calls are performed by a block v in G whose labeling λ_v contains the call instruction to G'. At runtime, the execution of the CFG block v is performed by executing the CFG block α of G'. When ω of G' is executed, the transaction represented by the execution of G' is finalized by committing any changes to the state variables. The execution is then resumed from v, mapping the return variables of f' to the expected local variables of f, and updating the local variables of f representing state variables to match the new values resulting from the commit just performed by the concluded transaction.

3.1 Model of a Contract Function

This section presents the rules for creating the CHC model of a function $f(a)$ of a contract having state variables s, returning variables r, and manipulating local variables l.

The CHCs are constructed given the control flow graph $\langle G, \alpha, \omega, \rho \rangle$ of the function f, where $G = (V, E, \lambda, \mu)$. For each CFG block v, the *Static Single Assignment (SSA) formula* $\mathsf{SSA}_{\lambda_v}(l, l')$, where $l' = \{x' \mid x \in l\}$, models the behavior of v by formalizing in logic the relation between x and x' for each $x \in l$, based on the execution of the instructions in λ_v. The formula $\mathsf{SSA}_{\mu_e}(l)$ of each jump e is the logical condition under which e is taken. For each CFG block $v \in V$, $\mathcal{P}_f^v(s, a, l)$ is a predicate symbol representing the states that are reachable in the block v. The set of rules representing the execution of f is defined as follows. For each jump $e = \langle v, u \rangle \in E$, the *jump rule* of e is the CHC

$$\mathcal{P}_f^u(s, a, l') \leftarrow \mathcal{P}_f^v(s, a, l) \wedge \mathsf{SSA}_{\lambda_v}(l, l') \wedge \mathsf{SSA}_{\mu_e}(l). \qquad (\mathsf{Jump}_{f,e})$$

The *entry rule* sets the local variables equal to the corresponding current values of state variables and passed arguments.

$$\mathcal{P}_f^\alpha(s, a, l) \leftarrow \bigwedge_{x \in s \cup a} x = \rho(x) \wedge \rho(\tilde{r}) = 0. \qquad (\mathsf{Entry}_f)$$

The variables in s and a are symbolically assigned in (Entry_f) and never changed throughout the jump rules $(\mathsf{Jump}_{f,e})$ of any $e \in E$. In case of reverting during execution, these variables provide the necessary information to revert to the state prior to the execution of f. A revert is caused a jump to ω setting the local variable

$\rho(\tilde{r})$ equal to the integer identifier of a safety property that failed. Initially, $\rho(\tilde{r})$ is set to zero. Let $\mathcal{S}_f(s, a, s', r)$ be the predicate symbol representing the *function summary* of the execution of f. The function summary expresses the relation between the input and the output of an execution of the function. In this context the input is represented by the function arguments a and state variables s prior execution, and the output is represented by the return values r and the state variables s' after the execution. The *summary rule* of f is the CHC

$$\mathcal{S}_f(s, a, s', r) \leftarrow \mathcal{P}_f^{\omega}(s, a, l) \wedge \hspace{3cm} (\text{Sum}_f)$$

$$\underbrace{(\rho(\tilde{r}) \neq 0 \implies \bigwedge_{x \in s} x' = x)}_{revert} \wedge \underbrace{(\rho(\tilde{r}) = 0 \implies \bigwedge_{x \in s} x' = \rho(x))}_{commit} \wedge \underbrace{\bigwedge_{x \in r} x = \rho(x)}_{returns}.$$

The *revert* constraints in (Sum$_f$) ensures that an execution is reverted when ω is reached having the local variable corresponding to $\tilde{r}$ set to the identifier of a safety property. Conversely, the mutually exclusive *commit* constraints store the local copy of the state in s', modeling a commit of the computed values. The *return* constraints equate the return variables r with the corresponding local variables.

Definition 1. *Given a contract function f, the set of CHC Π_f modeling f is the set consisting of the jump rule of e (Jump$_{f,e}$) for each control flow jump e of f, and the entry and summary rules from f (Entry$_f$) and (Sum$_f$).*

3.2 Function Calls

Let $e = \langle v, u \rangle$ be a control flow jump where λ_v contains a function call to $g(a_g)$ returning variables r_g. The summary of g is used to synchronize the local variables of f with the new state committed after g's execution terminates. Therefore, $\text{SSA}_{\lambda_v}(l, l')$ is defined as

$$\mathcal{S}_g(s', a_g, s'', r_g) \wedge \hspace{4cm} (\text{Call}_{g, \rho_{call}})$$

$$\underbrace{\bigwedge_{x \in a_g \cup r_g} x = \rho_{call}(x)}_{arguments\ and\ returns\ passing} \wedge \underbrace{\bigwedge_{x \in s} (x' = \rho(x) \wedge x'' = \rho(x)')}_{state\ set\ and\ update} \wedge \underbrace{\bigwedge_{x \in l \setminus l_{call}} x' = x}_{untouched\ locals}$$

where $\rho_{call} : a_g \to l, r_g \to l'$ is the mapping specific for this call that maps both arguments of g to l according to how they are passed, and the return variables of g to l' according to how they are assigned; $l_{call} = \rho_{call}(r_g) \cup \rho(s)$ is the set of local variables that can be affected by the call. We assume arguments are passed by value. Therefore local variables $\rho_{call}(a_g)$ corresponding to the arguments of g are not affected by the execution of the block. The *argument and return passing* uses ρ_{call} to match arguments and return variables to the respective local variables of the caller. The *state set and update* conjunction makes sure that the local variables in l' representing the state variables get updated according to the execution of the just-ended transaction. For each local variable not in l_{call}, the *untouched locals* constraint equates its primed and non-primed versions, modeling that its value is not affected by the block execution, and therefore remains unchanged after the jump. Note that the primed version of the local variables in l_{call} are set in the former constraints according to the effects of the call. This ensures that all variables in l', which are passed to the predicate $\mathcal{P}_f^u$, are constrained, modeling a deterministic execution. By applying $(\mathsf{Jump}_{f,e})$, the resulting CHC is non-linear because it contains the two predicates $\mathcal{P}_f^v$ and $\mathcal{S}_g$.

3.3   Contract's External Behaviour

Given a contract $C = \langle s, I(s), F \rangle$, a contract transaction is the execution of a public function. A single contract transaction is therefore modelled by the summaries of every function f in F^+, each proving the relation between state variables s, s' before and after a transaction performed by calling f. The *external behaviour* of the contract is defined as the transitive closure of contract transactions, modelling an arbitrary number of calls to any public function, in any order. The external behaviour provides the relation between state variables before and after any possible interaction with the contract performed by an external contract.

We define the predicate $\mathcal{E}_C(s, s')$ that models the external behavior of C inductively, where the base case is the CHC

$$\mathcal{E}_C(s, s) \leftarrow \top, \qquad\qquad (\mathsf{ExtBase}_C)$$

and the inductive steps are, for each function f in F^+, the CHCs

$$\mathcal{E}_C(s, s'') \leftarrow \mathcal{E}_C(s, s') \wedge \mathcal{S}_f(s', a, s'', r). \qquad (\mathsf{ExtInd}_{C,f})$$

The external behaviour of C can be used to model calls to a function of an external contracts D which source code in unknown before runtime. In this way, any possible transaction resulting from D interaction during runtime is considered. Every control flow jump $\langle v, u \rangle$ in C, where the block v contains a call to a function that is unknown before runtime, is modelled using $\mathcal{E}_C$ in place of the called function summary. The resulting $\mathsf{SSA}_{\lambda_v}(l, l')$ is built similarly to $(\mathsf{Call}_{g,\rho_{call}})$, with the difference of omitting the *argument and return passing* constraints. The local variables in ρ_{call} are unconstrained in order to nonde-terministically model any possible values returned by the unknown function. Specifically, the resulting $\mathsf{SSA}_{\lambda_v}(l, l')$ is

$$\mathcal{E}_C(s', s'') \wedge \underbrace{\bigwedge_{x \in s} (x' = \rho(x) \wedge x'' = \rho(x)')}_{\text{state set and update}} \wedge \underbrace{\bigwedge_{x \in l \setminus l_{call}} x' = x}_{\text{untouched locals}}. \qquad (\mathsf{ECall}_{\rho_{call}})$$

If a safety proof for this model can be obtained, then it is not possible to construct an external contract that can violate assertions in C by any sequence

Input : A contract $C = \langle s, I(s), F \rangle$.
Output : The set of CHC Π_C.
Initially: $\Pi_C = \{(\mathsf{Init}_C), (\mathsf{ExtBase}_C)\}$.

1 **foreach** $f = \langle G, \alpha, \omega, \epsilon, \rho \rangle \in F$ **do**
2 $\quad$ Let a, r, l respectively the arguments, returns and local variables of f.
3 $\quad$ Let $\Pi_f := \{(\mathsf{Entry}_f), (\mathsf{Sum}_f)\}$
4 $\quad$ Let $G = (V, E, \lambda, \mu)$
5 $\quad$ **foreach** $e = \langle v, w \rangle \in E$ **do**
6 $\quad\quad$ **if** v *contains a call to* $g(a_g) \to r_g$ **then**
7 $\quad\quad\quad$ Create ρ_{call} from λ_v
8 $\quad\quad\quad$ **if** (Sum_g) *is known* **then** $\mathsf{SSA}_{\lambda_v} := (\mathsf{Call}_{g,\rho_{call}})$;
9 $\quad\quad\quad$;
10 $\quad\quad\quad$ **else** $\mathsf{SSA}_{\lambda_v} := (\mathsf{ECall}_{\rho_{call}})$;;
11 $\quad\quad$ **else**
12 $\quad\quad\quad$ $\mathsf{SSA}_{\lambda_v}(l, l') := \mathrm{Model}(\lambda_v)$
13 $\quad\quad$ **end**
14 $\quad\quad$ $\mathsf{SSA}_{\mu_e} := \mathrm{Model}(\mu_e)$
15 $\quad\quad$ $\Pi_f := \Pi_f \cup \{(\mathsf{Jump}_{f,e})\}$
16 $\quad$ **end**
17 $\quad$ $\Pi_C := \Pi_C \cup \Pi_f$
18 $\quad$ **if** $f \in F^+$ **then**
19 $\quad\quad$ $\Pi_C := \Pi_C \cup \{(\mathsf{ExtInd}_{C,f}), (\mathsf{RootTr}_{C,f})\}$
20 $\quad$ **end**
21 **end**

Algorithm 1. The algorithm to construct Π_C.

of reentrant calls. A counterexample for such model implies that there exists a contract that can be designed specifically for violating one or more assertions, by calling one or more public functions in a particular order and returning specific values.

3.4 Checking Contract Safety

Let $\mathcal{C}(s)$ be the predicate representing the reachable values for the contract. The initial state is modeled by the CHC

$$\mathcal{C}(s) \leftarrow I(s). \tag{Init_C}$$

Every transition performed by a call to a public function is modeled by the *root transition rule*. For each public function $f \in F^+$,

$$\mathcal{C}(s') \leftarrow \mathcal{C}(s) \wedge \mathcal{S}_f(s, a, s', r) \wedge \tilde{r} = 0. \tag{$\mathsf{RootTr}_{C,f}$}$$

Definition 2. *Given a contract C, the set of CHC Π_C modeling any possible behavior of C is defined as the union of the initial rule (Init_C), the external base* *case rule (*ExtBase$_C$*), all the rules Π_f of every function $f \in F$, and for each public function $f \in F^+$ the root transition rule (*RootTr$_{C,f}$*) and the external inductive rule (*ExtInd$_{C,f}$*).*

Algorithm 1 gives an overall view of the modeling technique. Given as input a smart contract C, the algorithm returns the set Π_C of CHCs modeling C. Initially, Π_C consists only of the initial rule of C. Then, the loop from line 1 to 20 iterates over each contract function f, gradually producing the respective set Π_f that is finally merged with Π_C in line 16. The internal loop from line 5 to 15 iterates over every edge $\langle v, w \rangle$ of the CFG of f. The case where v is a block representing a function call is handled in lines 6 to 9, using either the summary of the called function or the external predicate. Otherwise, a formal model representing the block execution is generated in line 10, and used in the jump rule.

Definition 3 (Safety Rule). *The safety rule Σ_f for the CHC model of a public function f is $\bot \leftarrow C(s) \wedge S_f(s, a, s', r) \wedge \tilde{r} \neq 0$. The safety rule of a contract C is the set Σ_C of the safety rules of every public function of C.*

The safety rule ensures that a function f is safe, in the sense that every possible transaction of f does not revert, i.e. produce assertion violations. A contract C is safe if and only if the set $\Pi_C \cup \Sigma_C$ is satisfiable.

3.5 Counterexample Generation

The *refutation*, or proof of unsatisfiability, for $\Pi_C \cup \Sigma_C$ proves that a specific safety query in Σ_C can not be satisfied, i.e., $\Delta_\bot$ is non-empty. While our solving methodology can show satisfiability over unbounded executions through the use of over-approximation, we can only represent finite counterexamples. This, of course, is not a practical limitation since in real programs we are only interested in bugs that manifest themselves after a finite number of steps. While the description of how a counter-example is constructed in our solver is outside of the scope of this paper, we give here a short overview of the refutations themselves.

A refutation is a tree-shaped structure obtained by an unwinding of clauses. The nodes of the refutation are labeled with clauses. The root v_0 of the tree is labeled with a clause with $\bot$ as head. For each predicate P in the body of a clause c, we create a child labeled with a unique clause c' such that $head(c') = P$. The leaves of the tree are labeled with clauses with no predicates in the body. Let $v_0, \ldots, v_k$ be a path from the root to a leaf, labeled with clauses $c_0, \ldots, c_k$. Given a clause c of form (1), let $body_\phi(c)$ denote the constraint ϕ of c. Then in a refutation for all such paths it must hold that

$$\models_T body_\phi(c_0)(\boldsymbol{x_0}, \boldsymbol{x_1}) \wedge body_\phi(c_1)(\boldsymbol{x_1}, \boldsymbol{x_2}) \wedge \ldots \wedge body_\phi(c_k)(\boldsymbol{x_{k-1}}, \boldsymbol{x_k}). \quad (2)$$

A counterexample corresponds then to a first-order structure satisfying (2) as follows: The counterexample generation traverses the entire refutation tree and considers only the nodes that refer to the initial state rule (Init$_C$), the root transaction rule (RootTr$_{C,f}$), or the safety rule. The breath-first search results

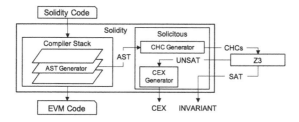

Fig. 1. Solicitous module inside the Solc compiler.

in a list of nodes that has the safety rule as first element (the root), a possibly empty list of elements representing root transaction rules, and finally a leaf representing an initial rule. The first-order structure satisfying (2) is used to produce a model of the initial state for the counterexample setup. Then, each following node represents the result of a transaction whose children model (i) the contract state prior the transaction, and (ii) a function call with given arguments that results in a new state. The last transaction involves a call to the function $\hat{f}$ that resulted in a revert. The arguments of each such function are then used to produce a trace of function calls which serves as the counterexample.

4   Implementation

Our approach is being implemented in collaboration with the engineers from the Ethereum Foundation, inside the SMTChecker component [2,8] of the Solidity compiler [18]. Specifically, the implementation of our work consists of the CHC model checking engine of SMTChecker, called Solicitous.

The Solicitous functionality can be enabled in the compilation by providing the corresponding *pragma* directive in the source file. Once enabled, the compiler provides the main Abstract Syntax Tree (AST) to Solicitous that generates the CHC model of the contract following Algorithm 1. The CHC model is then provided to the engine Spacer [29] of the SMT solver Z3 [35] for solving. In case an assertion failure is detected, Solicitous can provide a transaction trace as a witness to the failure, which can easily be checked by the developer. An overview of Solicitous and Solidity can be seen in Fig. 1.

The emphasis of this paper is in the modelling of the control flow of Solidity contracts. The control flow corresponds to AST nodes related to language constructs such as loops and conditional branches. Visiting these nodes triggers the creation of the corresponding clauses as described in Sect. 3. In addition, the AST nodes corresponding to Solidity expressions result in accumulating the constraint ϕ of the clauses. Each expression node introduces a new SMT variable of the type of the expression. As an implementation detail, the unique identifiers the compiler assigns to AST nodes are used for guaranteeing unique names for these variables.

Solidity offers two special types of functions: *modifiers* and *constructors*. Modifiers represent pieces of code that envelope a function body. Therefore, modifiers' definitions depend on the functions they envelope, and they are not encoded separately but instead in-lined to the functions. Constructors define the initialization procedure executed at deployment time of a contract. The constructor modeling is prepended by providing the initialization $I(s)$ where variables are either zeroed or given their explicit initial values. In contracts that inherit base classes, the inheritance order is obtained by the Solidity compiler using the C3 linearization [9]. In addition, each constructor is executed exactly once. In our implementation, the entire deployment procedure, which might include the inheritance linearization and state variable initialization, is in-lined into a single constructor function.

Solicitous currently supports a working subset of the Solidity language, including the complex control flow and arithmetic operators (except exponentiation), integers of all available sizes, Boolean variables, arrays, mappings access and assignment, and inheritance. Strings and structs are currently not supported, and their occurrences in ϕ are replaced by nondeterministic operations in order to maintain soundness. Continuous support and the addition of the remaining language features is a goal of the Ethereum Foundation, and the supported subset of language is therefore expected to grow.

5   Experiments

We evaluate the precision and language coverage of Solicitous on a set of real-world contracts from 17 month period, between the block 7 million, mined 2nd of January 2019 and the block 10 million, mined on 4th of May 2020. We took all contracts in that period that are written in Solidity v0.5 and v0.6, and are available through the Etherscan block explorer [1]. The benchmarks are available at https://scm.ti-edu.ch/repogit/verify-solidity-contracts.git.

We queried 1147850 addresses and obtained 136802 contract sources, of which 27887 are unique: 367 v0.6, 10301 v0.5, and 17219 of previous versions. We run the tools only on contracts containing assertions. However, we checked also assertions that were commented out. We believe that commented assertions are of special interest because developers might have removed them before deployment in order to reduce gas cost, believing them to always hold. In total, we obtained 6061 v0.5 contracts including 11076 assertions (the V5 benchmark set), and 77 v0.6 contracts including 163 assertions (the V6 benchmark set).

We compare Solicitous[2] against three other tools: Solc-Verify [24,25] and VeriSol [30] that verify Solidity source code, and Mythril [15] that verifies EVM bytecode. Mythril differs from the other tools in that it is a purely bounded checking engine of three transactions. Unlike Solicitous, Solc-Verify and VeriSol, Mythril does not produce safe inductive invariants, and contracts Mythril reports safe can be considered safe only up to three transactions after contract deployment. In this sense Mythril can report only unsafe results, and only if a counterexample within three transactions exists. It is also hard to make claims about the validity of its counterexamples, as Mythril authors do not provide any scientific

---

[2] Available at https://github.com/usi-verification-and-security/solc.

publication that explains their technique. Despite its limitations, Mythril is well known in the smart contracts community for having the best support for language features. In our comparative analysis, Mythril serves as a gold standard for the language support metric. To the best of our knowledge these tools are the only ones with which an automated comparison is possible.[3] Both Solc-Verify and VeriSol support only Solidity v0.5, thus for the comparative analysis using V5 we use a legacy version of Solicitous supporting v0.5 that has no support for counterexample generation. Solc-Verify, VeriSol and legacy Solicitous are sound but over-approximative. Specifically, while safe results are justified in these tools by an inductive invariant that proves safety, the tools do not justify unsafe results: in particular they do not provide an execution that would serve as a counterexample for the validity of an assertion. Therefore we distinguish between 'not safe' and 'unsafe', using the former when no or spurious counterexample is produced and the latter when a concrete counterexample proves a real bug. We separately evaluate the current Solicitous implementation using V6 to assess the concrete counter-example generation for proving unsafe results.

5.1   Counterexample Generation

The overall results for the V6 benchmark set is shown in Table 1. We run Solicitous with two different types of encodings where integer arithmetic is encoded both without and with modularity. The former allows arbitrarily large values, while the latter models overflow and underflow precisely. Mythril reports 13 safe contracts up to three transactions. Solicitous performs the best over this benchmark set, not only guaranteeing a good number of contracts to be safe, but also supporting the language features present in most contracts. The counterexamples of the 7 unsafe contracts reported by Solicitous were all checked to be concrete with the Ethereum evaluator HEVM [19]. Every counterexample leads to a runtime exception. Despite the small number of benchmarks due to Solidity v0.6 being very recent at the time of writing, our results show that Solicitous is capable of generating valuable witnesses of assertion failures that can help developers to prevent vulnerabilities.

In addition to its standard execution, in which a potential assertion failure is reported by mentioning its line number in the source file, Solicitous is also capable of generating concrete counterexamples to prove that the result is unsafe and not spuriously reported not safe due to the over-approximations of unsupported features. Unlike the fixed-size bounded approach of VeriSol and Mythril, Solicitous generates counterexamples of arbitrary length, reporting assertion failures that can happen at any point in the lifecycle of a contract.

5.2   Comparative Analysis

To get a better understanding of Solicitous performance on a larger benchmark set, we evaluated the 0.5 version of Solicitous, Solc-Verify, and VeriSol on V5. The

---

[3] We considered two other tools for the comparison, namely Zeus [28] and SAFEVM [7], but Zeus is not publicly available and SAFEVM only supports Solidity v0.4.

Table 1. Experimental results for the V6 benchmark set. INT and MOD stand for integer and modulo arithmetics. SOL and M respectively stand for Solicitous and Mythril. Verified shows the percentage of contracts with either Safe or Unsafe result.

	INT	MOD	
	SOL	SOL	M
Safe	32	27	–
Unsafe	7	7	1
Timeout	5	9	63
Error	33	34	0
Verified	50%	44%	18%

Table 2. Experimental results for the V5 benchmark set. INT and MOD stand for integer and modulo arithimetics. SOL, SV, VS, and M respectively stand for Solicitous, Solc-Verify, VeriSol and Mythril. The Verified row shows the percentage of contracts reported either Safe or Not safe. The best result in each category is highlighted. * These numbers refer to unsafe reports proved by a concrete counterexample.

	INT			MOD			
	SOL	SV	VS	SOL	SV	VS	M
Safe	**1720**	778	135	**1681**	54	117	–
Not safe	142	572	298 (46*)	93	515	198 (31*)	23*
Timeout	586	89	**37**	678	**56**	130	5426
Error	3613	4622	5591	3609	5436	5616	**33**
Verified	**30%**	22%	7%	**29%**	9%	5%	9%

results are shown in Table 2. Safe contracts are those for which all the assertions in the code are proved safe by safe inductive invariants. Not safe contracts have at least one assertion that is not proven safe. The timeout of each individual verification run is 60 s. Verification tasks halted for various types of errors are counted in the error row.

Solicitous reports the largest amount of safe inductive invariants for both arithmetic encodings. Regarding the not safe results, Solicitous can indistinguishably produce spurious and concrete results depending on whether unsupported features are present or not, since they are modelled as non-deterministic operations in order to preserve soundness. Similarly, Solc-Verify introduces overapproximations during its translation to Boogie that produce the same effect. VeriSol presents the same issue, however if no invariant is found it performs a further step creating a bounded model of length four. If the bounded check reports unsafe, VeriSol produces a concrete counterexample. In summary, VeriSol can prove an assertion unsafe only if it can fail within four transactions after contract deployment. The unsafe reports proved by a concrete counterexample are shown with an asterisk in Table 2.

The table also provides a comparison against Mythril. Due the tool limitations, the number of contracts reported safe (579) is not reported in Table 2. Our experiments show that Solicitous is the tool that guarantees the largest amount of contracts to be safe, and that it is also the one able to verify the largest amount of contracts in general. Regarding the coverage of language features, using the amount of errors as a proxy metric, we see that Mythril possesses the best support. Solicitous is closer to it than Solc-Verify or VeriSol. Given the positive results, aligned with the practical nature of the benchmarks set used, Solicitous stands as a valuable tool for Solidity developers.

6   Related Work

There is much interest in formally verifying Ethereum smart contracts, and several tools rely on different techniques to verify either Solidity or Vyper source code, or EVM bytecode. Oyente [31] is one of the pioneers in this field, and uses symbolic execution of EVM bytecode to find common vulnerabilities. Mythril [15] is a security tool based on control-flow analysis and concolic execution of EVM, supporting analysis of assertions up to a fixed bound of transactions. MAIAN [36] is also bounded in the number of transactions and searches EVM bytecode for three specific types of vulnerabilities. Securify [39] encodes EVM bytecode into Datalog to analyze programs, targeting specific types of bugs encoded as data patterns. VerX [37] verifies temporal properties written using a specification language for a particular class of contracts referred as *effectively external callback free*. It requires user intervention when the automatic inference of abstraction predicates fails. The tool is not publicly available. Manticore [34] has a symbolic execution engine for EVM that uses SMT to systematically explore the state space of the contract by repeatedly executing *symbolic transactions*. KEVM [26] is a formal specification of the EVM semantics written in the K-framework [38]. It provides an assisted theorem prover and a specification language for further analysis, including reachability. Similarly, KVyper [22] and KSolidity [21] are the Vyper and Solidity semantics expressed over the K-framework. KLAB [16] provides a specification language tailored for smart contracts that compiles to general K properties and a framework for proof debugging and counterexample analysis based on KEVM. SAFEVM [7] verifies EVM code produced by Solidity 0.4 through an intermediate translation to C that can be checked with three different backend C-verifiers. Zeus [28] translates Solidity into LLVM bitcode which is fed to the SeaHorn [23] model checker. A subset of Solidity not including loops is verified after a translation to F* [10]. Why3 [40] has also been used to verify translated Solidity programs. However, Why3 does not support many of the Solidity constructs and is no longer developed. Slither [20] translates Solidity to its own intermediate SSA language and performs bounded checks for several vulnerability classes. More recently, the tools Solc-Verify [25] from SRI and VeriSol [30] from Microsoft verify Solidity contracts using the language Boogie as intermediate representation. The estimation of gas consumption in order to cope with gas-related vulnerabilities is considered in [32].

7 Conclusions

We presented a formal technique for modeling smart contracts using CHCs. The constructed models (i) formally capture semantic features specific to smart contracts, (ii) enable fully-automated verification of safety properties, and (iii) are suitable for exploiting generic theorem provers in the task of analysis and contract invariants generation. We implemented our technique for the Solidity language and demonstrated its effectiveness through an extensive experimentation involving 6138 contracts specifying 11239 safety properties. Based on these experiments we believe that our technique represents an effective, highly promising avenue for smart contract verification.

Acknowledgements. The authors would like to thank Enrique Fynn and Fernando Pedone for their kind assistance in providing us with the addresses for the deployed Ethereum contracts used in the experiments. This work is partially supported by the SNSF grant 200021_185031 and by the ERC grant FP7-617805.

References

1. Etherscan. https://etherscan.io
2. Smtchecker documentation. https://solidity.readthedocs.io/en/v0.6.6/security-considerations.html#formal-verification
3. Solidity documentation. https://solidity.readthedocs.io
4. theDAO. https://etherscan.io/address/0xbb9bc244d798123fde783fcc1c72d3bb8c1 89413
5. Vyper documentation. https://vyper.readthedocs.io
6. Parity security alert (2017). https://www.parity.io/security-alert-2/
7. Albert, E., Correas, J., Gordillo, P., Román-Díez, G., Rubio, A.: SAFEVM: a safety verifier for Ethereum smart contracts. In: Proceedings of the ISSTA 2019, pp. 386–389 (2019)
8. Alt, L., Reitwiessner, C.: SMT-based verification of solidity smart contracts. In: Margaria, T., Steffen, B. (eds.) ISoLA 2018. LNCS, vol. 11247, pp. 376–388. Springer, Cham (2018). https://doi.org/10.1007/978-3-030-03427-6_28
9. Barrett, K., Cassels, B., Haahr, P., Moon, D.A., Playford, K., Withington, P.T.: A monotonic superclass linearization for Dylan. In: Proceedings of the OOPSLA 1996, pp. 69–82 (1996)
10. Bhargavan, K., et al.: Formal verification of smart contracts: short paper. In: Proceedings of the PLAS 2016, pp. 91–96 (2016)
11. Bjørner, N., Gurfinkel, A., McMillan, K., Rybalchenko, A.: Horn clause solvers for program verification. In: Beklemishev, L.D., Blass, A., Dershowitz, N., Finkbeiner, B., Schulte, W. (eds.) Fields of Logic and Computation II. LNCS, vol. 9300, pp. 24–51. Springer, Cham (2015). https://doi.org/10.1007/978-3-319-23534-9_2
12. Blass, A., Gurevich, Y.: Existential fixed-point logic. In: Börger, E. (ed.) Computation Theory and Logic. LNCS, vol. 270, pp. 20–36. Springer, Heidelberg (1987). https://doi.org/10.1007/3-540-18170-9_151
13. Blicha, M., Hyvärinen, A.E.J., Marescotti, M., Sharygina, N.: A cooperative parallelization approach for property-directed k-induction. In: Beyer, D., Zufferey, D. (eds.) VMCAI 2020. LNCS, vol. 11990, pp. 270–292. Springer, Cham (2020). https://doi.org/10.1007/978-3-030-39322-9_13

14. Bradley, A.R.: SAT-based model checking without unrolling. In: Jhala, R., Schmidt, D. (eds.) VMCAI 2011. LNCS, vol. 6538, pp. 70–87. Springer, Heidelberg (2011). https://doi.org/10.1007/978-3-642-18275-4_7
15. ConsenSys: Mythril (2018). https://github.com/ConsenSys/mythril
16. Erfurt, D., Lundfall, M., Hildenbrandt, E., Livnev, L.: Klab (2020). https://github.com/dapphub/klab
17. Ethereum Foundation: Ethereum: a secure decentralised generalised transaction ledger (2018). http://ethereum.github.io/yellowpaper/paper.pdf
18. Ethereum Foundation: Solidity compiler (2018). https://github.com/ethereum/solidity
19. Ethereum Foundation: HEVM Ethereum evaluator (2020). https://github.com/dapphub/dapptools/tree/master/src/hevm
20. Feist, J., Grieco, G., Groce, A.: Slither: a static analysis framework for smart contracts. arXiv e-prints arXiv:1908.09878, August 2019
21. kframework: Solidity semantics (2018). https://github.com/kframework/solidity-semantics
22. kframework: Vyper semantics (2018). https://github.com/kframework/vyper-semantics
23. Gurfinkel, A., Kahsai, T., Komuravelli, A., Navas, J.A.: The SeaHorn verification framework. In: Kroening, D., Păsăreanu, C.S. (eds.) CAV 2015. LNCS, vol. 9206, pp. 343–361. Springer, Cham (2015). https://doi.org/10.1007/978-3-319-21690-4_20
24. Hajdu, Á., Jovanović, D.: SMT-friendly formalization of the solidity memory model. ESOP 2020. LNCS, vol. 12075, pp. 224–250. Springer, Cham (2020). https://doi.org/10.1007/978-3-030-44914-8_9
25. Hajdu, Á., Jovanovic, D.: solc-verify: a modular verifier for solidity smart contracts. CoRR abs/1907.04262 (2019)
26. Hildenbrandt, E., et al.: KEVM: a complete formal semantics of the Ethereum virtual machine. In: Proceedings of the CSF 2018, pp. 204–217 (2018)
27. Hoare, C.A.R.: An axiomatic basis for computer programming. Commun. ACM 12(10), 576–580 (1969)
28. Kalra, S., Goel, S., Dhawan, M., Sharma, S.: ZEUS: analyzing safety of smart contracts. In: Proceedings of the NDSS 2018. The Internet Society (2018)
29. Komuravelli, A., Gurfinkel, A., Chaki, S.: SMT-based model checking for recursive programs. Formal Methods Syst. Des. 48(3), 175–205 (2016). https://doi.org/10.1007/s10703-016-0249-4
30. Lahiri, S.K., Chen, S., Wang, Y., Dillig, I.: Formal specification and verification of smart contracts for azure blockchain. CoRR abs/1812.08829 (2018)
31. Luu, L., Chu, D.H., Olickel, H., Saxena, P., Hobor, A.: Making smart contracts smarter. In: Proceedings of the CCS 2016, pp. 254–269. ACM (2016)
32. Marescotti, M., Blicha, M., Hyvärinen, A.E.J., Asadi, S., Sharygina, N.: Computing exact worst-case gas consumption for smart contracts. In: Margaria, T., Steffen, B. (eds.) ISoLA 2018. LNCS, vol. 11247, pp. 450–465. Springer, Cham (2018). https://doi.org/10.1007/978-3-030-03427-6_33
33. Marescotti, M., Gurfinkel, A., Hyvärinen, A.E.J., Sharygina, N.: Designing parallel PDR. In: Stewart, D., Weissenbacher, G. (eds.) Proceedings of the FMCAD 2017, pp. 156–163. IEEE (2017)
34. Mossberg, M., et al.: Manticore: a user-friendly symbolic execution framework for binaries and smart contracts. CoRR abs/1907.03890 (2019)

35. de Moura, L., Bjørner, N.: Z3: an efficient SMT solver. In: Ramakrishnan, C.R., Rehof, J. (eds.) TACAS 2008. LNCS, vol. 4963, pp. 337–340. Springer, Heidelberg (2008). https://doi.org/10.1007/978-3-540-78800-3_24

36. Nikolic, I., Kolluri, A., Sergey, I., Saxena, P., Hobor, A.: Finding the greedy, prodigal, and suicidal contracts at scale. CoRR abs/1802.06038 (2018)

37. Permenev, A., Dimitrov, D., Tsankov, P., Drachsler-Cohen, D., Vechev, M.: VerX: safety verification of smart contracts. In: Proceedings of the IEEE SSP 2020 (2020, to appear)

38. Rosu, G., Serbanuta, T.F.: An overview of the K semantic framework. J. Log. Algebraic Program. **79**(6), 397–434 (2010)

39. Tsankov, P., Dan, A., Drachsler-Cohen, D., Gervais, A., Bünzli, F., Vechev, M.: Securify: practical security analysis of smart contracts. In: Proceedings of the CCS 2018, pp. 67–82. ACM (2018)

40. Why3: Why3 (2018). http://why3.lri.fr/

Smart Derivatives: On-Chain Forwards for Digital Assets

Alfonso D. D. M. Rius[1](✉) and Eamonn Gashier[2]

[1] Department of Computing, Imperial College London, London, UK
`a.delgado17@imperial.ac.uk`
[2] Centre for Blockchain Technologies, University College London, London, UK
`eamonn@blockscholes.io`

Abstract. In this paper, we present a framework for the development of on-chain forwards (and futures). This utilises smart contracts to automate the custody of collateral and settlement of payouts on expiry. Importantly, our framework also enables forwards to be traded without counterparty risk or reliance on off-chain assets (such as fiat currencies). To achieve this, we build on our previous work on on-chain options and demonstrate how the relevant mathematical guarantees can be extended to forwards. In addition, we discuss recent trends in cryptoasset derivatives, capital requirements, and other design considerations (such as the use of split contracts). This paper will be of interest to academics and practitioners interested in financial smart contracts.

Keywords: Financial cryptography · Blockchain · Smart contracts · Derivatives

1 Introduction

The market for digital asset derivatives has grown rapidly over the past year, now exceeding \$15 billion in daily volume.[1] A derivative is a contract between two or more parties that derives its value from an underlying variable (the *underlying*) and is settled at a future date. The underlying will typically be an asset (e.g. Apple stock), an index (e.g. S&P 500) or an interest rate (e.g. LIBOR). As a result of this relationship, the price of a derivative is affected by fluctuations in the price (or state) of the underlying. The most common types of derivatives are options, forwards, futures and swaps.

Derivatives have been hailed as a fertile ground for smart contracts (Eskandari et al. [1]), though formal work in this area has been scarce (see e.g. Clack [2] and Fries and Kohl-Landgraf [3]). In our previous paper (the "**Options Paper**" [4]), we introduced a framework for the creation of on-chain call and put options, encompassing a series of design principles that are sensitive to the characteristics of distributed ledger technology (DLT). Amongst these characteristics

---

[1] Nominal value of notional traded, as reported by `Skew.com` (accessed 29 May 2020).

© Springer Nature Switzerland AG 2020
T. Margaria and B. Steffen (Eds.): ISoLA 2020, LNCS 12478, pp. 195–211, 2020.
https://doi.org/10.1007/978-3-030-61467-6_13

are the pseudonymity of participants, deterministic message-processing, and the inability to exercise (direct) control over off-chain assets. Through financial engineering, we were able to eliminate counterparty risk and to settle all payouts in cryptoassets (e.g. ether), removing the need for parties to use fiat currencies. We also showed how smart contracts can be used to automate the custody of collateral and settlement of obligations on expiry, with the potential to generate savings in cost and time vis-à-vis traditional (off-chain) trading venues. It is this capacity to automate aspects of the derivatives lifecycle that can be said to endow these contracts with a dose of "smartness".

In this paper, we wish to extend our framework to cover another type of derivative - *forwards*. These are contracts comprising an obligation to buy (or sell) an underlying (e.g. ether) at a future date (the *expiry*). The price at which this contract is bought is referred to as the *forward price*. Forwards and futures are equivalent contracts in terms of exposure to the underlying; the distinguishing feature is that forwards are traded *over-the-counter (OTC)*, whereas futures are *exchange-traded* contracts. As will be explained in this paper, our derivatives exhibit characteristics that are associated with each of these instruments.

This paper is structured as follows. In Sect. 2, we landscape the evolution of the derivatives market and mention some noteworthy new entrants. In Sect. 3, we show how forwards can be constructed from a combination of call and put options. This allows us to draw from the formulae in the Options Paper, with the corresponding mathematical guarantees, and reapply them in the construction of on-chain forwards. In Sect. 4, we evaluate the benefits and shortfalls of our design and highlights areas for future work (such as split contracts and stablecoin integration). We assume a general familiarity with DLT concepts and derivatives terminology. For a more detailed introduction to these topics, as well as the benefits and risks associated with trading derivatives, we gladly refer readers to the Options Paper.

2 Evolution of the Derivatives Market

When we completed our work on on-chain options in late 2018, the market for cryptoasset derivatives was in its infancy. The shortage of financial products and liquid trading venues made it difficult for market participants to obtain leverage and, more importantly, to hedge their exposure to adverse price moves. At the time of writing, cryptoassets remain highly volatile. For instance, bitcoin has a realised volatility of 89%, whereas ether's realised volatility is 105%.[2] We can contrast this to the S&P500's volatility, which notwithstanding the shocks induced by coronavirus pandemic, stands at 33%.[3] At the same time, cryptoassets are subject to price jumps; in statistical terms, the distribution of returns has

---

[2] Annualised standard deviation of daily returns over a 365 day window. Source: Skew.com (accessed 29 May 2020).

[3] Annualised standard deviation of daily returns for the S&P500 (Total Return) index, based on a 252 trading day window (as of 29 May 2020).

long tails.[4] Without the hedging properties of derivatives, market participants can be left in a very vulnerable position.

As anticipated in our previous paper, the derivatives market has expanded rapidly over the course of 2019 and 2020. Although the derivatives data offered by aggregators like Skew.com is currently limited and their methodology is not disclosed, we now have a starting point for the purpose of market sizing. At $15 billion in daily volume, the derivatives market overshadows the spot market (with just $0.8 billion in volume).[5] This characteristic is also observed in mature financial markets (see e.g. Deutsche Börse Group [6]).

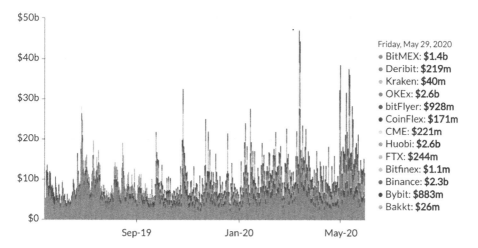

Fig. 1. Bitcoin forwards/futures volumes (May 19–May 20). Source: Skew.com

As Fig. 1 shows, the forwards/futures market is dominated by BitMEX and (to a lesser extent) Deribit.[6] These are both unregulated venues that do not require participants to disclose their identity, and settle all transactions in cryptoassets. Regulated exchanges, such as the Chicago Mercantile Exchange (CME) and Bakkt (a new entrant owned by the Intercontinental Exchange), are much lower in the pecking order.

---

[4] In a distribution of daily returns, high sigma moves for cryptoassets are far more frequent than those experienced in other asset classes (e.g. 8 instances of $+/-10\%$ daily moves for bitcoin in 2019).

[5] "Real" spot volume data from Bitwise [5] (accessed 29 May 2020). Note that derivatives volumes are inflated through leverage (that is, they reflect the contracts' notional). Nonetheless, they help us ascertain market participants' exposure to cryptoassets through derivatives (versus spot).

[6] The chart includes volumes for perpetual swaps (BitMEX's most popular product), though these are (as their name indicates) swaps designed to track spot prices through regular payments to parties that are ITM, as opposed to forwards or futures.

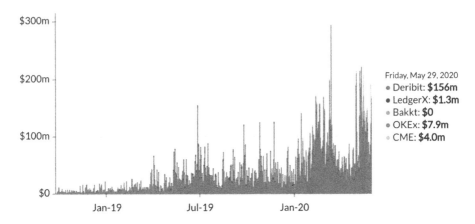

Fig. 2. Bitcoin option volumes (Sep 18–May 20). Source `Skew.com`

Figure 2 tells a similar story. The leading trading venue for options is Deribit (an unregulated venue). LedgerX, a regulated swap execution facility requiring full collaterisation and physical settlement, is a distant contender. Bakkt launched its options (on bitcoin futures) in late 2019, with CME entering this product line in early 2020. While still early to gauge how much liquidity these offerings will attract, both have yet to capture a significant size of the options market.

It is also worth considering a couple of developments in on-chain derivatives within the Decentralised Finance (DeFi) space. In early 2020, dYdX launched perpetual futures that rely on conventional margining. Similarly, the recently launched Opium Exchange enables parties to enter into on-chain futures, options and swaps through partial collaterisation. Although the DeFi space continues to grow, these products have attracted low volumes to date, which we think stems in part from their inability to eliminate counterparty risk and jump risk (as we noted in the Options Paper).[7] For criticisms of design choices within DeFi and technical constraints, see Samani [7] and Rius [8].

The fact that unregulated venues have managed to attract far more liquidity (in both forwards and options markets) cannot be attributed solely to the facilitation of tax avoidance and other illicit activities. In our view, it reflects inherent inefficiencies in the manner in which conventional trading venues operate, including the chain of intermediary brokers that traders are subjected to. At the same time, we think that the case for robust on-chain derivatives that eliminate counterparty risk and jump risk remains an attractive proposition.

---

[7] Defi Pulse reports that $130 million is locked up in on-chain derivatives (accessed 29 May 2020). However, we note that this includes Synthetix, a platform for trading tokenised assets, which are not derivatives in the common use of the term (as they have no settlement or expiry).

3   From Options to Forwards

3.1   Flashback: Our Design Principles

In the Options Paper, we presented a framework for the management of an option's lifecycle through the use of smart contracts. In laying out this framework, we were guided by the following design principles, which recognise the possibilities and constraints of DLT networks.

1. **Full collaterisation:** this allows us to eliminate both counterparty risk and jump risk; there is sufficient collateral to meet the payout in every state of the world, regardless of whether the price jumps to 0 or even infinity.
2. **Limited intervention:** we make use of a contract factory model to minimise the frictions involved in creating and trading derivatives.
3. **Minimising costs:** parties are not required to overcollaterise their positions and the smart contract will net out payments wherever possible to free up capital. In addition, no agency costs are incurred by trading these contracts. Since contracts are physically settled and the premium is paid in the underlying too, there is no need to handle fiat.
4. **Checks and balances:** parties can input or negotiate their choice of oracle and (if deemed fit) arbitrator.
5. **Managing systemic risk:** each derivative is a standalone child contract. We do not wish to escrow all collateral in a single smart contract to reduce systemic (i.e network-wide) risk if a vulnerability is identified or exploited.

In the Options Paper, we proved that the guarantee of a full payout would be upheld in every state of the world. In Sect. 3.3, we seek to build on the formulae introduced in said paper to build new products that retain this guarantee.

3.2   The Put-Call Parity

On expiry, a forward buyer will realise a gain/(loss) if the forward price is greater/(lower) than the spot price.[8] Intuitively, the buyer can generate a profit by receiving the underlying asset (for which they paid below the spot price) and then selling it in the market.

Options are flexible derivatives that can be combined to (synthetically) recreate the payoffs of other instruments, including forwards. A buyer can obtain the same exposure to the underlying by simultaneously buying a call option and selling a put option with the same strike price and expiry. The combined payoff, which is depicted in Fig. 4, is equivalent to the payoff for the buyer of a forward with the same expiry (Fig. 3). Note that a forward seller would be able to replicate their payoff by taking the opposite side to each option trade: derivatives are a zero-sum game.

---

[8] From the perspective of a forward seller, the payoff is the opposite: forward price - final spot price.

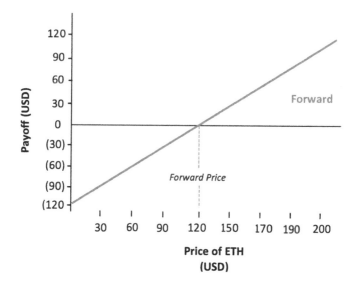

Fig. 3. Forward buyer's payoff: the payoff for the buyer at expiry is the difference between the forward price ($120 per ether) and the market price of ether at the time (the "final spot price").

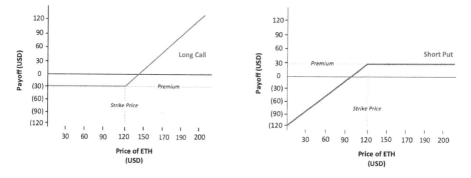

Fig. 4. Long call and short put payoffs: the premium paid for buying the call option is $30, which matches the premium received for selling the put. In both cases, the strike is $120 per ether.

It is perhaps helpful to elaborate on this equivalence further. In an efficient market, if an at the money (ATM) call option and an ATM put option with the same expiry were to have different premiums, an arbitrage opportunity would arise.[9] For instance, if the call option is trading with a $40 premium, then a risk-free profit could be earned by (1) buying the ATM call; (2) selling the ATM put; and (3) selling the forward. In this case, the buyer has neutralised their

---

[9] In this context, ATM indicates that the options' strike is (at the time of purchase) equal to the price of the forward with the same expiry (i.e. ATM forward).

exposure to the underlying, so as to no longer be affected by spot price moves, and generated a risk-free profit in the process. The converse applies if the put option has a higher premium than the call. This no-arbitrage relationship is referred to as the *Put-Call Parity* (see e.g. Hull [9]).[10]

3.3   Back to the Future

In our Options Paper, we introduced a design for on-chain call and put options. The associated formulae are set out in Appendix A and Appendix B, respectively. The important implication of the Put-Call Parity is that we can build on our earlier work to arrive at new formulae for physically-settled, fully-collaterised forwards. To achieve this, we need to combine the payment flows for call and put options (from the perspective of each forward party), both at inception of the options (i.e. $t = 0$) and at expiry. In doing so, and based on the foregoing discussion, we will reference the numbered equations in the appendices and replace references to the "strike price" with "forward price". A plus sign indicates an inflow (i.e. a credited sum), whereas a minus sign represents an outflow for the party.

Forward buyer at $t = 0$ (*i.e. equations c1 + p2*):

$$-call\ premium + put\ premium - notional * \frac{forward\ price}{spot} \tag{f1}$$

Forward seller at $t = 0$ (*i.e. equations c2 + p1*):

$$call\ premium - put\ premium - 2 * notional \tag{f2}$$

Before we repeat this exercise for the payment flows on expiry, we need to consider whether there is any room for netting. To do so, we need to distinguish between amounts that the smart contract must retain in escrow and those that will be forwarded to a counterparty. Following the logic outlined in our Options Paper, we know that if the smart contract holds (2 * notional), this will suffice to meet the full payout on forward contracts in every state of the world. Since the (notional * forward price/spot) that the buyer is posting would be forwarded to the seller, we can deduct this from the (2 * notional) that the seller would otherwise need to post for escrowing purposes.

It is helpful to divide the possible states of the world into two ranges to showcase how this netting would work in practice.

State Range 1: forward price < 2 * spot

Let us imagine that the spot price of ETH is $240. Bob (buyer) wishes to purchase a forward with a notional of 1 ETH and expiry in 1 year for $300.

---

[10] See e.g. this guide from CME: https://www.cmegroup.com/education/courses/introduction-to-options/put-call-parity.html.

Here, formula *f1* indicates that the buyer must transfer: $1 * (300/240) = 1.25$ ETH to the seller. We know from the formulae that the seller needs to transfer a total of (2 * notional) to the smart contract, and that this will satisfy the payouts in every state of the world. To avoid an unnecessary (and more capital intensive) back-and-forth between the seller and the smart contract, the smart contract can retain the buyer's payment (instead of forwarding it to the seller), and deduct this from the amount that the seller needs to post. In other words, the seller now only needs to transfer: $2 \text{ ETH} - 1.25 \text{ ETH} = 0.85$ ETH.

State Range 2: forward price $\geq$ (2 * spot)

This time round, the forward is trading at $500 and the spot price remains $240. If we were to apply equation *f1*, Bob would prima facie need to transfer $1 * (500/240) = 2.08$ ETH (equivalent to $499) to the seller. However, we know that the collateral that needs to be escrowed is merely 2 * 1 ETH (equivalent to $480). In this scenario, the smart contract would simply return the surplus amount ($19 in ETH) to the buyer to prevent a "payment overflow". Consequently, the seller does not need to transfer any collateral, as the payment that the buyer would otherwise make to the seller can be escrowed instead. Since the seller is not required to give up anything of value in this range of states, the buyer will not want to trade forwards at such high prices. In this range of states, our framework does not allow a trade to occur; we discuss the implications of this further in Sect. 4.4.

Based on this reasoning, and relying on the Put-Call Parity to cancel out the premiums, we arrive at the following modified formulae:

Forward buyer at t = 0 (after netting):

$$- \max(notional * \frac{forward\ price}{spot}, 2 * notional) \qquad \textbf{(f1*)}$$

Forward seller at t = 0 (after netting):

$$-(2 * notional - \textbf{\textit{f1*}}) \qquad \textbf{(f2*)}$$

Last, we can follow the same process of combining the formulae at expiry to arrive at the following payment flows.

Forward buyer (t = expiry):

if final price > forward price (*equations c3.1 + p4.2*):

$$[notional - notional * \frac{forward\ price}{final\ price}] + [notional * \frac{forward\ price}{final\ price}] = notional$$
(f3.1)

if final price ≤ forward price (*equations c3.2 + p4.1*):

$$[0] + [notional] = notional \qquad (f3.2)$$

Forward seller (t = expiry):

if final price > forward price (*equations c4.1 + p3.2*):

$$[notional * \frac{forward\ price}{final\ price}] + [notional - notional * \frac{forward\ price}{final\ price}] = notional$$
(f4.1)

if final price ≤ forward price (*equations c4.2 and p3.1*):

$$[notional] + [0] = notional \qquad (f4.2)$$

An interesting result arises from these calculations. Regardless of where the spot price lands on expiry, each party will receive the notional. In other words, the escrowed amount will always be split equally. While this might seem counterintuitive, we will now proceed to proof the validity of the results by calculating parties' overall (nominal) payoffs for the transaction with a practical example.

3.4   Practical Example

The following sequence of events illustrates the creation of a forward between Alice (seller) and Bob (buyer).

- Bob is willing to buy a forward contract as he has a positive outlook on the spot market. The spot price at the time is $214. He decides to set the notional at 10 ETH, the forward price at $218, and expiry in 1 months' time.
- Since we are within "State Range 1", Bob transfers: $10 * (218/214) = 10.2$ ETH to the smart contract. This amount will now be held in escrow.
- Alice is a miner who has a long position in ETH. In order to hedge her position against a drawdown in the market, she decides to accept Bob's offer. To post her part of the collateral (and meet the 2 * notional requirement), she transfers $20 - 10.2 = 9.8$ ETH to the smart contract. (Note that Fig. 6 reflects the unnetted flow of payments for simplicity; the smart contract would not forward the buyer's payment to the seller, instead retaining this in escrow).

Forward/Future

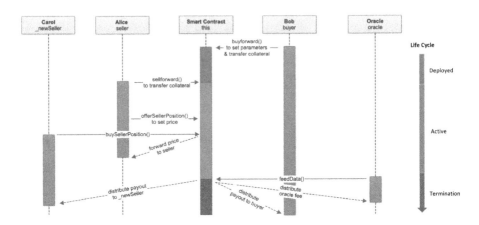

Fig. 5. Forwards' technical lifecycle: this diagram shows the workings of the smart contract functions and the associated calls from parties. For simplicity, we assume that only Alice will trade out of her position and that arbitration has not been opted into.

- The parties will be free to exit their position from that point onward, as the escrowed sum will cover the payout in every state of the world. In Fig. 5, we show the set of function calls and payout distributions in a scenario where Alice decides to trade out of her position.
- On expiry (in 1 months' time), the final price is fed by the oracle to the smart contract. Since this variable will determine the payouts, the parties can choose to opt into arbitration at inception to set out a means of resolving disputes. In the Options Paper, we detail how dispute resolution could be made to work in practice.
- If the final price is > \$218, say \$250, Bob will be in the money (ITM).[11] As we established in the previous section, he will receive 10 ETH (the nominal). At the prevailing spot price, and after accounting for the nominal value of his outflow at inception, this equates to a profit of \$320. Consequently, Alice has suffered a loss of \$320.
- On the other hand, if the final price is ≤ \$218, say \$150, Bob will be out of the money (OTM). At the prevailing spot price, and after accounting for the nominal value of his outflow at inception, this equates to a loss of \$680. As a result, Alice will earn a profit of \$680 from this trade.

A simple way to check the operations outlined above is to calculate: *dif(forward price, final price) * notional*. For the party that is ITM/(OTM), the resulting sum will constitute a profit/(loss). It is the fact that we are dealing with cryptoassets as collateral and eliminating the need for parties to post

---

[11] A buyer is ITM when the forward price is greater than the spot price (in which case, the seller is OTM). The converse holds true when the forward price is below the spot price.

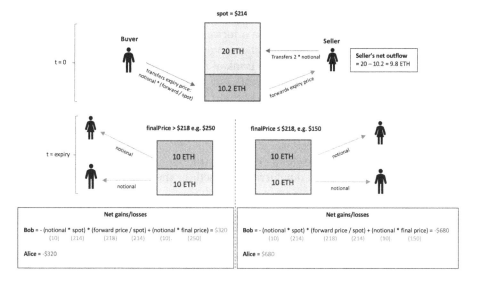

Fig. 6. Forward payoffs: this diagram shows the assets transferred into and out of the contract account at inception and expiry. The boxes at the bottom show the fiat-equivalent gains/losses, though all transfers are made in the underlying (ETH). We have excluded any oracle and arbitration fees for simplicity.

additional funds on expiry that complicates the maths. Our design requires us to determine the spot price of the underlying at the time of each transfer (i.e. at inception and expiry) in order to arrive at parties' nominal payoffs. To assist with this process, the calculation of distributions due on expiry is automated by the smart contract's embedded logic. It is the oracle's calling of the relevant function to feed the price that triggers the distribution in an atomic manner; as Fig. 5 indicates, parties need not lift a finger after transferring the collateral at inception. As the practical example shows, parties can be sure that the payoffs will add up to their entitlement in every state of the world.

4   Design Observations

4.1   Forwards or Futures?

As mentioned in the introduction, forward contracts are traded OTC, whereas futures are exchange-traded contracts. Both instruments offer the same exposure to the underlying (margining aside). However, parties' risk exposure may differ between forwards and futures, which can cause a disparity in their respective prices. In particular, futures are marked-to-market at the end of each trading session (e.g. on weekdays) and collateral is exchanged to reflect daily gains or losses. This is not necessarily the case for forwards, as parties are free to tailor the frequency of these collateral adjustments. As a result, futures reduce counterparty risk by regularly posting margin in response to the underlying's price moves. In addition, a party to a future contract usually faces a clearing-house (directly or indirectly), whereas a forward creates a bilateral relationship between two private parties. Clearinghouses are well capitalised entities with a very low probability of defaulting (see Bank of England [10]); in the post-Lehman world, the same cannot be said of investment banks offering OTC derivatives.

Like futures, our on-chain forwards could very well be listed in a regulated venue. Since counterparty risk is eliminated (through full collaterisation), the risk exposure is also closer to that of a future. On the other hand, the product is not designed to allow for collateral adjustments prior to expiry (as there is no need for this), which is more fitting of a forward. We leave it to future work to determine the fair pricing of our forwards based on these observations.

4.2 Split Contracts: Adding Natural Language

On-chain derivatives rely on smart contract code as a means of automating the operational aspects of the derivatives lifecycle, including the flow of value transfers and the feeding of spot prices. However, there will be instances in which parties will wish to protect themselves from errors in the code, cover a broader range of (off-chain) obligations, or otherwise facilitate dispute resolution off-chain. The non-operational parameters of a contract are better addressed through the use of (written) natural language. The natural language text can be linked to the code through the use of a hash (and vice versa), creating an inextricable link. Miller [11] refers to this construction of code, natural language and a cryptographic interface as a split contract.

As argued in Rius [8,12], split contracts are a powerful tool to increase effi-ciencies in derivatives markets. The use of smart contracts is particularly attrac-tive for assets that are native to a DLT network (such as BTC and ETH), as the network's own settlement efficiencies can be utilised. In relation to conven-tional asset classes, the International Swaps and Derivatives Association (ISDA) is already looking to combine the operational efficiencies of code with its natural language templates for OTC trading, which are used broadly by market par-ticipants (see [13,14]). We think that there may be room for extending ISDA's framework to cover on-chain instruments and intend to research this intersection in future work.

4.3 Capital Intensity

A challenge that we face when evaluating our on-chain forwards is that they are capital intensive. This is a challenge that our on-chain options themselves faced. By using these options as our building blocks, we inherit their strengths (in the form of mathematical guarantees that certain risks will be eliminated), but also their shortfalls.

We think that the lack of leverage is a small price to pay in view of the poten-tial to use on-chain forwards for hedging purposes. This is particularly important for miners, exchanges and other market participants which, by the nature of their operations, have a structural long position in an underlying cryptoasset.

Last, we wish to refer to an argument that we advanced in the Options Paper. Cryptoassets remain highly volatile and, as such, parties who have not fully collaterised their trade would need to set aside significant collateral to deal with margin calls. In the existing unregulated trading venues and DeFi applications, there is no guarantee that a counterparty will meet a margin call (either in time or at all). This means that losses must be "socialised", which entails clawing back profit from non-defaulting parties.[12] Further, because of cryptoassets' volatility and the need to set aside collateral, the opportunity cost of unused capital is far lower than it would be with other asset classes.

As observed in Rius [8], pseudonymous parties who do not wish to rely on intermediaries or clearinghouses must fully collaterise their trade, or otherwise stomach the heightened counterparty risk. Since it is hard to obtain legal recourse following a counterparty's default, there is little incentive for parties to post further collateral when prices move against them; any party can consciously default and walk away unscathed, without fear of enforcement.

4.4   Feasible Range of Pricing

As set out in Sect. 3.3, our framework does not support trades where the forward is being priced at above 2 * spot price (i.e. in State Range 2). Due to the way that the formulae operate, the seller would not be required to post anything of value, making the trade unattractive for the buyer (as they have nothing to gain).

Given the volatility of cryptoassets, it is conceivable that parties may want to enter into a forward contract with a distant expiry date (e.g. greater than 1 year), and that such a contract could perhaps command a forward price in State Range 2. After all, BTC returned approximately 94% 2019. A traditional trading venue like CME would be able to deal with this scenario through conventional margining, as the parties' identity is known and recourse against defaults is available. On the other hand, the DeFi applications examined would not be able to offer the same assurances to participants, severely limiting the effectiveness of the trade (particularly for hedgers).

4.5   Stablecoins: A New Hope

The use of stablecoins has accelerated in recent years. Apart from Tether's USDT, which has been associated with market manipulation and is presently not fully collaterised, new centralised alternatives have emerged from the likes of Circle (USDC), Gemini (GUSD) and Paxos (PAX). The Libra Association, which boasts of having several large corporations as its members, is planning to introduce a series of stablecoins within the Libra network (Libra [15]). Within

---

[12] For an overview of the socialised losses system in BitMEX, see https://blog.bitmex.com/bitmex-vs-cme-futures-guide/. On BitMEX's insurance fund, see https://blog.bitmex.com/the-bitmex-insurance-fund/.

the DeFi space, Maker [16] has introduced the DAI stablecoin, a decentralised (synthetic) alternative that is collaterised with Ethereum-based tokens.

Stablecoins are very interesting for our purposes. As set out above, the reason why the maths become so complex, and parties need to post significant collateral, is that we are trying to circumvent the need to rely on an off-chain payment instrument (fiat currencies). Stablecoins bring the fiat currency paradigm on-chain, thereby opening new possibilities for payment netting and collateral transfers. By using stablecoins, we would also be able to cover all possible pricing states, circumventing the limitation highlighted in the previous subsection. We leave it to future work to explore the benefits and risks of expanding our framework to integrate stablecoins.

5 Conclusion

Derivatives have been identified as a promising field for automation, with smart contracts being a worthy candidate for this task. In this paper, we presented a framework for the creation of on-chain forwards. By building on our previous work on on-chain options, we were able to extend a number of mathematical guarantees that ensure counterparty risk and jump risk are eliminated when trading forwards.

We also landscaped the current state of the derivatives market and covered a number of shortfalls in our design. In particular, our on-chain forwards remain capital intensive compared to products with conventional margining. In view of the volatility of cryptoassets, and the user pseudonimity that masks on-chain interactions, we regard this as a worthwhile sacrifice in exchange for a robust hedging instrument. With trading venues like BitMEX offering up to 100x leverage, the cryptoasset market is hardly in need of another leveraged product.

In future work, we plan to explore the benefits of linking natural language templates (such as those produced by ISDA) to our on-chain derivatives. We also intend to consider the use of stablecoins to make our products more efficient from a capital perspective. In the interim, we hope that this paper will drive further work by academics and businesses on on-chain financial instruments.

A   Appendix: Call Option

The diagram below shows the flow of payments for a physically settled, fully collaterised call option for 10 ETH (notional) with a strike price of $250, and a premium of 1.6 ETH (equivalent to $280 at the initial spot price).

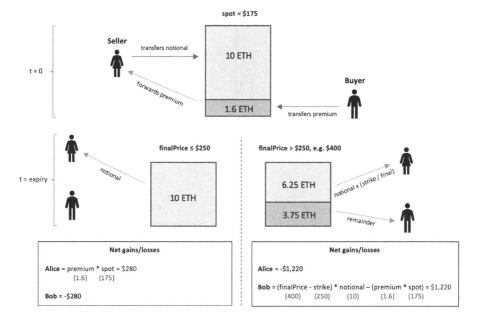

Inflows/outflows at t = 0:

$$Long\ call = -premium \qquad (c1)$$

$$Short\ call = premium - notional \qquad (c2)$$

Inflows/outflows at t = expiry, if call option is ITM (finalPrice > strike):

$$Long\ call = notional - (notional * \frac{strike}{finalPrice}) \qquad (c3.1)$$

$$Short\ call = notional * \frac{strike}{finalPrice} \qquad (c4.1)$$

Inflows/outflows at t = expiry, if call option is ATM/OTM (finalPrice ≤ strike):

$$Long\ call = 0 \qquad (c3.2)$$

$$Short\ call = notional \qquad (c4.2)$$

B   Appendix: Put Option

The diagram below shows the flow of payments for a physically settled, fully collaterised put option for 10 ETH (notional) with a strike price of $70, and a premium of 0.2 ETH (equivalent to $35 at the initial spot price).

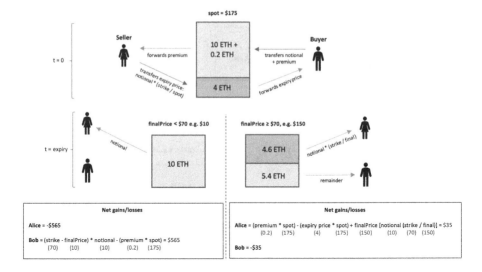

Inflows/outflows at t = 0:

$$Long\ put = -premium - notional \qquad (p1)$$

$$Short\ put = premium - notional * \frac{strike}{spot} \qquad (p2)$$

Inflows/outflows at t = expiry, if put option is ITM (finalPrice < strike):

$$Long\ put = 0 \qquad (p3.1)$$

$$Short\ put = notional \qquad (p4.1)$$

Inflows/outflows at t = expiry, if put option is ATM/OTM (finalPrice ≥ strike):

$$Long\ put = notional - (notional * \frac{strike}{finalPrice}) \qquad (p3.2)$$

$$Short\ put = notional * \frac{strike}{finalPrice} \qquad (p4.2)$$

References

1. Eskandari, S., Clark, J., Sundaresan, V., Adham M.: On the feasibility of decentralized derivatives markets. The Computer Research Repository (CoRR), abs/1802.04915 (2018). https://arxiv.org/abs/1802.04915
2. Clack, C.D., Bakshi, V.A., Braine, L.: Smart contract templates: foundations, design landscape and research directions. The Computer Research Repository (CoRR), abs/1608.007771 (2016). http://arxiv.org/abs/1608.00771

3. Fries, C.P., Kohl-Landgraf, P.: Smart derivative contracts (detaching transactions from counterparty credit risk: specification, parametrisation, valuation) (2018). https://doi.org/10.2139/ssrn.3163074
4. Delgado De Molina Rius, A., Gashier, E.: Smart derivatives: on-chain financial options for digital assets. Paper presented at the IEEE Crypto Valley Conference (2019). Shorturl.at/oFHVX
5. Bitwise: Economic and non-economic trading in bitcoin: exploring the real spot market for the world's first digital commodity (2019). https://www.sec.gov/comments/sr-nysearca-2019-01/srnysearca201901-5574233-185408.pdf
6. Deutsche Börse Group: The global derivatives market: a blueprint for market safety and integrity (2009)
7. Samani, K.: Defi's invisible asymptotes (2020). https://multicoin.capital/2020/06/04/defis-invisible-asymptotes/
8. Delgado De Molina Rius, A.: Smart contracts: taxonomy, transaction costs and design trade-offs (2020, forthcoming)
9. Hull, J.: Options, Futures, and Other Derivatives. Pearson, London (2014)
10. Rehlon, A., Nixon, D.: Central counterparties: what are they, why do they matter and how does the bank supervise them? Bank of England Quarterly Bulletin Q2 (2013)
11. Miller, M.S., Stiegler, M.: The digital path: smart contracts and the third world. In: Birner, J., Garrouste, P. (eds.) Markets, Information and Communication. Austrian Perspectives on the Internet Economy. Routledge (2003). https://doi.org/10.4324/9780203180419_chapter_3
12. Delgado De Molina Rius, A.: Split contracts: bridging smart contract code and legal prose (2018). (Unpublished manuscript)
13. ISDA and Linklaters: whitepaper: smart contracts and distributed ledger - a legal perspective (2017). https://www.isda.org/a/6EKDE/smart-contracts-and-distributed-ledger-a-legal-perspective.pdf
14. ISDA: Legal guidelines for smart derivatives contracts: introduction (2019). https://www.isda.org/a/MhgME/Legal-Guidelines-for-Smart-Derivatives-Contracts-Introduction.pdf
15. The Libra Association: Libra whitepaper (v2.0) (2020). https://libra.org/en-US/white-paper/
16. The Maker Foundation: MakerDAO's multi-collateral dai (MCD) system

The Good, The Bad and The Ugly: Pitfalls and Best Practices in Automated Sound Static Analysis of Ethereum Smart Contracts

Clara Schneidewind[✉], Markus Scherer[✉], and Matteo Maffei[✉]

TU Wien, Vienna, Austria
{clara.schneidewind,markus.scherer,matteo.maffei}@tuwien.ac.at
https://secpriv.wien/

Abstract. Ethereum smart contracts are distributed programs running on top of the Ethereum blockchain. Since program flaws can cause significant monetary losses and can hardly be fixed due to the immutable nature of the blockchain, there is a strong need of automated analysis tools which provide formal security guarantees. Designing such analyzers, however, proved to be challenging and error-prone. We review the existing approaches to automated, sound, static analysis of Ethereum smart contracts and highlight prevalent issues in the state of the art. Finally, we overview *eThor*, a recent static analysis tool that we developed following a principled design and implementation approach based on rigorous semantic foundations to overcome the problems of past works.

Keywords: Static analysis · Smart contracts · Formal methods

1 Introduction

Blockchain technologies are revolutionizing the distributed system landscape, providing an innovative solution to the consensus problem leveraging probabilistic guarantees and incentives. In particular, they allow for the secure execution of payments, and more in general computations, among mutually distrustful parties. While some cryptocurrencies, like Bitcoin [27] provide only a limited scripting language tailored to payments, others, like Ethereum [32], support a quasi Turing complete[1] smart contract language, allowing for advanced applications such as trading platforms [25,28], elections [26], permission management [7,11], data management systems [5,29], or auctions [13,17]. With the growing complexity of smart contracts, however, also the attack surface grows. This is particularly problematic as smart contracts control real money flows and hence constitute an attractive target for attackers. In addition, due to the immutable nature of blockchains, smart contracts cannot be modified once they are uploaded to the blockchain, which makes the effects of security vulnerabilities permanent. This is not only a theoretical threat, but a practical problem, as demonstrated by

---

[1] Supporting a Turing complete instruction set, Ethereum enforces termination by bounding the number of computation steps based on an prespecified resource limit.

© Springer Nature Switzerland AG 2020
T. Margaria and B. Steffen (Eds.): ISoLA 2020, LNCS 12478, pp. 212–231, 2020.
https://doi.org/10.1007/978-3-030-61467-6_14

infamous hacks, such as the DAO hack [1] or the Parity hacks [2,3] which caused losses of several millions of dollars. This state of affairs calls for reliable static analysis tools which are accessible to the users of the Ethereum system, that is, developers, who need to be able to verify their contracts before uploading them to the blockchain, and users interacting with existing smart contracts, who need tool assistance to assess whether or not those contracts (which are published in human unreadable bytecode format on the blockchain) are fraudulent.

State of the Art. The bug-finding tool Oyente [24] (published in 2016) pioneered the (automatic) static analysis of Ethereum smart contracts. This work highlighted, for the first time, generic types of bugs that typically affect smart contracts, and proposed a tool based on symbolic execution for the detection of contracts vulnerable to these bugs.

A particular compelling feature of Oyente is that it is a push-button tool that does not expect any interaction or deeper knowledge of the contract semantics from the user. On the downside, however, Oyente does not provide any guarantees on the reported results, being neither sound (absence of false negatives) nor complete (absence of false positives) and, thereby, yielding only a heuristic indication of contract security. Given the importance of rigorous security guarantees in this context, several approaches have been later proposed for the verification of Ethereum smart contracts. In particular, alongside tools that aim at machine-checked smart contract auditing [6,9,18,19], a line of work focused on automation in the verification process to ensure usability and broad adaption. Despite four years of intense research, however, until now only four works on such sound and fully automatic static analysis of Ethereum smart contracts have been published. Furthermore, all of these works exhibit shortcomings which ultimately undermine the security guarantees that they aim to provide.

Our Contributions. Motivated by these struggles, we overview the difficulties that arise in the design of sound static analysis for Ethereum smart contracts, and the pitfalls that so far hindered the development of such analyzers. To this end, we first give a short introduction to the Ethereum platform and its native smart contract language (Sect. 2). Afterwards, we illustrate the challenges in automated smart contract verification by overviewing existing works in this field with emphasis on their weak spots (Sect. 3 and 4). We conclude the paper summarizing our experiences in the design of *eThor* [30], a static analyzer for EVM bytecode we recently introduced, along with a breakdown of the components we deem crucial to achieve efficiency and soundness (Sect. 5).

2 Ethereum and the EVM Bytecode Language

Ethereum is (after Bitcoin) the second most widely used cryptocurrency with a market capitalization of over 14 billion U.S. dollars[2]. Compared to Bitcoin,

---

[2] As of the fourth quarter of 2019, see https://www.statista.com/statistics/807195/ethereum-market-capitalization-quarterly.

Ethereum stands out due its expressive scripting language, that enables the execution of arbitrary distributed programs, so called *smart contracts*. Ethereum smart contracts are stored on the blockchain in bytecode that is jointly executed by the network participants (also called *nodes*) according to the Ethereum Virtual Machine (EVM) – Ethereum's execution environment that is implemented in different clients[3]. Smart contract execution is part of Ethereum's consensus protocol: The state of the system is determined by a jointly maintained, tamper-resistant public ledger, the *blockchain*, that holds a sequence of transactions. Transactions do not only indicate money transfers, but can also trigger contract executions. To derive the state of the system, every node locally executes the transactions in the blockchain as specified by the EVM. For advancing the system, nodes broadcast transactions which are assembled into blocks and appended to the blockchain. While the correctness of the system is ensured by the nodes validating all blocks, fairness is established by a proof of work mechanism: Only nodes (called *miners*) capable of solving a computationally hard puzzle are eligible to propose a block. This adds randomness the selection of proposers and prevents a minority from steering the evolution of the system.

Ethereum Ecosystem. The state of the Ethereum system (called *global state*) consists of the state of all virtual accounts and their balances in the virtual currency *Ether*. Smart contracts are special account entities (*contract accounts*) that in addition to a balance hold persistent storage and the contract code. While non-contract (so called *external*) accounts can actively transfer fractions of their balance to other accounts, contract accounts are purely governed by their code: A contract account can be activated by a transaction from another account and then executes its code, possibly transferring money or stimulating other contracts. Similarly, a contract can be created on behalf of an external account or by another contract. We will in the following refer to such inter-contract interactions as *internal transactions*, as opposed to *external transactions* that originate from external accountexternal accounts and are explicitly recorded on the blockchain.

EVM Bytecode. The EVM bytecode language supports designated instructions to account for the blockchain ecosystem. These encompass primitives for different flavors of money transfers, contract invocations, and contract creations. Most prominently, the CALL instruction allows for transferring money to another account while at the same time triggering code execution in case the recipient is a contract account. Other domain-specific bytecodes include instructions for accessing the blockchain environment such as the instructions SSTORE and SLOAD for reading and writing the cells of the persistent contract storage. Further the instruction set contains opcodes for accessing information on the ongoing (internal) transaction (its caller, input, or value transferred along) and for

---

[3] Currently, a Go, a C++ and a Python implementation are distributed by the Ethereum Foundation: https://github.com/ethereum/wiki/wiki/Clients,-tools,-dapp-browsers,-wallets-and-other-projects.

computation: The EVM is a stack-based machine supporting standard instructions for arithmetic and stack manipulation. The control flow of a contract is also subject to the stack-based architecture: conditional and unconditional jump instructions allow for resuming execution at another program position that is determined by the value on the stack. While these features would make EVM bytecode Turing-complete, to enforce termination the execution of EVM smart contracts is bounded by an upfront-specified resource called *gas*. Every instruction consumes gas and the execution halts with an exception when running out of gas. The gas budget is set by the initiator of the transaction who will pay a compensation to the miner of the enclosing block for the effectively consumed amount of gas when executing the transaction. Due to the low-level nature of EVM bytecode, smart contracts are generally written in high-level languages (most prominently the *Solidity* [4] language) and compiled to EVM bytecode.

3   Related Work on Automated Sound Static Analysis of Ethereum Smart Contracts

We overview the state of the art in the automated static analysis of Ethereum smart contracts. So far there have been works on four static analyzers published that come with (explicit or implicit) soundness claims: the dependency analysis tool Securify [31] for EVM bytecode, the static analyzer ZEUS [22] for *Solidity*, the syntax-guided *Solidity* analyzer NeuCheck [23], and the bytecode-based reachability analysis tool EtherTrust [14]. By implicit soundness claim, we mean that the tool claims that a positive analysis result guarantees the contract's security (i.e., absence of false negatives with respect to a specific security property). While Securify, ZEUS, and EtherTrust implement semantic-based analysis approaches, NeuCheck is purely syntax-driven.

Securify supports data and control flow analysis on the EVM bytecode level. To this end, it reconstructs the control-flow graph (CFG) from the contract bytecode and transforms it into SSA-form. Based on this structured format, it models immediate data and control flow dependencies using logical predicates and establishes datalog-style logical rules for deriving transitive dependencies which are automatically computed using the enhanced datalog engine *Soufflé* [21]. For checking different security properties, Securify specifies patterns based on the derived predicates which shall be sufficient for either proving a property (compliance patterns) or for showing a property to be broken (violation patterns).

ZEUS analyzes *Solidity* contracts by first translating them into the intermediate language LLVM bitcode and then using off-the-shelf model checkers to verify different security properties. In the course of the translation, ZEUS uses another intermediate layer for the *Solidity* language which introduces abstractions and that allows for the insertion of assumptions and assertions into the program code which express security requirements on the contract. The security properties supported by ZEUS are translated to such assertion checks, possibly in conjunction with additional property-specific contract transformations.

NeuCheck analyzes *Solidity* contracts by pattern matching on the contract syntax graph. To this end, it translates *Solidity* source code into an XML parse tree. Security properties are expressed as patterns on this parse tree and are matched by custom algorithms traversing the tree.

EtherTrust implements a reachability analysis on EVM bytecode by abstracting the bytecode execution semantics into (particular) logical implications, so called Horn clauses, over logical predicates representing the execution state of a contract. Security properties are expressed as reachability queries on logical predicates and solved by the SMT solver *z3* [12]. EtherTrust was a first prototype that later evolved into the *eThor* analyzer, which we will discuss in Sect. 5.1.

All presented tools focus on generic (contract-independent) security properties for smart contracts. However, the underlying architectures allow for extending the frameworks with further properties. Foremost, the tool *eThor* supports general reachability properties and hence also functional properties characterized in terms of pre- and postconditions. For the soundness considerations in this paper we put the focus on the abstractions of generic security properties.

4   Challenges in Sound Smart Contract Verification

EVM bytecode exposes several domain-specific subtleties that turn out to be challenging for static analysis. Furthermore, even the definition itself of security properties for smart contracts is highly non-trivial and subject to ongoing research. Furthermore, characterizing relevant generic security properties for smart contracts is highly non-trivial and subject to ongoing research. We will examine both of these problems in the following.

4.1   Analysis Design

We summarize below the main challenges that arise when designing a performant and still sound analysis for Ethereum smart contracts:

- *Dynamic jump destinations:* Jump destinations are statically unknown and computed during execution. They might be influenced by the blockchain environment as well as the contract state. As a consequence, the control flow graph of a contract is not necessarily determinable at analysis time.
- *Mismatch between memory and stack layout:* The EVM has a (stack) word size of 256 bits while the memory (heap) is fragmented into bytes and addressed accordingly. Loading words from memory to the stack, and conversely writing stack values to memory, requires (potentially costly) conversions between these two value formats.
- *Exception propagation and global state revocation:* If an internal transaction (as, e.g., initiated by a CALL) fails, all effects of this transaction including those on the global state (e.g., writes to global storage) are reverted. However, such a failure is not propagated to the callee, who can continue execution in the original global state. Modeling calls must thus save the state before calling in order to account for global state revocation.

- *Native support for low-level cryptography:* The EVM supports a designated SHA3 instruction to compute the hash of some memory fraction. As a consequence, hashing finds broad adaption in Ethereum smart contracts, and the Solidity compiler bases its storage layout on a hash-based allocation scheme.
- *Dynamic calls:* The recipient of an (inter-contract) call is specified on the stack and hence subject to prior computation. Consequently, the recipient is not necessarily derivable at analysis time, resulting in uncertainty about the behavior of the callee and the resulting effects on the environment.
- *Dynamic code creation:* Ethereum supports the generation of new smart contracts during transaction execution: A smart contract can deploy another one at runtime. To do so, the creating smart contract reads the deployment code for the new contract from the heap. The newly created contract may hence be subject to prior computation and even to the state of the blockchain.

In order to effectively tackle these challenges, several contributions of independent interest are required, such as domain-specific abstractions (e.g., suitable over-approximations of unknown environment behavior); the preprocessing of the contract to reconstruct its control flow or call graph; (easily checkable) assumptions that restrict the analysis scope (e.g., restriction to some language fragment); and optimizations or simplifications in intermediate processing steps (e.g, contract transformations to intermediate representations). Altogether, these analysis steps enlarge the semantic gap between the original contract semantics and the analysis, making it harder to reliably ensure the soundness of the latter. In the following, we will review in more detail the tension between soundness and performance of the analysis, and how past works stumbled in this minefield.

Soundness. Ensuring the soundness of the analysis requires a rigorous specification of the semantics of EVM bytecode. The original semantics was written in the Yellow Paper [32]. This paper however, from the beginning exhibited flaws [15,18,19] and underspecified several aspects of bytecode execution. The ultimate truth of smart contract semantics could therefore only be extracted from the client implementations provided by the Ethereum foundation. In the course of time, several formal specifications of the EVM semantics have been proposed by the scientific community [15,18,19], leading the Yellow paper to be replaced by an executable semantics in the K framework [18][4].

For the high level language Solidity, despite first efforts within the scientific community [8,10,20,34,35], there exists at present no full and generally accepted formal semantics. Consequently the semantics of Solidity is only defined by its compilation to EVM bytecode. Since the compiler is subject to constant changes, Solidity constitutes a moving target.

The complexity and uncertainty about the concrete semantics made most works build on ad-hoc simplified versions of the semantics which do not cover all language features and disregard essential aspects of the EVM's execution model.

---

[4] Also called the Jello paper: https://jellopaper.org.

```
1 contract Test {
2   bool test = false;
3   function flipper () { if (msg.sender != 0){flip();} }
4   function flip () internal {test = !test;} }
```

Fig. 1. Simple contract highlighting an unsoundness in Securify's dependency analysis.

ZEUS [22], for instance, defines an intermediate goto language for capturing the core of Solidity. The semantics of this language, however, is inspired by the (ad-hoc) semantic modeling used in Oyente [24], inheriting an essential flaw concerning global state revocation: In case that an internal transaction returns with an exception, the effects on the global state are not reverted as they would be in real EVM (and Solidity) executions. Since the translation to the intermediate language is part of the analysis pipeline of [22], such a semantic flaw compromises the soundness of the whole analysis.

Also Securify [31] introduces an ad-hoc formalism for EVM bytecode semantics. This is not, however, related to the dependency predicates used for the analysis, but just serves for expressing security properties. It is hence unclear to which extent the dependency predicates faithfully reflect the control flow and value dependencies induced by the EVM semantics. Assessing the correctness of this approach is difficult, since no full logical specification of the dependency analysis is provided[5]. Indeed we found empirical indication for the unsoundness of the dependency analysis in the presence of complicated control flow. Consider the example contract depicted in Fig. 1. For better readability, we present the contract in the high-level language *Solidity*, a language inspired by *JavaScript*, that is centered around contracts which are used analogously to the concept of classes in object-oriented programming languages. The depicted contract `Test` has a global boolean field `test`. Global fields are reflected in the persistent storage of the contract and constitute the contract state. The public function `flipper()` allows every account but the one with address 0 to flip the value of the `test` field: For checking the restriction on the calling account, the `flipper()` function accesses the address of the caller using *Solidity*'s `msg.sender` construct. For writing the `test` field, the internal function `flip()` is called. Internal functions are not exposed to the public, but are only accessible by the contract itself and calls to such functions are compiled to local jumps. The use of internal functions consequently substantially complicates the control flow of a contract.

We identified a soundness issue affecting the conditional reachability of contract locations. We identified a correctness issue that affects both the soundness and completeness of Securify. This incorrectness becomes evident in the violation pattern that checks for unrestricted writes. An unrestricted write is a write access of the global storage that can be performed by any caller. The violation pattern states that such an unrestricted write is guaranteed to happen if there is a SSTORE instruction whose reachability does not depend on the caller of

---

[5] Only an excerpt is presented in [31], and the public implementation at https://github.com/eth-sri/securify intermingles specification and implementation.

the contract. This pattern should not be matched by the Testcontract since the only write access to the Test's sole variable test in function flip() is only reachable via the function flipper where it is conditioned on the caller (msg. sender). Hence not every contract can write the test variable, but the write access depends on the caller. Still Securify reports this contract to match the violation pattern, consequently proving the wrong statement that there is no dependency between writing the test field and the account calling the contract. Note that even though showing up in a violation pattern (hence technically producing false positives), the underlying issue also affects the soundness of the core dependency analysis[6]. Securify specifies a *may dependency* relation to capture (potential) abstract dependencies between program locations. For correctly (i.e. soundly) abstracting the dependencies in real programs, the absence of a may dependency should imply a corresponding independence in the real program. Since the may dependency relation is used in both compliance and violation patterns, without such a guarantee Securify can be neither sound nor complete. The example refutes this guarantee and thereby illustrates the importance of providing clear formal correctness (i.e. soundness) statements for the analysis.

These two examples show how the missing semantic foundations of the presented analysis approaches can lead to soundness issues in the core analysis design itself. These problems are further aggravated once additional stages are added to the analysis pipeline for increasing performance, since such additional stages are often not part of the correctness considerations.

Performance. For performance reasons, it is often unavoidable to leverage well-established and optimized analysis frameworks or solvers. This leaves analysis designers with the challenge to transform their analysis problem into a format that is expressible and efficiently solvable within the targeted framework while preserving the semantics of the original problem.

ZEUS [22] makes use of off-the-shelf model checkers for LLVM bitcode and hence requires a transformation of smart contracts to LLVM bitcode. The authors describe this step to be a 'faithful expression-to-expression translation' that is semantics preserving, but omit a proof for this property. The paper itself later contradicts this statement: The authors report on LLVM's optimizer impacting the desired semantics. This indicates that the semantics of the LLVM bitcode translation does not coincide with the one of the intermediate language, since it would otherwise not be influenced by (semantics-preserving) optimizations.

The Securify tool [31] makes use of several preprocessing steps in order to make EVM bytecode amenable to dependency analysis: First it reconstructs the control flow graph of a contract and based on that transforms the contract to SSA form. The correctness of these steps is never discussed. Indeed we found Securify's algorithm for control flow reconstruction to be unsound: The algorithm fails when encountering jump destinations that depend on blockchain information. In such a case the control flow should be considered to be non-reconstructable since a jump to such a destination may result in a valid jump at runtime or

---

[6] We illustrate the issue with a violation pattern for easier presentation and since the affected compliance pattern turned out not to be implemented in Securify.

```
1 contract DAO{                        1 contract Mallory{
2   mapping (address => uint) bal;     2   address DAO_ADDRESS = 0x...;
3                                       3   DAO dao = DAO(DAO_ADDRESS);
4   function invest () public payable{ 4
5     bal[msg.sender]+= msg.value;}     5   function investSmallAmount() public {
6                                       6①  dao.invest().value(1);}
7   function withdraw () public {       7
8     address a = msg.sender;           8②  function() paybable{
9     if (bal[a] > 0){                  9②  dao.withdraw();}
10      a.call.value(bal[a]);    ③      10④
11      bal[a] = 0;}}            ⑤
12 }
```

Fig. 2. Simplified DAO contract.

simply fail due to a non-existing jump destination. Securify's algorithm however does not report an error on such a contract, but returns a (modified) contract that does not contain jumps. Such an unsound preprocessing step again impacts the soundness of the whole analysis tool since it breaks the assumption that the contract semantics is preserved by preprocessing.

4.2   Security Properties

The Ethereum blockchain environment opens up several new attack vectors which are not present in standard (distributed) program execution environments. This is in particular due to the contracts' interaction with the blockchain which is in general controlled by unknown parties and hence needs to be considered hostile. It is a partly still open research question what characterizes a contract that is robust in such an environment. A well-studied property in this domain is robustness against reentrancy attacks. We will focus on this property in the following to illustrate the challenges and pitfalls in proving a contract to be safe.

Reentrancy Attacks. Reentrancy attacks became famous due to the DAO hack [1] in 2016 which caused a loss of over 60 Million dollars, and ultimately led to a hard fork (a change in the consensus to explicitly ignore this particular incident) of the Ethereum blockchain. The DAO was a contract implementing a crowd-funding mechanism which allowed users to invest and conditionally withdraw their invested money from the contract. An attacker managed to exploit a bug in the contract's withdraw functionality for draining the whole contract, stealing the money invested by other participants. We illustrate the main workings of this attack with a simplified example in Fig. 2.

The depicted DAO contract has a global field bal which is a mapping from account addresses to the payments that they made so far. The two (publicly accessible) functions of the contract allow arbitrary entities to invest and withdraw money from the contract. If an account with address a calls the invest function, the money transferred with this invocation is registered in the bal mapping. Similar to msg.sender, *Solidity* provides the variable msg.value to access the value transferred with the currently executed (internal) transaction.

The `withdraw` function when being called by a, will check the amount of money invested by a so far and in case of non-zero investments, transfer the whole amount of Ether (as recorded in `bal[a]`) back to a. This is done using Solidity's `call` construct for function invocations: it initiates a transaction to the specified address (here `a`) and allows for the specification of the value to be sent along (using `.value()`). The attack on the `DAO` contract can be conducted by an attacker that deploys a malicious contract `Mallory` to first make a small investment to the `DAO` contract (①) that they later withdraw (②). When the `withdraw` function of the `DAO` contract calls back to the sender (`Mallory`, ③), not only the corresponding amount of Ether is transferred, but also code of `Mallory` is executed. This is as in the case that not a specific (*Solidity*) function gets invoked with a contract call, the contract's *fallback function* (a function without name and arguments) is executed. `Mallory` implements this function to call the `DAO`'s `withdraw` function (④). Since at this point the balance of `Mallory` in the `bal` mapping has not been updated yet, another value transfer to `Mallory` will be initiated (⑤). By proceeding in this way, `Mallory` can drain all funds of the `DAO` contract.

The depicted attack is an example of how standard intuitions from (sequential) programming do not apply to smart contracts: In Ethereum one needs to consider that an internal transaction hands over the control to a (partly) unknown environment that can potentially schedule arbitrary contract invocations.

Formalizing Security Properties. While bug-finding tools typically make use of heuristics to detect vulnerable contracts, there have been two systematic studies that aim at giving a semantic characterization of what it means for a contract to be resistant against reentrancy attacks: The resulting security definitions are call integrity [15] and effective callback freedom [16].

Call integrity follows non-interference-style integrity definitions from the security community. It states that two runs of a contract in which the codes of the environment accounts may differ, should result in the same sequences of observable events (in this case outgoing transactions). In simpler words, another contract should not be able to influence how a secure contract spends its money. Intuitively, this property is violated by the `DAO` contract since an attacker contract can make the contract send out more money than in an honest invocation.

In contrast, effective callback freedom is inspired by the concept of linearizability from concurrency theory: It should be possible to mimic every (recursive) execution of a contract by a sequence of non-recursive executions. The `DAO` contract violates this property since the attack is only possible when making use of recursion (or callbacks respectively). After each callback-free execution, the `investments` mapping will be updated, so that a subsequent execution will prevent further withdraws by the same party.

While [15] shows how to over-approximate the hyperproperty call integrity by three simpler properties (the reachability property single-entrancy and two dependence properties), [16] does not indicate a way of statically verifying effective callback freedom, but proves this property to be undecidable. This leaves sound, and (efficiently) verifiable approximations an open research question.

```
 1 library Lib {
 2    struct Data { mapping (address => uint) map;}
 3    function write(Data storage self, address a, uint v) { self.map[a] = v;}
 4    function get(Data storage self, address a) returns (uint) {
 5      return (self.map[a]);} }
 6
 7 contract DAO {
 8    Lib.Data bal;
 9    function invest() public payable {
10      Lib.write(bal, msg.sender, Lib.get(bal, msg.sender) + msg.value);}
11    function withdraw () public {
12      address a = msg.sender;
13      if (Lib.get(bal, a) > 0){
14        a.call.value(Lib.get(bal, a));
15        Lib.write(bal, a, 0);}} }
```

Fig. 3. Simplified DAO contract using a library

Checking Security Properties. The state-of-the-art sound analyzers discussed so far do not build on prior efforts of semantically characterizing robustness against reentrancy attacks, but come up instead with own ad-hoc definitions.

Securify. Securify expresses security properties of smart contracts in terms of compliance and violation patterns over data flow and control flow dependency predicates. In [31] it is stated that Securify supports the analysis of a property called 'no writes after call' (NW) which is different from (robustness against) reentrancy, but still aims at detecting bugs similar to the one in the DAO. The NW property is defined using an ad-hoc semantic formalism, and it states that for any contract execution trace, the contract storage shall not be subject to modifications after performing a CALL instruction. Intuitively, this property should exclude reentrancy attacks by preventing that the guards of problematic money transfers are updated only after performing the money transferring call. However, this criterion is not sufficient e.g., since reentrancies can also be triggered by instructions other than CALL. For proving the NW property, the compliance pattern demands that a CALL instruction may not be followed by any SSTORE instruction. We found this pattern not to be sufficient for ensuring compliance with the NW property (nor robustness against reentrancy). We will illustrate this using a variation of the DAO contract in Fig. 3. This contract implements the exact same functionality as the one in Fig. 2. The only difference is that the access to the balance mapping is handled via the library contract Lib. Ethereum actively supports the use of library contracts in that it provides a specific call instruction, called DELEGATECALL, that executes another contract's code in the environment of the caller. When calling Lib.write in the withdraw function, such a delegated call to the (external) library contract is executed. Executing write in the context of contract DAO will then modify DAO's storage (instead of the one of the Lib contract). In order to let the write and the get functionality access the right storage position (where DAO stores the bal mapping), these functions take as first argument the reference to the corresponding storage location. Same as the version in Fig. 2, this contract is vulnerable to a reentrancy bug. Also, it violates the NW property: The storage of the contract

```
1 contract DAO{                            1 contract DAO{
2   mapping (address => uint) bal;         2   mapping (address => uint) bal;
3   uint lock = 0;                         3   uint lock = 0;
4   function withdraw () public {          4   function withdraw () public {
5     if(lock ==1){throw;}                 5     if(lock ==1){throw;}
6     lock=1;                              6     lock=1;
7     address a = msg.sender;              7     address a = msg.sender;
8     a.call.value(bal[a]);                8     a.call.value(bal[a]);
9     bal[a] = 0;                          9     bal[a] = 0;
10    lock=0;}                             10    lock=0;}
11  function switchLock () {
12    lock = 1-lock;} }
```

Fig. 4. Simple versions of the DAO contract with reentrancy protection.

can be changed after executing the call (when writing the `bal`) mapping. Still, this contract matches the compliance pattern (which should according to [31] guarantee the contract to satisfy the NW property), since it does not contain any explicit SSTORE instruction. This example illustrates how without a proven connection between a property and its approximation, the soundness of an analyzer can be undermined. This issue does not only constitute a singular case, but is a structural problem: There are counter examples for the soundness of 13 out of the 17 patterns presented in [31], as we detail out in [30].

ZEUS. In [22], the property to rule out reentrancy attacks is only specified in prose as a function being vulnerable 'if it can be interrupted while in the midst of its execution, and safely re-invoked even before its previous invocations complete execution.' This definition works on the level of functions, a concept which is only present on the *Solidity* level, and leaves open the question what it means for *a contract* to be robust against reentrancy attacks. The authors distinguish between 'same-function-reentrancy' and 'cross-function-reentrancy' attacks, but do not consider cross-function reentrancy (where a function reenters another function of the same contract) in the analyzer. We found that without excluding cross-function reentrancy also single-function reentrancy cannot be prevented.

Consider the versions of the DAO contract depicted in Fig. 4 that aim to prevent reentrancy using a locking mechanism. The global `lock` field tracks whether the `withdraw` function was already entered (indicated by value 1). In that case, the execution of `withdraw` throws an exception. Otherwise the `lock` is set and only released when concluding the execution of `withdraw`. While the two depicted contracts implement the exact same `withdraw` function, the first contract's function is vulnerable to a reentrancy attack, while the second one is safe. This is as the first contract implements a public `switchLock()` function that can be used by anyone to change the `lock` value. An attacker could hence mount the standard attack with the only difference that they would need to invoke the `switchLock()` function once before reentering to disable the reentrancy protection in line 5. Without exposing such functionality, the second contract is safe, since every reentering execution will be stopped in line 5. This example shows that ZEUS' approach of analyzing functions in isolation to exclude 'same-function-reentrancy' is not sound.

Another issue in the reentrancy checking of ZEUS is caused by the reentrancy property exceeding the scope of the analysis framework. For proving a function resistant against reentrancy attacks, ZEUS checks whether it is ever possible to reach a call when a function is recursively invoked by itself. However, the presented translation to LLVM bitcode only models non-recursive executions of a function. Consequently, the reentrancy property cannot be expressed as a policy (which could be translated to assertions in the program code), but requires to rewrite the contract under analysis to contain duplicate functions that mimic reentering function invocations. This contract transformation is not part of any soundness considerations. As a result, not only the previously discussed unsoundness due to the lacking treatment of cross-function reentrancies is missed, but it is also disregarded that *Solidity*'s `call` construct is not the only way to reinvoke a function. Indeed there are several other mechanisms (e.g., direct function calls) that allow for the same functionality. Still, ZEUS classifies contracts that do not contain an explicit invocation of the `call` construct to be safe by default.

NeuCheck. The NeuCheck tool formulates a syntactic pattern for detecting robustness against reentrancy attacks. The pattern checks for all occurrences of the `call` function whether they are followed by the assignment of a state variable. As discussed for Securify, the absence of explicit writes to the storage does not imply that the storage stays unchanged. Hence the example in Fig. 3 would also serve as a counter example for the soundness claim of NeuCheck. Also, as discussed for ZEUS, `call` is not the only way of invoking another contract, what reveals another source of unsoundness in this definition. Furthermore, neither the security properties that the tool aims for are specified nor any justifications for the soundness of this syntactic analysis approach are provided.

5   How to Implement a Practical, Sound Static Analysis?

After exposing the problems that can arise when designing a practical, sound static analysis, we discuss how we tackled them in developing *eThor* and the underlying static analysis specification framework *HoRSt* [30]. We then present the elements we identified as essential for designing an automated sound analysis: A semantic foundation, sound abstractions, and a principled implementation.

5.1   Overview of *eThor*

eThor was preceded by an earlier prototype, called *EtherTrust* [14]. *EtherTrust* implemented the rules of a formal abstract semantics in $Java^{TM}$ and exported them to *z3*. While this design showed promising preliminary results, it turned out to be too inflexible for our purposes: Changes in the abstract semantics had to be tediously translated to $Java^{TM}$ code; the non-declarative manner of specifying rules made them hard to write and review; and the lack of a proper intermediate representation made it difficult to implement custom optimizations before passing the verification task to *z3*.

These limitations are addressed by *HoRSt* [30], a dedicated high-level language for designing Horn clause based static analyses. *HoRSt* allows for the specification of Horn Clause based semantic rules in an declarative language and can apply different optimizations before translating them to *z3* formulae. Thus, the semantics specification and the tool implementation are logically separated and systematic experiments with different versions of the semantics are possible. Additionally, optimizations can be implemented independently from specific semantics, improving the overall performance in a robust fashion.

eThor [30] combines *HoRSt* with an abstract EVM semantics, a parser to read EVM bytecodes, and a set of EVM-specific preprocessing steps, including the reconstruction of the control flow and the propagation of constants. It supports general reachability analysis and in particular allows for (soundly) verifying that a contract is single-entrant (following the definition in [15]).

What distinguishes *eThor* from prior work discussed in Sect. 3 is its well defined analysis specification that is supported by rigorous formal soundness proofs, as well as its principle implementation design. Prior works do not come with thorough formalization and proofs what ultimately leads to soundness issues in the analyzers, as we confirmed empirically. In contrast, *eThor* lives up to its theoretical soundness guarantees in an extensive evaluation while still being practical in terms of runtime and precision. In the following, we will discuss in detail the semantic foundations, modular design and implementation of *eThor* as well as its empirical performance evaluation.

5.2   Semantic Foundations

A formal soundness guarantee requires a formal semantics of the system under analysis. Such a semantics might be specified on paper [33] or in an executable fashion [15,18], but in any case has to be precise enough to unambiguously capture all relevant aspects of the system. While semantics defined in prose tend to be more readable, executable semantics lend themselves to automated testing or tooling (e.g., the generation of interpreters or symbolic debuggers [18]). *eThor* builds on the semantics presented in [15] which consists of a logical specification as well as an executable F^* semantics that was rigorously tested for its compliance with the Ethereum client software.

Using a formal semantics, security properties can be precisely characterized. *eThor* bases its analysis for the absence of reentrancy attacks on the notion of single-entrancy [15]. Single-entrancy captures that the reentering execution of a contract should not initiate any further internal transactions. This property rules out reentrancy attacks and also contributes to the proof strategy for the more general call integrity property as detailed out in [15].

However, an executable semantics combined with precisely defined security properties alone does not yield a useful analysis tool. While these components allow experts to semi-automatically verify contracts (using frameworks such as [6,15,18,19]), automation generally requires abstractions to be feasible.

5.3   Sound Abstractions

A first step to reduce the complexity of the analysis problem, and hence to make it amenable to automation, is to over-approximate the target property. For *eThor*, we over-approximate the single-entrancy property by the simpler *call unreachability* [14] property. Call unreachability breaks down single-entrancy to a simple criterion on the execution states of a single contract, as opposed to reasoning about the structure and evolution of whole call stacks. Such over-approximations have to be proven sound – every program fulfilling the over-approximated property also has to fulfill the original property. A corresponding proof for single-entrancy is conducted in [14].

To further simplify the analysis task, the relevant parts of a contract's execution behavior need to be abstracted in a sound manner. In *eThor* for this purpose we devised an abstract semantics based on Horn clauses that we proved in [30] to soundly over-approximate the small step semantics in [15]. The abstract semantics simplifies and summarizes complex execution scenarios that may emerge due to the uncertain blockchain environment, as we exemplify in the following.

In the largely unknown blockchain environment it is infeasible to track constraints on all unknown values. Instead, following a standard technique in abstract interpretation, we enriched our domain of concrete computation values with a new value $\top$, signifying *all* possible values. This designated symbol over-approximate under-specified values while dropping constraints on them. Some computations, such as the SHA-3-computations or unaligned memory accesses in EVM, are due to their complexity over-approximated by $\top$ in *eThor*.

Further, we abstract the initial invocation of a contract and its reentering executions as they might be scheduled by (unknown) contracts which are called during execution. In *eThor* we ignore the call stack up until the first execution of the analyzed contract, and assume a contract to be called in an arbitrary environment instead. Also, we only distinguish between the first execution of a contract under analysis in a call chain and a reentering execution of such a contract. In this way we collapse all reentering executions while modeling relevant storage invariants with a sophisticated domain-specific abstraction.

For an extended discussion of the abstractions used in *eThor*, including those for inter-contract calls, gas treatment, and memory layout, we refer to [30].

In summary, *eThor* provides a reliable soundness guarantee for the single-entrancy property, proving that a contract labeled secure by *eThor* satisfies single-entrancy. This guarantee stems from the soundness of the abstract semantics with respect to the rigorously tested small step semantics and from the proof that call unreachability (formulated in terms of the abstract semantics) soundly approximates single-entrancy. The soundness of the abstract semantics further enables the sound verification of arbitrary reachability properties that are expressed in terms of the abstract semantics. In particular this holds for functional contract properties phrased as pre- and postconditions: *eThor* can prove that a contract starting in a state satisfying the precondition is never able to reach a state that does not satisfy the postcondition.

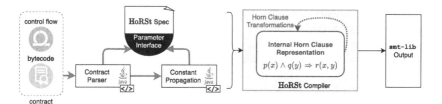

Fig. 5. Architecture of *eThor*

5.4   Implementation Strategies

To arrive at a fast and stable analysis implementation, the analysis task is usually reduced to a known problem supported by performant and well-maintained solvers. This does not only save implementation time and help performance, but it also adds an abstraction layer that facilitates reasoning. For *HoRSt* we decided to use *z3*, respectively Constrained Horn Clauses over `smt-lib`'s linear integer arithmetic fragment, as translation target. We chose *z3* since it is a state-of-the-art solver for program analysis and the fragment suffices to formulate reachability properties.

Architecture. In *eThor*, the generation of `smt-lib` code that models the abstract semantics of a contract is structured into separate and well-defined phases. As can be seen in Fig. 5, the input of *eThor* consists of a contract with reconstructed control flow. The bytecode of the contract is then parsed and constants are propagated within basic blocks. With this information, the abstract semantics (provided as a *HoRSt* specification) is instantiated to a set of Horn clauses which are, after several transformation steps, translated to `smt-lib` formulae.

Optimizations. The performant analysis of real-world programs might require the usage of different optimizations, such as leveraging domain-specific knowledge in a pre-processing step. Such preprocessing may include propagation of constants [30,31], reconstruction of the control flow [30,31], computation of memory offsets [31], and pruning of irrelevant parts of the input [30,31].

As mentioned in Sect. 4.1, unsoundness introduced in any optimization or preprocessing step (e.g., by using an unsound decompiler) immediately affects the soundness of the whole analysis. It is hence crucial to formally reason over each step. In *eThor* the control flow graph reconstruction of a smart contract is realized by symbolically computing the destinations of all jump instructions based on a simplified version of the sound abstract semantics used for the later reachability analysis. Therefore, all soundness considerations from the full abstract semantics carry over to the preanalysis. Since this version of the semantics falls into the datalog solvable fragment as implemented by the *Soufflé* solver, we encoded this simple abstract semantics as a *Soufflé* program. To automate the generation of such preprocessing steps in the future we plan to extend *HoRSt* with *Soufflé* as additional compilation target.

Evaluation. To ensure the correctness and perfomance of an analysis tool, it is inevitable to extensively and systematically test the tool implementation. To this end synthetic, well-understood inputs help to identify problems regarding precision, performance, and correctness early. These, however, may not be representative of the challenges that are found in real-world contracts. Data gathered from a real-world setting, on the other hand, might be difficult to classify manually (i.e. check for presence or absence of properties), making it difficult to check for correctness of the implementation, and may overtax earlier, non-optimized iterations of the analysis tool.be of uncertain ground truth or too complex to give guidance in early stages of the development. In our experience, an automated test suite with corpus of synthetic and real-world inputs is a significant help while experimenting with different formulations and optimizations, as implementation bugs can be found already at an early stage.

For *eThor* we leveraged the official EVM test suite and our own property-based test suite for assessing the correctness of of the abstract semantics and abstract properties. Out of 604 relevant EVM test cases, we terminated on 99%. All tests confirmed the tool's soundness and the possibility of specifying the test suite within *eThor* confirmed the versatility of our approach beyond reentrancy.

The correctness and precision of *eThor* for the single-entrancy property were assessed on a benchmark of 712 real-world contracts. Within a 10 min timeout, *eThor* delivered results for 95% of the contracts, with all of them confirming soundness, and yielding a specificity of 80%, resulting in an F-meassure of 89%. These results do not only demonstrate *eThor*'s practicability on real-world contracts, but also clearly improve over the state-of-the-art analyzer ZEUS. When run on the same benchmark, ZEUS yields a specificity of only 11.4% (challenging its soundness claim) and a specificity of 99.8%, giving an F-measure of 20.4%[7].

6   Future Challenges

To bring forward the robust design and implementation of sound static analyzers, we plan on extending *HoRSt* in multiple ways: We want to integrate *HoRSt* with proof assistants in order to streamline and partially automate soundness proofs. Further, we want to add support for additional compilation targets, and enrich the specification language and compilation to go beyond reachability analysis, and to support restricted classes of hyperproperties.

For the particular case of *eThor*, we want to improve the precision of the analysis, e.g., to include a symbolic treatment of hash values, and to enable the joint verification of multiple interacting contracts. Further, we strive to create a public benchmark of smart contracts exhibiting different security vulnerabilities, as well as mitigations. This would enable the community to systematically compare the performance, correctness, and precision of different tools.

---

[7] *eThor* was evaluated against ZEUS since this is the only tool to implement a property similar to single-entrancy.

Beyond that, we plan to transfer the presented techniques to other smart contract platforms, such a Libra, EOS, or Hyperledger Fabric, which exhibit domain-specific security properties and different semantics.

Acknowledgements. This work has been partially supported by the European Research Council (ERC) under the European Union's Horizon 2020 research (grant agreement 771527-BROWSEC); by the Austrian Science Fund (FWF) through the projects PROFET (grant agreement P31621) and the project W1255-N23; by the Austrian Research Promotion Agency (FFG) through the Bridge-1 project PR4DLT (grant agreement 13808694) and the COMET K1 SBA; and by the Internet Foundation Austria (IPA) through the netidee project EtherTrust (Call 12, project 2158).

References

1. The DAO smart contract (2016). http://etherscan.io/address/0xbb9bc244d798123fde783fcc1c72d3bb8c189413#code
2. The parity wallet breach (2017). https://www.coindesk.com/30-million-ether-reported-stolen-parity-wallet-breach/
3. The parity wallet vulnerability (2017). https://paritytech.io/blog/security-alert.html
4. Solidity (2019). https://solidity.readthedocs.io/
5. Adhikari, C.: Secure framework for healthcare data management using ethereum-based blockchain technology (2017)
6. Amani, S., Bégel, M., Bortin, M., Staples, M.: Towards verifying ethereum smart contract bytecode in isabelle/hol. In: Proceedings of the 7th ACM SIGPLAN International Conference on Certified Programs and Proofs, pp. 66–77 (2018)
7. Azaria, A., Ekblaw, A., Vieira, T., Lippman, A.: Medrec: using blockchain for medical data access and permission management. In: International Conference on Open and Big Data (OBD), pp. 25–30. IEEE (2016)
8. Bartoletti, M., Galletta, L., Murgia, M.: A minimal core calculus for solidity contracts. In: Pérez-Solà, C., Navarro-Arribas, G., Biryukov, A., Garcia-Alfaro, J. (eds.) DPM/CBT -2019. LNCS, vol. 11737, pp. 233–243. Springer, Cham (2019). https://doi.org/10.1007/978-3-030-31500-9_15
9. Bhargavan, K., et al.: Formal verification of smart contracts: short paper. In: Proceedings of the 2016 ACM Workshop on Programming Languages and Analysis for Security, pp. 91–96 (2016)
10. Crafa, S., Di Pirro, M., Zucca, E.: Is solidity solid enough? In: Bracciali, A., Clark, J., Pintore, F., Rønne, P.B., Sala, M. (eds.) FC 2019. LNCS, vol. 11599, pp. 138–153. Springer, Cham (2020). https://doi.org/10.1007/978-3-030-43725-1_11
11. Cruz, J.P., Kaji, Y., Yanai, N.: RBAC-SC: role-based access control using smart contract. IEEE Access **6**, 12240–12251 (2018)
12. de Moura, L., Bjørner, N.: Z3: an efficient SMT solver. In: Ramakrishnan, C.R., Rehof, J. (eds.) TACAS 2008. LNCS, vol. 4963, pp. 337–340. Springer, Heidelberg (2008). https://doi.org/10.1007/978-3-540-78800-3_24
13. Galal, H.S., Youssef, A.M.: Verifiable sealed-bid auction on the ethereum blockchain. In: Zohar, A., et al. (eds.) FC 2018. LNCS, vol. 10958, pp. 265–278. Springer, Heidelberg (2019). https://doi.org/10.1007/978-3-662-58820-8_18

14. Grishchenko, I., Maffei, M., Schneidewind, C.: Foundations and tools for the static analysis of ethereum smart contracts. In: Chockler, H., Weissenbacher, G. (eds.) CAV 2018. LNCS, vol. 10981, pp. 51–78. Springer, Cham (2018). https://doi.org/10.1007/978-3-319-96145-3_4

15. Grishchenko, I., Maffei, M., Schneidewind, C.: A semantic framework for the security analysis of ethereum smart contracts. In: Bauer, L., Küsters, R. (eds.) POST 2018. LNCS, vol. 10804, pp. 243–269. Springer, Cham (2018). https://doi.org/10.1007/978-3-319-89722-6_10

16. Grossman, S., et al.: Online detection of effectively callback free objects with applications to smart contracts. Proc. ACM Program. Lang. 2(POPL), 1–28 (2017)

17. Hahn, A., Singh, R., Liu, C.C., Chen, S.: Smart contract-based campus demonstration of decentralized transactive energy auctions. In: 2017 IEEE Power & Energy Society Innovative Smart Grid Technologies Conference (ISGT), pp. 1–5. IEEE (2017)

18. Hildenbrandt, E., et al.: KEVM: a complete formal semantics of the ethereum virtual machine, pp. 204–217. IEEE (2018). https://doi.org/10.1109/CSF.2018.00022. https://ieeexplore.ieee.org/document/8429306/

19. Hirai, Y.: Defining the ethereum virtual machine for interactive theorem provers. In: Brenner, M., et al. (eds.) FC 2017. LNCS, vol. 10323, pp. 520–535. Springer, Cham (2017). https://doi.org/10.1007/978-3-319-70278-0_33

20. Jiao, J., Kan, S., Lin, S.W., Sanan, D., Liu, Y., Sun, J.: Executable operational semantics of solidity. arXiv preprint arXiv:1804.01295 (2018)

21. Jordan, H., Scholz, B., Subotić, P.: SOUFFLÉ: on synthesis of program analyzers. In: Chaudhuri, S., Farzan, A. (eds.) CAV 2016. LNCS, vol. 9780, pp. 422–430. Springer, Cham (2016). https://doi.org/10.1007/978-3-319-41540-6_23

22. Kalra, S., Goel, S., Dhawan, M., Sharma, S.: ZEUS: analyzing safety of smart contracts. Internet Society (2018). https://doi.org/10.14722/ndss.2018.23082. https://www.ndss-symposium.org/wp-content/uploads/2018/02/ndss2018_09-1_Kalra_paper.pdf

23. Lu, N., Wang, B., Zhang, Y., Shi, W., Esposito, C.: Neucheck: a more practical ethereum smart contract security analysis tool. Pract. Exp. Softw.(2019)

24. Luu, L., Chu, D.H., Olickel, H., Saxena, P., Hobor, A.: Making smart contracts smarter. In: Proceedings of the 2016 ACM SIGSAC Conference on Computer and Communications Security, pp. 254–269 (2016)

25. Mathieu, F., Mathee, R.: Blocktix: decentralized event hosting and ticket distribution network (2017). https://blocktix.io/public/doc/blocktix-wp-draft.pdf

26. McCorry, P., Shahandashti, S.F., Hao, F.: A smart contract for boardroom voting with maximum voter privacy. In: Kiayias, A. (ed.) FC 2017. LNCS, vol. 10322, pp. 357–375. Springer, Cham (2017). https://doi.org/10.1007/978-3-319-70972-7_20

27. Nakamoto, S.: Bitcoin: a peer-to-peer electronic cash system (2008). http://bitcoin.org/bitcoin.pdf

28. Notheisen, B., Gödde, M., Weinhardt, C.: Trading stocks on blocks - engineering decentralized markets. In: Maedche, A., vom Brocke, J., Hevner, A. (eds.) DESRIST 2017. LNCS, vol. 10243, pp. 474–478. Springer, Cham (2017). https://doi.org/10.1007/978-3-319-59144-5_34

29. Panescu, A.T., Manta, V.: Smart contracts for research data rights management over the ethereum blockchain network. Sci. Technol. Libr. 37(3), 235–245 (2018)

30. Schneidewind, C., Grishchenko, I., Scherer, M., Maffei, M.: ethor: practical and provably sound static analysis of ethereum smart contracts. arXiv preprint arXiv:2005.06227 (2020)

31. Tsankov, P., Dan, A., Drachsler-Cohen, D., Gervais, A., Bünzli, F., Vechev, M.: Securify: practical security analysis of smart contracts, pp. 67–82. ACM (2018). https://doi.org/10.1145/3243734.3243780

32. Wood, G.: Ethereum: a secure decentralised generalised transaction ledger. Ethereum Proj. Yellow Paper **151**, 1–32 (2014)

33. Wood, G.: Ethereum: a secure decentralised generalised transaction ledger (2014)

34. Yang, Z., Lei, H.: Lolisa: formal syntax and semantics for a subset of the solidity programming language. arXiv preprint arXiv:1803.09885 (2018)

35. Zakrzewski, J.: Towards verification of ethereum smart contracts: a formalization of core of solidity. In: Piskac, R., Rümmer, P. (eds.) VSTTE 2018. LNCS, vol. 11294, pp. 229–247. Springer, Cham (2018). https://doi.org/10.1007/978-3-030-03592-1_13

Automated Verification of Embedded Control Software

Automated Verification of Embedded Control Software
Track Introduction

Dilian Gurov[1]([⊠]), Paula Herber[2]([⊠]), and Ina Schaefer[3]([⊠])

[1] KTH Royal Institute of Technology, Stockholm, Sweden
dilian@kth.se
[2] University of Münster, Münster, Germany
paula.herber@uni-muenster.de
[3] TU Braunschweig, Braunschweig, Germany
i.schaefer@tu-braunschweig.de

Abstract. Embedded control software is used in a variety of industries, such as in the automotive and railway domains, or in industrial automation and robotization. The development of such software is subject to tight time-to-market requirements, but at the same time also to very high safety requirements posed by various safety standards. To assure the latter, formal methods such as model-based testing and formal verification are increasingly used. However, the main obstacle to a more wide-scale adoption of these methods, and especially of formal verification, is the currently relative low level of automation of the verification process and integration in the general software development cycle. At present, writing formal specifications and annotating the embedded code is still a highly labour intensive activity requiring special competence and skills. In this track we address this challenge from various angles. We start by introducing the topic and then give a summary of the contributions.

1 Introduction to the Theme of the Track

The development of embedded control software is driven by high demands with respect to both cost efficiency and quality. The time-to-market is comparatively short, and the functionality volume is ever-increasing. For example, in 2005, the software in a modern car comprised about 70 MB. Since 2010, we usually have more than 1 GB (i.e., more than 100 million lines of code) distributed over more than a hundred microprocessors [2]. With the current trend towards autonomous driving and the Internet of Things, these numbers can be expected to further increase. At the same time, embedded control software components often have to meet the highest safety requirements. Beside functional requirements, non-functional requirements like real-time behaviour, memory and power consumption are crucial. For example, the control part of automotive software is typically classified on the highest Automotive Safety Integrity Levels, that is, ASIL C or ASIL D, according to the ISO 26262 standard for functional safety in road vehicle [7]. ISO 26262 strongly recommends that semi-formal and formal verification are used for such systems.

T. Margaria and B. Steffen (Eds.): ISoLA 2020, LNCS 12478, pp. 235–239, 2020.
https://doi.org/10.1007/978-3-030-61467-6_15

The major barrier for the adoption of semi-formal and formal verification in industrial practice is the limited degree of automation of formal methods. Formal specifications and models often need to be manually written, and scalable verification techniques typically require user annotations and interactions. The challenges of automated verification for embedded control software are multiplied by their heterogeneous nature and their coupling with dynamic and partially unknown environments. A recent survey by Gleirscher and Marmsoler [4] gives an overview about the potential and challenges of formal methods in industrial practice and shows future directions for formal methods research.

This track investigates how the degree of automation can be increased for the verification of embedded control software. It discusses advanced verification methods that ensure the safety of embedded control software and their applicability to industrial practice, and also addresses recent challenges like smart technologies, autonomous agents, and dynamically changing environments.

2   Summary of Contributions

Amendola et al. [1] (*A Model-Based Approach to the Design, Verification and Deployment of Railways Interlocking System*) present ongoing work on a formally well-founded, model-based development and verification process for interlocking systems. One of the key ideas of their approach is that domain experts can express specifications of interlocking systems in a special kind of natural language, namely the controlled natural language (CNL), which is close to the jargon domain experts typically use, but in contrast it is unambigious. From CNL, Amendola et al. automatically generate SysML models and C/Python code. In addition to that, the authors also propose to automatically extract formal properties from legacy relay circuits and use this to complement the SysML models and generated code. Verification is supported by various verification methods, including model checking, simulation, and boolean abstraction. The whole methodology is implemented as a toolchain and currently used by domain experts from the Italian railway signaling network.

Fränzle and Kröger [3] (*Guess What I'm Doing! Rendering Formal Verification Methods Ripe for the Era of Interacting Intelligent Systems*) address the formal verification of smart technologies, which incorporate elements of intelligence, cooperation, and adaptivity. The authors discuss and illustrate with two examples, one of a self-driving car and one of two ships that make a cooperative control decision, why classical hybrid-automata based approaches for modeling and verification are not adequate to model such smart technologies. They show that even for comparatively simple case studies, the results from an analysis based on hybrid automata are imprecise. The reason for this is, as stated by the authors, the inaptness of hybrid automata to represent rational decision making under uncertain information. The authors suggest an extension of hybrid automata with state distributions that represent state estimates and discuss automatic verification support for such an extended formalism.

Huisman and Monti [5] (*On the Industrial Application of Critical Software Verification with VerCors*) address the problem that software verification is still not used in typical industrial development processes. To encourage the integration of formal method into the industrial production cycle, they provide experience reports of projects where they have used formal verification in industrial design processes. In particular, they report on two projects on the verification of tunnel control software at Technolution, and on one project on the verification of a radio bearing antenna with Thales. In their case studies, the authors combine model checking using mCRL2 with deductive verification using VerCors. While they show that this combination is powerful, they also have derived several aspects where the tools could be improved. In particular, a broader support of the frontend languages would be desirable, for example, with floating point reasoning and structures in C. The authors also discuss other directions for future research that would help the adoption of formal verification in practice, for example, patterns and DSL languages to ease model-based verification and the automation of permission specifications.

Hungar [6] (*A Concept of Scenario Space Exploration with Criticality Coverage Guarantees*) addresses the problem of assuring the safety of an automated driving system in complex traffic situations via testing. As complete testing of all possible situations is usually not feasible in such systems, the author suggests a criterion to decide whether a scenario space has been sufficiently covered by simulation runs. The author considers scenario spaces in terms of sets of simulation runs with parametric behaviour for other traffic participants. He sketches an exploration procedure that may be used for coverage-driven test generation for the suggested criterion, and discusses under which conditions the criterion can be shown to imply sufficient coverage to assert safety of a given system under test. The elaboration, implementation and demonstration of the test generation procedure are subject to future work.

Liebrenz et al. [8] (*Towards Automated Service-oriented Verification of Embedded Control Software modeled in Simulink*) present a compositional, service-oriented verification approach for hybrid embedded control systems that are modeled in Simulink. The key idea of their approach is to automatically transform given Simulink models into differential dynamic logic and verify safety properties with the interactive theorem prover KeYmaeraX with a contract-based approach. In this paper, the authors present a new case study, namely a generic infusion pump, and discuss the challenges that arise during the verification process, in particular due to interactive verification. They discuss the manual effort necessary to verify the generic infusion pump, which is mainly due to the necessity to manually define invariants. Then, they propose to generate invariants automatically that can be derived from block parameters or the Simulink semantics. With that, they significantly reduce the verification effort and increase the practical applicability of their previously proposed verification process.

Meywerk et al. [9] (*Verifying Safety Properties of Robotic Plans Operating in Real-World Environments via Logic-based Environment Modeling*) address the verification of cognition-enabled robotic agents, which are increasingly finding their way into the personal environment of many people, for example as household assistants. To cope with constantly changing environments, autonomous robots need complex goal-driven control programs, so-called plans, that incorporate perception, manipulation, and navigation capabilities. The authors present an approach for the verification of robotic plans in dynamically changing environments. They assume that robotic plans are implemented in the CRAM Plan Language (CPL) and use the Discrete-Event Calculus (DEC) for environment modeling. Then, they use a combination of symbolic execution, SAT and SMT solving to show that a given plan satisfies a given set of properties. They illustrate their approach with the running example of an autonomous vacuum cleaner and show its practical applicability with the Shopping Demo from the CRAM respository, where a two-armed human-sized household robot is autonomously packing and unpacking a shelf.

Nyberg et al. [10] (*Formally Proving Compositionality in Industrial Systems with Informal Specifications*) present a methodology and a deductive system for proving compositionality, based on first-order logic. The methodology does not assume specifications to be formal logical sentences, but takes as input properties of specifications and, in particular, refinement relations. To cover general industrial heterogeneous systems, the chosen semantics is behavior-based, originating in previous work on contract-based design for cyber-physical systems. In contrast to the previous work, implementation of specifications is not required to be monotonic with respect to composition. That is, even though a specification is implemented by one component, its composition with other components may not implement the same specification. This kind of non-monotonicity is fundamentally important to support architectural specifications and so-called freedom-of-interference properties used in the design of safety critical systems.

Schlingloff [11] (*Validation of Collaborative Embedded Systems*) presents work in progress about the modelling of collaborative embedded systems, which are autonomous components of cyber-physical systems that cooperate with each other in order to accomplish a common goal. The contribution shows how to construct strategies for individual agents towards fulfilling the goals of a coalition, based on model checking for a new strategic temporal logic called Alternating Signal Temporal Logic (ASTL*). The author presents two examples, one for car platooning and the other for automated guided vehicles in industrial production.

References

1. Amendola, A., et al.: A model-based approach to the design, verification and deployment of railways interlocking system. In: Margaria, T., Steffen, B. (eds.) ISoLA 2020. LNCS, vol. 12478, pp. 240–254. Springer, Heidelberg (2020)
2. Charette, R.N.: This car runs on code. IEEE Spectr. **46**(3), 3 (2009)
3. Fränzler, M., Kröger, P.: Guess what I'm doing! Rendering formal verification methods ripe for the era of interacting intelligent systems. In: Margaria, T., Steffen, B. (eds.) ISoLA 2020. LNCS, vol. 12478, pp. 255–272. Springer, Heidelberg (2020)
4. Gleirscher, M., Marmsoler, D.: Formal methods: Oversold? Underused? A survey. Technical report, ArchivX - 1812.08815 (1812)

5. Huisman, M., Monti, R.: On the industrial application of critical software verification with VerCors. In: Margaria, T., Steffen, B. (eds.) ISoLA 2020. LNCS, vol. 12478, pp. 273–292. Springer, Heidelberg (2020)
6. Hungar, H.: A concept of scenario space exploration with criticality coverage guarantees. In: Margaria, T., Steffen, B. (eds.) ISoLA 2020. LNCS, vol. 12478, pp. 293–306. Springer, Heidelberg (2020)
7. ISO: Road vehicles - Functional safety (2011)
8. Liebrenz, T., Herber, P., Glesner, S.: Towards automated service-oriented verification of embedded control software modeled in Simulink. In: Margaria, T., Steffen, B. (eds.) ISoLA 2020. LNCS, vol. 12478, pp. 307–325. Springer, Heidelberg (2020)
9. Meywerk, T., Walter, M., Herdt, V., J. Kleinekathöfer, D. Große, and R. Drechsler. Verifying safety properties of robotic plans operating in real-world environments via logic-based environment modeling. In: Margaria, T., Steffen, B. (eds.) ISoLA 2020. LNCS, vol. 12478, pp. 326–347. Springer, Heidelberg (2020)
10. Nyberg, M., Westman, J., Gurov, D.: Formally proving compositionality in industrial systems with informal specifications. In: Margaria, T., Steffen, B. (eds.) ISoLA 2020. LNCS, vol. 12478, pp. 348–365. Springer, Heidelberg (2020)
11. Schlingloff, H.: Specification, synthesis and validation of strategies for collaborative embedded systems. In: Margaria, T., Steffen, B. (eds.) ISoLA 2020. LNCS, vol. 12478, pp. 366–385. Springer, Heidelberg (2020)

A Model-Based Approach to the Design, Verification and Deployment of Railway Interlocking System

Arturo Amendola[1], Anna Becchi[2], Roberto Cavada[2], Alessandro Cimatti[2(✉)], Alberto Griggio[2], Giuseppe Scaglione[1], Angelo Susi[2(✉)], Alberto Tacchella[2], and Matteo Tessi[1]

[1] RFI Rete Ferroviaria Italiana – Osmannoro, Firenze, Italy
amendola.arturo@yahoo.com, {m.tessi,g.scaglione}@rfi.it
[2] Fondazione Bruno Kessler – Povo, Trento, Italy
{abecchi,cavada,cimatti,griggio,susi,atacchella}@fbk.eu

Abstract. This paper describes a model-based flow for the development of Interlocking Systems. The flow starts from a set of specifications in Controlled Natural Language (CNL), that are close to the jargon adopted in by domain experts, but fully formal. From the CNL, a complete SysML specification is extracted, leveraging various forms of diagrams, and enabling automated code generation. Several formal verification methods are supported. A complementary part of the flow supports the extraction of formal properties from legacy Interlocking Systems designed as Relay circuits. The flow is implemented in a comprehensive toolset, and is currently used by railway experts.

Keywords: Model-based design · Interlocking Systems · Functional specifications · Code generation · Formal verification

1   Introduction

Functional specifications of complex embedded systems are often written in natural language, but can be ambiguous and subject to different interpretations. This phenomenon emerges in several domains such as avionics and automotive, and is particularly evident in the specification of railway Interlocking (IxL) systems. Different regulations and technical specifications expressed in natural language documents, together with complex legacy relay electrical diagrams, have to be reconciled and interpreted to design and evolve digital systems. Such representations usually fail to provide a high-level information about the overall system logics since the design and the actual implementation of the system is highly interconnected. Moreover, the work on these documents requires a strong legacy domain knowledge which is vanishing in these days.

All these aspects contribute to produce different interpretations by Interlocking system suppliers, making railway infrastructure managers weaken or even losing their knowledge of the systems, and ultimately get locked-in to the specific supplier providing the system instances.

© Springer Nature Switzerland AG 2020
T. Margaria and B. Steffen (Eds.): ISoLA 2020, LNCS 12478, pp. 240–254, 2020.
https://doi.org/10.1007/978-3-030-61467-6_16

In this paper, we propose a Model-Based, tool-supported methodology for the specification, implementation and verification of interlocking systems for the Italian Railway Signaling network. The aim is to ensure product standardization, smooth specification of requirements, and automated code generation and verification of the system. Moreover, this research is intended to support a systematic strategy for the migration of legacy relay systems to computer-based systems.

The approach has several distinguishing features. First, the approach relies on a Controlled Natural Language (CNL) to support railway experts having deep knowledge on regulations and provisions, who are not trained in formal methods, in writing the specification of interlocking procedures using their own language. The CNL, in fact, has been defined to be very close to the jargon adopted by domain experts, yet it is unambiguous. From the CNL, models in *SysML* and C/Python code are automatically generated, thus retaining full traceability. The methodology does not allow to manually modify the automatically generated models and code. Second, the interlocking logics are generic, i.e. specified on station types rather than on a single station. The configuration process with respect to a specific station, also model-based, is out of the scope of this paper. This poses the problem of analyzing not only the interlocking procedures once instantiated on a single station, but also the correctness of the generic procedures with respect to a class of stations. Third, in order to manage legacy, the approach supports the digitalization of relay circuit documents, and the automated extraction of formal models and properties, to allow model checking and co-simulation [2,6–8]. Finally, the validation of the interlocking logic is supported by a number of formal verification engines, ranging from CNL checkers, to single FSM analyzers, to different model checking engines.

The project is ongoing: the proposed methodology and support tools are currently in use by domain experts, and various kinds of verification engines are being integrated and optimized to specific properties of interest.

The paper is structured as follows. Section 2 introduces the overall approach. Section 3 covers the formalization of the railway specifications; Sect. 4 their modelling in *SysML*, Sect. 5 describes the transformation of *SysML* into code. Section 6 discusses the management of legacy relay *IxL*, and Sect. 7 outlines the verification approach. Section 8 concludes the paper.

2   The Specification and Validation Approach

The Model-Based approach aims at guiding and supporting the analyst from the definition of an informal specification of the system to its formalization, verification and validation and deployment. As shown in Fig. 1, it is based on two independent confluent flows. The entire process can be summarized in three main steps:

– Flow A on the left; the formalization of an input set of documents related to the Interlocking system, such as natural language specifications, topological and signalling data about railroad tracks and stations, performed by the

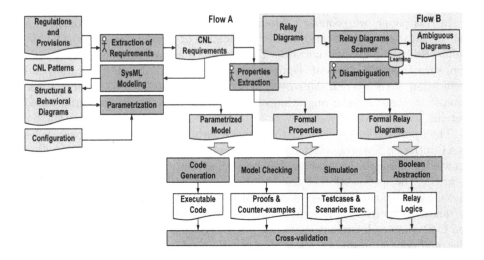

Fig. 1. The general approach

experts, the automated modelling of the requirements, the automated generation of code and its verification.

- Flow B on the right; the automated extraction and formalization of legacy relay logics, represented by line schematics.
- The artifacts produced in Flows A and B are then used by the analysis steps such as testing or simulation and cross-validation among the different artifacts.

The first step of Flow A aims at the elicitation of domain knowledge through the manual translation of informal textual railways regulations and provisions, into a set of specifications in CNL using a set of predefined specification patterns. The CNL specifications are then automatically formalized and modeled as Block Definition and State Machine *SysML* diagrams, to capture the overall taxonomy of railway elements (together with the structure of relationships among them), and the behavior of the railway logics, respectively. The definition of a computational model allows the specification of a formal semantics for the *SysML* model to enable formal verification, simulation and automatic code generation. The railway logic is abstract, i.e. not referring to a particular configuration of railway stations. Abstraction is allowed by parametric cardinalities in relations among functional blocks. An abstract logic has none or partial configuration, whilst a complete configuration makes the logic concrete. Concretization allows the generation of optimized code tailored for specific configurations, and the application of standard techniques for performing formal analysis such as verification. However, although very challenging, being able to perform formal analysis on abstract models is a prime project goal, as it allows for the distribution of formally verified models prior to their instantiation.

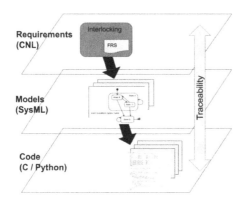

Fig. 2. The three levels development process

Flow B aims at eliciting the control logic that is implicitly implemented in legacy relay circuits. After its formalization, this knowledge is used to produce safety and functional properties, test cases and scenarios, a boolean representation of the relay logics. Given the complexity, size and number of relay diagrams, the formalization of these artifacts is performed using a semi-automatic approach based on a combination of image recognition techniques. This produces a formally defined model that allows the application of formal methods.

Finally, the artifacts produced in the two flows allow the co-simulation with formal model from flow A, and other cross-validation techniques.

The development process for the Interlocking system follows a *V* model and is based on three levels of activities and related artifacts as described in Fig. 2.

In the first level the Functional Requirements Specifications (FRS) are manually extracted from the domain documents, in the second level the *SysML* models are automatically derived from the CNL specification, at the third level the C/Python code is automatically produced from the models. A complete traceability is maintained among the artifacts in the three levels allowing the designer to connect the generated code to the requirements that originated it.

The entire process is supported by the AIDA toolchain, based on the Eclipse platform, that allows the specification of the requirements and their transformation into *SysML* models and code. The toolchain includes tools for the formal verification of the artifacts produced by the methodology and for the extraction, representation and formalization of relay circuits to support flow B.

3   Formalization of the Railway Specifications

The requirements for the *IxL* is extracted from a set of railway domain documents such as diagrams describing the structure of a railway station, railway regulations and provisions. The resulting Functional Requirements Specification (FRS) document consists of a set of cards each one containing the definition of the structure and behavior of a so called Class of Logic that is the representation

244 A. Amendola et al.

of the elements of a railway that are relevant for the *IxL*, such as the safety logics of physical devices (e.g. *Railroad Switch*, *Train Track*, different kinds of *Signal*s), or the safety logics of higher level entities (e.g. *Train Itinerary*, *Section Block*). The specification of the FRS is performed by domain experts carrying out three main activities:

- Analysis of the railway documents to identify the relevant aspects and concepts that should become part of the Functional Requirements Specifications;
- Specification of the FRS as a collection of classes using the CNL that allows the expert to specify in a textual form the structure of the class and its behavior through the definition of the associated Finite State Machine using a language that is very close to their jargon;
- Definition of tracing links between the resulting FRS and the railway documents from which it originated.

In order to guide the specification of the FRS, a set of CNL patterns have been defined also analysing specification documents produced by the experts in previous projects. In particular, a document describing a class contains two main sections: one for the definition of the attributes of the class, the other for describing the behavior in terms of the states and transitions of the Finite State Machine (*FSM*) of the class. Each transition in the *FSM* is described using the CNL and is characterized by a set of triggering conditions and a set of effects that specifies the actions to be performed by the class when changing its state. An example of triggering conditions and effects are:

```
conditions: verify that the control Position is not equal to Normal
            verify that cdb is free and not locked
            verify that the timer TOWait is expired
...
effects: assign to control Position the value Normal
         activate the timer TOWait
```

The specification of the FRS by the experts is supported by the modeling tool AIDA that provides an editor and a set of syntactic and semantic checks for the correct writing of the classes in CNL.

3.1 Architecture of the *IxL*

The *IxL* is made of a set of Class of Logic, each possibly interacting with:

- the environment: receiving *Manual Commands* which are asynchronous events sent by the user; sending state information for visualization; reading hardware signals from the station plant; writing actuations to the station plant.
- other classes: synchronously reading/writing state of linked classes; sending/receiving *Automatic Commands* which are asynchronous events possibly carrying data information.

The classes are organized hierarchically by linking them in a *use-a* relationship. Relations among links are possible within a class, e.g. class *Itinerary* having a pair ⟨*Signal, TrackSection*⟩. The hierarchy is made by constraining the possible interactions among the classes. Only higher-level classes can send *Automatic Commands* to lower-level classes; only classes at higher or same level can write state of same or lower-level classes; a class can read the state of all other classes.

3.2 Structure of a Class

Each class has an interface to rule the above described possible system interactions (*Manual Commands, Automatic Commands*, I/O from/to the plant), an internal state and a deterministic *FSM*. The internal state is made of: *configuration parameters* and *configuration lists* (which contain links to other class instances to implement *is-a* relationship), both of which are fixed when instantiating the class; variables, whose type can be boolean, integers, literal sets, ordered literal sets, timers and counters; the current state of the associated *FSM*. *functional macros* can be defined for the information-hiding of reading state. *procedural macros* can be defined for the information-hiding of writing state and sending *Automatic Commands*.

The *FSM* has a set of named states, a set of initial transitions to determine the initial state, and the set of transitions among states. Each transition is characterized by a *guard*, an *effect*, a *priority*. Guards are functions of reception of manual and automatic commands, the internal state (including visible state of linked instances and functional macros). Effects contain state assignments (including accessible sate of linked instances), sending of *Automatic Commands* and invocation of procedural macros. Priority setting is simplified for the modeler by defining four categories of priority (from the railways domain), and by associating each transition to a category.

3.3 Execution Model

The execution of the *IxL* logics is performed by a periodic task, which at each cycle performs the sequence depicted in Fig. 3:

1. Reads and latches inputs from the user (*Manual Commands*) and from the plant (I)
2. Executes the *IxL* logics (E)
3. Writes outputs for the user interface and for the plant (O)

The Execution phase (E) is carried out by a *Scheduler*, which executes all the active class instances according to three phases:

Manual Phase all instances that received one or more *Manual Command* are activated. Each instance can process a single *Manual Command* by executing a single transition, if the corresponding guards are enabled. If no transition can be executed, then the *Manual Command* is lost.

State Phase every instance having a transition enabled in the current state is activated. Each instance processes a single transition. The phase terminates when all activated instances have performed one state transition.

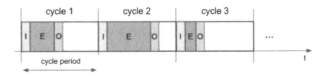

Fig. 3. Delta cycle

Automatic Phase all instances that received one or more *Automatic Command* are activated. Since in the effects of any transition other *Automatic Commands* can be sent, in this phase a given instance may get activated multiple times. If a command cannot be processed (as unexpected or as the truth value of guards do not enable any transition) the command is lost. This phase is repeated until fixpoint is reached, i.e. all instances reaches a quiescent state where no further *Automatic Commands* are sent.

The execution is deterministic. The three phases are executed in the same order; the instances in each phase are also fired in the same order, although this order is not known to the *IxL* designer. The execution of each *FSM* is also deterministic, as the priority uniquely determines the transitions that the scheduler activates. The execution runs to completion by construction: in the *Manual Phase* and in the *State Phase* at most one transition per instance is executed; in the *Automatic Phase*, structural constraints on the system hierarchy assure the absence of execution loops.

4 Automated *SysML* Model Generation

4.1 *SysML* for Model-Based System Engineering Applications

SysML (System Modeling Language - https://sysml.org/) is a generic language for architecture design widely adopted in Model-Based System Engineering (MBSE) applications It supports specification, analysis, design, verification and validation of a wide range of systems, such as hardware, software, information, processes, resources and structures. *SysML* is a dialect derived from *UML* 2, defined as a *UML* profile. In 2006 the Object Management Group (OMG) adopted OMG *SysML* as a standard, and manages it maintenance. The current version is OMG *SysML* 1.6. *SysML* diagrams also in *UML* are: *Activity*, *Block Definition* (*Class* in *UML*), *Internal Block* (*Composite Structure* in *UML*), *Sequence*, *State Machine*, and *Use Case*. Diagrams that are unique in *SysML* are *Requirement* and *Parametric*. Diagrams in *SysML* are mainly split into two groups:

Structural Diagrams. Allow the definition of the system entities to be modelled, relations among them, and their structural content, like properties, operations and other member attributes.

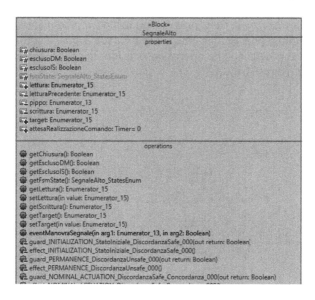

Fig. 4. Fragment of `SysML::Block`. Attributes' colors denote different typologies (Color figure online)

Behavioral Diagrams. Define the dynamic behaviour of the entities, both in terms of internal dynamics and interaction among them.

SysML allows meta-model extensions through the use of *stereotypes*, to create new elements of the meta-model derived from the existing ones.

4.2   Modeling of the Abstract *IxL* System

The abstract *IxL* system is modeled as an Object-Oriented system of classes communicating by mean of *Operations*, and whose execution is ruled by the Scheduler and scheduling schema described in Sect. 3.3.

The automatic translation process takes the FRS as input, and generates a *SysML* model as output. The structural part of each class is translated as `SysML::Block`. Each class attribute is translated to a block's `UML::Property`, which have been stereotyped to model its domain-specific typology, like *Manual Commands*, *Automatic Commands*, parameters, linked instances, variables, plant inputs and outputs, etc. Primitive types exploit basic *UML* types (boolean, integer, etc.), while the other types like Timer, Counter, Enumeratives, Records, etc. are generated into a dedicated `UML::Package`. A stereotyped `UML::Operation` is used to model each attribute's getter, setter, macro, guard function and effect procedure. Each *Manual Command* and *Automatic Command* is translated into a `UML::CallEvent`, and a `UML::Operation` get associated to the event to model its behaviour. Figure 4 shows a sample of a `SysML::Block` taken from the domain.

Each class's *FSM* is translated as a `UML::State Machine`, which is associated to the corresponding `SysML::Block`. Each state of the *FSM* is translated as a `UML::State`, each transition is translated with a `UML::Transition` extended with stereotypes that provide information about priority, its category and scheduling phase. The `UML::Transition`'s guard and effect consist of `UML::Operation` calls to the operation containing the guard expression and effect procedure, respectively (Fig. 5).

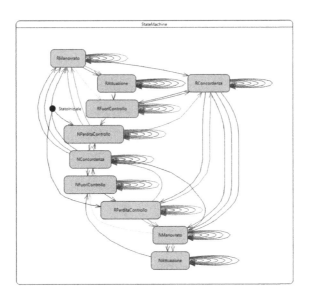

Fig. 5. `UML::State Machine` of the logics of a *Railroad Switch*. Transition colors denotes the typology (Color figure online)

Guards expressions and effects statements are translated into a concrete language that is formally-defined subset of C extended with an object-oriented notation, and corresponding Abstract Syntax Tree get attached to the *Operations* corresponding to each guard/effect. The following example shows a CNL guard and the automatically translated code:

```
all the following
 verify that the variable PowerSupply is equal to true
 verify that the control Position is not equal to Normal
 verify that cdb is free and not locked
 verify that the timer TOWait is expired

vvvvvvvvvvvvvvvvvvvvvvvvvvvvvvvvvvvvvvvvvvvvvvvvvvvvvv
return (
    (PowerSupply == true) &&
    (! (Position == Normal)) &&
    all(CdBRec iter: cdb, iter.cdb.getFree() && ! iter.cdb.getLocked()) &&
    TOWait.isExpired())
```

The evaluation context is the class instance containing the `UML::Operation` associated to the guard, so *PowerSupply, Position cdb* and *TOWait* are instance's attributes. Notice the Object-Oriented dotted notation to call linked instances' *Operations*, like in *cdb.getLocked()*. As *cdb* is a list of records, functional flavors for quantifiers (*all(...)*) are provided by the concrete language.

5   Automated Code Generation

The code generation process takes as input the *SysML* model and produces two different artifacts:

- A first version of the code, written in the Python programming language, is intended for debugging and simulation purposes, running on a host machine.
- The second version, written in the C programming language, is intended for deployment on the target platform and contains the code that will be effectively executed on the field.

The overall structure of the two versions is very similar and will be explained in the next subsection. The details of the two implementations are, of course, quite different: whereas the Python version fully leverages the dynamic nature of its execution environment, the C version allocates every data structure either statically or at initialization time, as soon as the configuration parameters are known.

5.1   Structure of the *IxL* Code

In both versions of the *IxL* code each Class of Logic is translated to a separate module. In the Python version, to each Class of Logic corresponds a single Python class derived from a common base class. In the C version, each Class of Logic is translated into a separate compilation unit, that is a .h/.c file pair.

The code generated for each Class of Logic implements the interface of the Class, as described in the corresponding Block Diagram of the *SysML* model, and the execution logic of the associated Finite State Machine. In more detail, each module contains:

- the declaration of the local variables of the state machines, as extracted from the *SysML* model;
- for each variable, a pair of getter and setter methods;
- the interface procedures **init** and **exec**, whose job is, respectively, to initialize the variables of the FSM and to pick the correct transition for the state machine, by checking the current state and the relevant guards in turn;
- for each transition specified by the state machine, a *guard* function that checks if the triggering conditions of that particular transition hold, and an *effect* procedure that performs the corresponding set of effects.

The generation process itself is driven by a template engine that operates on a data structure which is preliminarly populated directly from the *SysML* model.

The code produced by the generation process is parametric on the number of instances of each Class of Logic and on the inter-relationships between the various Classes. In order to be executed, this code must be instantiated according to a specific configuration, as described in Subsect. 5.3.

5.2   Execution of *IxL* Code

Each instance of a Class of Logic represents a distinct *process*. The execution of such processes is orchestrated by a *scheduler* whose code is generic, that is it does not depend on the specific station configuration.

The scheduler execution is based on a loop (delta cycle) with three distinct phases: *input reading*, *elaboration*, and *output writing*. At every cycle, the elaboration is performed on the inputs extracted from the snapshot taken at the previous step (input latching).

In the elaboration phase each process is activated in turn by the scheduler according to a fixed order, which is specified ahead of time and is part of the configuration data, so that it can be customized depending on the characteristic of each specific station.

The execution of the processes takes place according to a policy of *cooperative scheduling*: the scheduler halts its execution until each process yields back control. In this way, execution of the *IxL* is guaranteed to be deterministic and purely sequential, which eliminates every possible problem stemming from concurrency.

Inter-process communication is realized through the exchange of *Automatic Commands*, as described in Sect. 3. The scheduler is responsible for forwarding the *Automatic Commands* from the source process to the target one.

Each execution cycle is divided in the three phases described in Sect. 3.3: *manual phase*, *state phase*, and *automatic phase*.

5.3   The Code Configuration Mechanism

As pointed out above, the *IxL* code is parametric: the number of instances of each Class of Logic, and the mutual references between the various instances, are not known at code generation and must be supplied at a later time in order to instantiate the code for a particular station. This data is globally referred to as the "configuration".

The instantiation mechanism is different for Python and C code. In the first case, the Python runtime reads the configuration at startup from a JSON file and dynamically fills the corresponding data structures. This is appropriate for execution on a host machine, where access to a filesystem can be taken for granted. On the target platform, however, the resources available to the *IxL* code are minimal, and are provided by a tailor-made OS. In this case the configuration data is stored in a binary file with the same layout as a direct memory dump of the corresponding C data structures. This binary file is loaded at system initialization in a specific memory area which is subsequently marked as read-only. The initialization routine of the *IxL* code is then called to set up appropriately the pointers to the configuration data for each instance of a Class of Logic. Various checks are performed to ensure that no pointer remains uninitialized and that configuration data is correctly validated.

6 Automated Formalization of Relay Schematics

Relay diagrams are standard representations of networks of electro-mechanical components. We now describe how to extract the controlling logics left implicit in these circuits, hidden by non-trivial physical laws. The behaviour of the network is induced by the characteristics of the components, such as resistance values, and by both wired and remote connections. As an example, a relay can open or close a switch, possibly belonging to a different circuit, depending on the value of the induced magnetic field.

Firstly, a graphical front-end based on an extension of the DIA diagram editor (https://gitlab.gnome.org/GNOME/dia) allows for the digital modeling of relay schemata that are originally provided as paper-based sheets. Digital modeling is done by overlaying components and connections on the top of the scanned images of the original sheets. Components are picked from a palette which is context aware to help choosing from hundreds of components. Picking components, entering data (name and other properties) and construction of electrical connections, is aided by OCR, template matching and deep learning image recognition techniques.

Each component, such as power supplies, switches, resistors and electrically-controlled contacts, is mapped into the library of known electrical elements. Here, each symbol is associated with a set of parameters and specifications. The XML format provides a modular and flexible description for the connections and the remote-controlling interactions between the tagged elements. The front-end provides also some sanity checks on the status of the network, like dangling terminals or connections with incompatible symbols.

The subsequent step is to convert the circuit in a formalism amenable for verification. Following [3], we adopt a methodology to analyze and understand Relay Interlocking Systems, by reduction to a Switched Multi-Domain Kirchhoff Network which is compiled in a hybrid automaton. A compiler implements a component-based translation of the XML file into the HyDI language [5]. The resulting automaton is the synchronous composition of the models of the components: shared variables implement remote discrete interactions, while wired connections are handled locally, by imposing Kirchhoff conservation laws between the voltage and current values at every node.

The independent modeling of single components can be done with different levels of abstraction. Due to internal inertial electro-mechanical phenomena, some components exhibit transient states between stationary condition. The precise approach requires considering complex differential equations defining continuous variables.

A more pragmatic approach consists in extracting a hybrid automaton with a piecewise-linear abstraction of the dynamics. Namely, state changes of components exhibiting transient conditions, such as delayed relays, are modeled as discrete transitions happening within a constrained time interval.

The formalization of the relay diagram as a hybrid automaton allows for different kinds of analysis. The expected properties of both the components and the whole network can be checked with the HyCOMP back-end verifier [4]. In addition, it is possible to formally reason on the behaviours of the circuits as the language of the corresponding automata (or by one of their abstractions) for a more thorough comparison with the language of the generated code. The target of such a verification step is to check whether the legacy circuit, while being based on different internal electro-mechanical variables, responds on the railway elements in the same way of the digital implementation.

7   System Verification

The verification activities are carried out at three different levels: (i) verification of structural properties of the components, operating at the *SysML* level; (ii) verification of properties of the generated C code for a specific station/configuration; (iii) verification of properties of the abstract interlocking logic on a given set of configurations.

Structural Checks. The first level consists of a set of "light-weight" checks on the *SysML* model generated by the CNL translation. These checks are meant to verify structural properties of the model, that are independent from the actual application domain. Examples include absence of deadlock states in the state machines, mutual exclusion among different transition guards, absence of unreachable states and/or unreachable transitions (due e.g. to guards that are always true/false). These checks are essentially local to each generated state machine, and can typically be performed very efficiently. Although conceptually quite simple, they offer a very useful debugging aid to domain experts during the initial phases of development of new Classes of Logic.

Code Verification. The second level consists on the verification of the correctness of the automatically-generated implementation of the interlocking logic for a specific station with respect to a set of user-specified properties.

We follow an approach based on software model checking, in which the C implementation of the interlocking logic, combined with an abstraction of its execution environment and instantiated for a specific configuration, is translated into a symbolic transition system which can then be formally verified with state-of-the-art model checking tools such as nuXmv [1].

More specifically, the translation from the C implementation to the transition system for verification is performed as follows. First, the generated C code for the Classes of Logic is instantiated according to the specific configuration under verification. All dynamic data structures (e.g. lists and vectors whose size depends on configuration parameters) are statically allocated, and all indirect references (expressed as pointers in the C code) are statically resolved; Second, the code is simplified and specialized according to the configuration: static loops (with upper bounds depending on the configuration) are unrolled, dead code is eliminated, and methods of each Class of Logic are specialised for each of the instantiated objects. Then, a model of the execution environment (properly instantiated for the specific configuration) is added. This consists of a main scheduling loop that executes the different instances in a "scan cycle" mode: input acquisition (abstracted as nondeterministic assignment to the input variables), logic execution (according to the specified scheduling policy), output generation. Finally, the imperative program is compiled to a symbolic transition system using standard techniques: inlining of all functions, removal of side effects, generation of a SSA form, symbolic encoding of the control-flow-graph and the program statements into SMT constraints.

An advantage of approaches based on model checking is their capability of producing counterexample traces witnessing the violation of some property. In our flow, such traces are automatically translated into a high-level sequence of commands/controls from the environment (i.e. the actual train station) that can be used to drive the interactive simulator for the interlocking logic, so that the erroneous scenarios can be immediately visualized and understood by the domain experts. Moreover, the same approach can also be used for automatic test-case generation, given a target system state to reach.

The verification at the level of concrete/instantiated code has two drawbacks. First, scalability is a major issue. Even the smallest stations involve hundreds of instances, which quickly become thousands for medium-sized configurations. When performing full specialization of the code, the resulting transition system can significantly blow-up in size and become unmanageable for the model checker. As mitigation strategies, we are adopting various abstraction and simplification techniques, in which the transition system is generated incrementally, via a successive sequence of increasingly-precise approximations, guided by an analysis of the generated spurious counterexamples; ultimately however, the approach will still be limited by the size of the actual configuration. Second, the results of the verification are only valid for one specific configuration, and cannot be easily lifted to different configurations/stations.

Abstract Verification. The third level of verification consists in tackling the correctness of the interlocking logic independently from any specific configuration. From the formal point of view, this can be formalized as a parametric verification problem, in which each Class of Logic corresponds to a different process type. Although the problem of automatic verification of parametric systems has been extensively studied in the literature, the complexity of the task is significantly beyond the state of the art: current automatic techniques are typically focused on handling distributed protocols specifications, involving very few process types (on the order of 2–4) with a few tens of transition actions. In our context, instead, the parametric description consists of tens of different process types, with hundreds of transition actions. This is an extremely challenging activity, which however has the potential of offering significant advances to the state of the art.

8   Conclusions and Future Work

The paper presents a model-based methodology for the design, deployment and verification of Interlocking systems. The approach has several key feature. First, there is a strong connection among different abstraction levels of the design: Controlled Natural Language for requirements specification, and the automatically generated *SysML* models and C/Python code. Second, the verification is supported by various verification methods. Third, a strong connection with legacy systems: the specification documents of relay legacy systems are automatically modeled and formally analyzed to extract reference specifications.

The methodology is supported by tools that are currently being used by domain experts. In the future, we plan to add new verification and validation techniques specialized to the most common properties, to complement the formal verification techniques with model-based testing techniques for the generated code, and to address the problem of certification.

References

1. Cavada, R., et al.: The NUXMV symbolic model checker. In: Biere, A., Bloem, R. (eds.) CAV 2014. LNCS, vol. 8559, pp. 334–342. Springer, Cham (2014). https://doi.org/10.1007/978-3-319-08867-9_22

2. Cavada, R., Cimatti, A., Micheli, A., Roveri, M., Susi, A., Tonetta, S.: Othelloplay: a plug-in based tool for requirement formalization and validation. In: Bishop, J., Breitman, K.K., Notkin, D. (eds.) Proceedings of the 1st Workshop on Developing Tools as Plug-ins, TOPI 2011, Waikiki, Honolulu, HI, USA, 28 May 2011, p. 59. ACM (2011). https://doi.org/10.1145/1984708.1984728

3. Cavada, R., Cimatti, A., Mover, S., Sessa, M., Cadavero, G., Scaglione, G.: Analysis of relay interlocking systems via SMT-based model checking of switched multi-domain Kirchhoff networks. In: Bjørner, N., Gurfinkel, A. (eds.) 2018 Formal Methods in Computer Aided Design, FMCAD 2018, Austin, TX, USA, 30 October–2 November 2018, pp. 1–9. IEEE (2018). https://doi.org/10.23919/FMCAD.2018.8603007

4. Cimatti, A., Griggio, A., Mover, S., Tonetta, S.: HYCOMP: an SMT-based model checker for hybrid systems. In: Baier, C., Tinelli, C. (eds.) TACAS 2015. LNCS, vol. 9035, pp. 52–67. Springer, Heidelberg (2015). https://doi.org/10.1007/978-3-662-46681-0_4

5. Cimatti, A., Mover, S., Tonetta, S.: Hydi: a language for symbolic hybrid systems with discrete interaction. In: 37th EUROMICRO Conference on Software Engineering and Advanced Applications, SEAA 2011, Oulu, Finland, 30 August–2 September 2011, pp. 275–278. IEEE Computer Society (2011). https://doi.org/10.1109/SEAA.2011.49

6. Cimatti, A., Roveri, M., Susi, A., Tonetta, S.: Formalizing requirements with object models and temporal constraints. Softw. Syst. Model. **10**(2), 147–160 (2011). https://doi.org/10.1007/s10270-009-0130-7

7. Cimatti, A., Roveri, M., Susi, A., Tonetta, S.: Validation of requirements for hybrid systems: a formal approach. ACM Trans. Softw. Eng. Methodol. **21**(4), 22:1–22:34 (2012). https://doi.org/10.1145/2377656.2377659

8. Ferrari, A., Gori, G., Rosadini, B., Trotta, I., Bacherini, S., Fantechi, A., Gnesi, S.: Detecting requirements defects with NLP patterns: an industrial experience in the railway domain. Empir. Softw. Eng. **23**(6), 3684–3733 (2018). https://doi.org/10.1007/s10664-018-9596-7

Guess What I'm Doing!
Rendering Formal Verification Methods Ripe for the Era of Interacting Intelligent Systems

Martin Fränzle$^{(\boxtimes)}$ and Paul Kröger

Department of CS, C. v. Ossietzky Universität, 26111 Oldenburg, Germany
{martin.fraenzle,paul.kroeger}@uni-oldenburg.de

Abstract. Emerging smart technologies add elements of intelligence, cooperation, and adaptivity to physical entities, enabling them to interact with each other and with humans as systems of (human-) cyber-physical systems or (H)CPSes. Hybrid automata, in their various flavours, have been suggested as a formal model accurately capturing CPS dynamics and thus facilitating exhaustive behavioural analysis of interacting CPSes with mathematical rigour.

In this article, we demonstrate that despite their expressiveness, all flavours of hybrid automata fall short of being able to accurately capture the interaction dynamics of systems of well-engineered, rationally acting CPS designs. The corresponding verification verdicts obtained on the best possible approximations of the actual CPS dynamics are across the range of hybrid-automata models bound to be either overly optimistic or overly pessimistic, i.e., imprecise.

We identify inaptness to accurately represent rational decision-making under uncertain information as the cause of this deficiency. Such rational decision-making requires manipulation of state distributions representing environmental state estimates within the system state itself. We suggest a corresponding extension of hybrid automata and discuss the problem of providing automatic verification support.

1 Introduction

Not to be absolutely certain is, I think,
one of the essential things in rationality.   *(Bertrand Russell)*

Smart cities, automated transportation systems, smart health, and Industry 4.0 are examples of large-scale applications in which elements of intelligence, cooperation, and adaptivity are added to physical entities, enabling them to interact with each other and with humans as cyber-physical systems or, in the latter case, human-cyber-physical systems (CPSes or HCPSes). Due to the criticality of many of their application domains, such interacting cyber-physical systems

This research was supported by Deutsche Forschungsgemeinschaft through the grants DFG GRK 1765 "System Correctness under Adverse Conditions" and FR 2715/4-1 "Integrated Socio-technical Models for Conflict Resolution and Causal Reasoning".

© Springer Nature Switzerland AG 2020
T. Margaria and B. Steffen (Eds.): ISoLA 2020, LNCS 12478, pp. 255–272, 2020.
https://doi.org/10.1007/978-3-030-61467-6_17

call for rigorous analysis of their emergent dynamic behaviour w.r.t. a variety of design goals ranging from safety, stability, and liveness properties over performance measures to human-comprehensibility of their actions and absence of automation surprises. The model of hybrid (discrete-continuous) automata [1–3], in its various flavours, has traditionally been suggested as a formal model accurately capturing CPS dynamics and thus facilitating such analysis with mathematical rigour whenever the pertinent requirements can also be formalised, which applies at least for the safety, stability, convergence, and liveness properties.

Hybrid automata (HA) provide a mathematical abstraction of the interaction between decision making, continuous control, and continuous environments. They couple a finite-state control skeleton with a continuous state-space spanned by real-valued variables. The continuous state has its dynamics governed by differential equations selected depending on the current control-skeleton state (often called a *discrete mode*), and vice versa state dynamics of the control skeleton is controlled by predicates on the continuous state. Various flavours of HA have been suggested as a means to formally analyse different aspects of hybrid-state dynamical systems, among them deterministic HA facilitating reasoning about their normative behaviour, nondeterministic HA [1,2] under a demonic interpretation supporting worst-case analysis with respect to disturbances and measurement error, and stochastic HA enabling quantitative verification [3–9]. Encoding the dynamics of an actual cyber-physical system into one of the aforementioned modelling frameworks is in general considered a tedious, yet mostly straightforward activity: it is assumed that these frameworks are rich enough to accommodate adequate models of standard components, like sensors measuring physical quantities and actuators modifying such quantities, as well as standard models of physical dynamics, continuous control, and mode-switching control.

In this article, we demonstrate that despite their embracing expressiveness and contrary to the intuition underlying the above modelling pragmatics, all flavors of hybrid automata fall short of being able to accurately capture the interaction dynamics of systems of well-engineered, rationally acting CPS designs operating under aleatory uncertainty. We show that the corresponding verification verdicts obtained on the best possible approximations of the actual CPS dynamics are across the range of hybrid automata models bound to be either overly optimistic or overly pessimistic, i.e., imprecise.

We identify inaptness to adequately cover rational decision making under uncertain information as the cause of this deficiency of the hybrid-automaton model. As such rational decision making requires manipulation of environmental state estimates to be embedded into the system state itself, necessitating manipulation of state distributions rather than "just" discrete plus real-vector valued state within the CPS and its corresponding formal model, we suggest an appropriate extension of hybrid automata featuring mixture-based probability distributions in some of its state variables. It adopts from metrology the concept of processing noisy measurements by means of filtering and representing the result as a distribution over possible ground truth [10,11] and incorporates it into HA models. The resulting hybrid models can in general not be reduced to traditional HA featuring a finite-dimensional real-valued state vector, such that verification support remains an open issue that cannot be discharged by appropriate encoding into existing hybrid-automata verification approaches [12].

Organisation of the Paper. In the subsequent section, we discuss related work in order to identify a current lack of models for hybrid dynamics being able to directly accommodate inference mechanisms about uncertain state observation. This would, however, not necessarily imply that current models are too weak for producing precise verdicts on system correctness, as an encoding of pertinent methods for fusing measurements could well be possible within existing models. In Sect. 3.2, we therefore demonstrate by means of a running example that traditional hybrid-system models are bound to fail in providing the expected verification verdicts. This in turn motivates us to introduce filtering and state estimation into a revised model of hybrid automata. Section 3.3 demonstrates that this indeed leads to accurate verdicts adequately reflecting engineering practice, while Sect. 4 shows that an embedding of such environmental state estimation into traditional hybrid automata featuring real-vector state is in general impossible if the state estimation has to deal with states of other autonomous agents. Section 5 puts forward ideas on automatic verification support for the resulting rich class of hybrid automata, and Sect. 6 concludes the paper by shedding light on related problems in the field of interacting intelligent systems.

2   Related Work

An essential characteristic of cyber-physical systems is their hybrid discrete-continuous state-space, combining a continuous, real-vector state-space with a number of discrete modes determining the dynamics of the continuous evolution. Hybrid automata (HA) [1,2] have been suggested as a formal model permitting the rigorous analysis of such systems. In their deterministic or demonically non-deterministic form, HA support qualitative reasoning in the sense of exhaustive verification or falsification, over the normative behaviour or the worst-case behaviour of the system. Probabilistic or stochastic extensions of HA, so-called stochastic hybrid automata [7], enable deriving quantitative figures about the satisfaction of a safety target by considering probability distributions over uncertain choices. Several variants of such a quantification have been studied, e.g., HA with discrete [4,6] or continuous [8] distributions over discrete transitions as well as stochastic differential dynamics within a discrete mode [3].

HA models support the qualitative and quantitative analysis of systems subject to noise, yet lack pertinent means for expressing the effects of state estimation and filtering known to be central to rational strategies in games of incomplete information [13, Chapters 9-11] and thus in optimal control under uncertainty. Formal modelling of systems taking rational decisions based on best estimates of the uncertain and only partially observable state of other agents inherently requires to incorporate two levels of probabilism: first, in the model of system dynamics as probabilistic occurrences of sequences of observations;

second, as distributions representing the best estimates the embedded controller can gain about the state of its environment based on these noisy observations. Formal modelling of rational decision making consequently requires the estimations to be explicitly available in the state space of the controller for evaluations underlying decisions (e.g., in the evaluation of a transition guard in supervisory control) and secondly correlated observations have to be fused to obtain best estimates, e.g. in form of Bayes filters [14–16]. Such probabilistic filters are widely used in robotics, e.g. for the estimation of occupancy grids [17,18], in robust fault detection under noisy environment [19], or for estimating parameters of stochastic processes in biological tissues or molecular structures [20].

Aiming at approximating Maximum Likelihood Estimates for parameters of non-linear systems with non-Gaussian noise, Murphy [21] considers state estimation with switching Kálmán filters in presence of multiple linear dynamic models. In his setting, the time instances for switching to a certain linear dynamics are unknown up to a known stochastic distribution. In combination with stochastic state observations, this gives rise to state estimates in form of joint distributions, approximated by mixtures of Gaussian distributions. However, in addition to limited dynamics, switching between modes is based on Markovian dynamics, i.e., it is not possible to model switching based on probabilistic constraints on state estimates as necessary to model rational decisions about changing a mode as a response to observed states.

This lack of capabilites to model (rational) control decisions including discontinuous updates of the continuous state space is only partially resolved by the models underlying adaptive control theory, which is subject to comprehensive research [22–24]. In this context, the focus is on the identification of unknown (control) parameters of systems under imperfect observation. However, these approaches are not sufficient to analyse the behaviour of interacting intelligent systems as they are restricted to identifying the correct choice between a set of (possibly time-variant) dynamical models for the controlled process.

The consequential necessity of applying Bayesian filtering within hybrid systems implementing optimal control was already discovered by Ding et al. [25]. They present an approach to derive optimal control policies for partially observable discrete time stochastic hybrid systems, where optimality is defined in terms of achieving the maximum probability that the system remains within a set of safe states. In order to be able to apply dynamic programming in search for an optimal solution, Ding et al. replace the partially observable system by an equivalent perfect information system via a sufficient statistics in form of a Bayes filter. This is very close to our approach in mindset, as a sufficient statistics about a Bayesian estimate of the imperfectly known actual system state is at the heart of rational decisions in control under uncertainty. The main difference is that we are trying to formulate a general model facilitating the behavioural analysis of such optimal hybrid control systems, while Ding et al. aim at the construction of such controllers w.r.t. a given safety goal. The latter facilitates a decomposition of the design problem into obtaining a Bayesian filtering process and developing a—then scalar-valued—control skeleton. This renders a direct integration, as

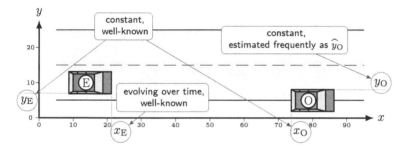

Fig. 1. A common traffic situation (taken from [26]): ego vehicle E shall decide between passing the parked obstacle O or halting.

pursued in this article, of state distributions and Bayesian inference mechanisms into the state space of an analytical model unnecessary.

3   Inadequacy of Existing Hybrid-Automata Models

Hybrid automata have been conceived in [1,2] as a formal model seamlessly integrating decision making with control, thus facilitating the modelling and analysis of the joint dynamics of these two layers pertinent to CPSes: discrete decisions, e.g. between the alternative manoeuvres of following a lead car or overtaking it in an autonomous car, do dynamically activate and deactivate continuous control skills, like an automatic distance control implementing the car-following manoeuvre. In HA, the former are described by a finite automaton featuring transitions guarded by (and possibly inducing side effects on) continuous state variables of the control path and the controller, while the latter are governed by differential equations attributed to (and thus changing in synchrony with) the automaton locations and ranging over the continuous state variables and thus describing the state dynamics of both the control path and the controller.

In reality, such CPSes have to operate and draw decisions under a variety of uncertainties stemming from their multi-component nature, as the latter requires mutual state observation between agents. Such sensing of non-local state inevitably induces uncertainties due to, a.o., the measurement inaccuracies inherent to sensor devices. In consequence, the decision making in real CPSes is bound to be rational decision-making under uncertainties. In this section, we demonstrate how existing hybrid-automata models fall short in taking account of such rational decision-making. To showcase the problem, we will in the following exploit a very simple example, mostly taken from [26], of a rational decision-making problem to be solved by a CPS.

3.1   An Example of a Control Decision Problem

Our example deals with a common traffic situation depicted in Fig. 1. Our own autonomous car, called the ego vehicle and denoted by E in the sequel, is driving along a road which features another vehicle O parked further down the road. Despite being parked on the roadside, car O may extend into the lane used by E. E cannot perform a lateral evasive manoeuvre due to dense oncoming traffic. E therefore has to decide between passing the car while keeping its lane and an emergency stop avoiding a collision. It obviously ought to decide for a pass whenever that option is safe due to a small enough intrusion of O into the lane, and it should stop otherwise.

The geometric situation can be described by four real-valued variables: three rigid variables x_O, y_O, and y_E describing the static longitudinal position of O and the static lateral positions of both cars, as well as a flexible, continuously evolving variable x_E representing the momentary longitudinal position of the ego car. For simplicity, we assume that all values except the environmental variable y_O are exactly known to the ego car E. The value of y_O has to be determined by sensing the environment via a possibly inaccurate measurement yielding an estimate $\widehat{y}_O$ for y_O. For the sake of providing a concrete instance, we assume a normally distributed measurement error, i.e., $\widehat{y}_O \sim \mathcal{N}(y_O, \sigma^2)$, though our findings do not hinge on that particular distribution. As a further simplification we assume that car E either drives with nominal speed ($\dot{x}_E = 1$) or is fully stopped ($\dot{x}_E = 0$) and that it switches between these two dynamics instantaneously.

The design goal is to design an ego car that is both safe and live—and the corresponding analysis goal consequently is to prove these two properties. Liveness in this context means that car E eventually passes car O whenever $y_E > y_O$. Safety is defined as the exclusion of the possibility of a collision, i.e., that $x_E < x_O$ stays invariant over time whenever $y_E \leq y_O$. These two properties can be formalised as follows using a straightforward extension of CTL featuring relational atoms over continuous signals akin to Signal Temporal Logic [27]:

$$\textbf{safe} := (y_E \leq y_O) \implies \textbf{AG}\,(x_E < x_O) \tag{1a}$$

$$\textbf{live} := (y_E > y_O) \implies \textbf{AF}\,(x_E \geq x_O) \tag{1b}$$

3.2   Hybrid Automata Models

Dealing with sensory observation of environmental variables and potentially reflecting the pertinent measurement inaccuracies within hybrid-automata models is a classical theme. Figure 2 represents the three standard means of dealing with sensory observation in HA models, exemplified on the example from the previous section: Automaton **Nominal** identifies environmental states with their measurements, thereby neglecting measurement error and claiming to draw control decision based on exact environmental entities. **Demonic** models measurement error as a bounded offset e between the actual value y_O and its measurement $\widehat{y}_O$, with the offset e non-deterministically chosen afresh upon every take of a measurement. It also employs the a safety margin δ within its decision making, passing only when the distance between y_E and $\widehat{y}_O$ is larger than the safety margin δ. **Stochastic**, finally, incorporates the faithful model of measurement noise

Nominal: $(x_E = 0) \wedge (y_E = 6.875) \wedge (x_O = 73.75) \wedge (\widehat{y}_O = y_O) \wedge (c = 0)$

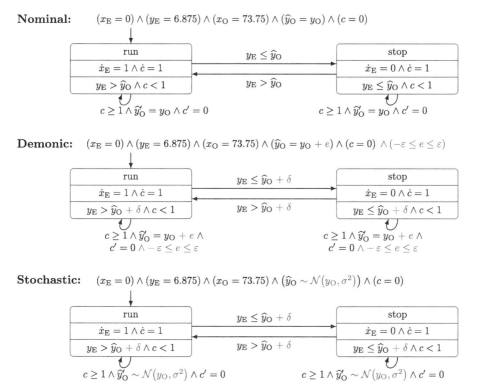

Fig. 2. Hybrid automata models for the scenario of Fig. 1 (refinements of [26])

by generating the measurement $\widehat{y}_O$ via a normal distribution $\mathcal{N}(y_O, \sigma^2)$ centered around y_O, where σ is the standard deviation of the measurement process.

Case analysis reveals that, depending on the relation between y_E and y_O and the safety margin δ, satisfaction of the two requirements formulae **safe** and **live** by the three models **Nominal**, **Demonic**, and **Stochastic** varies. Satisfaction applies as shown in Table 1.

None of these results seems particularly convincing. The nominal model, ignoring any measurement error in its analysis, optimistically claims its control to be both absolutely safe and live despite its decisions not even catering for adversarial measurement error impacting the non-robust guard $y_E > y_O$. The other two models pessimistically claim that it either is impossible to build any system satisfying any positive safety threshold ($p(\textbf{safe}) \to 0$ in **Stochastic**) or to achieve any liveness (**Demonic** $\not\models$ **live**). Given that building such controllers and achieving very high quantitative degrees of, though not absolute, liveness and safety is standard engineering practice, all the above verdicts are disappointing and show inherent deficiencies in our conventional hybrid-state models.

Table 1. Analysis results for the different models. $\to x$ denotes probabilities converging to x in the long-run limit.

	safe	live
$y_E > y_O$	trivial	sat
$y_E \leq y_O$	sat	trivial

Optimistic verdict, claiming perfect control possible despite the in reality inevitable uncertainty about environmental state.

(a) Analysis results for automaton **Nominal**

	safe	live
$y_E > y_O + \delta + \max(e)$	trivial	sat
$y_O + \delta + \varepsilon \geq y_E > y_O$	trivial	unsat
$y_E \leq y_O < y_E - \delta + \varepsilon$	unsat	trivial
$y_E - \delta + \varepsilon \leq y_O$	sat	trivial

Pessimistic verdict, rightfully claiming safety at risk whenever an inappropriate safety margin is selected (case 3 in the table), but also claiming liveness perfectly impossible to achieve.

(b) Automaton **Demonic** (case 3 arises only under insufficient safety margin $\delta < \varepsilon$)

	$p(\mathbf{safe})$	$p(\mathbf{live})$
$y_E > y_O$	1	$\to 1$
$y_E \leq y_O$	$\to 0$	1

Pessimistic verdict, claiming achievement of even marginal safety levels impossible over extended periods of time.

(c) Analysis results for automaton **Stochastic**

3.3   Adding Kálmán Filtering

The obvious problem is that the above, standard hybrid-automata models neglect the fact that repetition of noisy measurement processes accumulates increasingly better evidence about the true state of the observed entity, albeit always with a remaining uncertainty. While model **Nominal** ignores the impossibility of perfect knowledge, thus yielding inherently optimistic verdicts, models of the shapes **Stochastic** or **Demonic** do not correlate measurements across time series and thus fail to reflect the steady build-up of increasingly precise evidence about the true position y_O of the obstacle. Any form of truly rational decision-making would, however, take advantage of the latter fact; vice versa, any formal model neglecting it provides a coarse overapproximation of actual observational uncertainty resulting in correspondingly pessimistic verification verdicts relative to standard engineering practice employing filtering of measurements.

In the given case of a static obstacle O, as well as in the more general case of a physical process subject to purely linear differential dynamics, standard Kálmán filtering [10] manipulating normal distributions is the method of choice for obtaining best possible estimates of perceived state from independently normally distributed individual measurements. As normal distributions can be represented by a fixed number of parameters, namely their mean value and variance, these can still be incorporated into standard stochastic hybrid-automata models by means of extra variables: Retaining $\hat{y}_O$ as the variable representing the current estimate of the lateral position of O in the scenario from Fig. 1, one has to add a second variable representing the accuracy of the current estimate. This could be the standard deviation or the variance of the estimation error; for simplicity of

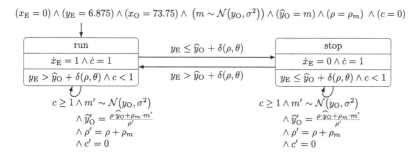

Fig. 3. A stochastic hybrid automaton incorporating Kálmán filtering for the measurements of O's position. $\delta(\rho, \theta)$ computes a safety margin yielding confidence θ when the precision is ρ, i.e., is defined by $\int_{-\infty}^{\delta(\rho,\theta)} \mathcal{N}(0, 1/\rho)(s)\mathrm{d}s = \theta$.

the update rules it is, however, customary to instead use the precision (i.e., the reciprocal of the variance). Adding a variable ρ representing the precision, the measurement transitions thus change to the usual Kálmán-filter update rules

$$m' = \mathcal{N}(y_O, 1/\rho_m),$$
$$\widehat{y}_O' = \frac{\rho \cdot \widehat{y}_O + \rho_m \cdot m}{\rho'},$$
$$\rho' = \rho + \rho_m,$$

where ρ_m is the precision of an individual measurement process and m the recent measurement. The guards governing the decision to move to mode run (as well as the invariant of that mode) change to threshold conditions on the probability mass $p_{x \sim \mathcal{N}(\widehat{y}_O, 1/\rho)}(y_E > x) \geq \theta$, checking for sufficient evidence that $y_E > y_O$ holds and thus confining the risk of erroneously moving the car forward when in fact $y_E \leq y_O$ applies to below $1 - \theta$. The resulting automaton is depicted in Fig. 3 and reflects the standard engineering practice of Kálmán filtering noisy measurements. As can be seen from the experimental results reported in Figs. 4 and 5, its control performance significantly exceeds all the verdicts for the standard models stated in Table 1.

4   Interacting and Cooperating Cyber-Physical Systems

From the above, it might seem that encoding of standard engineering practice into stochastic hybrid automata well is feasible. Issues do, however, get more involved when the perceived objects are subject to more complex dynamics than linear differential equations s.t. normal distributions or other distributions representable by a finite vector of scalar parameters do no longer suffice for encoding optimal state estimates. This applies for example when the observed agent itself is a hybrid or cyber-physical system, as we will show in this next section. The above encoding into a stochastic hybrid automaton with finite-dimensional state

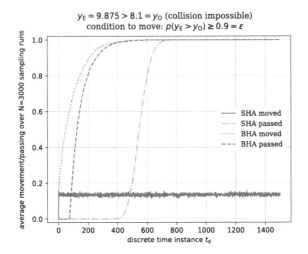

Fig. 4. Simulation results for the traffic example (Fig. 1) comparing automaton **Stochastic** (labelled SHA) with its Kálmán-filtered variant (BHA) in a safe situation ($y_E > y_O$). BHA moves steadier (dotted green vs. solid blue line) and passes earlier (red vs. orange). (Color figure online)

becomes infeasible then, instead requiring to embed complex probability distributions directly into the automaton's state space.

To demonstrate this problem induced by the cooperation of smart entities, which hinges on the additional necessity to mutually detect and reason about control decisions of the mutually other agents based on uncertain behavioural observations, we now move on to a slightly more complex scenario involving interaction between cyber-physical systems.

4.1   An Example of a Cooperative Control-Decision Problem

Imagine two ships approaching each other on a narrow channel permitting opposing traffic only within a designated passing place, as depicted in Fig. 6. The ship reaching the passing place first (ship O) is allowed[1] to draw a decision to which side it turns for mooring while the oncoming ship E enters the passing place. To complicate the issue, we forbid direct communication between the ships. In absence of means of negotiation, the ego ship E has to determine O's ensuing manoeuvre from observing the current lateral position of ship O and decides to move to a certain side as soon as its confidence that O will move to the opposite shore is above a specified threshold.

We assume that ship O has perfect knowledge about its own longitudinal (x_O) and lateral (y_O) position. Ship E, in turn, has perfect knowledge about its own position (x_E and y_E) while it maintains estimates $\widehat{x}_O$ and $\widehat{y}_O$ of O's position. The problem for E is to determine, based on these estimates, to which side O will

---

[1] Please note that this is a toy example ignoring all maritime rules such as COLREGs.

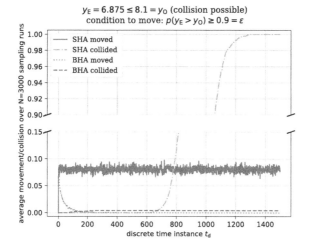

Fig. 5. Comparison in an unsafe situation ($y_E < y_O$) of the traffic example (Fig. 1). The Kálmán-filtered BHA enhances safety as it almost surely stops (dotted green line) and its collision probability saturates (dashed red), whereas the latter diverges for the SHA (dash-dotted orange) due to a constant rate of stuttering movement (solid blue). (Color figure online)

evade. Especially when O initially sails nearly centerline, this requires accumulation of evidence concerning O's decision from subsequent imprecise observation of its consequences, where the (partially) observable consequences stem from the different dynamics induced depending on O's decision. Filtering w.r.t. a single, known dynamics of O thus is no longer possible; instead, mixtures dealing with all possible decision alternatives (including the case that the decision is pending) have to be dealt with.

This obviously requires an extension of the stochastic hybrid automaton setting, as the estimates no longer constitute Gaussians due to the decision process itself, which is reflected by chopping the distributions at the evidence thresholds. That the underlying dynamics is non-linear only adds to the problem.

4.2 Formal Modelling of the Scenario

Given the complexity of the state estimation and rational decision processes sketched above, a decomposition of the overall problem into a set of interacting automata with dedicated functionalities seems appropriate. Figure 7 shows such a decomposition for the—still simple—case of unilateral observation, i.e., that ship O does not observe ship E and that their control behaviour consequently is not mutually recursive.

The roles of the various automata are as follows:

– *Observed automata (OA)* represent entities that are observed by the ego system. In the example, ship O is modeled by an observed automaton. As ship

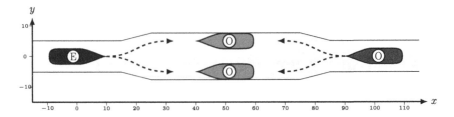

Fig. 6. Two ships approaching each other on a channel. The red ship (labelled O) decides to move to the right side of the passing place if its lateral position is larger than 0, and to the left otherwise. The ego ship (blue, labelled E) tries to determine O's manoeuvre and to move to the opposite side. (Color figure online)

O has perfect knowledge about its own state (and as its behaviour is independent from E's in the unilateral case), its automaton model is a traditional hybrid automaton of the same shape as **Deterministic** in Fig. 2.

- *Perception automata (PA)* cover the perception process, i.e. they reflect the (possibly error-afflicted) environmental perception of the ego system and update quantitative estimates $\widehat{x}$ of the observed parameters x. In simple cases, they will regularly at sampling intervals provide noisy copies $\widehat{x} \sim \mathcal{N}(x, 1/\rho_m)$ of the observed physical states.
- *Estimate automata (EA)* provide best estimates of O's current *hybrid* state to E. They extrapolate and update these estimates over time and refine them by incorporation of fresh measurements whenever such arrive. The steps involved in creating and updating the estimates thus are manifold:
  1. Temporal extrapolation starts with splitting the current estimate, i.e., state distribution for the observed entity O according to O's known mode selection dynamics. In the example, this would imply splitting the $\widehat{y}_O$ values of the part of the distribution that is associated to mode 'run' at 0 and associating its negative branch to mode 'left' and the non-negative to mode 'right'.

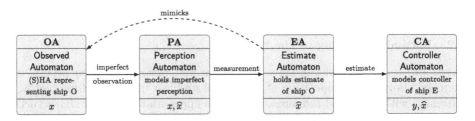

Fig. 7. Interplay between different automata modelling unilateral observation. Lowermost section lists types of variables accessed by the automata: x for system variables of the observed entity O, $\widehat{x}$ for state estimate variables associated to x within entity E, and y for system variables of the ego entity E.

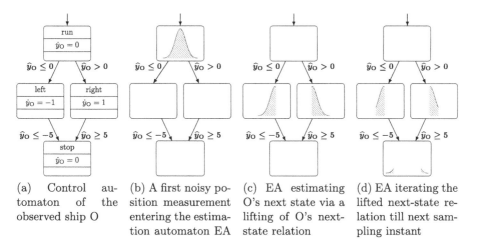

(a) Control au-tomaton of the observed ship O

(b) A first noisy po-sition measurement entering the estima-tion automaton EA

(c) EA estimating O's next state via a lifting of O's next-state relation

(d) EA iterating the lifted next-state re-lation till next sam-pling instant

Fig. 8. Estimating the observed ship's state within estimation automaton EA: A noisy position measurement corresponds to a distribution of possible positions for O (b), each of which would drive O's control automaton (a) to a specific state. EA reflects this by synchronously computing its estimate of O's hybrid state via a lifting of O's next-state relation to estimate distributions (b–d).

2. For each mode, extrapolate these "fragments" of the distribution associ-ated to the mode along the pertinent mode dynamics, which is followed for the duration of a single time-step.[2]

3. Repeat from step 1 if the inter-sample duration has not yet been reached. Else take the resulting extrapolated distribution of O's state, which now reflects the best possible estimate of O's state at the next measurement sampling time, and

4. Pursue a Bayesian update of each of the individual fragments of the "dis-sected" distribution with the fresh measurement.

5. Build the mixture of the resulting posterior "fragments" paired with their corresponding modes.

For a simple case, where the prior distribution merely stems from a single noisy measurement, the state extrapolation process of steps 1–3 is illustrated in Fig. 8b–8d.

– *Controller automata (CA)* represent the controller of the ego system, i.e. of ship E in the example. Such a CA accesses estimate variables provided by EA if control decisions to be drawn involve estimated parameters. The cor-responding decisions are "rational" in so far as safety-critical mode switches are based on sufficient confidence that the corresponding guard property is satisfied. Confidence here again relates to the probability that the guard con-dition gc holds true w.r.t. the estimated distributions: a critical transition is only taken if $p_{x \sim M}(gc) \geq \theta$, where θ denotes the required confidence and M the mixture representing the current estimate of O's state. A safe alternative

---

[2] For simplicity, we are assuming a discrete-time model here.

action (including a stay in the current mode iff its invariant bears sufficient evidence of being satisfied) has to be taken whenever no critical action can be justified with sufficient confidence.

Without digging into further detail of the above automata, it should be obvious that they go well beyond what can be encoded within hybrid automata models with their discrete plus finite-dimensional real-valued state-space:

1. As *controller automata* have to draw inferences about mixtures (representing state estimates) in order to evaluate their guards and invariants, such mixtures must be part of the state-space that controllers can observe.
2. As the state estimation by estimate automata involves active manipulation of such mixtures, these mixtures have to be part of their dynamic state.

State distributions therefore become first class members of the dynamic state themselves. As such state distributions can only rarely be encoded by finite-dimensional vectorial state (e.g., if they are bound to stay within a class of distributions featuring a description by a fixed set of parameters, like with normal distributions), this requires a completely fresh—and much more complex—set-up of the theory of hybrid automata extending beyond finite-dimensional vectorial state towards distributions as states. That this complication is necessary for obtaining accurate verdicts on control performance is witnessed by Figs. 4 and 5.

5   Automated Verification

While there is a strong body of research concerning state-exploratory methods for hybrid-system verification or falsification (for an overview cf. [12]), all of these methods are currently confined to finite-dimensional, hybrid discrete-continuous state. With complex, mixture-type distributions becoming part of the state-space of the system itself, these methods are no longer applicable: State-exploratory methods for stochastic hybrid automata [4,6,8,28] do, of course, manipulate complex mixtures over hybrid state, but as these stem from the stochastic transition dynamics rather than from the state-space itself, state-exploratory methods covering estimate automata inherently have to add another layer of mixtures (due to the iterated transition dynamics of estimate automata) ranging over state mixtures (themselves being part of the state of estimate automata). To the best of our knowledge, neither a comprehensive tool nor data structures facilitating such an analysis do currently exist.

Simulation faithfully reflecting the arising distributions in a frequentistic sense, however, seems feasible. This would facilitate rigorous statistical model-checking [29]. As mixtures of hybrid states are part of the state-space itself due to the hybrid-state estimation process (see Fig. 8), the underlying simulator, however, has to manipulate the corresponding mixtures as part of its state-space.

If all mixtures arising are linear combinations of interval-restrictions of normal distributions, as in Fig. 8, a length-unbounded list of such interval-restrictions suffices for representing the mixture part of the state space, which then has to be combined with the usual discrete and real-vector-valued states of hybrid automata. Each individual interval restriction of a (scaled) normal distribution can be represented by a five-tuple $(b, e, m, \sigma, \alpha)$ of real numbers encoding the density

$$d_{(b,e,m,\sigma,\alpha)}(x) = \begin{cases} \alpha \cdot \mathcal{N}(m, \sigma^2) & \text{if } b \leq x \leq e, \\ 0 & \text{otherwise,} \end{cases}$$

thus facilitating a computational representation of the corresponding mixtures as lists of such tuples. Evaluation of simple rational guards $p_{x \sim M}(x \sim k) \geq \theta$ over such a mixture M represented as a finite list, where k is a constant and $\sim$ denotes an inequality, is also computationally feasible. Hence, a probabilistic simulator could be built provided the distributions arising in the estimate automata remain mixtures of interval-restrictions of normal distributions, which, however, would severely confine the admissible dynamics of the observed processes: non-linear dynamics, deforming the (interval-restrictions of) normal distributions, would have to be excluded, and even affine rotations are cumbersome to deal with.

An obvious alternative is the approximation of the mixtures arising as states in the estimation automata by a set of particles, as in particle-filtering [30]. As the effect of the state extrapolation within the estimation process on each of these particles can be computed whenever the state dynamics of the observed process O can be computed, due to the extrapolation concerning a single particle coinciding exactly with O's state dynamics, simulation using such a particle approximation of the estimation mixtures is feasible even with non-linear dynamics. It should be noted, however, that extrapolation of the state of particles occurs at a different place here than in classical analysis of stochastic systems by particle-based simulation: within each state advancement step of a *single* simulation run of the overall system, we have to advance all particles representing the estimation component of the overall state-space.

Development of this technology for simulation and statistical model-checking is currently commencing in our group.

6 Summary

In the above, we have used two examples to argue that traditional hybrid-automata models, be they deterministic, nondeterministic, or stochastic, are insufficient for obtaining precise verdicts on the safety and liveness, etc., of interacting cyber-physical systems. We identified inaptness to represent rational decision-making under uncertain information as the cause of this deficiency. One may, however, argue that there might be other cures to the problem than the introduction of state estimation into the observing CPS and consequently also into its formal model, the latter necessitating a significant extension and complication of the model of hybrid automata and its related formal analysis techniques.

One such cure could be the introduction of communication within systems of interacting CPSes: the need for state estimation for an observed agent would vanish if all agents would actively communicate the local measurements that their decisions are based on (and optionally also communicate the decisions themselves) rather than having to estimate these from imprecisely observed physical behaviour. This is true, but does not provide a panacea. Not only may the mere cost as well as all kinds of reasons for data privacy and protection render such an approach undesirable, it is also bound to fail when we face socio-technical interaction within human-cyber-physical systems, as humans will neither be able nor willing to communicate a sufficiently complete representation of their perception to the CPS components. HCPSes will inherently have to rely on state estimation permitting technical systems to obtain an image of the humans' states and plans based on behavioural observations, neurophysiological measurements, etc. [31].

Another apparent cure would be the introduction of machine-learned components into the CPS for the sake of estimating (and possibly extrapolating into reasonable future) the state of observed entities. This would, however, not fundamentally change the problems induced to analysis and verification of such systems: the example of deep neural networks used for classification tasks indicates that such machine-learned state estimators manipulate "probabilities"[3] too, necessitating a very similar treatment in models and analysis engines when trying to reason rigorously about the interactive behaviour of mutually coupled systems featuring DNN components within environmental state assessment.

We conclude that the introduction of state estimation processes, with their associated complex state spaces, is a necessary addendum to the hybrid-automata framework in order render them ripe for the modelling and analysis demands of the era of interacting intelligent systems. The development of corresponding automatic verification technology, though constituting a mostly unsolved scientific challenge, is of utmost societal importance.

References

1. Alur, R., Courcoubetis, C., Henzinger, T.A., Ho, P.-H.: Hybrid automata: an algorithmic approach to the specification and verification of hybrid systems. In: Grossman, R.L., Nerode, A., Ravn, A.P., Rischel, H. (eds.) HS 1991-1992. LNCS, vol. 736, pp. 209–229. Springer, Heidelberg (1993). https://doi.org/10.1007/3-540-57318-6_30

2. Nerode, A., Kohn, W.: Models for hybrid systems: automata, topologies, controllability, observability. In: Grossman, R.L., Nerode, A., Ravn, A.P., Rischel, H. (eds.) HS 1991-1992. LNCS, vol. 736, pp. 317–356. Springer, Heidelberg (1993). https://doi.org/10.1007/3-540-57318-6_35

3. Hu, J., Lygeros, J., Sastry, S.: Towards a theory of stochastic hybrid systems. In: Lynch, N., Krogh, B.H. (eds.) HSCC 2000. LNCS, vol. 1790, pp. 160–173. Springer, Heidelberg (2000). https://doi.org/10.1007/3-540-46430-1_16

4. Sproston, J.: Decidable model checking of probabilistic hybrid automata. In: Joseph, M. (ed.) FTRTFT 2000. LNCS, vol. 1926, pp. 31–45. Springer, Heidelberg (2000). https://doi.org/10.1007/3-540-45352-0_5

---

[3] We are adding quotes here, as the "probability" assigned to a given label by a DNN classifier does not constitute a probability in a frequentistic sense or according to other conventional interpretations of probability theory.

5. Davis, M.: Markov Models and Optimization. Chapman and Hall, London (1993)
6. Fränzle, M., Hermanns, H., Teige, T.: Stochastic satisfiability modulo theory: a novel technique for the analysis of probabilistic hybrid systems. In: Egerstedt, M., Mishra, B. (eds.) HSCC 2008. LNCS, vol. 4981, pp. 172–186. Springer, Heidelberg (2008). https://doi.org/10.1007/978-3-540-78929-1_13
7. Kowalewski, S., et al.: Hybrid automata. In: Lunze, J., Lamnabhi-Lagarrigue, F., (eds.) Handbook of Hybrid Systems Control: Theory, Tools, Applications, pp. 57–86. Cambridge University Press (2009)
8. Fränzle, M., Hahn, E.M., Hermanns, H., Wolovick, N., Zhang, L.: Measurability and safety verification for stochastic hybrid systems. In: Caccamo, M., Frazzoli, E., Grosu, R. (eds.) Proceedings of the 14th ACM International Conference on Hybrid Systems: Computation and Control, HSCC 2011, Chicago, IL, USA, 12–14 April 2011, pp. 43–52. ACM (2011)
9. Bujorianu, L., Lygeros, J.: Toward a general theory of stochastic hybrid systems. In: Blom, H.A.P., Lygeros, J. (eds.) Stochastic Hybrid Systems. Lecture Notes in Control and Information Science, vol. 337, pp. 3–30. Springer, Heidelberg (2006). https://doi.org/10.1007/11587392_1
10. Kálmán, R.E.: A new approach to linear filtering and prediction problems. Trans. ASME-J. Basic Eng. **82**(Series D), 35–45 (1960)
11. Särkkä, S.: Bayesian Filtering and Smoothing. Cambridge University Press, New York (2013)
12. Fränzle, M., Chen, M., Kröger, P.: In memory of Oded Maler: automatic reachability analysis of hybrid-state automata. SIGLOG News **6**(1), 19–39 (2019)
13. Maschler, M., Solan, E., Zamir, S.: Game Theory. Cambridge University Press, Cambridge (2013)
14. Barber, D.: Bayesian Reasoning and Machine Learning. Cambridge University Press, Cambridge (2012)
15. Langseth, H., Nielsen, T.D., Rumí, R., Salmerón, A.: Inference in hybrid Bayesian networks. Reliab. Eng. Syst. Saf. **94**(10), 1499–1509 (2009)
16. Mahler, R.P.S.: Multitarget Bayes filtering via first-order multitarget moments. IEEE Trans. Aerosp. Electron. Syst. **39**(4), 1152–1178 (2003)
17. Elfes, A.: Using occupancy grids for mobile robot perception and navigation. Computer **22**(6), 46–57 (1989)
18. Coué, C., Pradalier, C., Laugier, C., Fraichard, T., Bessiere, P.: Bayesian occupancy filtering for multitarget tracking: an automotive application. Int. J. Robot. Res. **25**(1), 19–30 (2006). http://emotion.inrialpes.fr/bibemotion/2006/CPLFB06/
19. Combastel, C.: Merging Kalman filtering and zonotopic state bounding for robust fault detection under noisy environment. IFAC-PapersOnLine **48**(21) 289–295 (2015). 9th IFAC Symposium on Fault Detection, Supervision and Safety for Technical Processes SAFEPROCESS 2015
20. Sherlock, C., Golightly, A., Gillespie, C.S.: Bayesian inference for hybrid discrete-continuous stochastic kinetic models. Inverse Prob. **30**(11), 114005 (2014)
21. Murphy, K.P.: Switching Kalman filters. Technical report (1998)
22. Lavretsky, E.: Robust and adaptive control methods for aerial vehicles. In: Valavanis, K.P., Vachtsevanos, G.J. (eds.) Handbook of Unmanned Aerial Vehicles, pp. 675–710. Springer, Dordrecht (2015). https://doi.org/10.1007/978-90-481-9707-1_50
23. Gambier, A.: Multivariable adaptive state-space control: a survey. In: 2004 5th Asian Control Conference (IEEE Cat. No. 04EX904), vol. 1. pp. 185–191, July 2004

24. Narendra, K.S., Han, Z.: Adaptive control using collective information obtained from multiple models. IFAC Proc. **44**(1) 362–367 (2011). 18th IFAC World Congress
25. Ding, J., Abate, A., Tomlin, C.: Optimal control of partially observable discrete time stochastic hybrid systems for safety specifications. In: 2013 American Control Conference, pp. 6231–6236, June 2013
26. Fränzle, M., Kröger, P.: The demon, the gambler, and the engineer. In: Jones, C., Wang, J., Zhan, N. (eds.) Symposium on Real-Time and Hybrid Systems. LNCS, vol. 11180, pp. 165–185. Springer, Cham (2018). https://doi.org/10.1007/978-3-030-01461-2_9
27. Donzé, A., Maler, O.: Robust satisfaction of temporal logic over real-valued signals. In: Chatterjee, K., Henzinger, T.A. (eds.) FORMATS 2010. LNCS, vol. 6246, pp. 92–106. Springer, Heidelberg (2010). https://doi.org/10.1007/978-3-642-15297-9_9
28. Abate, A., Katoen, J., Lygeros, J., Prandini, M.: Approximate model checking of stochastic hybrid systems. Eur. J. Control **16**(6), 624–641 (2010)
29. Younes, H.L.S., Simmons, R.G.: Probabilistic verification of discrete event systems using acceptance sampling. In: Brinksma, E., Larsen, K.G. (eds.) CAV 2002. LNCS, vol. 2404, pp. 223–235. Springer, Heidelberg (2002). https://doi.org/10.1007/3-540-45657-0_17
30. Berntorp, K., Di Cairano, S.: Particle filtering for automotive: a survey. In: 22nd International Conference on Information Fusion, pp. 1–8, July 2019
31. Damm, W., Fränzle, M., Lüdtke, A., Rieger, J.W., Trende, A., Unni, A.: Integrating neurophysiological sensors and driver models for safe and performant automated vehicle control in mixed traffic. In: 2019 IEEE Intelligent Vehicles Symposium, pp. 82–89. IEEE (2019)
32. Grossman, R.L., Nerode, A., Ravn, A.P., Rischel, H. (eds.): HS 1991-1992. LNCS, vol. 736. Springer, Heidelberg (1993). https://doi.org/10.1007/3-540-57318-6

On the Industrial Application of Critical Software Verification with **VerCors**

Marieke Huisman[✉] and Raúl E. Monti[✉]

University of Twente, Enschede, The Netherlands
{m.huisman,r.e.monti}@utwente.nl

Abstract. Although software verification is evolving fast in both theoretical and practical aspects, it still remains absent from the actual industrial production cycle. Case studies can help to encourage these integrations. We report on our experiences applying software verification in several projects with industry. In particular, we report on two projects on the verification of tunnel control software at Technolution, where we go from a high-level design to concrete code. These case studies show the power of combining model checking (using mCRL2) and deductive verification (using VerCors) as complementary approaches. We also report on a project with Thales, where we looked at antenna bearing control software, and specified this based on their requirements documents. For all cases, we report on lessons learned and on directions for future work to improve both our tool and the industrial methodology for ensuring software correctness. Notably, our second case study involves the modelling and verification of critical software by a team of engineers from Technolution. This case study is an ongoing project; we describe our experience on the team's learning curve for this experiment and present the preliminary conclusions on the case study.

1 Introduction

Over the last years, software has become omnipresent in our daily lives, in a very wide range of different applications, such as games, business software, and embedded control software [29]. With the omnipresence of software, also the potential consequences of software failures have increased, while at the same time we see that all software contains bugs [15,26]. Thus, there is an urgent need for tools and techniques that can be used to easily identify and prevent bugs.

In this paper, we focus in particular on critical embedded control software, and we investigate how formal verification techniques can be used to improve the reliability of such control software. For this kind of software, reliability and the absence of bugs is even more important than for other applications, as the consequences of software errors can be very serious. To investigate how we can improve the reliability of such software, we consider several case studies of industrial control software, for tunnel and antenna bearing control, respectively, and we discuss how we analysed those using techniques supported by the VerCors

© Springer Nature Switzerland AG 2020
T. Margaria and B. Steffen (Eds.): ISoLA 2020, LNCS 12478, pp. 273–292, 2020.
https://doi.org/10.1007/978-3-030-61467-6_18

verifier for the verification of concurrent software [5]. The verification work on these case studies has been done in close collaboration with our industrial partners, Technolution and Thales. These companies have an elaborated software development process, involving meticulous pair review, enormous test suits for unit and integration testing, and a careful architectural design. However, the preliminary results of our case studies show that despite this careful process, we are still able to identify software errors using the VerCors verification technology.

The VerCors verification technology is mainly based on deductive verification, i.e. a user annotates the source code with suitable pre- and postconditions, and then from the specifications and the source code, the VerCors verifier generates proof obligations (using the intermediate language Viper [20]), which are suitable for automated first-order reasoning, using e.g. Z3 [12]. In addition, VerCors also provides techniques to reason about behavioural models of (concurrent) programs [23,24]. Concretely, the user defines a model and then uses a model checker (currently mCRL2 [16]) to reason about the model, while deductive verification is used to show that the source code implementation is a refinement of the model.

The goal of the investigations described in this paper is three-fold. First of all, we would like to demonstrate that it is indeed possible to use formal verification techniques on industrial software, and that formal verification is able to find errors in the software. Second, we would like to investigate what is needed to make formal verification part of the main-stream development process, i.e. what is needed to ensure that formal verification techniques become usable for non-experts. The outcomes w.r.t. this goal can be divided into two parts. Part of it is technical and related to the question how can we make formal verification techniques easier to use. We will discuss some ideas in this direction in this paper (see Sect. 4.3). Part of the outcome is also psychological, i.e. it has to do with how to *convince* our industrial partners that it is worthwhile to invest in the use of formal verification techniques. This is a long-term process, which requires to build up a trust relation. We started this process by inviting some of our industrial contacts for the *VerCors advisory board*. However in the mean time we realised it takes much more than just talking about what we are able to do. We also need to demonstrate this on examples that are of interest to *them*. Moreover, it involves identifying bugs and problems in the code they have developed, and which cannot easily be identified with the quality-control cycle that is already in place, i.e., the use of formal verification techniques really need to have *additional value*. Third, we use these case studies to identify new directions of work for the VerCors verifier, which need to be addressed to make sure that the verification techniques can handle the size and complexity of modern industrial software.

Notice that the VerCors verifier has originally been developed for the verification of concurrent software. In the case studies described in this paper, concurrency is not relevant. However as one of the goals of the VerCors project is to make verification of concurrent software accessible to non-verification experts, we feel that the case studies presented in this paper are an important first step in this direction. Moreover, the software components that we investigated here might be part of larger applications, where concurrency is used. Therefore, we believe that it is important that formal verification technology combines ease of use with support for a large range of language features, including concurrency.

Concretely, this paper describes three different case studies. The first case study (Sect. 3) describes work we did for Technolution on detecting a deadlock in tunnel control software. This case study has been described in detail elsewhere [25], but we include a high-level description here because it illustrates our point that incorporating formal verification in industrial software development is a long-term process. This first case study was done on existing software with a known bug. As we were able to identify the bug much faster, and in a systematic way, this led to the second case study described in Sect. 4, where we use formal verification techniques *in parallel* to the standard software development, and *in direct collaboration* with some Technolution employees. In both these case studies, we use our technique to specify a behavioural model, following Technolution's design documents, and to analyse these models using mCRL2, while using VerCors to show that their implementation adheres to the model. The third case study (Sect. 5) addresses the verification from a different perspective, as we encode a requirements document directly into pre- and postconditions, and then verify whether the code respects these pre- and postconditions.

For all case studies, we describe the lessons that we learned from the case study, and we also identify directions for future research. As mentioned above, future research is aimed at different directions: making verification technology easier to use for non-experts, and improving our verification technology to make it applicable to a larger range of applications.

Finally, this paper concludes with a discussion of related work in Sect. 6, where we compare our experiences with other experience reports discussing the use of formal verification in an industrial setting, and then concludes in Sect. 7 with the most important lessons that we learned from the case studies described in this paper.

2   Background

2.1   VerCors

VerCors [5] is a static verification tool that focuses on the verification of (concurrent) programs written in high level programming languages such as Java, OpenCL, OpenMP for C and its own prototypal verification language PVL. VerCors allows reasoning about data race freedom, memory safety, and functional properties of (possibly non-terminating) concurrent programs. Static verification in VerCors follows a design by contract approach: the user needs to specify the code with program-annotations in the form of pre- and post-conditions, following the style of JML [18]. VerCors then takes the program and its annotations and translates it into a problem for the intermediate language verifier Viper [20].

VerCors implements permission-based Separation Logic (PBSL) [1,6] to reason about different concurrency models, notably heterogeneous concurrency (e.g. Java programs) and homogeneous concurrency (e.g. GPU kernels). For this, the program specification needs to explicitly express heap ownership in the form of permission annotations.

Figure 1 shows an example of program specification for verification with Ver-Cors. The lines prepended with //@ present VerCors specifications. Keyword Perm is used to indicate heap ownership. For method inc we require that the thread executing this method should have write permission to variable x in order to change its value. This is done at line 5, where value 1 means full (write) permission. The logic of VerCors verifies that the sum of all granted permissions to a same heap location never exceeds 1, which ensures absence of data races in a verified program. Then, we can ensure that the final value of x will actually be the expected one (line 7). At line 6 we only ensure to return half (1\2) of the permissions we obtained for x, i.e. a read permission. Retaining half of the permission to x will actually cause the verification to fail at line 17, since we will not be able to provide the write permission required by the second call to inc.

```
1    class Foo{                         11
2                                       12    //@ requires Perm(x,1);
3      int x;                           13    //@ ensures Perm(x,1);
4                                       14    //@ ensures x == \old(x)+2;
5      //@ requires Perm(x,1);          15    void incx2(){
6      //@ ensures Perm(x,1\2);         16      inc();
7      //@ ensures x == \old(x)+1;      17      inc();
8      void inc(){                      18    }
9        x = x + 1;                     19
10     }                                20  }
```

Fig. 1. VerCors verification example.

Most interesting for the first two case studies in this work, VerCors features a model-based verification technique [23, 24]. This uses a process algebra language to capture the behaviour of a software system by abstracting its access to shared memory by means of actions. The model specifies the acceptable executions of the system, and this can be verified to fulfil behavioural properties by an external model checker. Our technique then allows to connect blocks of code from the implementation to the actions in the abstract model. VerCors is then capable of verifying if the model is actually an abstraction of the code, or equivalently, if the implementation refines the model.

A central aspect of this technique is a formally proven deduction system which allows to link the abstract modelled behaviour of the software and its actual implementation. With this, we fill the usual gap between the model and the implementation: (safety) properties that are proven valid in the model are by refinement also true for the code.

The VerCors Advisory Board. The VerCors Advisory Board consists of members of the Thales, BetterBe, Technolution, Rosen, and PolderValley, companies. It is intended to be a place to exchange interests and experience with the industrial side of software production. The members of the Advisory Board were selected based on former interactions with them, who approached the VerCors team presenting some interest in formal verification. It was also intended that they would represent an wide and diverse spectrum in the industrial application field for formal verification. The Advisory Board is intended to meet with the VerCors team twice a year. During the meetings we present our advances in support for formal verification and we get feedback, new ideas and case study proposals from the industrial side.

2.2   mCRL2

mCRL2 [8] is a state of the art tool set for model checking which offers an ACP-style process algebra as modelling language and allows to verify properties specified in modal μ-calculus with data. The tool set offers around sixty different tools to describe, manipulate and analyse the models.

Figure 2a shows an mCRL2 model of a producer/consumer protocol, where the producer generates messages of type A and B, queues them, and sends them to a consumer. Line 1 defines a new type T with constructors A and B. Line 3 defines several actions, parametrised by the type T. Lines 5 and 9 define process P and C respectively representing the producer and the consumer respectively. P is parametrised by an mCRL2 native type List, to queue up to two generated messages. In line 12, init indicates the initial setting of the system: allow defines the visible actions (opposite to usual hiding of actions) and comm renames the multi-action snd|rcv to com to indicate that P and C will communicate by both executing snd respectively rcv at the same time. Finally, line 16 defines that P and C should execute in parallel.

Figure 2b shows the labeled transition system of the producer/consumer model as presented by the ltsgraph tool from the mCRL2 tool chain. This tool allows to visually inspect the model described by the algebra. mCRL2 also allows to minimise the models against several bisimulation notions, to reduce the size of the generated state space.

3   Case Study 1: Tunnel Emergency Control Software

This section gives a high level overview of the first case study study [25] carried out between our group and Technolution [27], a Dutch software and hardware development company located in Gouda, with a recorded experience in developing safety-critical industrial software. The aim of this case study was to understand to what extent our formal verification tools could be applied in the context of Technolution's software development projects. The case study analysed an emergency control module from a traffic tunnel system, by (1) formalising and verifying the design by means of the mCRL2 model checker and (2) by demonstrating that the implementation is a refinement of the design by using our VerCors tool. The main goal of the case study was to explore if the mentioned combination of model checking and refinement by deductive verification could really be applied to a real-world software product, and to what extent this would be beneficial for the company involved, i.e. Technolution. We refer the curious readers to [25] and [23] for more details about this case study.

```
1    sort T = struct A | B;
2
3    act snd, rcv, new, com: T;
4
5    proc P(q:List(T)) =
6       (#q<2) -> sum x: T . new(x) . P(q<|x)
             +
7       (#q>0) -> snd(head(q)) . P(tail(q));
8
9    proc C =
10      sum x: T . rcv(x) . C;
11
12   init
13      allow({new, com},
14         comm({snd|rcv->com},
15            P([]) || C() ));
```

(a) mCRL2 model of prod/cons.   (b) ltsgraph visualisation of prod/cons.

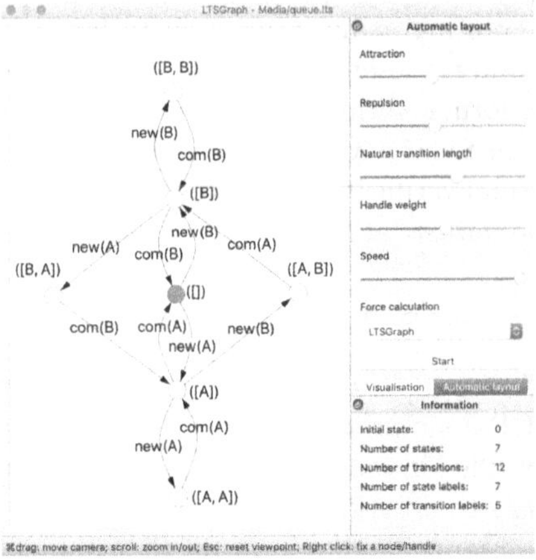

Fig. 2. mCRL2 model of a producer/consumer and its state space visualisation in the ltsgraph tool.

3.1 Formal Verification of an Industrial Safety-Critical Traffic Tunnel Control System

Technolution provided us with the specification and implementation of an already deployed *emergency control software* from a *traffic tunnel*. This control system is in charge of ensuring that the right measures are taken when any (possible) calamity is detected in the tunnel. These measures could be, for instance, enabling fire extinguishers, turning on visual notification for people to know how to get to a safe place, turning the fans in the right direction to expel the smoke out of the tunnel, etc. This software is considered to be highly critical and for this reason the Dutch government imposes very high reliability demands on it, which are specified in a document of requirements that is over 500 pages in length [21].

As expected, the development process of the traffic tunnel control system was executed as an elaborate process of quality assurance/control, to satisfy the high demands on reliability imposed by the Dutch government. Significant time and energy has been spent on software design and specification, code inspection, peer reviewing, unit and integration testing, etc. In particular, we were given a precise design of the system, assisted by pseudocode definitions for each functionality (see Fig. 3 for an excerpt of [21]) and detailed state machines indicating the possible state changes after executing these functionalities (see [25] for more details). However, even though precise, the specification was informal and could not be formally verified.

Our goal was to demonstrate how formal methods could aid the verification of this control software by answering two main questions: (1) Is the informal specification of the tunnel control system consistent, meaning that it does not

```
1    Evacueer()
2        Evacueer de aangegeven verkeersbuis.
3        (Overgang 6)
4
5        Conditie: #substate = calamiteit_volledig
6        Acties: #substate := calamiteit_evacuatie
7                NaarEvacuatie()
```

Fig. 3. Pseudo-code design of the Evacueer() function from the National Tunnel Standard [21].

reach undesired states such as deadlocks or present any dangerous behaviour? and (2) does the actual implemented code follow the pseudocode specification?

Our approach to address the verification of these properties followed a combination of verification techniques (see Fig. 4 for a graphical representation of the approach). To answer question (1), we used model checking, by developing a formal model from the informal specification and verifying appropriate properties on this model. Particularly, we used the model checker mCRL2 for this task. To answer question (2), we used the refinement technique developed for VerCors [23,24], mentioned above, to formally prove that the code implementing the controller followed the behaviour described by the model.

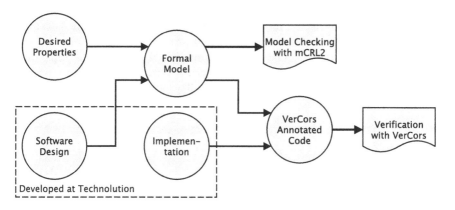

Fig. 4. Scheme of our model based deductive verification approach to code verification.

3.2   Model Checking the Design

To build the model for the control system, we followed the pseudocode descriptions of the intended functionalities and state machine diagrams describing the state jumps triggered by these functionalities. We also took into account interesting parts of the execution model, which slightly restricted the order of execution of the functionalities.

Although the initial model was too big to analyse, a series of abstraction iterations allowed us to arrive to a sufficiently expressive and concise model, small enough to verify. A couple dozen of properties elaborated by us after consulting the team of engineers from Technolution were verified on the model. During the verification we were able to identify a deadlock in the model, resulting from an intricate combination of times and events, which is very difficult to discover by methods traditionally implemented in industry. In fact, Technolution had discovered this error by chance, and had intensionally given us a faulty design to test our approach.

3.3   Code Verification by Refinement

Next, we used VerCors to prove deductively that the code developed by Technolution followed the formal specification of the tunnel, i.e. it refines the actual model. An important property of our refinement technique is that it preserves safety properties, such as deadlock freedom. The mCRL2 model is first translated to an intended equivalent model in the specification language of VerCors. The actions of the model can then logically be attached to sets of commands in the corresponding code by annotating blocks of code. The proof rules that VerCors implements allow to formally verify that the behaviour of the code follows the behaviour of the model [23,24]. Actually, we did not verify the Java implementation, but we translated it into equivalent code in our prototypal verification language (PVL), since at the moment this has a better support for the refinement verification. Although there is no formal proof of the equivalence between the original mCRL2 model and the VerCors model, the relation becomes quite evident from the proximity of the model structure. During the verification refinement we were able to conclude that the code followed the behaviour specified by the model.

3.4   Lessons Learned

During this first case study, in roughly 7 working days, with a single PhD student assigned to the project, we constructed a formal model of the informal specification of the tunnel control system, analysed it using mCRL2, and used VerCors to deductively prove that the implementation adheres to the specification. This resulted in the detection of undesired behaviour, preventing the control system from automatically starting the calamity procedure after an emergency has been detected. Even though Technolution was already aware of this behaviour, they only found it coincidentally, while we demonstrated that formal methods can indeed help to find such undesired behaviours in a structural manner, and within realistic time. It is our intention to continue investigating this technique in further case studies with Technolution and other companies. We believe that the success of this first step in the case study was highly influenced by the quality of the tunnel specification which, despite being informal, was well-structured, and therefore had the potential to be formalised within reasonable time.

Note that we did not find any discrepancies between the code and the specification by means of our refinement technique. We believe that this could be because we verified an implementation that was already deployed and thoroughly tested. This partly jeopardised our goal of demonstrating the usability of the technique, as the company only saw the extra effort, without any gain in the form of bugs found. Nevertheless they became aware of the potential of the technique and opened to new collaborations.

We also mentioned that we did not verify the actual Java implementation but an intended equivalent PVL implementation. On future case studies we would like to extend our tool support for the refinement technique to the rest of our front end languages, in order to verify the actual code. This is in fact a compulsory step for the systematic application of our technique in industry.

Finally, the experiences with this case study led to an idea to investigate if the pseudocode specification language can be formalised into a domain specific language (DSL), that can be automatically translated to mCRL2. We suspect that the specification of the pseudocode description in terms of this language would be a mechanical and straightforward activity. As a consequence, we expect that this language will greatly reduce the effort of adopting our technique for further verification at Technolution, in contrast to the steep learning curve necessary to use the mCRL2 modelling language.

4   Case Study 2: A New Tunnel Emergency Control Software

After the promising results of the first case study, we are currently working on a follow up project with Technolution. In contrast to our earlier collaboration, in this project we are working on the formal specification and verification *during* the development process of a new tunnel project. Moreover, a team of engineers from Technolution will be in charge of the formal modelling and model checking verification steps, while we advise them and work on the verification of code.

A main goal of this follow up project is to understand how much effort it will take the engineers at Technolution to learn formal verification and to what extent they can use this knowledge to verify their software. Furthermore, we want to obtain new insights and ideas on how to ease this process. Although not formally a goal of the project, we expect to be able to shape the characteristics of the DSL language as we mentioned as an insight from our previous case study with Technolution. Another main goal of this case study is to showcase our refinement verification with VerCors. We hope to increase the chances of finding bugs this time, by targeting the implementation in the earlier stages of development.

Figure 5 shows the steps we agreed upon before the start of the project: a team of two or three engineers from Technolution will use our help and expertise to learn the modelling principles surrounding mCRL2. They will try to model an interesting part of the tunnel specification by themselves, while only seeking for our help if really needed. Once the first version of the code for the selected components will become available to us, we will start the refinement verification against the mCRL2 model from the Technolution team using the VerCors tool.

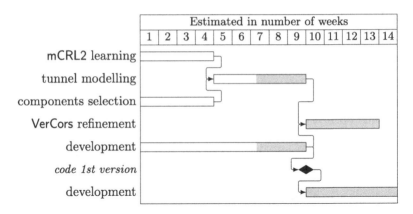

Fig. 5. Gantt chart of the steps of the project. White colour inside bars indicates the progress already made. (Color figure online)

4.1 Progress of the Project

We started the project by teaching mCRL2 modelling to the Technolution team. For this, we developed a series of slides presenting the main concepts of modelling, focusing on their applicability. We also used the mCRL2 web tutorial [19] for putting the learned concepts into practice. The other main standard source to learn mCRL2 is the book "Modeling and Analysis of Communicating Systems" [16]. Although the engineers working in the project initially dedicated considerable time to reading this book and understanding its concepts, they finally concluded that it was ineffective for their purpose. They claimed that the book assumes a thorough understanding of many formal mathematical concepts and notations, not common for outsiders in formal verification, and that the return on investment for understanding these concepts is not directly applicable to the modelling; they experienced quite some distance between the learned concepts and their application using the modelling language. They expect to have sources better aimed towards the application of the verification methodologies.

In between the teaching meetings, we had several extra modelling meetings, where we investigated the new tunnel specification and attempted to both figure out the differences with the former project and to choose interesting new aspects to model and verify. This turned to be beneficial in the sense that it also helped the engineers to analyse how the different concepts of modelling could match the different aspects of the system design.

When a good level of understanding of the modelling and verification concepts was reached, the Technolution team was ready to select the target modules to verify. The new tunnel differs from the former tunnel by being split into two consecutive sections. It consists of two parallel tubes both split in half by a joining lane (see Fig. 6 for clarification). This involves introducing new control units and protocols to coordinate each segment of the tubes. The engineering team decided to target these new modules for their verification.

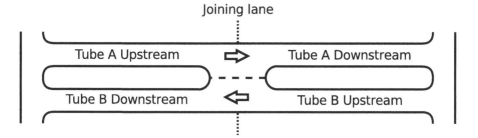

Fig. 6. The new tunnel topology.

In the current stage of the project, the Technolution team is attempting to model the selected modules. They are also defining the properties to verify and use these to decide upon the level of abstraction they should apply during the modelling. We expect the first version of the code to be available by August 2020. Then we will be able to start the verification by refinement with VerCors.

4.2   Lessons Learned Up to Now

Even though the project is still ongoing, we can already report on some important observations, mostly involving the learning curve of the modelling language.

We found that the official material, i.e. the web tutorial [19] and book [16], alone is not enough to learn the mCRL2 modelling language with an approach on application: the tutorial examples helped to get started but they focus mostly on covering each of the characteristics of the language, and miss a focus on real case studies concerning for instance of distributed systems and communication protocols. The book discusses the mathematical concepts behind the tool, and lacks the practical approach desired by the engineers. For the same reason, its language differs from the one used in practice and thus misguides the engineers when trying to apply what they learn.

We also realised that the modelling language is too low level and general for the usual purpose of the engineer. As an example, during some proof-of-concept designs that we developed with the Technolution team, we came up with many different solutions to the problem of communicating the state of a process to another process. Some of these solutions turned out to be more efficient than others, i.e. they generated a smaller state space for the same problem. Some were actually found to be wrong solutions. Finding and understanding which one is viable and more efficient could have been spared from us if this mechanism had been offered at a higher level of abstraction.

Furthermore, we experienced that the complexity of μ-calculus is highly unpractical for our purpose. Of course the property specification language is not necessary meant to be practical, but powerful. However, our experience was that explaining the initial concepts of the logic, without yet involving the fix-point modalities, already took a substantial amount of time and practice. The fixpoint modalities were presented from an application point of view as a way to express finite/infinite recursions on the propositional formulas, or liveness and safety properties respectively. Nevertheless the concept remains to be unclear, and the typical working mode right now is to use pre-built templates and modify them when needed to express a new property.

On a positive side, we experienced that with the current set-up for the case, the attitude of the engineers involved is much more proactive in comparison to our previous general experiences with students at university level. This makes it possible to compensate for the experienced difficulties, such as not completely understanding the intricacies of the modelling language.

4.3   Sketches on Future Directions

As mentioned before, we found that the complexity of the μ-calculus formulas are one of the weakest points in adapting our formal verification techniques to an industrial setting. As a workaround, it was discussed several times during our meetings that it would be convenient to prepare more template formulas, to avoid reworking them each time a similar property has to be defined. An important property of such patterns is that they can be tool independent, since they can be translated into different logics for property specification. Furthermore, if defined simple and intuitive, such patterns can reduce the learning curve for the use of formal logics for specification.

As an example, in the context of emergency control systems, it is very common to require properties about recoverability: *It is always possible to recover from a calamity state.* That is, we should always be able to take our system back to a normal execution after a calamity has been resolved. A common way of specifying such property by a μ-calculus formula would look like:

$$[true^*.enterCalamity]\,\nu.X($$
$$[\neg exitCalamity^*]\langle exitCalamity\rangle true\wedge \qquad (1)$$
$$[true^*.enterCalamity]X)$$

which is neither direct to understand nor to remember. Ideally, we would like to use a declarative version such as

$$\texttt{recover}(enterCalamity, exitCalamity)$$

which is automatically translated into the formula above.

Of course, ideas for adapting the logics for property specification into more suitable languages for a systematic use in industry are not new. For example, the Bandera tool for Model Checking Java code [10], defines the Bandera temporal specification language (BSL) [11]. The language consists of a set of common specification patterns corresponding to common classes of temporal requirements such as response, precedence or absence. For instance, a *response* property requires that the occurrence of a designated state or event is followed by another designated state or event in the execution. BSL also defines pattern scopes which restrict the fragments of execution where the property patterns are validated. For instance a *between* scope may define that a certain pattern is expected to be valid in between the occurrence of some pair of designated states or actions. For example, property (1) can be expressed in BSL by using a `leads to` pattern and a `globally` scope as follows:

$$exitCalamity \text{ \texttt{leads to} } enterCalamity \text{ \texttt{globally}}$$

The EVALUATOR3.5 tool from the CADP [14] project, defines a translation from BSL to μ-calculus [7].

Also SUGAR [4] presents an interesting approach to ease the specification of properties in temporal formalisms by defining syntactic sugar on top of CTL. As an example, a *next_event* operator, defined in terms of the weak until operator, refers to the next time an event may occur, in contrast to AX which refers to the next state. The language also defines a *within* operator to define properties to be expected between two states or actions, and syntactic sugar to introduce counters into the formulas. A similar approach is followed by the SALT [3] language, where several syntactic sugars are introduced inspired by relevant case studies on real-world specifications.

As an output of our case study, we plan to produce a list of interesting properties and patterns. We would like to analyse if some of the mentioned specification languages effectively covers this list, or if we would need some extension to them. An alternative direction would be defining a more specific language tailored to emergency control systems in general. In any case, we consider that it is important to still allow the use of the underlaying formalism for property specification (μ-calculus in the case of mCRL2), for a bigger expressive power whenever needed.

5   Case Study 3: Antenna Bearing Controller in C

Next we discuss a third case study, provided by the Thales group [28]. Thales is a world-scale software and hardware company specialised in defence technology, digital identity and security, and transportation among others.

The goal of this case study is to understand how VerCors can improve the quality of Thales' software development. A parallel goal is to investigate what needs to be improved in VerCors to be able to verify Thales' software projects in the future.

As part of our VerCors Advisory Board, a representative of Thales attended a presentation about the type of verification we target with our tool. As a result, they proposed us to verify a critical component of the control software for a radar. This component is in charge of validating the messages obtained from the sensors that measure the current position of the radar bearing.

5.1   Case Study Settings

The settings for this case study considerably differ from the two case studies discussed above. The code provided by Thales is completely written in C and instead of a design document a requirements document was provided. We investigated how can we use VerCors C support to validate the code against the requirements, and how to improve our support (if needed).

Structure of the Requirements. The bearing validation component can be divided into several smaller modules, which are each in charge of the validation of specific data included in the messages received from the sensors. For each of these modules, the requirement document defines a *general* requirement enumerating which *sub*-requirements have to be fulfilled in order to validate a specific property of the message assigned to this module (See Fig. 7 for clarification). The smaller requirements define conditions to be fulfilled by specific values in the message. These conditions are usually comparisons against predefined constants, or values in former messages, aiming to ensure the consistency of the newly arrived messages. The structure of messages and their fields are defined in a separate document and used in the conditions of the requirements.

Structure of the Code. On the implementation side, the messages from the sensors are represented by structures with field names that closely follow the ones defined in the requirements document. Other fields inside these same data structures allow the code to keep track of the validity verdict for the message. In particular, a `valid` field in the message structure indicates if the message is considered to be valid, i.e. if it is considered to fulfil all the validity conditions from the radar validation component. A few other fields are used as `flags` to indicate the cause of invalidation of the message.

A single C-file implements the code to validate each requirement from the validation component. The code follows the structure of the requirements document. There are *general* functions which validate the *general* requirements by

```
REQ_MODULE_0:
   MODULE_0 declares that
      message M is valid only
      if SUB_REQ_0 to SUB_REQ_N
      are validated.
```

```
SUB_REQ_0:
   The validation component
      shall verify that the
      value of field F from the
      message M lays between
      constants C and C'.
   ...
SUB_REQ_N:
   The validation component
      shall verify that ...
```

(a) A general requirement.   (b) Sub-requirements for (a).

Fig. 7. Structure of the requirements for the validation component. (Concrete names from the case study have been anonymised for confidentiality reasons).

```
void REQ_MODULE_0(struct Message *msg){
  SUB_REQ_0(msg);
  SUB_REQ_N(msg);
  ...
}

void SUB_REQ_0(struct Message *msg){
// set msg->flag0 to the result of validating SUB_REQ_0
// from the requirements document, and update msg->valid.
  ...
}
...
void SUB_REQ_N(struct Message *msg){
// set msg->flagN to the result of validating SUB_REQ_N
// from the requirements document, and update msg->valid.
  ...
}
```

Fig. 8. Structure of implementation code for 7

calling *sub*-functions which validate the *sub*-requirements. The message data structure travels through the function calls as a parameter and the verdict of the validations are written into it using the `valid` and `flags` fields (see Fig. 8 for clarification).

5.2 Approach to Verification with **VerCors**

To verify the implementation of the validation component, we translated each sub-requirement from the specification document to a postcondition for the function in charge of validating the corresponding sub-requirement. Figure 9 shows an example specification for SUB_REQ_0 from Fig. 7b.

```
\*@
  ...
  ensures (msg->valid && msg->flag_sub_req_0) ==
          (C <= \old(msg->F) && \old(msg->F) <= C');
@*\
void sub_req_0(struct Message *msg){
  ...
}
```

Fig. 9. Example of contract for verification of requirements.

To validate a general requirement, such as the one in Fig. 7a, we specified its corresponding function with the following postcondition:

`ensures` `msg->valid`$\wedge$`!msg->flag`$_0$ $\wedge \cdots \wedge$`!msg->flag`$_N$ $\Leftrightarrow$ `cond`$_0$ $\wedge \cdots \wedge$ `cond`$_N$;

where `cond`$_i$ encodes the conditions specified by sub-requirement i.

To showcase the approach we validated a single general requirement (and its sub-requirements) that was representative of the rest of them. We did not find any implementation errors during the validation. However, while inspecting the code, we found annotations in the form of comments indicating assumptions on the use of certain functions, such as an argument being positive, and we turned them into requirements of the alleged functions. During verification, we realised that one of these assumption was not met. Fortunately, the documented assumption was not considered in the implementation of the function and thus it did not evolve into an error in the code. However, the engineers from the Thales group considered this a useful discovery, because they claimed that most of the times developers would blindly follow the assumption and not implement a check inside the function in order to keep the code simple. Notice that these specifications in the form of comments are completely overlooked by the test suites which only involve testing the implementation code.

5.3 Lessons Learned

On the positive side, we discovered that even in relatively simple and well structured code, requirement inconsistencies can be overlooked by traditional testing techniques, while they are easily spotted by our tool.

On the other hand, a first limitation we found while working on this case study, is our poor support for the C language. For instance, support for structures and floating point numbers was missing. While we were able to add support for structures (in a limited fashion) quite easy, we decided in the meanwhile to abstract from floating point calculations by rounding every value to a close integer; the amount of work that it would take to add support for floats would have stalled the case study.

In this same direction, it was interesting to learn the discrepancies between the characteristics of the code used in industry and the one we imagine should be targeted while developing VerCors. In fact we are more used to focus on intricate algorithms with complex concurrency models, while this is usually the kind of code that industrial critical software tries to avoid. The risks of producing this kind of software, which is difficult to analyse, is too high. At the same time, we as developers of a verification tool, overlook other aspects such as the importance of having complete support of front end languages.

Another caveat we found in our tool is the amount of annotations needed to verify relatively simple properties. Actually, most of the annotations belong to permission-related constraints, inherent to VerCors' separation logic based verification. This problem was strengthened due the presence of large structures with many fields for which the precise access permissions have to be defined at each function contract.

5.4   Directions for Improving **VerCors**

A first direction of improvement we observe from this case study is to broaden our support for C. Some of this support can be added in a straightforward way, or by just applying some (substantial) engineering effort. Some other aspects, such as reasoning about floating point numbers will be a bigger challenge. We can find inspiration for this in other verification tools which already support these features, such as Why3 [30] or Frama-C [2].

We should also work on automating the annotations of contracts for verification. The amount of annotations the developer needs to manually introduce is sometimes overwhelming, and it makes the code difficult to read and maintain. During this case study the rate reached up to around 10 lines of specification code for each line of implementation code. A possible way to reduce this rate would be to extend our C frontend by defining predicates to encapsulate annotations, which are already present in our Java and PVL frontends. However, we believe that adding this support may not be sufficient by itself, since we have also found this problem in the other frontends before. A complementary solution would be to work on fully automated, or semi-automated user-assisted procedures to annotate permissions constraints. This solution will imply research work to develop and to figure out to what extent we can be apply these techniques.

6   Related Work

The lessons learned and the various discoveries during or case studies are of course not completely new to us, and we can find similar experiences in other works. In [22] the authors present several case studies on critical software, one of which is on deductive verification of a C program. They happened to find the same problem we have with floating point numbers which are pervasive in this kind of code. They also discus on the complexity of the verification languages and the struggles that non-expert personnel have to go through to come up with the right specifications to verify. They admit that even after 8 years of conducting case studies at the same company, they have not yet managed to introduce formal verification in a larger scale.

Dwyer et al. [13] hypothesise that a main cause of the difficulty of transitioning into industrial application of formal methods for verification is that practitioners are unfamiliar with specification processes and notations. They propose a pattern-based approach to property specification. We also discuss this, since it has actually been a concurrent request from the engineers involved in our case studies.

Larsen et al. [17] analyses 20 years of development of their model checking tool UPPAAL. They emphasise the importance of industrial case studies and collaborations, which they claim to have guided the construction of their tool. From the lessons learned in this process, they highlight that reaching an industrial impact of formal methods requires several iterations on collaboration with industrial partners and a coordinated evolution of both the tool and the industrial methods. They also emphasise that, although formal, the specification languages should be engineer-friendly in order to increase the chances of impact.

Cok [9] states that engaging the software developers responsible for code development directly in the specification and verification process is a current challenge. In this sense, we believe our work is making a valuable contribution, since we are presenting an actual experience where we have managed to involve the design engineering team of Technolution (as described in Sect. 4) in the tasks of modelling, specifying and verifying their software product. In fact, it is not easy to find similar case studies; in the big majority of cases, the experts in formal verification are in charge of the experimentation.

7   Conclusion

A first conclusion from our work is that it takes time to build a relation with industry that may result in the eventual adaption of formal verification into an industrial environment and its application as a successful way of verifying critical software. We noticed that our VerCors Advisory Board has been very helpful to generate this relation; it allows us to communicate what we can do to industrial partners, and to get proposals for case studies from them.

In our experience, case studies have been very useful. They helped us to understand what are the usual problems that industry faces when developing critical software, and they helped us to improve our tool to make it suitable to solve such problems. We noticed that even some small success in a case study can open further collaborations and experiments with the industrial partners, since it showcases for them that there exists a real possibility of applying formal methods in their industrial processes. We find that in general, they are interested in finding techniques that can help them to improve software quality, as long as there is a good trade-off between invested time and results.

From the case studies analysed in this work, we have derived several points for improvement of our tool. These involve broadening the support for our frontend languages by, for instance, supporting floating point reasoning, as well as structures in C. We would also like to investigate patterns and DSL languages for our model based verification, in order to ease its adoption, which is now quite limited by the learning curve of the mCRL2 tool. Finally it is worth to investigate automating the permissions specifications, which is currently an error prone unpleasant job for the developer.

In the future we would like to continue with these case studies and spin-offs that may emerge from them. We are looking forward to the results of our ongoing tunnel control software verification with Technolution, and we will look for new case studies on which to showcase our planned upgrades to the C frontend.

References

1. Amighi, A., Haack, C., Huisman, M., Hurlin, C.: Permission-based separation logic for multithreaded Java programs. Log. Methods Comput. Sci. **11**(1), 1–66 (2015)

2. Ayad, A., Marché, C.: Multi-prover verification of floating-point programs. In: Giesl, J., Hähnle, R. (eds.) IJCAR 2010. LNCS (LNAI), vol. 6173, pp. 127–141. Springer, Heidelberg (2010). https://doi.org/10.1007/978-3-642-14203-1_11

3. Bauer, A., Leucker, M., Streit, J.: SALT—structured assertion language for temporal logic. In: Liu, Z., He, J. (eds.) ICFEM 2006. LNCS, vol. 4260, pp. 757–775. Springer, Heidelberg (2006). https://doi.org/10.1007/11901433_41

4. Beer, I., Ben-David, S., Eisner, C., Fisman, D., Gringauze, A., Rodeh, Y.: The temporal logic sugar. In: Berry, G., Comon, H., Finkel, A. (eds.) CAV 2001. LNCS, vol. 2102, pp. 363–367. Springer, Heidelberg (2001). https://doi.org/10.1007/3-540-44585-4_33

5. Blom, S., Darabi, S., Huisman, M., Oortwijn, W.: The VerCors tool set: verification of parallel and concurrent software. In: Polikarpova, N., Schneider, S. (eds.) IFM 2017. LNCS, vol. 10510, pp. 102–110. Springer, Cham (2017). https://doi.org/10.1007/978-3-319-66845-1_7

6. Bornat, R., Calcagno, C., O'Hearn, P.W., Parkinson, M.J.: Permission accounting in separation logic. In: Palsberg, J., Abadi, M. (eds.) Proceedings of the 32nd ACM SIGPLAN-SIGACT Symposium on Principles of Programming Languages, POPL 2005, Long Beach, California, USA, 12–14 January 2005, pp. 259–270. ACM (2005)

7. The BSL to MU-calculus webpage. http://cadp.inria.fr/resources/evaluator/rafmc.html. Accessed June 2020

8. Bunte, O., et al.: The mCRL2 toolset for analysing concurrent systems. In: Vojnar, T., Zhang, L. (eds.) TACAS 2019. LNCS, vol. 11428, pp. 21–39. Springer, Cham (2019). https://doi.org/10.1007/978-3-030-17465-1_2

9. Cok, D.R.: Java automated deductive verification in practice: lessons from industrial proof-based projects. In: Margaria, T., Steffen, B. (eds.) ISoLA 2018. LNCS, vol. 11247, pp. 176–193. Springer, Cham (2018). https://doi.org/10.1007/978-3-030-03427-6_16

10. Corbett, J.C., et al.: Extracting finite-state models from Java source code. In: Ghezzi, C., Jazayeri, M., Wolf, A.L. (eds.) Proceedings of the 22nd International Conference on on Software Engineering, ICSE 2000, Limerick Ireland, 4–11 June 2000, pp. 439–448. ACM (2000)

11. Corbett, J.C., Dwyer, M.B., Hatcliff, J., Robby: A language framework for expressing checkable properties of dynamic software. In: Havelund, K., Penix, J., Visser, W. (eds.) Proceedings of the 7th International SPIN Workshop on SPIN Model Checking and Software Verification, Stanford, CA, USA, 30 August – 1 September 2000. LNCS vol. 1885, pp. 205–223. Springer, Heidelberg (2000). https://doi.org/10.1007/10722468_13

12. de Moura, L., Bjørner, N.: Z3: an efficient SMT solver. In: Ramakrishnan, C.R., Rehof, J. (eds.) TACAS 2008. LNCS, vol. 4963, pp. 337–340. Springer, Heidelberg (2008). https://doi.org/10.1007/978-3-540-78800-3_24

13. Dwyer, M.B., Avrunin, G.S., Corbett, J.C.: Property specification patterns for finite-state verification. In: Ardis. M.A., Atlee, J.M. (eds.) Proceedings of the Second Workshop on Formal Methods in Software Practice, 4–5 March 1998, Clearwater Beach, Florida, USA, pp. 7–15. ACM (1998)

14. Fernandez, J.-C., Garavel, H., Kerbrat, A., Mounier, L., Mateescu, R., Sighireanu, M.: CADP - a protocol validation and verification toolbox. In: Alur, R., Henzinger, T.A. (eds.) Proceedings of the 8th International Conference Computer Aided Verification, CAV 1996. LNCS, New Brunswick, NJ, USA, 31 July – 3 August 1996, vol. 1102, pp. 437–440. Springer (1996). https://doi.org/10.1007/3-540-61474-5_97

15. Ganapathi, A., Patterson, D.A.: Crash data collection: a windows case study. In: Dependable Systems and Networks (DSN), pp. 280–285. IEEE Computer Society (2005)
16. Groote, J.F., Mousavi, M.R.: Modeling and Analysis of Communicating Systems. MIT Press, Cambridge (2014)
17. Guldstrand Larsen, K., Lorber, F., Nielsen, B.: 20 years of *real* real time model validation. In: Havelund, K., Peleska, J., Roscoe, B., de Vink, E. (eds.) FM 2018. LNCS, vol. 10951, pp. 22–36. Springer, Cham (2018). https://doi.org/10.1007/978-3-319-95582-7_2
18. Leavens, G., Baker, A., Ruby, C.: JML: a notation for detailed design. In: Kilov, H., Rumpe, B., Simmonds, I. (eds.) Behavioral Specifications of Businesses and Systems, pp. 175–188. Springer, Boston (1999). https://doi.org/10.1007/978-1-4615-5229-1_12
19. mCRL2–Tutorials.   https://www.mcrl2.org/web/user_manual/tutorial/tutorial.html. Accessed May 2020
20. Müller, P., Schwerhoff, M., Summers, A.J.: Viper: a verification infrastructure for permission-based reasoning. In: Pretschner, A., Peled, D., Hutzelmann, T. (eds.) Dependable Software Systems Engineering, NATO Science for Peace and Security Series - D: Information and Communication Security, vol. 50, pp. 104–125. IOS Press (2017)
21. Landelijke Tunnelstandaard (National Tunnel Standard). http://publicaties.minienm.nl/documenten/landelijke-tunnelstandaard. Accessed May 2020
22. Nyberg, M., Gurov, D., Lidström, C., Rasmusson, A., Westman, J.: Formal verification in automotive industry: enablers and obstacles. In: Margaria, T., Steffen, B. (eds.) ISoLA 2018. LNCS, vol. 11247, pp. 139–158. Springer, Cham (2018). https://doi.org/10.1007/978-3-030-03427-6_14
23. Oortwijn, W.: Deductive techniques for model-based concurrency verification. Ph.D. thesis, University of Twente, Netherlands (2019)
24. Oortwijn, W., Gurov, D., Huisman, M.: Practical abstractions for automated verification of shared-memory concurrency. In: Beyer, D., Zufferey, D. (eds.) Proceedings of the 21st International Conference Verification, Model Checking, and Abstract Interpretation, VMCAI 2020. LNCS, New Orleans, LA, USA, 16–21 January 2020, volume 11990, pp. 401–425. Springer, Cham (2020). https://doi.org/10.1007/978-3-030-39322-9_19
25. Oortwijn, W., Huisman, M.: Formal verification of an industrial safety-critical traffic tunnel control system. In: Ahrendt, W., Tapia Tarifa, S.L. (eds.) IFM 2019. LNCS, vol. 11918, pp. 418–436. Springer, Cham (2019). https://doi.org/10.1007/978-3-030-34968-4_23
26. Ostrand, T.J., Weyuker, E.J., Bell, R.M.: Where the bugs are. In: 2004 ACM SIGSOFT International Symposium on Software Testing and Analysis (ISTTA), pp. 86–96. ACM (2004)
27. The Technolution webpage. https://www.technolution.eu. Accessed May 2020
28. The Thales webpage. https://www.thalesgroup.com/en. Accessed May 2020
29. van Genuchten, M., Hatton, L.: Metrics with impact. IEEE Soft. **30**, 99–101 (2013)
30. Why3 Floating point axiomatisation. http://why3.lri.fr/stdlib/floating_point.html. Accessed June 2020

A Concept of Scenario Space Exploration with Criticality Coverage Guarantees

Extended Abstract

Hardi Hungar[(⊠)]

Institute of Transportation Systems, German Aerospace Center, Lilienthalplatz 7,
38108 Brunswick, Germany
hardi.hungar@dlr.de

Abstract. Assuring the safety of an automated driving system is difficult, because a large, heterogeneous set of traffic situations has to be handled by the system. Systematic testing of the full system at the end of the development seems necessary to be able to reach the required level of assurance. In our approach, the set of potentially relevant, concrete test cases result by parameter instantiation from finitely many more abstract, so called logical scenarios. For nearly all interesting automation systems, even virtual testing via simulation can cover only a tiny fraction of this set of concrete test cases.

Here we present an approach by which a selection of test cases can be shown to be sufficient to assert the system's safety. For that, we make reasonable assumptions about the system's inner workings, and about the way safety of a traffic situation can be captured mathematically. Based on these assumptions a criterion for test coverage is derived. This criterion can be used in a simulation procedure exploring the scenario space as a stop condition. If some additional conditions are met, the criterion is shown to imply sufficient coverage to assert safety of the system under test. We discuss the extent and limitation of the resulting guarantee.

We plan to elaborate, implement, and demonstrate this procedure in the context of research projects which develop and apply simulation tools for the verification and validation of automated driving systems.

Keywords: Safety testing · Automated driving system · Simulation · Scenario exploration

This research was partially funded by the German Federal Ministry for Economic Affairs and Energy, Grant No. 19A18017 B (SET Level 4 to 5), based on a decision by the Parliament of the Federal Republic of Germany. The responsibility for the content lies with the author.

© Springer Nature Switzerland AG 2020
T. Margaria and B. Steffen (Eds.): ISoLA 2020, LNCS 12478, pp. 293–306, 2020.
https://doi.org/10.1007/978-3-030-61467-6_19

1 Problem Statement

It is widely accepted that it is very difficult to prove that an *automated driving system* (ADS) behaves in a safe manner in its entire *operational design domain* (ODD). Even if the ODD is restricted to a comparatively simple one, e.g. highway traffic, the challenge is substantial.

The goal of a safety argument must be to prove an absence of unacceptable risk, i.e., sufficient safety. Such an argument is based on *evidence*. Currently, it is expected that the bulk of the evidence about the safe behavior will come from various forms of testing. How testing can be judged to be sufficient, and how this can be realized, is the main question of this paper. This is not to say that other forms of evidence like results from FMEA (Failure Mode and Effect Analysis), tool qualification, etc. are not important or indispensable.

It is important, however, that in our opinion, the usual approach to develop safety-critical systems according to the ISO 26262 fails here. This approach relies on a full functional system specification being available in an early design stage phase, a thorough criticality analysis identifying most or all sources risk, and a stepwise development where the output of each step is thoroughly verified. An ADS is too complex to realize such a process, at least at the time being. This puts a large burden on late testing for safety, to make up for the uncertainty about risk inherited from earlier development phases.

Main challenges in late testing are

1. All relevant traffic scenarios from the ODD have to be addressed (completeness of the test specification)
2. Testing must cover the scenario space sufficiently well to identify all critical situations (full criticality identification)
3. The test results must enable to quantify the risk coming from the operation of the ADS (risk estimation)

We are concerned with the second challenge, here: criticality identification.
We assume that the first challenge is met by

1. A specification of the scenario space to be covered in the form of *logical scenarios*
2. A mathematical definition of criticality by suitable *criticality indicators*

We do not address the third challenge, either, but merely, with our solution to challenge two, provide an essential precondition to handle that.

A *logical scenario* is a parametric formalization of a set of traffic evolutions around an ego vehicle. The ego vehicle is not restrained in its behavior. Instantiating the logical scenario with a set of parameter values results in a *concrete scenario*. Semantically, a concrete scenario is a function from ego vehicle behavior to a fully defined traffic evolution. I.e., given an ego behavior, a concrete scenario provides trajectories for all participants.

A *criticality indicator* is a function which assigns, to a given traffic situation, a numerical value which is related to the criticality of that situation, i.e., how close it is to an accident.

Since even simple logical scenarios have a large number of concrete instances, and there will likely be a few hundred logical scenarios, the space to be covered by testing is very large. And it is inconceivable to cover this space with proving ground or field tests. The bulk of testing has to be done by simulation. Ignoring the validity problem of simulation, this offers the possibility to

1. Run a very large number of tests
2. Dynamically and flexibly select test cases to optimize coverage

The test object, called *ego vehicle* (E), is, in simulation, a model of the automated vehicle, including all components of the ADS like sensors, sensor fusion, situation evaluation and decision (Highly automated driving function, HADF), actuation, and dynamics control.

We can assume to have some insight into E, but not a full view of its inner state and function. That means, in at least one main instance of a late testing approach, we face a gray-box situation.

Main Goal. The main goal is to define a procedure which explores the space defined by a logical scenario and detects all its instances in which the ego behavior results in situations exceeding a given level of criticality.

2   Conceptual Approach

2.1   The Ego Vehicle

For a completely arbitrary ego, the problem stated in the previous section will be unsolvable. If the ego might change its behavior drastically without apparent reason in the external situation, no testing without deep insight into the inner workings can be complete. We must assume certain well-behavior.

As the ego will result from a thorough development geared towards avoiding bugs, such erratic actions resulting from software glitches can be assumed to be controlled. This results from the fact that a development process following the requirements and recommendations from the ISO 26262 as much as possible will be geared towards minimizing software bugs and component failures. System failures from the remaining errors can thus be assumed to be sufficiently rare. This reasoning does not apply to the overall functionality whose adequacy cannot be similarly ascertained.

Also, E should be deterministic, in principle predictable. Its reaction to a certain situation should always be the same, provided its mission is the same and the history leads to a similar assessment of the situation. The situation includes the road layout, furniture, infrastructure (e.g. traffic lights) state, traffic participants and their actions, weather, communication with the environment or other vehicle (V2X/X2V), and state information about the ego vehicle itself. State information might be available to the HADF (velocity etc.) or not (sensor malfunction). The mission of an ADS is given by route settings and other options like driving style etc. Situation assessment might depend on some limited history, to e.g. account for traffic participants which have temporarily left the field of view of the sensors. In the definition of test cases (scenarios), this must be taken care of by including a settling phase at the beginning.

A hybrid automaton should be able to model the behavior of the ego. Such automata can capture a control following the common "sense – plan –act" paradigm. Depending on the degree of precision of the simulation, the modeling of the driving physics will be more or less complex, but never leaving the capabilities of such automata. The automaton itself is *not* assumed to be known. In the light of the first assumption, the discrete conditions will depend in a not-too-fragile way on the external state, mission and other parameters, and scenario events (e.g. component failures).

Assumptions on the Ego Vehicle. We summarize our assumptions on the ego vehicle as follows

1. The ego vehicle E is (sufficiently) free from arbitrary, erratic behavior.
2. The behavior of E is deterministic, depending only on the external situation
3. Test scenarios are constructed so that pre-history has no impact on the behavior of E in the test-relevant scenario part
4. The behavior of E can be modeled faithfully by a hybrid automaton.

2.2 Criticality Indicators

The situations arising in the operation of the ego shall be evaluated for their criticality. There is no precise, universally applicable definition of criticality. Roughly, an accident has maximal criticality (not taking the severity of its consequences into account), a situation where all participants are well separated (keep their safety distance etc.) is uncritical.

Typical mathematical formalizations of the concept of criticality are function like *time to collision* (TTC) or *time headway* (THw). Such functions capture particular aspects of potential criticality. TTC applies to a situation where two trajectories would cross if both traffic participants keep their current speed and direction. E.g., if car B has velocity v_B, and follows car A (velocity v_A), in the same lane with $v_B > v_A$, and the respective positions are p_A and p_B, then

$$TTC(B,A) = (p_A - p_B)/(v_B - v_A)$$

Time headway applies to the same situation, but does not require $v_B > v_A$. It gives the time gap between A and B.

$$THw(B, A) = (p_A - p_B)/v_B$$

Both functions indicate criticality by a low numerical value – zero means accident (the definition of the gap as the position difference is only adequate for a very abstract modelling of the physical situation). In their raw form they are not calibrated. Both go towards infinity for more and more uncritical situations.

To be able to detect critical situations reliably, we require scaled and calibrated indicator functions. What we would like to have are (piecewise) continuously differentiable functions from the set of traffic situations to the interval [0,1] calibrated as follows:

- $0 < s < h < 1$ with
  - 0 absence of criticality
  - s: significant criticality
  - h: high criticality
  - 1: maximal criticality (accident)

Significant and high criticality should refer to standard detection goals: A *high* criticality shall be detected by the exploration. Any value below *significant* criticality is an indication that a situation is in the standard range and does not warrant further examination. These values enter the completeness criterion and guide the detection activities. There are some approaches to objectify the calibration criticality indicators, in particular in the Swedish Conflict Technique (Várhelyi and Laureshyn 2018). A future elaboration of the presented exploration procedure will take these into consideration.

Criticality Indicator. A *criticality indicator* (CI) is a piecewise continuously differentiable function from all situations in a given scenario space to [0, 1], with threshold values $s < h \in (0, 1)$.

Given that the scenario space is bounded, a CI is always Lipschitz continuous.

TTC and THw can be combined into such a CI, though this is not trivial. Doing that involves taking the reciprocal values, smoothing, scaling, and a softmax of both input values.

2.3   Scenario Space

Scenario according to (Ulbrich et al. 2015) is a very general notion. It may best be defined as a description of evolutions of road traffic. One may imagine a scenario as a movie storyboard. There are a number of snapshots which capture important intermediate steps, and evolutions – continuous in nature – between those snapshots. In physical reality, the traffic participants in a scenario follow continuous trajectories over time. A snapshot may be taken at any time, resulting in one particular *situation*. A simulation will compute a discretization of the physical reality, producing a finite number of situations. Besides continuous evolutions, there are discrete events which may have an impact on the participants' behavior.

The degree of precision of a scenario may vary considerably, from very abstract, so-called functional scenarios to fully defined concrete instances, with intermediate "logical" scenarios defining sets of concrete scenarios.

Only part of this broad domain is relevant to our method. We consider:

- Results of simulation runs. In those, all traffic participants including the ego vehicle have produced fully defined shown some behavior. These are *fully-defined concrete scenarios* (FCS).
- Definitions of a simulation run. These are, semantically, functions from ego behavior to FCSs. We call them *open concrete scenarios* (OCS).
- Definitions of *sets* of simulation runs, where the behavior of the non-ego participants is parameterized. These are *logical scenarios* (LS). Given a vector of concrete parameters, a logical scenario yields an OCS. It defines a *scenario space*. In this

paper, we consider only continuous parameters like thresholds in triggers and scaling factors for movements.

Formats. All these variants of scenarios can be expressed in practice by a combination of the formats OpenDRIVE (ASAM e. V., 2020) and OpenSCENARIO (ASAM e. V., 2020), resp., extensions of them. This has been done in the PEGASUS project PEGASUS (PEGASUS Project), and is continued in SET Level 4to5 and other projects.

Maneuvers. OCS and LS make use of pre-defined maneuvers ("change lane", "turn right", "follow lane", "accelerate", "keep distance" etc.) with triggers and adequate detailed parametrization to build up situations for the ego where its fitness is to be tested. A more detailed description of scenarios and their definition is given in (Hungar 2018).

Test Scenarios. The scenario space to be explored in testing is given by a number of logical scenario. In the test setting we consider here, the ego vehicle shall be subjected in a fully determined way to all possible evolutions which might come to pass in its ODD. The behavior of all non-ego traffic participants is completely specified in the maneuvers and triggers of the scenario definition. Of course, these triggers and maneuvers may include references to the ego behavior. E.g., some maneuver starts when the distance to the ego has reached a certain threshold, or, a vehicle adjusts its velocity dynamically to arrive at a crossing at the same time as the ego. That is, the scenario definition exerts full control over all aspects except the ego behavior. Other testing approaches, not considered here, might prefer a more indirect specification of the scenarios, for instance by using complex driver models to control other vehicles. Traffic evolutions would likely emerge from the interplay of the actors. We consider such loosening of control not to be too useful for safety testing.

Scenario Semantics. We assume a fully defined semantics for these three types of scenarios. For FCS, these are essentially timed trajectories within the context of the street scenery for all traffic participants. An OCS denotes a function from ego behavior to a full behavior of all participants. And an LS has further arguments for its set of parameters.

The semantical domains for the three types of scenarios may be presented as follows, leaving out details and assuming, wlog, a certain level of abstraction.

Semantical Domains. Let TP be a finite set of traffic participants, $E \notin TP$ the ego vehicle, and let the following domains be given: $TIME = [0, max]$ for time, POS for vehicle positions (including orientation), DYN for vehicle dynamics (e.g. velocity), STATE for control states of elements of TP and E, and PAR for logical scenario parameter values. Then

$$[[FCS]] \subset TP \cup E \rightarrow TIME \rightarrow (POS \times DYN \times STATE)$$

$$[[OCS]] \subset (E \rightarrow TIME \rightarrow (POS \times DYN \times STATE)) \rightarrow$$
$$TP \rightarrow TIME \rightarrow (POS \times DYN \times STATE)$$

$$[[LS]] \subset PAR \to (E \to TIME \to (POS \times DYN \times STATE)) \to$$
$$TP \to TIME \to (POS \times DYN \times STATE)$$

Explanations on the Semantical Domains. With the usual isometries, these domains can be presented differently (shuffling of arguments, currying and de-currying). Similarly, the semantics of an OCS or LS can be viewed as a parallel composition between the ego and the TP parts. A particular important view is

$$ocs\,(e) \in TP \to TIME \to (POS \times DYN \times STATE), \qquad (0)$$

for $osc \in OCS$ and a particular ego behavior $e \in TIME \to (POS \times DYN \times STATE)$. Or, retaining the behavior of E, we might write (abusing notation)

$$ocs\,(e) \in TP \cup E \to TIME \to (POS \times DYN \times STATE),$$

for $osc \in OCS$ and a particular ego behavior $e \in TIME \to (POS \times DYN \times STATE)$.

Depending on the level of abstraction of the modeling of TP and E, the domain POS may have two dimensions (position on a plane), three (adding orientation), or more (e.g., yaw and roll angles). DYN may include velocities, acceleration and other parameters. These are the most common attributes for car modeling, and they are observable from the outside. We do not include placeholders beyond POS and DYN for more attributes which may be used in more sophisticated simulations.

Semantical Properties (OCS, TP). As with E, we assume that each TP in an OCS can be described by a hybrid automaton. Different from E, we have full access to the internal discrete state of each TP, as this is fixed by the respective state of execution of the scenario. We also know the conditions which govern the discrete state changes of the TP during the execution of a scenario. These are assumed to be boolean combinations of formula literals. A literal is a comparison ($<$, $>$, …) between terms denoting continuous numerical functions. The function from TIME to POS is continuous for each TP.

Ego and TP Behavior. In the view (0) of the OCS semantics above, the full ego behavior $e \in TIME \to (POS \times DYN \times STATE)$ enters the semantical function as an argument. In practical testing, this behavior is of course produced by the system under test. If we test by simulation, the ego behavior is generated by an executable model of the real system.

Given a logical scenario ls, concrete parameters $par \in PAR$, and $t \in TIME$, this model provides the behavior of E in the continuation of the current state reached at time t, namely ls(par)(e) ([0, t]). And similarly, the scenario description defines how the TP behave from time t onwards, by interpreting the constructs of scenario language.

(Timed) Trajectory. The set of positions assigned to a TP or E in the semantics of an FCS form a *trajectory*. If we include only the planar coordinates, this is a two-dimensional curve. Adding the time coordinate yields a *timed trajectory*.

A criticality indicator at a point in time depends only on the visible behavior. We call it the domain of *(timed) situations.*

(Timed) Situation. If we take a snapshot of the evolution of an FCS, and ignore the internal states, we get a *situation*, an element of

$$(TP \cup E) \times POS \times DYN, \text{ or, equivalently}$$

$$(TP \times POS \times DYN) \times (E \times POS \times DYN)$$

A *timed situation* adds the current time to the situation.

A situation includes all what is externally observables of the TP and E. Criticality indicators are defined on the domain of situations. Given an FCS, a CI can be viewed as a function from TIME to [0, 1].

The completeness criterion will also take the internal states of the TP into account. The reason is their importance for answering scenario coverage. If, during the exploration of an LS, a situation arises which is very close to one already evaluated, it need not be evaluated for its CI value. But to decide whether already all continuations of the new situation have been investigated, one needs to know whether also the scenario is in the same execution state, i.e., whether the discrete state history is the same.

(Timed) Constellation. A constellation extends a situation by the sequence of internal states of the TP up the reaching the situation. Constellations are elements of

$$(TP \times POS \times DYN \times STATE^*) \times (E \times POS \times DYN)$$

A *timed constellation* additionally includes the current time.

The STATE components in (timed) constellations are discrete. We partition the constellations into *clusters*, those subsets sharing a common STATE history. Within a cluster, the semantical function from parameters of an LS to the resulting (timed or not) trajectories would be continuous, if the STATE component of E was known. This results from the role of parameters in the hybrid-automata view of the TPs and the respective assumption on E. Also, a CI would be a continuous function of parameters and time. Since the internal state of E is not assumed to be observable, we must subdivide clusters into *subclusters* to arrive at continuous relations from parameters to observables.

(Timed) Cluster. Given ls $\in$ LS and the behavior e of the ego vehicle E, the set of *(timed) clusters* of ls(e) is constructed by (a) partitioning the set of *(timed) constellations* into the sets of (timed) constellations sharing the same $STATE^*$ values, and (b) projecting the classes to their (timed) situation components (i.e., dropping the $STATE^*$ component).

(Timed) Subcluster. Each (timed) cluster can be partitioned into a finite set of *(timed) subclusters* s.t. each (timed) subcluster scs is the image of a connected subset PT of PAR $\times$ TIME under the semantic function ls(e), and ls(e) is continuously differentiable on PT. *Closed (timed) subclusters* result from topologically closing the (timed) subclusters. clsr(scs) denotes the closure of a subcluster scs.

Properties of Clusters and Subclusters. The existence of the partitioning into (timed) subclusters follows from the finiteness of the discrete control states of the ego vehicle: In a region where the hybrid automata producing the behavior of TP and E stay in the same discrete state, the evolutions are continuously differentiable. The number of subclusters is related to number of discrete states of the ego vehicle. Clusters and subclusters are bounded subsets of a vector space over $\mathfrak{R}$. The closure operation adds the boundary to subclusters.

A situation may belong to several clusters, depending on the history how the situation came to pass.

2.4 Problem Statement

We can now restate the exploration problem in a more precise form. Given are

- A logical scenario ls $\in$ LS with parameter space PAR
- An ego vehicle in the form of a model or program e
- A criticality indicator c

  Then

- H = {v $\in$ ls (PAR) (e) (TIME)|c (v) $\geq$ h } is the set of *highly critical situations for* ls (e).
- S = {v $\in$ ls (PAR) (e) (TIME)| c (v) < s } is the set of *insignificantly critical situations for* ls (e).

Goal: The exploration shall compute supersets $H^+ \supseteq H$ and $S^+ \supseteq S$ s.t.

$$H^+ \cap S = \varnothing \text{ and}$$

$$S^+ \cap H = \varnothing$$

Thus, H^+ over-approximates H, but does not include situations of insignificant criticality. Similarly, S^+ over-approximates S, but does not include highly critical situations. H^+ and S^+ might overlap, their intersection is a subset of points which are significantly critical, but not highly critical (Fig. 1).

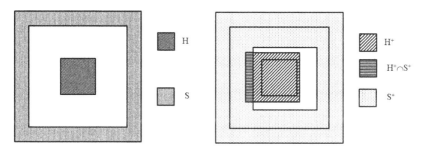

Fig. 1. Illustration of the coverage goal

Remark: Obviously, one might remove the intersection $H^+ \cap S^+$ from both sets, once they are computed. For simplicity, we do not include this step in the coverage requirement.

2.5   Simulation

The functionality of a simulation tool is to interpret a fully defined concrete scenario ls (e) (par) over time. The tool computes a discrete approximation of its semantics, which consists of a set of timed trajectories, one for each TP and E. We assume that the simulation operates with a fixed time step size. Since the maximal run time of a scenario is limited, there are a finite number of situations produced by each run. The situations occurring in such an approximation are witnesses of the semantics of the scenario.

Witness. A timed situations w = ls (par) (e) (t) generated by a simulation tool in the simulation of an instance OCS of some logical scenario ls(e), combined with the subcluster scs(w), to which this situation belongs, is called a *witness* of ls(e). If a set of witnesses W is given, then

$$W_h = \{w \in W \mid c(w) \geq h\} \text{ and } W_s = \{w \in W \mid c(w) < s\}$$

are the subsets of highly critical, resp., insignificantly critical witnesses in W.

The goal of the exploration of the parameter space of a scenario ls(e) is to find a witness for the criticality of every critical point of ls(e), and witnesses for the uncriticality of points which are not near any critical point.

2.6   Coverage Criterion

Let ls, e, and c be given as in the section "Problem Statement" above. The coverage criterion employs the Lipschitz continuity of c on every compact subset of the set of situations. In a given spatial context, let λ be the respective Lipschitz constant.

Lipschitz Neighborhood. For a situation v = ls (par) (e) (t), a λ-Lipschitz-neighborhood is a subset of the closure of its subcluster scs(ls (par) (e) (t)) s.t. the criticality indicator is λ-Lipschitz on the neighborhood. A λ-neighborhood is denoted by $\lambda - N(v)$. A λ-neighborhood containing only points of distance less than d is denoted as $\lambda - N_d(v)$.

(Vicinity) Coverage Criterion. A set of witnesses W *covers* the scenario ls(e) if

1. For each highly critical point (ls (par) (e) (t)) $\in$ H there is a witness w $\in W_h$ and some $\lambda - N(w)$ s.t..

$$(\text{ls(par) (e) (t)}) \in \lambda - N(w) \tag{1a}$$

$$\text{and} \quad c(w) - \lambda \, \text{dist}(w, (\text{ls (par) (e) (t)})) > s \tag{1b}$$

2. For each insignificantly critical point (ls (par) (e) (t)) $\in$ S there is a witness w $\in$ W$_s$ and some λ−N(w) s.t.

$$(\text{ls(par) (e) (t)}) \in \lambda - N(w) \tag{2a}$$

$$\text{and} \quad c(w) - \lambda \, dist(w, (\text{ls (par) (e) (t)})) < h \tag{2b}$$

The criterion distinguishes highly critical and insignificantly critical points by witnesses in their neighborhood. This motivates the name "Vicinity Criterion".

From the sets W$_h$ and W$_s$ and λ-neighborhoods of their elements, one can get H$^+$ and S$^+$:

1. H$^+$ can be made up from the union of some λ−N$_{(c(w)-s)}$(w) of w $\in$ W$_h$,
2. S$^+$ can be made up from the union of some λ−N$_{(h-c(w))}$(w) of w $\in$ W$_s$

Other criteria which more directly identify regions of interest may be formulated. For instance, one might be interested in a more direct, geometrical representation of an over-approximation of regions of highly critical points. E.g., one might define a concept of *container*, given by a number of defining points. The content of the container is then the convex hull of the defining points. Then, a solution to an adequately reformulated problem would consist in a number of containers whose union contains all highly critical points (and no insignificantly critical ones).

2.7   Exploration Procedure

To make use of the coverage criterion we have to define an exploration procedure which generates witness sets W$_h$ and W$_s$ satisfying the two respective conditions. We sketch a procedure which achieves this goal under the following assumption.

Assumption on Simulation Adequacy.   The criticality of the discrete-time FCS computed by the simulation is the same as continuous-time FCS of the semantics.

In practice, one may relax this assumption to permit (more realistically) a small deviation which can be accounted for by adjusting the h and s values.

Exploration Concept   The witnesses produced by the exploration procedure do not only cover the situation space as required by the criterion. They also cover PAR × TIME densely (in relevant areas). I.e., for some ls (par) (e) (t) in H or S, the respective witness will be ls (par') (e) (t') for some (par', t') with a small distance dist((par, t), (par', t')). The exploration starts with a rough sampling of PAR, and goes on to cover clusters and identify subclusters. Clusters are defined by the STATE components of the TP. Subclusters are identified by continuity breaches.

Cluster Coverage.   To cover all clusters resembles the problem of finding input values to activate paths in a program. Indeed, the scenario definition can be viewed a as program. It does not contain unbounded loops, also the maximal number of steps is bounded. Thus, one of the problems of test coverage (infinite number of paths) is avoided. On the other hand, the behavior of the ego is an uncontrollable input. But at least, bounds for the evolution of the ego vehicle are known (max acceleration etc.), and it does not change behavior patterns erratically. Thus, we expect that constraint solving and gradient-directed searches will greatly speed up the process of finding parameter values activating the trigger conditions necessary to visit all reachable clusters.

Subcluster Identification. Within a cluster, the (differentiable) continuous relation between parameters and situations is only disturbed by the influence of discrete state changes of the ego vehicle. These should be identifiable by systematically validating gradients inside the cluster, i.e., by comparing extrapolated changes in situations (using gradients computed on the neighborhood of a point) with observed changes. Drastic continuity breaches will be easy to identify, others will be discovered during the construction of a covering set of witnesses.

Criticality Coverage. Hand in hand with subcluster identification, computed situations are analyzed for their witness potential. Given some $w = ls\,(par')\,(e)\,(t')$ with $c\,(w) < s$, a neighborhood of (par', t') s.t. its image satisfies condition (2a) and (2b), using conservative approximations of Lipschitz conditions for $ls(e)$. Points of high criticalities are in the complement of the insignificantly critical ones, and witnesses for those are treated likewise. The search procedure stops when the set of witnesses satisfies (1, a&b) and (2, a&).

3   Discussion

Assuming adequacy of the simulation and a minimal relevant resolution of parameter values, the coverage problem is finite, but prohibitively large. This means, that any exploration must be incomplete, thus risking to overlook important (highly critical) situations. This work delineates an approach how this deficiency might be overcome. On the one hand, the amount of simulations must not be too large. On the other hand, nothing must be overlooked, or at least, the probability of anything being overlooked must be made very small. We think that the combination of Lipschitz-based extrapolations and systematic, semantics guided search for extrapolation boundaries (i.e. subcluster boundaries) has the potential to solve this problem.

A fine-grained resolution will only be necessary for regions of significant and high criticality, in particular at cluster or subcluster boundaries. Neighborhoods of situations with low criticality will tend to be large. Thus, we expect that relatively few witnesses will cover the vast majority of situations.

We consider it a higher challenge to ascertain that all breaches of continuity will be detected. For that, the assumption on the freedom from erratic behavior of E becomes important. If E might behave arbitrarily, each procedure not covering the full cluster will likely be incomplete. The procedure sketched in the paragraph on subcluster identification above is far from being defined precisely.

There are several ways to technically refine this assumption on the ego, which might help in getting to a concrete procedure definition. One might, for instance, require that state changes are triggered by conditions true for large subsets of the parameter space, if they are not criticality relevant. I.e., only in emergency situations, we have drastic variations in the reactions of E: Those can be found by the detailed coverage of the neighborhood of a critical situation, which is necessary anyhow. The robust conditions triggering changes in uncritical situations would be found by a more superficial parameter variation.

Still, a rigidly provable completeness might be difficult to achieve, even if the conditions on E are tightened. From the outside, the problem of reliable criticality coverage might even appear unsolvable, as it subsumes an instance of model checking of hybrid automata. But the setting of the application is rather specific. The automata producing the behavior of the TP are simple, they do not contain loops. And the actions of the TP on the one side and the ego vehicle on the other are only loosely coupled: The visible behavior on which the traffic participants interact has a high inertia. This is indirectly captured in the assumption on simulation adequacy: A discrete simulation with fixed, discrete step size would not be adequate to compute the effects of, say, a coordinated control of a platoon of cars. Thus, while there is no proof of the usefulness of the completeness criterion, there is also no simple argument for the opposite.

4 Conclusion

We have defined a coverage criterion for a scenario space sufficient to guarantee that highly critical situations and insignificantly critical ones can be reliably distinguished. And we have sketched how an exploration procedure may proceed to achieve this coverage, if a number of assumptions are satisfied[1]. A mathematically precise and practically useful definition of these assumptions will have to be based on practical experiments. From these, one would have to derive a characterization of the specific nature of the components which enables to better delineate the scope of the guarantee assertion.

We plan to go this road. We will implement variants of the exploration procedure sketched above, and try it on sample verification tasks of practical significance. Our hope is that a core method will indeed satisfy mathematically rigorous guarantee criteria. And even if this cannot be achieved, we expect to be able to find lines of argumentation for the significance of the coverage achieved to be able to strongly support a safety case by the simulation findings.

References

ASAM e. V., Von OpenDRIVE 1.6.0. https://www.asam.net/standards/detail/opendrive/abgerufen
ASAM e. V, OpenSCENARIO 1.0.0. https://www.asam.net/standards/detail/openscenario/. Accessed 13 Mar 2020

---

[1] It may be noted that the validity of the simulation results themselves is outside the scope of the guarantee. A fortiori, the assumption on simulation adequacy is even strengthening the validity requirement.

Hungar, H.: Scenario-based validation of automated driving systems. In: Margaria, T., Steffen, B. (eds.) ISoLA 2018. LNCS, vol. 11246, pp. 449–460. Springer, Cham (2018). https://doi.org/10.1007/978-3-030-03424-5_30

PEGASUS Project. (kein Datum). Abgerufen. https://www.pegasusprojekt.de/. Accessed 15 June 2020

SAE International: Surface Vehicle Recommended Practice: Taxonomy and Definitions for Terms Related to Driving Automation Systems for On_Road Motor Vehicles J3016-Jun2018 (2018)

Ulbrich, S., Menzel, T., Reschka, A., Schuldt, F., Maurer, M.: Defining and substantiating the terms scene, situation and scenario for automated driving. In: IEEE International Annual Conference on Intelligent Transportation Systems (ITSC) (2015)

Várhelyi, A., Laureshyn, A.: The SwedishTraffic Conflict Technique v. 1.0. (Lund University, Hrsg.) Von http://www.tft.lth.se/fileadmin/tft/images/Update_2018/Swedish_TCT_Manual.pdf. Accessed Apr 2018

Towards Automated Service-Oriented Verification of Embedded Control Software Modeled in Simulink

Timm Liebrenz[1]([✉]), Paula Herber[1], and Sabine Glesner[2]([✉])

[1] Embedded Systems Group, University of Münster, Münster, Germany
{timm.liebrenz,paula.herber}@uni-muenster.de
[2] Software and Embedded Systems Engineering Group, TU Berlin, Berlin, Germany
sabine.glesner@tu-berlin.de

Abstract. The verification of hybrid embedded control systems is a difficult and time intensive task. In previous work, we have presented a compositional, service-oriented verification approach for hybrid systems that are modeled in Simulink using differential dynamic logic and the interactive theorem prover KeYmaera X. In this paper, we discuss the challenges that arise during this verification process with a hybrid system from the medical domain, namely a generic infusion pump (GIP). We discuss the manual effort necessary to verify this (comparatively large) system and propose partial automations that reduce the effort and increase the practical applicability of the verification process.

Keywords: Hybrid systems · Compositional verification · Theorem proving · Model-driven development

1 Introduction

Hybrid embedded control systems, i.e., systems that combine both discrete and continuous behavior, are used in many different domains and the demands on their functionality are steadily increasing. Model-driven development languages like Matlab Simulink [1] are widely used to cope with the increasing complexity. Simulink enables modeling and simulation of hybrid systems and provides mature tool support for graphical editing, simulation, and automated code generation. It is increasingly used in a variety of industrial domains. In some of these domains, for example, in the automotive industry or in the medical domain, a failure may result in enormous cost or even endanger human lives. For such safety-critical systems, it is highly desirable to ensure their correctness with formal proofs.

The formal verification of hybrid control systems is, however, a time intensive task. The interaction between discrete and continuous components introduces an enormous complexity. In addition, a prerequisite to enable formal verification of hybrid embedded control systems is a formal model of the system under verification. The semantics of typical industrial modeling languages, like Simulink is, however, only informally defined by The Mathworks ®. There exist various

T. Margaria and B. Steffen (Eds.): ISoLA 2020, LNCS 12478, pp. 307–325, 2020.
https://doi.org/10.1007/978-3-030-61467-6_20

approaches to manually or automatically generate a formal representation of a given Simulink system for more or less restricted subsets, but the vast majority of these approaches only target a discrete subset of the Simulink language, or they do not scale for larger systems. In previous work [2,3], we have presented a compositional service-oriented verification approach to overcome these problems. The key ideas are twofold: First, we decompose a given system into services that are described by hybrid contracts and can be verified in a modular fashion. Second, we provide an automated transformation from a comparatively large subset of Simulink, including discrete and continuous modeling elements, into the formally well-defined and expressive differential dynamic logic ($d\mathcal{L}$) [4]. With that, we gain access to the powerful, interactive theorem prover for hybrid systems KeYmaera X [5]. KeYmaera X does, however, not provide these proofs fully automatically, but requires manual interactions from the user to provide proof ideas, invariants, and guide the verification process.

In this paper, we discuss the manual effort that is necessary to verify hybrid embedded control systems that are modeled in Simulink with our transformation from Simulink to $d\mathcal{L}$ and the interactive theorem prover KeYmaera X. To illustrate the verification process and the necessary manual interactions, we present a new case study from the medical domain, namely a generic infusion pump (GIP) [6]. Then, we present ideas and techniques to increase the automation. The key idea is to extract implicitly available information of the Simulink model, for example, data types and the semantics of blocks, to automatically generate invariants for the automatically generated $d\mathcal{L}$ model. The additional invariants simplify the interactive proof process and significantly decrease the necessary user interactions. Note that the automatically extracted information can, in some cases, also provide formal interface conditions that can be used as hybrid contracts and thus reduce the manual effort to define formal properties of a system or service. This further reduces the manual effort of compositional, service-oriented verification. With the presented extensions to our compositional, service-oriented verification process, the degree of automation to verify some crucial propertis of the GIP can be significantly increased.

This paper is structured as follows: In Sect. 2, we introduce Simulink and $d\mathcal{L}$. We discuss related work in Sect. 3. In Sect. 4 and Sect. 5, we briefly summarize our transformation from Simulink to $d\mathcal{L}$ [2] and our service-oriented verification approach [3]. We present our new case study and discuss the verification process in Sect. 6. In Sect. 7, we present our partial automations. We conclude in Sect. 8.

2   Preliminaries

In this section, we introduce Simulink and the differential dynamic logic $d\mathcal{L}$.

2.1   Simulink

MATLAB/Simulink [1] is a data flow oriented modeling language and integrated modeling tool. It enables the design and simulation of hybrid system. The basic building elements are blocks with input and output ports and signals

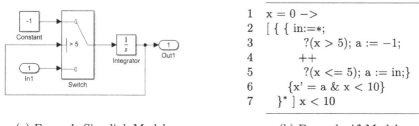

1	x = 0 ->
2	[{ { in:=*;
3	?(x > 5); a := −1;
4	++
5	?(x <= 5); a := in;}
6	{x' = a & x < 10}
7	}*] x < 10

(a) Example Simulink Model   (b) Example d$\mathcal{L}$ Model

Fig. 1. Example Models

that connect the ports of blocks. Blocks perform calculations on their input values and write the results to their outputs. Signals transfer the values of outputs to inputs. Blocks can be assigned to different groups, e.g., direct feed-through, time-discrete, time-continuous, and control flow.

Figure 1a shows a small example. The model provides the output of an *Integrator* block as output *Out1*. A *Switch* block controls the input for the integrator depending on its current value. If the value is larger than 5 a *Constant* of −1 is used as input. Otherwise, an input signal provided by the port *In1* is used. The input port *In1* and output port *Out1* connect the model to its environment.

2.2 Differential Dynamic Logic (d$\mathcal{L}$)

The d$\mathcal{L}$ [4] is a logic for specifying and verifying hybrid systems. A system is modeled in d$\mathcal{L}$ as a hybrid program. A *sequential execution* $\alpha; \beta$ describes that the hybrid program α is executed before β. A *nondeterministic choice* $\alpha ++ \beta$ means that either α or β can be executed. With a *nondeterministic repetition* α^*, α is executed an arbitrary number of times. A *discrete assignment* $x := \theta$ assigns a value θ to a variable x. A *nondeterministic assignment* $x := *$ assigns an arbitrary value to a variable x. In a *continuous evolution* $\{x'_1 = \theta_1, ..., x'_n = \theta_n \& H\}$ the variables $x_1, ..., x_n$ evolve continuously over time along their respective derivatives $\theta_1, ..., \theta_n$. This evolution is executed for an arbitrary amount of time if the conditions given by the evolution domain H hold. A test formula $?\phi$ continues the execution if ϕ holds and aborts it otherwise.

Figure 1b shows a hybrid program similar to the Simulink model in Fig. 1a. The variable x denotes the value of the Integrator, a the current gain of the Integrator, and *in* the input value. The simulation loop is modeled by a nondeterministic repetition $\{·\}^*$. The value of the input port is provided by the environment, therefore a nondeterministic value is assigned to it in every execution of the simulation loop. Depending on the value of x, the gain a is set to −1 or the current value of *in*. The variable x evolves continuously according to a derivative of a as long as its value is less than 10. The specification $[·]$ requires that under the precondition $x = 0$, after all possible executions, $x < 10$. The interactive theorem prover KeYmaera X [5] enables the deductive verification of hybrid systems modeled in d$\mathcal{L}$. It supports tactics for the partial automation of proofs.

3   Related Work

In this section, we discuss related work on the verification of Simulink models and on the verification of hybrid systems in general.

Simulink Verification. The semantics of Simulink is only informally defined in [1]. In [7], the authors define a formal Simulink semantics. However, their formalization does not provide an automated formalization of given models, but formalizes the execution semantics of Simulink. Furthermore, it is not connected to any existing formal verification tool. There also exist some approaches that enable formal verification of Simulink models using a transformation into some formal language, e.g. [8–10]. There also exists a solution for formal verification by The Mathworks, namely the Simulink Design Verifier [11], and the tool CLawZ [12] enables us to automatically prove code that is provided by code generation of a Simulink model. However, all of these approaches only consider discrete system behavior. In [13], Simulink models are transformed into sequential programs, and verified using a contract-based approach. However, while this approach supports multi-rate systems, it still supports only time-discrete systems. In [14], a toolbox for hybrid equations in Simulink is presented. However, it only extends the simulation capabilities and does not enable verification. The tool CheckMate [15] enables the modeling and verification of Simulink models using hybrid automata, and a transformation of hybrid Simulink models into a specific hybrid automata dialect (SpaceEx) is presented in [16]. This enables the use of reachability algorithms to check safety properties of the system. However, the state space increases exponentially in the number of concurrent blocks, and thus it does not scale well for larger systems. There exist approaches that use statistical model checking in to analyze the behavior of Simulink models. In [17], the authors combine their formalization of Simulink models with Petri nets to use them as input for the statistical model checker Cosmos [18]. The authors of [19] propose a transformation of Simulink blocks into a network of stochastic timed automata. These are used as input for statistical model checking with UPPAAL SMC [20]. However, statistical model checking is not able to ensure correct system behavior. Other approaches verify requirements for the C-code that can be generated from Simulink models. In [21], the BTC EmbeddedValidator is used to perform bounded model checking on C-code that is generated from Simulink models. It can be used to find program errors that violate requirements and these errors are traced back to the original Simulink models. However, due to the nature of bounded model checking it is difficult to ensure correct behavior of the system outside of the chosen bounds.

Hybrid System Verification. Hybrid systems model the interactions between discrete state changes and continuous evolutions. A widely used modeling technique for such systems is hybrid automata [22]. To cope with concurrent systems, approaches that are based on hybrid automata usually use some kind of parallel composition [23–25]. However, since the state space increases exponentially in the

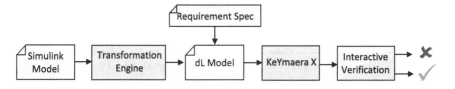

Fig. 2. Simulink to d$\mathcal{L}$ approach

number of concurrent processes of a parallel composition, these approaches suffer from the state space explosion problem. In [26] and [27], the authors present compositional analysis approaches for hybrid automata. However, no timing properties are considered. In [4], the *differential dynamic logic* (d$\mathcal{L}$) together with a compositional proof calculus is introduced, and embedded into a contract-based approach for the compositional verification of hybrid systems in [28]. We adopt the idea that system parts can be described by contracts defined in d$\mathcal{L}$ to enable compositional verification, and make heavy use of the underlying compositionality of the proof calculus implemented in the KeYmaera X theorem prover. Note that in [28], the authors assume that the system under verification has a classical controller-plant structure. In Simulink and other data flow or signal flow oriented languages, however, we have to cope with hierarchical subsystems and the resulting cascading control flow through multiple subsystems, that is, the controller might be distributed over multiple subsystems or services. Our service-oriented approach provides us with an elegant way to cope with the data flow oriented nature of Simulink models, as we do not reason about input and output states, but about the properties of the input and output trajectories.

4   Simulink to d$\mathcal{L}$ Transformation

In [2], we have presented a fully-automatic transformation of hybrid Simulink models into d$\mathcal{L}$. The overall approach is depicted in Fig. 2. Our transformation automatically generates a d$\mathcal{L}$ model from a given Simulink model, which can semi-automatically be verified using the interactive theorem prover KeYmaera X. This spares the designer the tedious task of formally defining a formal model, and gives access to the powerful verification techniques that KeYmaera X provides.

The key idea of our approach for the transformation from Simulink to d$\mathcal{L}$ is to define d$\mathcal{L}$ expressions that precisely capture the semantics of all Simulink blocks in a given model, connect them according to the signal lines, and expand control conditions such that assignments and evaluations are only performed if the control conditions are satisfied. To achieve this, we have defined transformation rules that map the semantics of individual Simulink blocks to d$\mathcal{L}$. We have introduced discrete state variables for time-discrete blocks that keep an inner state, continuous evolutions to model time-continuous blocks, and a sophisticated macro mechanism to represent stateless behavior, e.g. port connections, arithmetic calculations, and, in particular, control flow. To capture the combined

1	*Variable Declarations*
2	*Preconditions & Initializations* −>
3	[{ { *Discrete Assignments* } { *Continuous Evolutions* } } *] *Postcondition*

Listing 1.1. Structure of a transformed model

```
1  Integrator = INIT →
2  [{ smallstep:=0;
3     Out1:=Integrator;
4     In1:=∗;
5     ?(In1 < IN_MAX & In1 > IN_MIN);
6     {?(Integrator>5);
7        {Integrator'=−1, smallstep'=1 & (Integrator>5 | smallstep <= ϵ)}
8        ++
9        ?(Integrator<=5);
10        {Integrator'=In1, smallstep'=1 & (Integrator<=5 | smallstep <= ϵ)} }
11   }*] (true)
```

Fig. 3. Transformation of the Simulink Example in Fig. 1a

behavior of the whole model, we use a global simulation loop, which is modeled as a *nondeterministic repetition* in d$\mathcal{L}$. The structure of the transformed system is depicted in Listing 1.1. Since all macros are fully expanded during the transformation, our macro mechanism does not introduce additional variables in the final d$\mathcal{L}$ model, and since we keep the structure of the original model transparent to the designer using prefixing, the resulting models are compact and comprehensible. Note that our transformation from Simulink to d$\mathcal{L}$ requires that a given Simulink model uses no algebraic loop, no S-function blocks and no external scripts or libraries, and that there are some additional assumptions on the supported block set due to the current state of the implementation [2].

Illustrating Example. Figure 3 shows the d$\mathcal{L}$ model that results from a transformation of the Simulink model shown in Fig. 1a. The switch block is expanded to the conditions and evolution domains in Lines 6–10. The integrator block from the original Simulink model is represented by its initial condition in Line 1 and the continuous evolutions in Line 7 and 10. The switch condition is added to its evolution domain to ensure that the control conditions are reevaluated whenever the threshold is crossed. The input block is represented by the nondeterministic assignment in Line 4 together with the condition in Line 5, as it may provide arbitrary inputs between *IN_MIN* and *IN_MAX*. The variable *smallstep* is introduced to the continuous evolutions and evolution domains to take the approximative character of Simulink simulations into account. By restarting the simulation loop and reevaluating all conditions with a delay of at most ϵ time units, small deviations in the switching behavior are allowed. Thus, if we prove safety properties on the d$\mathcal{L}$ model, we ensure that they still hold if small delays in the switching behavior take place, for example due to numerical errors.

Discussion. With our transformation from Simulink to d$\mathcal{L}$, we define a formal semantics for Simulink in differential dynamic logic. Note that there is a semantic gap between the Simulation simulation semantics of Simulink, and the semantics of our d$\mathcal{L}$ models, where you have to trust in the correctness of our transformation. However, as the Simulink semantics is not formally defined in [29], this semantic gap would exist in any case. By choosing d$\mathcal{L}$ to formalize the Simulink semantics, we gain access to the mature and powerful verification tool KeYmaera X. At the same time, by precisely capturing the semantics of each block separately, we stay as close as possible at the original Simulink semantics, and thus keep the semantic gap small. We take the liberty to abstract from numerical errors quite roughly by allowing evaluations with an ϵ-delay, but we are confident that this is a good choice as it preserves the most important aspect of numerical errors (that a deviation may occur) while keeping the formal model manageable and comprehensible.

5   Service-Oriented Compositional Verification

In [3], we have presented a service-oriented verification approach for hybrid control systems modeled in Simulink. Our key idea to enable compositional verification is that we have introduced *services* in Simulink and *hybrid contracts* to abstractly capture the dynamic behavior of Simulink services.

In our compositional verification process, we firstly identify components that can be considered to be independent and configurable Simulink services, as we have defined them in [30], and create hybrid contracts for them. Then, secondly, we transform each service individually into a d$\mathcal{L}$ model using our transformation defined in [2]. Third, we use the interactive theorem prover KeYmaera X to verify that each service fulfills its contract. Fourth, we replace all services in a given hybrid system by their contracts, and thus enable the hierarchical abstraction from implementation details of services. Fifth and finally, we use the abstracted d$\mathcal{L}$ representation where services are replaced by their contracts to semi-automatically verify safety properties using KeYmaera X. We have demonstrated that our compositional, service-oriented verification approach significantly reduces the verification time with an industrial case study from the automotive industry. Note that the case study was too complex to be verified with the Simulink Design Verifier or KeYMaera X without the compositional approach. Our approach is sound in the sense that safety properties are preserved by our abstraction using hybrid contracts. Soundness is guaranteed by the verification of individual services and by correctly embedding services into the overall d$\mathcal{L}$ representation of a system [3]. Note that verified services can also be reused in other Simulink models without having to verify their contract again.

6   Compositional Verification of a Generic Infusion Pump

In this paper, we evaluate and discuss the manual interactions that are necessary in our service-oriented compositional verification process, and present some partial automations. In this section, we introduce a new case study, namely a Simulink model of a generic infusion pump (GIP), and the most crucial requirements this model has to satisfy. Then, we discuss contracts that can be used to compositionally verify the GIP model, and briefly summarize our key insights from the interactive verification with KeYmaera X.[1]

6.1   Generic Infusion Pump (GIP)

The generic infusion pump (GIP) project [6] is a research project to model and verify a wide range of infusion pump models. Typical components of the infusion pump are the infusion pump controller and the patient. The pump consists of sensors, input buttons, a tank, and the pump itself. The patient has a current concentration of the drug in her bloodstream and can generate input signals for the pump. An infusion pump has at least three different operation modes. First, the pump is turned off and no drug is injected. Second, a given basal rate is injected over a long time. Third, for a short time a high bolus rate is injected. The pump is controlled by the patient and can be programmed with different inputs. Note that a real pump could also be controlled by a doctor instead of the patient. The patient can set a basal and bolus rate for an infusion, change the batteries of the pump, change the tank with a full one or refill the tank. The basal rate is typically a continuous injection of a small drug amount over a longer time, while a bolus is the injection of a higher drug amount for a short time.

The safe operation of a GIP is important, since faulty behavior can harm the health of a patient. There are typically three major safety requirements: (1) No critical dosage should be administered. (2) To prevent overdose, if a critical concentration of the drug in the blood is measured, the administering of the drug should be stopped. (3) An alarm should be raised and the drug delivery should be stopped whenever the battery or the tank level is critically low.

6.2   GIP Model in Simulink

To develop a Simulink model of the GIP model in Simulink, we followed a strictly service-oriented approach. We have decomposed the system into independent components that can be independently modeled, and, in particular, also later be independently verified. A service-oriented modeling approach increases the reusability of the components, enables distributed and joint development, and generally makes the structure of the model more transparent and the overall system easier to comprehend. In total, we have defined nine services:

1. *ServiceInputGenerator* feeds input signals into the system.
2. *ServicePatientInput* prepares the input signal for the use by the controller.
3. *ServiceInputProcessing* processes the input signals.

---

[1] The Simulink model of the GIP and all d$\mathcal{L}$ models and proofs are available online: https://www.uni-muenster.de/EmbSys/research/projects/SoVer-HySiM.html.

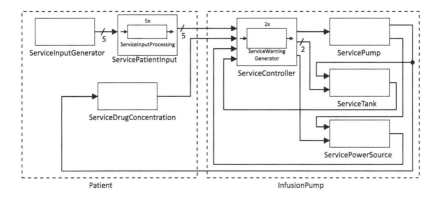

Fig. 4. Structure of the GIP model in Simulink

4. *ServiceDrugConcentration* represents the concentration of the drug in the blood of the patient and its absorption over time.
5. *ServiceController* determines the operating mode of the pump.
6. *ServiceWarningGenerator* generates a warning if battery or tank level are critically low.
7. *ServicePump* represents the pump that performs the infusion.
8. *ServiceTank* models the internal tank of the pump that contains the drug.
9. *ServicePowerSource* represents the power supply of the pump.

The resulting structure of the overall GIP model in Simulink is shown in Fig. 4. Note that *ServiceInputGenerator*, *ServicePatientInput*, and *ServiceDrugConcentration* model the behavior and dynamics of the patient, while all other services model the infusion pump itself. Furthermore, note that the service structure is hierarchical, i.e., some services contain inner services, e.g. *ServiceController*. Overall the system consists of nine different service types. The services *ServiceInputProcessing* and *ServiceWarningGenerator* are instanciated multiple times. The continuous dynamics are present by the services *ServiceDrugConcentration*, *ServiceTank* and *ServicePrwerSource*.

6.3 Hybrid Contracts

To compositionally verify the crucial safety properties of the Simulink model of the GIP described above, we have manually defined hybrid contracts for all services that are present in the design. The hybrid contracts capture the interface behavior of each service, but abstract from inner details like internal computation steps. To illustrate our approach, we discuss the Simulink models and the corresponding hybrid contracts of three services in more detail, namely *ServiceWarningGenerator*, *ServiceController*, and *ServiceDrugConcentration*.

Warning Generator. The *ServiceWarningGenerator* is used twice, to give a warning whenever the energy level is critically low and whenever the drug tank

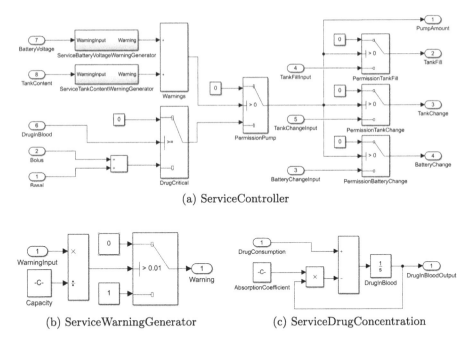

(a) ServiceController

(b) ServiceWarningGenerator   (c) ServiceDrugConcentration

Fig. 5. Simulink models of Warning Generator, Controller and Drug Concentration

is critically low. The Simulink model is depicted in Fig. 5b. The value *Capacity* denotes the capacity of the tank or the battery. The value *CapacityWarning* denotes the percentage of the capacity at which the warning should be issued, i.e. at which the outgoing signal is set to 1. The contracts that describe the desired behavior of the warning generator are shown in the upper part of Table 1. *NoWarning* ensures that no warning is produced if the current value is above the critical value. *OutputWarning* guarantees that the warning output is set to 1 if the input value drops below the critical value. *BinaryOutput* guarantees that the output signal is binary and either has a value of 0 or 1.

Controller. The *ServiceController* is the main controller of the infusion pump. Figure 5a shows the Simulink model. The controller has eight input signals and provides four output signals. *Basal* and *Bolus* represent the currently set basal rate and bolus. *DrugInBlood* represents the current concentration of the drug in the blood. *TankContent* represents the amount of drug in the tank, and *Battery-Voltage* the voltage of the power supply. *BatteryChangeInput, TankChangeInput, TankFillInput* are user inputs that signal that a battery change, a change of the drug tank or a refill of the drug tank is requested. *PumpAmount* determines the current rate of infusion, *BatteryChange, TankChange* and *TankFill* signal that the battery or tank can be changed or refilled, respectively. The controller determines the current mode of operation and checks that no critical states are reached, like a low content of the drug tank. The change of the battery or tank,

Table 1. Contracts of Warning Generator, Controller and Drug Concentration

Contract	Assumptions	Guarantees
Warning Generator		
NoWarning	WarningInput > CapacityWarning · Capacity	Warning = 0
OutputWarning	WarningInput ≤ CapacityWarning · Capacity	Warning = 1
BinaryOutput	true	Warning = 0 ∨ Warning = 1
Controller		
CriticalConcentration	DrugInBlood ≥ DrugCritical	PumpAmount = 0
ValidPumping	Basal > 0 ∧ Bolus ≥ 0 ∧ DrugInBlood < DrugCritical ∧ BatteryVoltage > VoltCritical ∧ TankContent > TankCritical	PumpAmount > 0 ∧ BatteryChange = 0 ∧ TankChange = 0 ∧ TankFill = 0
Drug Concentration		
NoInfusion	DrugConsumption = 0	DrugInBlood_Start ≥ DrugInBlood
ConcentrationIncrease	DrugConsumption > DrugInBlood * AbsorptionCoefficient	DrugInBlood_Start ≤ DrugInBlood
ConcentrationDecrease	DrugConsumption < DrugInBlood * AbsorptionCoefficient	DrugInBlood_Start ≥ DrugInBlood
ConcentrationPositive	DrugConsumption ≥ 0	DrugInBlood ≥ 0

or refilling, is only possible if there is no ongoing infusion. The contracts that
describe the desired behavior of the controller are shown in the middle part
of Table 1. *CriticalConcentration* ensures that there is no pumping in progress
when the drug concentration in the blood of the patient exceeds a critical value.
ValidPumping states that the pump is only turned on if no critical states are
reached, if there is actually a basal or bolus requested by the user, and if there
is currently no battery change, tank change or tank refill in progress.

Drug Concentration. The *ServiceDrugConcentration* models the concentration
of the drug in the bloodstream of the patient. Figure 5c shows the Simulink
model. The current drug concentration in the blood of the patient is calculated
by an integration over the sum of the newly administered drug value (*DrugCon-
sumption*) and the current concentration reduced by the absorption of the drug
by body tissue. The signal *DrugInBloodOutput* provides the current concentration of the drug in the blood. Note that we use *DrugInBlood_Start* to denote
the drug concentration at the beginning of each simulation loop, and thus can
reason about changes in the drug concentration during one cycle. The contracts
that describe the desired behavior of the drug concentration are shown in the

lower part of Table 1. *NoInfusion* ensures that the concentration of the drug in the blood of the patient decreases if the pump is inactive. *ConcentrationIncrease* and *ConcentrationDecrease* ensure the concentration of the drug increases if the currently administered drug amount is larger that the absorption and vice versa. *ConcentrationPositive* ensures that the concentration of the drug in the blood is always larger than zero if some drug is administered.

6.4   Compositional Verification

To verify that the crucial safety requirements defined above are satisfied under all circumstances by our GIP model, we have used our service-oriented compositional verification process [3]. To this end, we have written down contracts for all services, and we have also captured the system requirements in a contract of the overall system. Note that for our GIP, the system requirements defined in Sect. 6.1 directly correspond to the guarantees of the service contracts defined in Table 1. Thus, the contract of the overall system is a conjuction of these service guarantees. For compositional verification, we have used our Simulink to d$\mathcal{L}$ transformation together with KeYmaera X to interactively verify that each service satisfies its contract. Finally, we have built an abstract d$\mathcal{L}$ model of the overall system where all services are replaced by their contract to verify the system requirements. While the Simulink model uses fixed values for model parameters, e.g., the tank capacities and the possible pumping range, we have verified that the safety properties hold for arbitrary values for these parameters. To this end, we have replaced the corresponding fixed values by variables and added the assumption that describe these parameters, like that the capacities are greater than zero and that the pumping values are always in a certain range.

Challenges. The overall system behavior of the GIP model arises from the composition of the nine services described above, with no additional atomic blocks between these services. A major challenge in the interactive verification process is to specify contracts such that all behavior is captured that is necessary to prove the system requirements and at the same time to make sure that the provided abstractions are strong enough such that the verification can be completed in acceptable time. The verification of the system consists of two parts. First, the verification of the individual services, where we show that each service adheres to its contract. Second, the verification of the overall system, where we use the service contracts to prove system properties. At first, this sounds straightforward. However, both parts of the verification process are intertwined. The service contracts are needed for the system verification, but at the same time only during the overall system verification, we notice whether the chosen service contracts are expressive enough to prove the system properties. If it is not possible to find a proof for a system property, this can have different causes. For example, if the model does not fulfill the system property, this means that either the model contains an error or the system property needs to be changed. If the contracts of the services are not expressive enough to infer the system property, more details need to be added. If a contract refers to values that are not considered by other services, additional contracts are needed.

Interactive Verification. The overall structure of d$\mathcal{L}$ models that result from an automatic transformation of a Simulink model with our approach is a non-deterministic repetition as shown in Listing 1.1. This makes KeYmaera's *loop induction proof rule* the most important proof rule for transformed systems. The definition of loop invariants is generally the verification step where human insight is most needed [31]. The loop induction proof rule specifies that a nondeterministic repetition fulfills its guarantees if three conditions are fulfilled: First, the *loop invariant* must be fulfilled before the simulation loop is executed. Second, if the *loop invariant* holds before one execution of the loop, it must hold after one execution of the loop. Third, the guarantees can be provided if we can show that the *loop invariant* implies the desired guarantees. As d$\mathcal{L}$ models that result from our Simulink to d$\mathcal{L}$ transformation always have a nondeterministic repetition representing the global simulation loop as outermost statement, the guarantees that can be proven directly correspond to the invariants of this loop and vice versa. Overall, the interactive verification process has the following structure:

1. Define some guarantees for any individual service.
2. Perform the proof in KeYmaera X.
3. If the proof can not be completed, use the open proof goals to infer necessary restrictions on the input signals. Add these as assumptions and go to 2.
4. Redo step 1 to 3 for all services. It often makes sense to propagate assumption of some services as guarantees for other services or vice versa.
5. Perform the compositional system verification.
6. If the proof can not be completed, infer additional service contracts from the open proof goals.

In our experiences with previous case studies, we found that it is often helpful to start with signal bounds on input or output signals: a signal is zero, a signal is not equal to zero, a signal has negative values, a signal has positive values, the value of a signal increases over time, the value of a signal decreases over time. Signal bounds can be used both as assumptions on input values and as guarantees on output values. Further assumptions and guarantees can often be infered from the system requirements. This requires some domain expertise, since the effect of a service on the system behavior is often non-trivial. To ease the manual definition of hybrid contracts, we have presented property templates for range properties, timing properties, and dynamic properties in [3].

Manual Effort. With the interactive verification in KeYmaera X, we have proven that our GIP model satisfies the safety requirements defined in Sect. 6.1. The second column of Table 2 shows the total amount of invariants that we have defined for the interactive verification of the GIP. In total, we have defined 59 invariants. The overall interactive verification of the GIP model took 25 person hours. Note that some of the invariants were only needed to generalize the proof for arbitrary parameter values of the pump. The input generator can produce arbitrary signals that are processed by the patient input service. Output signals without any guarantees represent arbitrary signals, therefore the input generator service has no invariants.

Table 2. Interactive Verification Results

Service	Total Invariants	Automatically Generated Invariants
Warning Generator	3	2
Input Processing	2	2
Controller	14	11
Pump	8	6
Tank	8	4
Power Source	5	2
Input Generator	0	0
Patient Input	10	10
Drug in Blood	9	7
Total	59	44

7 Automated Invariant Generation

As stated above, the definition of loop invariants is generally the verification step where human insight is most needed [31]. In our d$\mathcal{L}$ models, invariants capture relations between state variables that hold before and after each execution of the global simulation loop. Such relations are generally hard to find. However, some invariants can directly be derived from data or signal types, or from the block semantics in a given Simulink model. For example, many blocks restrict the range of their output signals, or an integrator block will never decrease its value if the input is positive. Such invariants can be viewed as contracts on the very fine-granular level of individual Simulink blocks, and they are implicitly introduced into the model whenever the corresponding block type is used. In this section, we propose to exploit this implicitly available information and enrich it with knowledge about the block semantics that needs to be defined by the designer only once and then can be reused for every model that uses these blocks.

Signal Bounds. Many blocks in Simulink restrict the range of their output singals. For example, for a unit delay block, optional block parameters *upperBound* and *lowerBound* may be defined by the designer. If they are set, the output signal is always kept in the given range. To automatically generate invariants that exploit and capture this information, we perform an analysis where we collect the range of each signal at each block input or output. An example for the invariants that we automatically generate as a result is shown in Table 3.

Block Semantics. In some cases, the behavior of a block can be described as a fine-granular contract individually. For example, an integrator block will never decrease its value if the input is positive (and vice versa), or a switch block will always put one of its inputs through to the output, depending on the control condition. Although this information is already (implicitly) encoded into the d$\mathcal{L}$ model that is automatically generated from a given Simulink model with our

Table 3. Example Signal Bound Invariants

Block	Parameter	Signal bound
value $\longrightarrow$ out	value	$out \leq value \wedge\ out \geq value$
$in \longrightarrow \frac{1}{s} \longrightarrow out$	upperBound(optional), lowerBound(optional)	$out \leq upperBound \wedge\ out \geq lowerBound$
$1 \longrightarrow out$	User defined	$out \geq low_1 \wedge out \leq up_1$

Table 4. Example Block Invariants

Block	Parameter	Dependency
$in \longrightarrow \frac{1}{s} \longrightarrow out$ state		$(in > 0 \rightarrow state_{start} \leq state) \wedge$ $(in < 0 \rightarrow state_{start} \geq state) \wedge$ $(in = 0 \rightarrow state_{start} = state)$
in_1, c_{in}, in_2 $\rightarrow c_{switch} \rightarrow out$	c_{switch}	$(in_2 > c_{switch} \rightarrow switch = in_1) \wedge$ $(\neg(in_2 > c_{switch}) \rightarrow switch = in_3)$
in_1, in_2, in_n AND $\rightarrow out$	c_{logic}	$(c_{logic}(in_1, in_2, ...in_n) \rightarrow logic = 1) \wedge$ $(\neg c_{logic}(in_1, in_2, ...in_n) \rightarrow logic = 0)$
$in \longrightarrow \sqcap \longrightarrow out$	$up, low,$ out_{up}, out_{low}	$(in_1 > up \rightarrow relay = out_{up}) \wedge$ $(in_1 < low \rightarrow relay = out_{low})$
in_1, in_2 $\geq \rightarrow out$	$c_{relation}$	$c_{relation}(in_1, in_2) \rightarrow relation = 1 \wedge$ $\neg c_{relation}(in_1, in_2) \rightarrow relation = 0$

transformation from Simulink to dL, it significantly eases the verification process if the underlying relation between state variables is explicitly captured as an invariant. Examples for such invariants, which can directly be derived from the block semantics, are shown in Table 4. Note that the derivation of such invariants is not trivial and depends on the specific semantics of the block. However, once such fine-granular contracts of individual blocks are defined, they can be reused whenever the corresponding block type is used.

Delay Propagation. Many discrete-time blocks in Simulink delay a given input signal according to their sample time. If the same input signal is fed into multiple discrete blocks that also have the same sample time, the internal state of these blocks will change to the same value exactly at the same simulation steps. To capture this, we perform an analysis where we track the number of delay samples for each signal, and automatically generate invariants whenever state variables hold the same signals that are delayed for the same number of simulation steps. For example, for the Simulink model shown in Fig. 6, we automatically infer the invariant $delay1\_state0 = z\_order1\_out = delay2\_state0$. In other words, the

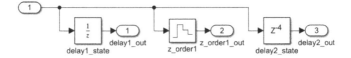

Fig. 6. Example Delay Propagation

input signal delayed by one simulation step is exactly the same if it is propagated to the internal state variable of a unit block on one path (*delay1_state0*), delayed by a zero order hold and written to its ouput on a second path (*z_order1_out*), or propagated to the first internal state variable in a delay block with four delays slots on a third path (*delay2_state0*). We detect such equivalences automatically and generate the corresponding invariants to ease the verification process.

Error Checking. There exist some general conditions that are often desirable to guarantee fault free behavior, for example the absence of errors from well-known error-classes like *overflows* and *division-by-zero*. An overflow can be produced by arithmetic operations if the result does not fit into the underlying hardware data type. To account for this, we provide user-defined constants that may define lower and upper bounds on all signals. We automatically generate invariants that check for overflows whenever arithmetic operations are performed, e.g. at sum, product, and integrator blocks. Similarly, we automatically generate invariants that prohibit a division by zero for all blocks that perform a division.

Automated Invariant Generation for the GIP. To evaluate our partial automations, we have implemented the automated invariant generation and used it to generate invariants for our GIP model. The third column of Table 2 shows the number of automatically generated and manually added invariants for each service. The automated generation of invariants significantly eased the verification process. In total, 44 out of 59 invariants were automatically generated. For 2 out of 9 services, the automated invariant generation even provided all information about the contracts that are necessary to prove the properties for the whole system. Note that 3 invariants were added for generalization.

8   Conclusion

In this paper, we have presented and discussed an approach for service-oriented compositional verification of hybrid systems that are modeled in Simulink with the interactive theorem prover KeYmaera X. By using a state-of-the-art contract-based approach with assume-guarantee reasoning, the scalability of our approach is increased compared to traditional full system verification approaches. However, the scalability is counteracted by the manual verification effort the interactive verification in KeYmaera X requires. Our main contributions in this paper are threefold: First, we provide a compact summary of our previous papers on the transformation from Simulink into differential dynamic logic (d$\mathcal{L}$) and on service-oriented compositional verification of hybrid systems with KeYmaera X. Second, we have presented and discussed a new case study for our approach from the medical domain, namely a generic infusion pump (GIP). In particular, we have discussed the manual efforts and user interactions that are necessary to verify some crucial safety properties of the GIP using our transformation from Simulink to d$\mathcal{L}$ and our service-oriented compositional verification approach with KeYmaera X. Third, and finally, we have presented an approach to increase the degree of automation in service-oriented compositional verification. To achieve this, we have exploited implicit information like signal ranges and block semantics to automatically generate invariants. We use these invariants to enrich hybrid contracts with additional assumptions and guarantees that can be automatically infered. This significantly eases the verification process and reduces the amount of hand-written contracts that are necessary to prove crucial safety properties.

In future work, we plan to evaluate the manual and automated verification effort with more and larger case studies. Furthermore, we plan to investigate best practices to write good contracts for Simulink services, which significantly reduce the verification effort on the one hand but still enable the compositional verification of a wide set of system properties on the other hand.

References

1. MathWorks: MATLAB Simulink. www.mathworks.com/products/simulink.html
2. Liebrenz, T., Herber, P., Glesner, S.: Deductive verification of hybrid control systems modeled in Simulink with KeYmaera X. In: Sun, J., Sun, M. (eds.) ICFEM 2018. LNCS, vol. 11232, pp. 89–105. Springer, Cham (2018). https://doi.org/10.1007/978-3-030-02450-5_6
3. Liebrenz, T., Herber, P., Glesner, S.: A service-oriented approach for decomposing and verifying hybrid system models. In: Arbab, F., Jongmans, S.-S. (eds.) FACS 2019. LNCS, vol. 12018, pp. 127–146. Springer, Cham (2020). https://doi.org/10.1007/978-3-030-40914-2_7
4. Platzer, A.: Differential dynamic logic for hybrid systems. J. Autom. Reason. **41**(2), 143–189 (2008)
5. Fulton, N., Mitsch, S., Quesel, J.-D., Völp, M., Platzer, A.: KeYmaera X: an axiomatic tactical theorem prover for hybrid systems. In: Felty, A.P., Middeldorp, A. (eds.) CADE 2015. LNCS (LNAI), vol. 9195, pp. 527–538. Springer, Cham (2015). https://doi.org/10.1007/978-3-319-21401-6_36
6. Generic infusion pump research project. https://rtg.cis.upenn.edu/gip/. Accessed 18 May 2020
7. Bouissou, O., Chapoutot, A.: An operational semantics for Simulink's simulation engine. ACM SIGPLAN Notices **47**(5), 129–138 (2012)
8. Herber, P., Reicherdt, R., Bittner, P.: Bit-precise formal verification of discrete-time MATLAB/Simulink models using SMT solving. In: 2013 Proceedings of the International Conference on Embedded Software (EMSOFT), pp. 1–10. IEEE (2013)
9. Araiza-Illan, D., Eder, K., Richards, A.: Formal verification of control systems' properties with theorem proving. In: 2014 UKACC International Conference on Control (CONTROL), pp. 244–249. IEEE (2014)

10. Reicherdt, R., Glesner, S.: Formal verification of discrete-time MATLAB/Simulink models using Boogie. In: Giannakopoulou, D., Salaün, G. (eds.) SEFM 2014. LNCS, vol. 8702, pp. 190–204. Springer, Cham (2014). https://doi.org/10.1007/978-3-319-10431-7_14

11. MathWorks: White Paper: Code Verification and Run-Time Error Detection Through Abstract Interpretation. Technical report (2008)

12. O'Halloran, C.: Automated verification of code automatically generated from Simulink®. Autom. Softw. Eng. **20**(2), 237–264 (2013)

13. Boström, P.: Contract-based verification of Simulink models. In: Qin, S., Qiu, Z. (eds.) ICFEM 2011. LNCS, vol. 6991, pp. 291–306. Springer, Heidelberg (2011). https://doi.org/10.1007/978-3-642-24559-6_21

14. Sanfelice, R., Copp, D., Nanez, P.: A toolbox for simulation of hybrid systems in Matlab/Simulink: hybrid equations (HyEQ) toolbox. In: 16th International Conference on Hybrid Systems: Computation and Control, pp. 101–106. ACM (2013)

15. Chutinan, A., Krogh, B.H.: Computational techniques for hybrid system verification. IEEE Trans. Autom. Control **48**(1), 64–75 (2003)

16. Minopoli, S., Frehse, G.: SL2SX translator: from Simulink to SpaceEx models. In: 19th International Conference on Hybrid Systems: Computation and Control, pp. 93–98. ACM (2016)

17. Barbot, B., Bérard, B., Duplouy, Y., Haddad, S.: Integrating Simulink Models into the Model Checker Cosmos. In: Khomenko, V., Roux, O.H. (eds.) PETRI NETS 2018. LNCS, vol. 10877, pp. 363–373. Springer, Cham (2018). https://doi.org/10.1007/978-3-319-91268-4_19

18. Ballarini, P., Barbot, B., Duflot, M., Haddad, S., Pekergin, N.: HASL: a new approach for performance evaluation and model checking from concepts to experimentation. Perform. Eval. **90**, 53–77 (2015)

19. Filipovikj, P., Mahmud, N., Marinescu, R., Seceleanu, C., Ljungkrantz, O., Lönn, H.: Simulink to UPPAAL statistical model checker: analyzing automotive industrial systems. In: Fitzgerald, J., Heitmeyer, C., Gnesi, S., Philippou, A. (eds.) FM 2016. LNCS, vol. 9995, pp. 748–756. Springer, Cham (2016). https://doi.org/10.1007/978-3-319-48989-6_46

20. David, A., Larsen, K.G., Legay, A., Mikučionis, M., Poulsen, D.B.: UPPAAL SMC tutorial. Int. J. Softw. Tools Technol. Transfer **17**(4), 397–415 (2015)

21. Berger, P., Katoen, J.-P., Ábrahám, E., Waez, M.T.B., Rambow, T.: Verifying auto-generated C code from Simulink. In: Havelund, K., Peleska, J., Roscoe, B., de Vink, E. (eds.) FM 2018. LNCS, vol. 10951, pp. 312–328. Springer, Cham (2018). https://doi.org/10.1007/978-3-319-95582-7_18

22. Alur, R., Courcoubetis, C., Henzinger, T.A., Ho, P.-H.: Hybrid automata: an algorithmic approach to the specification and verification of hybrid systems. In: Grossman, R.L., Nerode, A., Ravn, A.P., Rischel, H. (eds.) HS 1991-1992. LNCS, vol. 736, pp. 209–229. Springer, Heidelberg (1993). https://doi.org/10.1007/3-540-57318-6_30

23. Henzinger, T.A., Ho, P.H., Wong-Toi, H.: HyTech: a model checker for hybrid systems. Int. J. Softw. Tools Technol. Transfer **1**(1–2), 110–122 (1997). https://doi.org/10.1007/s100090050008

24. Frehse, G.: PHAVer: algorithmic verification of hybrid systems past HyTech. In: Morari, M., Thiele, L. (eds.) HSCC 2005. LNCS, vol. 3414, pp. 258–273. Springer, Heidelberg (2005). https://doi.org/10.1007/978-3-540-31954-2_17

25. Aştefănoaei, L., Bensalem, S., Bozga, M.: A compositional approach to the verification of hybrid systems. In: Ábrahám, E., Bonsangue, M., Johnsen, E.B. (eds.) Theory and Practice of Formal Methods. LNCS, vol. 9660, pp. 88–103. Springer, Cham (2016). https://doi.org/10.1007/978-3-319-30734-3_8
26. Cubuktepe, M., Ahmadi, M., Topcu, U., Hencey, B.: Compositional analysis of hybrid systems defined over finite alphabets. IFAC-PapersOnLine **51**(16), 115–120 (2018)
27. Benvenuti, L., Bresolin, D., Collins, P., Ferrari, A., Geretti, L., Villa, T.: Assume-guarantee verification of nonlinear hybrid systems with ARIADNE. Int. J. Robust Nonlinear Control **24**(4), 699–724 (2014)
28. Müller, A., Mitsch, S., Retschitzegger, W., Schwinger, W., Platzer, A.: Change and delay contracts for hybrid system component verification. In: Huisman, M., Rubin, J. (eds.) FASE 2017. LNCS, vol. 10202, pp. 134–151. Springer, Heidelberg (2017). https://doi.org/10.1007/978-3-662-54494-5_8
29. MathWorks: MATLAB   Simulink.   https://mathworks.com/help/simulink/referencelist.html?type=block
30. Liebrenz, T., Herber, P., Göthel, T., Glesner, S.: Towards service-oriented design of hybrid systems modeled in Simulink. In: IEEE 41st Annual Computer Software and Applications Conference (COMPSAC), 2017. vol. 2, pp. 469–474. IEEE (2017)
31. Mitsch, S., Platzer, A.: The KeYmaera X proof IDE: concepts on usability in hybrid systems theorem proving. In: 3rd Workshop on Formal Integrated Development Environment. Volume 240 of Electronic Proceedings in Theoretical Computer Science, pp. 67–81. Open Publishing Association (2017)

Verifying Safety Properties of Robotic Plans Operating in Real-World Environments via Logic-Based Environment Modeling

Tim Meywerk[1]([envelope]), Marcel Walter[1], Vladimir Herdt[2],
Jan Kleinekathöfer[1,2], Daniel Große[2,3], and Rolf Drechsler[1,2]

[1] Research Group of Computer Architecture,
University of Bremen, Bremen, Germany
{tmeywerk,m_walter,ja_kl,drechsler}@uni-bremen.de
[2] Cyber Physical Systems, DFKI GmbH, Bremen, Germany
vherdt@uni-bremen.de, daniel.grosse@jku.at
[3] Chair of Complex Systems, Johannes Kepler University Linz, Linz, Austria

Abstract. These days, robotic agents are finding their way into the personal environment of many people. With robotic vacuum cleaners commercially available already, comprehensive cognition-enabled agents assisting around the house autonomously are a highly relevant research topic. To execute these kinds of tasks in constantly changing environments, complex goal-driven control programs, so-called *plans*, are required. They incorporate perception, manipulation, and navigation capabilities among others. As with all technological innovation, consequently, safety and correctness concerns arise.

In this paper, we present a methodology for the verification of safety properties of robotic plans in household environments by a combination of environment reasoning using *Discrete Event Calculus* (DEC) and *Symbolic Execution* for effectively handling symbolic input variables (e. g. object positions). We demonstrate the applicability of our approach in an experimental evaluation by verifying safety properties of robotic plans controlling a two-armed, human-sized household robot packing and unpacking a shelf. Our experiments demonstrate our approach's capability to verify several robotic plans in a realistic, logically formalized environment.

Keywords: Cognition-Enabled Robotics · Household Robots · Formal Verification · Symbolic Execution · Discrete Event Calculus

The research reported in this paper has been supported by the German Research Foundation DFG, as part of Collaborative Research Center (Sonderforschungsbereich) 1320 *EASE – Everyday Activity Science and Engineering*, University of Bremen (http://www.ease-crc.org/). The research was conducted in sub-project P04.

T. Margaria and B. Steffen (Eds.): ISoLA 2020, LNCS 12478, pp. 326–347, 2020.
https://doi.org/10.1007/978-3-030-61467-6_21

1   Introduction

These days, robotic agents are finding their way into the personal environment of many people; for example in the form of autonomous vacuum cleaner robots. Ambitious research is conducted in the direction of fully autonomous household robots solving complex tasks like tea serving [20] or cooking [1]. In contrast to their ancestors—industrial robots that were only utilized for repetitive and physically strenuous work—these household robots operate in highly complex, constantly changing environments. To achieve their goals, more than a simple pre-programmed action sequence is required to control them. There is a need for cognitive mechanisms that allow robotic agents to interact with their environments based on the execution of general tasks. These include, but are not limited to, reasoning about spatial relations of objects and, based on that, deciding which action leads to the intended environment manipulation. Approaches based on cognitive mechanisms have proven their usefulness and, as a consequence, learning, knowledge processing, and action planning found entry into robot control programs, which are usually called (robotic) *plans*. For programming plans, many high-level *planning languages* have been developed. Some examples are RPL [5], RMPL [30], and CPL [2]. These languages combine a rich, Turing-complete semantic with the ability to natively call low-level subroutines like perception, navigation, and manipulation. The *CRAM Plan Language* (CPL) in particular is an extension of the *Common Lisp* programming language and part of the *Cognitive Robot Abstract Machine* (CRAM) toolbox [2]. CRAM provides a multitude of environment interaction and reasoning modules.

With such complex software systems and challenging tasks in real-world household environments, reliability is more important than ever. Since simulation and testing quickly reach their limits in guaranteeing this reliability, formal safety verification methods become indispensable. Recently, in [16], we have proposed a procedure based on *Symbolic Execution* [3,10] for the verification of CPL code that we called *SEECER*. As shown in that paper, reasoning about the robotic plan by itself offers only limited benefits. Instead, the plan must be related to its intended environment. In particular, interaction between the robot and the environment needs to be taken into account to produce comprehensive verification results. In [16], the relatively abstract *Wumpus World* [24] has been used as an environment model. To allow easier integration with the CPL, the environment was modeled directly in the Common Lisp programming language. However, environment models in Common Lisp have to be specifically adjusted to the plan under verification. Therefore, each plan requires its own environment model, which can be used for no other purpose than the plan verification. Yet, there are several logical formalisms specialized in the modeling of environments and actions, for example, *Situation Calculus* and its predecessors [14] and *(Discrete) Event Calculus* [11,17,19,26]. They are regularly used to model household environments and robotic actions [18,25]. These formalisms have several advantages over a model in Common Lisp, such as their well-defined semantics and a plethora of environment descriptions and reasoning procedures proposed in the literature.

In this paper, we propose a safety verification methodology of robotic plans written in a high-level planning language—we use CPL as a running example—with respect to a logically formalized environment description. Our formalism of choice is the *Discrete Event Calculus* (DEC) due to its high expressiveness and simultaneous decidability that we combine with symbolic execution. Our contribution in this paper is threefold. We first present a decision procedure for the verification of simple branching-free *action sequences* with respect to a DEC environment model. This is achieved via a reduction to a pure DEC reasoning problem. To the best of our knowledge, such a reduction has not been proposed before. Additionally, our procedure serves as an important building block for our second and major contribution, namely the verification of more complex robotic plans in combination with a DEC environment model and symbolic execution. Our third contribution is the verification of several plans (that are taken from the CRAM repository) in a detailed household environment and the modeling of this very environment in DEC. Our experiments demonstrate our approach's capability to verify several robotic plans in a realistic, logically formalized environment.

The remainder of this paper is structured as follows: Sect. 2 reviews preliminaries necessary to keep this work self-contained. Section 3 introduces our safety verification methodology. In Sect. 4, we evaluate the applicability of our approach by verifying safety properties of CPL plans controlling a two-armed, human-sized robot packing and unpacking a shelf. Section 5 concludes the paper.

2   Preliminaries

In this section, we discuss all the necessary preliminaries to keep this paper self-contained. We give an overview of the CPL in Sect. 2.1 first, and discuss our recent approach for symbolic execution of the CPL in Sect. 2.2. Afterwards, we introduce DEC in Sect. 2.3.

2.1   CRAM Plan Language

Many AI and robotics systems utilize the *Lisp* programming language to this day because libraries and frameworks written in or at least mainly supporting Lisp are available. The *Cognitive Robot Abstract Machine* (CRAM) [2] is a prominent example as it is written in *Common Lisp*, a dialect of the Lisp programming language. CRAM provides an interface for perception modules, belief states, knowledge bases, and navigation and manipulation actuators to be used in robotic systems. Additionally, it exposes the *CRAM Plan Language* (CPL) which allows writing high-level plan descriptions in Common Lisp. An abstract overview of the architecture of the CRAM stack can be seen in Fig. 1. The execution is controlled by the CPL plan, which interacts with the environment through perception, manipulation, and navigation subroutines. To reason about the next action to be taken, a belief state and knowledgebase can be consulted through a query-answer interface.

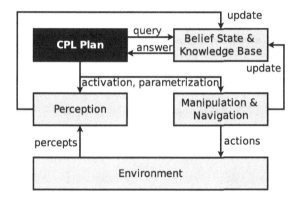

Fig. 1. Overview of the CRAM stack architecture

In CPL, plans describe desired behavior in terms of hierarchies of goals, rather than fixed sequences of actions that need to be performed. All exchange of information with parts of the CRAM stack, e. g., the perception modules or knowledge bases, as well as interaction with actuators to manipulate the environment, works via *designators* which are a common concept among reasoning and planning systems. Designators thereby often encapsulate high-level descriptions that are familiar to humans but abstract to robots like a *location* or a *motion*. Classes of designators available in CPL are for instance

- *location designators*: physical locations under constraints like reachability, visibility, etc.,
- *object designators*: real-world objects on a semantic level like what they are and what they could be used for,
- *human designators*: description of a human entity in an environment, and
- *motion and action designators*: actions that can be performed by a robot.

In CPL, an action designator contains the action type to perform (like detecting or grasping) and several parameters. It can be passed to the **perform** function, which breaks it down to sub-tasks and takes care of their execution. Both, action designators and the **perform** function, are particularly important for this work and will be utilized in Sect. 3. The following example illustrates a typical use of different designators.

Example 1. Figure 2 shows a typical snippet taken from a CPL plan that uses multiple different designators to indicate action, motion, and location. In CPL, the designators are generated using the **a** and **an** macros. The plan snippet performs a motion to turn the robot's head to look at a specified target position and places the robot's arm to the same location in parallel (indicated by the **par** function). As shown here, designators may be nested, i. e., contain other designators such as the location designators contained within an action and a motion designator respectively.

```
1 (defun place−object (?target−pose ?arm)
2   (par
3     (perform (a motion (type looking)
4         (target (a location (pose ?target−pose)))))
5     (perform (an action (type placing)
6         (arm ?arm) (target (a location (pose ?target−pose)))))))
```

Fig. 2. Designator usage in CPL code

In the following section, we review our recent approach to verify properties of CPL plans.

2.2 Symbolic Execution for the CRAM Plan Language

In [16], we utilized a technique known as *Symbolic Execution* [3,10] to verify annotated assertions on plans written in CPL. Due to the high abstraction level, the CPL plans were first translated to an Assembly-like intermediate language that we called *Intermediate Plan Verification Language* (IPVL). The CPL-to-IPVL compiler that we implemented also integrated an environment model that had to be written in Common Lisp as well. This model was then also compiled to IPVL code. Safety properties were also modeled in Common Lisp in the form of `assert` instructions. All designators included in the plan were mocked by the environment model to abstract from underlying sensor and actuator operations. To handle this IPVL code, we implemented the symbolic interpreter *SEECER* (Symbolic Execution Engine for Cognition-Enabled Robotics).

SEECER analyzes the plan path-wise while managing a set of *symbolic execution states*. A symbolic execution state is a 3-tuple (pc, ip, α). Here, pc is the *path condition*, which encapsulates all restrictions that are imposed on the execution state; ip is the *instruction pointer*, which points to the next instruction to be executed; and α is the *variable map*, which maps plan variables to their symbolic value. Non-control flow instructions (e.g. arithmetic instructions) update α by changing the target variable to its new value and increment ip by 1. Branching instructions of the form `if C goto i` with a conditional C and instruction i are evaluated as follows: the feasibility of both branches is checked using an SMT solver, i.e. the formulas $pc \wedge C$ and $pc \wedge \neg C$ are checked for satisfiability. If only one of the formulas is satisfiable, the respective branch is taken and ip is updated accordingly. If both formulas are satisfiable however, the execution state is duplicated. One copy follows the jump, i.e. the path condition pc is updated to $pc \wedge C$ and ip is set to i. The other copy appends $\neg C$ to the path condition and resumes with the next instruction. Whenever SEECER encounters an `assert(a)` instruction, the satisfiability of $pc \wedge \neg a$ is evaluated. A satisfying assignment corresponds to an error in the plan. If the symbolic execution terminates without finding such an error, the plan is proven to be safe.

Finally, we conducted a case study on the rather simplistic *Wumpus World* [24] environment that we modeled in Common Lisp to demonstrate the general feasibility of our approach.

While this paper uses some concepts from our previous work [16], we focus on more real-world scenarios in this paper. Furthermore, as an environment model, we rely on a logic formalism called *Discrete Event Calculus* (DEC) due to its high expressiveness and simultaneous decidability. Since we use DEC in this paper for modeling environments as well as verifying action sequences and plans, we give an overview on DEC in the following section.

2.3 Discrete Event Calculus

The *event calculus* [11,17,26] is an established formalism to model and reason about events and their consequences. It allows for the modeling of non-determinism, conditional effects of events, state constraints, and gradual change, among others. A domain description modeled in the event calculus follows the *commonsense law of inertia*. Intuitively, this means that the properties of the world do not change over time unless there is an explicit reason for the change. The modeler may however choose to *release* certain properties from this law. Furthermore, the event calculus allows us to state that a predicate must be false unless explicitly required to be true. This is known as *default reasoning* and can be used e. g. to limit the occurrences of events. Default reasoning is usually realized through *circumscription* and denoted as CIRC$[\phi; P]$. Here, all occurrences of predicate P in ϕ are false unless specifically required by ϕ to be true.

The event calculus has been used to model robotic sensors [27], traffic accidents [4], diabetic patients [8] and smart contracts [12].

In [19] a discrete version of the original event calculus has been introduced. This section recaps this *Discrete Event Calculus* (DEC). For simplicity, a version without gradual change axioms is presented.[1]

Overview. The DEC is based on many-sorted first-order logic with equality, supporting the sorts of *events*, *fluents*, *integers*, *timepoints* and arbitrary user-defined sorts (e. g. for domain objects). Events are occurrences in the modeling domain and can be divided into *actions*, which are deliberately executed by an agent, or *triggered events*, which happen as a result of a change in the world. In this paper, we will focus mostly on actions and will, therefore, use event and action synonymously. There exists no notion of preconditions of an action, i. e., any action may happen in any state. The effects of an action can, however, vary depending on the state of the world. Consequently, the same action could lead to the desired effect, an erroneous effect, or no effect at all depending on the surrounding environment. Fluents describe the state of some property of the world through time. At any given point in time, a fluent may be either *true* or *false*. Timepoints in the DEC as opposed to classical event calculus are bounded to the integer domain. Sorts may be *reified*, i. e. taking other sorts as arguments. Examples of this are the action *going*(*location*) or the fluent *isAt*(*object, location*).

---

[1] Gradual change allows to model properties that change over time after an initial action, e. g., an object falling and eventually hitting the ground after it has been dropped.

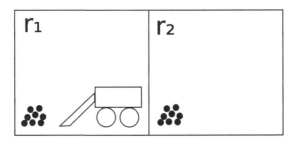

Fig. 3. Visualization of the vacuum world ($n = 2$)

DEC descriptions are built using a set of predicates to formalize the state of the world at different timepoints as well as the occurrences and effects of actions. These predicates include:

- *Happens*(a, t): Action a happens at timepoint t.
- *HoldsAt*(f, t): Fluent f is true at timepoint t.
- *ReleasedAt*(f, t): Fluent f is released from the commonsense law of inertia at timepoint t.
- *Initiates*(a, f, t): When action a happens at timepoint t, then fluent f will be true at timepoint $t + 1$.
- *Terminates*(a, f, t): When action a happens at timepoint t, then fluent f will be false at timepoint $t + 1$.
- *Releases*(a, f, t): When action a happens at timepoint t, then fluent f will be released from the commonsense law of inertia at timepoint $t + 1$.
- Arbitrary user-defined predicates.

Additionally, the predicates $\neq, \leq, <, \geq, >$ and the functions $+, -, \cdot, \div$ are defined over integers with their usual extensions. To illustrate how these predicates may be used to model robotic environments, consider the following example:

Example 2. Consider the modeling of a simple robotic environment inspired by the *vacuum world* [23]. The environment is composed of a finite number of rooms $r_1, \ldots, r_n$, which are each either dirty or clean. The rooms are arranged in a row, i.e. room r_i is left of room r_{i+1} and right of room r_{i-1}. In the initial state, a vacuum cleaner robot is positioned in one of the rooms. The robot can move through the rooms and clean the room it is currently in. A possible state of the vacuum world with $n = 2$ is visualized in Fig. 3. In this case the robot is located in room r_1 and both rooms are dirty.

Our DEC description for the vacuum world includes the sort *room*, which is a sub-sort of the integers, the actions *Left*, *Right* and *Clean* and the fluents *RobotInRoom*(*room*) and *Dirty*(*room*).

At first, we require that the *RobotInRoom* fluent is functional, i.e. the robot is in exactly one room at any given time:

$$\forall t : \exists r : \big(HoldsAt(RobotInRoom(r), t)\big)$$
$$\forall t, r_i, r_j : \big(HoldsAt(RobotInRoom(r_i), t) \wedge HoldsAt(RobotInRoom(r_j), t) \implies$$
$$r_i = r_j\big)$$

After that we describe the effects of the robot's actions. The *Left* and *Right* action will move the robot in the respective adjacent room and remove it from its current room, unless it is already in the leftmost (r_1) or rightmost (r_n) room:

$$\forall t, r : \big(HoldsAt(RobotInRoom(r), t) \wedge r \neq r_1 \implies$$
$$Initiates(Left, RobotInRoom(r-1), t) \wedge$$
$$Terminates(Left, RobotInRoom(r), t)\big)$$
$$\forall t, r : \big(HoldsAt(RobotInRoom(r), t) \wedge r \neq r_n \implies$$
$$Initiates(Right, RobotInRoom(r+1), t) \wedge$$
$$Terminates(Right, RobotInRoom(r), t)\big)$$

The *Clean* action will result in the robot's current room being clean (i.e. not dirty):

$$\forall t, r : \big(HoldsAt(RobotInRoom(r), t) \implies Terminates(Clean, Dirty(r), t)\big)$$

To ensure that these predicates have the intended logical consequences, a set of axioms is necessary. These axioms are given below.

Axioms. Following the notation from [19], all free variables are assumed to be universally quantified.

Axioms DEC1 through DEC4 deal with gradual change and are therefore omitted here. The axioms DEC5 through DEC8 enforce the commonsense law of inertia, i.e. if a fluent is not released and no action happens to change its value, then the fluent will retain its value from the last timepoint. Additionally, if no action happens to release the fluent, it will remain unreleased. If a fluent is released and no action happens to set it to either truth value, it will remain released.

AXIOM DEC5
$$\big(HoldsAt(f, t) \wedge \neg ReleasedAt(f, t+1) \wedge$$
$$\neg \exists a : \big(Happens(a, t) \wedge Terminates(a, f, t)\big)\big) \implies$$
$$HoldsAt(f, t+1)$$

AXIOM DEC6
$$\big(\neg HoldsAt(f, t) \wedge \neg ReleasedAt(f, t+1) \wedge$$
$$\neg \exists a : \big(Happens(a, t) \wedge Initiates(a, f, t)\big)\big) \implies$$
$$\neg HoldsAt(f, t+1)$$

Axiom Dec7

$$(ReleasedAt(f,t) \land$$
$$\neg \exists a : (Happens(a,t) \land (Initiates(a,f,t) \lor Terminates(a,f,t)))) \implies$$
$$ReleasedAt(f,t+1)$$

Axiom Dec8

$$(\neg ReleasedAt(f,t) \land$$
$$\neg \exists a : (Happens(a,t) \land Releases(a,f,t))) \implies$$
$$\neg ReleasedAt(f,t+1)$$

The axioms Dec9 through Dec12 ensure the correct consequences of actions. That is, if some action happens that initiates (terminates) a fluent, that fluent will be set to true (false) at the next timepoint. The fluent will also no longer be released from the commonsense law of inertia. If some action happens that releases a fluent, that fluent will be released at the next timepoint.

Axiom Dec9

$$(Happens(a,t) \land Initiates(a,f,t)) \implies HoldsAt(f,t+1)$$

Axiom Dec10

$$(Happens(a,t) \land Terminates(a,f,t)) \implies \neg HoldsAt(f,t+1)$$

Axiom Dec11

$$(Happens(a,t) \land Releases(a,f,t)) \implies ReleasedAt(f,t+1)$$

Axiom Dec12

$$(Happens(a,t) \land (Initiates(a,f,t) \lor Terminates(a,f,t))) \implies \neg Released(f,t+1)$$

Let the conjunction of axioms Dec5 to Dec12 be Ax_{DEC}.

Reasoning. The following example showcases a possible reasoning problem in the DEC.

Example 3. Consider again the DEC description from Example 2. We will now use this description to reason about the vacuum world with two rooms ($n = 2$). We require that the robot starts in the left room:

$$HoldsAt(RobotInRoom(r_1), 0)$$

We additionally specify an action that is executed by the robot:

$$Happens(Right, 0)$$

When combining this extended description with the Ax_{DEC} axioms, we can infer $HoldsAt(RobotInRoom(r_2), 1)$ as a logical consequence. Please note that this consequence is true and can be deduced even though we did not specify some aspects of the initial state, namely the dirtiness of the rooms.

The former is an example of the *deduction* reasoning task. Deduction asks whether a certain goal state follows from a (partial) initial state and a set of actions. Other notable reasoning problems are *abduction* which asks for a sequence of actions that lead from a given initial state to a given goal state, and *model finding* which asks for complete models of partially specified DEC descriptions.

Since most interesting reasoning tasks in first-order logic are generally undecidable, reasoning in the classical event calculus has to be done either manually [18,29] or automatically in highly restricted settings [28]. The DEC on the other hand allows for fully automated reasoning by restricting all domains, including the timepoints, to a finite set. We call these descriptions *bounded DEC descriptions*. One way to reason about such bounded DEC descriptions is a translation into *Boolean satisfiability* (SAT). For this purpose, universal (existential) quantifiers are replaced by a conjunction (disjunction) over all objects of the respective sort and the resulting quantifier-free formula is converted into *Conjunctive Normal Form* (CNF). This together with efficient computation of circumscription and simplification techniques was implemented in the Discrete Event Calculus Reasoner (DEC reasoner) [19]. The resulting Boolean formula can then be solved by state-of-the-art SAT solvers, yielding a set of models, which can be translated back into models for the original DEC description.

Comparison to Other Formalisms. Over the years, several formalisms for the description of actions and their effects have been proposed. Prominent examples are the action languages $\mathcal{A}$ [6], ADL [21] and PDDL [15] and their extensions. In contrast to DEC, these formalisms have a restricted expressive power which allows for efficient reasoning. In many cases, properties can be proven even for an unrestricted time period. On the other hand, this limited expressive power also limits the environments that can be modeled. For instance, non-determinism, ramification constraints, gradual change, or multiple agents can all be expressed in the DEC, but are often problematic for the aforementioned action languages. In the context of this paper, reasoning about an environment is combined with symbolic execution on a Turing-complete planning language. In this scenario, reasoning is only possible over a finite number of timepoints anyway, making the use of a restricted action language unnecessary.

A closer relative of the (discrete) event calculus is the situation calculus [13, 22]. The two formalisms are very similar in that they both reason about actions and change. Their differences are rather subtle. The major reason why we choose the DEC over the situation calculus for this work is the ability to easier model the exact time at which an action occurs, including concurrent actions. Even though this ability is not extensively used in this publication, we expect it to prove its usefulness in future works.

3   DEC-Based Verification of Robotic Plans

In this section, we propose a novel methodology for verification of robotic plans with respect to environment descriptions formalized in DEC. We give an

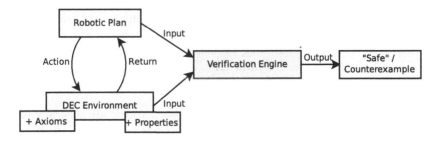

Fig. 4. Abstract view on the considered verification problem

overview of the considered topics and the structure of this part in the following Sect. 3.1. In Sect. 3.2, we first cover the verification of simple action sequences and in Sect. 3.3, we present our verification approach, which is based on symbolic execution, for complex plans written in CPL.

3.1 Overview

Robotic agents operating in complex and changing household environments can impose a safety risk on both the environment and themselves. To verify the safety of plans operating in these environments, we present an approach that combines symbolic execution and DEC reasoning. The problem that we are tackling is depicted in Fig. 4 and intuitively reads as follows: given a robotic plan and a DEC description consisting of an environment description formulated in DEC, the DEC axioms and a set of safety properties; is it possible to pick values for the free (input) variables (e. g. the position of certain objects) such that any of the safety properties do not hold? The approach that we are proposing implements the verification engine shown in Fig. 4 via a combination of symbolic execution and DEC reasoning and either returns "Safe", stating the plan's safety under all possible free variable assignments, or an execution trace and a sequence of environment states as a counterexample leading to the violation of at least one property. An important building block of our approach is a procedure for the verification of action sequences, i. e. a finite, branching-free sequence of atomic actions that are executed in order by a robotic agent. This building block is implemented by the means of a reduction to a pure DEC reasoning problem. Since action sequences are still widely used e. g. in manufacturing tasks, it is also useful as a stand-alone technique. In the overall approach for the verification of CPL plans, this procedure is used repeatedly during symbolic execution. We first introduce the verification approach for action sequences in the following section and, afterward, present our combined approach for complex plans.

3.2 Verification of Action Sequences

Verification of action sequences can be reduced to a pure DEC deduction problem, as we will show in the following. Given the DEC axiomatization Ax_{DEC}, an environment description Env, a sequence of actions $a_1, \ldots, a_k$ and a set of properties $P_1, \ldots, P_l$, we want to prove that the conjuction of DEC axioms, environment description and action occurrences entails the safety properties, i.e.

$$\text{Ax}_{\text{DEC}} \wedge Env \wedge \text{CIRC}[\bigwedge_{i=1}^{k} Happens(a_i, i-1); Happens] \models \bigwedge_{j=1}^{l} P_j.$$

Here, CIRC is the circumscription operator introduced in Sect. 2.3. In this case, it ensures that only the actions $a_1, \ldots, a_k$ are occurring.

Since most reasoners for DEC, including the DEC reasoner introduced in Sect. 2.3, do not directly support deduction, we formulate the deduction problem given above as a model finding problem instead. To this end, we perform model finding on the following conjunction

$$\text{Ax}_{\text{DEC}} \wedge Env \wedge \text{CIRC}[\bigwedge_{i=1}^{k} Happens(a_i, i-1); Happens] \wedge$$

$$\text{CIRC}[\bigwedge_{j=1}^{l} (\neg P_j \implies U); U] \wedge U,$$

where U (short for *unsafe*) is a new 0-ary predicate symbol. Since the final action occurs at timepoint $k-1$, it is sufficient to consider the timepoints 0 to k. This allows to encode the verification problem in a bounded DEC description and to solve it using the SAT-based DEC reasoner from [19]. If a model is found, it contains concrete states for all timepoints together with the failed properties. This can be helpful when debugging the action sequence. If no model is found, the action sequence is proven to be safe.

Example 4. Consider again the vacuum world with $n = 2$ from the previous examples. Consider further the following action sequence: *Left, Clean, Right, Clean*. Assume that we want to verify that this action sequence results in all rooms being cleaned. We express this by the property $P_1 = \forall r : (\neg HoldsAt(Dirty(r), 4))$. The verification is now conducted by model finding on the following conjunction:

$$\text{Ax}_{\text{DEC}} \wedge Vac_2 \wedge \text{CIRC}[Happens(Left, 0) \wedge Happens(Clean, 1) \wedge$$
$$Happens(Right, 2) \wedge Happens(Clean, 3); Happens] \wedge$$
$$\text{CIRC}[\exists r : (HoldsAt(Dirty(r), 4)) \implies U; U] \wedge U,$$

where Vac_2 is the DEC description of the vacuum world described in Example 2 with $n = 2$. When giving this conjunction to the DEC reasoner, no model will be returned, therefore proving the safety of the action sequence with respect to P_1.

3.3   Verification of Complex Robotic Plans

In the previous section, we discussed how simple action sequences can be verified with respect to a set of properties using DEC reasoning. This approach is however

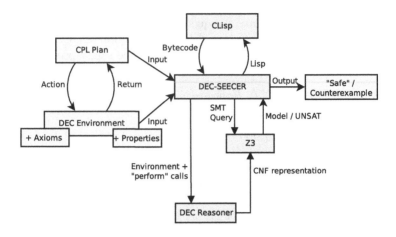

Fig. 5. DEC-centric architectural view

no longer sufficient to solve the verification task for arbitrary plans written in Turing-complete planning languages. In this section, we therefore combine this procedure with symbolic execution. We present our approach utilizing CPL as a running example. We would like to point out, however, that our approach works for any robotic planning language, as long as a suitable symbolic execution engine is available.

Figure 5 shows an overview of our architecture. The inputs to the verification problem are a CPL plan and the DEC environment description, that interacts with the plan through actions and their respective return values. The environment description is further extended with the DEC axioms and the safety properties, forming a single joint DEC description. The core of our approach is the symbolic execution engine *DEC-SEECER*, which is an extension of the CRAM symbolic execution engine SEECER, which we have previously presented in [16]. We extended SEECER by the capability to handle DEC descriptions and to reason about them in combination with the SMT constraints for the path condition that arise during symbolic execution. An important part of this extension is the interface to the DEC reasoner, which receives DEC descriptions and translates them into Boolean CNF formulas. These formulas can be combined with other SMT constraints and solved by the SMT solver *Z3*. Like in [16], a `perform` mock is used to abstract from low-level effects like motor control. In contrast to our previous work, however, this mock is not hand-written for each environment, but can instead handle arbitrary DEC descriptions, thus supporting a multitude of different environments. To facilitate this more general `perform` mock, we decided to replace the intermediate representation IPVL from [16] with a more general and mature intermediate representation, namely the *CLISP bytecode* generated by the Common Lisp implementation *CLISP* [7].

In the remainder of this section, we describe DEC-SEECER and especially the integration between symbolic execution and DEC reasoning in more detail.

Integration Between DEC and Symbolic Execution. The CLISP byte-code is executed symbolically by DEC-SEECER. The general symbolic execution operates similar to the version described in Sect. 2.2 by managing several execution states. These execution states are however represented by a 4-tuple (pc, ip, α, E), where pc, ip and α are the path condition, instruction pointer and variable map known from Sect. 2.2, respectively. The DEC description E is added to allow combined reasoning about the plan and its environment. This description is built in a very similar way to the one in Sect. 3.2. The DEC description of the initial state is given as

$$E_0 = \mathrm{Ax_{DEC}} \wedge Env \wedge \mathtt{CIRC}[\bigwedge_{j=1}^{l} (\neg P_j \implies U); U]$$

and combines the $\mathrm{Ax_{DEC}}$ axioms, environment description and safety properties.

During the symbolic execution of the plan, we differentiate between three types of instructions: the first type are non-control flow Common Lisp instructions, e. g., arithmetic instructions, or string manipulations. These update the execution state in the usual way and do not affect E. The second type are **perform** instructions, which add an action occurrence to E via a respective *Happens()* conjunct. Like in Sect. 3.2, these *Happens()* conjuncts are subject to circumscription. **perform** instructions also increase the instruction pointer ip by 1, but do not affect pc and α. The third type, branching instructions, lead to a feasibility check of both branches. To account for effects from the environment, the DEC description is incorporated in this feasibility check as follows. E is translated into CNF by the DEC reasoner. We denote this translation by $DECR(E)$. Since the SAT variables in this CNF are disjunct from the plan variables, they need to be related via a mapping. This mapping is implemented by the conjunction of equivalence constraints $m(E)$. DEC-SEECER now evaluates the satisfiability of both $C \wedge pc \wedge DECR(E) \wedge m(E)$ and $\neg C \wedge pc \wedge DECR(E) \wedge m(E)$. Here, C and pc are the branching condition and path condition, as before.

To ensure the plan's safety concerning the properties, a similar satisfiability check is used. After executing any action, the following conjunction is checked for satisfiability:

$$pc \wedge DECR(E) \wedge DECR(U) \wedge m(E)$$

Any assignment satisfying this formula corresponds to a counterexample, i. e. an instance of a safety property being violated by the plan. Consequently, if all such checks return *UNSAT* during the symbolic execution, the plan's safety is proven. The following example illustrates our approach.

Example 5. Consider once again the vacuum world from the previous examples. We extend this world by an additional action *Detect* that is supposed to detect dirt in the robot's current room. Since this action returns information to the plan, we need an additional fluent *ReturnVal()*. We also add constraints expressing that *Detect* will set *ReturnVal()* to true if the robot's current room is dirty, and to false otherwise. We denote this extended environment description by *Vac'*.

```
1 (perform (an action (type left)))
2 (let ((dirty (perform (an action (type detect))))))
3   (if dirty
4     (perform (an action (type clean)))))
5 (perform (an action (type right)))
6 (let ((dirty (perform (an action (type detect))))))
7   (if dirty
8     (perform (an action (type clean)))))
```

Fig. 6. CPL plan for the vacuum world

Assume we want to verify the safety of the CPL plan shown in Fig. 6. This plan is more complex than the action sequence presented in Example 4 because it considers the state of the environment in Line 3 and 3 before executing certain actions. Namely, the robot only cleans a room if it detects dirt in that room. Again, we would like to verify the plan's safety using the property P_1 from Example 4. Additionally, we would like to prove that the robot will never attempt to clean an already cleaned room. This is expressed by the safety property

$$P_2 = \forall t, r : \big(\neg HoldsAt(Dirty(r), t) \wedge$$
$$HoldsAt(RobotInRoom(r), t) \implies \neg Happens(Clean, t)\big).$$

The initial symbolic execution state can now be written as the 4-tuple $(true, 0, \emptyset, E_0)$ with

$$E_0 = \text{Ax}_{\text{DEC}} \wedge Vac'_2 \wedge \text{CIRC}[\exists r : \big(HoldsAt(Dirty(r), t_{max})\big) \implies U \wedge$$
$$\exists t, r : \big(\neg HoldsAt(Dirty(r), t) \wedge HoldsAt(RobotInRoom(r), t) \wedge$$
$$Happens(Clean, t)\big) \implies U; U].$$

Figure 7 shows parts of the execution tree imposed by the symbolic execution. Each node in the tree represents an execution state composed of the path condition, the instruction pointer (denoted by the respective line number in Fig. 6), variable mapping, and DEC description. Since each instruction except for the conditional branch performs an action, the DEC descriptions and assignments are updated as follows:

$$E_1 = E_0 \wedge \text{CIRC}[Happens(Left, 0); Happens]$$
$$E_2 = E_0 \wedge \text{CIRC}[Happens(Left, 0) \wedge Happens(Detect, 1); Happens]$$
$$\alpha_2 = \{\texttt{dirty} \mapsto DECR(HoldsAt(ReturnVal()), 2)\}$$

After every action being performed, the plans' safety is checked via an SMT solver call. For example, after the *Clean* action (which is performed in the node on the bottom left), the following conjunction is checked for satisfiability:

$$\alpha_2(\text{dirty}) \wedge DECR(E_2) \wedge DECR(U) =$$
$$DECR(HoldsAt(ReturnVal()), 2) \wedge DECR(E_2) \wedge DECR(U)$$

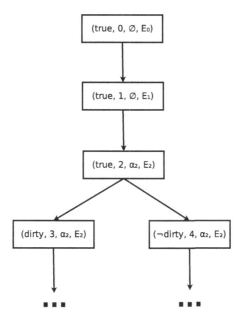

Fig. 7. Execution tree of the symbolic execution

This formula is unsatisfiable. In fact, every such formula during the symbolic execution of this plan is unsatisfiable, thus proving safety of said plan.

Since verification of Turing-complete programs is undecidable in general, there are cases in which our approach will not terminate or terminate with an inconclusive result. In particular, this is caused by non-terminating CRAM plans or complex arithmetic conditions in the plan. These results are exclusively due to the symbolic execution part of our approach, since DEC-based environment descriptions can always be grounded to pure Boolean SAT problems. Because of the undecidability of program verification, termination could only be guaranteed by severely restricting the robotic plans under verification.

In the following section, we show that our approach can nonetheless handle many practically relevant robotic plans. Here, we evaluate our approach on a real-world scenario.

4   Experimental Evaluation

We implemented DEC-SEECER using the DEC reasoner version 1.0, the SMT solver Z3 version 4.8.4, and CLISP version 2.49.93+ as back-end. To evaluate our approach, we used several variations of the *Shopping Demo* plan taken from the official CRAM repository [2]. The Shopping Demo plan involves a two-armed human-sized robot operating in a supermarket environment consisting of a shelf and a table. The robot is supposed to move several objects between the two locations. The shelf is wider than the robot's reach, making it necessary for

```
 1 (when (>= (y ?object−position ) 0.8)
 2          (setf ?grasping−arm :left )
 3          (perform (an action
 4                   (type going)
 5                   (target (a location
 6                           (pose ?grasp−pose−left ))))))
 7 (when (< (y ?object−position ) −0.8)
 8          (setf ?grasping−arm :right )
 9          (perform (an action
10                   (type going)
11                   (target (a location
12                           (pose ?grasp−pose−right ))))))
13 (perform (an action
14                   (type picking−up)
15                   (arm ?grasping−arm )
16                   (object ?newobject )))
```

Fig. 8. Excerpt of the Shopping Demo plan

the robot to determine a suitable position in front of the shelf for grasping certain objects. However, positions directly in front of the shelf cannot be used for detection, because parts of the shelf may obstruct the robot's view. It is, therefore, necessary that the robot first obtains an overview from a suitable position. We modeled these restrictions in an environment description in DEC.

To evaluate our approach, we used several variations of the existing Shopping Demo plan in combination with the DEC description. In the following Sect. 4.1, we discuss all plans in detail. In Sect. 4.2, we present our DEC environment and the safety properties. Finally, in Sect. 4.3, we show our experimental results and discuss them.

4.1 Robotic Plans

For the experimental evaluation, a total of six plans have been evaluated. They are listed below.

Shopping Demo. The original Shopping Demo plan attempts to move a set of predefined objects from the shelf to the table. The robot moves to a predefined position from where it has an overview of the whole shelf and tries to detect all objects. Afterward, it repeats the following operations for each object. First, the robot moves to a central position in front of the shelf. If the object is already in reach, it is then grasped with the closest gripper. Otherwise, the robot needs to move to a different position to its left or right. Once the object is grasped, it is transported to the table and placed onto the tabletop. Over the course of the execution, certain positions on the table are filling up. To avoid collisions, the robot computes a new free position after setting an object and uses that position for the next object.

Figure 8 shows an excerpt of the Shopping Demo. The plan compares an object's position with predefined boundaries (Line 1 and Line 7). Depending on that position, the robot either moves to the left (Lines 2–6), to the right (Lines 9–12), or stays in its current position. Afterwards, the robot attempts to grasp the object (Lines 13–16).

Modified Shopping Demo 1. This plan is a modified version of the Shopping Demo. A small error was deliberately inserted to test our approach's bug-finding capabilities. By replacing the >= in Line 1 of Fig. 8 with a <=, the robot chooses the wrong grasping position for some objects. We expect this change to result in an error for some initial environment states.

Modified Shopping Demo 2. This plan is another erroneous modification of the original Shopping Demo, too. Here, the plan does not move the robot to the designated detection pose at the start of the plan but instead attempts to detect all objects from the robot's initial position. We expect this to result in some objects not being detected, which would mean that some objects remain on the shelf not fulfilling the plan's goal.

Shelf Filling. The *Shelf Filling* plan has the reverse goal of the Shopping Demo. A set of objects is located anywhere in the environment and the robot's goal is to pick up these objects and put them onto the shelf. This plan simulates the automatic refilling of supermarket shelves by a robotic agent. Here, each object has an associated row, onto which it has to be placed on the shelf. The plan achieves this by grabbing the objects one by one and placing them in an unoccupied spot in their respective shelf. To this end, it needs to maintain a belief state of objects that have already been placed onto the shelf. This procedure is repeated until there are no more objects left. In some cases, however, it is necessary to omit certain objects, because some positions on the shelf are initially occupied. Placing these objects is tried again at the end of the plan. This plan is deliberately more complex with a higher amount of branching logic compared to the Shopping Demo plan.

Modified Shelf Filling 1. We again constructed erroneous versions of the original plan. In this version, whenever an object is omitted, it is simply removed from the list of objects and not moved to the end. We expect this error to result in objects being left in the environment and, therefore, in the wrong position after the plan's termination.

Modified Shelf Filling 2. This modified version of the Shelf Filling plan does not take certain occupied positions on the shelf into account, resulting in possible collisions of objects.

All plans presented in this section are evaluated in the DEC environment description, which we explain next.

4.2   Environment Description and Safety Properties

All plans presented in the previous section operate in the same environment consisting of a shelf and a table. We modeled this environment in the DEC. The shelf consists of three rows (top, middle, bottom) and four sections in each row (far left, left, right, far right). Objects may be located in any of the sections in any row, resulting in a total of twelve positions on the shelf per object. There are three positions for the robot in front of the shelf and a fourth one a little further away. These positions are suitable for reaching parts of the shelf or detecting objects on the shelf, respectively. The table is also partitioned into several sections. This allows us to model the limited space available. The table can again be reached from a dedicated position in front of it. Our model uses sorts for the movable objects in the world, the positions, and other aspects like the robot's arms or different heights. We use several fluents modeling the position of objects and the robot, grasps, detection status, and others. The whole environment model consists of 56 logical sentences.

To ensure the plan's safety, a set of safety properties was also formalized in DEC. These safety properties ensure that (1) the robot never reaches an internal error state, (2) all actions produce their desired effects[2], and (3) no two objects are ever placed in the same position. This last property detects possible collisions that, in the real world, would result in the robot damaging its environment. Additionally, we added properties that require (1) that at the end of the Shopping Demo, all objects are placed on the table, and (2) that at the end of the Shelf Filling plan all objects are placed onto their associated shelf rows.

4.3   Experimental Results

We ran our proposed verification approach on all plans presented in Sect. 4.1. All Shopping Demo plans had two objects in their initial state. The objects' positions were not restricted which means that the plan was verified for any possible initial placement of objects. The initial state for the Shelf Filling plans includes three objects. Their positions, both on the table and on the shelf, were again left fully symbolic. In all scenarios, the robot's initial position, arm positioning and torso height was left symbolic to account for all possible starting states. All experiments have been conducted on a Linux machine with an Intel Xeon CPU with 3.5 GHz clock rate.

Table 1 summarizes our experimental results. Here, each row represents a run of one plan. We report (from left to right) the plan's name, the number

---

[2] Note that this does not necessarily hold by design of the environment model. E. g. a grasping action will not result in the desired result if the robot is too far away from the object or the gripper is already occupied.

Table 1. Verification results

Plan's name	#LOC	Verdict	#Paths	Time (s)	Time gen. (s)
Shopping Demo	338	Safe	16	2144	1967
Modified Shopping Demo 1	338	Unsafe	2	343	300
Modified Shopping Demo 2	327	Unsafe	1	176	152
Shelf Filling	914	Safe	123	31370	30708
Modified Shelf Filling 1	823	Unsafe	10	2823	2767
Modified Shelf Filling 2	911	Unsafe	11	3326	3262

of lines of the respective CLISP bytecode (#LOC), the verification verdict, the number of paths in the symbolic execution tree (#Paths), the total runtime, and the time spent on generating SAT instances by the DEC reasoner. All times are reported in seconds.

As can be seen, our approach always returned the expected verification result. All errors in the modified plans were found and both unmodified plans were proven to be safe with respect to the specified safety properties. Moreover, the three versions of the Shopping Demo were verified with only a few paths and in less than 40 min. This is due to the fact that only the branching logic in the plan itself affected the number of symbolic execution paths. Any conditional construct in the environment itself was instead translated into a conditional CNF representation and solved by the SMT solver. The Shelf Filling plans, which were designed to involve a lot more branching, led to more symbolic execution paths and thus to a significantly higher runtime. Even the unmodified Shelf Filling plan was however verified in under 9 hours. Verifying the modified versions of both plans took a fraction of the runtime of their unmodified counterparts. This is because DEC-SEECER terminates after the first property violation has been found. The right-most column reports the runtime that was spent on the generation of the SAT instance by the DEC reasoner. As one can see, this procedure was responsible for the majority of the overall runtime (86–98%). The solving process was a lot faster in comparison. This indicates that the generation procedure of the DEC reasoner is inefficient compared to the solving capabilities of modern state-of-the-art engines. In fact, a number of more efficient grounding procedures have been developed since then (c. f. [9] for an overview). Furthermore, the DEC reasoner does not generate CNF instances iteratively.

In summary, our experiments show DEC-SEECER's capability to verify the safety of robotic plans such as the Shopping Demo. Even a more complex plan, namely the Shelf Filling plan, was verified correctly and within an adequate time. To further improve our approach's runtime, a dedicated reasoner for DEC could be developed with state-of-the-art grounding techniques and support for the incremental unrolling of environments.

5   Conclusion

The verification of safety properties of robotic plans is an indispensable prerequisite for using autonomous robotic agents in everyday scenarios. Although this task is of paramount importance, it is also extremely difficult, since one is dealing with Turing-complete high-level plans operating in constantly changing environments.

In this paper, we presented a methodology that addresses this problem. We were able to verify plans operating in household environments by combining Discrete Event Calculus and symbolic execution. This integration allows for the formal verification of general robotic plans in arbitrary environments modeled in DEC. We exemplary showed, by means of experimental evaluation, that we can verify safety properties of several plans controlling a two-armed human-sized household robot packing and unpacking a shelf.

While we could demonstrate the general applicability of our proposed approach by the means of an experimental evaluation, it also indicated that there is room for performance improvements. In future work, we, therefore, want to rebuild the current DEC reasoner from scratch incorporating state-of-the-art grounding techniques and an incremental approach.

References

1. Beetz, M., et al.: Robotic roommates making pancakes. In: IEEE-RAS International Conference on Humanoid Robots (2011)
2. Beetz, M., Mösenlechner, L., Tenorth, M.: CRAM-a cognitive robot abstract machine for everyday manipulation in human environments. In: Intelligent Robots and Systems, pp. 1012–1017. IEEE (2010)
3. Cadar, C., Sen, K.: Symbolic execution for software testing: three decades later. Commun. ACM **56**(2), 82–90 (2013)
4. Chisalita, I., Shahmehri, N., Lambrix, P.: Traffic accidents modeling and analysis using temporal reasoning. Conf. Intell. Transp. Syst. (ITSC) **7**, 378–383 (2004)
5. Drabble, B.: EXCALIBUR: a program for planning and reasoning with processes. Artif. Intell. **62**(1), 1–40 (1993)
6. Gelfond, M., Lifschitz, V.: Representing action and change by logic programs. J. Logic Program. **17**(2), 301–321 (1993)
7. Haible, B., Stoll, M., Steingold, S.: Implementation notes for GNU CLISP (2010)
8. Kafali, Ö., Romero, A.E., Stathis, K.: Agent-oriented activity recognition in the event calculus: an application for diabetic patients. Comput. Intell. **33**(4), 899–925 (2017)
9. Kaufmann, B., Leone, N., Perri, S., Schaub, T.: Grounding and solving in answer set programming. AI Mag. **37**(3), 25–32 (2016)
10. King, J.C.: Symbolic execution and program testing. Commun. ACM **19**(7), 385–394 (1976)
11. Kowalski, R., Sergot, M.: A logic-based calculus of events. New Gener. Comput. **4**, 67–95 (1986)
12. de Kruijff, J., Weigand, H.: Formalising commitments using the event calculus. In: VMBO (2020)

13. McCarthy, J.: Situations, actions, and causal laws. Technical report (1963)
14. McCarthy, J., Hayes, P.J.: Some philosophical problems from the standpoint of artificial intelligence. In: Meltzer, B., Michie, D. (eds.) Machine Intelligence, vol. 4, pp. 463–502. Edinburgh University Press (1969)
15. McDermott, D., et al.: PDDL–the planning domain definition language (1998)
16. Meywerk, T., Walter, M., Herdt, V., Große, D., Drechsler, R.: Towards formal verification of plans for cognition-enabled autonomous robotic agents. In: Euromicro Conference on Digital System Design (DSD), pp. 129–136 (2019)
17. Miller, R., Shanahan, M.: Some alternative formulations of the event calculus. In: Kakas, A.C., Sadri, F. (eds.) Computational Logic: Logic Programming and Beyond. LNCS (LNAI), vol. 2408, pp. 452–490. Springer, Heidelberg (2002). https://doi.org/10.1007/3-540-45632-5_17
18. Morgenstern, L.: Mid-sized axiomatizations of commonsense problems: a case study in egg cracking. Studia Logica **67**, 333–384 (2001)
19. Mueller, E.T.: Event calculus reasoning through satisfiability. J. Logic Comput. **14**(5), 703–730 (2004)
20. Okada, K., Kojima, M., Tokutsu, S., Mori, Y., Maki, T., Inaba, M.: Task guided attention control and visual verification in tea serving by the daily assistive humanoid hrp2jsk. In: 2008 IEEE/RSJ International Conference on Intelligent Robots and Systems (IROS), pp. 1551–1557 (2008)
21. Pednault, E.P.D.: ADL: exploring the middle ground between strips and the situation calculus. In: Proceedings of the First International Conference on Principles of Knowledge Representation and Reasoning, pp. 324–332 (1989)
22. Reiter, R.: The frame problem in the situation calculus: a simple solution (sometimes) and a completeness result for goal regression. In: Artificial and Mathematical Theory of Computation, pp. 359–380 (1991)
23. Russell, S., Norvig, P.: Artificial Intelligence: A Modern Approach. 3rd edn. (2009)
24. Russell, S.J., Norvig, P.: Artificial Intelligence: A Modern Approach. Pearson Education Limited, Malaysia (2016)
25. Schiffer, S., Ferrein, A., Lakemeyer, G.: Reasoning with qualitative positional information for domestic domains in the situation calculus. J. Intell. Robot. Syst. **66**, 273–300 (2012)
26. Shanahan, M.: A circumscriptive calculus of events. Artif. Intell. **77**, 249–284 (1995)
27. Shanahan, M.: Robotics and the common sense informatic situation. Eur. Conf. Artif. Intell. (ECAI) **12**, 684–688 (1996)
28. Shanahan, M.: An abductive event calculus planner. J. Logic Programm. **44**(1), 207–240 (2000)
29. Shanahan, M.: An attempt to formalise a non-trivial benchmark problem in common sense reasoning. Artif. Intell. **153**(1), 141–165 (2004)
30. Williams, B.C., Ingham, M.D., Chung, S.H., Elliott, P.H.: Model-based programming of intelligent embedded systems and robotic space explorers. Proc. IEEE **91**(1), 212–237 (2003)

Formally Proving Compositionality in Industrial Systems with Informal Specifications

Mattias Nyberg[✉], Jonas Westman, and Dilian Gurov

Royal Institute of Technology (KTH), Stockholm, Sweden
{matny,jowestm,dilian}@kth.se
https://www.kth.se/itm/rigorous-systems-engineering

Abstract. Based upon first-order logic, the paper presents a methodology and a deductive system for proving compositionality. Typical specifications found in industry are not expressed in any formal notation; rather most often in natural language. Therefore, the methodology does not assume specifications to be formal logical sentences. Instead, the methodology takes as input, properties of specifications and in particular, refinement relations. To cover general industrial heterogeneous systems, the semantics chosen is behavior based, originating in previous work on contract-based design for cyber-physical systems. In contrast to the previous work, implementation of specifications is non-monotonic with respect to composition. That is, even though a specification is implemented by one component, a composition with a second component may not implement the same specification. This kind of non-monotonicity is fundamentally important to support architectural specifications and so-called freedom-of-interference used in design of safety critical systems.

1 Introduction

To enable verification of large scale systems, the need for *compositional verification* is well known [5,13,14]. The survey paper [14], one of the most cited ones in the area of compositional verification, describes the principle of *compositional verification* of software programs as presented below, but here by using the notation and terminology of the present paper.

Consider $\mathbf{c}$ to be a component being a composition of a set of components $\mathbf{c}_1, \ldots \mathbf{c}_n$. According to [14], to ensure by *compositional verification* that $\mathbf{c}$ implements a specification $\mathbf{S}$ amounts to the following steps:

a) Find specifications $\mathbf{S}_1, \ldots \mathbf{S}_n$ for $\mathbf{c}_1, \ldots \mathbf{c}_n$ such that steps (b) and (c) below can be executed.
b) Prove that any component c implements $\mathbf{S}$ whenever c is composed of any components c_i implementing specifications $\mathbf{S}_i$, $i = 1, \ldots n$. This is called the *compositionality proof problem* and involves the specifications $\mathbf{S}_1, \ldots \mathbf{S}_n$ and $\mathbf{S}$ only.
c) Verify that each $\mathbf{c}_i$, $i = 1, \ldots n$, implements specification $\mathbf{S}_i$.

T. Margaria and B. Steffen (Eds.): ISoLA 2020, LNCS 12478, pp. 348–365, 2020.
https://doi.org/10.1007/978-3-030-61467-6_22

In [14], all the specifications $\mathbf{S}$ and $\mathbf{S}_i$, $i = 1, \ldots n$, are assumed to be expressed using *logical sentences only*. It is also assumed that specifications are composed using a composition operator op^S such that, given that each component $\mathbf{c}_i$ implements $\mathbf{S}_i$, the composition of components implements $op^S(\mathbf{S}_1, \ldots, \mathbf{S}_n)$. Then, the compositionality proof problem reduces to showing that $op^S(\mathbf{S}_1, \ldots, \mathbf{S}_n)$ logically entails $\mathbf{S}$.

The problem we are solving in the present paper is the *compositionality proof problem*, but with the following generalizations and modifications in relation to [14].

- We consider the general domain of heterogeneous systems. That is, a component may be a software program, as in [14], but we allow also mechanical and electrical components.
- Specifications are industrial engineering objects, and as such we do not presume these to be expressed in any logical language. The motivation is that a typical specification found in industry is not expressed in any formal notation; instead it is most often informally expressed in natural language [11].

Exactly like [14], we deal with the compositionality proof problem, i.e. the problem of proving that the composition of a given set of specifications $\mathbf{S}_1, \ldots \mathbf{S}_n$ "implies" another given specification $\mathbf{S}$. However, *due to that we do not assume specifications to be expressed as logical sentences*, in contrast to [14], we can not rely on a solution based on proving that the composition $op^S(\mathbf{S}_1, \ldots, \mathbf{S}_n)$ *logically entails* $\mathbf{S}$. Instead, we represent specifications formally as constant symbols, and rather than formalizing the content of the specifications, we formalize refinement relations between specifications and certain properties of the specifications. These formalizations are then used to prove compositionality.

Our aim is industrial software-intensive heterogeneous systems, meaning the solution needs to support both discrete and continuous systems. We have therefore chosen a *behavior based semantics* of components and specifications originating in previous work developed to support "contract-based design for cyberphysical systems" [1,2,15–17].

The previous frameworks for contracts-based design [1,2,15,16] also give some support for proving compositionality in the form of their definition of "parallel composition" as a condition on the involved specifications. However, their condition is based upon the assumption that *implementation is monotonic with respect to component composition*. In contrast to these previous works, the present paper does *not* make this assumption; instead we support the case when *implementation is non-monotonic with respect to composition* [17]. That is, even though a component $\mathbf{c}_1$ implements a specification $\mathbf{S}$, it should *not* hold generally that the composition of $\mathbf{c}_1$ with another component $\mathbf{c}_2$ also implements $\mathbf{S}$.

A support for this kind of non-monotonicity is important since architectural specifications typically state that components shall not read and not write any other signals than those included in a defined interface. This is inherently a "nonmonotonic property" since, for example, consider a component $\mathbf{c}_1$ that does not write to a signal x, but another component $\mathbf{c}_2$ does. Component $\mathbf{c}_1$ clearly implements the specification "Signal x shall not be written to." but when composed with component c_2, this specification is no longer implemented. Thus, implementation is non-monotonic with respect to composition. The property that certain components shall not read or write certain variables is also fundamental when designing safety critical systems and in those cases referred to as *freedom of interference* [9]. In conclusion, any framework for proving compositionality, and that is capable of including also architectural specifications, needs to support the case when implementation is non-monotonic with respect to composition. The proposed solution generally supports the non-monotonic case, but it also gives specific support to, and can explicitly utilize, the case when implementation is indeed monotonic with respect to component composition, which is still a common case for normal functional specifications.

With all these observations in mind, we propose as a first contribution of the paper, a *formal framework* that enables formal reasoning about relationships between components and specifications, and most importantly, it does not require specifications to be formally expressed. The framework is based upon first-order predicate logic and consists of a *formal language*, presented in Sect. 2, a *formal semantics*, presented in Sect. 3, and a number of *derived formal properties*, presented in Sect. 4. Based upon the proposed formal framework, Sect. 5 presents the second contribution of the paper, a *methodology and a deductive system for proving compositionality*. Proofs of propositions and theorem in the paper have been left out but can be found in the report [12].

2   Syntax

In the framework of first-order predicate logic [8], this section presents the grammars defining the syntactic categories used in the class of languages considered. This forms a formal syntax for the contracts theory in [17] and is part of the proposed formal framework, i.e. the first contribution of the paper. We consider languages parameterized by two disjoint sets of symbols $\mathbb{C}$ and $\mathbb{S}$. A *component term* is formed by the grammar

$$c ::= \mathbf{c} \mid c \times c \mid q$$

where $\mathbf{c} \in \mathbb{C}$ and $\mathbb{C}$ is a set of component constant symbols, $\times$ is a component composition function symbol, and q ranges over component variables.

A *specification term* is formed by the grammar

$$S ::= \mathbf{S} \mid S \sqcap S \mid (S, S) \mid S \| S \mid V$$

where $\mathbf{S} \in \mathbb{S}$ and $\mathbb{S}$ is a set of specification constants; $\sqcap$, $(\cdot, \cdot)$, and $\|$ are specification composition function symbols; and V ranges over specification variables. A specification term of the kind $S_1 \sqcap S_2$ will be referred to as *conjunction* of specifications. A specification term of the kind (S_1, S_2) will be referred to as *assume-guarantee contract*, or for short, *contract*. The first specification term in (S_1, S_2) is called *assumption* and the second *guarantee*. A specification term of the kind $S_1 \| S_2$ will be referred to as *parallel composition* of specifications.

As an extension to the contracts theory in [17], we introduce two new types of specification constants, namely ©, called the *compatibility specification*, and $\top_{\|}$, called the *top specification*. As will be explained in detail in Sect. 3 and 4, the compatibility specification © is used to enforce composed components to be compatible with each other, and the top specification $\top_{\|}$ is used to allow contracts to be a most general form of specification. Both © and $\top_{\|}$ are included among the specification constants $\mathbb{S}$.

We introduce three predicate symbols; the only ones considered in the paper. First, *implementation* written $c : S$, which reads c implements S. Second, *refinement* written $S_1 \sqsubseteq S_2$, which reads S_1 refines S_2. Third, Assertional(S), which is a new concept and an extension of the contracts theory in [17]. As will be explained in detail in Sect. 3 and 4, the purpose of Assertional(S) is to give explicit support for cases when implementation is monotonic with respect to component composition, since in general, the proposed framework otherwise assumes non-monotonicity.

As usual in predicate logic [8], *formulas* are recursively built by combining the three kind of predicates with the first-order logical symbols $\forall$, $\exists$, $\neg$, $\wedge$, $\vee$, $\rightarrow$, and $=$. Furthermore, a *sentence* is a formula without free variables.

In summary, we have introduced a class of formal languages in which each language, denoted $\mathcal{L}_{\mathbb{C},\mathbb{S}}$, has the *signature*, i.e. non-logical symbols:

– the function symbols $\times$, $\sqcap$, $\|$, and $(\cdot, \cdot)$
– the predicate symbols $:$, $\sqsubseteq$, and Assertional$(\cdot)$
– component constant symbols instantiated by a set $\mathbb{C}$
– specification constant symbols instantiated by a set $\mathbb{S}$, which includes the two specification constant symbols © and $\top_{\|}$.

As seen each language is completely specified by the disjoint sets $\mathbb{C}$ and $\mathbb{S}$.

3   Semantics

In order to formally reason about compositionality, and as part of the proposed formal framework, the present section introduces semantics for the syntactic categories given in the previous section.

In a given engineering context, component terms and specification terms represent real-world components and specifications respectively. When reasoning about whether real-world components implement real-world specifications, we are not so interested in the components and specifications themselves. Instead, of relevance are only the *behaviors* of components and behaviors that specifications specify. Therefore, given an engineering context, we define a *semantics* based upon *behavior of a real-world component* and *behavior set of real-world specification*. Formally, the engineering context is represented by a *model* $\mathcal{M}$. Since our interest is only the behaviors, the model $\mathcal{M}$ "bypasses" the real-world objects and provides a mapping directly from terms to behaviors and behavior sets, and from predicate symbols to relations between behaviors and behavior sets.

The first subsection below defines *behavior* formally, by reusing concepts from previous work in [1, 2, 16] and [17]. The next subsections then use this definition of behavior to define the semantics of terms and predicates. Many more detailed explanations and motivations follow later in Sect. 4.

3.1   Behavior and Behavior Set

Let *the universal set of variables* $\Xi = \{x_1, \ldots, x_{N_v}\}$, $N_v \geq 1$, denote the set of variables considered. These variables represent measurable or immeasurable quantities of interest in the context studied. As such, a variable is typically a function of time representing the fact that its value changes over a time window. Next, in accordance with [16], let a *run* be a vector, with the elements being variables in Ξ. For example, a run can be a *trace* [3, 4, 18] or an *execution* [10].

Let Ω denote the considered set of possible runs over the variables Ξ. Note that for the same set of variables Ξ, infinitely many different sets Ω can be chosen by varying the domain of each variable and the time window over which runs are defined. Now, a *behavior* B is a, possibly empty, set of runs, i.e. B $\subseteq \Omega$. A *behavior set* $\mathcal{Q}$ is a, possibly empty, set of behaviors, i.e. $\mathcal{Q} \subseteq \mathcal{P}(\Omega)$, where $\mathcal{P}$ denotes *power set*.

3.2   The Model Class *Behavior Semantics*

In general and according to standard predicate logic [8], a model $\mathcal{M}$ for a language $\mathcal{L}$ is a pair of an *interpretation* for the language $\mathcal{L}$ and a *domain of discourse* $\mathcal{D}$.

For a given arbitrary set Ω, we will here consider a class of models $\mathbb{M}_{\Omega,\mathbb{C},\mathbb{S}}$ for the language $\mathcal{L}_{\mathbb{C},\mathbb{S}}$. The class is defined by the following two constraints applying to each model in $\mathbb{M}_{\Omega,\mathbb{C},\mathbb{S}}$:

- The domain of discourse is $\mathcal{D}_\Omega = \mathcal{P}(\Omega) \cup \mathcal{P}(\mathcal{P}(\Omega))$, i.e. $\mathcal{D}_\Omega$ is the union of the set of all possible behaviors and the set of all possible behavior sets.
- The interpretation conforms to a set of constraints (1), (2), and (3), presented in the next section.

Let *behavior semantics* refer to the class $\mathbb{M}_{\mathbb{C},\mathbb{S}}$ that we define to be the union of all model classes $\mathbb{M}_{\Omega,\mathbb{C},\mathbb{S}}$ for all possible sets Ω.

3.3   Constraints on the Interpretation

We will below introduce constraints applying to the interpretation of each model $\mathcal{M} \in \mathbb{M}_{\Omega,\mathbb{C},\mathbb{S}}$. As stated above, each such model $\mathcal{M}$ has a domain of discourse generated by the set Ω. Furthermore, since $\mathcal{M}$ is a model for some language $\mathcal{L}_{\mathbb{C},\mathbb{S}}$, the interpretation is a mapping from each of the symbols in $\mathcal{L}_{\mathbb{C},\mathbb{S}}$, as presented in Sect. 2, to $\mathcal{D}_\Omega$.

The interpretation of component constant symbols is a mapping from component constant symbols to behaviors. The interpretation of the function symbol *component composition* $\times$ is a function from $(\mathcal{P}(\Omega))^2$ to $\mathcal{P}(\Omega)$. That is,

$$q^{\mathcal{M}} \qquad \in \mathcal{P}(\Omega) \tag{1a}$$

$$\mathsf{B}_1 \times^{\mathcal{M}} \mathsf{B}_2 = \mathsf{B}_1 \cap \mathsf{B}_2. \tag{1b}$$

The interpretation of the component composition symbol reveals that it is associative, commutative, and idempotent, i.e. $(c_1 \times c_2) \times c_3 = c_1 \times (c_2 \times c_3)$, $c_1 \times c_2 = c_2 \times c_1$ and $c \times c = c$ respectively.

The interpretation of specification constant symbols is a mapping from specification constant symbols to behavior sets. The interpretation of the function symbols *specification conjunction*, *specification parallel composition*, and *contract* are functions from $(\mathcal{P}(\mathcal{P}(\Omega)))^2$ to $\mathcal{P}(\mathcal{P}(\Omega))$. The interpretation of specification parallel composition is defined using a *double intersection of sets*, i.e. $\mathcal{Q}_1 \cap\!\!\!\cap \mathcal{Q}_2 = \{\mathsf{B}_1 \cap \mathsf{B}_2 | \, \mathsf{B}_1 \in \mathcal{Q}_1, \mathsf{B}_2 \in \mathcal{Q}_2\}$.

$$p^{\mathcal{M}} \qquad \in \mathcal{P}(\mathcal{P}(\Omega)) \tag{2a}$$

$$\top_{\|}^{\mathcal{M}} \qquad = \{\Omega\} \tag{2b}$$

$$\copyright^{\mathcal{M}} \qquad = \{\mathsf{B} \in \mathcal{P}(\Omega) | \, \mathsf{B} \neq \emptyset\} \tag{2c}$$

$$\mathcal{Q}_1 \sqcap^{\mathcal{M}} \mathcal{Q}_2 = \mathcal{Q}_1 \cap \mathcal{Q}_2 \tag{2d}$$

$$\mathcal{Q}_1 \|^{\mathcal{M}} \mathcal{Q}_2 = \mathcal{Q}_1 \cap\!\!\!\cap \mathcal{Q}_2 \tag{2e}$$

$$(\mathcal{A}, \mathcal{G})^{\mathcal{M}} = \{\mathsf{B} \in \mathcal{P}(\Omega) | \, \forall \mathsf{B}' \in \mathcal{A}. \, \mathsf{B} \cap \mathsf{B}' \in \mathcal{G}\} \tag{2f}$$

We can note that both the interpretations of the conjunction and parallel composition symbols are associative, commutative, and idempotent. However, the interpretation of contract has none of these properties.

As common in predicate logic, we extend the interpretation to non-constant terms, e.g. $(c_1 \times c_2)^{\mathcal{M}} = c_1^{\mathcal{M}} \times^{\mathcal{M}} c_2^{\mathcal{M}}$ and $(\mathcal{A}, \mathcal{G})^{\mathcal{M}} = (\mathcal{A}^{\mathcal{M}}, \mathcal{G}^{\mathcal{M}})^{\mathcal{M}}$.

Next, we consider the interpretation of the three predicate symbols. In predicate logic, interpretation of each predicate is usually defined by a relation over $\mathcal{D}^n$ where n is the arity of the predicate. Using this principle, the interpretation of the three predicate symbols is as follows:

$$:^{\mathcal{M}} \qquad = \{(\mathsf{B}, \mathcal{Q}) \in \mathcal{P}(\Omega) \times \mathcal{P}(\mathcal{P}(\Omega)) | \, \mathsf{B} \in \mathcal{Q}\} \tag{3a}$$

$$\sqsubseteq^{\mathcal{M}} \qquad = \{(\mathcal{Q}_1, \mathcal{Q}_2) \in \mathcal{P}(\mathcal{P}(\Omega)) \times \mathcal{P}(\mathcal{P}(\Omega)) | \, \mathcal{Q}_1 \subseteq \mathcal{Q}_2\} \tag{3b}$$

$$\text{Assertional}^{\mathcal{M}} = \{\mathcal{Q} \in \mathcal{P}(\mathcal{P}(\Omega)) | \, \mathcal{Q} \text{ is downward closed}\} \tag{3c}$$

where *downward closed* refers to the general set property that for each $\mathsf{B} \in \mathcal{Q}$, it holds that each subset $\mathsf{B}' \subseteq \mathsf{B}$ is also in $\mathcal{Q}$, i.e. $\mathsf{B}' \in \mathcal{Q}$.

3.4 Evaluation

As standard in predicate logic, given a model $\mathcal{M}$ for a language $\mathcal{L}_{\mathbb{C},\mathbb{S}}$, evaluation of a *sentence* ϕ in $\mathcal{L}_{\mathbb{C},\mathbb{S}}$, is done by first using the interpretation of the constants to find the corresponding concrete elements in $\mathcal{D}_\Omega$, i.e. behaviors and behavior sets. If ϕ is a single predicate, by iteratively using the interpretation of the function symbols, we compute one element, or a pair of elements, depending on the arity of the actual predicate symbol. The element(s) are then checked in the relation obtained from the interpretation of the predicate symbol. If and only if the element(s) are in the relation, we say that $\mathcal{M}$ *satisfies* ϕ, or ϕ is *true* in $\mathcal{M}$, and write $\mathcal{M} \models \phi$. If ϕ is a formula built with several predicates combined by logical symbols, it is evaluated by using the standard usage of the logical symbols, e.g. $\mathcal{M} \models \phi_1 \vee \phi_2$ if and only if $\mathcal{M} \models \phi_1$ or $\mathcal{M} \models \phi_2$.

A set of formulas $\Psi = \{\psi_1, \ldots \psi_N\}$ *semantically entails* a formula ϕ, denoted $\Psi \models \phi$, if it holds that any model $\mathcal{M}$ that satisfies each formula $\psi_i \in \Psi$ also satisfies the formula ϕ.

3.5   Theory

According to standard first order logic, we use the concept of *theory* [6] in order to obtain a syntactical characterization of the model class considered. Let $T_{\mathbb{C},\mathbb{S}}$ be the *theory* of model class $\mathbb{M}_{\mathbb{C},\mathbb{S}}$. That is, $T_{\mathbb{C},\mathbb{S}}$ is the set of all first-order sentences such that each sentence is satisfied by every model in $\mathbb{M}_{\mathbb{C},\mathbb{S}}$. The following proposition explains how general semantical-entailment properties can be proven by refering to the theory $T_{\mathbb{C},\mathbb{S}}$, and is the basis for all other propositions and theorem in the paper.

Proposition 1. *Let* $\phi_i(t_1, ..., t_m)$, $i = 1..n$, *and* $\varphi(t_1, ..., t_m)$ *represent sentences in* $\mathcal{L}_{\mathbb{C},\mathbb{S}}$. *If for each model* $\mathcal{M} \in \mathbb{M}_{\mathbb{C},\mathbb{S}}$, *such that* $\mathcal{M} \models \phi_i(t_1, ..., t_m)$, *it holds also* $\mathcal{M} \models \varphi(t_1, ..., t_m)$, *then* $T_{\mathbb{C},\mathbb{S}}, \phi_1(t_1, ..., t_m), \ldots, \phi_n(t_1, ..., t_m) \models \varphi(t_1, ..., t_m)$. $\square$

4   Explanations and Connection to Real-World Engineering

This section presents more detailed explanations of and motivations for the behavior semantics presented in Sect. 3. We also present a number of propositions stating important properties of the proposed formal framework, i.e. the first contribution of the paper. In the sequel, most results and discussions will be presented *without* reference to a specific language $\mathcal{L}_{\mathbb{C},\mathbb{S}}$. Still, it means that each result is valid only for a given implicit language $\mathcal{L}_{\mathbb{C},\mathbb{S}}$, but since that language is arbitrary in the class considered, the results and discussions will be valid for all such languages.

We consider *real-world components* and *real-world specifications* to be engineering artifacts existing in an engineering context. In the following three subsections, with the ambition to strive for clarity, we carefully distinguish between component *terms*, *real-world* components that are represented by component terms, and *behavior* of real-world components represented by the interpretation of the terms. Similarly we carefully distinguish between specification terms, real-world specifications, and behavior sets. However, in the rest of paper, when the context is sufficiently precise, we will often refer to just *component* or *specification*.

4.1   Components and Component Compositions

We are considering an engineering context represented by a model $\mathcal{M}$. The component constant symbol $\mathbf{c}$ represents a real-world component in that context. The interpretation $\mathbf{c}^{\mathcal{M}}$ is the behavior of this real-world component. As seen, the real-world component is not explicit in our formalism, although we could have introduced a second interpretation containing a mapping from the symbols $\mathbb{C}$ to real-world components. However, since all our reasoning is about *behavior* components, such a second interpretation would not bring any extra usefulness.

The real-world component, represented by the symbol $\mathbf{c}$, has the behavior $\mathbf{c}^{\mathcal{M}}$. In accordance with Sect. 3.1, this behavior captures, through the runs it includes, the dynamic and static constraints imposed by the real-world component on the variables in Ξ, independent of constraints imposed by other real-world components.

Example 1. Consider an electrical amplifier that takes an input signal u and creates an output signal y, with amplification factor 2. The relationship between the input u and output y can be described by the equation $y = 2u$. Let $\Xi = \{u, y\}$, where u and y are real variables. For simplicity, we consider only one point in time, i.e. each run is a vector of values, not a vector of functions of time. The behavior of the amplifier is then the infinite set of all vectors (u, y) that are solutions to $y = 2u$. That is $\mathsf{B} = \{(0,0), (0.1, 0.2), (1, 2), (2, 4), (15, 30), \dots\}$.   □

Example 2. Let $\Xi = \{x, y\}$, where x and y are Boolean variables. For simplicity, we consider only one point in time. Examples of behaviors are $\mathsf{B}_1 = \{(0,0)\}$, $\mathsf{B}_2 = \{(0,1)\}$, $\mathsf{B}_3 = \{(0,0), (0,1)\}$, $\mathsf{B}_4 = \{(0,0), (1,1)\}$, and $\mathsf{B}_5 = \emptyset$.   □

Example 3. Let $\Xi = \{x, y\}$, where u and y are real variables. Examples of runs are $\omega_1 = (x(t), y(t)) = (t, e^t)$ and $\omega_2 = (t, 2e^t)$ defined on a time window $[0, 10]$. These two runs can be combined to form four different behaviors $\mathsf{B}_1 = \{\}$, $\mathsf{B}_2 = \{(t, e^t)\}$, $\mathsf{B}_3 = \{(t, 2e^t)\}$, and $\mathsf{B}_4 = \{(t, e^t), (t, 2e^t)\}$.   □

Conceptually, composing two real world components means combining the constraints imposed individually by the components. Thus the behavior $(\mathbf{c}_1 \times \mathbf{c}_2)^{\mathcal{M}}$ captures the combined dynamic and static constraints imposed by both real world components. That is, the first real world component allows the runs $\mathbf{c}_1^{\mathcal{M}}$ and the second allows the runs $\mathbf{c}_2^{\mathcal{M}}$. Together, the two real world components allow only runs that are in both $\mathbf{c}_1^{\mathcal{M}}$ and $\mathbf{c}_2^{\mathcal{M}}$. Thus, the behavior of the composed real world component is the intersection $(\mathbf{c}_1 \times \mathbf{c}_2)^{\mathcal{M}} = \mathbf{c}_1^{\mathcal{M}} \cap \mathbf{c}_2^{\mathcal{M}}$.

In the paper, we will mostly write expressions involving general component terms. A term c may therefore be either a constant symbol or a composition of constant symbols. If it is a composition, it represents a corresponding composition of real-world components. Even though the term c is a composition, representing a real-world composition, we will refer to it as a real-world component. That is, we always consider a composition of real-world components to be a new real-world component even though there may be no explicit component constant symbol representing this composed real-world component.

4.2   Specification

Real-world specifications are usually defined in some requirements management system. A specification constant symbol $\mathbf{S}$ represents such a real-world specification. A real-world specification expresses, formally or informally, an *intended property* in terms of the variables Ξ. Typical examples are functional requirements or interface requirements. Note that, regardless of if a real-world specification is expressed formally or informally in natural language, we presume that the specified intended property is *unambiguous*, in line with standards on requirements engineering e.g. [9].

The intended property is in our framework characterized by $\mathbf{S}^{\mathcal{M}}$, which is the set of behaviors consistent with the intended unambiguous property. For example, if a real world specification represented by $\mathbf{S}$ is expressed as "The signal x shall be larger than zero.", then the behavior set $\mathbf{S}^{\mathcal{M}}$ consists of all behaviors in which all runs have the value of the variable x larger than 0 at all time points.

Example 4. Let $\Xi = \{x, y, z\}$ where each variable is Boolean, and consider only one point in time. Consider a real-world specification represented by $\mathbf{S}_1$ and expressed as "The variable x shall be 0, y shall be constrained to either 0 or 1, and z shall not be constrained at all.". Consider also real-world specification represented by $\mathbf{S}_2$ and expressed as "Either x shall be 0 and z not be constrained, or z shall be 0 and x not be constrained. In both cases, y shall be 1.". This corresponds to the behavior sets

$$\mathbf{S}_1^{\mathcal{M}} = \{\{(0,0,0), (0,0,1)\}, \{(0,1,0), (0,1,1)\}\} \tag{4a}$$

$$\mathbf{S}_2^{\mathcal{M}} = \{\{(0,1,0), (0,1,1)\}, \{(0,1,0), (1,1,0)\}\} \tag{4b}$$

$\square$

As seen in the example, the framework allows specifications that specify properties, both of the kind that variables shall take certain values, but also of the kind stating that some variables shall *not* be constrained. The latter is a typical property enforced by architecture specifications and requirements of freedom of interference, and as further discussed in the following sections, closely related to implementation being non-monotic with respect to composition.

4.3   Implementation

As stated above, a real world component, represented by a term c, has a behavior $c^{\mathcal{M}}$ that is the set of all runs that are possible with the constraints imposed by the component. A real world specification, represented by a symbol S, expresses an intended property, and the behavior set $S^{\mathcal{M}}$ is the set of all behaviors consistent with this intended property. Based upon these notions, a real-world component, represented by c, *implements* a real-world specification, represented by S, if the behavior $c^{\mathcal{M}}$ is in the set $S^{\mathcal{M}}$. We express this as $\mathcal{M} \models c\colon S$.

Example 5. Consider again the real-world specifications represented by $\mathbf{S}_1$ and $\mathbf{S}_2$ from Example 4. Consider also three real-world components represented by $\mathbf{c}_3$, $\mathbf{c}_4$, and $\mathbf{c}_5$, having behaviors $\mathbf{c}_3^{\mathcal{M}} = \{(0,0,0),(0,0,1)\}$, $\mathbf{c}_4^{\mathcal{M}} = \{(0,1,0),(0,1,1)\}$, and $\mathbf{c}_5^{\mathcal{M}} = \{(0,1,0),(1,1,0)\}$ respectively. Notably, it holds that $\mathcal{M} \models \mathbf{c}_3 : \mathbf{S}_1$ and $\mathcal{M} \models \mathbf{c}_4 : \mathbf{S}_1$, but since $\mathbf{c}_3^{\mathcal{M}} \cap \mathbf{c}_4^{\mathcal{M}} = \emptyset \notin \mathbf{S}_1^{\mathcal{M}}$, it does *not* hold that $\mathcal{M} \models \mathbf{c}_3 \times \mathbf{c}_4 : \mathbf{S}_1$. Furthermore, it holds that $\mathcal{M} \models \mathbf{c}_4 : \mathbf{S}_2$ and $\mathcal{M} \models \mathbf{c}_5 : \mathbf{S}_2$, but since $\mathbf{c}_4^{\mathcal{M}} \cap \mathbf{c}_5^{\mathcal{M}} = \{(0,1,0)\} \notin \mathbf{S}_2^{\mathcal{M}}$, it does *not* hold that $\mathcal{M} \models \mathbf{c}_4 \times \mathbf{c}_5 : \mathbf{S}_2$. □

Example 5 highlights the fact that even though two real-world components individually satisfy the same real-world specification, their composition does in general *not*. That is, *implementing a specification is non-monotonic with respect to composition.*

4.4 Refinement

From now on, we will stop being so careful in the dinstinction between terms and real-world objects.

In general, *refinement* is the single most important property used to prove compositionality, as will be further highlighed in Sect. 5.1. Refinement means, in words, that if any component c implements specification S_1, and S_1 *refines* S_2, then c will implement also S_2. The following proposition confirms that the interpretation constraints (2) and (3) match this notion of refinement.

Proposition 2 (Refinement Elimination (re) and Introduction). *It holds*

$$a)\ T_{\mathbb{C},\mathbb{S}}, c\colon S_1, S_1 \sqsubseteq S_2 \models c\colon S_2 \quad and \tag{re}$$
$$b)\ T_{\mathbb{C},\mathbb{S}}, \forall q(q\colon S_1 \to q\colon S_2) \models S_1 \sqsubseteq S_2\ . \qquad □$$

4.5 Assertional Specification

The proposed framework, as noted many times by now, supports generally the case when implementation is non-monotonic with respect to component composition. However, in many cases, implementation of a specification S is indeed monotonic and in order to support reasoning utilizing this fact, the framework incorporates the predicate $\mathsf{Assertional}(S)$. If a specification S is assertional and a component c_1 implements S, i.e. $c_1 : S$, then any composition with any other component c_2 will also implement S, i.e. $c_1 \times c_2 : S$. Thus, if a specification S is assertional, then implementation of S will be monotonic with respect to component composition. This relationship is indeed a consequence of the interpretation constraints (1), (2), and (3), as confirmed by the following proposition.

Proposition 3 (Assertional vs Monotonic (am)). *It holds*

a) $T_{\mathbb{C},\mathbb{S}}, \forall q_1 \forall q_2 (q_1:S \rightarrow q_1 \times q_2:S) \models \mathsf{Assertional}(S)$ *and*
b) $T_{\mathbb{C},\mathbb{S}}, \mathsf{Assertional}(S), c_1:S \models c_1 \times c_2:S$.   (am)

□

Consider a specification **S** expressing an intended property of the kind of a simple relation between variables in Ξ, e.g. "x shall be larger than y". According to Sect. 4.2 the behavior set $\mathbf{S}^{\mathcal{M}}$ contains all behaviors consistent with the relation, which means all behaviors in which each run respects the relation. Since any subset, including the empty set, of such a behavior will also have all its runs respecting the relation, any such subset is also a behavior in $\mathbf{S}^{\mathcal{M}}$. Recall from Sect. 3.3 that this corresponds to the definition of downward-closed set and the interpretation of $\mathsf{Assertional}(S)$. Thus, in general it holds that any property of individual runs lifted to sets of runs, is assertional. This includes all properties that are expressible in linear-time temporal logic. In particular, a specification becomes assertional if it is possible to express the specification as a simple relation between variables in Ξ, or a combination of such relations, and this should be the case for a majority of industrial specifications. Note however, that the empty behavior is rarely a desired behavior, but it can be excluded simply by means of the specification ⓒ as will be explained in Sect. 4.8.

An important exception is specifications expressing architectural contraints, e.g. "signal x shall not be sent out" or "memory location 0x2AF3 shall not be written to", sometimes refered to as a requirement on *freedom of interference* [9]. The specifications $\mathbf{S}_1$ and $\mathbf{S}_2$ in Example 4 are two examples of specifications that are not assertional. This can be seen by studying the behavior sets (4) and also by observing that their natural language formulations include the phrase "not constrained" which is a type of architectural specification.

4.6   Conjunction and Parallel Composition of Specifications

Conjunction of two specifications simply means that the component shall implement both specifications, as confirmed by the following proposition. The following proposition confirms that the interpretation constraints (2) and (3) match this notion of refinement.

Proposition 4 (Conjunction Introduction (⊓i) and Elimination (⊓e)). *It holds*

a) $T_{\mathbb{C},\mathbb{S}}, c:S_1, c:S_2 \models c:S_1 \sqcap S_2$ *and*   (⊓i)
b) $T_{\mathbb{C},\mathbb{S}}, c:S_1 \sqcap S_2 \models c:S_1$.   (⊓e)

□

Parallel composition of two specifications means that, if a component c implements $S_1 \| S_2$, the behavior of the component is possible to "factorize" into two behaviors $\mathsf{B}_1 \in S_1^{\mathcal{M}}$ and $\mathsf{B}_2 \in S_2^{\mathcal{M}}$ such that $c^{\mathcal{M}} = \mathsf{B}_1 \cap \mathsf{B}_2$. In practice, parallel composition of specification $S_1 \| S_2$ is typically used as part of a refinement relation $S_1 \| S_2 \sqsubseteq S$, which means that, if the refinement relation holds, we can check that components c_1 and c_2 implement S_1 and S_2 respectively, and then it follows that the composition $c_1 \times c_2$ implements S. The following proposition confirms that the interpretation constraints (1), (2), and (3) match both these views of parallel composition.

Proposition 5 (Parallel Specification Composition). *It holds*

a) $T_{\mathbb{C},\mathbb{S}}, c : S_1 \| S_2 \models \exists q_1, q_2 (q_1 : S_1 \wedge q_2 : S_2 \wedge q_1 \times q_2 = c)$ *and*
b) $T_{\mathbb{C},\mathbb{S}}, c_1 : S_1, c_2 : S_2 \models c_1 \times c_2 : S_1 \| S_2$. $\qquad\qquad\qquad\qquad\qquad$ □

The following proposition investigates the relationship between conjunction and parallel composition.

Proposition 6 (Conjunction vs Parallel Composition). *It holds*

a) $T_{\mathbb{C},\mathbb{S}} \models S_1 \sqcap S_2 \sqsubseteq S_1 \| S_2$ *and*
b) $T_{\mathbb{C},\mathbb{S}}, \mathsf{Assertional}(S_1), \mathsf{Assertional}(S_2) \models S_1 \| S_2 \sqsubseteq S_1 \sqcap S_2$. $\qquad\quad$ □

Part (b) of the proposition is interesting since it, in the case S_1 and S_2 are assertional, provides an indirect way to prove $S_1 \| S_2 \sqsubseteq S$ from knowing that $S_1 \sqcap S_2 \sqsubseteq S$, which in some cases might be simpler to prove.

4.7   Contracts

Traditionally in the literature, e.g. see [1,2,15,16], an assume-guarantee contract (A, G) is defined by the property that: a component c_2 implements a contract (A, G) if for any component c_1 that implements A, the composition $c_1 \times c_2$ implements G. The following proposition confirms that our way of defining contract *as the constraint* (2f) *on the interpretation*, leads to this property used as definition in the previous literature.

Proposition 7 (Contract Elimination (ce) and Introduction (ci)). *It holds*

a) $T_{\mathbb{C},\mathbb{S}} \models A \| (A, G) \sqsubseteq G$ *alternatively expressed as*
$\qquad T_{\mathbb{C},\mathbb{S}}, c_1 : A, c_2 : (A, G) \models c_1 \times c_2 : G$,$\qquad\qquad\qquad\qquad$ (ce)
b) $T_{\mathbb{C},\mathbb{S}}, \forall q_1 (q_1 : A \rightarrow q_1 \times c_2 : G) \models c_2 : (A, G)$.$\qquad\qquad\qquad$ (ci)
$\qquad\qquad\qquad\qquad\qquad\qquad\qquad\qquad\qquad\qquad\qquad\qquad\qquad\qquad\qquad$ □

As noted in Sect. 1, and as will be seen in Sect. 5.1, contracts are of particular importance when proving compositionality. Therefore, results in Sect. 5.1 will be derived assuming that all specifications are contracts. However, this is no limitation according to the following proposition.

Proposition 8 (Generality of Contracts).
It holds that $T_{\mathbb{C},\mathbb{S}} \models S = (\top_\|, S)$. $\qquad\qquad\qquad\qquad\qquad\qquad\qquad\qquad$ □

Thus, any specification S can always be written as the contract $(\top_\|, S)$. In fact, this is the reason why the specification constant symbol $\top_\|$ was introduced in the syntax in Sect. 2.

According to Proposition 3, assertional specifications are tightly connected with implementation being monotonic with respect to component composition.

This monotonicity is highly useful for proving compositionality, as will be seen in Sect. 5.1. Therefore, it is important to know if a contract is assertional, and according to the following proposition, a contract is in fact assertional if its guarantee is assertional.

Proposition 9 (Assertional Contracts). *It holds*
$T_{\mathbb{C},\mathbb{S}}, \mathsf{Assertional}(G) \models \mathsf{Assertional}((A, G))$.   □

4.8   Compatibility Specification ©

Two components may impose constraints incompatible with each other. This corresponds to that there is no single run that is in both behaviors of the components, i.e. $c_1^{\mathcal{M}} \cap c_2^{\mathcal{M}} = \emptyset$. We want to be able to reason about this case, in order to avoid it. Therefore we need support in the syntax to express and specify that components shall be compatible, and to express that components are or are not compatible. This syntactic support is provided by the specification constant symbol © whose interpretation, according to (2), is the set of all behavior sets except the empty set. Consequently, for any model $\mathcal{M} \in \mathbb{M}_{\mathbb{C},\mathbb{S}}$, it holds $\mathcal{M} \models c_1 \times c_2 : ©$ if and only if $c_1^{\mathcal{M}} \cap c_2^{\mathcal{M}} \neq \emptyset$.

Note that even though the purpose of the notion of compatible components is to avoid *two or more* components to get the behavior empty set. However, in the framework, the notion of compatibility is formally a property of *general* component terms, including *single* components. Therefore we will simply refer to compatible or incompatible *components*, irrespective of whether the component is a composition or not.

Note that an assertional specification will always accept an incompatible component, i.e. an incompatible component will always implement any assertional specification, since the interpretation of an assertional specification is a downward-closed set, which always includes the empty set as one of the elements. Therefore, the specification © comes in handy in conjunction with assertional specifications, i.e. $S \sqcap ©$ allows S to be assertional while at the same time enforces compatibility.

5   Compositionality

With grammar and behavior semantics defined, this section will present the second contribution of the paper: a methodology and a deductive system for proving compositionality without presuming specifications to be expressed formally. We start by defining compositionality formally.

Definition 1 (Compositionality). *Consider a model $\mathcal{M}$ such that $\mathcal{M} \in \mathbb{M}_{\mathbb{C},\mathbb{S}}$. In the model $\mathcal{M}$, the specifications $S_1, \ldots S_N$ are composable into the specification S, or equivalently, the specification S is decomposable into the specifications $S_1, \ldots S_N$, if*
$$\mathcal{M} \models S_1 \| \ldots \| S_N \sqsubseteq S . \tag{5}$$
     □

Note that in Definition 1, compositionality is defined for a specific model $\mathcal{M}$. In fact, in the framework of the paper, we *can not* define compositionality to be a property only of the specifications $S_1, \ldots, S_N, S$ such as

$$T_{\mathbb{C},\mathbb{S}} \models S_1 \| \ldots \| S_N \sqsubseteq S$$

since this relation does *not* hold in general. It holds in some particular cases, such as $T_{\mathbb{C},\mathbb{S}} \models A \| (A, G) \sqsubseteq G$. However it does not hold if $S_1, \ldots, S_N, S$ are distinct constant terms, i.e. $T_{\mathbb{C},\mathbb{S}} \models \mathbf{S}_1 \| \ldots \| \mathbf{S}_N \sqsubseteq \mathbf{S}$ does *never* hold, since there is always possible to find one model that does not satisfy $\mathbf{S}_1 \| \ldots \| \mathbf{S}_N \sqsubseteq \mathbf{S}$.

The reference to a model in Definition 1 stands in contrast to [14], in which specifications themselves are expressed as formulas of predicates, meaning that in [14], no reference to a specific model $\mathcal{M}$ is needed to define or evaluate compositionality. This difference is further highlighted in the following example.

Example 6. Consider an engineering context represented by a model $\mathcal{M}_1$ in which the specification constant symbol $\mathbf{S}$ represents a real-world specification expressed as "The value of signal y shall be two times the value of signal u.". That is, the interpretation $\mathbf{S}^{\mathcal{M}_1}$ is the behavior set of all behaviors matching this natural-language specification. Furthermore, $\mathbf{S}_1$ represents a specification expressed as "The value of signal x shall equal the value of signal u.", and $\mathbf{S}_2$ represents a specification expressed as "The value of signal y shall be two times the value of signal x." In this model $\mathcal{M}_1$, it holds $\mathcal{M}_1 \models \mathbf{S}_1 \| \mathbf{S}_2 \sqsubseteq \mathbf{S}$. However, we can not say anything about any *other* model $\mathcal{M}_2$ since we do not know the interpretation of $\mathbf{S}_1, \mathbf{S}_2$, and $\mathbf{S}$ in any such model. For example, in $\mathcal{M}_2$, it might be the case that $\mathbf{S}_1, \mathbf{S}_2$, and $\mathbf{S}$ represents real-world specifications "x shall equal 0.", "y shall equal 0.", and "z shall equal 0" respectively. Thus, it does not hold generally that $\models \mathbf{S}_1 \| \mathbf{S}_2 \sqsubseteq \mathbf{S}$. □

5.1 Proving Compositionality

Even though compositionality is a property of a model, we want to utilize standard methods and tools, developed for first-order logic, and these work solely on a syntactic level. Thus, when proving compositionality, we need a way to avoid making reference to a particular model.

To solve this problem, we below present a theorem, which explains how compositionality can be proven without reference to any model $\mathcal{M}$. To remove the model $\mathcal{M}$ from the reasoning, we abstract it into a set Γ of sentences that $\mathcal{M}$ satisfy. More specifically, the sentences in Γ represent given knowledge about *refinement relations* between specifications, and also given knowledge that some specifications are *assertional*. The theorem refers to a hypothetical deductive system that is *strongly* sound for $T_{\mathbb{C},\mathbb{S}}$, which means that, for any sentence ϕ, if $T_{\mathbb{C},\mathbb{S}} \vdash \phi$, then also $T_{\mathbb{C},\mathbb{S}} \models \phi$.

Theorem 1. (Proving Contract Compositionality). *Let Γ be a set of sentences where each sentence is either in the form $\sqcap_j \alpha_j \sqsubseteq \beta$ or $\mathsf{Assertional}(\gamma)$, where each α_j, β, and γ is a specification term. If there is a proof of*

$$\Gamma, \ q_1{:}(A_1, G_1), \ldots, \ q_N{:}(A_N, G_N) \vdash q_1 \times \ldots \times q_N{:}(A, G), \tag{6}$$

in a deductive system, strongly sound for $T_{\mathbb{C},\mathbb{S}}$, then it holds

$$T_{\mathbb{C},\mathbb{S}}, \Gamma \models (A_1, G_1)\|\ldots\|(A_N, G_N) \sqsubseteq (A, G). \tag{7}$$

$$\square$$

Note that (7) means, according to Definition 1, that in any model $\mathcal{M} \in \mathbb{M}_{\mathbb{CS}}$, satisfying Γ, the specifications $(A_1, G_1), \ldots (A_N, G_N)$ are composable into the specification (A, G).

To illustrate how the theorem can be used in an engineering context, assume that the specifications $A_1, G_1, \ldots, A_N, G_N, A, G$ are stored in a requirements management system. Assume also that the requirements management system contains the knowledge of refinement relations between the specifications and of which specifications that are assertional. This knowledge can be based on manual informal analysis made by engineers, which is the only option when specifications are informal, or it can be based upon formal analysis. However, it is important to note that any such formal analysis is done outside the proposed framework and outside the scope of Theorem 1. This allows using the most appropriate analysis technique for the problem at hand, e.g. non-linear analysis in case specifications are expressed as non-linear differential equations.

Whatever analysis methods that are used, manual or formal, the obtained knowledge is taken as input to the compositionality proof problem by inserting it as sentences in the set Γ. Then a theorem prover such as HOL4 can be used with a deductive system to find a proof of the sequent (6). That a proof has been found means formally that in any model $\mathcal{M} \in \mathbb{M}_{\mathbb{C},\mathbb{S}}$, such that $\mathcal{M}$ satisfies each sentence in Γ, the contract (A, G) is decomposable into the contracts (A_i, G_i). Note that the model $\mathcal{M}$ is the mathematical object representing the engineering context but it is not needed explicitly. Instead we can express the conclusion simply as: in the engineering context considered, the contract (A, G) is decomposable into the contracts (A_i, G_i).

5.2 Deductive System for Proving Compositionality

Theorem 1 presented the solution to prove compositionality (5) by finding a proof of the sequent (6). In order to find such proofs, we consider a deductive system for the language $\mathcal{L}_{\mathbb{C},\mathbb{S}}$, having no axioms but a set of inference rules R. We choose R to include seven rules based upon the propositions in Sect. 4: $R = \{\mathsf{re}, \mathsf{am}, \sqcap\mathsf{i}, \sqcap\mathsf{e}, \mathsf{ce}, \mathsf{ci}, \mathsf{cre}\}$. The first six match exactly the corresponding proposition and rule cre is a rule derived by combining $\sqcap\mathsf{e}$, re, and $\sqcap\mathsf{i}$. Two examples of the inference rules are Contract Elimination (ce), based upon Proposition 2a, and the derived rule Conjunction Refinement Elimination (cre):

$$\frac{c_1 : S_1 \quad c_2 : (S_1, S_2)}{c_1 \times c_2 : S_2} \; \mathsf{ce} \qquad\qquad \frac{c : S_1 \sqcap S_2 \quad S_2 \sqsubseteq S_3}{c : S_2 \sqcap S_3} \; \mathsf{cre}.$$

Each rule in R is not sound generally, but according to the underlying propositions 2, 3, 4, and 7, which have all been proven using HOL4, see [7], each rule is sound when $T_{C,S}$ is added to the premises. This means that each rule is strongly sound for $T_{C,S}$, and consequently, the deductive system is strongly sound for $T_{C,S}$.

In general, more inference rules can be needed to prove compositionality. For instance, the utilization of interface specifications is highly useful but this is out of the scope of the present paper. However, for the example presented in Sect. 5.3 below, the seven rules in R are sufficient.

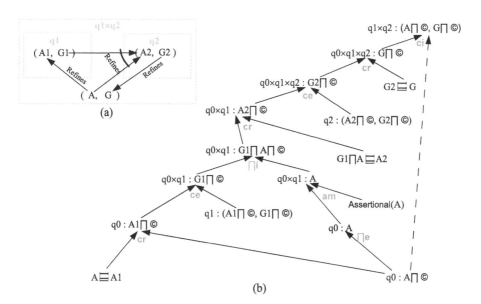

Fig. 1. (a) A compositionality problem with refinement relations in (8) illustrated as a directed graph. (b) A proof DAG for a proof of the sequent (9) corresponding to the compositionality problem in (a) but with Ⓒ added to each contract.

5.3   Compositionality Proof Example

We consider an example of a basic compositionality problem as illustrated in Fig. 1a, where arrows represent known refinement relations, and component terms in the sequent to prove (9) are represented as dashed boxes. The refinement relations and a known fact that the specification A is assertional are collected in

$$\Gamma = \{\text{Assertional}(A), A \sqsubseteq A_1, A \sqcap G_1 \sqsubseteq A_2, G_2 \sqsubseteq G\}. \tag{8}$$

To ensure compatibility as explained in Sect. 4.8, we add the compatibility specification Ⓒ to the assumption and guarantee of each contract. According to

Theorem 1, this gives us the following sequent to prove:

$$\Gamma, \; x_1 : (A_1 \sqcap \copyright, G_1 \sqcap \copyright), x_2 : (A_2 \sqcap \copyright, G_2 \sqcap \copyright) \; \vdash \; x_1 \times x_2 : (A \sqcap \copyright, G \sqcap \copyright). \quad (9)$$

The deductive system has been implemented in the theorem prover HOL4, as further explained in [7], and by using this implementation, we automatically obtain a proof of the sequent (9). The proof is shown in Fig. 1 as a proof DAG in which arrows point from the premises used in the inference rule shown at the corresponding arrow head. The dashed arrow illustrates that $q_0 : A \sqcap \copyright$ is temporarily assumed when applying the rule contract introduction ci.

6   Conclusions

Based upon first-order predicate logic, the paper has presented a formal framework and methodology for proving compositionality. To support general heterogeneous systems, the semantics chosen is behavior based, originating in previous work on contract-based design for cyber-physical systems [1,2,15,16]. However, in contrast to the previous work, we treat implementation of specifications to be *non-monotonic* with respect to composition. That is, even though a specification is implemented by one component, a composition with a second component may not implement the same specification. This kind of non-monotonicity is fundamentally important to support architectural specifications and so called freedom of interference used in design of safety critical systems.

With the contributions of the paper, i.e. the framework and methodology for proving compositionality, it is now possible to prove compositionality for industrial systems, even though specifications themselves are not formal objects. Instead, we rely on given *refinement* relations between specifications and the property *assertional* of the specifications.

Our view is that in industrial heterogenuous systems, there is in general a mix between informal and formal specification. Furthermore, for the specifications that indeed are formal, the kind of formalism differ between different parts of the system, e.g. one part might be described by differential equations, while another by linear-time logic. Therefore, within each formalism, some individual refinement relations may indeed be possible to prove, although there is no universal formalism in which all refinement relations can be proven and certainly not the whole compositionality. In this case, the proposed framework provides a unifying framework allowing reasoning utilizing the *results from* individual refinement proofs, and also *results from* informal analyses, in order to prove compositionality.

References

1. Benveniste, A., Caillaud, B., Ferrari, A., Mangeruca, L., Passerone, R., Sofronis, C.: Multiple viewpoint contract-based specification and design. In: de Boer, F.S., Bonsangue, M.M., Graf, S., de Roever, W.-P. (eds.) FMCO 2007. LNCS, vol. 5382, pp. 200–225. Springer, Heidelberg (2008). https://doi.org/10.1007/978-3-540-92188-2_9

2. Benveniste, A., Caillaud, B., Passerone, R.: Multi-viewpoint state machines for rich component models. In: Model-Based Design for Embedded Systems, pp. 487–518. Taylor & Francis (2009)

3. Brookes, S.D., Hoare, C.A.R., Roscoe, A.W.: A theory of communicating sequential processes. J. ACM **31**(3), 560–599 (1984)

4. Dill, D.L.: Trace theory for automatic hierarchical verification of speed-independent circuits. In: Proceedings of the fifth MIT Conference on Advanced Research in VLSI, pp. 51–65. MIT Press, Cambridge, MA, USA (1988)

5. Furia, C.A.: A Compositional World - a survey of recent works on compositionality in formal methods. Technical Report 22, Dipartimento di Elettronica e Informazione, Politecnico di Milano (2005)

6. Galton, A.: Logic for Information Technology. John Wiley & Sons Inc., Hoboken (1990)

7. Hedengren, G.: Verifying Correctness of Contract Decompositions. Master's thesis, Royal Institute of Technology (KTH) (2020)

8. Huth, M., Ryan, M.: Logic in Computer Science: Modelling and Reasoning about Systems. Cambridge University Press, Cambridge (2004)

9. ISO 26262: "Road vehicles - Functional safety" (2018)

10. Negulescu, R.: Process spaces. In: Palamidessi, C. (ed.) CONCUR 2000. LNCS, vol. 1877, pp. 199–213. Springer, Heidelberg (2000). https://doi.org/10.1007/3-540-44618-4_16

11. Nyberg, M., Gurov, D., Lidström, C., Rasmusson, A., Westman, J.: Formal verification in automotive industry: enablers and obstacles. In: Margaria, T., Steffen, B. (eds.) ISoLA 2018. LNCS, vol. 11247, pp. 139–158. Springer, Cham (2018). https://doi.org/10.1007/978-3-030-03427-6_14

12. Nyberg, M., Westman, J., Gurov, D.: Formally proving compositionality in industrial systems with informal specifications. Technical report, Royal Institute of Technology (KTH) (2020). http://www.kth.se/profile/matny

13. Peng, H., Tahar, S.: A survey on compositional verification. Technical report, Department of Electrical and Computer Engineering, Concordia University, Montreal, Canada, November 1998

14. Roever, W.-P.: The need for compositional proof systems: a survey. In: de Roever, W.-P., Langmaack, H., Pnueli, A. (eds.) COMPOS 1997. LNCS, vol. 1536, pp. 1–22. Springer, Heidelberg (1998). https://doi.org/10.1007/3-540-49213-5_1

15. Sangiovanni-Vincentelli, A.L., Damm, W., Passerone, R.: Taming Dr. Frankenstein: contract-based design for cyber-physical systems. Eur. J. Control **18**(3), 217–238 (2012)

16. Westman, J., Nyberg, M.: Conditions of contracts for separating responsibilities in heterogeneous systems. Formal Methods Syst. Des. **52**(2), 147–192 (2017). https://doi.org/10.1007/s10703-017-0294-7

17. Westman, J., Nyberg, M.: Preserving contract satisfiability under non-monotonic composition. In: Baier, C., Caires, L. (eds.) FORTE 2018. LNCS, vol. 10854, pp. 181–195. Springer, Cham (2018). https://doi.org/10.1007/978-3-319-92612-4_10

18. Wolf, E.S.: Hierarchical Models of Synchronous Circuits for Formal Verification and Substitution. Ph.D. thesis, Stanford University, Stanford, CA, USA (1996)

Specification, Synthesis and Validation of Strategies for Collaborative Embedded Systems

Bernd-Holger Schlingloff[1,2(✉)]

[1] Humboldt-Universität zu Berlin, Berlin, Germany
hs@informatik.hu-berlin.de
[2] Fraunhofer FOKUS, Berlin, Germany

Abstract. A collaborative embedded system is an autonomous component of a cyber-physical system which cooperates with other such systems in order to accomplish a common goal. In this paper, we report on approaches for the validation of such collaborative embedded systems. We describe specification methods for hierarchies of goals and targets. Using model checking of alternating signal temporal logic, we show how to construct strategies for the satisfaction of goals and targets. For run-time validation of safety properties, we give a robust monitoring procedure which can flag potential problems in advance. Our two examples are car platooning and automated guided vehicles in industrial production. In the car platooning example, autonomous vehicles collaborate to enable high-speed driving at short distances. The fleet of transport robots collaborates in loading and unloading of production machines.

1 Introduction

The validation of embedded systems is of increasing importance, since we more and more rely on their correct functioning. It is estimated that every European citizen on average owns more than 100 such systems. In a single modern car, there are between 50 and 100 electronic control units (ECU), which provide various services and driver assistance functions. An ongoing trend is that these devices are increasingly interconnected. This holds both on the level of tightly coupled systems, such as the ECU within a vehicle, and on the level of system-of-systems, such as a group of vehicles. In order to be able to adapt to changing demands and environments, systems are given more and more autonomy in their decisions. For example, even a simple robot vacuum cleaner and lawn mower can navigate autonomously within their dedicated areas. More sophisticated industrial transport robots have complex path planning components, circumventing obstacles and road blocks. In the railway and automotive domains, autonomous driving is a major innovation factor.

Autonomous systems can increase their performance, if they join forces and form collaborative groups. For example, a group of assembly robots in an industrial production cell can collaborate and distribute the required tasks amongst themselves, to jointly minimize the assembly time. As another example, a group

© Springer Nature Switzerland AG 2020
T. Margaria and B. Steffen (Eds.): ISoLA 2020, LNCS 12478, pp. 366–385, 2020.
https://doi.org/10.1007/978-3-030-61467-6_23

of autonomous trucks can form a platoon, travelling in close distance to one another in order to minimize fuel consumption. We call such a strategic alliance a *collaborative system group* (CSG), and each member of the group a *collaborative embedded system* (CES).

A defining criterion of a CSG is that all CES in the group work together to perform a common function. Thus, they share a common objective, to which each individual contributes. This is in contrast to competitive behaviour, where two or more agents have conflicting or even contradictory objectives. As an example with both cooperation and competition, consider robot soccer as practised in the annual RoboCup tournament: In each match, the two teams compete, whereas within each team the robots cooperate.

Even if several CES share a common objective, this does not exclude the possibility that each system also has individual objectives. In the platooning example, each vehicle in the platoon may have an individual destination. Conflicting objectives may result in an overall behaviour which is hard to predict. For example, we would not want a car in the middle of a platoon to follow its own route; however, at the end of a platoon such a behaviour can be acceptable.

Thus, there is a need for design methods which guarantee a reliable and safe operation of CES in a collaborating group. In this paper, we describe several approaches for informal and formal specification and validation of CSG objectives. Starting with two use cases, we describe a stepwise formalization approach for specifications: Starting from a statement of the system purposes, via the objectives of a collaborating group, to the strategies each collaborative system should follow. In order to formalize the requirements, we define a temporal specification logic as a blend of signal temporal logic and alternating-time temporal logic. Then, we use model checking and machine learning to synthesise collaboration strategies. Furthermore, we monitor properties to predict behaviour which might lead to problems.

The paper is structured as follows: First, we give some pointers to related work (Sect. 2). Then, we describe our two use cases (Sect. 3). After that (Sect. 4), we describe objectives for these systems. To formalize these objectives, we define our specification logic ASTL* (Sect. 5). Subsequently, we show how this logic can be used for strategy synthesis (Sect. 6) and online monitoring (Sect. 7).

2   Related Work

Collaborative embedded systems emerge as a rather new paradigm in the German CrESt project [BBK+20]. For the more general multi-agent systems, there is a long research history with an extensive literature [Woo02]. The CrESt design methodology for collaborative embedded systems is based on a similar one for embedded systems, developed in two volumes [PHA+12, PBD+16]. Alternative approaches for cyber-physical systems can be found in [Hu13] and [LS11].

For an introduction to logical aspects of multi-agent systems, see [SL-B08]. Our logic is based on a combination of signal temporal logic [Don13] and alternating temporal logic [KV96]. Following the definition of ATL, many other game-related modal logics have been defined. For example, strategy logic [CHP10] treats strategies in two-player games as explicit first-order objects, which is similar to our treatment of signals. Strategy logic subsumes ATL* and other such logics, whereas we have not yet investigated the expressiveness of our logic.

Synthesis of strategies for multi-agent logics is discussed in [JM14] and, for strategic logic with epistemic aspects, in [CSS10]. We are aiming at algorithms which are computationally much simpler.

Online monitoring and runtime verification are concerned with the analysis of the dynamic behaviour of systems. A survey can be found in [GP10]. Our approach for robust monitoring (parts of) our logic was developed from the one originally proposed for metric temporal logic monitoring [TR05, HOW14] and is described in detail in [LS18].

3   Use Cases

Our first example is from the automotive domain. Highly automated cars can collaborate to form a platoon which travels together at high speed in short distance to one another. This reduces the air resistance for each individual car, and allows a better use of highway space. Figure 1 depicts the model cars we designed for this use case.

Fig. 1. Model cars for platoon driving

The model cars recognize their environment via camera, ultrasonic sensors and wheel encoders. They communicate via WLAN. There are two ECU on board: The vehicle ECU handles low-level driving functions such as adjusting the motor speed and steering direction, whereas the advanced driver assistance ECU is responsible for collaboration, image processing, and other higher-level functions. The purpose of the collaborative adaptive cruise control (CACC) software on this ECU is to control the velocity and trajectory of the vehicles such that they can safely drive in a platoon.

As our second example, we use a fleet of autonomous, collaborating transport robots in a factory environment. A detailed description of this case study can be found in [SSJ16]. Figure 2 depicts some of the available robots [ProAnt].

Robots navigate in a production plant, using laser scanners to recognize their environment. They have a built-in floor map which allows self-localisation by comparing scan data and map data. In Fig. 3, a typical map from an actual factory is shown. Robots are only allowed to move in the area enclosed by the grey area. The current destination of the robot is indicated by a line.

Fig. 2. Transport robots for factory automation

The purpose of the robots is to load and unload production machines. Machines issue requests for being served, either if they are in need for new input material, or if the output buffer of produced goods is full. Robots receive the requests and decide amongst themselves which one should take the transport job. The main objective of the fleet is that every request is served in time. However, robots also have individual goals, for example never to run out of energy.

4   Natural Language Specifications

In a systematic design process, a first step consists of a systematic description of the functions a system shall provide. This is often done in specification documents in natural language. We describe a stepwise process which we applied for the case studies.

User Stories

For specifying the different aspects of a CSG, we use controlled natural language. *User stories* [Coh04] describe the system from the viewpoint of human stakeholders. A user story describes a purpose which a user in a certain role can achieve by applying the system at a certain time, as well as the reasons for pursuing this purpose. User stories may then be exemplified via use case descriptions and scenarios, formalized in UML use case diagrams and sequence charts. We use a template sentence to formulate user stories.

As a [actor/role] *I want the system to* do [function] *whenever* [trigger] occurs, *such that* [rationale] holds.

For example, the user story "Decentralized order management" describes how the robots determine which one of them accepts an order. It can be formulated as follows.

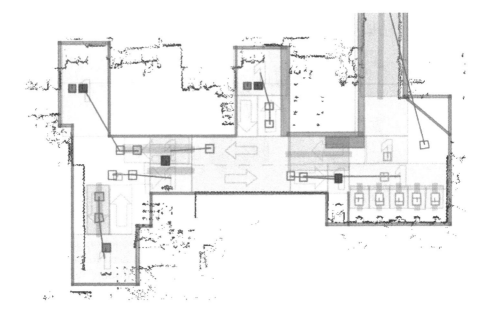

Fig. 3. Scanned oor plan with roads, robots, and docking points

As a transport system operator *I want the system to* decide autonomously which robot accepts a transport job *whenever* a job is issued by a machine, *such that* there is no need of a central control.

For the platooning use case, a typical top-level user story is the following.

As a driver *I want the system to* drive automatically together with other vehicles in a platoon at close distance *whenever* a sufficiently large common route exists, *such that* fuel consumption decreases and a better traffic flow is maintained.

A subordinate user story is about leaving a platoon:

As a driver *I want the system to* leave the platoon and hand over control to me *whenever* I request it, *such that* I can drive to a different destination than the platoon.

Objectives: Goals and Targets

From such user stories, objectives for the systems can be derived. An *objective* is a specific requirement describing a specific intention for the system, contribution to the realization of the system's purposes. Objectives can be structured into a hierarchy, where lower levels support higher levels. Moreover, they can be ordered according to their importance, or level of contribution to the topmost objective.

For cyber-physical systems consisting of several independent agents, we have to distinguish between objectives for the collaborative system group (CSG) and for the individual collaborative embedded system (CES). The individual objectives should support the group objectives.

Later on, we will distinguish between objectives which are goals and those which are targets. Intuitively, targets are "soft goals" which can be approximated, whereas "hard goals" must be reached to fulfil a system's purposes. A rough ontology of these terms is given in Fig. 4 below.

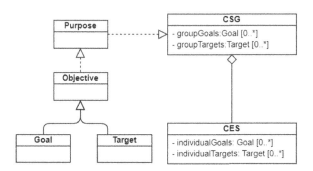

Fig. 4. Purposes, objectives, goals, and targets

For the platooning use case, the purposes of driving in close distance are to save fuel and make better use of highway space. A target of the group realizing this purpose is to minimize the maximal distance between any two consecutive vehicles in the platoon. A group goal is to never let the minimal distance in the group fall below a certain safety threshold, to avoid rear end collisions. A high-priority individual goal for each car is to decrease or increase its speed if told so by the platoon leader. An individual target would be to avoid accelerating and breaking within a short time period (e.g., one second), in order to avoid a waste of fuel.

In the transport robot case study, the purpose of the CSG is to provide transport services to machines. The most important high-level objective is to serve each request issued by a machine in time. That is, the main goal for the system is to keep the maximal waiting time of each machine below a given threshold. That is, if the machine emits a request for a transport job, then it will be served by exactly one robot within this threshold. The rationale is that production machines often have a buffer for incoming and outgoing materials. If the input buffer is empty or the output buffer is full, the machine will stop its operation. This needs to be avoided. A related high-level target is to minimize the average waiting time of machines, in order to cope with varying production speed. Low-level objectives include

- *robustness and fault tolerance*, e.g., being able to deal with failures of (unloaded) robots, being able to circumvent temporary road blocks;
- *scalability and flexibility*, e.g., being able to dynamically integrate new robots into the fleet, and being able to adapt to changes in the factory topology;
- *efficiency and durability*, e.g., balancing the usage of robots for equal wear and tear; and
- *security*, e.g., ensuring that intruders and traitors cannot bring down the system.

These fleet-related objectives must be complemented with individual objectives for each CES. The topmost goal for each robot is to accomplish each transport job it has accepted, if this is within its capabilities. A related target is to accomplish the accepted transport jobs as fast as possible.

In order to support the topmost global goal "each request will be serviced", corresponding objectives for the individual robots must be set. For example, an individual target could be to service as many requests as possible. However, in isolation, this target might be too coarse, as it might lead robots to "self-destructive" behaviour such as neglected charging, extensive wear and tear, congestion of roads in the factory, etc. As an example, consider the case when a robot has a low battery level which would allow to finish one more transport job, but it would risk running out of energy on the subsequent way to a charging station. Here, we have a conflict between different individual objectives. Should the robot prioritize the target of servicing as many requests as possible over the goal of never running out of battery? This shows that the targets must be refined with an appropriate strategy which takes all objectives into respect.

Further objectives include

- keeping within designated floor areas,
- being able to cope with obstacles and road blocks,
- keeping battery level at 40–70%,
- minimizing the occupation time of docking and charging points,
- minimizing the number and length of empty trips, and
- avoiding rests outside designated parking areas.

Our industrial partner InSystems Automation GmbH, now ASTI Mobile Robotics, formulated a number of objectives which refines and extends this list [ZDS+17]. Analysing these objectives, we see that there are two types: Some are "sharp", for an actual implementation it is clear whether it has been reached or not. For example, requirement "Load factor" enforces that production machines are always adequately provided materials. If it is violated, machines will simply stop working.

However, most objectives are "soft" or "fuzzy", in the sense that they can be reached more or less. An example is the requirement "Minimising non-value-creating processes", which implies that the number of robots should be as low as possible. Thus, a solution with 10 robots is better than one with 20. However, a solution where 12 robots are employed may also be acceptable, it offers more options in unexpected circumstances.

We call an objective with a clear criterion whether it has been reached or not a *goal*. In analogy to an archery target disk with concentric circles, which can be hit more or less in the centre, we call soft requirements *targets* for the system. In other words, a target is an objective which can be partially met, to a higher or lower degree.

This categorization of objectives into *goals* and *targets* is essential for the design. A goal is described as a certain state of affairs which an agent strives to reach or maintain, whereas a target is a rough set of states which can be approximated more or less. An agent can be close to a target, but being close to a goal is the same as missing it. Therefore, goals usually have a long-term character, whereas targets are frequently re-evaluated.

Scenarios

Goals and targets were operationalized via so-called *scenarios*. These are procedural descriptions of sequences of actions, which illustrate one particular sequence of events within the operation of the system. There is a huge body of literature on different ways to denote scenarios, see, e.g., [Coc01]. In our framework, each step is described by a consecutive number, the name of the agent, the action performed, the potential trigger for the action, and the rationale for the step.

An example is the distributed order management, which describes how autonomous cooperating robots are able to determine which one of them fulfils an order for transportation. If a new order is given and several robots are able to take it, it must somehow be decided which one of these robots actually will carry out the task. This is accomplished via a "bidding" or "consensus" process in which each available robot calculates its factors playing into this task, e.g. how far it is currently away from the pick-up area or how high or low its battery charging status currently is. It then sends these combined factors as information to the group as a bid. Depending on which robots can offer the most practical circumstances, it is decided which robot takes the job. The respective scenario is given in Table 1; for more information, see [Sch20].

The specific notation we use for scenarios is adapted from the CrESt methodology, see [BBK+20]. The first four columns are necessary for subsequent formalization steps, whereas the "why" column is for documentation purposes only.

5   Formal Specification

For an automated validation of system requirements, it is mandatory that these are denoted in a suitable formal specification language.

Temporal Logics: LTL, MTL, WMTL, STL

For the formal specification of goals, temporal logics can be used. In contrast to more graphical specification languages, temporal logics are closer to textual

Table 1. Scenario for decentralized order management

	Who?	What?	When?	Why?
1	Machine	Broadcasts transportation need to robots	Every time a machine has support or dispose need (may be in advance and/or may be with priority)	The production process of the machine is not allowed to stop
2	Every Robot	Calculates a bid for this transport (may be based on individual cost and/or other criteria)	When a new transport need is notified	To get the information which robot fits the best for this transport
3	Every Robot	Determine winner by distributed leader election algorithm. If two robots bid the exact same amount, the winner is selected randomly	After bidding	
4	Robot	Bid winner adds the transport to its own transport queue	When won a bid	That the transport need is satisfied

representations. A classical example is the property "for every request there is a subsequent response". This is written in linear temporal logic (LTL, [GPSS80]) as follows[1].

$$\mathbf{G}(request \rightarrow \mathbf{F} \ response)$$

In our setting, properties refer to real-time values. Therefore, timed temporal logics are necessary. The property that every request for service by a machine is fulfilled within 60 time units by some robot can be written in metric temporal logic (MTL, [Koy90]) as follows[2].

$$\mathbf{G} \, \forall m_i (request(m_i) \rightarrow \mathbf{F}_{(0,60)} \exists r_k \ at(m_i, r_k))$$

Other goals need spacial, epistemic, or strategic operators for formalization. It is much harder to express quantitative targets in classical or modal logics. If the bounds are made explicit (as in the example formula above), we can use these bounds in formulas. For example, we can specify performance in Weighted Metric Temporal Logic (WMTL, [BDL+12]). This logic contains an operator $\mathcal{P}$ which returns the probability of a statement within a certain time period. As an example, let the response time be the time difference between the time when a job is created and the time when the job is finished. The property "The response time within the first 1000 time units shall be less than 450 time units in 80% of all requests" can be written in WMTL as follows.

$$(\mathcal{P}_{(0,1000)}(\mathbf{G}(Job.active \rightarrow (Job.clock \leq 450))) \geq 0.8)$$

---

[1] As a remark, this formula does not require that for each request there is a *corresponding* subsequent response, which cannot be expressed in LTL.

[2] In this formula, the universal and existential quantifiers can be replaced by finite conjunction and disjunction, since sets m_i and r_k of machines and robots are finite.

However, these specification logics do not allow to adequately translate the natural-language formulation of the targets. The numerical borders (1000 time units, 450 time units, 80%) are introduced artificially for the purpose of specification, they do not appear in the original target.

In order to formalize also targets, we need a logic which allows to reason about vagueness and strategies. Thus, we define a suitable variant of robust signal temporal logic (STL) for this purpose [DM10]. Signal temporal logic was invented to monitor the value of continuous signals in time. For example, if x is the distance of a robot to some no-go-area, then $\mathbf{G}(x \geq 10)$ means that the robot always keeps at least 10 units distance to this area. As another example, if v is the desired and y is the actual speed of the car, then $\mathbf{F}_{[0,3]}(y = v)$ requires that within 5 time units the desired speed is reached. The robustness value of a formula indicates the quality with which a formula is satisfied. A positive value means that the formula is true, with the indicated robustness. For example, the formula $(x \geq 10)$ is both true if $x = 10$ and if $x = 1000$, but in the latter case with higher robustness.

Alternating Signal Temporal Logic ASTL*: Syntax

We now define a new logic called alternating signal temporal logic (ASTL^*) which is tailored for the specification of collaborative embedded systems. ASTL^* is a canonical extension of both signal temporal logic (STL, [Don13]) and alternating-time temporal logic $(\text{ATL}^*$, see [AHK02]). It is inspired by the synthesis approach for STL in [RDS+15]. In this section, we are using only the STL-part of ASTL^*; strategic reasoning will be used in Sect. 6.

Let Σ_0 be an alphabet of *primary signals*, some of which can be *controlled* and some *observed*. For example, a variable v to adjust the speed of a motor is a controlled signal, whereas a sensor d signalling the distance to the next obstacle is an observed signal. The set of controlled variables is called Σ_c. Furthermore, let $\mathcal{F} = \{+, -, *, \sqrt{\cdot}, ...\}$ be a set of *primitive functions* on signals. We assume that $\mathcal{F}$ also contains constant functions, e.g., $0, 1, 3.14$, etc. A *derived signal* is a term built from primary signals with primitive functions. For example, if d_x and d_y are primary signals indicating the distance of an object to an origin in cartesian coordinates, then $d = \sqrt{d_x * d_x + d_y * d_y}$ is a derived signal indicating its absolute distance. The set Σ of signals consists of all primary and derived signals. An *atomic proposition* is an inequality $s \geq 0$, where s is a signal; the set of atomic propositions is denoted by $\mathbf{P}$. The syntax of ASTL is defined as follows.

$$\varphi ::= \mathbf{P} \mid \mid \perp \mid (\varphi \to \varphi) \mid (\varphi \, \mathbf{U}_I \, \varphi) \mid \langle\!\langle \Sigma_c \rangle\!\rangle \, \varphi$$

Here, I is a closed or open interval of $\mathbb{R}^+$, and in the formula $\langle\!\langle s \rangle\!\rangle\, \varphi$, $s \in \Sigma_c$ is a controlled variable[3]. As usual, $\neg\varphi = (\varphi \to \bot)$, $\top = \neg\bot$, $(\varphi \vee \psi) = (\neg\varphi \to \psi)$, etc. $\mathbf{F}_I\,\varphi$ is short for $(\top \mathbf{U}_I\,\varphi)$, $\mathbf{G}_I\,\varphi$ for $\neg\mathbf{F}_I\,\neg\varphi$. The unconstrained temporal operator $(\varphi\mathbf{U}\psi)$ stands for $(\varphi\mathbf{U}_{(0,\infty)}\,\psi)$, and similar for $\mathbf{F}\varphi$ and $\mathbf{G}\varphi$. Propositions $s < 0$, $s \le c$, $s = 0$, etc., can be defined as $\neg s \ge 0$, $c - s \ge 0$, and $(s \ge 0 \wedge s \le 0)$, respectively.

Alternating Signal Temporal Logic ASTL*: Semantics

In the semantics, each signal $s \in \Sigma_0$ is interpreted as a real-valued function over the time domain. That is, a model $\mathcal{M}$ consists of a set of functions $s^{\mathcal{M}} : \mathbb{R}^+ \to \mathbb{R}$. From the interpretation of primary signals, the interpretation of derived signals can be deduced. Satisfaction of a formula φ at time t in model $\mathcal{M}$ is defined as follows.

- $(\mathcal{M}, t) \models s \ge 0$ iff $s^{\mathcal{M}}(t) \ge 0$
- $(\mathcal{M}, t) \not\models \bot$, and $(\mathcal{M}, t) \models (\varphi \to \psi)$ iff $(\mathcal{M}, t) \models \varphi$ implies $(\mathcal{M}, t) \models \psi$
- $(\mathcal{M}, t) \models (\varphi\mathbf{U}_I\,\psi)$ iff for some $t_1 \in t + I$, $(\mathcal{M}, t_1) \models \psi$, and for all t_2 such that $t < t_2 < t_1$ it holds that $(\mathcal{M}, t_2) \models \varphi$.
- $(\mathcal{M}, t) \models \langle\!\langle s \rangle\!\rangle\varphi$ iff there is a function $s' : \mathbb{R}^+ \to \mathbb{R}$ such that $(\mathcal{M}', t) \models \varphi$, where $s^{\mathcal{M}'} = s'$ and $r^{\mathcal{M}'} = r^{\mathcal{M}}$ for all $r \ne s$.

From this definition, it follows that

- $(\mathcal{M}, t) \models \mathbf{F}_I\,\varphi$ iff for some $t_1 \in t + I$, $(\mathcal{M}, t_1) \models \varphi$.
- $(\mathcal{M}, t) \models \mathbf{G}_I\,\varphi$ iff for all $t_1 \in t + I$, $(\mathcal{M}, t_1) \models \varphi$.

In the definition of the specification logic, we are more concerned with the pragmatic, i.e., the ability to easily formulate objectives, than with questions about expressiveness and complexity.

We write $\mathcal{M} \models \varphi$ iff $(\mathcal{M}, 0) \models \varphi$. Thus, the above clauses assign a boolean truth value to a formula in a model. STL is famous for its *robust* semantics, (see, [AVM19] and [LD18]). Where the "truth value" is a numerical value. Let $\overline{\mathbb{R}} = \mathbb{R} \cup \{\infty, -\infty\}$ and $(\overline{\mathbb{R}}, \le)$ be its closure with the usual ordering relation. Further let $\sqcup : \overline{\mathbb{R}} \times \overline{\mathbb{R}} \to \overline{\mathbb{R}}$ and $\sqcap : \overline{\mathbb{R}} \times \overline{\mathbb{R}} \to \overline{\mathbb{R}}$ be the maximum and minimum functions on the extended domain, i.e., $(x \sqcup \infty) = (\infty \sqcup y) = \infty$, $(x \sqcup -\infty) = (-\infty \sqcup x) = x$, $(x \sqcap -\infty) = (-\infty \sqcap y) = -\infty$, $(x \sqcap \infty) = (\infty \sqcap x) = x$ and for $x, y \notin \{\infty, -\infty\}$, we have $(x \sqcup y) = \max(x, y)$ and $(x \sqcap y) = \min(x, y)$. Furthermore, for any subset $X \subseteq \overline{\mathbb{R}}$, let $\bigsqcup$ and $\bigsqcap$ be the supremum and infimum functions over the set X, with $\bigsqcup \overline{\mathbb{R}} = \infty$ and $\bigsqcap \overline{\mathbb{R}} = -\infty$. The *score*, also called *spatial robustness*, of a formula with respect to a model is defined as follows.

- $\rho(\mathcal{M}, t, s \ge 0) = s^{\mathcal{M}}$
- $\rho(\mathcal{M}, t, \bot) = -\infty$
- $\rho(\mathcal{M}, t, (\varphi \to \psi)) = (-\rho(\mathcal{M}, t, \varphi) \sqcup \rho(\mathcal{M}, t, \psi))$

---

[3] In strategic logics such as ATL the modality is typically labelled by a set of agents which collaborate; in ATL*, this is unnecessary since $\langle\!\langle s, t \rangle\!\rangle\,\varphi \iff \langle\!\langle s \rangle\!\rangle\langle\!\langle t \rangle\!\rangle\,\varphi$.

- $\rho(\mathcal{M}, t, (\varphi \mathbf{U}_I \psi)) = \bigsqcup_{t_1 \in t+I} \{\rho(\mathcal{M}, t_1, \psi), \bigsqcap_{t_2 \in t+I, t_2 < t_1} \rho(\mathcal{M}, t_2, \varphi)\}$
- $\rho(\mathcal{M}, t, \langle\langle s \rangle\rangle \varphi) = \bigsqcup \{\rho(\mathcal{M}', t, \varphi) \mid r^{\mathcal{M}'} = r^{\mathcal{M}} \text{ for all } r \neq s\}$

This gives

- $\rho(\mathcal{M}, t, \neg\varphi) = -\rho(\mathcal{M}, t, \varphi)$
- $\rho(\mathcal{M}, t, (\varphi \vee \psi)) = (\rho(\mathcal{M}, t, \varphi) \sqcup \rho(\mathcal{M}, t, \psi))$
- $\rho(\mathcal{M}, t, (\varphi \wedge \psi)) = (\rho(\mathcal{M}, t, \varphi) \sqcap \rho(\mathcal{M}, t, \psi))$
- $\rho(\mathcal{M}, t, \mathbf{F}_I \varphi) = \bigsqcup \{\rho(\mathcal{M}, t_1, \varphi) \mid t_1 \in t + I\}$
- $\rho(\mathcal{M}, t, \mathbf{G}_I \varphi) = \bigsqcap \{\rho(\mathcal{M}, t_1, \varphi \mid t_1 \in t + I)\}$

Robust and classical semantics are connected by the fact that $\rho(\mathcal{M}, t, \varphi) \geq 0$ iff $(\mathcal{M}, t) \models \varphi$. The score of a specification formula enables us to reason about goals and targets of a system.

Alternating Signal Temporal Logic ASTL*: Examples

Using ASTL*, we can formalize some of the goals and targets for the transport robot use case given in the previous section. For example, if *Batt.lvl* is an observable signal indicating the current battery level, then

$$\mathbf{G}(Batt.lvl \geq 0.4 \wedge Batt.lvl \leq 0.7)$$

formalizes the requirement that the battery level should be always between 40 and 70%. In each model $\mathcal{M}$, the score of this statement at time t_0 is

$$\bigsqcap \{(Batt.lvl^{\mathcal{M}}(t + t_0) - 0.4), (0.7 - Batt.lvl^{\mathcal{M}}(t + t_0)) \mid t \in \mathbb{R}^+\}.$$

If this score falls below zero, then the requirement is violated and the design of the robots must be changed.

Similarly, the score of the target

$$\mathbf{G}(Job.active \rightarrow Job.clock \leq 450)$$

which corresponds to the requirement "response time should be less than 450 time units" indicates by a numerical value whether the deadline has been kept. Here, *Job.active* is a boolean variable indicating whether a service has been requested, and *Job.clock* is a clock variable which starts to count whenever it becomes active. Such clock variables can serve to formulate also other requirements, notably "minimizing the occupation times of docking points", "minimizing the number and length of empty trips", and "avoiding rests outside of parking areas".

Alternating Signal Temporal Logic ASTL*: Application

A model for ASTL* consists of an interpretation of signals by real-valued functions. In order to generate such an interpretation which reflects the working of an actual system, we need to model it[4]. In general, a model of a collaborative system group consists of three parts:

- A model of the collaborating systems,
- a model of the static environment, and
- a model of the dynamic use of the system.

For the platooning use case, we need to model

- the CACC function,
- the road including lanes, traffic signs, etc., and
- traffic situations and platooning scenarios.

In the transport robot use case, components of the system model are

- the behaviour of each robot,
- the map, including no-go-areas, location of machines, charging points, etc., and
- the load, i.e., the transport jobs which are issued.

These components can be formulated in a suitable modelling language. We use hybrid automata, as realized in the Simulink® modelling language.

For the platooning use case, the CACC function of a follower vehicle takes as input commands from the lead vehicle as well as the current vehicle speed and distance to the predecessor, and determines the acceleration or deceleration. The road model determines speed limits at certain locations. The model of a traffic situation includes, e.g., a description of new vehicle joining the platoon.

For the transport robot use case, the control algorithm of the robots is a diagram representing the behaviour and decisions. It is described in the next section. The map is represented by a two-dimensional table, and the load is a list of transport jobs, each with an ID, starting time, origin, and destination.

In general, the model of the collaborating system provides a mapping from observed to controlled signals. For systems with a certain level of autonomy, this mapping can be nondeterministic. E.g., in the platooning use case, each vehicle decides on the optimal acceleration or deceleration, depending on the commands from the leader vehicle and the distance to its predecessor. In the transport robot use case, each robot decides on the amount to bid for a certain job. Since Simulink does not allow nondeterministic models, we have to provide a "default" strategy in the model.

Since the system model is a deterministic hybrid automaton, for every setup there is exactly one (infinite) run. This run defines a model for the ASTL* specification. It is represented as a discrete linear sequence of states and transitions. This sequence is directly obtained from a run of the Simulink model. For model checking such a sequence, a time-discrete semantics for ASTL* can be defined.

---

[4] Unfortunately, the word "model" is used in two different meanings: as a structure to evaluate logical formulas, and as an abstraction of a physical system. Both of these uses of the word are well-established, the meaning should be clear from context.

In such a time-discrete semantics, the score of a formula is evaluated up to a certain state. Whenever the formula contains no strategic operators, the evaluation is linear in the length of the formula and the length of the run. Given a sufficiently fast computer, it can be done on-line, while the simulation is running. This approach is called *monitoring* and is elaborated in Sect. 7.

If the formula contains strategic operators, several alternative runs of the system need to be checked in order to determine whether the formula holds in the model. Since there may be an infinite number of alternatives, monitoring is not sufficient. In the next section, we discuss the automatic construction of strategies for a given system model and ASTL* specification.

6   Strategy Synthesis

The control algorithm for the robots consists of a three-layered architecture. The bottom layer contains low-level control functions such as the evaluation of sensor data and driving of motors. We call this layer the *reactions* layer. In this layer, self-localization and mapping is handled: laser scan data and odometry daty are combined to calculate a most likely position for the robot in the factory. Commands to move to a specific target are translated into motor settings, and continually supervised during the movement of each robot. If an obstacle is sensed, the robot stops; if a deviation of the actual trajectory from the planned path is detected, it is corrected.

The mid-layer deals with regulations for the behaviour, such as the planning of optimal paths according to the map and current situation, maintaining a queue of assigned jobs, and navigating only in dedicated roads. This layer is called the *rules* layer.

The topmost layer deals with principles and priorities which govern the overall behaviour, such as goals and targets. In our terminology, we call this the *principles* layer. It determines the strategy according to which each robot bids for a job, or decides to drive to a power outlet.

This three-layered architecture, depicted in Fig. 4 below, reflects a generic scheme for reliable autonomous systems as elaborated in [FMR+20].

We wish to derive strategies for the principles layer. For example, a strategy supporting the topmost goal of servicing each machine in time consists of an auctioning mechanism for issued transport requests, see Table 1. This strategy can be formulated in natural language as follows.

Each robot maintains a local queue of accepted transport jobs and estimated completion times. If a machine issues a new request, the robot calculates an estimated arrival time at this machine. The job mileage is the distance between the last position in this list and the location of the machine. The estimated arrival time is the estimated completion time of the last job in the task queue and the estimated travel time for the job mileage. Based on the estimated arrival time and the deadline of the job, the robot places the job mileage as a bid. Then, the robot waits and collects other bids. After all bids are placed, the robot selects and communicates the lowest bid. If more than one lowest bid arrived, one of the

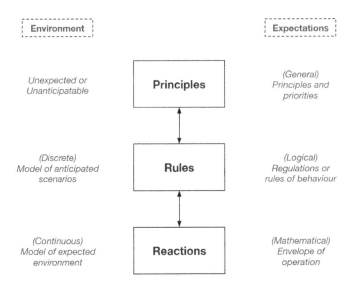

Fig. 5. A reference three-layer autonomy framework (from [FMR+20])

lowest bids is selected randomly. Otherwise, if the robot has placed the lowest bid itself, the job is appended to the task queue (Fig. 5).

This strategy does not take into respect power consumption, battery charging, wear and tear, and other targets. Further strategies are, e.g., the following.

- Random: In the bidding, each robot bids a randomly chosen amount.
- First-come-first-served: Each robot bids the estimated completion time of its current task list.
- Shortest time: Each robot bids the estimated earliest arrival time at the machine.
- Highest energy: Each robots bid its current battery level (highest bid wins). A variant is to bid the estimated energy after completing the last job in the task list.
- Mileage: The bidding sum is a function of the job mileage, and the total mileage of the robot.

The bidding process is decisive for the performance of the whole fleet. In simulation runs, one can observe that the fleet behaviour changes significantly with the bidding strategy [Sit18]. The strategy of each robot culminates in the question which amount to bid if a new request is issued. In general, this is a function of

- current task list,
- current traffic situation,
- battery level, and
- individual history and future of the robot.

Our aim is to find a bidding strategy which satisfies the requirements for the fleet. This is where strategic quantifiers of ASTL* come into play. They allow to formulate requirements without resorting to a specific strategy.

Specifically, if $bid.i.j$ is the amount robot i bids on task j, then $\langle\!\langle bid.i.j \rangle\!\rangle \varphi$ denotes that there is a way for robot i to bid for a job leading to the satisfaction of goal φ. We assume that $bid.i.j$ is a controlled variable which can be set by robot i. With a concrete formula φ,

$$\langle\!\langle bid.i.j \rangle\!\rangle \mathbf{G} \, \forall k(waitingtime(m_k) \leq 100)$$

denotes that there is a bidding strategy which restricts the maximal waiting time of all machines m_k to 100 time units. Likewise, for the platooning use case, the formula

$$\langle\!\langle accel.i \rangle\!\rangle \mathbf{G}(dist.i \geq 30 \wedge dist.i \leq 70)$$

describes that there is a way for vehicle i to accelerate such that the distance to its predecessor is between 30 and 70 space units.

In lieu of a dedicated model checker for ASTL*, we used MCMAS [LQR17] on a scenario similar to the transport robot use case. MCMAS is a tool for model checking of strategic epistemic logic with multi-agent systems. It has been successfully applied to several academic examples.

We do not (yet) have a detailed Simulink model of the use cases. Instead, we modelled a scenario which is similar to the transport robot use case, however, not involving real-time constraints. Our scenario is similar to the well-known "Pac-man" game, where agents are trying to pick up rewards on a two-dimensional grid. Strategic choices for an agent in each situation are whether to move north, south, east or west. From this, complex group strategies emerge. For example, it may not be optimal to always move towards the nearest reward, if another agent is also heading to pick it up. As expected, a state explosion occurs with the size of the board and the number of agents. Specifically, we were able to synthesize strategies for up to three robots on an 8×8 grid.

This is far from the size required for realistic industrial scenarios. Therefore, we are using machine learning techniques to find an optimal strategy. The `MAgent` research platform for many-agent reinforcement learning [ZYC+17] allows to train systems with hundreds to millions of agents. We compared the quality of supervised strategy learning with reinforcement learning of strategies. In supervised learning, the MCMAS model checker guides the learning process. Since this is computationally very expensive, the technique can only be applied for off-line synthesis. In reinforcement learning, each agent starts with a random strategy and learns from previous matches. Our experiments show some results which were surprising to us. Supervised learning scales better if only few learning iterations are allowed. However, after a few thousands of iterations, reinforcement learning results in better strategies. This is consistent with results obtained for learning games such as Go, Chess and Shogi by the `AlphaZero` program.

7   Online Monitoring

Online monitoring is a technique where the observed traces of a system are compared to a formal specification. Traces can be obtained from a prototypical implementation, or from a simulation as described above. As mentioned before, monitoring requires that there is a unique system run; hence is can be used to assert that a strategy automatically synthesized from a model behaves as expected also in reality. A challenge is to design a monitoring system which can detect and flag problems early, ideally even before they occur. That is, the monitor should raise an alarm even while the system is acting normally, if it has a tendency to drift into the exceptional behaviour.

To this end, we extended the semantics of ASTL*. Basically, we consider traces of finite length, which are processed one step after the other. A formula in a timed trace at a certain instant not only can be *true* or *false*, but the truth value additionally can be any real number. As long as the truth value of a formula in a model is not determined according to the standard semantics, we assign it a "likelihood" of being satisfied. This "likelihood" is calculated from the distance of the deadlines in the formula to the end of the trace, and the respective values for the sub-formulas.

We implemented an algorithm for monitoring our extended semantics [LS18]. For the evaluation of this algorithm, we collected traces from (a centralized version of) our transport robot case study. These traces covered a duration of several days up to a week of operation, and contained more than 10^6 timed events. By analysing the response time of the transport system to issued requests, we found a quite high variance of this value (between 1 and 100 min). Evaluating the MTL response property given above (every job will be fulfilled within 60 sec) revealed that property violation tended to "build up": several "near misses" were followed by a definite miss. This could not have been found by classical boolean-valued monitoring methods.

8   Conclusion and Further Work

We presented results in the specification and verification of collaborative embedded systems. As case studies, we described platooning of highly-automated vehicles, and an indoor logistics system consisting of autonomous transport robots in factories. For the specification of the systems, we used a stepwise refinement approach: From purposes via objectives to strategies. We specified the aims of the system with user stories in controlled natural language, augmented by scenarios as sequences of steps. From this, we derived formal objectives for the system. We categorized the objectives as goals or targets, depending on whether they are purely qualitative or also quantitative. Furthermore, we showed how to formalize the goals in various temporal logics. Then, we identified strategies supporting the defined goals and targets. We formalized the strategies in different state-transition-based modelling formalisms, and used simulation and model checking to analyse these models. Finally, we showed how to apply monitoring techniques to analyse long execution traces of the system for the accumulation of problems.

From our results, we can draw the following conclusions. Firstly, there is no "one size fits all" method for the formal analysis of such complex systems. We used different methods, e.g., timed automata, for different verification goals, e.g., correct timing. For the defined targets, we used quantitative analysis methods such as stochastic simulation and probabilistic model checking. However, these methods forced us to introduce artificial bounds. Therefore, we employed robust semantics which can give precise results also for fuzzy requirements and approximative targets.

Secondly, our analysis was facilitated by the fact that we were dealing with collaborative rather than competitive systems. In this paradigm, the individual strategy of each agent contributes to the aims of the whole system. The environment has no "strategy" to adverse the outcome. Therefore, by an individual optimization, the performance of the collaborative group increases. We believe that this observation is typical for a large number of similar systems. It remains further work to make this statement precise, i.e., to show that the complexity of collaborative strategy synthesis is lower than in the competitive case.

There are several other directions for further work. The complexity of our specification logic is unnecessarily high, since it employs full second-order quantification on functions. It remains to be investigated whether suitable sublanguages yield a lower complexity. Furthermore, we have not elaborated a dedicated model checking algorithm for our logic with a specific modelling framework. Hybrid automata and Simulink are very expressive formalisms which might be suitably restricted. Our hope is to find a "small" framework which is nevertheless sufficiently rich to model all important aspects of collaboration.

Furthermore, strategy learning in the context of CSG validation is a topic which needs further consideration. Although our experiments indicate that there is no "easy" way to combine model checking and machine learning for strategy synthesis, there are a number of directions we did not yet explore. Thus, the future remains exciting.

Acknowledgements:. This paper is an extended and revised version of our preliminary report [Sch18]. The research was supported by the German BMBF project "CrESt" on collaborative embedded systems, FKZ 01|S16043G/E. The author would like to thank the industrial partner InSystems Automation GmbH/ASTI mobile robotics for providing the transport robot case study, and the two anonymous referees for helpful comments and suggestions.

References

[AHK02] Alur, R., Henzinger, T.A., Kupferman, O.: Alternating-time temporal logic. JACM (2002)

[AVM19] Abbas, H., Pant, Y.V., Mangharam, R.: Temporal logic robustness for general signal classes. In: Proceedings of the ACM HSCC conference (HSCC-2019), pp. 45–56 (2019)

[BBK+20] Böhm, W., Broy, M., Klein, C., Pohl, K., Rumpe, B., Schröck, S. (eds.): Collaborative Embedded Systems. Springer, Heidelberg (2020, to appear)

[BDL+12] Bulychev, P., David, A., Larsen, K.G., Legay, A., Li, G., Poulsen, D.B.: Rewrite-based statistical model checking of WMTL. In: Qadeer, S., Tasiran, S. (eds.) RV 2012. LNCS, vol. 7687, pp. 260–275. Springer, Heidelberg (2013). https://doi.org/10.1007/978-3-642-35632-2_25

[CHP10] Chatterjee, K., Henzinger, T., Piterman, N.: Strategy logic. Inf. Comput. **208**(6), 677–693 (2010)

[Coc01] Cockburn, A.: Writing Effective Use Cases. Addison-Wesley, Boston (2001)

[Coh04] Cohn, M.: User Stories Applied for Agile Software Development. Addison-Wesley, Boston (2004)

[CSS10] Calta, J., Shkatov, D., Schlingloff, H.: Finding uniform strategies for multi-agent systems. In: Dix, J., Leite, J., Governatori, G., Jamroga, W. (eds.) CLIMA 2010. LNCS (LNAI), vol. 6245, pp. 135–152. Springer, Heidelberg (2010). https://doi.org/10.1007/978-3-642-14977-1_12

[DM10] Donzé, A., Maler, O.: Robust satisfaction of temporal logic over real-valued signals. In: Chatterjee, K., Henzinger, T.A. (eds.) FORMATS 2010. LNCS, vol. 6246, pp. 92–106. Springer, Heidelberg (2010). https://doi.org/10.1007/978-3-642-15297-9_9

[Don13] Donzé, A.: On signal temporal logic. In: Legay, A., Bensalem, S. (eds.) RV 2013. LNCS, vol. 8174, pp. 382–383. Springer, Heidelberg (2013). https://doi.org/10.1007/978-3-642-40787-1_27

[FMR+20] Fisher, M., et al.: Towards a Framework for Certification of Reliable Autonomous Systems. Preprint, arXiv:2001.09124v1, January 2020

[GP10] Goodloe, A., Pike, L.: Monitoring distributed real-time systems - a survey and future directions, NASA report cr-2010-216724 (2010)

[GPSS80] Gabbay, D., Pnueli, A., Shelah, S., Stavi, J.: On the temporal analysis of fairness. In: Proceedings of the 7th ACM POPL, pp. 163–173 (1980)

[HOW14] Ho, H.-M., Ouaknine, J., Worrell, J.: Online monitoring of metric temporal logic. In: Bonakdarpour, B., Smolka, S.A. (eds.) RV 2014. LNCS, vol. 8734, pp. 178–192. Springer, Cham (2014). https://doi.org/10.1007/978-3-319-11164-3_15

[Hu13] Hu, F.: Cyber-Physical Systems. Integrated Computing and Engineering Design. CRC Press (2013)

[JM14] Jamroga, W., Murano, A.: On module checking and strategies. In: Proceedings 13th Autonomous Agents and Multiagent Systems (AAMAS 2014) (2014)

[Koy90] Koymans, R.: Specifying real-time properties with metric temporal logic. Real-time Syst. **2**(4) (1990)

[KV96] Kupferman, O., Vardi, M.Y.: Module checking. In: Alur, R., Henzinger, T.A. (eds.) CAV 1996. LNCS, vol. 1102, pp. 75–86. Springer, Heidelberg (1996). https://doi.org/10.1007/3-540-61474-5_59

[LD18] Lindemann, L., Dimarogonas, D.V.: Robust Control for Signal Temporal Logic Specifications using Discrete Average Space Robustness. Preprint submitted to Automatica, December 2018

[LQR17] Lomuscio, A., Qu, H., Franco, R.: MCMAS, an open-source model checker for the verification of multi-agent systems. Int. J. Softw. Tools Technol. Transf. **19**, 9–30 (2017)

[LS11] Lee, E., Seshia, S.: Introduction to Embedded Systems: A Cyber-physical Systems Approach. MIT Press, Cambridge (2011)

[PHA+12] Pohl, K., Hönninger, H., Achatz, R., Broy, M. (eds.): Model-Based Engineering of Embedded Systems - The SPES 2020 Methodology. Springer, Heidelberg (2012). https://doi.org/10.1007/978-3-642-34614-9

[PBD+16] Pohl, K., Broy, M., Daembkes, H., Hönninger, H. (eds.): Advanced Model-Based Engineering of Embedded Systems - Extensions of the SPES 2020 Methodology. Springer, Heidelberg (2016). https://doi.org/10.1007/978-3-319-48003-9

[ProAnt] http://www.insystems.de/en/produkte/proant-transport-roboter/

[RDS+15] Raman, V., Donzé, A., Sadigh, D., Murray, R.M., Seshia, S.A.: Reactive synthesis from signal temporal logic specifications. In: HSCC 2015 (2015)

[Sch18] Schlingloff, B.-H.: Specification and verification of collaborative transport robots. In: Proceedings of the EITEC 2018 (2018)

[Sch20] Schlingloff, B.-H.: CrESt Use Cases. Chapter 4 in [BBK+20], Springer, Heidelberg (2020, to appear)

[Sit18] Sitzmann, F.: Simulation und Vergleich der Effektivität verschiedener Job-Scheduling-Verfahren für autonome Transportroboter. Bachelor's Thesis, Humboldt Universität zu Berlin, Institut für Informatik (2018)

[SL-B08] Shoham, Y., Leyton-Brown, K.: Multiagent Systems - Algorithmic, Game-Theoretic, and Logical Foundations. Cambridge University Press, Cambridge (2008)

[LS18] Lorenz, F., Schlingloff, H.: Online-monitoring autonomous transport robots with an R-valued temporal logic. In: CASE 2018 (2018)

[SSJ16] Schlingloff, B.-H., Stubert, H., Jamroga, W.: Collaborative embedded systems - a case study. In: Proceedings of the EITEC 2016–3rd International Workshop on Emerging Ideas and Trends in Engineering of Cyber-Physical Systems. CPS-Week, Wien, April 2016

[TR05] Thati, P., Rosu, G.: Monitoring algorithms for metric temporal logic specifications. In: ENTCS, vol. 113 (2005)

[Woo02] Wooldridge, M.: An Introduction to MultiAgent Systems. Wiley, Hoboken (2002)

[ZDS+17] Zernickel, J.S., Dannat, S., Schmiljun, A., Stubert, H., Samuel, J.: CrESt UC.AP4.D1. Internal report, InSystems Automation GmbH, Berlin (2017)

[ZYC+17] Zheng, L., Yang, J., Cai, H., Zhang, W., Wang, J., Yu, Y.: MAgent: a many-agent reinforcement learning platform for artificial collective intelligence. In: AAAI 2018 (2018). https://github.com/geek-ai/MAgent

Formal methods for DIStributed COmputing in future RAILway systems

Formal Methods for Distributed Computing in Future Railway Systems

Alessandro Fantechi[1,2]($\boxtimes$), Stefania Gnesi[2]($\boxtimes$), and Anne E. Haxthausen[3]($\boxtimes$)

[1] DINFO Università degli Studi di Firenze, Via S. Marta 3, Florence, Italy
`alessandro.fantechi@unifi.it`
[2] Istituto di Scienza e Tecnologie dell'Informazione "A. Faedo" CNR,
Via Moruzzi 1, Pisa, Italy
`stefania.gnesi@isiti.cnr.it`
[3] DTU Compute, Technical University of Denmark, Lyngby, Denmark
`aeha@dtu.dk`

1 Motivation

The growingly wide deployment of ERTMS-ETCS systems on high speed lines as well as on freight corridors is already a witness to the possible achievement of high safety standards by means of distributed control algorithms, that span over geographical areas and are able to safely control large physical systems. In ERTMS-ETCS the guarantee of global properties (such as safety) emerges from the conformance of the subsystems to well-established communication protocols and standards.

Formal methods are already one of the technologies used within railway industries, and the Shift2Rail program insists on the synergy of formal methods and standardised interfaces for a seamless connection of independent (formally specified) equipments and devices through well-defined interfaces, a synergy that can guarantee global dependability properties.

Most of the crucial decisions needed to guarantee safety are still taken at centralized places (such as the Radio Block Centre RBC), and the topology of such systems can be considered as a two layers network, the lower layer being just a connection of mobile systems with a centralized unit (the RBC), while the higher layer connects through a fixed network the RBCs with each other and the traffic management systems.

Following an increasingly popular trend for Cyber-Physical Systems, a more dynamic network connection among mobile components can be envisaged, in which decisions are actually taken in a distributed fashion. An example is given by proposals of fully distributed interlocking systems, where the route reservation is a global concept to be negotiated between the nodes [5,6,10]. Another example is the virtual coupling concept, in which the strict cross-control between coupled trains has to be negotiated locally, while the global behavior of the set of coupled trains has to follow the rules dictated by the ETCS control system [9,15].

Pros and Cons of distributing vital decisions is a matter of active research, especially considering that the increasing importance of communication raises

© Springer Nature Switzerland AG 2020
T. Margaria and B. Steffen (Eds.): ISoLA 2020, LNCS 12478, pp. 389–392, 2020.
https://doi.org/10.1007/978-3-030-61467-6_24

the need of uncertainty being taken into account in a railway control system: is the same safety level achievable by distributed decisions w.r.t. centralised ones? How formal methods can guarantee safety in such context?

2   Goals

The adoption of formal methods in railway signalling has been already the subject of two tracks of past ISOLA conferences. The track on "Formal Methods for Intelligent Transportation Systems" held at ISOLA 2012 [3], was actually focused mostly on railway applications, and this was indeed a recognition on how much already the railway signalling sector had been a source of success stories about the adoption of formal methods. The more railway-focused track "Formal Methods and Safety Certification: Challenges in the Railways Domain" held at ISOLA 2016 [4] aimed at presenting advanced results and at addressing the challenges posed by the increasing scale and complexity of railway systems.

In 2019, a specific workshop colocated with the DisCoTec federated conference on distributed computing, DisCoRail 2019, was set up with the aim of discussing how distributed computing was affecting the railway signalling domain. It has soon appeared evident that the high expectations on safety, but also on availability and performance of future railway signalling systems, in presence of a high degree of distribution, could be addressed only by a systematic adoption of formal methods in their definition and development. For this reason DisCoRail has joined ISOLA, and inherits at this regard some traits of the two mentioned past tracks.

Hence the aim of this track is to discuss (1) how distributed computing can change, and is actually changing, the domain of railway signaling and train control systems, and (2) how formal methods can help to address challenges arising from this change.

3   Contributions

Two contributions [2,12] discuss two different frameworks in which an established formal method in the railway domain, B, is extended to deal with distributed applications in an industrial setting.

Two other contributions of this track focus on formal verification by model checking of distributed interlocking systems [7,11], considering different modelling and verification strategies, and evaluating the scalability of formal verification, typically affected by state explosion problems when dealing with systems dealing with large station and network layouts.

The paper [14] presents a completely different view on how distributed computing can be exploited to achieve better performance/cost ratio of signalling equipment, that is, moving to the cloud the (safety-related) data that constitute the digital twin of the physical plants: the problems raised by this revolutionary proposal are discussed in detail.

Given the importance recognized by the Shift2Rail program to the very topics of this track, a session dedicated to presentations of running Shift2Rail projects contributes to the track program. The session includes paper [1] on the 4SECU-Rail project, aimed at providing a demonstrator of state-of-the-art formal methods and tools, applied on a railway signalling subsystem described by means of standard interfaces. Further to the contribution presented in this volume the actual discussion at the conference is expected to include interventions coming from other Shift2Rail projects, such as the RAILS project [8], aimed at investigating the potential of AI in the rail sector in continuity with ongoing research in railways, and from parallel running projects such as FORMASIG [13] aimed as well at formal definition of standardized interfaces. Further to the contributions presented in this volume the actual discussion at the conference is expected to include interventions coming from other Shift2Rail projects.

It is our opinion that, notwithstanding the limited space available, the contributions to the track succeed to give a glance of the state of the art and of the opportunities of the application of formal techniques to the distributed systems of systems represented by the future railway signalling systems.

References

1. Basile, D., et al.: Designing a demonstrator of formal methods for railways infrastructure managers. In: Margaria, T., Steffen, B. (eds.) ISoLA 2020. LNCS, vol. 12478, pp. 467–485. Springer, Heidelberg (2020)
2. Collart-Dutilleul, S., Bon, P.: A modular design framework to assess intelligent trains. In: Margaria, T., Steffen, B. (eds.) ISoLA 2020. LNCS, vol. 12478, pp. 404–414. Springer, Heidelberg (2020)
3. Fantechi, A., Flammini, F., Gnesi, S.: Formal methods for intelligent transportation systems. In: Margaria, T., Steffen, B. (eds.) ISoLA 2012. LNCS, vol. 7610, pp. 187–189. Springer, Heidelberg (2012). https://doi.org/10.1007/978-3-642-34032-1_19
4. Fantechi, A., Ferrari, A., Gnesi, S.: Formal methods and safety certification: challenges in the railways domain. In: Margaria, T., Steffen, B. (eds.) ISoLA 2016. LNCS, vol. 9953, pp. 261–265. Springer, Cham (2016). https://doi.org/10.1007/978-3-319-47169-3_18
5. Fantechi, A., Gnesi, S., Haxthausen, A., van de Pol, J., Roveri, M., Treharne, H.: SaRDIn - a safe reconfigurable distributed interlocking. In: Proceedings of 11th World Congress on Railway Research, WCRR. Ferrovie dello Stato Italiane, Milano (2016)
6. Fantechi, A., Haxthausen, A.E.: Safety interlocking as a distributed mutual exclusion problem. In: Howar, F., Barnat, J. (eds.) FMICS 2018. LNCS, vol. 11119, pp. 52–66. Springer, Cham (2018). https://doi.org/10.1007/978-3-030-00244-2_4
7. Geisler, S., Haxthausen, A.E.: Model checking a distributed interlocking system using k-induction with RT-Tester. In: Margaria, T., Steffen, B. (eds.) ISoLA 2020. LNCS, vol. 12478, pp. 449–466. Springer, Heidelberg (2020)
8. https://www.utwente.nl/en/eemcs/fmt/research/projects/formasig/. Accessed 10 Oct 2020
9. Flammini, F., Marrone, S., Nardone, R., Petrillo, A., Santini, S., Vittorini, V.: Towards railway virtual coupling. In: International Transportation Electrification Conference (ITEC). IEEE, Nottingham (2018). https://doi.org/10.1109/ESARS-ITEC.2018.8607523

10. Haxthausen, A.E., Peleska, J.: Formal development and verification of a distributed railway control system. IEEE Trans. Softw. Eng. **26**(8), 687–701 (2000). https://doi.org/10.1109/32.879808

11. Laursen, P.L., Trinh, V.A.T., Haxthausen, A.E.: Formal modelling and verification of a distributed railway interlocking system using UPPAAL. In: Margaria, T., Steffen, B. (eds.) ISoLA 2020. LNCS, vol. 12478, pp. 415–433. Springer, Heidelberg (2020)

12. Lecomte, T., Comptier M., Molinero, J., Sabatier, D.: Ensuring safety with system level formal modelling. In: Margaria, T., Steffen, B. (eds.) ISoLA 2020. LNCS, vol. 12478, pp. 393–403. Springer, Heidelberg (2020)

13. https://rails-project.eu. Accessed 10 Oct 2020

14. Peleska, J.: New Distribution paradigms for railway interlocking. In: Margaria, T., Steffen, B. (eds.) ISoLA 2020. LNCS, vol. 12478, pp. 434–448. Springer, Heidelberg (2020)

15. UIC: Virtually coupled trains. http://www.railway-energy.org/static/Virtually_coupled_trains_86.php. Accessed 12 Aug 2020

Ensuring Safety with System Level Formal Modelling

Thierry Lecomte[(⊠)], Mathieu Comptier, Julien Molinero, and Denis Sabatier

ClearSy, 320 avenue Archiméde, Aix en Provence, France
thierry.lecomte@clearsy.com

Abstract. During the last five years, Event-B formal modelling has been successfully applied to various railway systems to demonstrate safety early in the design process or once systems are in operation. This approach is aimed at formalising a safety reasoning instead of modelling every bit of the system. This approach is intrinsically fit to scale up to large systems (or system of systems), hence able to handle centralised or distributed systems.

Keywords: B method · Safety platform · Automated proof

1 Introduction

Railway signalling systems, legacy, new, and/or forthcoming, are complex systems, difficult to validate and certify. A large number of works have been reported over years, taking into account exploitation procedure [7], interlocking design data [6], hybrid systems [10], distributed systems [4,5]. Some projects report difficulties to scale up or to properly transmit knowledge through the very formal models.

Since several years, CLEARSY has driven large projects about using formal proofs at system level for railway signalling systems. The fundamental goal in these projects is, instead of modelling all the components of a signalling system, to extract the rigorous reasoning that establishes that the considered system ensures its requested properties, and to assert that this reasoning is correct and fully expressed. The concerned systems were either under preliminary specification, under design or already existing.

This paper makes clear the recent advances in the domain of system-level modelling aimed at demonstrating the safety of railways signalling systems, that remains manageable by the signalling engineer and understandable by the recipient of the study.

This paper is structured in six parts. Section 2 introduces the Terminology. Section 3 briefly introduces the B method. Section 4 presents the methodological framework. Section 5 presents some applications on real signalling systems performed the last years.

© Springer Nature Switzerland AG 2020
T. Margaria and B. Steffen (Eds.): ISoLA 2020, LNCS 12478, pp. 393–403, 2020.
https://doi.org/10.1007/978-3-030-61467-6_25

2 Terminology

This section contains specific definitions, concepts, and abbreviations used throughout this paper.

Atelier B is an Integrated development environment (IDE) supporting the B method and the B language for software development, and Event-B for system-level analysis.

B0 is a subset of the B language that must be used at implementation level. It contains deterministic substitutions and concrete types. B0 definition depends on the target hardware associated to a code generator.

Safety refers to the control of recognized hazards in order to achieve an acceptable level of risk.

SIL put for Safety Integrity Level [11], is a relative level of risk-reduction provided by a safety function. Its range is usually between 0 and 4, SIL4 being the most dependable and used for situations where people could die.

3 Introduction to the B Method

B [1] is a method for specifying, designing, and coding software systems. It covers central aspects of the software life cycle (Fig. 1): the writing of the technical specification, the design by successive refinement steps and model decomposition (layered architecture), and the source code generation.

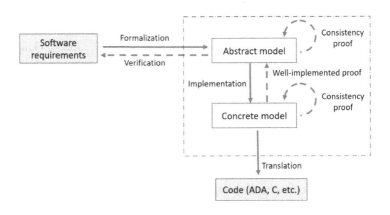

Fig. 1. A typical B development cycle, from requirements to code.

B is also a modelling language that is used for both specification, refinement (Fig. 2), and implementation. It relies on substitution calculus, first order logic and set theory. All modelling activities are covered by mathematical proof that finally ensures that the software system is correct.

B is structured with modules and refinements. A module is used to break down a large software into smaller parts. A module has a specification (called a machine) where are formalized both a static and a dynamic description of the requirements. It defines a mathematical model of the subsystem concerned:

– an abstract description of its state space and possible initial states,
– an abstract description of operations to query or modify the state.

This model establishes the external interface for that module: every implementation will conform to this specification. Conformance is assured by proof during the formal development process. A module specification is refined. It is re-expressed with more information: adding some requirements, refining abstract notions with more concrete notions, getting to implementable code level. Data refinement consists in introducing new variables to represent the state variables for the refined component, with their linking invariant. Algorithmic refinement consists in transforming the operations for the refined component. A refinement may also be refined. The final refinement of a refinement column is called the implementation, it contains only B0-compliant models. In a component (machine, refinement, or implementation), sets, constants, and variables define the state space while the invariant define the static properties for its state variables. The initialisation phase (for the state variables) and the operations (for querying or modifying the state) define the way variables are modified. From these, proof obligations are computed such as: the static properties are consistent, they are established by the initialisation, and they are preserved by all the operations. Atelier B contains a model editor merging model and proof (Fig. 3) by displaying the number of proof obligations associated to any line of a B model, its current proof status (fully proved or not) and the body of the related proof obligations. An Event-B project is a project containing one refinement column (one specification machine refined several times) and possibly context machines (machines containing only constants and sets definitions). Instead of B operations called sequentially, Event-B components contains atomic events which may be triggered when their enabling condition holds. An Event-B model represents the specification of a system (a device, a procedure, a business rule, etc.) with asynchronous transitions from one state to an other. Similarly to B models,

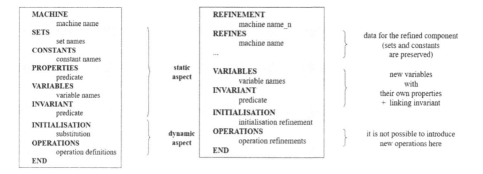

Fig. 2. Structure of MACHINE and REFINEMENT components.

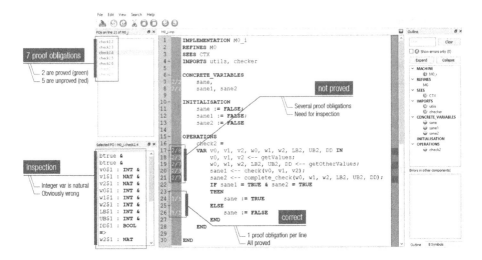

Fig. 3. Atelier B model editor showing proof status.

Event-B models have to verify their invariant properties: initialisation should establish invariant, and for each event fired, if the invariant was true before then it remains true after the execution of the event.

4   Methodology

The methodology described is issued from [2, 3, 8]. Figure 4 illustrates its different stages, which can be called "the ideal formal world" and which makes it possible to obtain a system that is guaranteed to be zero-defect.

The left side of the diagram represents the "formal proof of correct interoperability". The aim is to ensure that if the individual sub-systems making up the overall solution are implemented in accordance with their specifications, then the safety of the overall system is guaranteed. This proof enables the entity responsible for the integrated system to ensure that there are no hidden safety bugs in the subsystem breakdown.

The right side of the schema could be named "formal proof of correct design". It is a question of guaranteeing that a given implementation (RBC for example) is designed in such a way that the safety expectations expressed in the specifications are effectively met. This part is not included in the project as it is not required and is only provided for illustration.

The "formal proof of correct interoperability" is in three steps, detailed below.

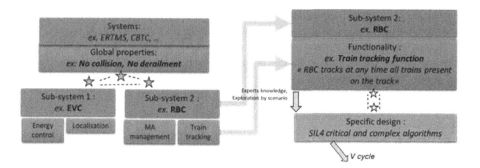

Fig. 4. The complete picture of the formal approach for safe systems.

4.1 Overall Safety Study, Roles and Responsibilities of the Subsystems

The objective is to acquire sufficient knowledge of the selected architecture and of the functional decomposition planned (or anticipated) within the framework of the target project.

It allows more concretely to identify the different actors involved in the security of the global systems as a first analysis of the security principles distributed within these subsystems. This analysis leads to a first version of a set of sub-properties resulting from the breakdown of the global non-collision and non-derailment properties to be respected by the subsystems through their different functionalities. This first phase also enables listing the different functionalities of the subsystems involved in safety and on which the formal proof has to be applied.

4.2 Formal Safety Demonstration Against the Risks of Collision and Derailment

This phase is the core of the formal proof of correct interoperability. It comprises a formalisation stage, i.e. a stage where all the elements involved in the safety demonstration (software variables, trains, signal states, points, etc.) are transformed into unambiguous mathematical objects.

4.2.1 Formalizing the Global Properties

The first activity consists in formalizing the global properties (mainly anti-collision and non-derailment) as well as the expected properties of the different subsystems in natural language (English) but with the precision of the mathematical language, which allows to obtain a definition without any possible ambiguity.

For example, sets can be a possible representation of trains and moving blocks. In this case the anti-collision property can be formalized as follows

$$\forall\, t_1,\, t_2 \in trains_{id} \Rightarrow t_1 \cap t_2 = \emptyset$$

where t_1 and t_2 represent the locations covered by each train. They are typed as sets. The anti-collision property implies that their intersection is empty.

Let us imagine that during the first phase of the study, it was identified that safety with regard to anti-collision is based on the principle of blockage, i.e. at any given moment, there is at most one train per block, so the anti-collision property can be refined by this principle of blockage:

$$\forall c_i \in blocks_{id} \Rightarrow (\exists! \, t_i \in trains_{id} \wedge t_i \cap c_i \neq \emptyset)$$

It reads that there exists only one train intersecting with a block (given that, implicitly, blocks do not intersect among themselves).

As long as the blocks do not intersect (reasoning hypothesis taken), it is possible to prove the anti-collision property mathematically from the refined property. In the same way, this property describing the blockage principle can be refined into sub-properties directly applicable to the subsystems.

For example, the ERTMS Blocking Principle will only be possible if the RBC has a correct train tracking (i.e. all trains on the track are tracked by the RBC at all times) but also if its Movement Authority (MA) management function is correct (i.e. the RBC never sends an MA to a train beyond a block already occupied by another train).

4.2.2   Performing an Irrefutable Mathematical Demonstration

The second activity consists of performing an irrefutable mathematical demonstration that the various subsystems meet the expected refined properties. Each functionality of each subsystem is analysed in order to verify that the requirements described in the specifications are sufficient to demonstrate the preservation of the expected properties. This demonstration shall be based on a set of explicit and justified assumptions, i.e. accompanied by the description of worst-case scenarios in case of non-compliance with these assumptions.

For example, the mathematical demonstration of the previous property requiring that a RBC never sends an MA to a train beyond a block already occupied by another train may be based on the assumption that the RBC never extends an MA from a train beyond a restrictive signal.

Assumptions thus obtained will have to be directly described in the specification or will be sub-properties requiring sub-demonstrations based in turn on other assumptions.

The outputs of the steps are:

- A formal safety demonstration (or correct interoperability) with regard to the risks of collision and derailment, described in natural language and formalised in mathematical language.
- The complete list of the so-called safety assumptions: all those used in the previous demonstration, together with their justification (worst-case scenario in case of non-compliance).

4.3 Modelling, Proof, and Animation of Event-B Models with Atelier B and ProB Tools

Atelier B is a tool for system modeling and proof of invariant properties of the modeled system. This modelling is done in a mathematical language: the B language. An "invariant" property is a property that is true at all times. In practice, the aim is to prove the invariance of the negation of the dreaded event (meaning that the opposite situation to the dreaded event is always true, e.g. "no collision").

The proof of invariant properties is based on the principle of induction: there is no evolution of the system leading to the invariant not being respected. The proof is obtained by demonstrating that the initial state of the system conforms to the expected properties, and each of the possible transitions of this same system preserves these properties (assuming the true properties at the input of the function).

The objective here is to model with Atelier B the reasoning conducted in the first two phases described in the two previous paragraphs. The production of these B models, accompanied by formal proof via the Atelier B tool, will ensure that the reasoning carried out on paper does not contain any logical errors and that all the security hypotheses have been expressed (no implicit hypothesis forgotten during the "paper" reasoning).

The outputs are:

– A proof model written in the B language, encapsulating the core concepts and the formal safety reasoning and associated safety concepts;
– A formal proof of important safety properties (no collision, no derailment, etc.) conducted within Atelier-B;
– Various instances of the proof model for animation with ProB, to ensure consistency and functionality. The models will be accompanied by various scenario files, to ensure that the formal models can implement various use cases;
– Vizualisations to ensure that domain experts can inspect the formal model without having to understand the B language (Fig. 5);
– An executable demonstrator for running more extensive functionality tests.

5   Applications

The methodology above have been used at several occasions:

– **Formal proof of the safety properties for the NYCT Line 7 Modernization Project** [9]. The New York City Transit Authority has included formal proofs at system level as part of the safety assessment for its New York subway Line 7 modernization project (Fig. 6), based on the CBTC from Thales Toronto. The main goal was to obtain a formal proof for the main safety properties of the system: no collision and no over-speeding. A book of assumptions was built up, covering every relevant aspect of the system, from

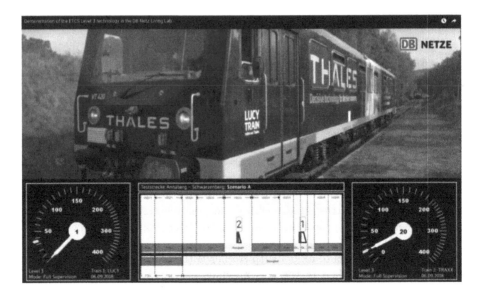

Fig. 5. Formal B model of Hybrid Level 3 Principles running in real-time. Source: Deutsche Bahn, https://www.youtube.com/watch?v=FjKnugbmrP4

internal design to external conditions. Safety properties were then obtained by pure logical reasoning only from these well defined assumptions. This study revealed all assumptions needed and reached a "proof level" confidence for the system properties.

- **Safety Analysis of the Octys CBTC System** [2]. RATP was going to upgrade their subway lines with driver with Octys, with the objective to improve throughput and safety by ensuring continuous train speed control, to participate in ensuring the safety of passenger transfers through the train and platform screen doors, to diminish the headway and to reduce wayside signaling requirements. Octys relies on multi-sourcing and interchangeability. The system is split in different sub-parts that are to be developed by different suppliers and interchangeable in the sense that any compliant sub-part, whatever its brand, shall fit seamlessly in the system. Octys had been deployed successively on Paris lines 3, 5 and 9; two other lines were scheduled to be equipped in the near future. The formal safety analysis consisted in expressing properties that are key to the safety of the system both in natural language and mathematical notation, and in constructing formal proofs that these properties hold. The conclusion was that such system level proof is feasible for a system like the Octys CBTC, with the appropriate level of independence with the intricate but out of scope interlocking. The findings (not disclosed) provided their benefits. The output results were expected to be reused as input properties for subsystem formal analysis performed by RATP.

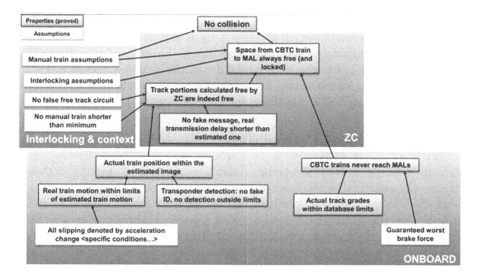

Fig. 6. NYCT line 7 modernization project - the structure of the formal proof for the main safety properties of the system: no collision and no over-speeding.

- **Validation of a CBTC zone controller** [3]. The analyzed CBTC is a flagship product of Alstom that is already in operation for over 95 metro lines worldwide. The formal analysis was applied at the software design level. The objective was to prove that a software specification and its implementation satisfy the expected system properties. The functional part of the analyzed software was developed with the B Method. A formal model of the software components was created, then formally refined and finally formally implemented. With the validation of the high-level specification of each component of a CBTC, we wanted to guarantee system-wide safety properties in light of evolving requirements specification of the components, and taking into account optimization to increase availability of the system. The following results were obtained:

  • Retrieve and/or explain clearly the fundamental design principles.
  • Exhibit and explain formally the assumptions made about the studied function inputs.
  • Retrieve and formalize the historical reasoning of the designers and keep track of their justification.
  • Identify complexity that is not necessary to maintain the properties and has become useless or obsolete, providing opportunities for functional improvements and performance gains.
  • Possibly detect corner cases where the properties are not fulfilled, providing the safety teams the elements necessary to analyze the consequences.
  • Propose design improvements.

From the point of view of the system teams at the origin of the design, it is no longer necessary to try to imagine all possible combinations of functions.

In return, any newly developed function must preserve the invariant properties. An implemented function is safe as long as it preserves the key invariant properties as exhibited by the study. To validate the safety of an evolution, it is therefore sufficient to require a formal demonstration, and to ensure that it does not contain logical errors. Any evolution can be mathematically proven even before it enters the traditional software development cycle.

6   Conclusion and Perspectives

Formally proving railway signalling systems is a very challenging activity, whether the system is centralized (this is the case of many legacy systems) or distributed. In this paper, we proposed a novel approach. We successfully experimented with the approach on several real-size systems, already in exploitation or to be deployed for the first time. Instead of modelling the different parts of the railway system, the approach extracts the rigorous reasoning that establishes that the considered system ensures its requested properties, and to assert that this reasoning is correct and fully expressed. This approach supports large systems without problem, is able to deliver understandable outputs in natural language as well as graphical model animation to exhibit key scenarios. This approach seems to be adequate for both centralized and distributed signalling systems. Several other experiments are on-going in several European countries for the main lines (ERTMS) that will be reported in the future.

References

1. Abrial, J.: The B-book - Assigning Programs to Meanings. Cambridge University Press, Cambridge (2005)
2. Comptier, M., Déharbe, D., Perez, J., Mussat, L., Pierre, T., Sabatier, D.: Safety analysis of a CBTC system: a rigorous approach with event-B. In: Fantechi, A., Lecomte, T., Romanovsky, A. (eds.) RSSRail 2017. LNCS, vol. 10598, pp. 148–159. Springer, Cham (2017). https://doi.org/10.1007/978-3-319-68499-4_10
3. Comptier, M., Leuschel, M., Mejia, L.-F., Perez, J.M., Mutz, M.: Property-based modelling and validation of a CBTC zone controller in Event-B. In: Collart-Dutilleul, S., Lecomte, T., Romanovsky, A. (eds.) RSSRail 2019. LNCS, vol. 11495, pp. 202–212. Springer, Cham (2019). https://doi.org/10.1007/978-3-030-18744-6_13
4. Geisler, S., Haxthausen, A.: Stepwise development and model checking of a distributed interlocking system using raise. Formal Aspects Comput. (2020)
5. Hei, X., Takahashi, S., Nakamura, H.: Distributed interlocking system and its safety verification, pp. 8612–8615 (2006)
6. Iliasov, A., Stankaitis, P., Adjepon-Yamoah, D.: Static verification of railway schema and interlocking design data. In: Lecomte, T., Pinger, R., Romanovsky, A. (eds.) RSSRail 2016. LNCS, vol. 9707, pp. 123–133. Springer, Cham (2016). https://doi.org/10.1007/978-3-319-33951-1_9
7. Metayer, C., Clabaut, M.: DIR 41 case study. In: Börger, E., Butler, M., Bowen, J.P., Boca, P. (eds.) ABZ 2008. LNCS, vol. 5238, pp. 357–357. Springer, Heidelberg (2008). https://doi.org/10.1007/978-3-540-87603-8_44

8. Sabatier, D.: Using formal proof and B method at system level for industrial projects. In: Lecomte, T., Pinger, R., Romanovsky, A. (eds.) RSSRail 2016. LNCS, vol. 9707, pp. 20–31. Springer, Cham (2016). https://doi.org/10.1007/978-3-319-33951-1_2

9. Sabatier, D., Burdy, L., Requet, A., Guéry, J.: Formal proofs for the NYCT line 7 (flushing) modernization project. In: Derrick, J., Fitzgerald, J., Gnesi, S., Khurshid, S., Leuschel, M., Reeves, S., Riccobene, E. (eds.) ABZ 2012. LNCS, vol. 7316, pp. 369–372. Springer, Heidelberg (2012). https://doi.org/10.1007/978-3-642-30885-7_34

10. Stankaitis, P., Iliasov, A.: Theories, techniques and tools for engineering heterogeneous railway networks. In: Fantechi, A., Lecomte, T., Romanovsky, A. (eds.) RSSRail 2017. LNCS, vol. 10598, pp. 241–250. Springer, Cham (2017). https://doi.org/10.1007/978-3-319-68499-4_16

11. Wikipedia contributors: Safety integrity level - Wikipedia, the free encyclopedia (2020). https://en.wikipedia.org/wiki/Safety_integrity_level. Accessed 08 May 2020

A Modular Design Framework to Assess Intelligent Trains

Simon Collart-Dutilleul$^{(\boxtimes)}$ and Philippe Bon

Université Gustave Eiffel, 20 rue Elisée reclus, 59666 Villeneuve D'Ascq, France
Collart-Dutilleul@univ-Eiffel.fr,
Philippe.bon@univ-effeil.fr

Abstract. The paper studies the use of formal methods in system design engineering in railways. Starting from the use of formal methods in French metro lines, the paper analyses various steps of dissemination of this know-how for main traffic lines. The case study of the ERTMS developments in France is presented for high speed lines and ETCS level 2. A study for an implementation in French regions is also considered. The last project to be analysed is the autonomous train of the IRT Railenium for the SNCF (the French railway national company). The system analysis shows that the old design assumptions are not valid anymore, as the system requires the autonomous trains to process a lot of data. All these industrial needs lead to specify a new approach based on a new semantic link between subsystems: REFSEES. The main target is to make it possible to focus on a given subsystem refinement while preserving global invariants.

Keywords: Formal methods · Composition by refinement · Railway safety

1 Introduction

In Europe, railway principles and standards used to be validated at the national level by National Safety Agencies (NSA). Historically, each country has its own requirements for managing trains on its network. As the multiplicity of national safety processes was impeding its economic development, the European Union introduced a new solution called the ERTMS (European Railway Traffic Management System) creating a common and standardized management of rail traffic and signaling in Europe. ERTMS is a new technological framework embedding specific technical building blocks like GSMR communication and specific Automatic Train Protection (ATP) using braking curves.

Assessing the implementation of a brand new system is difficult to achieve using existing processes. One of these approaches, known as the burocratic approach, is presented in the PhD Thesis of Helene Cecilie Blakstad [1]. It implies a single person mastering all the connected knowledge domains and able to make synthesis and compromises. It is an evidence that a drawback of this approach is that it is difficult to apply with radically new technologies. Obviously, it is close to impossible to find an expert of railway technology mastering all the connected knowledge, like, for instance the knowledge of railway safety, telecommunications and human factors.

An alternative approach uses a set of dedicated experts. The weakness of this solution is that each field of expertise comes with its own specific semantics, which

© Springer Nature Switzerland AG 2020
T. Margaria and B. Steffen (Eds.): ISoLA 2020, LNCS 12478, pp. 404–414, 2020.
https://doi.org/10.1007/978-3-030-61467-6_26

makes the communication between these fields error prone. Furthermore, dedicated experts do not have a mental representation of the impact of their technical choices outside of their domain. There is also a need of knowledge projection on a specific view of an industrial application. Considering this last point, model engineering will propose interesting contributions.

Let us consider the following definition:

A model is a simplification of a system built with an intended goal in mind. The model should be able to answer questions in place of the actual system [2].

Building a model means representing the real world focusing on specific aspects. The model is relevant because it provides an operational abstraction of a given knowledge, focusing on its impacts on a given structure. Finally, using a dedicated model for the formal projection of a specific knowledge regarding a given aspect is quite efficient from a conceptual point of view.

The paper presents the need of formal tools assisting a modular design of railway systems. The second section analyses formal studies, based on the ERTMS development in France. The third section focuses on frameworks developed around the B method [3]. It explains the need of a modular system design, assisted by formal methods, and highlights a specific semantic solution. The last section concludes on the project proposition and proposes some future works.

2 Formal Engineering in French Railways

2.1 The Leading Role of the RATP

Based on a track record of 25 years using formal methods, the RATP (Paris public transport network) noticed that the use of the PERF Approach instead of validation tests, reduces the overall workload by a proportion of 25% [4] (Fig. 1).

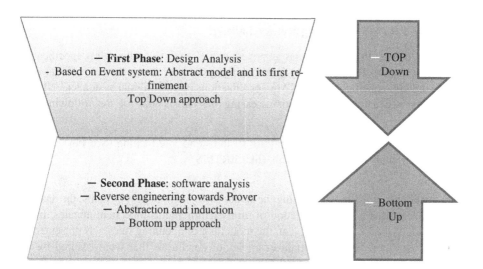

Fig. 1. PERF approach used by RATP

PERF is an approach, in continuous improvement, maintained by RATP. It is based on two main phases.

– The first one uses B method or Event B depending on the nature of the project. It is a top-down design process. Its main goal is as follow: *"Explicits the safety requirements (related to the sub-systems and configuration data) allowing to prove the mitigations of hazards by means of system design features"* [5]. A second step adds details of implementations to get closer to the concrete system while respecting the principles of architecture. As it is possible to specify discrete sets without specifying the bound, the approach can model a discrete system, "as close as we wish to a continuous system" [6].
– The second phase of PERF is a bottom up approach based on model checking, induction and abstraction. This work is performed at a software level, considering that the lower level product are software entities.

Works considered in the present paper are clearly related to the first phase, as they mainly deal with design choices embedding procedural, automation and software parts. It is to be noted that formal works led by RATP mainly focused on urban transport like metro lines. In this case, except particular zones dedicated to passenger trans boarding, the infrastructure is closed and the main scenarios are considered as deterministic.

From a formal design point of view, this means that the train is executing a mission defined by the control center, which may consult all the sensors which are put on the tracks, in order to know where the trains are. Moreover, the control center knows all the signal states and most of the device states. Finally, the control center sets points and signals, and the trains execute their missions, respecting signals and rolling on paths defined by points. The relation between train and control centers is like a master/slave one and no state information is transmitted from the train to the control center. Consequently, the formal architecture for assessing the train and control center collaboration is rather easy to define.

2.2   The ERTMS Operating Rules Challenge

A project, called "PERFECT", was launched in 2012 to develop the safety specification and verification of French railway interlocking systems in the context of national rules and of the implementation of ERTMS specifications on the original systems [7–9]. The study proposes a methodology for assessing the consistency of the following two aspects:

– the operating rules of local signalling systems and interlocking (See Fig. 2).
– the additional safety requirements (like ERTMS).

This methodology allows addressing the safety assessment of new systems, the analysis of given scenarios and the evaluation of safety requirements of system updates. In the framework of the PERFECT project, the modelling of operating rules was presented by Rahma Ben-Ayed [10]. Two main examples of conditions that were ensured by the means of invariants are:

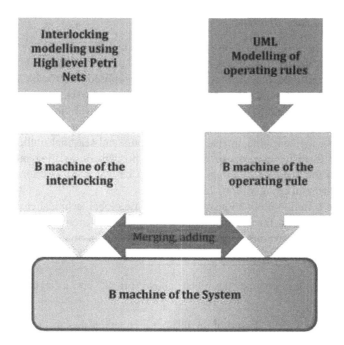

Fig. 2. Formal modelling process of railway systems for the assessment of operating rules

- non collision between trains when they respect signals. A single train should be on a single block of the railway track.
- past reception of the specific authorisation from the control center when going through a closed signal.

In this last case, the safety reasoning is that people of the control center are aware of the global state of the railway system. The control center may authorise safely to go through a closed signal. As an example, when a locomotive connects to a set of wagons, it has to enter a section which is already occupied by the wagons. Their presence automatically triggers a closed signal protecting the occupied track section, but the control signal delivers an authorisation to the locomotive driver to cross this signal. All these exceptional behaviors are controlled through interactions between the train and the control center. These interactions are specified in the operating rules.

From a formal analysis point of view, there was no feedback information flow from the train to the control center. It is a choice of the infrastructure manager to get the position of trains only using track devices (mainly track circuits). These train positions are discrete variables, because they belong to a finite set of values. The possibility of using some ERTMS packets to send back the train odometers (i.e. the continuous value of the train position registered in the train by a coding wheel) and to describe a continuous position on the control room screens was not considered. In this configuration, train and control centers mainly share messages. The information flow starts from the control center towards trains.

2.3   Regional Lines Diversity

The Nextregio project focused on the French regional lines. It is a project of IRT Railenium with "SNCF réseau" as main users, but the ARF (Association of French regions) was consulted too. The scientific work proposed to provide tools for the analysis of the system safety including operating rules and track devices.

Different kinds of traffic are considered: freight, passenger and mixed traffic. The variation of the need in terms of capacity may vary from a line to another. The need integrates some regional phenomena, like peak hours and seasonal traffic.

This wide diversity in terms of needs has to be built on existing infrastructures, inherited from the history of the region: they may be oversized, overloaded, more or less automatized and using various technologies.

One of the common motivations for changing the global technical environment for controlling the regional lines is that human workers mainly remaining in the railway stations perform a lot of controls and operations. This kind of organisation increases the cost of the global exploitation of the line, and decreases possibilities of building a good business plan.

Scientifically, the context described above brings out a certain number of difficulties:

- a methodology for the design of an abstract architecture has to be constructed;
- exploitation of this abstract architecture, for example by changing or refining a component, will raise the question of compliance with the requirements materialized by system invariants.

In the Nextregio project, building blocks of the abstract architecture are based on the functions expressed by the railway infrastructure manager in the expression of needs document [11]. Then the design works consist in refining these elementary functions and combining them in order to achieve production goals. Using the RBAC Profile and the B4MSecure Tool, an Event B model is produced, containing the functional specification and the safety restrictions [12] (see Fig. 3).

Let us now consider the railway system of a set of regional lines. This system can be broken out into subsystems constrained by contexts which are quite different. The presence of a skiing resort or the existence of a dense manufacturing area may completely change the need in terms of traffic for the railway stations in the vicinity. Moreover, this important traffic may justify heavy investments.

Therefore, all subsystem have to provide the same functions, but the constraints and the means to achieve the functions are quite different from a subsystem to another, whereas global properties of the whole system have to be guaranteed. This specification led to introduce the Prescom project of Railenium (meaning: Global safety proofs for modular design).

The whole railway system has to guarantee a set of global invariants. At the same time, this system is broken out into several components that can be refined independently. As an evidence, a sub-system cannot be handled independently if it has a coupling with other subsystems. A proposition is to provide a mathematical characterization of couplings: this would allow to study a sub-system implementation without representing the whole system It is an operational need to be able to model a railway

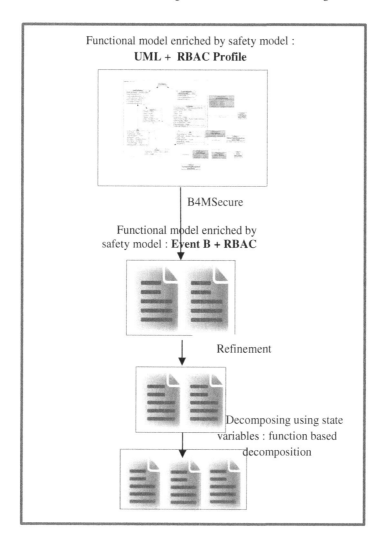

Fig. 3. Modelling process

station and its surroundings without modelling the entire system, that is, refining the system by decomposing it into several sub-systems. Taking one of these sub-systems, with its added proof obligations, which characterise the couplings between the sub-system and the other sub-systems, should allow focusing locally on the refinement of the considered component.

The conditions embedded into invariants are the same as in the Perfect project. The only difference is that on small stations, track occupancy is partially checked by a human operator in the station. In other words, functions and states are similar to those of the high speed line of the Perfect project, but they are broken out in different manners, depending on the level of automation of the lines.

Expressing the system structure in a formal modelisation point of view, track occupancy interconnecting local railway stations are shared variables between railways station component models. The implementation of the occupancy function is implementend (in other words: the corresponding variable is updated) in different manners.

Considering the relationship between infrastructure and trains, the investigation of virtual balises usage led to break an old architecture assumption: when the position of the train is known using GNSS, the train sends the position information towards the RBC (Radio Block Center) [13, 14]. The information flows began to be bidirectional.

2.4   The Autonomous Freight Train: An IRT Railenium Project of SNCF Freight

A dedicated task of the Autonomous Freight Train project focuses on needs engineering by the means of formal methods. Obviously, there does not exist a holistic approach for designing Autonomous Freight Trains from a high-level architecture to a formal specification where it can be possible to check the compliance with system requirements.

In the scope of this project [15], the train stores and analyses a lot of data (including continuous position provided by a composed system mixing odometry, GNSS and accelerometers). An autonomous train has many states, which may be taken into account by the control railway center in order to manage the whole system.

Moreover, in the safety analysis, the autonomous train may provide some safety critical information from its industrial vision system to the control railway center: detection of obstacle on the line, detection of obstacle on adjacent lines, detection of broken rail, detection of damaged catenary system, detection of people near the track area, etc.

All this information will trigger dedicated procedures in the control center. Finally, the relationship between infrastructure and trains are not of the master/slave type, and the information and control flows are bidirectional There are clearly shared variables and shared events between them.

From a formal assessment architecture point of view, it looks non-tractable to validate a new kind of autonomous train including its model into a huge model of the infrastructure. A modular process is needed, allowing implementing locally a specification, but the associated tools and methodologies have to be introduced.

3   Decomposition by refinement

Industrial railway needs led to increase the Event B semantics, proposing a new REFSEES clause [16]. The need corresponds to the possibility of refining a component which is coupled with other ones in order to allow an independent implementation synthesis. Added proof obligations corresponding to this new clause in order to focus on a component design keeping the insurance of not breaking global invariants must be specified [17].

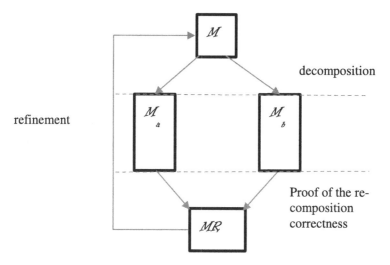

Fig. 4. The decomposition by refinement framework

The idea is to decompose a system into a set of components (see Fig. 4). These components may be refined afterwards. Then the re-composition of all the set elements should be a refinement of the initial system.

There are several kinds of decomposition in event B. Among others there are mainly:

- Decomposition with shared variable [18], called A-style, distributes events of a system in several sub-systems. Events handled by sub-systems may use shared variables and have specific signatures in the sub-systems.
- Decomposition with shared event [19], called B-style, is based on the variables partition, distributing variables in the set of sub-system.

Partitioning variables in the system components may lead to intellectual deadlocks within the design phase of a system. Since the autonomous train builds the state of the system through interdependent data analysis, the above-stated intellectual deadlock may lead to an industrial deadlock.

This approach looks well adapted for the classical urban line design: in a master/slave relationship, the central component can access all the data it needs and trigger actions. In other words, the more clever the train is, i.e. participates into building data that is used to trigger actions in the global system, the more difficult it is to find a design providing a partition of variables.

For A-style, the shared variables shouldn't be refined. Considering the diversity to be handled in regional line projects, this is a strong drawback. Actually, the needed structure of a variable may change, with a different context.

With this type of decomposition, the invariants involving the shared variables are not considered in the sub-systems. Yet it is an evidence that the global safety invariants have to be proved for a regional system involving the various local implementations that are the railway stations.

The technical limitation of A-style and B-Style have been already detailed [16]. The present paper mainly aims at providing an idea of the engineering impact of these limitations.

Starting from the identified engineering needs, a new approach was proposed [15]. It keeps the semantic link between the system and sub-systems resulting from the decomposition: the aim is to preserve global invariants (used for ensuring safety properties for example). Preserving the semantic link leads to defining a new link between the sub-systems, named REFSEES, allowing a cross visibility between sub-systems: the state of the private variables, the corresponding invariants, the constants, the sets and the properties. However, some proof obligations need to be added to specific components, for the sake of liveness, atomicity etc.

4   Conclusion

Starting from the strong know-how developed by the RATP for the use of formal methods in system design engineering in railways, the paper analyses various steps of dissemination of this know-how for main traffic lines.

The case study of the ERTMS developments in France is presented for high speed lines and ETCS level 2, but a study for an "ERTMS-Regional like" implementation in French regions is also considered. Specific needs in terms of architecture design are illustrated in both cases. The last project to be analysed is the autonomous train of the IRT Railenium for the SNCF (the French railway national company). The system analysis shows that the old design assumption are not valid anymore, as the autonomous train processes a lot of data which is needed for the global management of the system.

The first system analysis mainly identified differences between a train and a metro. The train drivers handle many interactions informally: the classical train is clever, because of the driver.

All these industrial needs lead us to specify a new approach based on a new semantic link between sub-systems named REFSEES. The main target is allowing to focus on a given sub-system refinement while preserving global invariants, without forbidding that a component modifies a shared variable belonging to another component. In French regional railway stations, occupancy of blocks of the track are shared variables that are usually modified by another component. In the BMVU ("bloc manuel voie unique") systems, the worker of the first station knows that the exit track is free, when the worker of the next station calls him, saying that the corresponding train with the corresponding number of wagon has arrived at his station. This industrial configuration corresponds to 3000 km of French railway tracks.

Future works consider the integration of the new propositions in industrial tools. Considering the benefit in the framework of a global model-engineering problem is to be considered in a second step.

References

1. Blakstad, H.C.: Revising rules and reviving knowledge. Adapting hierarchical and risk based approaches to safety rule modifications in the Norwegian Railway System. Fakultet for samfunnsvitenskap og teknologiledelse (2006)
2. Bézivin, J., Gerbé, O.: Towards a precise definition of the OMG/MDA framework. In: Proceedings 16th Annual International Conference on Automated Software Engineering (ASE 2001), pp. 273–280. IEEE (2001)
3. Abrial, J.-R.: The B-book - Assigning Programs to Meanings, pp. I–XXXIV, 1–779. Cambridge University Press (1996). ISBN 978-0-521-02175-3
4. Benaissa, N., Bonvoisin, D., Feliachi, A., Ordioni, J.: The PERF approach for formal verification. In: Lecomte, T., Pinger, R., Romanovsky, A. (eds.) RSSRail 2016. LNCS, vol. 9707, pp. 203–214. Springer, Cham (2016). https://doi.org/10.1007/978-3-319-33951-1_15
5. Bonvoisin, D.: 25 Years Of Formal Methods At Ratp. International Railway Safety Council (IRSC2016), Paris, 2–7 October (2016)
6. Mussat, L., Sabatier, D.: Modelling and proof of safety of Railway transportation systems. 13ème congrès de maitrise des risques et sureté de fonctionnement, Dijon 12 et 13 octobre 2014, France (2014)
7. Bon, P., Collart-Dutilleul, S., Sun, P.: International Conference on Industrial Engineering and Systems Management (IESM 2013), 28 October–30 October 2013, Rabat, Morocco (2013)
8. Sun, P., Collart-Dutilleul, S., Bon, P.: A formal modeling methodology of the French railway interlocking system via HCPN. Computers in Railways XIV (COMPRAIL 2014), ROMA, Italy, June 2014
9. Sun, P., Bon, P., Collart-Dutilleul, S.: A joint development of coloured petri nets and the B method in critical systems. J. Univ. Comput. Sci. **21**(12), 1654–1683 (2015). Impact Factor: 0.466 in 2014
10. Ben Ayed, R., Collart-Dutilleul, S., Bon, P., Idani, A., Ledru, Y.: B formal validation of ERTMS/ETCS railway operating rules. In: Ait Ameur, Y., Schewe, K.D. (eds.) Abstract State Machines. Lecture Notes in Computer Science, vol. 8477, pp. 124–129. Springer, Heidelberg (2014). https://doi.org/10.1007/978-3-662-43652-3_10
11. Ben-Ayed, R., Collart-Dutilleul, S., Prun E.: Formal method to tailored solution for single track low traffic French lines. In: International Railway Safety Council (IRSC 2016), 2–7 October 2016, Paris (2016)
12. Bougacha, R., Wakrime, A.A., Kallel, S., Ayed, R.B., Collart-Dutilleul, S.: A model-based approach for the modeling and the verification of railway signaling system. In: ENASE 2019 Conference, 4–5 May 2019, Heraklion, Crete-Greece (2019)
13. Ait Wakrime, A., Ben Ayed, R., Collart-Dutilleul, S., Ledru, Y., Idani, A.: Formalizing railway signaling system ERTMS/ETCS using UML/Event-B. In: Abdelwahed, E.H., Bellatreche, L., Golfarelli, M., Méry, D., Ordonez, C. (eds.) MEDI 2018. LNCS, vol. 11163, pp. 321–330. Springer, Cham (2018). https://doi.org/10.1007/978-3-030-00856-7_21
14. Boudi, Z., Ait Wakrime, A., Collart-Dutilleul, S., Haloua, M.: Petri nets to Event-B: handling mathematical sequences through an ERTMS L3 case. In: Abdelwahed, E.H., et al. (eds.) MEDI 2018. CCIS, vol. 929, pp. 50–62. Springer, Cham (2018). https://doi.org/10.1007/978-3-030-02852-7_5
15. Blin, C.: Scientific & technological obstacles to achieve the autonomy. In: Keynote Speech, International Conference on Reliability, Safety and Security of Railway Systems, Lille, 4–6 June (2019)

16. Kraibi, K., Ben-Ayed, R., Rehm, J., Collart-Dutilleul, S., Bon, P., Petit, D.: Event-B decomposition analysis for systems behavior modeling. In: ICSOFT 2019, 14th International Conference on Software Technologies, July 2019, Prague, France (2019)

17. Kraibi, K., Ben Ayed, R., Rehm, J., Collart-Dutilleul, S., Bon, P., Petit, D.: Towards a method for the decomposition by refinement in Event-B. In: Sekerinski, E., et al. (eds.) FM 2019. LNCS, vol. 12233, pp. 358–370. Springer, Cham (2020). https://doi.org/10.1007/978-3-030-54997-8_23

18. Abrial, J.-R., Hallerstede, S.: Refinement, decomposition, and instantiation of discrete models: application to Event-B. Fundam. Inform. **77**(1–2), 1–28 (2007)

19. Butler, M.: Decomposition structures for Event-B. In: Leuschel, M., Wehrheim, H. (eds.) IFM 2009. LNCS, vol. 5423, pp. 20–38. Springer, Heidelberg (2009). https://doi.org/10.1007/978-3-642-00255-7_2

Formal Modelling and Verification of a Distributed Railway Interlocking System Using UPPAAL

Per Lange Laursen[✉], Van Anh Thi Trinh[✉],
and Anne E. Haxthausen[✉]

DTU Compute, Technical University of Denmark, Kongens Lyngby, Denmark
perlangelaursen@gmail.com, anh-van@live.com, aeha@dtu.dk

Abstract. This paper investigates the modelling and model checking of a real-world distributed railway interlocking system algorithm using UPPAAL. Interlocking systems for specific railway networks are verified by instantiating a generic (re-configurable) model with configuration data that describes the network and involved trains. There are three variants of the generic model: (1) The first variant includes the minimum required operations such as reserving a segment for a train, locking a point in a fixed position, and moving a train. (2) A restricted variant that uses a more strict operational order. (3) A variant that extends the first variant with a cancel operation that removes reservations and locks. Verification experiments are carried out on instances of all variants in order to check their correctness and compare their performance. The scalability of the three variants has been investigated with networks of varying sizes. Finally, for a real-world railway network, instances of the three model variants have been successfully verified.

Keywords: Distributed systems · Railway interlocking systems ·
Formal verification · Model Checking · UPPAAL

1 Introduction

The aim of this paper is to report on the experiences using UPPAAL [4] for model checking a real-world distributed railway interlocking system.

Background. A railway interlocking system is a signalling system component responsible for controlling the switching of points in a railway network and the issuing of movement authorities to the trains running in that network, such that train collisions and derailments are avoided. Usually, interlocking systems are *centralised* control systems. For small local railways, this can be a quite expensive solution, so it has long been of interest to examine the possibilities of using *distributed* interlocking systems, as discussed in [9]. In distributed interlocking systems, the control is delegated to a collection of control components physically

© Springer Nature Switzerland AG 2020
T. Margaria and B. Steffen (Eds.): ISoLA 2020, LNCS 12478, pp. 415–433, 2020.
https://doi.org/10.1007/978-3-030-61467-6_27

distributed along the tracks and inside the trains. These components each have their own state space for storing relevant data. With this approach, the components communicate with each other in order to cooperate in controlling the trains and the switch points in the railway network. For a survey over different distributed control algorithms, see [11]. Although being a less expensive solution, the required communication also makes it more difficult to verify the safety of trains in the system. For that, the CENELEC standard EN 50128 [5] strongly recommends to use formal verification methods.

Contribution and Related Work. There are many examples of formal verification of railway control systems, see e.g. [1,2,6,8,13,15,16,18,21], but only very few for *distributed* interlocking systems, see e.g. [10,12,14].

The distributed interlocking concept considered in this paper is based on the RELIS 2000 interlocking system of INSY GmbH. This system was first modelled and verified in [14] using RSL [20] and the RAISE theorem prover. As verification by means of theorem proving is rather time consuming, while verification by means of model checking is fully automated, the use of the latter was later, in [12], investigated for the same case study. In [12], RSL* and the SAL symbolic model checker were used only for a proof of concept, and hence efficiency was here of less concern. It actually turned out that the tool did not scale up well for larger networks, in which case compositional reasoning was used instead.

The main goal of our study is to investigate whether UPPAAL has better scaling, such that larger networks can be verified. UPPAAL has been chosen, as it uses a symbolic on-the-fly verification technique, which has generally proved very efficient for many applications, see for instance [19,22]. UPPAAL additionally comes with an appealing graphical user interface, which may affect the modelling experience positively compared to modelling and model checking through a terminal for instance. Furthermore, we will investigate what it means for the verification performance if the control algorithm is restricted to a variant having a more specific execution order. We also use the opportunity to model additional functionality not included in [12]: an operation for cancelling reservations. Finally, we will also examine how well suited UPPAAL is as a modelling tool compared to RSL* and SAL.

Our control algorithm variants are similar to the ones presented in [12,14], but our models differ of course wrt the choice of data types as UPPAAL offers fewer data types than RSL and RSL*. They also differ from [12] by using channels instead of shared variables for modelling the communication between control components. A major difference from [12] is: For improved efficiency, a train in our models (like in [14]) only reserves route segments and locks points in the order that they are needed, leading to some simplifications. Furthermore, in contrast to [12,14], points are modelled in more detail, taking into account that a point can be in a switching state.

A totally different algorithm for a distributed interlocking system based on a two-phase commit protocol was modelled and verified in [10] using UMC [3].

Overview. First, in Sects. 2 and 3, short, informal introductions to the UPPAAL modelling language and the case study are given. Then, in Sects. 4 and 5, models of three different variants of the interlocking system are described. The first variant (later referred to as the 'First model') describes each of the different operations that a train control computer can perform, i.e. reserve a segment, switch and lock a point, and move the train to a new segment. Each of these different operations can be attempted in any order by the train control computer. The second variant restricts the execution sequence of the different operations to a more ideal sequence, while the third variant includes an additional operation for cancelling reservations and locks. Desired properties are then presented in Sect. 6 and used for the experiments described in Sect. 7[1]. A conclusion on the modelling and verification experiences is given in Sect. 8.

2   The UPPAAL Modelling Language

This section gives a very short, informal introduction to the major UPPAAL modelling language constructs used in this paper. The reader is assumed familiar with the theory of timed automata and temporal logics. For more details, especially on the semantics of the concurrency construct, the reader should consult [4].

In UPPAAL, a system is modelled as a network of parallel timed automata (called processes), which are finite-state machines extended with (1) time in the form of real-valued clocks that progress synchronously and (2) data variables of simple data types (bounded integers, arrays, etc.). Even though UPPAAL can use real-valued clocks as a part of an automaton, it is still possible to define and work with untimed automata. In that case, time will not affect the resulting state space of an automaton. The models that are described as a part of this paper are all untimed.

The specification of a system model consists of (1) templates for timed automata, (2) declarations of clocks, data variables, constants, channels, and functions, which can be used in the templates, and (3) a system declaration, which is a parallel composition of processes, which are instances of the templates. The processes can communicate asynchronously via shared variables or synchronously via unicast channels and broadcast channels.

Fig. 1. An example of a timed automaton in UPPAAL. (Colour figure online)

---

[1] The experiment models and the verified properties can be found at https://github.com/perlangelaursen/DistributedRailwayControl.

A timed automaton consists of locations and edges. In the graphical representation of timed automata (for an example, see Fig. 1), locations are shown as circles and may have a name shown in purple colour. The *initial* location is shown by a double circle. A location may be labelled with an *invariant* (shown in pink colour), which is a Boolean expression over variables and clocks. The process can stay in that location and let time pass as long as the invariant is satisfied, but when the invariant becomes false, it must leave the location.

Edges are shown as arrows. An edge may be labelled with (1) some parameters of the form *id : type* (shown in light green colour), (2) a guard (shown in green colour), which is a Boolean expression over variables and clocks determining when the edge is enabled and can be fired, (3) updates of variables and clocks (shown in blue colour), which are executed when the edge is fired, and (4) synchronisations of the form c? or c! over a channel c (shown in light blue colour). For a unicast channel c, an edge labelled with c! in one process (the sender) may synchronise with an edge labelled with c? in another process (the receiver) provided that both edges are enabled. For a broadcast channel c, an enabled edge labelled with c! in one process may synchronise with all enabled edges labelled with c? in other processes. If there are no receivers, then the sender can still execute the c! action. A channel may be declared to be *urgent*. Whenever an enabled edge is able to synchronise over an urgent channel, this edge must be fired without any delay.

For the specification of desired properties, UPPAAL uses a subset of Timed Computation Tree Logic (TCTL) [4], where the outer-most formula must be an application of one of the two quantifiers A (along all paths) or E (along at least one path) or the leads-to operator -->, and these must not be nested.

3 Case Study

In this section, the considered case study from [14] is described informally.

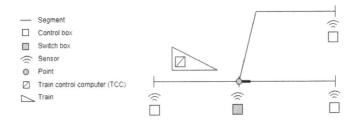

Fig. 2. Railway network with control components and train components.

Railway Network. A railway network (see Fig. 2) is composed of a series of *segments*, *points*, and *sensors*. A segment is a linear section of a railway track.

Each of its two ends can be connected to another segment. A point allows for two different connections to the same segment when the railway branches into two different directions. The segment that can be connected to two different segments is called the *stem* segment while the other two are the *plus* and *minus* segments. The stem segment can only be connected to one of the two other segments at a time. To change the connection, the point must be switched. Each point also has a sensor, which is used to detect a train passing the critical section of the point.

Control Components. The distributed railway interlocking system consists of a *train control computer* (TCC) in each train and a *control box* (CB) at each place where segments can be connected (see Fig. 2). Control boxes placed at points are also called *switch boxes* since they are responsible for switching and locking their associated points.

Control Task. The task of the control system is to ensure the safety of trains in the railway network under control. The trains are considered *safe* if they never *collide* or *derail*. Two trains (potentially) collide with each other if they occupy the same segment at the same time, and a train (potentially) derails if it is passing a switching point or if it enters a point from the wrong side (an unconnected branch).

Overall Control Strategy. The control strategy to ensure safety is as follows. Collisions are prevented by requiring that a train must obtain a *reservation* of a segment before it is allowed to enter it. This means that the train gets exclusive access to the segment, and therefore a segment may only be reserved by one train at a time. Derailment is prevented by requiring that a train obtains a *lock* of a point in the correct position for its route before it is allowed to pass it. Locking a point prevents the point from being switched, so a point can only be switched if no train has obtained a lock for it.

Distributed State Space. Information about obtained reservations and locks are stored in the state space of a train's TCC, which also has information about the train's route and its current position in the route. TCCs obtain these reservations and locks by sending requests to control boxes (see Fig. 3).

In the state space of a control box, the control box stores information about reservations of its associated segments. If the control box is a switch box (i.e. has an associated point), it also stores information about which sections are currently connected by the point and whether the point is locked for a train.

Reserving a Segment. A control box is associated with and responsible for the segments that it is placed by. If a train wishes to request a reservation of a segment, it should send this request to the control boxes placed at each end of that segment. This means that a *full reservation* of a segment is obtained by

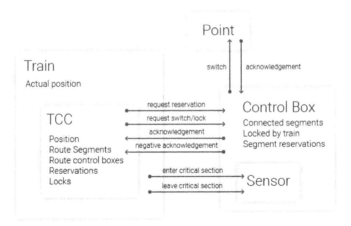

Fig. 3. Interactions between control components and point components.

requesting and successfully receiving the reservation of the segment at each of the segment's two control boxes.

A train only requests a reservation of a segment in its route at a control box in its route. It will only do so if it does not currently have that reservation. Different from [12], three additional conditions have been added:

– The train does not yet have the maximum allowed number of reservations,
– it has reserved all the segments between its current position and the segment in question and
– it always reserves a segment at the control box closest to its position first.

The first mentioned condition makes it possible to experiment with different values when figuring out how to improve the verification process. The two other conditions reduce the number of possible execution sequences by only allowing reservations to be made in the order that the train needs them while moving along its route.

When a control box receives a request for reserving a segment, it checks that

– it is in fact associated with that segment and
– the segment is not already reserved by another train.

If reservation is possible, the control box returns a positive acknowledgement to the requesting TCC, otherwise a negative acknowledgement is returned. If a request is positively acknowledged, both the control box and the TCC update their state spaces accordingly.

Locking a Point. To prevent a train from moving between unconnected segments or passing a switching point, it is necessary to first lock the point in the correct position.

A train sends a lock request to a switch box with the IDs of the segment that it is currently on and the segment that it wants to move to. It only requests locks in its route that it does not already have, and for connections of segments that are adjacent in the route and for which it already has the reservations at the switch box. Similarly to reservations, additional conditions have been added in order to improve the verification process:

- The train does not yet have the maximum allowed number of locks and
- it has already obtained the necessary locks between its current position and the switch box.

The receiving switch box will then check that

- it has not locked its point for another train,
- the received segments are the stem segment and either the plus or the minus segment and
- the received segments have been reserved by the requesting train.

If locking is possible, the switch box will switch the point if the segments are not already connected. It will then lock it and finally return a positive acknowledgement to the requesting train and both will update their state spaces. Otherwise, it will return a negative acknowledgement.

Releasing Reservations and Locks. Sensors detect trains in their critical sections by becoming *active*, and if no train is in the critical section, *passive*. When a sensor goes from active to passive, it triggers the release of reservations and locks at the associated control box. A TCC either uses the Global Positioning System (GPS) or track components signalling their location to know when it should release its reservations and lock data.

4 First Model

Our UPPAAL models have been designed to be re-configurable, so that they can be reused for a whole class of railway networks by only instantiating them with some configuration data: A model instance consists of (1) declarations of constants (provided as configuration data) defining a railway network, control parameters, and initial data of the control components, (2) channels, (3) functions, (4) templates, and (5) a system. The four last items are the same for all instances of the same model, and the same holds for the constant names, but the values of the constants are individual for each instance.

This section describes our first model. Details can be found in the report [17].

Configuration Data. Configuration data consists of (1) integer constants NTRAIN, NCB, NPOINT, NSEG, and NROUTELENGTH defining the number of trains, control boxes, points, segments, and route lengths, respectively, (2) constants resLimit and lockLimit defining the limits of how many reservations and locks each train is allowed to have at a time, and (3) constant arrays defining the railway network and initial data for the state spaces of the TCCs and CBs. For example, the array segRoutes

```
const segV_id segRoutes[NTRAIN][NROUTELENGTH] = {{...},...};
```

stores in segRoutes[i] an array of the segments of the route of the train with ID i. (All components of a specific kind are given an integer ID in the interval $[0; N-1]$, where N is the number of components of that kind.)

Templates. The templates for the railway components are: Train, CB and Point. These templates each have a single parameter named id, which can be instantiated with the ID of a train, a control box, and a point, respectively, resulting in a process modelling the behaviour of the entity with that ID. In addition, an Initializer template and an urgent broadcast channel, start, is used for initiating the initialisation of the instances of the other templates.

Sensors could also have been modelled as instances of a Sensor template and channel synchronisation could then have been used to model a sensor's sensing of passing trains and the forwarding of its status to its associated control box. However, both the communication between a train and a sensor and the communication between a sensor and a control box (which is a wired connection) can be seen as taking no time. Hence, one can model this communication as a single synchronisation directly between the train and the control box, so there is no need for a separate Sensor template.

System Declaration. The generic system declaration

```
system Initializer, Train, CB, Point;
```

creates automatically one Initializer process, a Train(t) process for each train/TCC t, a CB(cb) process for each control box cb, and a Point(p) process for each point p.

Channels. In addition to the broadcast channel used in the initialisation step, eight types of unicast channels, one for each of the interaction arrows shown in Fig. 3, are declared for binary communication between components.

```
chan reqSeg[NCB][NTRAIN][NSEG];
chan reqLock[NCB][NTRAIN][NSEG][NSEG];
chan OK[NTRAIN];
chan notOK[NTRAIN];
chan pass[NCB];
chan passed[NCB];
chan switchPoint[NPOINT];
chan OKp[NCB];
```

For instance, when a train t wants to send a request to a control box cb for a reservation of segment seg, it needs to send its own ID and the segment ID along in the request. This request can be modelled as an output on the channel reqSeg[cb][t][seg]. The control box cb can synchronise with that by making an input on that channel. The channels OK[t] and notOK[t] can then

be used by the control box to send a positive and negative acknowledgement to
t, respectively. pass[cb] and passed[cb] can be used by a train to signal to
a control box cb that it has started and finished passing the sensor associated
with that control box, respectively. switchPoint[p] can be used by a control
box cb to request point p to switch to its other position and OKp[cb] can then
be used by the point to notify that it has been locked in the requested position.

Synchronous communication of data over channels rather than via shared
variables as in [12], ensures that data is never lost or altered before it is received.

The Initializer Template. The Initializer automaton has one edge from
its initial location to its only other location. On this, it synchronises on an
urgent broadcast channel, start, with all Train and CB instances to initiate
their initialisation.

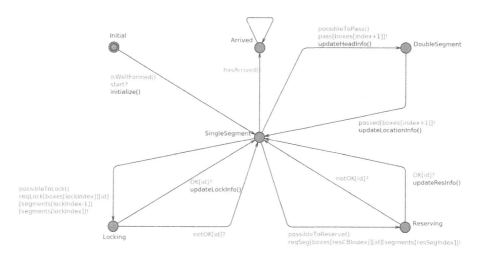

Fig. 4. The first model's Train template.

The Train Template. The Train template declares local variables (1) for
storing the distributed state information described in Sect. 3 for a TCC and
(2) for storing the actual position of the train itself. Below, the most important
variables are explained.

- routeLength stores the number of segments in the train's route.
- segments and boxes are arrays in which the IDs of the segments and the
  control boxes along the train's route are stored, respectively.
- index stores the index of the segment in segments that the train *believes*
  that it is occupying.

- resSegIndex stores the index of the segment in **segments** that needs to be reserved next, and **resCBIndex** stores the index of the control box in **boxes** at which this segment should be reserved for the train.[2] Hence, the next reservation should be of segment **segments[resSegIndex]** at **boxes[resCBIndex]**.
- **lockIndex** stores the index of the control box in **boxes** that needs its associated point to be locked next.
- **curSeg** and **headSeg** stores the IDs of segments *actually* occupied by the train.[3] If the train is only occupying one segment, the ID of that is stored in **curSeg** while **headSeg = -1**. If it is occupying two segments, the segment IDs occupied by the rear and the front of the train are stored in **curSeg** and **headSeg**, respectively. These variables are not used by the controller, but only for formulating the safety properties that should be verified in terms of the train's actual position.

The **Train** automaton for a train with ID **id** can be seen in Fig. 4.

The outgoing edge from the **Initial** location synchronises with **Initilizer** on the **start** channel and then copies configuration data to its local variables. The edge is only enabled if the data are wellformed.

After initialisation, it enters the location **SingleSegment**, which indicates that the train is located on a single segment.

From **SingleSegment**, there are two outgoing (request) edges used for requesting a segment reservation and for requesting a switching/locking of a point at a control box. These edges are guarded by functions that ensure that an operation is only initiated if the conditions stated in Sect. 3 are fulfilled. For instance, the guard for a reservation request is defined by the following function:

```
bool possibleToReserve() {
    return resSegIndex < routeLength && resSegIndex - 1 - index < resLimit;
}
```

This function states that a segment reservation should only be requested if (1) there are more segments in the route that the train has not yet reserved, and (2) the maximum number of allowed reservations will not be exceeded by a reservation.

If a guard is true, the train can send its request to the control box by a synchronisation on the channel intended for that. E.g. for a reservation request, it will be **reqSeg[boxes[resCBIndex]][id][segments[resSegIndex]]**.

After that, the train waits for the control box to either send a positive or negative acknowledgement by synchronisation on **OK[id]** or **notOK[id]**, respectively. After a positive acknowledgement, it also updates its state space. In the case of a reservation, the update is made by the following function:

```
void updateResInfo(){
    resBit = resBit^1;
    resSegIndex = (resBit==0) ? resSegIndex+1 : resSegIndex;
    resCBIndex = (resBit==1) ? resCBIndex+1 : resCBIndex;
}
```

---

[2] As segment reservations and locks of points are made in sequential order in contrast to [12], no data structures for explicitly storing reservations and locks are needed – they can be derived from **resSegIndex**, **resCBIndex**, and **lockIndex**.

[3] Trains are assumed to reside on at most two segments.

Since a segment must be reserved at two control boxes, `resSegIndex` should not be incremented every time a reservation has been obtained, but only every second time. `resBit` stores an integer ranging from 0 to 1, which is flipped every time a reservation has been obtained. `resSegIndex` is then only incremented whenever `resBit` is 0. Similarly, `resCBIndex` should only be incremented every second time: whenever `resSegIndex` is not.

From `SingleSegment`, there is also an edge to `DoubleSegment` and one back from that to `SingleSegment`, for modelling that the train starts and finishes passing a control box. The first edge is guarded by a function checking that the passing is only initiated if the conditions stated for that in Sect. 3 are fulfilled. On both edges the location information of the train is updated.

Finally, there is an edge from `SingleSegment` to the `Arrived` location. This is fired when the train has arrived at its destination, i.e. is on the last segment of its route.

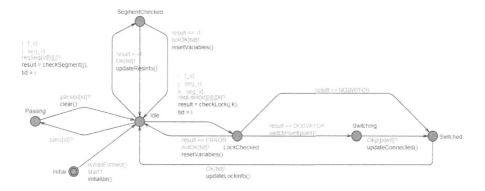

Fig. 5. The first model's CB template.

The CB Template. The CB template declares local variables for storing the distributed state at control boxes as described in Sect. 3. For instance, there is a `segments` array for storing the IDs of up to three segments that can be reserved at that CB, and an array, `res`, of the same length, which in `res[i]` stores the reservation status of the segment in `segments[i]`: The status is −1 if the segment is not reserved by a train, and otherwise it is the ID of the train that has reserved the segment.

The CB automaton for a control box with ID `id` can be seen in Fig. 5.

After initialisation, the CB enters the location `Idle`. From that, there is an outgoing edge on which it waits for a reservation request by synchronisation on a channel intended for that. After a synchronisation, it checks whether the conditions stated in Sect. 3 for granting the requested reservation are fulfilled. Based on the result of that check, it sends either a positive or negative acknowledgement back to the requesting train, `tid`, by synchronisation on `OK[tid]` or `notOK[tid]`, respectively. If the request is granted, the CB updates its own state space and returns to the `Idle` location. The mentioned check is expressed using the following function:

```
int[-1,2] checkSegment(seg_id sid) {
    for(i:int[0,2]) {
        if(segments[i] == sid && res[i] == -1) {
            return i; // sid exists and is not reserved
        }
    }
    return -1; //sid either not found or already reserved
}
```

This function call (`checkSegment(j)`) checks whether it can find the requested segment `j` among the CB's associated segments and that it is not reserved. If the reservation is possible, the index of the segment is returned, otherwise -1 is returned.

From the `Idle` location, there are other similar loops for handling a locking request from a train and for releasing reservations and locks for a train at the control box when the train passes it. The handling of locking requests is more complicated as that may also involve the switching of a point. Due to space limitations, the interested reader is referred to [17] for details.

Note that a CB cannot synchronise for a request from a train or with a passing train, when it is not in `Idle` (i.e. it is already processing a request or being passed by a train). This design ensures that a control box can only communicate with one train at a time.

5   Other System Variants

Two additional variants of the model described in Sect. 4 have been developed to explore how the model can be *restricted* and also *extended*. While the restricted model enforces a more restricted sequence of operations, the extended model introduces a new *cancel* operation, which can be used to cancel reservations and locks.

Restricted Operation Sequence. Although `Trains` are free to request segments and locks and pass CBs whenever they wish as long as the guards are true, it is not always beneficial to do so. For example, if a `Train` has not yet obtained its maximum allowed number of segment reservations or locks, it may choose to either reserve more segments or request the locking of connections of segments that it has already reserved. Hence, to further reduce the number of possible execution sequences, this variant should limit the number of choices a `Train` has.

An example of such a restricted sequence could be formulated as follows: Obtain as many reservations as possible, obtain as many locks as possible and finally move forward in the route for as long as possible.

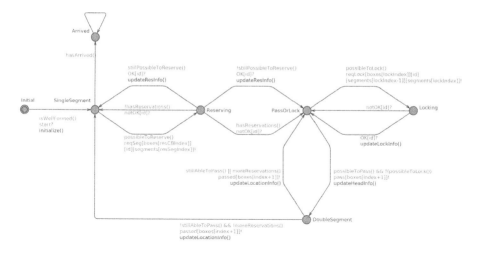

Fig. 6. The `Train` template with restricted options.

To ensure the deterministic execution path, the `SingleSegment` location has been divided into several locations: `SingleSegment`, `Reserving`, `PassOrLock` and `Locking` as seen in Fig. 6. Each of these locations will at most have one enabled edge to another location by considering both the current state and the potential future state of a `Train`. An example of this is when a `Train` is reserving a segment. It will make the reservation request and transition to the `Reserving` location. If the reservation was *successful*, it will go to either the `SingleSegment` location or the `PassOrLock` location depending on whether it can make more reservations or not. If the reservation was *unsuccessful*, then it will also go to either the `PassOrLock` location or the `SingleSegment` location this time depending on whether it already has at least one full reservation or not. The other operations are designed in the same manner by analysing what is possible in the next location before actually transitioning to it.

Extension with Cancel Operation. A situation that has not yet been discussed in the first model is the situation in which a train is unable to proceed on its route due to livelocks. This situation can for instance arise if a `Train` gets the reservation of a segment at one of the segment's associated CBs, while another `Train` gets the reservation of the same segment at the other associated CB. This prevents either of the two `Train`s to get the full reservation of the segment. Therefore, it may be beneficial to have a cancel operation that will allow a `Train` to cancel its obtained reservations and locks if needed.

The general strategy of the cancel operation is that a `Train` cancels reservations and locks in the opposite order of how it obtained them. For a description of how the cancel operation has been implemented, see [17].

6   Verification Properties

This section shows examples of the formalisation in TCTL of safety properties and other relevant properties to be verified. The complete list of properties and their formalisation can be found in [17].

Safety Properties. The safety properties to be verified are 'no collision' and 'no derailment'. Here we show how the former of these is formalised.

'No collision' means that at any time, no two different `Train` instances occupy any of the same segments. This property is formalised as:

```
A[] forall(i:t_id) forall(j:t_id) Initializer.Initialized && i != j imply
    (Train(i).curSeg != Train(j).curSeg) &&
    (Train(i).DoubleSegment imply Train(i).headSeg != Train(j).curSeg) &&
    (Train(i).DoubleSegment && Train(j).DoubleSegment imply Train(i).
        headSeg != Train(j).headSeg)
```

The query states that in all paths, for all states after the initialisation step (i.e when the `Initializer` automaton has reached the location `Initialized`), two `Train` instances with different IDs, i and j, have positions that do not include the same segments. With two position variables (`curSeg` and `headSeg`) for each `Train`, it should be checked that the values of these for one train are different from the values of these for the other train, but the value of `headSeg` for a train should only be checked when the train occupies two segments, i.e. if its automaton is in location `DoubleSegment`, which for a train with ID = i can be checked by the formula `Train(i).DoubleSegment`.

Other Properties. We have formulated other relevant properties to be verified. For example, *consistency properties*, which express the consistency between `Train` state spaces and `CB` state spaces, e.g. that whenever a `Train` has stored a segment reservation at a control box, the corresponding `CB` has stored the same segment as reserved for that train.

We have also formalised a *liveness property* that expresses that there exists a path in which all trains eventually arrive at their destinations:

```
E<> forall(i:t_id) Train(i).Arrived
```

7   Verification Experiments

A series of experiments has been conducted in order to determine whether the properties presented in Sect. 6 can be verified for instances of the three generic models for some specific networks having a typical RELIS 2000 layout[4] and what the verification resource usage is[5]. Furthermore, a comparison of verification metrics of UPPAAL and SAL has been made.

---

[4] The RELIS 2000 system was intended for local railways with up to 20 stations with 1–2 track segments each, connected by single lines, and operated by 2–3 trains.

[5] The experiment models and the verified properties can be found at https://github.com/perlangelaursen/DistributedRailwayControl.

The first set of networks focuses on the scalability of the system where the number of stations varies. A general description can be seen in Fig. 7 where two trains are positioned in each end of a network with n stations. Train t0's route is shown as a dashed line, while the route of t1 is shown as a dotted line.

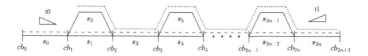

Fig. 7. Network with n stations.

Fig. 8. Nærumbanen with two trains.

The second set of networks is based on the local railway network *Nærumbanen* in Denmark. There are two separate situations for this network. The first situation represents the regular traffic where two trains start in each end of the network while their destinations are in the opposite ends as seen in Fig. 8. The second situation represents the rush hour traffic with an additional train t2. t0 starts at segment s0 with destination at s18, t1 starts at s18 with destination at s10 and t2 starts at s10 with destination at s0.

For each model instance, each of the properties have been verified[6] three times and the averages of the elapsed time and resident memory usage peaks (extracted from UPPAAL's model checker) have been calculated.

Table 1 shows the elapsed time and resident memory usage peaks for verification of the 'no collision' property for both experiment series for each of the model variants (with the limit control parameters set to 2).

The results show that the time and memory usage increases when the size of the network increases. The reason for the exponential growth is due to the increasing number of places where trains can pass each other, which results in more states that need to be checked. The results also show (as expected) that the restricted model generally has the lowest time and memory usage, and that the model including the cancel operation has the highest time and memory usage. This is because the restricted model has fewer interleavings than the other model variants, while the model with the cancel operation has additional states.

---

[6] The experiments were performed with UPPAAL version 4.1.19 on a machine with Arch Linux OS, an AMD Ryzen 2700X processor clocked at 4.0 GHz and 64 GB RAM memory clocked at 2666 MHz.

Table 1. Verification metrics for 'No collision': elapsed time in seconds on the left-hand side of a column and memory usage peak in KB on the right-hand side. All models use limits = 2. Verifications that lasted longer than 24 h (86400 s) were stopped.

Configuration	First model	Restricted model	Model with cancel
Station One	0,013/6515	0,021/8508	0,046/8727
Station Two	0,195/9944	0,127/12579	0,894/16641
Station Four	8/41508	2/39384	34/139527
Station Six	176/152875	48/122787	951/680333
Station Eight	1145/422327	277/276996	6587/2104345
Station Ten	4344/955109	1064/560651	23912/5207884
Station Twelfth	17905/3436440	3151/1360780	71971 / 11269876
Station Fourteen	47898/5680072	8540/2043916	stopped
Station Sixteen	stopped	26376/3225156	
Station Twenty		72986/6961996	
Nærumbanen (2T)	112/122196	20/113553	251/238945
Nærumbanen (3T)	4700/1834129	395/313881	9697/3638703

Within 24 h, the restricted model was verifiable for up to 20 stations, while the two others had to be stopped for 16 and 14 stations, respectively.

It could be interesting to compare our UPPAAL results with the SAL results in [12] for some common network. The railway network in Fig. 13 on P. 30 in [12] can be used for that, as it is the same as our *Station One*. The third model variant in [12] uses the Just-In-Time principle to reserve segments and lock points, which is close to our 'First model' with the limit parameters set to 1, but it differs by being less restrictive with respect to the order of reservations. For a more fair comparison of the verification performance, we have adapted the model from [12] to a new model (Model 4) that follows our more restricted order. Table 2 shows a comparison of the verification performance using the UPPAAL and the SAL model checkers, respectively, for these two models instantiated with the *Station One* network.[7] As it can be seen, UPPAAL had a much better performance only spending 0.017 seconds and 9.5 MB RAM to verify the UPPAAL model, whereas SAL spent around 6 seconds and 105–110 MB RAM for the RSL* model. The same was tried for the *Station Ten* network. In this case, UPPAAL spent 1858 seconds and 675 MB, while RSL*-SAL did not scale up to that.

---

[7] The verification using UPPAAL was this time kindly performed by Signe Geisler on her machine used in [12] to make the comparison possible. In [12], an Intel(R) Core(TM) i7-8650U CPU clocked 1.90 GHz with 31GB of memory was used.

Table 2. Verification metrics for verifying 'No collision' for *Station One* using SAL and UPPAAL.

Model Checker	Model	Time (sec)	Memory (MB)
SAL	RSL* Model 4	6.03–6.18	105–110
UPPAAL	UPPAAL First model with limit 1	0.017	9.5

8   Conclusion

This paper described the modelling and verification of three variants of a real-world distributed railway control system algorithm using UPPAAL.

Having modelled the first variant, it was easy to refine it to one enforcing a more restricted operation sequence, which improved the verification metrics and scalability significantly compared to the former. Extending the first model with an additional operation was even more straightforward than refining it since no changes to existing locations or edges were made, but only new locations and edges were added. Verification of the extended model costs more in terms of space and time than for the two other models, but the new operation introduced in this model is required in real-world systems to prevent livelocks. In conclusion, the first model was modelled in such a way that it was easy to both improve the verification process by refining it, but also extend it if new functionalities were to be introduced. One could also attempt to combine the two new variants by extending the restricted version with a cancel operation. The algorithm should then be re-specified, for example by allowing cancellations as a special operation at any time possible. This would introduce more interleavings, but still be more restricted than the extended model.

Compared to the use of RSL* and SAL in [12], some concepts have been more difficult to express in UPPAAL, which led to some less elegant solutions, e.g. the use of -1 as a filler because no list data structure of variable length was available. On the other hand, UPPAAL's model checker is significantly faster and less memory consuming than the SAL symbolic model checker, and consequently the use of UPPAAL scaled up to larger networks much better. Furthermore, UPPAAL's graphical tool generally made the modelling process more visual and straightforward, while the simulator and diagnostic trace function also made it simple to debug and test the different model variants.

In future work, we wish to explore the use of other tools, e.g. UMC, nuXmv, SPIN, and mCRL2, to model and verify the same railway control system and compare with that. It could also be interesting to experiment with variants of the UPPAAL models using shared variables for communication instead of channels, and to extend the model with the possibility of message loss (due to wireless communication) and check that the system still remains safe. Furthermore, it could be interesting to experiment with stochastic variants of the UPPAAL models and use UPPAAL STRATEGO [7] to synthesise schedulers.

Acknowledgements. We would like to express our gratitude to Jan Peleska from whom the case study originates and with whom the second author had the great pleasure to verify the same case study by theorem proving [14]. We are grateful to Signe Geisler for repeating some of our experiments on her laptop making it possible to compare the verification performance of some of our verification experiments using UPPAAL with some of her experiments using SAL. Finally, we would like to thank the anonymous reviewers for useful suggestions for the presentation.

References

1. Basile, D., et al.: On the industrial uptake of formal methods in the railway domain - a survey with stakeholders. In: Furia, C.A., Winter, K. (eds.) Integrated Formal Methods, pp. 20–29. Springer, Heidelberg (2018). https://doi.org/10.1007/978-3-319-98938-9_2
2. Basile, D., ter Beek, M.H., Ferrari, A., Legay, A.: Modelling and analysing ERTMS L3 moving block railway signalling with Simulink and UPPAAL SMC. In: Larsen, K.G., Willemse, T. (eds.) FMICS 2019. LNCS, vol. 11687, pp. 1–21. Springer, Cham (2019). https://doi.org/10.1007/978-3-030-27008-7_1
3. ter Beek, M.H., Fantechi, A., Gnesi, S., Mazzanti, F.: A state/event-based model-checking approach for the analysis of abstract system properties. Sci. Comput. Program. 76(2), 119–135 (2011)
4. Behrmann, G., David, A., Larsen, K.G.: A tutorial on UPPAAL. In: Bernardo, M., Corradini, F. (eds.) SFM-RT 2004. LNCS, vol. 3185, pp. 200–236. Springer, Heidelberg (2004). https://doi.org/10.1007/978-3-540-30080-9_7
5. CENELEC - European Committee for Electrotechnical Standardization: EN 50128:2011 - Railway applications - Communications, signalling and processing systems - Software for railway control and protection systems (2011)
6. Comptier, M., Deharbe, D., Perez, J.M., Mussat, L., Pierre, T., Sabatier, D.: Safety analysis of a CBTC system: a rigorous approach with Event-B. In: Fantechi, A., Lecomte, T., Romanovsky, A. (eds.) Reliability, Safety, and Security of Railway Systems. Modelling, Analysis, Verification, and Certification. LNCS, vol. 10598, pp. 148–159. Springer, Heidelberg (2017). https://doi.org/10.1007/978-3-319-68499-4_10
7. David, A., Jensen, P.G., Larsen, K.G., Mikučionis, M., Taankvist, J.H.: UPPAAL STRATEGO. In: Baier, C., Tinelli, C. (eds.) TACAS 2015. LNCS, vol. 9035, pp. 206–211. Springer, Heidelberg (2015). https://doi.org/10.1007/978-3-662-46681-0_16
8. Fantechi, A.: Twenty-five years of formal methods and railways: what next? In: Counsell, S., Núñez, M. (eds.) SEFM 2013. LNCS, vol. 8368, pp. 167–183. Springer, Cham (2014). https://doi.org/10.1007/978-3-319-05032-4_13
9. Fantechi, A., Gnesi, S., Haxthausen, A., van de Pol, J., Roveri, M., Treharne, H.: SaRDIn - a safe reconfigurable distributed interlocking. In: Proceedings of 11th World Congress on Railway Research (WCRR 2016). Ferrovie dello Stato Italiane, Milano (2016)
10. Fantechi, A., Haxthausen, A.E., Nielsen, M.B.R.: Model checking geographically distributed interlocking systems using UMC. In: 25th Euromicro International Conference on Parallel, Distributed and Network-Based Processing (PDP), pp. 278–286 (2017). https://doi.org/10.1109/PDP.2017.66

11. Fantechi, A., Haxthausen, A.: Safety interlocking as a distributed mutual exclusion problem. In: Howar, F., Barnat, J. (eds.) Formal Methods for Industrial Critical Systems. LNCS, vol. 11119, pp. 52–66. Springer, Heidelberg (2018). https://doi.org/10.1007/978-3-030-00244-2_4

12. Geisler, S., Haxthausen, A.E.: Stepwise development and model checking of a distributed interlocking system using RAISE. Formal Aspects Comput. 1–39 (2020). https://doi.org/10.1007/s00165-020-00507-2

13. Hansen, H.H., Ketema, J., Luttik, B., Mousavi, M.R., van de Pol, J.: Towards model checking executable UML specifications in mCRL2. Innov. Syst. Softw. Eng. 6(1), 83–90 (2010). https://doi.org/10.1007/s11334-009-0116-1

14. Haxthausen, A.E., Peleska, J.: Formal development and verification of a distributed railway control system. IEEE Trans. Softw. Eng. 26, 687–701 (2000)

15. Hoang, T.S., Butler, M., Reichl, K.: The hybrid ERTMS/ETCS level 3 case study. In: Butler, M., Raschke, A., Hoang, T.S., Reichl, K. (eds.) ABZ 2018. LNCS, vol. 10817, pp. 251–261. Springer, Cham (2018). https://doi.org/10.1007/978-3-319-91271-4_17

16. James, P., et al.: Verification of scheme plans using CSP∥B. In: Counsell, S., Núñez, M. (eds.) SEFM 2013. LNCS, vol. 8368, pp. 189–204. Springer, Cham (2014). https://doi.org/10.1007/978-3-319-05032-4_15

17. Laursen, P.L., Trinh, V.A.T.: Formal modelling and verification of distributed railway control systems. Technical report, DTU Compute, Technical University of Denmark (2019). https://github.com/perlangelaursen/DistributedRailwayControl/blob/master/s144449s144456-MSc-Thesis.pdf

18. Limbrée, C., Cappart, Q., Pecheur, C., Tonetta, S.: Verification of railway interlocking - compositional approach with OCRA. In: Lecomte, T., Pinger, R., Romanovsky, A. (eds.) RSSRail 2016. LNCS, vol. 9707, pp. 134–149. Springer, Cham (2016). https://doi.org/10.1007/978-3-319-33951-1_10

19. Mazzanti, F., Ferrari, A.: Ten diverse formal models for a CBTC automatic train supervision system. In: Gallagher, J.P., van Glabbeek, R., Serwe, W. (eds.) Proceedings Third Workshop on Models for Formal Analysis of Real Systems and Sixth International Workshop on Verification and Program Transformation. EPTCS, vol. 268, pp. 104–149 (2018). https://doi.org/10.4204/EPTCS.268.4, http://arxiv.org/abs/1803.08668

20. RAISE Language Group: The RAISE Specification Language. The BCS Practitioners Series, Prentice Hall Int. (1992)

21. Vu, L.H., Haxthausen, A.E., Peleska, J.: Formal modelling and verification of interlocking systems featuring sequential release. Sci. Comput. Program. 133(Part 2), 91–115 (2017). http://www.sciencedirect.com/science/article/pii/S0167642316300570, https://doi.org/10.1016/j.scico.2016.05.010

22. Yi, W., Pettersson, P., Daniels, M.: Automatic verification of real-time communicating systems by constraint-solving. Formal Description Techniques VII. IAICT, pp. 243–258. Springer, Boston (1995). https://doi.org/10.1007/978-0-387-34878-0_18

New Distribution Paradigms for Railway Interlocking

Jan Peleska[✉]

Department of Mathematics and Computer Science,
University of Bremen, Bremen, Germany
peleska@uni-bremen.de

Abstract. We discuss a new "flavour" of distributed interlocking systems, where the proper interlocking logic is allocated on cloud computers using conventional (i.e. commercial-off-the-shelf) multi-core hardware and operating systems. The servers in the cloud communicate with intelligent track elements over internet connections. Interlocking logic may even be geographically distributed on more than one server farm, introducing a new dimension of fault tolerance. This technology has been announced 2018 by Siemens Mobility, and the certification is currently underway. In this paper, it is analysed how the new distribution concept affects verification, validation, and certification. In particular, the complexity of the cloud system suggests to create a collection of scenario models instead of a single comprehensive model specifying the expected behaviour of the system. The use of scenario models is well known from the autonomous vehicle domain, but, to our best knowledge, it is the first time that this approach is also applied in the railway domain. We discuss verification-related and test-related implications of the scenario approach. In particular, solutions are proposed for determining whether a collection of scenario models is complete, and for deciding whether sufficient test coverage has been achieved for a given scenario. The material presented here is based on a collaboration between Siemens and Verified Systems International, a company specialised on verification and validation of safety-critical systems.

Keywords: Railway interlocking systems · Distributed systems · Cloud-computing · Safety · Verification

1 Introduction

1.1 Motivation

The introduction of new technologies for railway control systems may yield significant advantages regarding cost reduction, availability, or traffic throughput, but they always introduce new challenges regarding verification and validation

---

This work has been partially funded by the Deutsche Forschungsgemeinschaft (DFG, German Research Foundation) – project number 407708394.

T. Margaria and B. Steffen (Eds.): ISoLA 2020, LNCS 12478, pp. 434–448, 2020.
https://doi.org/10.1007/978-3-030-61467-6_28

(V&V) and certification effort. On the other hand, the modernisation of the European railway network certainly requires innovation to reach the ambitious goals defined by the European Union for both rolling stock and passenger transportation [1]. Therefore, clinging to the current state of practise in order to avoid the V&V-related and certification-related issues is certainly not an option.

In this light, we analyse a new distribution paradigm for railway control systems which has been designed by Siemens Mobility [28]. By allocating the railway control logic on server farms in the cloud, using COTS hardware and COTS operating systems, obvious availability and scalability advantages are gained. The interlocking logic allocated in the cloud communicates with intelligent track element controllers over internet connections. The controllers operate points, signals, and serve as track vacancy detectors, and they control their local safety constraints. The service software supporting this approach is called *Distributed Smart Safe System DS^3* and its certification is currently underway.

1.2   Main Contributions

The main contributions of this paper are threefold.

- We report on the DS^3 system design and highlight some complex techniques needed to guarantee safety despite the utilisation of COTS hardware and operating systems.
- It is explained how the resulting system complexity leads to the elaboration of a *scenario model collection* instead of a global comprehensive model specifying expected DS^3 behaviour. We advocate this approach since it has been shown in the domain of autonomous vehicles that this is unavoidable for systems of a certain system complexity.
- The scenario-based approach is studied from the testing perspective. We show how testing can help to check the completeness of the scenario collection, and how per-scenario test suites with adequate test strength can be constructed.

This contribution is intended as a position paper, where future developments are predicted and suitable methods are advocated. We refrain from presenting many technical details, but try to highlight the crucial aspects of our chain of arguments in an informal way that seems adequate to stimulate the important discussion concerning these future trends.

1.3   Overview

In Sect. 2, the DS^3 system by Siemens is presented, and some of its design features are highlighted. The V&V-related and certification-related challenges resulting from this novel system design are described in Sect. 3. In Sect. 4, it is explained how to overcome some of the main challenges. Section 5 contains the conclusion.

Throughout the text, we refer to related work where appropriate.

2   Cloud-Based Railway Control

2.1   Overall Concept

The *Distributed Smart Safe System DS*^{3} has been designed by Siemens Mobility [28]. Its main characteristic is the separation of global railway control logic and local track element control, such that the former can be deployed on cloud servers, while only the latter are located in the field (see Fig. 1). DS^3 is intended as a universal service layer, so that all variants of railway control logic, such as radio block centres (RBC), interlocking (IXL), occupation control systems (OCS) can be integrated as safe applications into the DS^3 service layer.

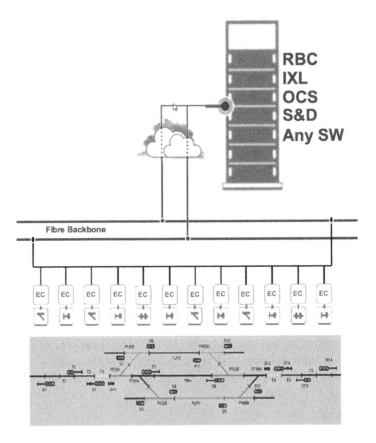

RBC
IXL
OCS
S&D
Any SW

Fibre Backbone

Fig. 1. DS^3 system architecture (from [28]).

The obvious advantages of cloud-based railway control are

– Increased availability through fault tolerance mechanisms inside a server farm. The field of fault-tolerant distributed computing has been thoroughly researched since the 1980ies [7]. Load balancing, standby and switchover techniques in case of server failure, as well as dynamic addition of memory and CPU cores to stressed applications are considered as standard in today's cloud service layers.

- Increased availability through *interaction between server farms.* DS^3 is capable of synchronising the control logic across *several* server farms, with the intention to provide geographically distributed backup and standby capabilities.
- Improved performance through utilisation of latest server hardware.
- Increased scalability through addition of servers.
- Reduced hardware costs and software costs through COTS servers and use of conventional operating systems, as well as standard software libraries for non-critical application components.
- Independence from specific hardware architectures through virtualisation.
- Re-use of legacy software is simplified by running it in emulators. This type of execution is enabled by the high performance of cloud servers.

A prerequisite for this approach is that the track element controllers have Ethernet-based communication interfaces and possess local fail-stop capabilities. This allows for geographical distribution of the overall railway control system and relieves the cloud applications from safety-related monitoring of track-side components. These capabilities have been introduced by Siemens to all wayside element controllers (point controllers, signal controllers, track vacancy detectors, level crossing controllers)[1].

It should be emphasised that this distribution concept differs significantly from other solutions, where the *control logic* is distributed over trains and wayside controllers, aiming to avoid centralised control (see, for example, [10]): in DS^3, the *view* on the control logic remains centralised. The distribution on many cloud servers and even on several server farms is made only to achieve safety by redundancy and to enhance availability and scalability. The *visible* distribution consists in the removal of the control logic from the train stations to remote data centres in the cloud.

2.2   Design Aspects

Coded Monoprocessor Principle. From the perspective of railway safety and the applicable software-related standard [2], the approach to run safety-relevant railway control logic on standard hardware and standard operating systems is unusual. For good reasons, no attempt is made to certify COTS hardware and the underlying standard operating systems (Windows and Linux). Instead, the essential method for achieving safety guaranties is by systematic exploitation of redundancy. Safety-related application software is executed concurrently in cyclic

---

[1] See, for example, https://www.mobility.siemens.com/global/en/portfolio/rail/auto mation/signaling-on-board-and-crossing-products/axle-counting-systems.html, where 2-out-of-2 track vacancy detectors are described.

fashion on redundant emulators implementing the concept of the *coded mono-processor* [8,19]. In DS^3, the redundant emulators executing a critical application run on different cores in virtual machines with different operating systems and store corresponding data at different addresses (Fig. 2). The results calculated by the redundant application code are enhanced by

- work flow digest values (did both applications run through the same path of the control flow graph?),
- dynamic data signatures (do the redundant results refer to the same processing cycle?), and
- encryption with complementary keys (the result can only be used if both applications calculated the corresponding complementary values).

As a result, two-redundant applications will together realise one fail-stop component. Increasing the degree of redundancy enables the creation of fault-tolerant and safe applications.

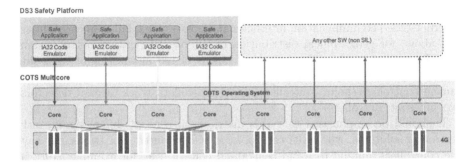

Fig. 2. Application of the coded mono processor principle in DS^3 (from [28]).

Clock Synchronisation. To solve synchronisation issues, a system-wide logical clock tick is distributed. This tick corresponds to emulator execution cycles, so that emulators running the same application process corresponding cycles between two given ticks. Based on the logical clock, it is ensured that corresponding emulators receive input in the same sequence. For railway control systems, the logical clock needs to a have a well-defined correspondence to a physical clock, since real-time events need to be supervised. For example, the actual speed of approaching trains, braking curves, and the point in time for switching signals or blocking level crossings to traffic and pedestrians needs to be supervised in real time. As a consequence, the logical clock tick must have a fixed relationship to physical time. In particular, drift of the logical clock in comparison to real physical time must be avoided. To this end, redundant clocks (local computer time and remote NTP time sources) are evaluated and a clock synchronisation and drift detection algorithm similar to Cristian's algorithm [4] is applied.

Safe and Secure Communication Protocols. For communicating control decisions to wayside elements and for receiving status data from the latter, safe and secure protocols are executed between the cloud gateways and the wayside controllers. No assumptions about the dependability of the *"grey channel"*, that is, the internet connection between cloud and wayside controllers are made. The application-level protocols apply session keys, encryption, safety codes, and redundant transmission.

Since the cloud intranet is based on COTS hardware and software, it also has to be considered as a new variant of a grey channel. Therefore, a novel message protocol format for local cloud communication has been designed, allowing to detect data corruption, data from corrupt servers, and outdated messages. Since very many messages are exchanged between railway control applications and DS^3 services, the message broker, publisher, and subscriber paradigm has been applied.

Configuration and Dynamic Re-configuration. An important part of the DS^3 service software has the task to provide configuration services. Additionally, services supporting re-configuration after fail-stop events or whole server failures are provided.

Safety Pattern Library. To facilitate the re-use of software designs ensuring fail-stop behaviour, a library of generic safety-patterns has been designed. New safety-related applications are created by first instantiating a suitable pattern from the library and then adding the application-specific code.

3   Challenges Regarding V&V and Certification

Main Challenge. It is not surprising that the advantages of cloud-based railway control solutions listed above come with a downside concerning V&V, safety case construction, and certification effort: the design features listed above indicate that the DS^3 software is highly non-trivial and has considerable size.

The main problem affecting the effort for V&V and certification is one currently discussed mainly in the context of autonomous systems, but – to our best knowledge – quite new in the field of railway control:

> *The DS^3 complexity suggests to use a collection of scenario models for specifying expected system behaviour, because the elaboration of a comprehensive formal (or at least formalised) model of the required system behaviour seems to be infeasible.*

Impact of the Scenario-Based Approach. Though at first glance surprising, this assessment is well-justified, mainly because the different techniques used in the system design and implemented in the DS^3 software affect each other. For example, a reconfiguration process due to a failed server affects the execution of the redundant fail-stop applications, and both are affected by a clock drift detected in parallel.

The utilisation of scenario models has considerable impact on the effort to analyse which normal behaviour system tests should be designed: for example, is it sufficient to verify the behaviour of a redundant application alone, or should the system test always consider concurrent re-configurations and/or concurrent clock adjustments which are specified in different scenarios? Regarding exceptional behaviour, how many simultaneous faults in different DS^3 components should be considered during verification? How many variants of hardware and operating system faults should be simulated for verifying fail-stop behaviour?

Consequences. Due to the absence of a comprehensive specification model, the effort to elaborate suitable integration and system test suites is very high. In particular, the validation effort regarding the comprehensiveness of the test suites and justifying this comprehensiveness in front of the certification authorities is quite costly. The collection of scenario models is hard to check with respect to completeness, and the system test elaboration is more complex as soon as the tests cannot be constrained to a single scenario.

These observations raise the question whether formal mechanised V&V approaches can help to decrease this effort while still guaranteeing at least the same level overall system quality (in particular, safety). This is discussed in the next section.

4   V&V Solutions

4.1   Scenario-Based Testing Approach

From our experience with safety-relevant avionic, automotive, and railway systems, we expect that the growing complexity of these systems will make the switch from comprehensive models to collections of scenario models unavoidable in the near future. For the autonomous vehicle domain, this seems to be accepted already today [9,17], and we can adopt testing approaches from there to other domains where the construction of comprehensive reference models has become infeasible as well.

A scenario model is a formal structural and behavioural model which is usually parameterised in the style of a template, allowing for different instantiations [17]. Since these models are formal, they allow for automated model-based test case generation which can also handle the identification of relevant instantiations with different parameter combinations [18,22,23]. Scenario models, however, only describe *subsets* of behaviours that may occur when the target system is executed in its operational environment. The input/output languages of different scenario models may have non-empty intersections: one scenario, for example, may describe how redundant DS^3 emulators behave under normal conditions, another scenario describes how they are affected by another emulator joining the redundant configuration during a re-configuration action. The input/output interfaces involved in these two scenarios obviously have a non-empty intersection. Moreover, input/output traces observable in one scenario may also be part of the other. This is the crucial distinction between scenario models and multiple models specifying the expected behaviour of a very large system. In the latter case, the models refer to disjoint behaviours of different system functions with no or just a few interfaces in between.

As pointed out in [9], two main aspects need to be considered in the scenario-based testing approach:

1. Is the library of scenarios complete, or could there still be a situation occurring during real operation which is not covered by any scenario and therefore still remains untested?
2. For a given scenario model: do the test cases result in sufficient test strength, that is, are they well suited to uncover deviations of the system implementation from the expected behaviour specified in the scenario model?

We will discuss these crucial aspects in the paragraphs to follow.

4.2   Validation of Scenario Completeness

Validation by Requirements Tracing. A first obvious step for checking the completeness of scenario collections is performed by *requirements tracing*. Every system requirement needs to be captured in at least one scenario. Formalised modelling languages like SysML [20] support the tracing of requirements to model elements, facilitating the verification of complete requirements coverage over all scenario models. This, however, is not sufficient for systems where comprehensive formal models are infeasible: in these cases, we can expect that also the requirements capture has been incomplete, or at least that the applicability of a requirement has not been fully specified for relevant situations.

Validation by Random Testing. To solve this problem, we advocate a solution suggested in [9] for testing autonomous vehicles, with adaptations to the railway control domain. The adaptations are necessary because in autonomous vehicle testing, sample data from many driving experiments is already available, while for a new system development such as DS^3, this data has first to be created.

To this end, we consider stochastically independent random input sequences to the DS^3 system and associate them with the sequence of *observed* DS^3 outputs. The resulting I/O-sequence π is called a *random test*. The test *matches* with a scenario model Sc_i, if π is in the I/O-language of Sc_i for a given parameterisation. Assume that each known scenario Sc_i matches with some probability p_i with a random test π. If the complete collection of scenarios were known, say $Sc_1, \ldots, Sc_n$, then the sum of these matching probabilities would be 1, that is, $\sum_{i=1}^{n} p_i = 1$. We now consider a random test as a *sample* of a statistical experiment **SE**:

- Creating a random test π corresponds to drawing a sample.
- Each drawn sample is matched with the scenarios $Sc_1, \ldots, Sc_n$.
- The experiment determines the number of samples we need to draw in order to match at least once with every scenario.

Let X be a random variable stating the number of independent random tests that we need to perform such that every scenario matches with at least one test. Then the expected value $E(X)$ of X gives us an estimate for how many samples would be needed to match with all the scenarios. The variance σ of X gives us an indication about the quality of the estimate $E(X)$. This expected value and its variance also need to be determined experimentally, by performing **SE** several times and calculating the mean value $\overline{X}$ of the X-values obtained in each experiment, thereby also obtaining an estimate for σ. The resulting values come with a *confidence level* depending on how many repetitions of experiment **SE** have been performed.

Suppose now that a test *fails* in the sense that it cannot be matched with any scenario. Then either

- a failure in the system under test (i.e. the DS^3 system) has been detected, or
- the behaviour is correct according to some scenario that has not yet been identified.

The decision whether a test fails or not (the component taking this decision is often called the *test oracle*) can be performed automatically, as soon as formal scenario models are available: failure occurs when a fragment of the observed input/output trace is not contained in *any* of the scenario model I/O-languages.[2] In contrast to this, the question whether the failed test indicates an error in the system being tested or a missing scenario having this fragment in its I/O-language requires manual analysis. We consider the effort for these analyses, however, to be considerably less than the effort required to elaborate one comprehensive model for expected system behaviour. It should also be taken into account, that – even in the case where the construction of a comprehensive model is feasible – effort is required to validate this model with respect to its correct representation of all system requirements. In model-based testing, when a test generated from the model fails while being executed against the target system, it always has to be checked whether this is not a *false alarm*: it may be the case that the underlying requirements have not been correctly represented in the mode used for test generation, while the implementation is correct with respect to these requirements.

Since failing tests are useful for either revealing system failures or missing scenarios, we exploit this fact in a slightly modified experiment, where there is some unknown scenario, say Sc_n, among the $Sc_1, \ldots, Sc_n$, so that our current collection $Sc_1, \ldots, Sc_{n-1}$ is not yet aware of Sc_n's existence. If there is a hypothesis about the matching probability p_n of Sc_n with a given random test, the expected value $E(X)$ tells us again after how many samples a test would fail

---

[2] More details about the model-based construction of test oracles are explained in [21].

and indicate Sc_n's existence. This is possible since $E(X)$ does not depend on whether we are aware of Sc_n or not, but only on Sc_n's occurrence probability p_n. Conversely, if no tests fail for $E(X)$ many samples, we can say that with a certain confidence level obtained for the calculation of $E(X)$, *there is no further scenario, or its matching probability p_n is smaller than assumed.*

The experiment **SE** is an instance of the *Coupon Collector's Problem (CCP)*[3] For the CCP (and therefore, for our experiment **SE**), the expected value of X can be calculated according to [6] by

$$E(X) = \int_0^\infty \left(1 - \prod_{i=1}^n (1 - e^{-p_1 x})\right) dx$$

In [9], it is recommended to used Monte Carlo simulations for executing multiple versions of experiment **SE** and determine $E(X)$ and its confidence level. Obviously, the confidence level for having captured all scenarios is improved with the number of executed solutions, and small occurrence probabilities p_n require more simulations to achieve a given confidence level.

Summarising, random test experiments of the form described above can reveal any missing scenario, if we perform these tests long enough. Since we need to complete the tests at a certain point in time, it is reassuring that we can at least say that the absence of missing scenarios has been verified with a given confidence level, under the hypothesis that the occurrence probability of any missing scenario is greater or equal to some value p_n. The tests to be performed for this purpose have "dual use", since they may also reveal violations by the system under test against the behaviour specified in some known scenario.

4.3 Complete Per-scenario Test Suites

The question how to decide whether a scenario model has been sufficiently covered by the test cases performed can be adequately answered by means of the theory of *complete test suites*. A test suite is complete if it is able to uncover any violation of behaviour specified in a reference model, and if every correct behaviour is accepted. For practical application, a *fault domain* is specified describing the possible deviations of the SUT from the given reference model. Typically, a fault domain specifies hypotheses about

- how many more distinguishable states may be contained in the SUT, when compared to the reference model,
- the minimal solution size of branch conditions over floating point data types[4], or
- which mutations of the reference model may have been (involuntarily) implemented in the SUT.

---

[3] The name is motivated by the collection of soccer player pictures provided with some product and the question how many products need to be bought in order get at least one picture of every player.

[4] For example, condition $0 < x \wedge x < 10$ has size 10.

The completeness assertion is then made under the hypothesis that the true SUT behaviour is captured by one behaviour contained in the fault domain.

The check of behavioural correctness is usually based on a *conformance relation*, such as I/O-language equivalence, language inclusion, or some other refinement relation. With fault domain and conformance relation at hand, *finite* complete test suites can be constructed for reference models given in many different modelling formalisms, such as finite state machines [3,5,12,27,29], labelled transition systems and associated process algebras [24], symbolic state machines, Kripke structures, and other formalisms offering more than just discrete data types [14,26]. As an alternative to model conformance, completeness can also be specified in relation to given requirements expressed by the reference model [13]. For symbolic methods with conceptually infinite state spaces, finite complete test suites are obtained by means of equivalence class constructions, reducing the state space of the reference model without "losing" any behavioural variants [15]. The symbolic methods used for test case and test data generation can also deal with parameterised specifications [22].

The smaller size of scenario models in comparison to comprehensive models facilitates the application of complete test suites, which were often criticised in the past for leading to test suites of infeasible size. The improved understanding of equivalence class constructions [14,15,26], however, has shown that typical scenario models as used for DS^3 can be adequately handled when selecting a suitable complete test generation method. This claim has been experimentally supported by case studies from the railway domain [25] and other fields of embedded control [16].

Since completeness guarantees for finite test suites are only given with respect to certain fault hypotheses, it remains to

- discuss how to ensure that the SUT is really part of the specified fault domain, or
- analyse the remaining test suite strength in situations where the fault hypotheses are not fulfilled by the SUT.

Ensuring the adequateness of the fault domain is possible, as soon as the SUT software code is available – this is also the case of the DS^3 system, where all development artefacts, including code, have been analysed during V&V. Using suitable static analysers, questions about the number of internal states or the size of branch conditions can be easily extracted from the code. If, however, the fault domain has been specified by means of a finite set of mutants, the questions whether the SUT behaves correctly or like one of these mutants is much harder to answer. If the mutant behaviour could be transformed into code, then, in principle, the SUT code could be model checked against the mutant code, using tools like CBMC[5]. If this were feasible, however, the SUT code could also be model checked against the reference model instead against a mutant, and then the mutants would be superfluous. We conclude from this discussion that mutation-based fault domains are less useful for our purposes.

---

[5] https://www.cprover.org/cbmc/.

If it cannot be decided whether the SUT is really part of the fault domain, it is reassuring to know that, when combining complete equivalence class construction methods with random input data selections from each class, the resulting test strength when checking an SUT outside the fault domain is – while no longer being complete – still significantly higher than that obtained by random test suites [16].

4.4   Cloud-Based Testing

In the context of autonomous systems, it is considered as an accepted fact that the number of test cases to be checked in order to verify safety-aspects of an autonomous system is too high to be executed on the target system alone [9]. We expect the same for railway control systems of the near future, in particular when autonomous rolling stock trains will be allowed to pass the same routes as passenger trains. It is advocated to perform these tests in the cloud, exploiting the availability of many CPU cores and sufficient memory. There is a critical question associated with cloud-based testing.

> How can we get certification credit for tests claimed to have been passed by the SUT, but which have run on cloud servers instead of the original hardware?

For DS^3, the answer is simple: the systems runs on cloud servers anyway, so testing it on such servers does not change the operational environment. The situation is different for wayside controllers. These run on specialised hardware, so that the machine code running in the target system usually differs from the code executed in the cloud for test purposes.

A promising approach to solve this problem is given by *virtual prototypes (VP)* [11]: The cloud server executes an emulator simulating CPU cores, registers, cache and memory of the original hardware, so that the original machine code of the embedded control can be executed in the emulator with its original memory address map. While this approach is technically feasible and quite promising, it remains to be shown that the VP can also be *validated* for certification purposes according to the requirements of the standard [2, 6.7.4.5]: it has to be shown that the VP does not simplify the real hardware environment and will not mask any failures that would be revealed on the target hardware.

5   Conclusion

We have presented a new distributed railway control system designed by Siemens Mobility, which is currently being certified. The main characteristic of this system is the deployment of the railway control logic (for RBC, IXL and other applications) on cloud server farms, running on COTS hardware and operating systems. It has been explained how safety can still be guaranteed in such an "unconventional" setting by exploiting redundancy in a systematic way. This leads, however, to a highly non-trivial system design and associated software which in turn affects the costs for V&V and certification.

In this light, we have discussed the benefits of scenario model collections as an alternative to the construction of one comprehensive model specifying the expected system behaviour. The scenario-based approach is currently the preferred method for specifying autonomous systems, and we predict that the growing complexity of railway control systems will also make this technique unavoidable in the railway domain.

Focusing on testing as the main task of V&V, it has been shown how the completeness of scenario model collections can be checked and how per-scenario test suites with adequate test strength can be created. We predict a considerable increase of test suite sizes for future railway control systems. Therefore it is useful to consider testing in the cloud, so that very large test suites can be executed in shorter time. It is expected that the technique of virtual prototypes will be crucial to obtain certification credit for these tests.

References

1. Roadmap to a Single European Transport Area - Towards a competitive and resource efficient transport system. Technical report, European Union - EUR-Lex (2011). https://eur-lex.europa.eu/legal-content/EN/TXT/?uri=celex: 52011DC0144, white paper
2. CENELEC: EN 50128:2011 Railway applications - Communication, signalling and processing systems - Software for railway control and protection systems (2011)
3. Chow, T.S.: Testing software design modeled by finite-state machines. IEEE Trans. Softw. Eng. **SE-4**(3), 178–186 (1978)
4. Cristian, F.: Probabilistic clock synchronization. Distrib. Comput. **3**(3), 146–158 (1989). https://doi.org/10.1007/BF01784024
5. Dorofeeva, R., El-Fakih, K., Yevtushenko, N.: An improved conformance testing method. In: Wang, F. (ed.) FORTE 2005. LNCS, vol. 3731, pp. 204–218. Springer, Heidelberg (2005). https://doi.org/10.1007/11562436_16
6. Ferrante, N., Saltalamacchia, M.: The coupon collector's problem. Materials matemàtics, pp. 1–35 (2014). http://mat.uab.cat/matmat_antiga/PDFv2014/v2014n02.pdf
7. Gärtner, F.C.: Fundamentals of fault-tolerant distributed computing in asynchronous environments. ACM Comput. Surv. **31**(1), 1–26 (1999). https://doi.org/10.1145/311531.311532
8. Gülker, J.: Certification of the coded monoprocessor as ATP according to European standards. In: Proceedings of the 7th International Conference on Automated People Movers 1999, pp. 96–101. IDA (1999)
9. Hauer, F., Schmidt, T., Holzmüller, B., Pretschner, A.: Did we test all scenarios for automated and autonomous driving systems? In: 2019 IEEE Intelligent Transportation Systems Conference, ITSC 2019, Auckland, New Zealand, 27–30 October 2019, pp. 2950–2955. IEEE (2019). https://doi.org/10.1109/ITSC.2019.8917326
10. Haxthausen, A.E., Peleska, J.: Formal development and verification of a distributed railway control system. IEEE Trans. Softw. Eng. **26**(8), 687–701 (2000)

11. Herdt, V., Große, D., Drechsler, R.: Fast and accurate performance evaluation for RISC-V using virtual prototypes. In: 2020 Design, Automation & Test in Europe Conference & Exhibition, DATE 2020, Grenoble, France, 9–13 March 2020, pp. 618–621. IEEE (2020). https://doi.org/10.23919/DATE48585.2020.9116522

12. Hierons, R.M.: Testing from a nondeterministic finite state machine using adaptive state counting. IEEE Trans. Comput. **53**(10), 1330–1342 (2004). https://doi.org/10.1109/TC.2004.85. http://doi.ieeecomputersociety.org/10.1109/TC.2004.85

13. Huang, W., Özoguz, S., Peleska, J.: Safety-complete test suites. Softw. Qual. J. **27**(2), 589–613 (2019). https://doi.org/10.1007/s11219-018-9421-y

14. Huang, W., Peleska, J.: Complete model-based equivalence class testing for nondeterministic systems. Formal Aspects Comput. **29**(2), 335–364 (2017). https://doi.org/10.1007/s00165-016-0402-2

15. Huang, W., Peleska, J.: Model-based testing strategies and their (in)dependence on syntactic model representations. STTT **20**(4), 441–465 (2018). https://doi.org/10.1007/s10009-017-0479-9

16. Hübner, F., Huang, W., Peleska, J.: Experimental evaluation of a novel equivalence class partition testing strategy. Softw. Syst. Model. **18**(1), 423–443 (2019). https://doi.org/10.1007/s10270-017-0595-8, published online 2017

17. Hungar, H.: Scenario-based validation of automated driving systems. In: Margaria, T., Steffen, B. (eds.) ISoLA 2018. LNCS, vol. 11246, pp. 449–460. Springer, Cham (2018). https://doi.org/10.1007/978-3-030-03424-5_30

18. Kuhn, D.R., Kacker, R.N., Lei, Y.: Introduction to Combinatorial Testing. CRC Press (2013)

19. Lardennois, R.: Safety: single coded processor architecture combined with ASIC provide a cost efficient and flexible solution to safety issues. IFAC Proc. Volumes **27**(12), 971–976 (1994). http://www.sciencedirect.com/science/article/pii/S1474667017476002, iFAC Symposium on Transportation Systems: Theory and Application of Advanced Technology, Tianjin, PRC, 24–26 August. https://doi.org/10.1016/S1474-6670(17)47600-2

20. Object Management Group: OMG Systems Modeling Language (OMG SysML), Version 1.6. Technical report, Object Management Group (2019). http://www.omg.org/spec/SysML/1.4

21. Peleska, J.: Industrial-strength model-based testing - state of the art and current challenges. In: Petrenko, A.K., Schlingloff, H. (eds.) Proceedings Eighth Workshop on Model-Based Testing, Rome, Italy, 17th March 2013. Electronic Proceedings in Theoretical Computer Science, vol. 111, pp. 3–28. Open Publishing Association (2013). https://doi.org/10.4204/EPTCS.111.1

22. Peleska, J.: Model-based avionic systems testing for the airbus family. In: 23rd IEEE European Test Symposium, ETS 2018, Bremen, Germany, 28 May–1 June 2018, pp. 1–10. IEEE (2018). https://doi.org/10.1109/ETS.2018.8400703

23. Peleska, J., Brauer, J., Huang, W.: Model-based testing for avionic systems proven benefits and further challenges. In: Margaria, T., Steffen, B. (eds.) ISoLA 2018. LNCS, vol. 11247, pp. 82–103. Springer, Cham (2018). https://doi.org/10.1007/978-3-030-03427-6_11

24. Peleska, J., Huang, W., Cavalcanti, A.: Finite complete suites for CSP refinement testing. Sci. Comput. Program. **179**, 1–23 (2019). https://doi.org/10.1016/j.scico.2019.04.004. http://www.sciencedirect.com/science/article/pii/S0167642319300620

25. Peleska, J., Huang, W., Hübner, F.: A novel approach to HW/SW integration testing of route-based interlocking system controllers. In: Lecomte, T., Pinger, R., Romanovsky, A. (eds.) RSSRail 2016. LNCS, vol. 9707, pp. 32–49. Springer, Cham (2016). https://doi.org/10.1007/978-3-319-33951-1_3
26. Petrenko, A., Timo, O.N., Ramesh, S.: Test generation by constraint solving and FSM mutant killing. In: Wotawa, F., Nica, M., Kushik, N. (eds.) ICTSS 2016. LNCS, vol. 9976, pp. 36–51. Springer, Cham (2016). https://doi.org/10.1007/978-3-319-47443-4_3
27. Simão, A., Petrenko, A., Yevtushenko, N.: On reducing test length for FSMs with extra states. Softw. Test. Verification Reliab. 22(6), 435–454 (2012). https://doi.org/10.1002/stvr.452. https://onlinelibrary.wiley.com/doi/abs/10.1002/stvr.452
28. Steffens, S., Siemens Mobility GmbH: Safety@COTS Multicore, Distributed Smart Safe System DS3. In: Innovationstag ETCS Stellwerk smartrail 4.0. pp. 35–47 (2018). https://www.google.com/url?sa=t&rct=j&q=&esrc=s&source=web& cd=&ved=2ahUKEwjTnZe9tfXqAhVOeMAKHWmuBn4QFjAAegQIARAB& url=https%3A%2F%2Fwww.smartrail40.ch%2Fservice%2Fdownload.asp %3Fmem%3D0%26path%3D%255Cdownload%255Cdownloads%255C2018 %252011%252013%2520Innovationstag%2520ETCS%2520Stellwerk_smartrail %25204.0.pdf&usg=AOvVaw0UXmG4VZsVLc-HqG6e3ZOJ, presentation slides
29. Vasilevskii, M.P.: Failure diagnosis of automata. Kibernetika (Transl.) 4, 98–108 (1973)

Model Checking a Distributed Interlocking System Using k-induction with RT-Tester

Signe Geisler[✉] and Anne E. Haxthausen[✉]

DTU Compute, Technical University of Denmark, Kongens Lyngby, Denmark
{sgei,aeha}@dtu.dk

Abstract. This paper investigates the use of k-induction with RT-Tester for tackling the challenge of verifying the safety of a distributed railway interlocking system. For a real-world case study, it is described how a generic and reconfigurable model of the system is modelled in a new extension of the RAISE Specification Language (RSL). The generic model is instantiated with concrete data sets and subsequently model checked with respect to safety properties using the k-induction facilities in RT-Tester. The performance metrics of the verification with k-induction are additionally compared with the metrics of verifying the same system model with the SAL model checker.

Keywords: Model checking · RAISE · Railway interlocking systems · Distributed systems · k-induction · RT-Tester

1 Introduction

This paper considers how to use k-induction to tackle the challenge of formally verifying the safety of a real-world geographically distributed interlocking system, RELIS 2000. This system was originally developed by INSY GmbH Berlin and first described in [14].

Railway interlocking systems are responsible for controlling the track side equipment and granting movement authorities to trains in a railway network such that derailments and collisions of trains are avoided. Traditionally, such systems are centralised. The interlocking system we consider in this paper, however, is geographically distributed: there are multiple control components which have been deployed at specific points along the tracks and in the trains, respectively. The control components must communicate and collaborate to control the track side equipment and grant movement authorities to trains in a safe manner.

We have previously investigated the formal specification and model checking of this interlocking system [13]. We used a stepwise development method where we incrementally added details to the model specification. For the verification of the interlocking system we used model checking, since the verification process is fully automated with this method.

We were using RSL⋆, an extension to RSL-SAL, which itself is an extension of RSL – the *RAISE Specification Language* [20]. RSL is a formal specification

© Springer Nature Switzerland AG 2020
T. Margaria and B. Steffen (Eds.): ISoLA 2020, LNCS 12542, pp. 449–466, 2020.
https://doi.org/10.1007/978-3-030-61467-6_29

language, allowing several different styles of formulating modular specifications. RSL-SAL [19] extends the functionality of RSL with constructs for the specification of transition systems in a guarded command style. RSL-SAL specifications can be translated by the RSL tool set (*rsltc*) and subsequently model checked using the SAL model checker [2]. Therefore, we used the SAL model checker as a proof of concept, but found that the scalability was limited in terms of for how large railway networks the model could be verified.

In a previous study [23], k-induction with RT-Tester [18,22] was used for proving the safety of a centralised interlocking system with great efficiency and scaling. Our goal in this paper is to investigate whether the scalability of the verification of the distributed interlocking system in [13] can also be improved by using k-induction.

Therefore, we have equipped *rsltc* with functionality for translating RSL⋆ specifications into model representations in RT-Tester such that k-induction with RT-Tester can be used to prove the safety of models of the distributed interlocking system considered in [13].

1.1 Related Work

Formal verification of railway interlocking systems is a well-researched topic. An overview of recent trends can be found in [4,9].

Centralised systems are the tradition for railway interlocking, and therefore a great part of the literature on formal verification of interlocking systems focuses on these. However, there are sources which cover the formal verification of distributed interlocking systems: The case study considered in this paper, was previously investigated in [14], but the behavioural model in [14] was expressed using the RSL process algebra instead of the RSL⋆ guarded command language that we are using, and the verification used the RAISE theorem prover rather than model checking. Another example can be found in [11], where a geographically distributed railway interlocking system was formally modelled and verified using the UMC model checker [1,6], although with a very different control protocol than the one used in this paper. A discussion of advantages and challenges of distributed interlocking can be found in [10].

The k-induction technique with RT-Tester that we are exploring is the same as used by Vu et al. in [23], but they used it for verifying a centralised interlocking system, and the modelling language was not a general-purpose language like RSL⋆, but a domain-specific railway modelling language.

There are examples of using many other model checking tools such as Simulink and UPPAAL [5], SPIN and nuSMV [12], proB [3], mCRL2 [7], and FDR [16] for the verification of railway control systems. For a comparative study, see [15].

1.2 Paper Overview

In Sect. 2, we introduce the background for the verification scheme. In Sect. 3, we introduce the case study under consideration in this paper, and in Sect. 4, we outline the generic model specification we have created of the interlocking system from the case study. Section 5 presents our verification efforts and discusses the scalability of our verification approach. Finally, Sect. 6 gives a conclusion and ideas for future work.

2   RT-Tester and k-induction

In this section we introduce some mathematical foundations for the applied verification approach. We briefly explain how a system model can be expressed and then describe the k-induction verification scheme.

Model Representations in RT-Tester. In RSL⋆ a system model is specified by a set of variable declarations (defining the state space), an initialisation constraint and a collection of transition rules in guarded command style. Using *rsltc*, such a system model can be translated to RT-Tester's [22] internal representation, where the model is expressed as a Kripke structure. In the Kripke structure, the initial state and the transition relation are expressed in propositional form over the states of the system:

$\mathcal{I}(s_0)$ is a proposition which holds for a state s_0, if s_0 is an initial state.

$\Phi(s, s')$ is a proposition which holds for a pair of states (s, s'), if there is a transition from s to s' in the model.

k-induction. k-induction [17,21] is a verification scheme which can be used to prove a state invariant ϕ in two steps: a *base case* and an *induction step*, both of which can be formulated as bounded model checking problems. This makes it possible to use RT-Tester's integrated bounded model checker to perform k-induction.[1]

In the *base case*, it should be proved that the property ϕ holds in every state of every acyclic path of length $k > 0$ starting from every initial state. This is formulated as a bounded model checking problem by searching for violations of the base case, i.e. searching for a witness for the following formula:

$$\mathcal{I}(s_0) \wedge \pi^=(s_0, \ldots, s_{k-1}) \wedge \neg \bigwedge_{i=0}^{k-1} \phi(s_i) \tag{1}$$

where $\pi^=(s_0, \ldots, s_{k-1})$ is a proposition expressing that $s_0, \ldots, s_{k-1}$ is an acyclic path in the model, and $\phi(s_i)$ denotes that ϕ holds in the state s_i. Thus, if a solution is found, there is a state which is reachable within k steps from one of the initial states and which does not satisfy ϕ.

In the *induction step*, it should be proved that if ϕ holds in every state of every acyclic path of length $k > 0$ starting from an arbitrary state, then ϕ also

---

[1] The facilities in RT-Tester that enable k-induction were originally developed by Linh Hong Vu in collaboration with Jan Peleska and his team [23] based on the work presented in [17,21] and using the bounded model checker of RT-Tester.

holds in any $k + 1$th state. This is formulated as a bounded model checking problem by searching for violations of the induction step, i.e. searching for a witness for the following formula:

$$\pi^= (s_n, \ldots, s_{n+k}) \wedge \bigwedge_{i=0}^{k-1} \phi(s_{n+i}) \wedge \neg\phi(s_{n+k}) \tag{2}$$

If a solution is found, there is a path of length $k + 1$ for which ϕ holds for the first k states, but not for the last state in the path.

If violations are neither found for the base case nor for the induction step (i.e. no witness was found for either of the above formulae), ϕ is an invariant.

If a violation is found in the base case, ϕ is not an invariant.

If a violation is found in the induction step, this might be a false negative, if the considered path starts in an unreachable state. To eliminate such *spurious* violations, one can (1) define a *strengthening invariant* ψ that is not satisfied in that unreachable start state, and then try to prove $\phi \wedge \psi$ instead of just ϕ, or (2) one can re-try the induction with a higher value of k (incremental k-induction).

Incremental k-induction works by first attempting to prove the base case starting at $k = 1$ and, if this is successful, attempting to prove the induction step for the same k. If the induction step fails, the value of k is incremented by one and the attempt to prove the base case and the induction step is repeated for the new value of k. The proof terminates unsuccessfully if the base case fails (or if the upper limit set for k is reached). The proof terminates successfully when the base case and induction step are proved for some value of k.

In principle, the incremental approach has the advantage that the process is automated. However, for some systems, with this approach k will reach such large values that it will take too much memory or unreasonably long time to explore the necessary subset of the state space. In such cases, it will be more efficient to invent and use strengthening invariants such that a lower value of k (e.g. $k = 1$) can be used.

3   Case Study

This section presents the considered interlocking system from [14]. This description of the case study is from [13].

The *control strategy* of the system must ensure the safety of the system by preventing derailment and collision of trains. In this engineering concept, safety is achieved by only allowing one train on each track segment at the same time and ensuring that points are locked in correct position while trains are passing them. To this end, trains must *reserve* track segments before entering them and *lock* points in correct position before passing them.

The *control components* of the system are responsible for implementing the control strategy. Each train is equipped with a *train control computer*. In the railway network, several *switchboxes* are distributed, each associated with a single point or an endpoint of the network. These components communicate with each other in order to collaboratively control the system. Each control component has its own, local state space for keeping track of the relevant information. As can be seen from Fig. 1, each of the train control computers has information about the train's route (a list of track segments) with its switchboxes, the train position, and the reservations and locks it has achieved. Each switchbox has information about its associated sensor (used to detect whether a train is passing the critical area close to the point), which segments are connected at its associated point (if any), for which train the point is locked (if any), and for which train each of the associated segments is reserved (if any).

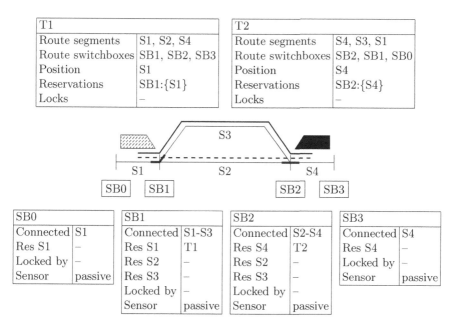

T1	
Route segments	S1, S2, S4
Route switchboxes	SB1, SB2, SB3
Position	S1
Reservations	SB1:{S1}
Locks	–

T2	
Route segments	S4, S3, S1
Route switchboxes	SB2, SB1, SB0
Position	S4
Reservations	SB2:{S4}
Locks	–

SB0	
Connected	S1
Res S1	–
Locked by	–
Sensor	passive

SB1	
Connected	S1-S3
Res S1	T1
Res S2	–
Res S3	–
Locked by	–
Sensor	passive

SB2	
Connected	S2-S4
Res S4	T2
Res S2	–
Res S3	–
Locked by	–
Sensor	passive

SB3	
Connected	S4
Res S4	–
Locked by	–
Sensor	passive

Fig. 1. An example system, adapted from [13].

The basic idea of the control strategy is as follows:

1. *Permission to enter a segment:* For a train control computer (TCC) to decide whether it is legal to enter the next segment of its route, the TCC must observe its local state space and check whether it has the needed reservations and locks. More precisely, the following must hold:
   - the next segment must have been reserved for the train at the two upcoming switchboxes, and
   - the point must have been switched in the direction for the train route and locked for the train at the next switchbox.

   In the scenario shown in Fig. 1, for the train $T1$, this means that it must have reservations for segment $S2$ at both the switchboxes $SB1$ and $SB2$, and a lock for the point at $SB1$, and $S1$ must be connected to $S2$ at $SB1$, before it can be allowed to enter $S2$.

2. *Making reservations and locks:* Reservations and locks are made by the trains by issuing requests to the relevant switchboxes. Depending on its local state, a switchbox may or may not comply with a request from a train. The switchbox can only fulfil a segment reservation request if the segment is not already reserved at the switchbox. Similarly, a switchbox can only lock a point (after potentially having switched the point in the direction for the train route), if the point is not already locked. Additionally, a request for locking a point can only be made if the train has reservations for the two segments in its route on either side of the point to be locked. In the scenario shown in Fig. 1, for the train $T1$, this means that it must have a reservation for segments $S1$ and $S2$ at the switchbox $SB1$, before it can request to switch and lock the point at $SB1$.

   If a switchbox can meet a request, it will update its state space accordingly. In any case, the switchbox will send a response to the train, based on which the train can determine whether the request has been met and, thereby, whether the train should update its state space as well.

3. *Release of reservations and locks:* When a train enters the critical area of a switchbox, the sensor associated with the switchbox will become *active*, and when the train later leaves the critical area of the switchbox, the sensor will become *passive* which in turn causes both the lock and reservations for that train at that switchbox to be *released* in the state space of the switchbox. When the train leaves the critical area of the switchbox, also the lock and reservations at that switchbox will be *released* in the state space of the train.

4   Generic Model and Verification Obligations

In this section, we will outline the model specification of the distributed interlocking system and the specification of proof obligations. The interlocking system is modelled as a *generic model*, which can later be instantiated with configuration data. An example instantiation of the full model corresponding to Fig. 1 can be found online.[2]

The specification can be divided into several different parts:

- Types for the network configuration data.
- Types and values for the static control component data.
- Types and state variables for the dynamic control component data.
- Interface and communication variables.
- Transition system rules.
- Functions for describing invariants of the system.

---

[2] https://github.com/raisetools/rslstar/tree/master/spec-examples/dracos/discorail2020.

The verification obligations (expressing the safety properties and other desired invariants) are specified as LTL assertions, which use the functions describing invariants of the system.

In Sect. 4.1 we give a brief overview of the adaptations we have made to the model from [13]. Then, in the following sections, we will elaborate on the different parts of the adapted model and the verification obligations.

Note that the original transition system model in [13] was developed in a stepwise manner and with translation to SAL in mind. More details about this can be found in our paper [13]. The final model of the stepwise development process resulted in the specification of a control system adhering to a *just-in-time* allocation principle, where each train can only make the immediately necessary reservations and locks at any point in time. This means that the train must only make reservations of its next segment (at the two upcoming switchboxes along its route) and that it must only lock the point at the next upcoming switchbox. It is this variant of the control algorithm that we are considering in this paper.

4.1   Overview of Adaptations

Since the subset of RSL⋆ translatable to SAL differs from the subset translatable to RT-Tester, it has been necessary to adapt the original specification from [13] in order to be able to translate it into RT-tester. For instance, the original specification uses RSL⋆ maps and sets which are translatable to SAL, but not to RT-Tester. These data structures have been replaced with RSL⋆ arrays, which are translatable to RT-Tester. As arrays can also be translated to SAL, it has actually been possible to create a specification which is translatable both to RT-Tester and to SAL, allowing us to compare the performance results from both model checkers on the same system model.

In order to use less space for data, we also made some additional adaptions of the model.

4.2   Network Configuration Data

The network configuration consists of data about the segments, switchboxes and trains in the network. Each segment, switchbox and train is given a unique identifier by specifying a type for each of them. In the generic model, the types are not further specified, but the intention is that the types enumerate the concrete identifiers for each component when the model is instantiated. Each identifier type must at least include a special *none* value: *seg_none* for segments, *sb_none* for switchboxes and *t_none* for trains. For each of the types, we also specify subtypes which do not include the special *none* values.

type
    SegmentID == seg_none | _,
    SegmentID_prime = {| s : SegmentID • s ≠ seg_none|}
    SwitchboxID == sb_none | _,
    SwitchboxID_prime = {| sb : SwitchboxID • sb ≠ sb_none |}

TrainID == t_none | _,
TrainID_prime = {| t : TrainID • t ≠ t_none |},

4.3   Static Control Component Data

In Sect. 3, we introduced the information that each switchbox and each train must keep track of. Some of this data is static: the route information for each train in the network and segments adjacency information for each switchbox in the network. In the generic model, this static data is modelled by generic constants. For instance, the following declaration states that for each train t in the type *TrainID_prime* (i.e. for each train in the network), there is a constant *route[t]* storing the train's route (of type *Route*).

value
   route[t : TrainID_prime] : Route

The type *Route* is defined as follows:

type
   Route = **array** RouteIndex **of** SegmentID,
   RouteIndex = {| i : **Int** • i ≥ 0 ∧ i < max_route_length + 1 |}

As it can be seen, a route is modelled as an array of segment identifiers. The index type of the array, the *RouteIndex* type, is an integer range from zero to the maximum route length (the value of which depends on the initialisation of the model).

To store the segments adjacent to each switchbox, we declare the following generic variable.

value
   sbSegments[sb : SwitchboxID_prime] : SbSegments

The type *SbSegments* is defined as follows:

type
   SbSegments = **array** SbIndex **of** SegmentID,
   SbIndex = {| i : **Int** • i ≥ 0 ∧ i < 3 |}

The adjacent segments are modelled as an array of segment identifiers. The index type of the array, the *SbIndex* type, is an integer range from zero to two (such that there is an entry for each of the up to three segments with which a switchbox may be associated).

When the model is instantiated, for each t in *TrainID_prime*, a concrete value for *route[t]* must be specified, and for each *sb* in *SwitchboxID_prime*, a concrete value for *sbSegments[sb]* must be specified as configuration data.

4.4   Dynamic Control Component Data

Most of the data that the trains and switchboxes must keep track of is dynamic. The trains store their position, their reservations and locks. The switchboxes similarly store their reservations and locks along with data about the associated sensor and information about which of its adjacent segments are currently connected.

In the generic model, this dynamic data is modelled by generic variables in a similar way as static data was modelled by generic constants. For instance, the following generic variable is used for storing reservations at each of the switchboxes sb.

variable
    sbReservations[sb : SwitchboxID_prime] : SbReservation

type
    SbReservation = **array** SbIndex **of** TrainID,
    SbIndex = {| i : **Int** • i $\geq$ 0 $\wedge$ i < 3 |}

As it can be seen, a switchbox reservation is modelled as an array of *TrainID*s with an index in the same range as used for the *SbSegments* arrays (such that there is an entry for each of the up to three segments with which a switchbox may be associated). Hence, *sbReservations[sb][i]* = *t* models that switchbox *sb* has recorded a reservation for train *t* of the segment which can be found at index *i* in the *sbSegments[sb]* array.

When the generic model is instantiated, initial values for all the resulting variables must be specified as configuration data.

4.5   Interface and Communication Variables

The control components must collaborate on making reservations and locks, so they must be able to communicate. The communication between the components is modelled as a simple request-acknowledge protocol, where the train is the initiating party. A train will consider its own state and can send a request to a switchbox if its state fulfils the requirements. If a switchbox receives a request, it will consider its own state to decide whether the request can be fulfilled. Depending on this, the switchbox sends a positive or negative acknowledgement to the train. If the switchbox can accommodate the request it will also update its state accordingly, as will the train when it receives a positive acknowledgement. If the switchbox sends a negative acknowledgement, neither the state of the switchbox nor the train is updated. We model the communication, i.e. the requests, acknowledgements and data sent as part of a request, by shared variables.

We declare three different generic variables to keep track of the requests and acknowledgements. For example, if a train *t* has sent a request to a switchbox *sb*, then *req[t]* = *sb*.

variable
    req[t : TrainID_prime] : SwitchboxID,
    ack[sb : SwitchboxID_prime] : TrainID,
    nack[sb : SwitchboxID_prime] : TrainID

We declare data variables for storing data sent as part of a request – for example, the segment to be reserved:

variable
  reqSeg : SegmentID

In addition, we declare event variables which describe which kind of event is taking place (*reserve at the next switchbox, reserve at the switchbox after the next switchbox* and *lock at the next switchbox*). For example, we declare a variable:

variable
  reserveNextEvent : **Bool**

This variable is set to true as soon as a train sends a request for reserving a segment at its next switchbox. The variable is set to false as soon as the train has received an acknowledgement (negative or positive).

4.6   Transition System Rules

In RSL*, the possible behaviour of a system is specified by state transition system rules. Each rule consists of a guard and an effect. The guard is a boolean expression over the state variables. It determines in which states the effect of the rule may occur. The effect of the rule is a collection of variable updates of the form $x' = value$, where the primed variable name x' refers to the variable x in the post state. Rules may be combined by using the non-deterministic choice operator $[]$.

In the specification of our generic model, we use 15 generic transition system rules. A generic rule is a shorthand for a non-deterministic choice over a set of rules of the same form, only differing by one or more parameters. For example, we have the following generic rule expressing for any switchbox sb, the sending of a positive acknowledgement to a train **t** that it has reserved the segment at index i for **t**:

($[]$ sb : SwitchboxID_prime, t : TrainID_prime, i : SbIndex •
  [switchbox_ack_reservation]
  (reserveNextEvent ∨ reserveNextNextEvent) ∧ req[t] = sb ∧
  sbSegments[sb][i] = reqSeg ∧
  sb_can_reserve(sbReservations[sb][i])
  $\longrightarrow$
  ack'[sb] = t,
  req'[t] = sb_none,
  sbReservations'[sb][i] = t
)

This rule represents the non-deterministic choice of the set of rules that are obtained by replacing the parameters sb, t and i with each of the possible combinations of the possible concrete values for each parameter.

In the rule effects, an acknowledgement is sent to the train t from the switchbox sb, the request from the same train is consumed (by setting the variable to the special value sb_none), and the reservations in the same switchbox is updated to have a reservation for t of the segment at its index i. The guard expresses that this can only happen if (1) there is a reservation event going on and the train t has sent a request to the switchbox sb, (2) the segment $reqSeg$ to be reserved is the one at index i of the switchbox, and (3) the segment is not already reserved. The latter is expressed by the following auxiliary function:

sb_can_reserve : TrainID $\rightarrow$ **Bool**
sb_can_reserve(res) $\equiv$ res = t_none,

4.7 Safety Invariants

We have specified two safety invariants to be proved. They describe that trains do not collide and trains do not derail, respectively. The specification of the former is as follows:

($\forall$ **distinct** tid1, tid2 : TrainID_prime •
    G(no_collide(hdPos[tid1], tlPos[tid1], hdPos[tid2], tlPos[tid2])))

where $hdPos[t]$ and $tlPos[t]$ is the head, respectively tail, position of a train t[3] and $no\_collide$ is a function defined as follows:

no_collide : SegmentID × SegmentID × SegmentID × SegmentID $\rightarrow$ **Bool**
no_collide(hdPos1, tlPos1, hdPos2, tlPos2) $\equiv$
    hdPos1 $\neq$ hdPos2 $\wedge$ hdPos1 $\neq$ tlPos2 $\wedge$ tlPos1 $\neq$ hdPos2 $\wedge$ tlPos1 $\neq$ tlPos2

Supplied with the head position and tail position of two $distinct$[4] trains, the function checks that there are no overlaps in the trains' position.

4.8 Strengthening Invariants

As a part of the verification process, we have added several strengthening invariants in order to prove the safety invariants by 1-induction.

Many of the strengthening invariants we have added are adaptions of the consistency properties that we have previously proved for earlier variants of the system [13]. These invariants express agreement between the train data and the switchbox data. For example, one of the strengthening invariants express that each reservation or lock possessed by a train is also found in the reservations/locks of the corresponding switchbox[5].

---

[3] For the considered local railway, trains are shorter than any segment, so they will at most occupy two segments at a time.

[4] The quantification with the $distinct$ keyword generates only distinct combinations of the parameters – in this case distinct pairs of train identifiers.

[5] Note that this property is indeed invariant, even though the updates to the train and switchbox reservations/locks happen in separate transitions, because the update to switchbox reservations/locks always happens before the update to the train reservations/locks. Note therefore also that the converse of the property is not invariant and only holds if the system is not in the middle of making a reservation/lock.

We also added several strengthening invariants relating to the interface variables used for the communication between train control computers and switchboxes. For example, one of the strengthening invariants expresses that a switchbox never sends both a positive and negative acknowledgement to a train simultaneously:

($\forall$ sb : SwitchboxID_prime •
  (ack[sb] $\neq$ t_none $\lor$ nack[sb] $\neq$ t_none) $\Rightarrow$ ack[sb] $\neq$ nack[sb])

5   Verification

In this section, we present our experiences using k-induction with RT-Tester to verify the safety of instances of our generic model. In particular we show the performance metrics (time and memory usage) for verifying the safety properties of models having configurations of increasing size (in terms of number of stations). Furthermore, we compare these results with the performance measures for the same configurations when verifying with the SAL model checker.

The RELIS 2000 system was intended for local railways having stations with 1–2 track segments, each connected by single lines and operated by 2–3 trains. Therefore, in our verification we consider configurations of the model which are representative for this class of local railways.

5.1   Bounded Model Checking

Before performing the k-induction, we used bounded model checking for quick detection of bugs in the considered model instances.

Bounded model checking can be used to find bugs in the specification within the first n transition steps. Given a bound n, the bounded model checker only explores the paths of the transition system of lengths up to the bound. Therefore, bounded model checking can be much quicker than global model checking or k-induction (with a large k) to find bugs.

Bounded model checking (with a bound ≥ 1) can in particular be used to check that the initial state (specified in the configuration data) of a certain model instance adheres to the safety and strengthening invariants. This is especially useful for large networks, where there is some risk of making errors in the configuration data.

The bounded model checker can also be used to show that a system progresses. We used it for proving that there exists at least one path where all trains can reach their destination, (but there might still be other paths for which a livelock or a deadlock may occur).[6] Selecting a path without deadlocks and livelocks is a task for the scheduler, rather than for the interlocking system. Our aim is to ensure that there exists a possible schedule (i.e. at least one path where

---

[6] This was done by asserting that it is never the case that all trains have reached their destination. This is expected to produce a counter-example showing the transition steps to a state where the trains indeed did reach their destinations.

all trains reach their destinations). For the bound for these experiments, we calculated the minimum number of transition steps needed for all trains to reach their final destination (for example, it takes three transition steps to finalise a reservation).

5.2 k-induction

First we tried to use incremental k-induction to verify the safety invariants without any strengthening invariants. Even for a small system instantiation with just one station (as in Fig. 1), the value of k eventually had to be increased to such a degree that the base case took an unreasonable amount of time to prove: After a total of fifty-three hours, the value of k had been increased to fifty-four and we manually terminated the execution.

Therefore, instead, we decided to add strengthening invariants until we obtained a property that is provable by k-induction with $k = 1$. As mentioned in Sect. 2, the strengthening invariants are conjuncted with the safety properties such that the k-induction should now attempt to prove the safety properties *and* the added strengthening invariants. The strengthening invariants were found by inspecting the counter-examples that resulted from failed induction steps and taking inspiration from the consistency properties of an earlier variant of the model [13].

5.3   System Instantiations

As our main goal is to investigate the scalability of using k-induction with RT-Tester, we have instantiated[7] the generic model with configurations of increasing size (in terms of the number of segments and stations in the network). The configurations follow the typical patterns of real-world systems in the class of railway networks we are considering.

Fig. 2. An example of a typical local railway network (from [13]).

For the class of networks we are considering, the configuration pattern illustrated in Fig. 2 is very typical. Two trains start at either end of the network driving in opposite directions and using distinct track segments at the stations such that they are able to pass each other there (the train routes are illustrated with lines, where the dashed line is the route of the striped train and the solid line is the route of the black train). We use instantiations of the system model

---

[7] To instantiate a model, configuration data for types, values and variables must be specified as explained in Sect. 4.2, Sect. 4.3, and Sect. 4.4, respectively.

with configurations of increasing size (with one, two, five, ten, fifteen, and twenty stations) for comparing the verification performance of SAL and RT-Tester.

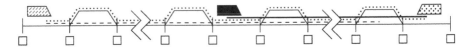

Fig. 3. An example of a typical local railway network with an extra train (from [13]).

Another typical configuration pattern is illustrated in Fig. 3, where an additional train has been added somewhere between the other two trains which are starting at each respective end of the network. We also use instantiations of the system model with configurations following this pattern with ten, fifteen and twenty stations, respectively.

5.4   Results and Verification Metrics

As mentioned previously, the model can be translated to both RT-Tester and SAL. This allows us to compare the performance of the two model checkers when verifying the safety properties of the same model. Note, however, that the k-induction proves the added strengthening invariants along with the safety properties, whereas SAL solely proves the two safety properties.

Below we present the time and memory consumption for verifying the safety properties by k-induction with RT-Tester and with the SAL model checker, respectively. The results were measured using GNU Time[8] on a machine with a Intel(R) Core(TM) i7-8650U CPU @ 1.90 GHz and 31 GiB of memory.

We firstly present the verification metrics for the instances following the configuration pattern shown in Fig. 2, i.e. with two trains driving in opposite directions from either end of the network. Table 1 shows the time and memory usage for verifying both of the safety properties with RT-Tester and SAL, respectively. For the smaller instantiations with one and two stations, SAL and RT-Tester have approximately the same time and memory usage. However, for the instantiation with five stations RT-Tester uses less than three minutes to verify the properties, whereas SAL uses more than an hour and a half. The memory consumption of RT-Tester is also much lower than that of SAL. For the instantiation with ten stations, the SAL execution was terminated by the operating system after almost seventeen hours due to memory exhaustion. Therefore we did not attempt to verify the safety of larger instantiations with SAL. In contrast to that, we successfully verified the properties with RT-Tester for instantiations with ten, fifteen, and twenty stations.

We now present the verification metrics for the instances following the configuration pattern shown in Fig. 3, i.e. with two trains driving in opposite directions

---

[8] https://www.gnu.org/software/time/.

Table 1. Time (hh:mm:ss) and memory (MB) usage for verifying the safety properties for the different instances of the system model with the initial state shown in Fig. 2.

# of stations	Time		Memory	
	RT-Tester	SAL	RT-Tester	SAL
1	00:00:06	00:00:06	118	113
2	00:00:18	00:00:17	187	165
5	00:02:20	01:42:57	678	5,076
10	00:33:02	*	2,860	*
15	02:10:53	†	7,493	†
20	10:04:09	†	16,232	†

* The execution was terminated by the operating system due to memory exhaustion.
† This experiment was not run.

from either end of the network and a third train starting roughly midway between the other two trains. Table 2 shows the time and memory consumption for verifying both of the safety properties with RT-Tester.

As it can be seen, the addition of a third train increased the time and memory usage. We again successfully verified the properties for instantiations with ten and fifteen stations, but for twenty stations the execution was this time terminated by the operating system due to memory exhaustion. SAL was not able to verify any of these instantiations.

Table 2. Time (hh:mm:ss) and memory (MB) usage for verifying the safety properties for the different instances of the system model with the initial state shown in Fig. 3.

# of stations	RT-Tester	
	Time	Memory
10	8:32:11	7,905
15	41:25:47	22,813
20	*	*

* The execution was terminated by the operating system due to memory exhaustion.

6   Conclusion and Future Work

In this paper we have shown the specification of a generic system model of a real-world geographically distributed interlocking system and successfully verified the safety of model instances representative for the class of local railway networks for which this interlocking system is intended.

We performed the verification using k-induction with RT-Tester. In order to make the proof within reasonable time, we found it was necessary to add several strengthening invariants and make the induction for $k = 1$ rather than use incremental k-induction. We successfully verified model instances for typical, real-world network configurations for the considered local railways.

We also verified the system model with the SAL model checker, and in general found k-induction with RT-Tester to be much more efficient – both in terms of time and memory consumption. The scalability of verifying the distributed interlocking system with RT-Tester was found to be substantially better compared to the SAL model checker, as it was possible to verify much larger networks with RT-Tester before reaching memory exhaustion. A main reason for this is that k-induction is based on bounded model checking. In contrast to this, SAL is performing global symbolic model checking and thus must explore the full state space in order to verify properties.

For future work, it would be interesting to automate the addition of strengthening invariants, for example using some of the strategies presented in [8]. We would also like to further optimise the system model in terms of how the data of the control components is stored and investigate whether the method can scale to even larger systems. In addition, it would be interesting to investigate k-induction with RT-Tester for other system models specified in RSL⋆ – of railway interlocking systems or even other safety-critical systems.

Acknowledgements. The authors would express their gratitude to Jan Peleska for wonderful inspiration and discussions, and for hosting the first author on several research stays and granting access to the RT-Tester source code, without which this paper would not have been possible. The authors would also like to acknowledge the work of Linh Hong Vu, in collaboration with Jan Peleska and his team, who originally implemented the k-induction facilities in RT-Tester, and whose work has been very valuable to us. In addition, Jan Peleska, Niklas Krafczyk, and Linh Hong Vu deserve many thanks for their technical help with the RT-Tester source code. The authors would also like to thank Chris George for valuable input during the development of the RSL⋆ extension to RSL. Finally, thanks go to the anonymous reviewers for helpful comments concerning the presentation.

References

1. UMC. http://fmt.isti.cnr.it/umc/V4.2/umc.html
2. Symbolic Analysis Laboratory, SAL (2001). http://sal.csl.sri.com
3. de Almeida Pereira, D.I., Deharbe, D., Perin, M., Bon, P.: B-specification of relay-based railway interlocking systems based on the propositional logic of the system state evolution. In: Collart-Dutilleul, S., Lecomte, T., Romanovsky, A. (eds.) RSSRail 2019. LNCS, vol. 11495, pp. 242–258. Springer, Cham (2019). https://doi.org/10.1007/978-3-030-18744-6_16
4. Basile, D., et al.: On the industrial uptake of formal methods in the railway domain - a survey with stakeholders. In: Furia, C.A., Winter, K. (eds.) IFM 2018. LNCS, vol. 11023, pp. 20–29. Springer, Cham (2018). https://doi.org/10.1007/978-3-319-98938-9_2
5. Basile, D., ter Beek, M.H., Ferrari, A., Legay, A.: Modelling and analysing ERTMS L3 moving block railway signalling with Simulink and UPPAAL SMC. In: Larsen, K.G., Willemse, T. (eds.) FMICS 2019. LNCS, vol. 11687, pp. 1–21. Springer, Cham (2019). https://doi.org/10.1007/978-3-030-27008-7_1

6. ter Beek, M.H., Fantechi, A., Gnesi, S., Mazzanti, F.: A state/event-based model-checking approach for the analysis of abstract system properties. Sci. Comput. Program. **76**(2), 119–135 (2011). https://doi.org/10.1016/j.scico.2010.07.002

7. Bouwman, M., Janssen, B., Luttik, B.: Formal modelling and verification of an interlocking using mCRL2. In: Larsen, K.G., Willemse, T. (eds.) FMICS 2019. LNCS, vol. 11687, pp. 22–39. Springer, Cham (2019). https://doi.org/10.1007/978-3-030-27008-7_2

8. Bradley, A.R., Manna, Z.: Property-directed incremental invariant generation. Formal Aspects Comput. **20**(4–5), 379–405 (2008)

9. Fantechi, A.: Twenty-five years of formal methods and railways: what next? In: Counsell, S., Núñez, M. (eds.) SEFM 2013. LNCS, vol. 8368, pp. 167–183. Springer, Cham (2014). https://doi.org/10.1007/978-3-319-05032-4_13

10. Fantechi, A., Gnesi, S., Haxthausen, A., van de Pol, J., Roveri, M., Treharne, H.: SaRDIn - a safe reconfigurable distributed interlocking. In: Proceedings of the 11th World Congress on Railway Research (WCRR 2016), Ferrovie dello Stato Italiane, Milano (2016)

11. Fantechi, A., Haxthausen, A.E., Nielsen, M.B.R.: Model checking geographically distributed interlocking systems using UMC. In: 2017 25th Euromicro International Conference on Parallel, Distributed and Network-based Processing (PDP), pp. 278–286 (2017). https://doi.org/10.1109/PDP.2017.66

12. Ferrari, A., Magnani, G., Grasso, D., Fantechi, A.: Model checking interlocking control tables. In: Schnieder, E., Tarnai, G. (eds.) FORMS/FORMAT 2010 - Formal Methods for Automation and Safety in Railway and Automotive Systems, pp. 107–115. Springer, Heidelberg (2010). https://doi.org/10.1007/978-3-642-14261-1_11

13. Geisler, S., Haxthausen, A.E.: Stepwise development and model checking of a distributed interlocking system using RAISE. Formal Aspects Comput. 1–39 (2020). https://doi.org/10.1007/s00165-020-00507-2

14. Haxthausen, A.E., Peleska, J.: Formal development and verification of a distributed railway control system. IEEE Trans. Softw. Eng. **26**(8), 687–701 (2000)

15. Mazzanti, F., Ferrari, A.: Ten diverse formal models for a CBTC automatic train supervision system. In: Gallagher, J.P., van Glabbeek, R., Serwe, W. (eds.) Proceedings Third Workshop on Models for Formal Analysis of Real Systems and Sixth International Workshop on Verification and Program Transformation. EPTCS, vol. 268, pp. 104–149 (2018). https://doi.org/10.4204/EPTCS.268.4. http://arxiv.org/abs/1803.08668

16. Moller, F., Nguyen, H.N., Roggenbach, M., Schneider, S., Treharne, H.: Defining and model checking abstractions of complex railway models using CSP‖B. In: Biere, A., Nahir, A., Vos, T. (eds.) HVC 2012. LNCS, vol. 7857, pp. 193–208. Springer, Heidelberg (2013). https://doi.org/10.1007/978-3-642-39611-3_20

17. de Moura, L., Rueß, H., Sorea, M.: Bounded model checking and induction: from refutation to verification. In: Hunt, W.A., Somenzi, F. (eds.) CAV 2003. LNCS, vol. 2725, pp. 14–26. Springer, Heidelberg (2003). https://doi.org/10.1007/978-3-540-45069-6_2

18. Peleska, J.: Industrial-strength model-based testing - state of the art and current challenges. In: Petrenko, A.K., Schlingloff, H. (eds.) Proceedings 8th Workshop on Model-Based Testing, Rome, Italy. Electronic Proceedings in Theoretical Computer Science, vol. 111, pp. 3–28. Open Publishing Association (2013)

19. Perna, J.I., George, C.: Model checking RAISE applicative specifications. In: Proceedings of the Fifth IEEE International Conference on Software Engineering and Formal Methods, pp. 257–268. IEEE Computer Society Press (2007)

20. RAISE Language Group: George, C., et al.: The RAISE Specification Language. The BCS Practitioners Series, Prentice Hall Int. (1992)
21. Sheeran, M., Singh, S., Stålmarck, G.: Checking safety properties using induction and a SAT-solver. In: Hunt, W.A., Johnson, S.D. (eds.) FMCAD 2000. LNCS, vol. 1954, pp. 127–144. Springer, Heidelberg (2000). https://doi.org/10.1007/3-540-40922-X_8
22. Verified Systems International GmbH: RT-Tester Model-Based Test Case and Test Data Generator - RTT-MBT - User Manual (2013). http://www.verified.de
23. Vu, L.H., Haxthausen, A.E., Peleska, J.: Formal modelling and verification of interlocking systems featuring sequential release. Sci. Comput. Program. **133**, Part 2, 91–115 (2017). https://doi.org/10.1016/j.scico.2016.05.010. http://www.sciencedirect.com/science/article/pii/S0167642316300570

Designing a Demonstrator of Formal Methods for Railways Infrastructure Managers

Davide Basile[1(✉)], Maurice H. ter Beek[1], Alessandro Fantechi[1,2],
Alessio Ferrari[1], Stefania Gnesi[1], Laura Masullo[3], Franco Mazzanti[1],
Andrea Piattino[3], and Daniele Trentini[3]

[1] ISTI–CNR, Pisa, Italy
{d.basile,m.terbeek,a.ferrari,s.gnesi,f.mazzanti}@isti.cnr.it
[2] Università di Firenze, Firenze, Italy
alessandro.fantechi@unifi.it
[3] SIRTI S.p.A., Genova, Italy
{l.masullo,a.piattino,d.trentini}@sirti.it

Abstract. The Shift2Rail Innovation Programme (IP) is focussing on innovative technologies to enhance the overall railway market segments. Formal methods and standard interfaces have been identified as two key concepts to reduce time-to-market and costs, while ensuring safety, interoperability and standardisation. However, the decision to start using formal methods is still deemed too risky. Demonstrating technical and commercial benefits of both formal methods and standard interfaces is necessary to address the obstacles of learning curve and lack of clear cost/benefit analysis that are hindering their adoption, and this is the goal of the 4SECURail project, recently funded by the Shift2Rail IP. In this paper, we provide the reasoning and the rationale for designing the formal methods demonstrator for the 4SECURail project. The design concerns two important issues that have been analysed: (i) the usefulness of formal methods from the point of view of the infrastructure managers, (ii) the adoption of a semi-formal SysML notation within our formal methods demonstrator process.

1 Introduction

The European public-private Joint Undertaking (JU) for rail research Shift2Rail (S2R)[1], acting under the broad umbrella of the EU Research and Innovation programme H2020, aims to improve the state-of-the-art of rail technology and revolutionise rail as a mode of transport making it a backbone of future mobility.

The Shift2Rail Innovation Programme 2 is focussing on innovative technologies with a view to enhance the overall railway market segments. Two key concepts that have been identified to reduce the time for developing and delivering railway signalling systems are formal methods and standard interfaces. They are

---

[1] http://www.shift2rail.org.

© Springer Nature Switzerland AG 2020
T. Margaria and B. Steffen (Eds.): ISoLA 2020, LNCS 12478, pp. 467–485, 2020.
https://doi.org/10.1007/978-3-030-61467-6_30

also useful to reduce high costs for procurement, development, and maintenance. Standard interfaces are needed to increase market competition and standardisation, and to reduce long-term life cycle costs, whereas formal methods are needed to ensure correct behaviour, interoperability, and safety. The Shift2Rail initiative plans to demonstrate technical and commercial benefits of formal methods and standard interfaces, applied on selected applications, with the goal of widening the industrial uptake of these key aspects. However, the decision to start using formal methods is often deemed too risky by management, and the railway sector is notoriously cautious about the adoption of technological innovations compared with other transport sectors [3]. Thus, demonstrating technical and commercial benefits of formal methods and standard interfaces is necessary to address the obstacles of learning curve and lack of clear cost/benefit analysis.

This paper presents the first results of the Shift2Rail project 4SECURail², and in particular of the workstream 1 named: "Demonstrator development for the use of Formal Methods in Railway Environment". This workstream aims to provide a *demonstrator* of state-of-the-art formal methods and tools, applied on a railway signalling subsystem described by means of standard interfaces. This demonstrator will be used to evaluate the learning curve and to perform a cost/benefit analysis of the adoption of formal methods in the railway industry. In this paper, we discuss the overall process to follow for the rigorous construction of system specifications (the formal methods demonstrator process), together with the suitability criteria for the supporting tools and the description of the architecture of the demonstrator itself. The main contributions are:

- a description of the planned architecture of the demonstrator, e.g., the expected types of (semi-)formal models to develop during the process;
- a discussion on the role of UML/SysML [42,44] as standardised notation within the demonstrator and the role of the internally generated (semi-)formal models with respect to the final system requirements specification that the demonstrator process is expected to define;
- an identification of the kind of data about the cost of the approach that needs to be assessed, having as target the cost-benefit analysis.

The paper is organised as follows. In Sect. 2, the 4SECURail project is recalled. Sections 3, 4 and 5 describe the point of view of the infrastructure managers, the architecture of the demonstrator, and the adoption of standard notations. Finally, Sect. 6 discusses conclusions and future work.

2   The 4SECURail Project

Despite several success stories on railway applications of formal methods (cf., e.g., [5,15,22–24,27]) these mathematically-based methods and tools for system development still find significant *obstacles* to their adoption in railway software industry.

---

² https://www.4securail.eu/.

Obstacles to the Adoption of Formal Methods. The major obstacle is the high learning curve; formal methods have the image of being too difficult to apply for ordinary engineers [3, 5, 29]. Other significant obstacles include the fact that applicable standards, such as CENELEC EN 50128 [21] do recommend formal methods, but do not provide sufficiently clear guidelines on how to use them in a cost-effective way and there is no clear picture of what can be achieved using formal methods (in terms of benefits, both technical and economical). This leads to the transition to formal methods being deemed too risky by the management.

Another obstacle to the widespread use of formal methods is the lack of commercial tools, easily integrated in the software development process and working on open standard formats [29]. In fact, the current state of the art of the development tools market either offers industry-ready, well maintained and supported tools working on closed proprietary formats, or open source tools working on standard open formats, but offering low levels of support and maintenance.

Formal Methods Demonstrator, Standard Interfaces and Cost-Benefit Analysis. To address these obstacles, 4SECURail foresees the development of a demonstrator of state-of-the-art formal methods to be used as a benchmark to demonstrate technical and commercial benefits of formal methods application on a selected application (a railway subsystem). The formal development demonstrator prototype will consist of the detailed description of the process that will be followed to provide a rigorously verified model of the application under development, together with the list of the tools to be employed. The demonstrator will also take into due account the adoption of *standard interfaces* among the components of the selected applications. The role of standard interfaces have also been investigated in a previous Shift2Rail project, named X2Rail-2[3].

Interested Railway Stakeholders. In the railway domain, it is expected that the following stakeholders will be interested in the use of formal methods.

- Systems designers: formal methods will contribute to the early validation of the consistency of captured requirements and the check of compliance of design solutions with user and safety requirements.
- System and product developers: formal methods will provide an environment for developing the project and the possibility of using simulators for testing.
- Infrastructure managers: main railway networks are under responsibility of independent *Infrastructure Managers* whose interest is in increasing the interoperability among different equipment suppliers, improving their competitiveness and maximizing safety and reliability, at the same time reducing life-cycle cost of signalling system: all goals supported by the adoption of formal methods and standard interfaces.

4SECURail will address the views of these stakeholders, with special focus on the infrastructure managers, exactly because it is expected that they will benefit most, both in terms of safety and of cost, from the adoption of formal methods and standard interfaces.

---

[3] https://projects.shift2rail.org/s2r_ip2_n.aspx?p=X2RAIL-2.

4SECURail Roadmap. 4SECURail will be based on the results and indications provided by the X2Rail-2 project to select suitable tools for supporting the development of a formal model and its verification. Moreover, tools and languages for the description of standard interfaces (e.g., Standard UML, SysML, etc.) of the selected railway subsystem will also be considered and integrated in the demonstrator framework. The exercising of the demonstrator on an identified railway subsystem will address the current obstacles and the lack of a clear cost/benefit analysis for the appraisal of the application of formal methods. This implies the assessment of different learning curves, the collection of relevant data about cost and benefits, and provide results about the financial feasibility and economic sustainability of the adoption of formal methods at micro and EU level. The above goal will be achieved by implementing the following activities, implemented in a specifically deployed Work Package (WP2) of 4SECURail.

- Development of the **formal development demonstrator prototype**, that will consist in the identification of the overall process to be followed, phase after phase, for the formal development, and establishing the criteria for suitability of tools supporting each phase. In particular, the formal development demonstrator will be based on the use case developed in X2Rail-2 [38, Sect. 5.4.1]. The definition of the architecture of the demonstrator will include the choice and integration of appropriate formal methods and tools, taking into account the results produced by the Shift2Rail projects ASTRail and X2Rail-2. Moreover, in this activity we will identify the tools for the description in standard interfaces of the railway subsystem.
- Selection of the railway signalling subsystem and its use for the **exercising of the formal development demonstrator prototype**.
- **Cost-benefit analysis**, and identification of learning curve scenarios (and related cost) connected to the adoption of formal methods. The cost-benefit analysis will identify the financial feasibility and the economic impact of the implementation of formal methods against the baseline scenario, made by processes which do not exploit formal methods.

3   The Point of View of the Infrastructure Manager

An Infrastructure Manager (IM) has to provide a validated specification of a desired equipment to the Manufacturers. In a classical client/developer scenario (see Fig. 1 left) the common practice is the generation of—usually informal—system requirements document. This document can then be used by the developer to build an initial executable specification of the system, and then refine it (possibly using formal or correct-by-construction methods) into a final product.

The scenario in case of railway IMs is slightly different, since the main interest is in providing the same rigorous/verifiable specification not just to single developers, but to possibly multiple different developers that should produce equivalent products (see Fig. 1 right). This is precisely the case described by the X2Rail-2 use case (see Sect. 2), where defining a standard/rigorous/verifiable specification of the system to be developed becomes the IM's responsibility.

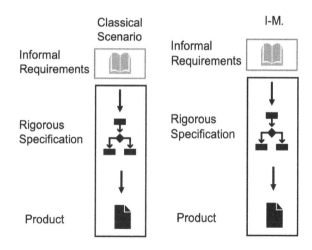

Fig. 1. The classical client/developer scenario (left) and the client/multiple developers scenario (right)

Actually, in the case of railway IMs, the scenario is even more complex. In fact, the railway infrastructure is constituted by a multitude of *subsystems* (each one possibly developed by a different supplier) that must correctly interact among them. In this case, the problem of building rigorous/formal/verifiable specifications should extend also to the verification of the interactions between these components (see Fig. 2). Clearly this does not hold only for railway IMs, but also for any other kind of complex infrastructures (e.g., telecommunications).

This introduces a further dimension of complexity. For example, safety properties can often be verified by reasoning at the level of single subsystems (e.g., ensuring that independently from the possible external interactions, no unsafe conditions are even reached), but the same cannot be said for specific properties related to the composite behaviour of several subsystems (e.g., liveness, absence of deadlocks, or missing desired execution paths involving the behaviour of several subsystems). A special case of these scenarios is when the produced specification takes the role of "standard specification" supported by international organisations (like the International Union of Railways (UIC)[4], the European Union Agency for Railways (ERA)[5], or UNISIG[6]), an industrial consortium to develop ERTMS/ETCS technical specifications), defined with the aim of creating interoperable railways in the whole of Europe (Single European Railway Area, SERA). For example, Fig. 2 depicts interoperability between Radio Block Centre (RBC) and Interlocking (IXL) by means of the RBC-IXL standard interface; and between IXL and Level Crossing (LX) by means of the IXL-LX standard interface.

---

[4] https://uic.org/.
[5] https://www.era.europa.eu/.
[6] http://www.ertms.net/wp-content/uploads/2014/09/ERTMS_Factsheet_8_UNISIG.pdf.

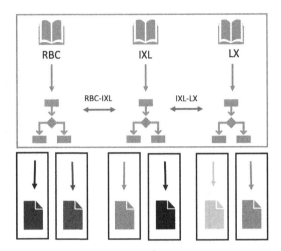

Fig. 2. The client/multiple developers scenario within a complex infrastructure

The Role of Standard(ised) Interfaces. The goal of our demonstrator related to the adoption of "standard interfaces" includes two standardisation aspects, since it aims at exploiting the use of formal methods for the definition of *standardised interfaces* (goal: interoperability) described in *standard notation* (e.g. SysML) (goals: uniformity, understandability, non-ambiguity). A very detailed presentation of the expected benefits from the adoption of standard notations for standardised signalling interfaces can be found in [13].

4   The Overall Structure of the Demonstrator Process

We now describe the overall structure of a demonstrator process aimed at employing formal methods to support IMs, distinguishing three possible cases. The next section will be dedicated to the specific instantiation of this process in the 4SECU-Rail context. The overall structure of a generic software development process targeted to the definition of rigorous system specifications which exploits the use of formal methods (our demonstrator) can be described as in Fig. 3.

First Case (with Requirements Elicitation). Starting from some input describing the initial IM requirements of the system, we start an *agile*[7] development phase in which the requirements are transformed into "formal simulatable models". These models are developed incrementally, and continuously analysed by means of formal verification, simulation, animation, and test case generation. These abstract formal models can also be refined by adding additional details into "refined simulatable models" that may help in validating the system behaviour, possibly through simulation and animation. Once these formal models are sufficiently stable, they represent the base for the construction of the demonstrator output (the official system requirements specification), in the form of description of "abstract system requirements", "safety requirements", "detailed system

---

[7] https://www.agilealliance.org/.

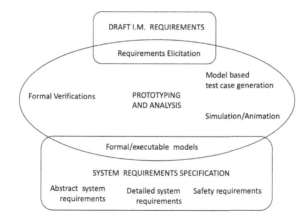

Fig. 3. Overall generic structure of demonstrator (first case)

requirements" (see Fig. 3). The resulting system requirements are still likely to be expressed in natural language, but enriched ·with tables and diagrams extracted from the (semi-)formal models. The (semi-)formal models themselves might be made available as complementary documentation.

On one hand, the construction of multiple, different semi-formal/simulatable/ formally verifiable models allows to obtain a deep understanding of the system design from many points of view and many levels of abstraction. On the other hand, this multiplicity raises the problem of keeping these models somewhat "synchronised". For example, if, for any reason, one of the models needs to be modified because of the discovery of some defect, the impact of the change on the other models surely cannot be ignored. This may require the construction and maintenance of some kind of cross-references between these artifacts, and probably also between the artifacts of the final "system requirements specification" resulting from the process. The effort needed for keeping all the different artifacts well synchronised should not be underestimated and might play a non-trivial role in deciding how many "points of view" to take into account.

Second Case (without Requirements Elicitation). The whole schema still holds in the case in which the input of the overall demonstrator process is not constituted by *Draft IM Requirements*, but by an already consolidated/official set of system requirements/safety requirements, that should be the object of more rigorous analysis. In this case, we simply would not have the *Requirements Elicitation* activity oriented to the consolidation of the *Draft IM Requirements* (i.e., the upper block in Fig. 3 is not present). In this second case, given that the starting point is an already consolidated specification, the modelling activities (in terms of tools and methods) might be somewhat different from the incremental prototyping activity driven by a rigorous/formal *Requirements Elicitation* phase.

Third Case. The same overall schema might also work in the mixed case in which an already consolidated set of system requirements/safety requirements might have to be extended/updated by an additional set of new user requirements (somewhat of a composition of the previous two cases). In these cases, the availability of previous formal simulatable artifacts would be of great help for the process. We consider as already acknowledged (cf., e.g., the related Shift2Rail surveys in [3,5,26,38]), that there is not a single formal method or tool that can fit all the possibly desired verification and modelling needs in the railway field [28,39]. Therefore, the whole *Modelling and Analysis* activity is supported at its best by a rich integrated ecosystem of tools and methodologies, rather than a single monolithic, usually closed, and tied to single specific methodologies framework. We recognise, however, that at least in the first case, where a classical V-shaped process might be followed covering all the steps from *Requirement Elicitation* to *Official Requirements Specification generation and verification*, a reference modelling framework might actually help in building and maintaining all the documentation related to the various artifacts being generated.

The Expected Output of the Demonstrator Process. The set of artifacts in output from the formal methods demonstrator process are represented in our overall generic model by the final "System Requirements Specification". Actually, these artifacts might be of different nature and with different purposes, we identify four cases:

- A *rigorous natural language textual description*, possibly enriched with standard diagrams and tables, that may constitute the legal document associated to the specification;
- A simulatable *semi-formal* system description: this artifact might be considered as a very useful complement that might be made available to the developers for checking their correct understanding of the system to be developed;
- *Formal* verifiable specifications, allowing the developers to possibly exploit these models for "correct-by-construction" code generation, and allowing the IMs to maintain, further verify, and possibly improve the system specification itself;
- A *set of tests* generated and successfully applied for the analysis of the various models, that can provide developers with guidance and early verification for the testing of the ongoing product development.

4.1 The Architecture of the 4SECURail Demonstrator

There are four points that directly affect the definition of the architecture of the demonstrator: (i) how the semi-formal models describing the system requirement specification are constructed for being analysed, (ii) how the simulatable models of the system are constructed, (iii) how the formal models of the system are contructed and verified, (iv) how the case study selected for the exercising the demonstrator may affect its architecture. In the remainder of this section we will discuss these four points.

Specification with Standard Notations. It is important to adopt as reference for the demonstrator a standardised notation for systems specification, considering the indications of the EULYNX[8] and X2Rail projects, which have chosen UML/SysML diagrams (in particular their behavioural state machines and sequence diagrams). The ideal approach to system specification should rely on an advanced support framework allowing to construct diagrams that are clear, graphically appealing, rich of content and possibly interactive. Starting from these, interactive simulation to explore the possible non-deterministic alternatives present in the behaviour would be possible, allowing the formal verification of system properties. Unfortunately, this ideal approach is still far from the current state of the art. In practice, if we really want to construct diagrams that are clear, graphically appealing and rich of content, it is necessary to make use of specific drawing-oriented tools (e.g., in ASTRail, the Graphviz[9] Graph Visualization Software has been used for this purpose) that do not support simulation and verification. Instead, diagrams automatically generated by UML/SysML-based frameworks are often of a not sufficient graphical quality and may not contain all the useful detailed information (e.g., the abstract events that relate a system transition to one or more system requirements). At the same time, however, they may be directly used to perform simulation and verification. The use of UML/SysML-based frameworks allows the progress from system design to code generation in a rather smooth way as well. This is usually of interest to developers but of less interest to the point of view of IMs. It is therefore likely, unless more experience comes out from the actual demonstrator experimentation, that a graphical SysML design will be adopted in our demonstrator without any predetermined relation with a specific UML/SysML-based framework.

Frameworks for Simulatable Modelling. As described above, the UML/SysML state diagrams descriptions might be exploited in the demonstrator not only as graphical designs with documentation purposes, or as a basis for translation into formal verifiable notations, but also as simulatable models suitable for experimenting the actual system behaviour. This requires the exploitation of much more complex (to learn, to use, to acquire) frameworks supporting execution and simulation of composite systems based on interacting state machines. The survey on semi-formal tools presented in X2Rail-2 deliverable D5.1 [38] indicates as preferred frameworks for system simulation the following ones:

- PTC Integrity Modeler (now Windchill Modeler SySim)[10];
- Sparx Systems Enterprise Architect[11];
- No Magic Cameo Systems Modeller (now Dassault 3DS Cameo Systems Modeller)[12].

---

[8] https://eulynx.eu/.

[9] https://www.graphviz.org/.

[10] https://www.ptc.com/en/products/plm/plm-products/windchill/modeler/sysim.

[11] https://sparxsystems.com/products/ea/index.html.

[12] https://www.nomagic.com/products/cameo-systems-modeler.

Although we intend to follow this indication, at the current stage of the 4SECU-Rail project, we still need to acquire some hands-on initial experience on the chosen case study to be able to select one of these tools.

In the context of the 4SECURail demonstrator, the exploitation of a framework allowing to directly simulate the designed behavioural models, in agreement with the official OMG fUML semantics [47], it would allow to ensure that the designed graphical models actually reflect the expected system behaviour in an unambiguous way.

Formal Verification by Model Checking. One of the project's main goals is to transform these standard UML/SysML designs, whatever supporting tool is chosen, into verifiable formal models. Theorem proving and model checking can be considered the two most used approaches to system verification, also in railway related contexts [3,5,15,28]. However, theorem proving, for instance as supported by Atelier B, fits better a specification refinement process that guides the correct-by-construction generation of code starting from an initial formal design. Theorem proving moreover scales well to infinite state systems and can help identify inductive properties. Model checking instead fits better a model-based approach in which the behaviour of a simulatable design is explored and exhaustively verified. In 4SECURail we follow the model-checking approach, partly because we are not interested in code generation. We will take advantage of the experience gained within the ASTRail project [2], where UML state machine descriptions were translated into Event-B state machines and subsequently analysed and verified by model checking with the ProB tool[13] [7].

ProB is an animator and model checker for the B-Method. It allows animation of many B specifications, and can be used to systematically check a specification for a range of errors. ProB is one of the tools also recommended by X2Rail-2 for formal verifications. Some of the reasons for the successful experience of its use in the ASTRail project, which suggest to reuse it in 4SECURail as well, are the following: (i) it is a free, open source product whose code is distributed under the EPL v1.0 license[14]; (ii) it is actively maintained and commercial support is available from Formal Mind[15]; (iii) it runs on Linux, Windows, and MacOS environments; (iv) it has several nice, very usable graphical interfaces, but it can also be used from the command line; (v) it is well integrated in the B/Event-B ecosystem (Rodin, Atelier B, iUML, B Toolkit); (vi) it allows construction, animation and visualisation of non-deterministic systems; (vii) it allows formal verification through different techniques like constraint solving, trace refinement checking, and model checking.

Instead, the following are some known weak points of the use of ProB [1]. (i) It does not allow the explicit modelling of multiple mutually interacting state machines. The only way to achieve that is to merge all the separate machines into a global one. (ii) Event-B state machines are different from UML/SysML state machines. At the current state of the art several proposals of translations from

---

[13] https://www3.hhu.de/stups/prob/.

[14] http://www.eclipse.org/org/documents/epl-v10.html.

[15] http://www.formalmind.com/.

UML to ProB state machines have been made, but as far as we know, no industrially usable product currently supports that mapping. (iii) Model checking does not support compositional approaches based on bisimulation equivalences which are congruences with respect to parallel composition operations. In simpler words, the verification approach does not scale when the system is composed by many interacting asynchronous state machines.

Modelling the behaviour of a system through the design of a single state machine has the advantage that this design can often be translated into the notations supported by formal verification frameworks with a reasonable effort. However, if we have to verify properties that depend on the behaviour of more interacting asynchronous systems, the situation becomes more difficult. If the components are not too complex, or not too many, a possibility is to merge all of them into a unique "global" system modelled again as a single state machine. Increasing the complexity and the number of components raises the state-space explosion problem.

One solution is to constrain the verification to a not full, but rich set of scenarios. That is, verifying the system under reasonable assumptions (e.g., absence of fatal errors in certain components, only one/two/three trains moving from one RBC to another, limited presence of communication errors, just to mention some). The other solution is to exploit alternative formal notations, more oriented towards the design and verification of asynchronous interacting systems and supported by specialised theoretical basis, such as process algebras.

We are unable at the current time to evaluate the overall final complexity of the chosen case study, and whether model checking within the ProB framework will be sufficient for its formal verification. In any case our approach does not prevent the experimentation with alternative translations towards verification engines more oriented to the analysis of "parallel asynchronous systems" (e.g., mCRL2[16] [14, 20], CADP[17] [18], FDR4[18] [31]), in the style of [36].

The overall execution flow embedding the three points discussed above is represented in Fig. 4.

The Case Study. The fourth point concerns the case study chosen to test the 4SECURail demonstrator: the RBC/RBC protocol, as specified by the UNISIG documents RBC/RBC Handover [52] and Safe Communication Interface [51].

In the ERTMS/ETCS train control system, a Radio Block Center (RBC) is responsible for controlling the separation of trains on the part of a line under its supervision. A handover procedure is needed to manage the interchange of train control supervision between two neighbour RBCs: when a train is approaching the end of the area supervised by one handing over RBC, an exchange of information with the accepting RBC takes place to manage the transaction of responsibilities. Since the two neighbouring RBCs may have been manufactured by different providers, the RBC/RBC interface is a typical product where development pro-

---

[16] https://www.mcrl2.org/.
[17] https://cadp.inria.fr/.
[18] https://cocotec.io/fdr/index.html.

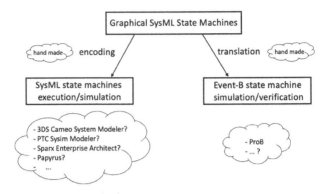

Fig. 4. Execution flow of the demonstrator prototype

cesses of different supplier meet, and is therefore an optimal choice to investigate how natural language specification may create the possibility of diverging interpretations, leading to interoperability issues. Being UNISIG SUBSET-039 and SUBSET-098 already consolidated standards, the overall structure of our demonstrator process will reflect the second point of view of those described in Sect. 4 (second case) and illustrated in Fig. 4. This is the case of the formal methods demonstrator process used for just analysing, verifying, and possibly improving an already existing standard specification.

In our particular architecture, being the input requirements an already stable official UNISIG standard, we will not rewrite it using again a natural language notation, even in the case that the rewriting could appear as more precise or complete. We can however complement it with annotations, if found useful, and/or enrich it with further artifacts developed with the demonstrator process, such as SysML models, animatable modes, formal model, test cases, and the required cross references among these components.

4.2 Input for the Cost/benefit Analysis and Learning Curve Evaluation

During the experimentation of our demonstrator process with its application to the selected case study, it will be important to assess as much data as possible about the costs of our approach. These costs might be related to actual monetary costs incurred (like the academic/research costs for acquiring some tool licence), or costs not actually incurred, but meaningful for the cost/benefit analysis (like the cost of full commercial licence for the same tool, or the cost for commercial support and training even if not activated, or cost of licence for alternative tools with respect to the ones used in the demonstrator). These costs might also be measured in terms of Man Month efforts and put in relation to the effort needed to learn a specific tool and methodology (learning curve), or to the time/effort needed to generate the animatable SysML specification, to generate the formally verifiable models, to select, design and perform the verifications of the properties of interest, to maintain the various model well synchronized.

It will also be important to put in evidence the differential of the cost associated with the demonstrator between the cases with-or-without the exploitation of formal methods. This final exercise of the consolidated demonstrator will be the basis for studying the cost/benefit analysis of the approach and the evaluation of the learning curve for the use of the selected methodologies and tools.

5   The Adoption of a Standard Notation

UML is a standardised modeling language consisting of an integrated set of graphical diagrams, developed to help system and software developers for specifying, visualizing, constructing, and documenting the artifacts of software systems [53]. UML, in its SysML version, has been adopted also in the EULYNX project within its underlying methodology for the development of standard interfaces. A detailed analysis of this approach is well described in [13]. Graphical designs do actually often convey information to the reader with a wider band than just text, and require less effort in the reader for receiving it. However, a textual representation readable/writeable by humans is equally important for the simpler way in which it can be produced, shared, translated, modified, and communicated. We believe that both kinds of representation should be made available, and they should be and remain in synch.

It is also important for the designer to be able to simulate the UML behavioural models (e.g., state machines) to obtain initial feedback on the correctness of the design with respect to the intended requirements. Otherwise models risk being precise, but wrong. A prerequisite for a reasonable introduction of UML as reference notation inside a formal methods demonstrator process is that the meaning of the UML designs shall not be ambiguous or uncertain. Since its origins, this has been recognised as a major problem for some of the behavioural diagrams of UML like state machines. The main known problems with this behavioural notation are in fact: uncertainties in the semantics, absence of standard action language, and lots of implementation freedom (cf., e.g., [25,49]).

Several studies and proposals have been conducted in the recent years with the goal of associating a formal semantics to the UML behavioural diagrams (cf., e.g., [12,19,37]), but none of these actually succeeded in solving the problems. An important step forward to overcome this problem has been achieved by the OMG (Object Management Group) with the standardisation of fUML (*Foundational Subset for Executable UML Models*) [47], which is also associated with an official reference implementation [40]. This definition of fUML is complemented with the definition of textual syntax for its action language *Alf* [46], and by the definition of PSCS (*Precise Semantics of UML Composite Structure*) [43]. The purpose of this fUML effort is the definition of an initial subset of UML that is free from the semantic uncertainties affecting the full standard and that might define a rigorous model of computation for the UML behavioural diagrams.

The remaining limits of this effort are that the fUML definition is still described in natural language, and that the "reference implementation" (that might play the role of unambiguous operational semantics) is currently being implemented only with respect to activity diagrams [40]. The Alf definition itself, when considered in conjunction with the state machine notation, is currently defined just through an "Informative Annex" [46] with no normative role. Within the demonstrator process, UML can play three different roles: (i) as complementary graphical *documentation* of specific aspects of the system requirements definition; (ii) as a direct notation for the execution and *simulation* of system models; (iii) as *baseline for translations* towards other formal notations supported by strong verification capabilities.

The use of UML for system *design* and *documentation* is supported by an extremely rich set of tools. If we were interested in the generation of diagrams for complementing the natural language description of a system, we might find it useful to use UML tools exploiting more immediate and user-friendly textual encoding able to automatically generate their corresponding diagrams. Support for the use of UML for *execution/simulation* of the system behaviour is limited.

None of the "industry-ready" UML tools allow direct *verification* of behavioural models; as far as we know, only a few academic prototypes have been developed for this purpose (e.g., UMC[19] [4]). Therefore, we are left with the possibility of performing the translation from the UML models into other formal notations supported by verification frameworks. The literature reports numerous translation attempts [8–11, 16, 17, 32–35, 41, 45, 48, 50, 54, 55], but none of them seems to be well supported and integrated inside "industry-ready" UML frameworks.

Given the focus on formal methods of the 4SECURail demonstrator, the major interest is in the possibility of translating UML for verification, although using UML for (*documentation* and *simulation*) may play a relevant role inside the demonstrator. From this point of view our preferred choice would be the use of an even stricter subset of the fUML state machine diagrams, defining a very simple state machine structure that would allow a direct translation into the main formalisms adopted by verification and simulation tools, such as Event-B[20] [1], LNT [30], and Uppaal[21] [6].

Concluding this section, the criteria that will be applied for selecting specific UML/SysML tools can be summarised as:

- unambiguity and standard quality of the supported notations;
- openness of the framework, i.e., how easy it is to import/export/translate the notations versus other frameworks;
- usability of the tool user interface;
- degree of support for non-deterministic aspects in the design and
- degree and cost of support and training by the tool providers.

---

[19] http://fmt.isti.cnr.it/kandisti/.

[20] http://www.event-b.org/.

[21] http://www.uppaal.org/.

6   Conclusions and Future Work

We have defined the rationale and the choices performed in terms of structure, methods, and tools selection, for the definition of a (semi-)formal software development process (demonstrator) targeted to the construction of clear, rigorous, and verifiable system specifications. In particular, two important issues deserve a specific analysis and discussion: (i) the clarification of the usefulness of formal methods from the point of view of the Infrastructure Managers, (ii) the role that the semi-formal SysML notation should play within our formal methods demonstrator process.

This defined process will be exercised for the specification and analysis of the identified case study fragment. After possible revision due to the experience gained during this first exercising of the demonstrator, a consolidated version will be used for the analysis and verification of the full case study. This final exercising of the consolidated demonstrator will be the basis for the study of the cost/benefit analysis of the approach and the evaluation of the learning curve for the use of the selected methodologies and tools.

Acknowledgements. This work has been partially funded by the 4SECURail project. The 4SECURail project received funding from the Shift2Rail Joint Undertaking under the European Union's Horizon 2020 research and innovation programme under grant agreement No 881775 in the context of the open call S2R-OC-IP2-01-2019, part of the "Annual Work Plan and Budget 2019", of the programme H2020-S2RJU-2019. The content of this paper reflects only the authors' view and the Shift2Rail Joint Undertaking is not responsible for any use that may be made of the included information.

We also would like to thank the Italian MIUR PRIN 2017FTXR7S project IT MaT-TerS (Methods and Tools for Trustworthy Smart Systems).

References

1. Abrial, J.R.: Modeling in Event-B: System and Software Engineering. Cambridge University Press, Cambridge (2010)
2. ASTRail Deliverable D4.3: Validation Report. http://astrail.eu/download.aspx?id=d7ae1ebf-52b4-4bde-b25e-ae251fd906df
3. Basile, D., et al.: On the industrial uptake of formal methods in the railway domain. In: Furia, C.A., Winter, K. (eds.) IFM 2018. LNCS, vol. 11023, pp. 20–29. Springer, Cham (2018). https://doi.org/10.1007/978-3-319-98938-9_2
4. ter Beek, M.H., Fantechi, A., Gnesi, S., Mazzanti, F.: A state/event-based model-checking approach for the analysis of abstract system properties. Sci. Comput. Program. 76(2), 119–135 (2011). https://doi.org/10.1016/j.scico.2010.07.002
5. ter Beek, M.H., et al.: Adopting formal methods in an industrial setting: the railways case. In: ter Beek, M.H., McIver, A., Oliveira, J.N. (eds.) FM 2019. LNCS, vol. 11800, pp. 762–772. Springer, Cham (2019). https://doi.org/10.1007/978-3-030-30942-8_46
6. Behrmann, G., et al.: UPPAAL 4.0. In: Proceedings of the 3rd International Conference on the Quantitative Evaluation of SysTems (QEST 2006), pp. 125–126. IEEE (2006). https://doi.org/10.1109/QEST.2006.59

7. Bendisposto, J., et al.: ProB 2.0 tutorial. In: Butler, M., Hallerstede, S., Waldén, M. (eds.) Proceedings of the 4th Rodin User and Developer Workshop. TUCS Lecture Notes, Turku Centre for Computer Science (2013)

8. Berglehner, R., Rasheeq, A.: An approach to improve SysML railway specification using UML-B and EVENT-B. In: Poster at the 3rd International Conference on Reliability, Safety, and Security of Railway Systems: Modelling, Analysis, Verification, and Certification (RSSRail 2019) (2019). https://doi.org/10.13140/RG.2.2.21925.45288

9. Bernardi, S., et al.: Enabling the usage of UML in the verification of railway systems: the DAM-rail approach. Rel. Eng. Syst. Saf. **120**, 112–126 (2013). https://doi.org/10.1016/j.ress.2013.06.032

10. Besnard, V., Brun, M., Jouault, F., Teodorov, C., Dhaussy, P.: Unified LTL verification and embedded execution of UML models. In: Proceedings of the 21th ACM/IEEE International Conference on Model Driven Engineering Languages and Systems (MoDELS 2018), pp. 112–122. ACM (2018). https://doi.org/10.1145/3239372.3239395

11. Bhaduri, P., Ramesh, S.: Model Checking of Statechart Models: Survey and Research Directions. CoRR cs.SE/0407038 (2004). http://arxiv.org/abs/cs.SE/0407038

12. Broy, M., Crane, M.L., Dingel, J., Hartman, A., Rumpe, B., Selic, B.: 2nd UML 2 semantics symposium: formal semantics for UML. In: Kühne, T. (ed.) MODELS 2006. LNCS, vol. 4364, pp. 318–323. Springer, Heidelberg (2007). https://doi.org/10.1007/978-3-540-69489-2_39

13. Bui, N.L.: An analysis of the benefits of EULYNX-style requirements modeling for ProRail. Ph.D. thesis, Technische Universiteit Eindhoven (2017). https://research.tue.nl/files/91220589/2017_09_28_ST_Bui_L.pdf

14. Bunte, O., et al.: The mCRL2 toolset for analysing concurrent systems. In: Vojnar, T., Zhang, L. (eds.) TACAS 2019. LNCS, vol. 11428, pp. 21–39. Springer, Cham (2019). https://doi.org/10.1007/978-3-030-17465-1_2

15. Butler, M., et al.: The first twenty-five years of industrial use of the B-method. In: ter Beek, M.H., Ničković, D. (eds.) FMICS 2020. LNCS, vol. 12327, pp. 189–209. Springer, Cham (2020). https://doi.org/10.1007/978-3-030-58298-2_8

16. Caltais, G., Leitner-Fischer, F., Leue, S., Weiser, J.: SysML to NuSMV model transformation via object-orientation. In: Berger, C., Mousavi, M.R., Wisniewski, R. (eds.) CyPhy 2016. LNCS, vol. 10107, pp. 31–45. Springer, Cham (2017). https://doi.org/10.1007/978-3-319-51738-4_3

17. Chen, J., Cui, H.: Translation from adapted UML to Promela for CORBA-based applications. In: Graf, S., Mounier, L. (eds.) SPIN 2004. LNCS, vol. 2989, pp. 234–251. Springer, Heidelberg (2004). https://doi.org/10.1007/978-3-540-24732-6_17

18. Coste, N., Garavel, H., Hermanns, H., Lang, F., Mateescu, R., Serwe, W.: Ten years of performance evaluation for concurrent systems using CADP. In: Margaria, T., Steffen, B. (eds.) ISoLA 2010. LNCS, vol. 6416, pp. 128–142. Springer, Heidelberg (2010). https://doi.org/10.1007/978-3-642-16561-0_18

19. Crane, M.L., Dingel, J.: UML vs. classical vs. RHAPSODY statecharts: not all models are created equal. In: Briand, L., Williams, C. (eds.) MODELS 2005. LNCS, vol. 3713, pp. 97–112. Springer, Heidelberg (2005). https://doi.org/10.1007/11557432_8

20. Cranen, S., et al.: An overview of the mCRL2 toolset and its recent advances. In: Piterman, N., Smolka, S.A. (eds.) TACAS 2013. LNCS, vol. 7795, pp. 199–213. Springer, Heidelberg (2013). https://doi.org/10.1007/978-3-642-36742-7_15

21. European Committee for Electrotechnical Standardization: CENELEC EN 50128 – Railway applications - Communication, signalling and processing systems - Software for railway control and protection systems, June 2011. https://standards.globalspec.com/std/1678027/cenelec-en-50128
22. Fantechi, A.: Twenty-five years of formal methods and railways: what next? In: Counsell, S., Núñez, M. (eds.) SEFM 2013. LNCS, vol. 8368, pp. 167–183. Springer, Cham (2014). https://doi.org/10.1007/978-3-319-05032-4_13
23. Fantechi, A., Ferrari, A., Gnesi, S.: Formal methods and safety certification: challenges in the railways domain. In: Margaria, T., Steffen, B. (eds.) ISoLA 2016. LNCS, vol. 9953, pp. 261–265. Springer, Cham (2016). https://doi.org/10.1007/978-3-319-47169-3_18
24. Fantechi, A., Fokkink, W., Morzenti, A.: Some trends in formal methods applications to railway signaling. In: Gnesi, S., Margaria, T. (eds.) Formal Methods for Industrial Critical Systems: A Survey of Applications, chap. 4, pp. 61–84. Wiley (2013). https://doi.org/10.1002/9781118459898.ch4
25. Fecher, H., Schönborn, J., Kyas, M., de Roever, W.-P.: 29 new unclarities in the semantics of UML 2.0 state machines. In: Lau, K.-K., Banach, R. (eds.) ICFEM 2005. LNCS, vol. 3785, pp. 52–65. Springer, Heidelberg (2005). https://doi.org/10.1007/11576280_5
26. Ferrari, A., et al.: Survey on formal methods and tools in railways: the ASTRail approach. In: Collart-Dutilleul, S., Lecomte, T., Romanovsky, A. (eds.) RSSRail 2019. LNCS, vol. 11495, pp. 226–241. Springer, Cham (2019). https://doi.org/10.1007/978-3-030-18744-6_15
27. Ferrari, A., Fantechi, A., Gnesi, S., Magnani, G.: Model-based development and formal methods in the railway industry. IEEE Softw. **30**(3), 28–34 (2013). https://doi.org/10.1109/MS.2013.44
28. Ferrari, A., Mazzanti, F., Basile, D., ter Beek, M.H., Fantechi, A.: Comparing formal tools for system design: a judgment study. In: Proceedings of the 42nd International Conference on Software Engineering (ICSE), pp. 62–74. ACM (2020). https://doi.org/10.1145/3377811.3380373
29. Garavel, H., ter Beek, M.H., van de Pol, J.: The 2020 expert survey on formal methods. In: ter Beek, M.H., Ničković, D. (eds.) FMICS 2020. LNCS, vol. 12327, pp. 3–69. Springer, Cham (2020). https://doi.org/10.1007/978-3-030-58298-2_1
30. Garavel, H., Lang, F., Serwe, W.: From LOTOS to LNT. In: Katoen, J.-P., Langerak, R., Rensink, A. (eds.) ModelEd, TestEd, TrustEd. LNCS, vol. 10500, pp. 3–26. Springer, Cham (2017). https://doi.org/10.1007/978-3-319-68270-9_1
31. Gibson-Robinson, T., Armstrong, P.J., Boulgakov, A., Roscoe, A.W.: FDR3: a parallel refinement checker for CSP. Int. J. Softw. Tools Technol. Transf. **18**(2), 149–167 (2016). https://doi.org/10.1007/s10009-015-0377-y
32. Grumberg, O., Meller, Y., Yorav, K.: Applying software model checking techniques for behavioral UML models. In: Giannakopoulou, D., Méry, D. (eds.) FM 2012. LNCS, vol. 7436, pp. 277–292. Springer, Heidelberg (2012). https://doi.org/10.1007/978-3-642-32759-9_25
33. Hvid Hansen, H., Ketema, J., Luttik, B., Mousavi, M.R., van de Pol, J., dos Santos, O.M.: Automated verification of executable UML models. In: Aichernig, B.K., de Boer, F.S., Bonsangue, M.M. (eds.) FMCO 2010. LNCS, vol. 6957, pp. 225–250. Springer, Heidelberg (2011). https://doi.org/10.1007/978-3-642-25271-6_12
34. Jussila, T., Dubrovin, J., Junttila, T., Latvala, T., Porres, I.: Model checking dynamic and hierarchical UML state machines. In: Proceedings of the 3rd International Workshop on Model Development, Validation and Verification (MoDeVa 2006), pp. 94–110. University of Queensland (2006)

35. Knapp, A., Merz, S., Rauh, C.: Model checking timed UML state machines and collaborations. In: Damm, W., Olderog, E.-R. (eds.) FTRTFT 2002. LNCS, vol. 2469, pp. 395–414. Springer, Heidelberg (2002). https://doi.org/10.1007/3-540-45739-9_23

36. Lang, F., Mateescu, R., Mazzanti, F.: Sharp congruences adequate with temporal logics combining weak and strong modalities. TACAS 2020. LNCS, vol. 12079, pp. 57–76. Springer, Cham (2020). https://doi.org/10.1007/978-3-030-45237-7_4

37. Liu, S., et al.: A formal semantics for complete UML state machines with communications. In: Johnsen, E.B., Petre, L. (eds.) IFM 2013. LNCS, vol. 7940, pp. 331–346. Springer, Heidelberg (2013). https://doi.org/10.1007/978-3-642-38613-8_23

38. Löfving, C., Borälv, A: X2Rail-2 Deliverable D5.1, Formal Methods (Taxonomy and Survey), Proposed Methods and Applications, May 2018. https://projects.shift2rail.org/download.aspx?id=b4cf6a3d-f1f2-4dd3-ae01-2bada34596b8

39. Mazzanti, F., Ferrari, A., Spagnolo, G.O.: Towards formal methods diversity in railways: an experience report with seven frameworks. Int. J. Softw. Tools Technol. Transf. **20**(3), 263–288 (2018). https://doi.org/10.1007/s10009-018-0488-3

40. ModelDriven: The fUML Reference Implementation. https://github.com/ModelDriven/fUML-Reference-Implementation/blob/master/README.md

41. Ober, I., Graf, S., Ober, I.: Validation of UML models via a mapping to communicating extended timed automata. In: Graf, S., Mounier, L. (eds.) SPIN 2004. LNCS, vol. 2989, pp. 127–145. Springer, Heidelberg (2004). https://doi.org/10.1007/978-3-540-24732-6_9

42. Object Management Group: Unified Modelling Language, December 2017. https://www.omg.org/spec/UML/About-UML/

43. Object Management Group: Precise Semantics of UML Composite Structure (PSCS), March 2018. https://www.omg.org/spec/PSCS/1.1/PDF

44. Object Management Group: OMG Systems Modeling Language (OMG SysML), November 2019. http://www.omg.org/spec/SysML/1.6/

45. Oliveira, R., Dingel, J.: Supporting model refinement with equivalence checking in the context of model-driven engineering with UML-RT. In: Burgueño, L., et al. (eds.) Proceedings of the 20th International Conference on Model Driven Engineering Languages and Systems (MoDELS 2017) – Satellite Events. CEUR Workshop Proceedings, vol. 2019, pp. 307–314. CEUR-WS.org (2017). http://ceur-ws.org/Vol-2019/modevva_2.pdf

46. OMG: Action Language for Foundational UML (Alf) – Concrete Syntax for a UML Action Language, July 2017. https://www.omg.org/spec/ALF/1.1

47. OMG: Semantics of a Foundational Subset for Executable UML Models (fUML), December 2018. https://www.omg.org/spec/FUML/1.4/PDF

48. Pétin, J.F., Evrot, D., Morel, G., Lamy, P.: Combining SysML and formal methods for safety requirements verification. In: Proceedings of the 22nd International Conference on Software & Systems Engineering and their Applications (ICSSEA 2010) (2010). https://hal.archives-ouvertes.fr/hal-00533311/document

49. Simons, A.J.H., Graham, I.: 30 things that go wrong in object modelling with UML 1.3. In: Kilov, H., Rumpe, B., Simmonds, I. (eds.) Behavioral Specifications of Businesses and Systems. SECS, vol. 523, pp. 237–257. Springer, Heidelberg (1999). https://doi.org/10.1007/978-1-4615-5229-1_17

50. Snook, C., Savicks, V., Butler, M.: Verification of UML models by translation to UML-B. In: Aichernig, B.K., de Boer, F.S., Bonsangue, M.M. (eds.) FMCO 2010. LNCS, vol. 6957, pp. 251–266. Springer, Heidelberg (2011). https://doi.org/10.1007/978-3-642-25271-6_13

51. UNISIG: RBC-RBC Safe Communication Interface – SUBSET-098, February 2012. https://www.era.europa.eu/sites/default/files/filesystem/ertms/ccs_tsi_annex_a_-_mandatory_specifications/set_of_specifications_3_etcs_b3_r2_gsm-r_b1/index063_-_subset-098_v300.pdf
52. UNISIG: FIS for the RBC/RBC Handover – SUBSET-039, December 2015. https://www.era.europa.eu/sites/default/files/filesystem/ertms/ccs_tsi_annex_a_-_mandatory_specifications/set_of_specifications_3_etcs_b3_r2_gsm-r_b1/index012_-_subset-039_v320.pdf
53. Visual Paradigm: What is Unified Modeling Language (UML)?. https://www.visual-paradigm.com/guide/uml-unified-modeling-language/what-is-uml/
54. Yeung, W.L., Leung, K.R.P.H., Wang, J., Dong, W.: Improvements towards formalizing UML state diagrams in CSP. In: Proceedings of the 12th Asia-Pacific Software Engineering Conference (APSEC 2005), pp. 176–184. IEEE (2005). https://doi.org/10.1109/APSEC.2005.70
55. Zhang, S.J., Liu, Y.: An automatic approach to model checking UML state machines. In: Proceedings of the 4th International Conference on Secure Software Integration and Reliability Improvement (SSIRI-C 2010), pp. 1–6. IEEE (2010). https://doi.org/10.1109/SSIRI-C.2010.11

Author Index

Printed in the United States
By Bookmasters